RACE PROFILES

FLAT 2010

RACE PROFILES
FLAT 2010

Dr Peter May

Published in 2010 by Raceform
Compton, Newbury, Berkshire, RG20 6NL

Copyright © Peter May 2010

The right of Peter May to be identified as the author of this work has been asserted by him in accordance with the Copyright, Designs and Patents Act 1988.

All rights reserved. No part of this publication may be reproduced, stored in a retrieval system, or transmitted in any form or by any means, electronic, mechanical, photocopying, recording, or otherwise, without the prior written permission of the publishers.

A catalogue record for this book is available from the British Library.

ISBN 978-1-906820-48-0

Designed by Fiona Pike

Printed in the UK by Thomson Litho, Glasgow

Contents

Introduction	**7**

Race Profiles

Juvenile Races	**9**
All Group Races	9
Listed Races	17
Conditions Stakes	25
Maiden Races	35
Claiming Races	43
Selling Races	51
Handicaps	59
Three-Year-Old Races	**68**
Group 1 Races	68
Group 2 & 3 Races	77
Listed Races	86
Conditions Stakes	96
Maiden Races	104
Claiming Races	113
Selling Races	122
Handicaps (Class 1..3)	131
Handicaps (Class 4..7)	140
All Age races	**150**
Group 1 Races	150
Group 2 & 3 Races	160
Listed Races	170
Conditions Stakes	180
Maiden Races	189
Claiming Races	198
Selling Races	208
Handicaps (Class 1..3)	218
Handicaps (Class 4..7)	228

For each race classification the profile for all races is supplemented by profiles over the four main distances: sprint, mile, middle distances, staying distances as well as profiles by going and field size.

Introduction

The book is essentially a reference guide allowing readers to identify the most likely winner of each race based on the historical profiles of similar events.

Race Profiling

Unlike Form Study, race profiling does not attempt to quantify the ability of a horse. Instead it extracts the key characteristics of the race and uses these features to generate a profile of the most likely race winner. These profiles can have few or many attributes depending on the significance of the features and the depth of data supporting each one. Some races do not lend themselves to profiling and it is difficult to find a reliable profile for the likely winner. This may be due to a lack of historical data, on which to base the profile, or simply that the race is won by a wide range of horses without favouring a specific type. However many races have very exact profiles and are won on a regular basis by horses that exhibit a specific set of qualities.

The logic underlying the Race Profiling method concerns the dominance of horses with certain characteristics in specific races. Often races are won by a particular type of horse, with others having only a minimal chance. For instance, age is often a key factor. Jumps races are often won by the younger horses, however there are cases where a very narrow age range can be associated with a race. Under such circumstances the horses lying outside this range can be considered unlikely winners, and if one or more happens to be a short price, then it may be possible to return a good profit by not only backing the horses with positive traits, but by laying those animals possessing negative profiles.

Specific Race Profiles

Essentially there are two types of profile: a Specific Race Profile and a General Race Profile. The former is most commonly applied to the main races of the year in the form of five year- or ten year- trends. In order to generate a specific race profile the credentials of the recent winners of the race are examined and the key trends extracted.

Unfortunately this sample only constitutes a small proportion of the ever expanding pool of races run each season and an alternative approach is required for the other events. One Class 4 maiden race, for instance, is very much like another, so extracting the details for a particular maiden race run at Newmarket in June may not be that informative or reliable. However given the degree of similarity between these less prominent events it is possible to analyse all similar races to generate a profile of the likely winner based on a large sample of events. For instance when considering a 2 mile handicap race at Newbury it may be helpful to find the profile of the most likely winner of all long distance handicaps. And given the amount of data available, this could be further restricted to a similar field size, the same race class, or to races run on a similar surface or a similar track. Consequently a more general approach, as opposed to the specific ten-year trends, is more applicable to the majority of races run each season.

General Race Profiles

General race profiles, as the title suggests, are based on a wide range of races, as opposed to a single event. It is possible to create a turf sprint race handicap profile, for instance, based on all such races run in a specific country. Whilst this is a very general profile it can be further restricted by the main discriminating factors such as race distance, going, time of year, race class and track. Using these additional inputs the profile can be structured to provide the information required based on the largest possible sample of races. Consequently it becomes more robust than a single race profile and hence more reliable.

The main advantage of general race profiles is their applicability. Few races can be profiled in isolation, whereas general profiles will apply to the remaining majority. Furthermore changing trends are more likely to be apparent from an analysis of several races as opposed to a single event. For instance, increased competitiveness in a specific sector of racing may reduce the proportion of events won by the favourite. When analysing a single race this may become obvious after a reasonable time period and number of races, but in a general profile it will be visible sooner, allowing the bettor to take advantage of the changing pattern and structure his/her bets accordingly.

This text presents a set of these general race profiles for all of the flat race classifications run in Great Britain and can be used to establish the key qualities a horse needs to possess in order to win a particular event.

Notation

In the main profile tables four columns of data are presented. The first, headed by "Prop" shows the proportion of races won by the horses in each of the categories; the next two columns show the number of winners and the number of runners. Column three, Wins%, is the overall win rate (winners divided by runners) expressed as a percentage. The "£" column shows the average profit at starting price to a level £1 stake on all runners in that category. For the *Other Factors* and *Trainer Analysis* sections just the number of wins, runners and average profit are displayed.

To qualify as a beaten favourite the horse had to be the sole market leader on its latest run in a flat race (turf or all weather); to be top-rated by the BHA the horse has to be clear of the other runners in the race based on this rating, joint-top-rated runners do not qualify. Class movement is determined by race class. So a horse moving from a class 4 race to a class 3 race would be considered, for this analysis, to be moving up in class. For class 1 races, Group 1 is considered to be the highest classification, followed by Group 2, Group 3, Listed Races and handicaps. So a horse which last ran in a class 1 handicap and today is running in a non-handicap Listed race would be considered to be moving up in class. The *seven day winners* classification groups together all horses which won their latest flat race within the last seven days.

In order to generate the profiles, only races from Great Britain run during the last five years have been used, however previous race performances in Ireland are included.

Race Profiles

Race Classifications

Included in Race Title	Equivalent Race Profile Classification
Group 1	Group 1 races
Group 2	Group 2 and 3 races
Group 3	Group 2 and 3 races
Listed	Listed races
Listed Handicap	Handicap races
Listed Rated Stakes Handicap	Handicap races
Conditions Stakes	Conditions races
Amateur Stakes	Conditions races
Selling Race	Sellers
Maiden Selling Stakes	Sellers
Claiming Stakes	Claimer
Amateur Claiming Stakes	Claimer
Maiden Claiming Stakes	Claimer
Classified Claiming Stakes	Claimer
Claiming Handicap	Handicap races
Selling Handicap	Handicap races
Maiden Handicap	Handicap races
Maiden Stakes	Maiden races

All Group Races

2-Y.O Races: All Group Races

ANALYSIS BY BHA RATING

Rating	Prop	Win	Runs	Wins%	£
120..139	0%	0	1	0.0%	-1.00
110..119	2%	4	40	10.0%	-0.41
100..109	23%	38	274	13.9%	-0.03
90..99	11%	18	246	7.3%	-0.15
70..89	5%	8	164	4.9%	-0.32
50..69	0%	0	3	0.0%	-1.00
..49	0%	0	0	0.0%	0.00
Unrated	60%	100	1030	9.7%	-0.27

ANALYSIS BY WEIGHT CARRIED

Weight	Prop	Win	Runs	Wins%	£
10-01+	0%	0	0	0.0%	0.00
9-8..10-00	0%	0	0	0.0%	0.00
9-0..9-07	36%	60	617	9.7%	-0.36
8-8..8-13	64%	108	1141	9.5%	-0.15
8-0..8-07	0%	0	0	0.0%	0.00
..7-13	0%	0	0	0.0%	0.00

ANALYSIS BY DAYS SINCE LAST RUN

Days	Prop	Win	Runs	Wins%	£
1..7	4%	6	56	10.7%	0.04
8..14	14%	23	314	7.3%	-0.46
15..28	46%	77	766	10.1%	-0.09
29..60	29%	48	506	9.5%	-0.33
61..100	7%	12	79	15.2%	0.12
101+	0%	0	13	0.0%	-1.00
Unraced	1%	2	24	8.3%	-0.52

ANALYSIS BY TODAY'S STARTING PRICE

Price	Prop	Win	Runs	Wins%	£
Odds On	6%	10	19	52.6%	-0.11
Ev-2/1	13%	22	75	29.3%	-0.25
9/4-4/1	32%	53	203	26.1%	0.09
9/2-6/1	14%	23	189	12.2%	-0.24
13/2-10/1	17%	28	314	8.9%	-0.18
11/1-16/1	10%	17	341	5.0%	-0.28
18/1-33/1	8%	14	343	4.1%	0.08
40/1+	1%	1	274	0.4%	-0.81

ANALYSIS BY STARTING PRICE LAST TIME

Price	Prop	Win	Runs	Wins%	£
Odds On	14%	23	179	12.8%	-0.22
Ev-2/1	19%	32	249	12.9%	0.04
9/4-4/1	23%	38	351	10.8%	-0.28
9/2-6/1	16%	27	235	11.5%	-0.04
13/2-10/1	10%	16	289	5.5%	-0.47
11/1-16/1	10%	17	207	8.2%	-0.08
18/1-33/1	6%	10	168	6.0%	-0.42
40/1+	2%	3	56	5.4%	-0.36
Unraced	1%	2	24	8.3%	-0.52

ANALYSIS BY DISTANCE BEATEN LAST TIME

Lengths	Prop	Win	Runs	Wins%	£
..-10	1%	1	7	14.3%	-0.46
-10..0	54%	90	823	10.9%	-0.30
0.1..2	24%	41	361	11.4%	0.08
2.1..5	12%	20	280	7.1%	-0.12
5.1..10	5%	9	181	5.0%	-0.53
10.1..20	3%	5	70	7.1%	-0.25
20.0..30	0%	0	10	0.0%	-1.00
30.1+	0%	0	2	0.0%	-1.00
Not Compl	0%	0	0	0.0%	0.00
Unraced	1%	2	24	8.3%	-0.52

ANALYSIS BY RUN NUMBER

Run No	Prop	Win	Runs	Wins%	£
FTO	1%	2	24	8.3%	-0.52
2nd Run	15%	26	266	9.8%	-0.37
3rd Run	30%	51	458	11.1%	-0.01
4th+ Run	53%	89	1010	8.8%	-0.27

ANALYSIS BY POSITION LAST TIME

Pos LT	Prop	Win	Runs	Wins%	£
Won	54%	91	830	11.0%	-0.31
2nd or 3rd	28%	47	432	10.9%	0.05
Unplaced	17%	28	471	5.9%	-0.32
Not Compl	1%	2	25	8.0%	-0.54

OTHER FACTORS (WINS-RUNS, £)

Course Winner:	18-167	£0.03
Distance Winner:	93-944	-£0.32
Going Winner:	55-531	-£0.11
Beaten Favourite:	23-140	£0.59
BHA Top Rated:	25-143	£0.48
Up in class:	122-1393	-£0.22
Same class:	34-240	-£0.08
Down in class:	10-101	-£0.50
7-Day Winners:	4-21	£0.33
Colts and Geldings:	95-924	-£0.25
Fillies:	7-88	-£0.51
Absolute Favourites:	52-157	-£0.03

TRAINERS (WINS-RUNS, £)

M R Channon 11-102 £0.64; E J O'Neill 4-28 £0.75; P W Chapple-Hyam 8-38 £0.46; B Smart 4-34 £0.42; J S Bolger 5-17 £0.82; A P O'Brien 13-87 £0.16; K A Ryan 7-52 £0.20; A P Jarvis 1-17 £0.53; C G Cox 2-15 £0.30; R Hannon 15-142 £0.02; E A L Dunlop 1-15 £0.13.

Race Profiles

2-Y.O Races: All Group Races – 2 to 7 runners

ANALYSIS BY BHA RATING

Rating	Prop	Win	Runs	Wins%	£
120..139	0%	0	0	0.0%	0.00
110..119	3%	1	10	10.0%	-0.50
100..109	29%	10	48	20.8%	0.29
90..99	6%	2	34	5.9%	-0.44
70..89	9%	3	24	12.5%	0.25
50..69	0%	0	1	0.0%	-1.00
..49	0%	0	0	0.0%	0.00
Unrated	54%	19	109	17.4%	0.09

ANALYSIS BY WEIGHT CARRIED

Weight	Prop	Win	Runs	Wins%	£
10-01+	0%	0	0	0.0%	0.00
9-8..10-00	0%	0	0	0.0%	0.00
9-0..9-07	34%	12	74	16.2%	0.07
8-8..8-13	66%	23	152	15.1%	0.02
8-0..8-07	0%	0	0	0.0%	0.00
..7-13	0%	0	0	0.0%	0.00

ANALYSIS BY DAYS SINCE LAST RUN

Days	Prop	Win	Runs	Wins%	£
1..7	3%	1	8	12.5%	1.63
8..14	14%	5	38	13.2%	0.14
15..28	49%	17	110	15.5%	0.11
29..60	26%	9	54	16.7%	-0.33
61..100	9%	3	13	23.1%	-0.06
101+	0%	0	1	0.0%	-1.00
Unraced	0%	0	2	0.0%	-1.00

ANALYSIS BY TODAY'S STARTING PRICE

Price	Prop	Win	Runs	Wins%	£
Odds On	14%	5	9	55.6%	-0.08
Ev-2/1	14%	5	23	21.7%	-0.45
9/4-4/1	31%	11	40	27.5%	0.19
9/2-6/1	17%	6	42	14.3%	-0.08
13/2-10/1	6%	2	38	5.3%	-0.54
11/1-16/1	11%	4	37	10.8%	0.49
18/1-33/1	6%	2	24	8.3%	1.29
40/1+	0%	0	13	0.0%	-1.00

ANALYSIS BY STARTING PRICE LAST TIME

Price	Prop	Win	Runs	Wins%	£
Odds On	11%	4	28	14.3%	-0.39
Ev-2/1	17%	6	42	14.3%	-0.18
9/4-4/1	23%	8	34	23.5%	0.78
9/2-6/1	23%	8	38	21.1%	0.24
13/2-10/1	11%	4	36	11.1%	-0.50
11/1-16/1	9%	3	24	12.5%	0.00
18/1-33/1	6%	2	18	11.1%	0.83
40/1+	0%	0	4	0.0%	-1.00
Unraced	0%	0	2	0.0%	-1.00

ANALYSIS BY DISTANCE BEATEN LAST TIME

Lengths	Prop	Win	Runs	Wins%	£
..-10	0%	0	1	0.0%	-1.00
-10..0	60%	21	113	18.6%	0.09
0.1..2	17%	6	46	13.0%	-0.18
2.1..5	6%	2	36	5.6%	-0.44
5.1..10	14%	5	16	31.3%	2.08
10.1..20	3%	1	9	11.1%	-0.52
20.0..30	0%	0	3	0.0%	-1.00
30.1+	0%	0	0	0.0%	0.00
Not Compl	0%	0	0	0.0%	0.00
Unraced	0%	0	2	0.0%	-1.00

ANALYSIS BY RUN NUMBER

Run No	Prop	Win	Runs	Wins%	£
FTO	0%	0	2	0.0%	-1.00
2nd Run	14%	5	31	16.1%	0.47
3rd Run	23%	8	51	15.7%	-0.29
4th+ Run	63%	22	142	15.5%	0.07

ANALYSIS BY POSITION LAST TIME

Pos LT	Prop	Win	Runs	Wins%	£
Won	60%	21	114	18.4%	0.08
2nd or 3rd	20%	7	50	14.0%	-0.11
Unplaced	20%	7	60	11.7%	0.11
Not Compl	0%	0	2	0.0%	-1.00

OTHER FACTORS (WINS-RUNS, £)

Course Winner:	5-30	£1.03
Distance Winner:	17-117	-£0.03
Going Winner:	13-72	£0.30
Beaten Favourite:	4-23	-£0.13
BHA Top Rated:	5-38	£0.16
Up in class:	25-178	-£0.03
Same class:	9-41	£0.45
Down in class:	1-5	-£0.42
7-Day Winners:	0-1	-£1.00
Colts and Geldings:	24-149	£0.16
Fillies:	0-3	-£1.00
Absolute Favourites:	10-33	-£0.35

TRAINERS (WINS-RUNS, £)

M R Channon 2-12 £1.99; K A Ryan 2-11 £1.36; R Hannon 2-18 £0.19.

All Group Races

2-Y.O Races: All Group Races – 8 to 14 runners

ANALYSIS BY BHA RATING

Rating	Prop	Win	Runs	Wins%	£
120..139	0%	0	1	0.0%	-1.00
110..119	2%	2	22	9.1%	-0.66
100..109	23%	26	197	13.2%	-0.05
90..99	12%	14	189	7.4%	-0.07
70..89	4%	5	125	4.0%	-0.35
50..69	0%	0	2	0.0%	-1.00
..49	0%	0	0	0.0%	0.00
Unrated	58%	66	648	10.2%	-0.34

ANALYSIS BY WEIGHT CARRIED

Weight	Prop	Win	Runs	Wins%	£
10-01+	0%	0	0	0.0%	0.00
9-8..10-00	0%	0	0	0.0%	0.00
9-0..9-07	35%	39	407	9.6%	-0.43
8-8..8-13	65%	74	777	9.5%	-0.17
8-0..8-07	0%	0	0	0.0%	0.00
..7-13	0%	0	0	0.0%	0.00

ANALYSIS BY DAYS SINCE LAST RUN

Days	Prop	Win	Runs	Wins%	£
1..7	4%	5	37	13.5%	0.00
8..14	15%	17	214	7.9%	-0.50
15..28	47%	53	512	10.4%	-0.11
29..60	26%	29	347	8.4%	-0.39
61..100	6%	7	48	14.6%	0.17
101+	0%	0	10	0.0%	-1.00
Unraced	2%	2	16	12.5%	-0.28

ANALYSIS BY TODAY'S STARTING PRICE

Price	Prop	Win	Runs	Wins%	£
Odds On	4%	5	10	50.0%	-0.13
Ev-2/1	14%	16	47	34.0%	-0.12
9/4-4/1	33%	37	141	26.2%	0.07
9/2-6/1	12%	13	124	10.5%	-0.36
13/2-10/1	19%	22	232	9.5%	-0.12
11/1-16/1	10%	11	241	4.6%	-0.34
18/1-33/1	8%	9	229	3.9%	0.03
40/1+	0%	0	160	0.0%	-1.00

ANALYSIS BY STARTING PRICE LAST TIME

Price	Prop	Win	Runs	Wins%	£
Odds On	13%	15	117	12.8%	-0.22
Ev-2/1	18%	20	159	12.6%	-0.10
9/4-4/1	23%	26	246	10.6%	-0.41
9/2-6/1	15%	17	153	11.1%	-0.09
13/2-10/1	9%	10	203	4.9%	-0.53
11/1-16/1	12%	13	144	9.0%	0.10
18/1-33/1	6%	7	110	6.4%	-0.47
40/1+	3%	3	36	8.3%	0.00
Unraced	2%	2	16	12.5%	-0.28

ANALYSIS BY DISTANCE BEATEN LAST TIME

Lengths	Prop	Win	Runs	Wins%	£
..-10	1%	1	5	20.0%	-0.25
-10..0	51%	58	553	10.5%	-0.36
0.1..2	27%	31	243	12.8%	0.24
2.1..5	12%	13	180	7.2%	-0.30
5.1..10	4%	4	134	3.0%	-0.74
10.1..20	4%	4	48	8.3%	0.01
20.0..30	0%	0	3	0.0%	-1.00
30.1+	0%	0	2	0.0%	-1.00
Not Compl	0%	0	0	0.0%	0.00
Unraced	2%	2	16	12.5%	-0.28

ANALYSIS BY RUN NUMBER

Run No	Prop	Win	Runs	Wins%	£
FTO	2%	2	16	12.5%	-0.28
2nd Run	16%	18	163	11.0%	-0.37
3rd Run	30%	34	305	11.1%	-0.12
4th+ Run	52%	59	700	8.4%	-0.29

ANALYSIS BY POSITION LAST TIME

Pos LT	Prop	Win	Runs	Wins%	£
Won	52%	59	558	10.6%	-0.36
2nd or 3rd	31%	35	283	12.4%	0.08
Unplaced	15%	17	326	5.2%	-0.37
Not Compl	2%	2	17	11.8%	-0.32

OTHER FACTORS (WINS-RUNS, £)

Course Winner:	12-117	-£0.10
Distance Winner:	64-641	-£0.34
Going Winner:	36-355	-£0.16
Beaten Favourite:	16-88	£0.26
BHA Top Rated:	19-99	£0.58
Up in class:	80-912	-£0.26
Same class:	23-180	-£0.16
Down in class:	8-76	-£0.45
7-Day Winners:	4-19	£0.47
Colts and Geldings:	64-664	-£0.28
Fillies:	6-55	-£0.39
Absolute Favourites:	38-106	£0.08

TRAINERS (WINS-RUNS, £)

P W Chapple-Hyam 6-26 £0.98; R Hannon 12-96 £0.22; J S Bolger 4-10 £1.85; B Smart 3-26 £0.66; A P Jarvis 1-13 £1.00; C G Cox 2-12 £0.63; M Johnston 6-39 £0.18; P F I Cole 3-23 £0.21; M A Jarvis 3-15 £0.18; J Noseda 6-30 £0.08; E J O'Neill 1-16 £0.06.

Race Profiles

2-Y.O Races: All Group Races – 15 runners or more

ANALYSIS BY BHA RATING

Rating	Prop	Win	Runs	Wins%	£
120..139	0%	0	0	0.0%	0.00
110..119	5%	1	8	12.5%	0.38
100..109	10%	2	29	6.9%	-0.41
90..99	10%	2	23	8.7%	-0.39
70..89	0%	0	15	0.0%	-1.00
50..69	0%	0	0	0.0%	0.00
..49	0%	0	0	0.0%	0.00
Unrated	75%	15	273	5.5%	-0.24

ANALYSIS BY WEIGHT CARRIED

Weight	Prop	Win	Runs	Wins%	£
10-01+	0%	0	0	0.0%	0.00
9-8..10-00	0%	0	0	0.0%	0.00
9-0..9-07	45%	9	136	6.6%	-0.37
8-8..8-13	55%	11	212	5.2%	-0.23
8-0..8-07	0%	0	0	0.0%	0.00
..7-13	0%	0	0	0.0%	0.00

ANALYSIS BY DAYS SINCE LAST RUN

Days	Prop	Win	Runs	Wins%	£
1..7	0%	0	11	0.0%	-1.00
8..14	5%	1	62	1.6%	-0.66
15..28	35%	7	144	4.9%	-0.18
29..60	50%	10	105	9.5%	-0.13
61..100	10%	2	18	11.1%	0.11
101+	0%	0	2	0.0%	-1.00
Unraced	0%	0	6	0.0%	-1.00

ANALYSIS BY TODAY'S STARTING PRICE

Price	Prop	Win	Runs	Wins%	£
Odds On	0%	0	0	0.0%	0.00
Ev-2/1	5%	1	5	20.0%	-0.52
9/4-4/1	25%	5	22	22.7%	0.08
9/2-6/1	20%	4	23	17.4%	0.13
13/2-10/1	20%	4	44	9.1%	-0.16
11/1-16/1	10%	2	63	3.2%	-0.54
18/1-33/1	15%	3	90	3.3%	-0.10
40/1+	5%	1	101	1.0%	-0.50

ANALYSIS BY STARTING PRICE LAST TIME

Price	Prop	Win	Runs	Wins%	£
Odds On	20%	4	34	11.8%	-0.10
Ev-2/1	30%	6	48	12.5%	0.69
9/4-4/1	20%	4	71	5.6%	-0.34
9/2-6/1	10%	2	44	4.5%	-0.11
13/2-10/1	10%	2	50	4.0%	-0.24
11/1-16/1	5%	1	39	2.6%	-0.79
18/1-33/1	5%	1	40	2.5%	-0.84
40/1+	0%	0	16	0.0%	-1.00
Unraced	0%	0	6	0.0%	-1.00

ANALYSIS BY DISTANCE BEATEN LAST TIME

Lengths	Prop	Win	Runs	Wins%	£
..-10	0%	0	1	0.0%	-1.00
-10..0	55%	11	157	7.0%	-0.40
0.1..2	20%	4	72	5.6%	-0.26
2.1..5	25%	5	64	7.8%	0.60
5.1..10	0%	0	31	0.0%	-1.00
10.1..20	0%	0	13	0.0%	-1.00
20.0..30	0%	0	4	0.0%	-1.00
30.1+	0%	0	0	0.0%	0.00
Not Compl	0%	0	0	0.0%	0.00
Unraced	0%	0	6	0.0%	-1.00

ANALYSIS BY RUN NUMBER

Run No	Prop	Win	Runs	Wins%	£
FTO	0%	0	6	0.0%	-1.00
2nd Run	15%	3	72	4.2%	-0.75
3rd Run	45%	9	102	8.8%	0.43
4th+ Run	40%	8	168	4.8%	-0.48

ANALYSIS BY POSITION LAST TIME

Pos LT	Prop	Win	Runs	Wins%	£
Won	55%	11	158	7.0%	-0.40
2nd or 3rd	25%	5	99	5.1%	0.05
Unplaced	20%	4	85	4.7%	-0.39
Not Compl	0%	0	6	0.0%	-1.00

OTHER FACTORS (WINS-RUNS, £)

Course Winner:	1-20	-£0.65
Distance Winner:	12-186	-£0.45
Going Winner:	6-104	-£0.22
Beaten Favourite:	3-29	£2.17
BHA Top Rated:	1-6	£0.83
Up in class:	17-303	-£0.22
Same class:	2-19	-£0.53
Down in class:	1-20	-£0.70
7-Day Winners:	0-1	-£1.00
Colts and Geldings:	7-111	-£0.60
Fillies:	1-30	-£0.70
Absolute Favourites:	4-18	-£0.10

TRAINERS (WINS-RUNS, £)

M R Channon 3-17 £3.00; A P O'Brien 2-19 £0.99; K A Ryan 2-10 £0.25.

All Group Races

2-Y.O Races: All Group Races – good or faster going

ANALYSIS BY BHA RATING

Rating	Prop	Win	Runs	Wins%	£
120..139	0%	0	0	0.0%	0.00
110..119	3%	3	26	11.5%	-0.52
100..109	19%	21	155	13.5%	-0.17
90..99	7%	8	127	6.3%	-0.14
70..89	5%	6	99	6.1%	0.03
50..69	0%	0	3	0.0%	-1.00
..49	0%	0	0	0.0%	0.00
Unrated	66%	74	788	9.4%	-0.31

ANALYSIS BY WEIGHT CARRIED

Weight	Prop	Win	Runs	Wins%	£
10-01+	0%	0	0	0.0%	0.00
9-8..10-00	0%	0	0	0.0%	0.00
9-0..9-07	38%	42	456	9.2%	-0.38
8-8..8-13	63%	70	742	9.4%	-0.17
8-0..8-07	0%	0	0	0.0%	0.00
..7-13	0%	0	0	0.0%	0.00

ANALYSIS BY DAYS SINCE LAST RUN

Days	Prop	Win	Runs	Wins%	£
1..7	1%	1	36	2.8%	-0.83
8..14	13%	14	191	7.3%	-0.42
15..28	48%	54	557	9.7%	-0.15
29..60	29%	32	338	9.5%	-0.31
61..100	8%	9	54	16.7%	0.21
101+	0%	0	5	0.0%	-1.00
Unraced	2%	2	17	11.8%	-0.32

ANALYSIS BY TODAY'S STARTING PRICE

Price	Prop	Win	Runs	Wins%	£
Odds On	7%	8	13	61.5%	0.08
Ev-2/1	13%	15	52	28.8%	-0.24
9/4-4/1	33%	37	132	28.0%	0.19
9/2-6/1	12%	13	129	10.1%	-0.37
13/2-10/1	17%	19	207	9.2%	-0.17
11/1-16/1	8%	9	223	4.0%	-0.41
18/1-33/1	10%	11	241	4.6%	0.26
40/1+	0%	0	201	0.0%	-1.00

ANALYSIS BY STARTING PRICE LAST TIME

Price	Prop	Win	Runs	Wins%	£
Odds On	13%	15	116	12.9%	-0.17
Ev-2/1	20%	22	174	12.6%	-0.11
9/4-4/1	23%	26	255	10.2%	-0.29
9/2-6/1	17%	19	151	12.6%	-0.01
13/2-10/1	7%	8	196	4.1%	-0.48
11/1-16/1	12%	13	136	9.6%	0.08
18/1-33/1	5%	6	120	5.0%	-0.59
40/1+	1%	1	33	3.0%	-0.73
Unraced	2%	2	17	11.8%	-0.32

ANALYSIS BY DISTANCE BEATEN LAST TIME

Lengths	Prop	Win	Runs	Wins%	£
..-10	1%	1	5	20.0%	-0.25
-10..0	51%	57	578	9.9%	-0.33
0.1..2	28%	31	245	12.7%	0.14
2.1..5	13%	14	183	7.7%	-0.14
5.1..10	4%	4	110	3.6%	-0.74
10.1..20	3%	3	50	6.0%	-0.34
20.0..30	0%	0	9	0.0%	-1.00
30.1+	0%	0	1	0.0%	-1.00
Not Compl	0%	0	0	0.0%	0.00
Unraced	2%	2	17	11.8%	-0.32

ANALYSIS BY RUN NUMBER

Run No	Prop	Win	Runs	Wins%	£
FTO	2%	2	17	11.8%	-0.32
2nd Run	18%	20	206	9.7%	-0.40
3rd Run	34%	38	337	11.3%	-0.06
4th+ Run	46%	52	638	8.2%	-0.30

ANALYSIS BY POSITION LAST TIME

Pos LT	Prop	Win	Runs	Wins%	£
Won	52%	58	583	9.9%	-0.33
2nd or 3rd	32%	36	301	12.0%	-0.00
Unplaced	14%	16	297	5.4%	-0.33
Not Compl	2%	2	17	11.8%	-0.32

OTHER FACTORS (WINS-RUNS, £)

Course Winner:	11-109	£0.15
Distance Winner:	62-654	-£0.32
Going Winner:	49-448	-£0.00
Beaten Favourite:	16-92	£0.40
BHA Top Rated:	14-76	£0.46
Up in class:	82-972	-£0.23
Same class:	22-157	-£0.25
Down in class:	6-52	-£0.49
7-Day Winners:	1-15	-£0.60
Colts and Geldings:	59-598	-£0.31
Fillies:	5-44	-£0.41
Absolute Favourites:	37-107	£0.04

TRAINERS (WINS-RUNS, £)

M R Channon 8-69 £0.39; B Smart 2-24 £0.63; A P Jarvis 1-13 £1.00; J S Bolger 2-10 £1.27; R Hannon 12-106 £0.10; E A L Dunlop 1-13 £0.31; A P O'Brien 5-54 £0.06; M Johnston 7-35 £0.08; E J O'Neill 1-16 £0.06; J Noseda 7-42 £0.01.

Race Profiles

2-Y.O Races: All Group Races – good to soft or softer going

ANALYSIS BY BHA RATING

Rating	Prop	Win	Runs	Wins%	£
120..139	0%	0	1	0.0%	-1.00
110..119	2%	1	14	7.1%	-0.21
100..109	30%	17	119	14.3%	0.16
90..99	18%	10	119	8.4%	-0.17
70..89	4%	2	65	3.1%	-0.85
50..69	0%	0	0	0.0%	0.00
..49	0%	0	0	0.0%	0.00
Unrated	46%	26	242	10.7%	-0.15

ANALYSIS BY WEIGHT CARRIED

Weight	Prop	Win	Runs	Wins%	£
10-01+	0%	0	0	0.0%	0.00
9-8..10-00	0%	0	0	0.0%	0.00
9-0..9-07	32%	18	161	11.2%	-0.29
8-8..8-13	68%	38	399	9.5%	-0.12
8-0..8-07	0%	0	0	0.0%	0.00
..7-13	0%	0	0	0.0%	0.00

ANALYSIS BY DAYS SINCE LAST RUN

Days	Prop	Win	Runs	Wins%	£
1..7	9%	5	20	25.0%	1.60
8..14	16%	9	123	7.3%	-0.52
15..28	41%	23	209	11.0%	0.07
29..60	29%	16	168	9.5%	-0.36
61..100	5%	3	25	12.0%	-0.08
101+	0%	0	8	0.0%	-1.00
Unraced	0%	0	7	0.0%	-1.00

ANALYSIS BY TODAY'S STARTING PRICE

Price	Prop	Win	Runs	Wins%	£
Odds On	4%	2	6	33.3%	-0.52
Ev-2/1	13%	7	23	30.4%	-0.26
9/4-4/1	29%	16	71	22.5%	-0.08
9/2-6/1	18%	10	60	16.7%	0.05
13/2-10/1	16%	9	107	8.4%	-0.20
11/1-16/1	14%	8	118	6.8%	-0.05
18/1-33/1	5%	3	102	2.9%	-0.33
40/1+	2%	1	73	1.4%	-0.30

ANALYSIS BY STARTING PRICE LAST TIME

Price	Prop	Win	Runs	Wins%	£
Odds On	14%	8	63	12.7%	-0.32
Ev-2/1	18%	10	75	13.3%	0.39
9/4-4/1	21%	12	96	12.5%	-0.25
9/2-6/1	14%	8	84	9.5%	-0.10
13/2-10/1	14%	8	93	8.6%	-0.46
11/1-16/1	7%	4	71	5.6%	-0.39
18/1-33/1	7%	4	48	8.3%	0.01
40/1+	4%	2	23	8.7%	0.17
Unraced	0%	0	7	0.0%	-1.00

ANALYSIS BY DISTANCE BEATEN LAST TIME

Lengths	Prop	Win	Runs	Wins%	£
..-10	0%	0	2	0.0%	-1.00
-10..0	59%	33	245	13.5%	-0.24
0.1..2	18%	10	116	8.6%	-0.04
2.1..5	11%	6	97	6.2%	-0.06
5.1..10	9%	5	71	7.0%	-0.21
10.1..20	4%	2	20	10.0%	-0.03
20.0..30	0%	0	1	0.0%	-1.00
30.1+	0%	0	1	0.0%	-1.00
Not Compl	0%	0	0	0.0%	0.00
Unraced	0%	0	7	0.0%	-1.00

ANALYSIS BY RUN NUMBER

Run No	Prop	Win	Runs	Wins%	£
FTO	0%	0	7	0.0%	-1.00
2nd Run	11%	6	60	10.0%	-0.27
3rd Run	23%	13	121	10.7%	0.12
4th+ Run	66%	37	372	9.9%	-0.23

ANALYSIS BY POSITION LAST TIME

Pos LT	Prop	Win	Runs	Wins%	£
Won	59%	33	247	13.4%	-0.24
2nd or 3rd	20%	11	131	8.4%	0.17
Unplaced	21%	12	174	6.9%	-0.28
Not Compl	0%	0	8	0.0%	-1.00

OTHER FACTORS (WINS-RUNS, £)

Course Winner:	7-58	-£0.19
Distance Winner:	31-290	-£0.33
Going Winner:	6-83	-£0.69
Beaten Favourite:	7-48	£0.96
BHA Top Rated:	11-67	£0.50
Up in class:	40-421	-£0.20
Same class:	12-83	£0.24
Down in class:	4-49	-£0.52
7-Day Winners:	3-6	£2.67
Colts and Geldings:	36-326	-£0.14
Fillies:	2-44	-£0.61
Absolute Favourites:	15-50	-£0.18

TRAINERS (WINS-RUNS, £)

M R Channon 3-33 £1.15; K A Ryan 4-21 £1.10; E J O'Neill 3-12 £1.67; P W Chapple-Hyam 3-19 £1.01; A P O'Brien 8-33 £0.32; S Kirk 2-10 £0.10; Sir Michael Stoute 2-12 £0.07.

All Group Races

2-Y.O Races: All Group Races – 5 to 6 furlong races

ANALYSIS BY BHA RATING

Rating	Prop	Win	Runs	Wins%	£
120..139	0%	0	0	0.0%	0.00
110..119	3%	3	20	15.0%	-0.01
100..109	26%	22	141	15.6%	-0.02
90..99	6%	5	94	5.3%	-0.55
70..89	3%	3	66	4.5%	-0.34
50..69	0%	0	2	0.0%	-1.00
..49	0%	0	0	0.0%	0.00
Unrated	62%	53	666	8.0%	-0.38

ANALYSIS BY WEIGHT CARRIED

Weight	Prop	Win	Runs	Wins%	£
10-01+	0%	0	0	0.0%	0.00
9-8..10-00	0%	0	0	0.0%	0.00
9-0..9-07	29%	25	292	8.6%	-0.57
8-8..8-13	71%	61	697	8.8%	-0.23
8-0..8-07	0%	0	0	0.0%	0.00
..7-13	0%	0	0	0.0%	0.00

ANALYSIS BY DAYS SINCE LAST RUN

Days	Prop	Win	Runs	Wins%	£
1..7	2%	2	42	4.8%	-0.69
8..14	13%	11	182	6.0%	-0.54
15..28	42%	36	420	8.6%	-0.26
29..60	31%	27	282	9.6%	-0.33
61..100	9%	8	40	20.0%	0.26
101+	0%	0	7	0.0%	-1.00
Unraced	2%	2	16	12.5%	-0.28

ANALYSIS BY TODAY'S STARTING PRICE

Price	Prop	Win	Runs	Wins%	£
Odds On	6%	5	8	62.5%	0.16
Ev-2/1	14%	12	41	29.3%	-0.23
9/4-4/1	33%	28	97	28.9%	0.23
9/2-6/1	16%	14	98	14.3%	-0.11
13/2-10/1	14%	12	154	7.8%	-0.27
11/1-16/1	12%	10	198	5.1%	-0.28
18/1-33/1	5%	4	212	1.9%	-0.50
40/1+	1%	1	181	0.6%	-0.72

ANALYSIS BY STARTING PRICE LAST TIME

Price	Prop	Win	Runs	Wins%	£
Odds On	15%	13	96	13.5%	-0.20
Ev-2/1	21%	18	142	12.7%	0.14
9/4-4/1	28%	24	204	11.8%	-0.26
9/2-6/1	9%	8	132	6.1%	-0.70
13/2-10/1	8%	7	144	4.9%	-0.57
11/1-16/1	9%	8	117	6.8%	-0.10
18/1-33/1	6%	5	104	4.8%	-0.57
40/1+	1%	1	34	2.0%	-0.82
Unraced	2%	2	16	12.5%	-0.28

ANALYSIS BY DISTANCE BEATEN LAST TIME

Lengths	Prop	Win	Runs	Wins%	£
..-10	1%	1	3	33.3%	0.25
-10..0	52%	45	428	10.5%	-0.33
0.1..2	24%	21	202	10.4%	-0.10
2.1..5	13%	11	176	6.3%	-0.32
5.1..10	5%	4	112	3.6%	-0.68
10.1..20	2%	2	45	4.4%	-0.59
20.0..30	0%	0	7	0.0%	-1.00
30.1+	0%	0	0	0.0%	0.00
Not Compl	0%	0	0	0.0%	0.00
Unraced	2%	2	16	12.5%	-0.28

ANALYSIS BY RUN NUMBER

Run No	Prop	Win	Runs	Wins%	£
FTO	2%	2	16	12.5%	-0.28
2nd Run	14%	12	145	8.3%	-0.62
3rd Run	33%	28	252	11.1%	0.18
4th+ Run	51%	44	576	7.6%	-0.49

ANALYSIS BY POSITION LAST TIME

Pos LT	Prop	Win	Runs	Wins%	£
Won	53%	46	431	10.7%	-0.32
2nd or 3rd	24%	21	249	8.4%	-0.17
Unplaced	20%	17	293	5.8%	-0.50
Not Compl	2%	2	16	12.5%	-0.28

OTHER FACTORS (WINS-RUNS, £)

Course Winner:	7-69	-£0.28
Distance Winner:	58-609	-£0.36
Going Winner:	27-325	-£0.54
Beaten Favourite:	10-86	£0.37
BHA Top Rated:	11-61	£0.59
Up in class:	59-779	-£0.36
Same class:	20-130	-£0.04
Down in class:	5-64	-£0.63
7-Day Winners:	1-15	-£0.73
Colts and Geldings:	45-476	-£0.45
Fillies:	6-74	-£0.49
Absolute Favourites:	29-80	£0.14

TRAINERS (WINS-RUNS, £)

M R Channon 6-64 £0.35; B Smart 4-27 £0.79; A P Jarvis 1-10 £1.60; M Johnston 4-19 £0.46; E J O'Neill 2-17 £0.47; K A Ryan 6-40 £0.03; J Noseda 6-37 £0.02.

Race Profiles

2-Y.O Races: All Group Races – 7 to 8 furlong races

ANALYSIS BY BHA RATING

Rating	Prop	Win	Runs	Wins%	£
120..139	0%	0	1	0.0%	-1.00
110..119	1%	1	20	5.0%	-0.81
100..109	20%	16	133	12.0%	-0.03
90..99	16%	13	152	8.6%	0.10
70..89	6%	5	98	5.1%	-0.31
50..69	0%	0	1	0.0%	-1.00
..49	0%	0	0	0.0%	0.00
Unrated	57%	47	364	12.9%	-0.07

ANALYSIS BY WEIGHT CARRIED

Weight	Prop	Win	Runs	Wins%	£
10-01+	0%	0	0	0.0%	0.00
9-8..10-00	0%	0	0	0.0%	0.00
9-0..9-07	43%	35	325	10.8%	-0.17
8-8..8-13	57%	47	444	10.6%	-0.02
8-0..8-07	0%	0	0	0.0%	0.00
..7-13	0%	0	0	0.0%	0.00

ANALYSIS BY DAYS SINCE LAST RUN

Days	Prop	Win	Runs	Wins%	£
1..7	5%	4	14	28.6%	2.21
8..14	15%	12	132	9.1%	-0.35
15..28	50%	41	346	11.8%	0.12
29..60	26%	21	224	9.4%	-0.34
61..100	5%	4	39	10.3%	-0.03
101+	0%	0	6	0.0%	-1.00
Unraced	0%	0	8	0.0%	-1.00

ANALYSIS BY TODAY'S STARTING PRICE

Price	Prop	Win	Runs	Wins%	£
Odds On	6%	5	11	45.5%	-0.30
Ev-2/1	12%	10	34	29.4%	-0.26
9/4-4/1	30%	25	106	23.6%	-0.03
9/2-6/1	11%	9	91	9.9%	-0.37
13/2-10/1	20%	16	160	10.0%	-0.09
11/1-16/1	9%	7	143	4.9%	-0.29
18/1-33/1	12%	10	131	7.6%	1.02
40/1+	0%	0	93	0.0%	-1.00

ANALYSIS BY STARTING PRICE LAST TIME

Price	Prop	Win	Runs	Wins%	£
Odds On	12%	10	83	12.0%	-0.25
Ev-2/1	17%	14	107	13.1%	-0.09
9/4-4/1	17%	14	147	9.5%	-0.31
9/2-6/1	23%	19	103	18.4%	0.80
13/2-10/1	11%	9	145	6.2%	-0.38
11/1-16/1	11%	9	90	10.0%	-0.05
18/1-33/1	6%	5	64	7.8%	-0.18
40/1+	2%	2	22	9.1%	0.36
Unraced	0%	0	8	0.0%	-1.00

ANALYSIS BY DISTANCE BEATEN LAST TIME

Lengths	Prop	Win	Runs	Wins%	£
..-10	0%	0	4	0.0%	-1.00
-10..0	55%	45	395	11.4%	-0.28
0.1..2	24%	20	159	12.6%	0.32
2.1..5	11%	9	104	8.7%	0.24
5.1..10	6%	5	69	7.2%	-0.30
10.1..20	4%	3	25	12.0%	0.36
20.0..30	0%	0	3	0.0%	-1.00
30.1+	0%	0	2	0.0%	-1.00
Not Compl	0%	0	0	0.0%	0.00
Unraced	0%	0	8	0.0%	-1.00

ANALYSIS BY RUN NUMBER

Run No	Prop	Win	Runs	Wins%	£
FTO	0%	0	8	0.0%	-1.00
2nd Run	17%	14	121	11.6%	-0.08
3rd Run	28%	23	206	11.2%	-0.25
4th+ Run	55%	45	434	10.4%	0.01

ANALYSIS BY POSITION LAST TIME

Pos LT	Prop	Win	Runs	Wins%	£
Won	55%	45	399	11.3%	-0.29
2nd or 3rd	32%	26	183	14.2%	0.34
Unplaced	13%	11	178	6.2%	-0.01
Not Compl	0%	0	9	0.0%	-1.00

OTHER FACTORS (WINS-RUNS, £)

Course Winner:	11-98	£0.26
Distance Winner:	35-335	-£0.27
Going Winner:	28-206	£0.56
Beaten Favourite:	13-54	£0.94
BHA Top Rated:	14-82	£0.39
Up in class:	63-614	-£0.05
Same class:	14-110	-£0.13
Down in class:	5-37	-£0.27
7-Day Winners:	3-6	£3.00
Colts and Geldings:	50-448	-£0.04
Fillies:	1-14	-£0.64
Absolute Favourites:	23-77	-£0.21

TRAINERS (WINS-RUNS, £)

R Hannon 6-57 £0.75; M R Channon 5-38 £1.13; A P O'Brien 10-59 £0.53; P W Chapple-Hyam 2-14 £1.57; J S Bolger 4-13 £1.24; E J O'Neill 2-11 £1.18; K A Ryan 1-12 £0.75; M A Jarvis 3-13 £0.37; S Kirk 2-10 £0.10; J H M Gosden 8-28 £0.00.

Listed Races

2-Y.O Races: Listed Races

ANALYSIS BY BHA RATING

Rating	Prop	Win	Runs	Wins%	£
120..139	0%	0	0	0.0%	0.00
110..119	0%	0	1	0.0%	-1.00
100..109	16%	22	78	28.2%	0.01
90..99	11%	15	213	7.0%	-0.50
70..89	16%	21	293	7.2%	0.12
50..69	0%	0	10	0.0%	-1.00
..49	0%	0	0	0.0%	0.00
Unrated	57%	76	744	10.2%	-0.09

ANALYSIS BY WEIGHT CARRIED

Weight	Prop	Win	Runs	Wins%	£
10-01+	0%	0	0	0.0%	0.00
9-8..10-00	0%	0	0	0.0%	0.00
9-0..9-07	46%	61	494	12.3%	0.17
8-8..8-13	51%	69	782	8.8%	-0.29
8-0..8-07	3%	4	61	6.6%	-0.03
..7-13	0%	0	2	0.0%	-1.00

ANALYSIS BY DAYS SINCE LAST RUN

Days	Prop	Win	Runs	Wins%	£
1..7	4%	6	77	7.8%	-0.61
8..14	28%	37	322	11.5%	-0.11
15..28	46%	61	590	10.3%	-0.08
29..60	19%	26	266	9.8%	0.01
61..100	1%	2	38	5.3%	-0.29
101+	0%	0	9	0.0%	-1.00
Unraced	1%	2	37	5.4%	0.03

ANALYSIS BY TODAY'S STARTING PRICE

Price	Prop	Win	Runs	Wins%	£
Odds On	4%	6	14	42.9%	-0.31
Ev-2/1	19%	25	71	35.2%	-0.12
9/4-4/1	25%	34	160	21.3%	-0.08
9/2-6/1	19%	26	147	17.7%	0.06
13/2-10/1	14%	19	259	7.3%	-0.32
11/1-16/1	8%	11	243	4.5%	-0.29
18/1-33/1	7%	9	252	3.6%	-0.09
40/1+	3%	4	193	2.1%	0.21

ANALYSIS BY STARTING PRICE LAST TIME

Price	Prop	Win	Runs	Wins%	£
Odds On	7%	10	74	13.5%	-0.32
Ev-2/1	10%	13	152	8.6%	-0.52
9/4-4/1	22%	30	245	12.2%	0.30
9/2-6/1	18%	24	176	13.6%	0.10
13/2-10/1	19%	25	228	11.0%	-0.13
11/1-16/1	10%	14	178	7.9%	-0.61
18/1-33/1	10%	13	180	7.2%	-0.06
40/1+	2%	3	69	4.3%	0.13
Unraced	1%	2	37	5.4%	0.03

ANALYSIS BY DISTANCE BEATEN LAST TIME

Lengths	Prop	Win	Runs	Wins%	£
..-10	0%	0	0	0.0%	0.00
-10..0	51%	68	524	13.0%	-0.16
0.1..2	18%	24	241	10.0%	-0.21
2.1..5	22%	30	259	11.6%	0.47
5.1..10	6%	8	189	4.2%	-0.43
10.1..20	1%	2	68	2.9%	-0.54
20.0..30	0%	0	13	0.0%	-1.00
30.1+	0%	0	8	0.0%	-1.00
Not Compl	0%	0	0	0.0%	0.00
Unraced	1%	2	37	5.4%	0.03

ANALYSIS BY RUN NUMBER

Run No	Prop	Win	Runs	Wins%	£
FTO	1%	2	37	5.4%	0.03
2nd Run	21%	28	238	11.8%	-0.34
3rd Run	25%	33	305	10.8%	0.14
4th+ Run	53%	71	759	9.4%	-0.15

ANALYSIS BY POSITION LAST TIME

Pos LT	Prop	Win	Runs	Wins%	£
Won	51%	68	524	13.0%	-0.16
2nd or 3rd	22%	29	319	9.1%	0.07
Unplaced	26%	35	457	7.7%	-0.19
Not Compl	1%	2	39	5.1%	-0.03

OTHER FACTORS (WINS-RUNS, £)

Course Winner:	6-54	-£0.31
Distance Winner:	82-665	-£0.06
Going Winner:	36-321	-£0.05
Beaten Favourite:	7-90	-£0.52
BHA Top Rated:	17-73	-£0.22
Up in class:	85-954	-£0.18
Same class:	14-166	-£0.09
Down in class:	33-182	£0.17
7-Day Winners:	2-21	-£0.60
Colts and Geldings:	75-670	£0.08
Fillies:	17-229	-£0.49
Absolute Favourites:	40-122	-£0.09

TRAINERS (WINS-RUNS, £)

J R Best 1-15 £5.73; J S Moore 3-18 £2.25; C E Brittain 4-22 £1.07; B Smart 7-29 £0.74; S Kirk 3-15 £1.17; P W Chapple-Hyam 4-13 £1.12; M A Jarvis 3-15 £0.53; R Hannon 19-104 £0.07; E J O'Neill 1-15 £0.40; K R Burke 3-32 £0.17; K A Ryan 5-46 £0.09; J H M Gosden 3-16 £0.13; J L Dunlop 3-14 £0.01.

Race Profiles

2-Y.O Races: Listed Races – 2 to 7 runners

ANALYSIS BY BHA RATING

Rating	Prop	Win	Runs	Wins%	£
120..139	0%	0	0	0.0%	0.00
110..119	0%	0	0	0.0%	0.00
100..109	17%	6	14	42.9%	0.34
90..99	6%	2	38	5.3%	-0.53
70..89	14%	5	33	15.2%	0.29
50..69	0%	0	1	0.0%	-1.00
..49	0%	0	0	0.0%	0.00
Unrated	63%	22	132	16.7%	-0.18

ANALYSIS BY WEIGHT CARRIED

Weight	Prop	Win	Runs	Wins%	£
10-01+	0%	0	0	0.0%	0.00
9-8..10-00	0%	0	0	0.0%	0.00
9-0..9-07	71%	25	123	20.3%	-0.03
8-8..8-13	26%	9	91	9.9%	-0.36
8-0..8-07	3%	1	4	25.0%	1.50
..7-13	0%	0	0	0.0%	0.00

ANALYSIS BY DAYS SINCE LAST RUN

Days	Prop	Win	Runs	Wins%	£
1..7	6%	2	19	10.5%	-0.16
8..14	26%	9	51	17.6%	0.07
15..28	51%	18	97	18.6%	-0.06
29..60	17%	6	42	14.3%	-0.40
61..100	0%	0	5	0.0%	-1.00
101+	0%	0	0	0.0%	0.00
Unraced	0%	0	4	0.0%	-1.00

ANALYSIS BY TODAY'S STARTING PRICE

Price	Prop	Win	Runs	Wins%	£
Odds On	14%	5	8	62.5%	-0.02
Ev-2/1	29%	10	26	38.5%	-0.07
9/4-4/1	14%	5	43	11.6%	-0.52
9/2-6/1	17%	6	32	18.8%	0.11
13/2-10/1	17%	6	40	15.0%	0.35
11/1-16/1	9%	3	37	8.1%	0.22
18/1-33/1	0%	0	26	0.0%	-1.00
40/1+	0%	0	6	0.0%	-1.00

ANALYSIS BY STARTING PRICE LAST TIME

Price	Prop	Win	Runs	Wins%	£
Odds On	9%	3	9	33.3%	-0.29
Ev-2/1	9%	3	26	11.5%	-0.47
9/4-4/1	26%	9	40	22.5%	0.29
9/2-6/1	17%	6	31	19.4%	0.16
13/2-10/1	23%	8	39	20.5%	0.08
11/1-16/1	9%	3	33	9.1%	-0.68
18/1-33/1	6%	2	24	8.3%	-0.29
40/1+	3%	1	12	8.3%	-0.17
Unraced	0%	0	4	0.0%	-1.00

ANALYSIS BY DISTANCE BEATEN LAST TIME

Lengths	Prop	Win	Runs	Wins%	£
..-10	0%	0	0	0.0%	0.00
-10..0	69%	24	104	23.1%	0.00
0.1..2	17%	6	35	17.1%	-0.35
2.1..5	9%	3	35	8.6%	0.29
5.1..10	6%	2	23	8.7%	-0.33
10.1..20	0%	0	15	0.0%	-1.00
20.0..30	0%	0	0	0.0%	0.00
30.1+	0%	0	2	0.0%	-1.00
Not Compl	0%	0	0	0.0%	0.00
Unraced	0%	0	4	0.0%	-1.00

ANALYSIS BY RUN NUMBER

Run No	Prop	Win	Runs	Wins%	£
FTO	0%	0	4	0.0%	-1.00
2nd Run	26%	9	38	23.7%	-0.45
3rd Run	23%	8	51	15.7%	0.13
4th+ Run	51%	18	125	14.4%	-0.13

ANALYSIS BY POSITION LAST TIME

Pos LT	Prop	Win	Runs	Wins%	£
Won	69%	24	104	23.1%	0.00
2nd or 3rd	20%	7	47	14.9%	-0.15
Unplaced	11%	4	63	6.3%	-0.31
Not Compl	0%	0	4	0.0%	-1.00

OTHER FACTORS (WINS-RUNS, £)

Course Winner:	3-14	£0.36
Distance Winner:	25-106	£0.03
Going Winner:	10-62	-£0.11
Beaten Favourite:	2-11	£0.48
BHA Top Rated:	3-16	-£0.53
Up in class:	28-155	-£0.01
Same class:	2-25	-£0.70
Down in class:	5-34	-£0.24
7-Day Winners:	1-8	-£0.38
Colts and Geldings:	29-154	£0.00
Fillies:	3-43	-£0.42
Absolute Favourites:	14-35	-£0.17

TRAINERS (WINS-RUNS, £)

R Hannon 8-26 £0.34; M R Channon 2-17 £0.26.

Listed Races

2-Y.O Races: Listed Races – 8 to 14 runners

ANALYSIS BY BHA RATING

Rating	Prop	Win	Runs	Wins%	£
120..139	0%	0	0	0.0%	0.00
110..119	0%	0	1	0.0%	-1.00
100..109	17%	15	52	28.8%	0.04
90..99	15%	13	145	9.0%	-0.39
70..89	15%	13	188	6.9%	0.14
50..69	0%	0	6	0.0%	-1.00
..49	0%	0	0	0.0%	0.00
Unrated	53%	46	482	9.5%	-0.33

ANALYSIS BY WEIGHT CARRIED

Weight	Prop	Win	Runs	Wins%	£
10-01+	0%	0	0	0.0%	0.00
9-8..10-00	0%	0	0	0.0%	0.00
9-0..9-07	33%	29	243	11.9%	-0.18
8-8..8-13	66%	57	613	9.3%	-0.23
8-0..8-07	1%	1	18	5.6%	-0.39
..7-13	0%	0	0	0.0%	0.00

ANALYSIS BY DAYS SINCE LAST RUN

Days	Prop	Win	Runs	Wins%	£
1..7	5%	4	46	8.7%	-0.69
8..14	30%	26	210	12.4%	-0.06
15..28	41%	36	380	9.5%	-0.16
29..60	22%	19	179	10.6%	-0.21
61..100	1%	1	23	4.3%	-0.74
101+	0%	0	6	0.0%	-1.00
Unraced	1%	1	30	3.3%	-0.87

ANALYSIS BY TODAY'S STARTING PRICE

Price	Prop	Win	Runs	Wins%	£
Odds On	1%	1	6	16.7%	-0.70
Ev-2/1	17%	15	42	35.7%	0.17
9/4-4/1	32%	28	105	26.7%	0.17
9/2-6/1	22%	19	106	17.9%	0.08
13/2-10/1	14%	12	186	6.5%	-0.40
11/1-16/1	7%	6	169	3.6%	-0.42
18/1-33/1	5%	4	160	2.5%	-0.36
40/1+	2%	2	100	2.0%	-0.08

ANALYSIS BY STARTING PRICE LAST TIME

Price	Prop	Win	Runs	Wins%	£
Odds On	8%	7	44	15.9%	0.00
Ev-2/1	11%	10	95	10.5%	-0.37
9/4-4/1	17%	15	162	9.3%	-0.43
9/2-6/1	18%	16	120	13.3%	-0.07
13/2-10/1	18%	16	145	11.0%	-0.12
11/1-16/1	13%	11	110	10.0%	-0.46
18/1-33/1	11%	10	124	8.1%	0.05
40/1+	1%	1	44	2.3%	0.16
Unraced	1%	1	30	3.3%	-0.87

ANALYSIS BY DISTANCE BEATEN LAST TIME

Lengths	Prop	Win	Runs	Wins%	£
..-10	0%	0	0	0.0%	0.00
-10..0	47%	41	347	11.8%	-0.19
0.1..2	18%	16	159	10.1%	-0.07
2.1..5	26%	23	170	13.5%	0.02
5.1..10	6%	5	121	4.1%	-0.47
10.1..20	1%	1	36	2.8%	-0.72
20.0..30	0%	0	6	0.0%	-1.00
30.1+	0%	0	5	0.0%	-1.00
Not Compl	0%	0	0	0.0%	0.00
Unraced	1%	1	30	3.3%	-0.87

ANALYSIS BY RUN NUMBER

Run No	Prop	Win	Runs	Wins%	£
FTO	1%	1	30	3.3%	-0.87
2nd Run	20%	17	175	9.7%	-0.37
3rd Run	23%	20	196	10.2%	-0.38
4th+ Run	56%	49	473	10.4%	-0.06

ANALYSIS BY POSITION LAST TIME

Pos LT	Prop	Win	Runs	Wins%	£
Won	47%	41	347	11.8%	-0.19
2nd or 3rd	21%	18	202	8.9%	-0.22
Unplaced	31%	27	294	9.2%	-0.19
Not Compl	1%	1	31	3.2%	-0.87

OTHER FACTORS (WINS-RUNS, £)

Course Winner:	3-33	-£0.45
Distance Winner:	52-431	-£0.05
Going Winner:	23-177	£0.08
Beaten Favourite:	5-52	-£0.47
BHA Top Rated:	13-51	-£0.15
Up in class:	51-612	-£0.28
Same class:	10-106	£0.10
Down in class:	25-126	-£0.04
7-Day Winners:	1-11	-£0.68
Colts and Geldings:	36-332	-£0.19
Fillies:	12-123	-£0.39
Absolute Favourites:	25-76	£0.02

TRAINERS (WINS-RUNS, £)

C E Brittain 3-16 £1.44; K A Ryan 4-28 £0.70; K R Burke 3-22 £0.70; P W Chapple-Hyam 3-10 £0.75; B Smart 6-14 £0.52; J H M Gosden 2-12 £0.38; Saeed Bin Suroor 3-13 £0.06; H R A Cecil 3-13 £0.04.

Race Profiles

2-Y.O Races: Listed Races – 15 runners or more

ANALYSIS BY BHA RATING

Rating	Prop	Win	Runs	Wins%	£
120..139	0%	0	0	0.0%	0.00
110..119	0%	0	0	0.0%	0.00
100..109	8%	1	12	8.3%	-0.46
90..99	0%	0	30	0.0%	-1.00
70..89	25%	3	72	4.2%	-0.01
50..69	0%	0	3	0.0%	-1.00
..49	0%	0	0	0.0%	0.00
Unrated	67%	8	130	6.2%	0.87

ANALYSIS BY WEIGHT CARRIED

Weight	Prop	Win	Runs	Wins%	£
10-01+	0%	0	0	0.0%	0.00
9-8..10-00	0%	0	0	0.0%	0.00
9-0..9-07	58%	7	128	5.5%	1.02
8-8..8-13	25%	3	78	3.8%	-0.70
8-0..8-07	17%	2	39	5.1%	-0.03
..7-13	0%	0	2	0.0%	-1.00

ANALYSIS BY DAYS SINCE LAST RUN

Days	Prop	Win	Runs	Wins%	£
1..7	0%	0	12	0.0%	-1.00
8..14	17%	2	61	3.3%	-0.46
15..28	58%	7	113	6.2%	0.16
29..60	8%	1	45	2.2%	1.24
61..100	8%	1	10	10.0%	1.10
101+	0%	0	3	0.0%	-1.00
Unraced	8%	1	3	33.3%	10.33

ANALYSIS BY TODAY'S STARTING PRICE

Price	Prop	Win	Runs	Wins%	£
Odds On	0%	0	0	0.0%	0.00
Ev-2/1	0%	0	3	0.0%	-1.00
9/4-4/1	8%	1	12	8.3%	-0.69
9/2-6/1	8%	1	9	11.1%	-0.28
13/2-10/1	8%	1	33	3.0%	-0.70
11/1-16/1	17%	2	37	5.4%	-0.19
18/1-33/1	42%	5	66	7.6%	0.94
40/1+	17%	2	87	2.3%	0.63

ANALYSIS BY STARTING PRICE LAST TIME

Price	Prop	Win	Runs	Wins%	£
Odds On	0%	0	21	0.0%	-1.00
Ev-2/1	0%	0	31	0.0%	-1.00
9/4-4/1	50%	6	43	14.0%	3.06
9/2-6/1	17%	2	25	8.0%	0.79
13/2-10/1	8%	1	44	2.3%	-0.34
11/1-16/1	0%	0	35	0.0%	-1.00
18/1-33/1	8%	1	32	3.1%	-0.34
40/1+	8%	1	13	7.7%	0.31
Unraced	8%	1	3	33.3%	10.33

ANALYSIS BY DISTANCE BEATEN LAST TIME

Lengths	Prop	Win	Runs	Wins%	£
..-10	0%	0	0	0.0%	0.00
-10..0	25%	3	73	4.1%	-0.25
0.1..2	17%	2	47	4.3%	-0.59
2.1..5	33%	4	54	7.4%	2.00
5.1..10	8%	1	45	2.2%	-0.36
10.1..20	8%	1	17	5.9%	0.24
20.0..30	0%	0	7	0.0%	-1.00
30.1+	0%	0	1	0.0%	-1.00
Not Compl	0%	0	0	0.0%	0.00
Unraced	8%	1	3	33.3%	10.33

ANALYSIS BY RUN NUMBER

Run No	Prop	Win	Runs	Wins%	£
FTO	8%	1	3	33.3%	10.33
2nd Run	17%	2	25	8.0%	-0.01
3rd Run	42%	5	58	8.6%	1.90
4th+ Run	33%	4	161	2.5%	-0.42

ANALYSIS BY POSITION LAST TIME

Pos LT	Prop	Win	Runs	Wins%	£
Won	25%	3	73	4.1%	-0.25
2nd or 3rd	33%	4	70	5.7%	1.05
Unplaced	33%	4	100	4.0%	-0.12
Not Compl	8%	1	4	25.0%	7.50

OTHER FACTORS (WINS-RUNS, £)

Course Winner:	0-7	-£1.00
Distance Winner:	5-128	-£0.16
Going Winner:	3-82	-£0.30
Beaten Favourite:	0-27	-£1.00
BHA Top Rated:	1-6	£0.08
Up in class:	6-187	£0.03
Same class:	2-35	-£0.21
Down in class:	3-22	£2.05
7-Day Winners:	0-2	-£1.00
Colts and Geldings:	10-184	£0.65
Fillies:	2-63	-£0.73
Absolute Favourites:	1-11	-£0.66

TRAINERS (WINS-RUNS, £)

B Smart 1-12 £1.42.

JUVENILE RACES

Listed Races

2-Y.O Races: Listed Races – good or faster going

ANALYSIS BY BHA RATING
Rating	Prop	Win	Runs	Wins%	£
120..139	0%	0	0	0.0%	0.00
110..119	0%	0	1	0.0%	-1.00
100..109	13%	11	41	26.8%	0.05
90..99	9%	8	127	6.3%	-0.46
70..89	11%	10	177	5.6%	0.10
50..69	0%	0	5	0.0%	-1.00
..49	0%	0	0	0.0%	0.00
Unrated	67%	59	592	10.0%	-0.01

ANALYSIS BY WEIGHT CARRIED
Weight	Prop	Win	Runs	Wins%	£
10-01+	0%	0	0	0.0%	0.00
9-8..10-00	0%	0	0	0.0%	0.00
9-0..9-07	47%	41	374	11.0%	0.33
8-8..8-13	50%	44	508	8.7%	-0.32
8-0..8-07	3%	3	59	5.1%	-0.17
..7-13	0%	0	2	0.0%	-1.00

ANALYSIS BY DAYS SINCE LAST RUN
Days	Prop	Win	Runs	Wins%	£
1..7	6%	5	45	11.1%	-0.37
8..14	28%	25	238	10.5%	-0.11
15..28	45%	40	428	9.3%	-0.05
29..60	17%	15	167	9.0%	0.09
61..100	1%	1	26	3.8%	-0.19
101+	0%	0	8	0.0%	-1.00
Unraced	2%	2	31	6.5%	0.23

ANALYSIS BY TODAY'S STARTING PRICE
Price	Prop	Win	Runs	Wins%	£
Odds On	3%	3	8	37.5%	-0.41
Ev-2/1	18%	16	44	36.4%	-0.07
9/4-4/1	25%	22	106	20.8%	-0.10
9/2-6/1	18%	16	95	16.8%	0.03
13/2-10/1	14%	12	181	6.6%	-0.39
11/1-16/1	9%	8	160	5.0%	-0.21
18/1-33/1	8%	7	193	3.6%	-0.05
40/1+	5%	4	156	2.6%	0.50

ANALYSIS BY STARTING PRICE LAST TIME
Price	Prop	Win	Runs	Wins%	£
Odds On	9%	8	59	13.6%	-0.23
Ev-2/1	8%	7	114	6.1%	-0.68
9/4-4/1	17%	15	172	8.7%	0.35
9/2-6/1	18%	16	116	13.8%	0.06
13/2-10/1	19%	17	159	10.7%	-0.13
11/1-16/1	10%	9	123	7.3%	-0.65
18/1-33/1	14%	12	122	9.8%	0.36
40/1+	2%	2	47	4.3%	0.45
Unraced	2%	2	31	6.5%	0.23

ANALYSIS BY DISTANCE BEATEN LAST TIME
Lengths	Prop	Win	Runs	Wins%	£
..-10	0%	0	0	0.0%	0.00
-10..0	49%	43	369	11.7%	-0.21
0.1..2	17%	15	164	9.1%	-0.21
2.1..5	22%	19	177	10.7%	0.68
5.1..10	8%	7	143	4.9%	-0.28
10.1..20	2%	2	47	4.3%	-0.34
20.0..30	0%	0	8	0.0%	-1.00
30.1+	0%	0	4	0.0%	-1.00
Not Compl	0%	0	0	0.0%	0.00
Unraced	2%	2	31	6.5%	0.23

ANALYSIS BY RUN NUMBER
Run No	Prop	Win	Runs	Wins%	£
FTO	2%	2	31	6.5%	0.23
2nd Run	23%	20	169	11.8%	-0.26
3rd Run	25%	22	232	9.5%	0.14
4th+ Run	50%	44	511	8.6%	0.09

ANALYSIS BY POSITION LAST TIME
Pos LT	Prop	Win	Runs	Wins%	£
Won	49%	43	369	11.7%	-0.21
2nd or 3rd	20%	18	228	7.9%	0.11
Unplaced	28%	25	313	8.0%	-0.02
Not Compl	2%	2	33	6.1%	0.15

OTHER FACTORS (WINS-RUNS, £)
Course Winner:	3-34	-£0.44
Distance Winner:	55-464	£0.01
Going Winner:	25-269	-£0.04
Beaten Favourite:	4-65	-£0.56
BHA Top Rated:	9-37	-£0.22
Up in class:	55-676	-£0.18
Same class:	9-111	£0.18
Down in class:	22-125	£0.32
7-Day Winners:	2-14	-£0.39
Colts and Geldings:	54-530	£0.19
Fillies:	11-166	-£0.57
Absolute Favourites:	27-80	-£0.03

TRAINERS (WINS-RUNS, £)
J R Best 1-13 £6.77; J S Moore 3-13 £3.50; B Smart 5-22 £1.03; S Kirk 3-12 £1.71; K R Burke 2-21 £0.52; J H M Gosden 3-13 £0.39; C E Brittain 2-13 £0.15.

Race Profiles

2-Y.O Races: Listed Races – good to soft or softer going

ANALYSIS BY BHA RATING

Rating	Prop	Win	Runs	Wins%	£
120..139	0%	0	0	0.0%	0.00
110..119	0%	0	0	0.0%	0.00
100..109	24%	11	37	29.7%	-0.02
90..99	15%	7	86	8.1%	-0.55
70..89	24%	11	116	9.5%	0.15
50..69	0%	0	5	0.0%	-1.00
..49	0%	0	0	0.0%	0.00
Unrated	37%	17	152	11.2%	-0.41

ANALYSIS BY WEIGHT CARRIED

Weight	Prop	Win	Runs	Wins%	£
10-01+	0%	0	0	0.0%	0.00
9-8..10-00	0%	0	0	0.0%	0.00
9-0..9-07	43%	20	120	16.7%	-0.34
8-8..8-13	54%	25	274	9.1%	-0.24
8-0..8-07	2%	1	2	50.0%	4.00
..7-13	0%	0	0	0.0%	0.00

ANALYSIS BY DAYS SINCE LAST RUN

Days	Prop	Win	Runs	Wins%	£
1..7	2%	1	32	3.1%	-0.94
8..14	26%	12	84	14.3%	-0.14
15..28	46%	21	162	13.0%	-0.18
29..60	24%	11	99	11.1%	-0.14
61..100	2%	1	12	8.3%	-0.50
101+	0%	0	1	0.0%	-1.00
Unraced	0%	0	6	0.0%	-1.00

ANALYSIS BY TODAY'S STARTING PRICE

Price	Prop	Win	Runs	Wins%	£
Odds On	7%	3	6	50.0%	-0.18
Ev-2/1	20%	9	27	33.3%	-0.19
9/4-4/1	26%	12	54	22.2%	-0.04
9/2-6/1	22%	10	52	19.2%	0.13
13/2-10/1	15%	7	78	9.0%	-0.16
11/1-16/1	7%	3	83	3.6%	-0.43
18/1-33/1	4%	2	59	3.4%	-0.20
40/1+	0%	0	37	0.0%	-1.00

ANALYSIS BY STARTING PRICE LAST TIME

Price	Prop	Win	Runs	Wins%	£
Odds On	4%	2	15	13.3%	-0.68
Ev-2/1	13%	6	38	15.8%	-0.02
9/4-4/1	33%	15	73	20.5%	0.16
9/2-6/1	17%	8	60	13.3%	0.16
13/2-10/1	17%	8	69	11.6%	-0.11
11/1-16/1	11%	5	55	9.1%	-0.50
18/1-33/1	2%	1	58	1.7%	-0.97
40/1+	2%	1	22	4.5%	-0.55
Unraced	0%	0	6	0.0%	-1.00

ANALYSIS BY DISTANCE BEATEN LAST TIME

Lengths	Prop	Win	Runs	Wins%	£
..-10	0%	0	0	0.0%	0.00
-10..0	54%	25	155	16.1%	-0.04
0.1..2	20%	9	77	11.7%	-0.21
2.1..5	24%	11	82	13.4%	0.01
5.1..10	2%	1	46	2.2%	-0.88
10.1..20	0%	0	21	0.0%	-1.00
20.0..30	0%	0	5	0.0%	-1.00
30.1+	0%	0	4	0.0%	-1.00
Not Compl	0%	0	0	0.0%	0.00
Unraced	0%	0	6	0.0%	-1.00

ANALYSIS BY RUN NUMBER

Run No	Prop	Win	Runs	Wins%	£
FTO	0%	0	6	0.0%	-1.00
2nd Run	17%	8	69	11.6%	-0.53
3rd Run	24%	11	73	15.1%	0.12
4th+ Run	59%	27	248	10.9%	-0.26

ANALYSIS BY POSITION LAST TIME

Pos LT	Prop	Win	Runs	Wins%	£
Won	54%	25	155	16.1%	-0.04
2nd or 3rd	24%	11	91	12.1%	-0.04
Unplaced	22%	10	144	6.9%	-0.57
Not Compl	0%	0	6	0.0%	-1.00

OTHER FACTORS (WINS-RUNS, £)

Course Winner:	3-20	-£0.10
Distance Winner:	27-201	-£0.21
Going Winner:	11-52	-£0.13
Beaten Favourite:	3-25	-£0.41
BHA Top Rated:	8-36	-£0.21
Up in class:	30-278	-£0.18
Same class:	5-55	-£0.63
Down in class:	11-57	-£0.15
7-Day Winners:	0-7	-£1.00
Colts and Geldings:	21-140	-£0.32
Fillies:	6-63	-£0.28
Absolute Favourites:	13-42	-£0.21

TRAINERS (WINS-RUNS, £)

R Hannon 9-25 £0.83; K A Ryan 2-14 £0.89.

Listed Races

2-Y.O Races: Listed Races – 5 to 6 furlong races

ANALYSIS BY BHA RATING

Rating	Prop	Win	Runs	Wins%	£
120..139	0%	0	0	0.0%	0.00
110..119	0%	0	1	0.0%	-1.00
100..109	17%	14	48	29.2%	-0.02
90..99	13%	11	155	7.1%	-0.49
70..89	13%	11	193	5.7%	0.18
50..69	0%	0	6	0.0%	-1.00
..49	0%	0	0	0.0%	0.00
Unrated	57%	48	495	9.7%	-0.02

ANALYSIS BY WEIGHT CARRIED

Weight	Prop	Win	Runs	Wins%	£
10-01+	0%	0	0	0.0%	0.00
9-8..10-00	0%	0	0	0.0%	0.00
9-0..9-07	48%	40	338	11.8%	0.34
8-8..8-13	50%	42	506	8.3%	-0.31
8-0..8-07	2%	2	52	3.8%	-0.27
..7-13	0%	0	2	0.0%	-1.00

ANALYSIS BY DAYS SINCE LAST RUN

Days	Prop	Win	Runs	Wins%	£
1..7	6%	5	61	8.2%	-0.69
8..14	32%	27	239	11.3%	-0.06
15..28	46%	39	393	9.9%	-0.06
29..60	12%	10	151	6.6%	0.08
61..100	1%	1	26	3.8%	-0.19
101+	0%	0	9	0.0%	-1.00
Unraced	2%	2	19	10.5%	1.00

ANALYSIS BY TODAY'S STARTING PRICE

Price	Prop	Win	Runs	Wins%	£
Odds On	5%	4	9	44.4%	-0.27
Ev-2/1	23%	19	45	42.2%	0.07
9/4-4/1	24%	20	94	21.3%	-0.10
9/2-6/1	17%	14	92	15.2%	-0.10
13/2-10/1	10%	8	163	4.9%	-0.54
11/1-16/1	10%	8	170	4.7%	-0.26
18/1-33/1	8%	7	173	4.0%	0.05
40/1+	5%	4	152	2.6%	0.54

ANALYSIS BY STARTING PRICE LAST TIME

Price	Prop	Win	Runs	Wins%	£
Odds On	8%	7	49	14.3%	-0.13
Ev-2/1	6%	5	96	5.2%	-0.76
9/4-4/1	24%	20	170	11.8%	0.31
9/2-6/1	19%	16	111	14.4%	0.25
13/2-10/1	18%	15	162	9.3%	-0.28
11/1-16/1	10%	8	120	6.7%	-0.66
18/1-33/1	11%	9	127	7.1%	0.16
40/1+	2%	2	44	4.5%	0.55
Unraced	2%	2	19	10.5%	1.00

ANALYSIS BY DISTANCE BEATEN LAST TIME

Lengths	Prop	Win	Runs	Wins%	£
..-10	0%	0	0	0.0%	0.00
-10..0	45%	38	317	12.0%	-0.24
0.1..2	20%	17	171	9.9%	-0.08
2.1..5	23%	19	182	10.4%	0.54
5.1..10	7%	6	142	4.2%	-0.37
10.1..20	2%	2	50	4.0%	-0.38
20.0..30	0%	0	11	0.0%	-1.00
30.1+	0%	0	6	0.0%	-1.00
Not Compl	0%	0	0	0.0%	0.00
Unraced	2%	2	19	10.5%	1.00

ANALYSIS BY RUN NUMBER

Run No	Prop	Win	Runs	Wins%	£
FTO	2%	2	19	10.5%	1.00
2nd Run	17%	14	127	11.0%	-0.36
3rd Run	21%	18	197	9.1%	0.18
4th+ Run	60%	50	555	9.0%	-0.12

ANALYSIS BY POSITION LAST TIME

Pos LT	Prop	Win	Runs	Wins%	£
Won	45%	38	317	12.0%	-0.24
2nd or 3rd	23%	19	223	8.5%	0.16
Unplaced	30%	25	337	7.4%	-0.11
Not Compl	2%	2	21	9.5%	0.81

OTHER FACTORS (WINS-RUNS, £)

Course Winner:	1-30	-£0.82
Distance Winner:	63-539	-£0.05
Going Winner:	28-221	£0.13
Beaten Favourite:	5-71	-£0.68
BHA Top Rated:	13-39	£0.12
Up in class:	49-622	-£0.18
Same class:	11-127	£0.06
Down in class:	22-130	£0.22
7-Day Winners:	2-14	-£0.39
Colts and Geldings:	48-441	£0.25
Fillies:	7-157	-£0.75
Absolute Favourites:	29-78	£0.01

TRAINERS (WINS-RUNS, £)

J R Best 1-13 £6.77; J S Moore 2-13 £2.65; B Smart 5-23 £0.74; K R Burke 3-29 £0.29; E J O'Neill 1-13 £0.62; Tom Dascombe 2-13 £0.29; B W Hills 2-12 £0.21.

Race Profiles

2-Y.O Races: Listed Races – 7 to 8 furlong races

ANALYSIS BY BHA RATING

Rating	Prop	Win	Runs	Wins%	£
120..139	0%	0	0	0.0%	0.00
110..119	0%	0	0	0.0%	0.00
100..109	17%	8	30	26.7%	0.06
90..99	8%	4	57	7.0%	-0.52
70..89	19%	9	91	9.9%	-0.01
50..69	0%	0	4	0.0%	-1.00
..49	0%	0	0	0.0%	0.00
Unrated	56%	27	244	11.1%	-0.24

ANALYSIS BY WEIGHT CARRIED

Weight	Prop	Win	Runs	Wins%	£
10-01+	0%	0	0	0.0%	0.00
9-8..10-00	0%	0	0	0.0%	0.00
9-0..9-07	42%	20	149	13.4%	-0.19
8-8..8-13	56%	27	269	10.0%	-0.24
8-0..8-07	2%	1	8	12.5%	0.38
..7-13	0%	0	0	0.0%	0.00

ANALYSIS BY DAYS SINCE LAST RUN

Days	Prop	Win	Runs	Wins%	£
1..7	2%	1	15	6.7%	-0.27
8..14	19%	9	76	11.8%	-0.28
15..28	44%	21	193	10.9%	-0.17
29..60	33%	16	113	14.2%	-0.08
61..100	2%	1	11	9.1%	-0.45
101+	0%	0	0	0.0%	0.00
Unraced	0%	0	18	0.0%	-1.00

ANALYSIS BY TODAY'S STARTING PRICE

Price	Prop	Win	Runs	Wins%	£
Odds On	4%	2	4	50.0%	-0.24
Ev-2/1	13%	6	26	23.1%	-0.43
9/4-4/1	27%	13	65	20.0%	-0.12
9/2-6/1	25%	12	52	23.1%	0.41
13/2-10/1	21%	10	90	11.1%	0.01
11/1-16/1	6%	3	70	4.3%	-0.33
18/1-33/1	4%	2	79	2.5%	-0.38
40/1+	0%	0	40	0.0%	-1.00

ANALYSIS BY STARTING PRICE LAST TIME

Price	Prop	Win	Runs	Wins%	£
Odds On	6%	3	25	12.0%	-0.69
Ev-2/1	17%	8	54	14.8%	-0.07
9/4-4/1	19%	9	72	12.5%	0.25
9/2-6/1	17%	8	65	12.3%	-0.17
13/2-10/1	21%	10	62	16.1%	0.34
11/1-16/1	13%	6	56	10.7%	-0.48
18/1-33/1	8%	4	52	7.7%	-0.61
40/1+	0%	0	22	0.0%	-1.00
Unraced	0%	0	18	0.0%	-1.00

ANALYSIS BY DISTANCE BEATEN LAST TIME

Lengths	Prop	Win	Runs	Wins%	£
..-10	0%	0	0	0.0%	0.00
-10..	60%	29	200	14.5%	-0.06
0.1..2	15%	7	67	10.4%	-0.51
2.1..5	21%	10	74	13.5%	0.29
5.1..10	4%	2	47	4.3%	-0.60
10.1..20	0%	0	16	0.0%	-1.00
20.0..30	0%	0	2	0.0%	-1.00
30.1+	0%	0	2	0.0%	-1.00
Not Compl	0%	0	0	0.0%	0.00
Unraced	0%	0	18	0.0%	-1.00

ANALYSIS BY RUN NUMBER

Run No	Prop	Win	Runs	Wins%	£
FTO	0%	0	18	0.0%	-1.00
2nd Run	29%	14	110	12.7%	-0.31
3rd Run	27%	13	102	12.7%	-0.02
4th+ Run	44%	21	196	10.7%	-0.19

ANALYSIS BY POSITION LAST TIME

Pos LT	Prop	Win	Runs	Wins%	£
Won	60%	29	200	14.5%	-0.06
2nd or 3rd	19%	9	93	9.7%	-0.18
Unplaced	21%	10	115	8.7%	-0.39
Not Compl	0%	0	18	0.0%	-1.00

OTHER FACTORS (WINS-RUNS, £)

Course Winner:	4-23	£0.15
Distance Winner:	19-125	-£0.06
Going Winner:	8-97	-£0.44
Beaten Favourite:	2-18	£0.17
BHA Top Rated:	4-32	-£0.58
Up in class:	35-319	-£0.16
Same class:	2-37	-£0.66
Down in class:	11-52	£0.06
7-Day Winners:	0-6	-£1.00
Colts and Geldings:	26-217	-£0.21
Fillies:	9-69	-£0.03
Absolute Favourites:	10-42	-£0.36

TRAINERS (WINS-RUNS, £)

C E Brittain 2-13 £1.50; R Hannon 6-38 £0.38; M R Channon 5-30 £0.27; J H M Gosden 3-12 £0.51; J L Dunlop 3-10 £0.41; H R A Cecil 3-10 £0.35; S Kirk 2-10 £0.15; B J Meehan 2-10 £0.10.

Conditions Stakes

2-Y.O Races: Conditions Stakes

ANALYSIS BY BHA RATING

Rating	Prop	Win	Runs	Wins%	£
120..139	0%	0	0	0.0%	0.00
110..119	0%	0	0	0.0%	0.00
100..109	3%	13	43	30.2%	-0.14
90..99	8%	34	204	16.7%	-0.24
70..89	14%	63	505	12.5%	-0.18
50..69	0%	1	63	1.6%	-0.86
..49	0%	0	9	0.0%	-1.00
Unrated	75%	326	2428	13.4%	-0.17

ANALYSIS BY WEIGHT CARRIED

Weight	Prop	Win	Runs	Wins%	£
10-01+	0%	0	0	0.0%	0.00
9-8..10-00	0%	1	11	9.1%	-0.27
9-0..9-07	44%	192	926	20.7%	-0.07
8-8..8-13	45%	197	1572	12.5%	-0.20
8-0..8-07	11%	47	698	6.7%	-0.30
..7-13	0%	0	45	0.0%	-1.00

ANALYSIS BY DAYS SINCE LAST RUN

Days	Prop	Win	Runs	Wins%	£
1..7	8%	34	204	16.7%	-0.26
8..14	27%	118	709	16.6%	-0.04
15..28	35%	153	1087	14.1%	-0.31
29..60	18%	78	574	13.6%	-0.28
61..100	3%	12	99	12.1%	0.38
101+	0%	1	22	4.5%	-0.94
Unraced	9%	41	557	7.4%	-0.12

ANALYSIS BY TODAY'S STARTING PRICE

Price	Prop	Win	Runs	Wins%	£
Odds On	19%	85	141	60.3%	-0.06
Ev-2/1	23%	101	279	36.2%	-0.10
9/4-4/1	24%	104	519	20.0%	-0.20
9/2-6/1	11%	48	303	15.8%	-0.00
13/2-10/1	13%	58	465	12.5%	0.12
11/1-16/1	4%	19	441	4.3%	-0.37
18/1-33/1	4%	17	535	3.2%	-0.28
40/1+	1%	5	569	0.9%	-0.41

ANALYSIS BY STARTING PRICE LAST TIME

Price	Prop	Win	Runs	Wins%	£
Odds On	9%	38	147	25.9%	0.29
Ev-2/1	14%	59	259	22.8%	-0.14
9/4-4/1	19%	84	523	16.1%	-0.27
9/2-6/1	13%	55	291	18.9%	0.03
13/2-10/1	14%	63	473	13.3%	-0.12
11/1-16/1	10%	44	379	11.6%	-0.42
18/1-33/1	8%	36	362	9.9%	-0.18
40/1+	4%	17	261	6.5%	-0.61
Unraced	9%	41	557	7.4%	-0.12

ANALYSIS BY DISTANCE BEATEN LAST TIME

Lengths	Prop	Win	Runs	Wins%	£
..-10	0%	0	3	0.0%	-1.00
-10..0	44%	194	895	21.7%	-0.11
0.1..2	18%	77	405	19.0%	-0.11
2.1..5	16%	71	460	15.4%	-0.16
5.1..10	9%	40	510	7.8%	-0.39
10.1..20	3%	12	320	3.8%	-0.23
20.0..30	0%	1	75	1.3%	-0.72
30.1+	0%	1	27	3.7%	-0.74
Not Compl	0%	0	0	0.0%	0.00
Unraced	9%	41	557	7.4%	-0.12

ANALYSIS BY RUN NUMBER

Run No	Prop	Win	Runs	Wins%	£
FTO	9%	41	557	7.4%	-0.12
2nd Run	31%	134	678	19.8%	-0.20
3rd Run	23%	100	660	15.2%	-0.03
4th+ Run	37%	162	1357	11.9%	-0.30

ANALYSIS BY POSITION LAST TIME

Pos LT	Prop	Win	Runs	Wins%	£
Won	44%	194	899	21.6%	-0.11
2nd or 3rd	23%	101	583	17.3%	-0.08
Unplaced	23%	101	1212	8.3%	-0.35
Not Compl	9%	41	558	7.3%	-0.12

OTHER FACTORS (WINS-RUNS, £)

Course Winner:	24-134	-£0.45
Distance Winner:	194-1061	-£0.16
Going Winner:	87-474	-£0.24
Beaten Favourite:	36-199	-£0.20
BHA Top Rated:	37-163	-£0.34
Up in class:	179-1452	-£0.24
Same class:	97-612	-£0.17
Down in class:	120-631	-£0.17
7-Day Winners:	17-57	£0.09
Colts and Geldings:	305-2090	-£0.18
Fillies:	83-757	-£0.22
Absolute Favourites:	183-416	-£0.05

TRAINERS (WINS-RUNS, £)

G M Moore 2-18 £3.28; R M Beckett 4-35 £1.22; A P Jarvis 1-18 £1.83; B J Meehan 15-95 £0.34; J H M Gosden 6-27 £1.05; A M Balding 8-40 £0.66; M P Tregoning 5-18 £1.19; J G Portman 3-16 £1.23; M W Easterby 3-15 £1.30; G G Margarson 2-13 £1.46; J R Jenkins 2-12 £1.43; W J Haggas 7-24 £0.59; Eve JohnsonHoughton 3-10 £1.25; R Hannon 53-283 £0.04; T P Tate 1-13 £0.62; P D Evans 14-61 £0.13; T D Easterby 5-56 £0.12; Mrs L Stubbs 4-22 £0.23; J Noseda 8-26 £0.17; Mrs A Duffield 6-20 £0.20

Race Profiles

2-Y.O Races: Conditions Stakes – 2 to 7 runners

ANALYSIS BY BHA RATING

Rating	Prop	Win	Runs	Wins%	£
120..139	0%	0	0	0.0%	0.00
110..119	0%	0	0	0.0%	0.00
100..109	3%	9	23	39.1%	-0.04
90..99	8%	24	110	21.8%	-0.18
70..89	14%	44	218	20.2%	-0.10
50..69	0%	0	13	0.0%	-1.00
..49	0%	0	5	0.0%	-1.00
Unrated	75%	230	1273	18.1%	-0.08

ANALYSIS BY WEIGHT CARRIED

Weight	Prop	Win	Runs	Wins%	£
10-01+	0%	0	0	0.0%	0.00
9-8..10-00	0%	1	10	10.0%	-0.20
9-0..9-07	48%	148	574	25.8%	-0.09
8-8..8-13	42%	130	761	17.1%	-0.07
8-0..8-07	9%	28	289	9.7%	-0.16
..7-13	0%	0	8	0.0%	-1.00

ANALYSIS BY DAYS SINCE LAST RUN

Days	Prop	Win	Runs	Wins%	£
1..7	7%	23	105	21.9%	-0.06
8..14	26%	81	376	21.5%	-0.11
15..28	38%	116	559	20.8%	-0.20
29..60	17%	51	269	19.0%	-0.26
61..100	3%	9	45	20.0%	1.23
101+	0%	1	9	11.1%	-0.85
Unraced	8%	26	279	9.3%	0.08

ANALYSIS BY TODAY'S STARTING PRICE

Price	Prop	Win	Runs	Wins%	£
Odds On	24%	74	121	61.2%	-0.06
Ev-2/1	26%	81	225	36.0%	-0.12
9/4-4/1	23%	71	363	19.6%	-0.23
9/2-6/1	9%	28	165	17.0%	0.09
13/2-10/1	11%	35	250	14.0%	0.26
11/1-16/1	3%	10	191	5.2%	-0.26
18/1-33/1	2%	6	192	3.1%	-0.31
40/1+	1%	2	135	1.5%	-0.13

ANALYSIS BY STARTING PRICE LAST TIME

Price	Prop	Win	Runs	Wins%	£
Odds On	9%	27	77	35.1%	0.27
Ev-2/1	15%	46	138	33.3%	-0.05
9/4-4/1	16%	50	250	20.0%	-0.35
9/2-6/1	12%	38	160	23.8%	-0.16
13/2-10/1	15%	47	230	20.4%	-0.12
11/1-16/1	11%	34	195	17.4%	-0.15
18/1-33/1	8%	26	185	14.1%	0.13
40/1+	4%	13	128	10.2%	-0.41
Unraced	8%	26	279	9.3%	0.08

ANALYSIS BY DISTANCE BEATEN LAST TIME

Lengths	Prop	Win	Runs	Wins%	£
..-10	0%	0	2	0.0%	-1.00
-10..0	46%	142	524	27.1%	-0.13
0.1..2	17%	52	177	29.4%	0.15
2.1..5	16%	48	240	20.0%	-0.05
5.1..10	10%	32	236	13.6%	-0.18
10.1..20	2%	6	131	4.6%	-0.28
20.0..30	0%	0	37	0.0%	-1.00
30.1+	0%	1	16	6.3%	-0.56
Not Compl	0%	0	0	0.0%	0.00
Unraced	8%	26	279	9.3%	0.08

ANALYSIS BY RUN NUMBER

Run No	Prop	Win	Runs	Wins%	£
FTO	8%	26	279	9.3%	0.08
2nd Run	33%	102	423	24.1%	-0.08
3rd Run	21%	66	358	18.4%	-0.26
4th+ Run	37%	113	582	19.4%	-0.10

ANALYSIS BY POSITION LAST TIME

Pos LT	Prop	Win	Runs	Wins%	£
Won	46%	142	526	27.0%	-0.14
2nd or 3rd	23%	71	271	26.2%	0.13
Unplaced	22%	68	565	12.0%	-0.26
Not Compl	8%	26	280	9.3%	0.08

OTHER FACTORS (WINS-RUNS, £)

Course Winner:	16-79	-£0.45
Distance Winner:	133-557	-£0.14
Going Winner:	63-245	-£0.06
Beaten Favourite:	23-86	-£0.08
BHA Top Rated:	33-109	-£0.14
Up in class:	121-641	-£0.27
Same class:	69-346	£0.04
Down in class:	91-376	-£0.06
7-Day Winners:	13-30	£0.46
Colts and Geldings:	213-1072	-£0.11
Fillies:	61-382	-£0.08
Absolute Favourites:	145-292	-£0.01

TRAINERS (WINS-RUNS, £)

A P Jarvis 1-13 £2.92; B J Meehan 9-31 £0.83; A M Balding 4-20 £0.74; P D Evans 10-32 £0.44; T P Tate 1-11 £0.91; E J O'Neill 7-20 £0.49; D Nicholls 2-11 £0.82; B Smart 11-34 £0.25; R Charlton 7-14 £0.53; J S Moore 7-23 £0.26; H R A Cecil 6-11 £0.40; J H M Gosden 3-10 £0.30; M Johnston 19-66 £0.04; J A Osborne 7-19 £0.05; K R Burke 6-33 £0.03; D M Simcock 2-10 £0.08; Mrs A Duffield 4-10 £0.04.

Conditions Stakes

2-Y.O Races: Conditions Stakes – 8 to 14 runners

ANALYSIS BY BHA RATING

Rating	Prop	Win	Runs	Wins%	£
120..139	0%	0	0	0.0%	0.00
110..119	0%	0	0	0.0%	0.00
100..109	2%	2	7	28.6%	0.46
90..99	6%	6	39	15.4%	-0.02
70..89	14%	13	109	11.9%	-0.10
50..69	0%	0	24	0.0%	-1.00
..49	0%	0	2	0.0%	-1.00
Unrated	78%	75	699	10.7%	-0.30

ANALYSIS BY WEIGHT CARRIED

Weight	Prop	Win	Runs	Wins%	£
10-01+	0%	0	0	0.0%	0.00
9-8..10-00	0%	0	1	0.0%	-1.00
9-0..9-07	39%	37	227	16.3%	-0.14
8-8..8-13	53%	51	483	10.6%	-0.17
8-0..8-07	8%	8	163	4.9%	-0.77
..7-13	0%	0	6	0.0%	-1.00

ANALYSIS BY DAYS SINCE LAST RUN

Days	Prop	Win	Runs	Wins%	£
1..7	10%	10	55	18.2%	-0.19
8..14	32%	31	201	15.4%	-0.28
15..28	27%	26	264	9.8%	-0.40
29..60	16%	15	132	11.4%	-0.29
61..100	2%	2	23	8.7%	0.35
101+	0%	0	3	0.0%	-1.00
Unraced	13%	12	202	5.9%	-0.20

ANALYSIS BY TODAY'S STARTING PRICE

Price	Prop	Win	Runs	Wins%	£
Odds On	10%	10	18	55.6%	-0.05
Ev-2/1	19%	18	48	37.5%	-0.03
9/4-4/1	29%	28	136	20.6%	-0.19
9/2-6/1	15%	14	96	14.6%	-0.10
13/2-10/1	16%	15	136	11.0%	0.00
11/1-16/1	5%	5	128	3.9%	-0.40
18/1-33/1	5%	5	152	3.3%	-0.29
40/1+	1%	1	166	0.6%	-0.69

ANALYSIS BY STARTING PRICE LAST TIME

Price	Prop	Win	Runs	Wins%	£
Odds On	7%	7	35	20.0%	-0.13
Ev-2/1	9%	9	55	16.4%	-0.26
9/4-4/1	24%	23	117	19.7%	0.05
9/2-6/1	14%	13	64	20.3%	0.05
13/2-10/1	13%	12	126	9.5%	-0.38
11/1-16/1	9%	9	103	8.7%	-0.53
18/1-33/1	7%	7	99	7.1%	-0.42
40/1+	4%	4	79	5.1%	-0.66
Unraced	13%	12	202	5.9%	-0.20

ANALYSIS BY DISTANCE BEATEN LAST TIME

Lengths	Prop	Win	Runs	Wins%	£
..-10	0%	0	1	0.0%	-1.00
-10..0	41%	39	223	17.5%	-0.24
0.1..2	16%	15	94	16.0%	-0.23
2.1..5	19%	18	105	17.1%	0.06
5.1..10	6%	6	114	5.3%	-0.59
10.1..20	5%	5	107	4.7%	-0.53
20.0..30	1%	1	26	3.8%	-0.19
30.1+	0%	0	8	0.0%	-1.00
Not Compl	0%	0	0	0.0%	0.00
Unraced	13%	12	202	5.9%	-0.20

ANALYSIS BY RUN NUMBER

Run No	Prop	Win	Runs	Wins%	£
FTO	13%	12	202	5.9%	-0.20
2nd Run	31%	30	197	15.2%	-0.28
3rd Run	27%	26	195	13.3%	-0.31
4th+ Run	29%	28	286	9.8%	-0.32

ANALYSIS BY POSITION LAST TIME

Pos LT	Prop	Win	Runs	Wins%	£
Won	41%	39	224	17.4%	-0.24
2nd or 3rd	21%	20	130	15.4%	-0.28
Unplaced	26%	25	324	7.7%	-0.36
Not Compl	13%	12	202	5.9%	-0.20

OTHER FACTORS (WINS-RUNS, £)

Course Winner:	8-36	-£0.17
Distance Winner:	44-249	-£0.01
Going Winner:	20-124	-£0.33
Beaten Favourite:	7-37	-£0.13
BHA Top Rated:	3-30	-£0.67
Up in class:	41-368	-£0.31
Same class:	22-160	-£0.37
Down in class:	21-150	-£0.20
7-Day Winners:	3-15	-£0.29
Colts and Geldings:	71-582	-£0.16
Fillies:	14-184	-£0.67
Absolute Favourites:	29-93	-£0.25

TRAINERS (WINS-RUNS, £)

A M Balding 3-13 £0.78; K A Ryan 3-27 £0.33; R A Fahey 5-20 £0.42; B J Meehan 3-29 £0.28; P D Evans 4-18 £0.26.

JUVENILE RACES

Race Profiles

2-Y.O Races: Conditions Stakes – 15 runners or more

ANALYSIS BY BHA RATING

Rating	Prop	Win	Runs	Wins%	£
120..139	0%	0	0	0.0%	0.00
110..119	0%	0	0	0.0%	0.00
100..109	6%	2	13	15.4%	-0.65
90..99	12%	4	55	7.3%	-0.52
70..89	18%	6	178	3.4%	-0.33
50..69	3%	1	26	3.8%	-0.65
..49	0%	0	2	0.0%	-1.00
Unrated	62%	21	456	4.6%	-0.24

ANALYSIS BY WEIGHT CARRIED

Weight	Prop	Win	Runs	Wins%	£
10-01+	0%	0	0	0.0%	0.00
9-8..10-00	0%	0	0	0.0%	0.00
9-0..9-07	21%	7	125	5.6%	0.16
8-8..8-13	47%	16	328	4.9%	-0.55
8-0..8-07	32%	11	246	4.5%	-0.13
..7-13	0%	0	31	0.0%	-1.00

ANALYSIS BY DAYS SINCE LAST RUN

Days	Prop	Win	Runs	Wins%	£
1..7	3%	1	44	2.3%	-0.83
8..14	18%	6	132	4.5%	0.54
15..28	32%	11	264	4.2%	-0.46
29..60	35%	12	173	6.9%	-0.31
61..100	3%	1	31	3.2%	-0.84
101+	0%	0	10	0.0%	-1.00
Unraced	9%	3	76	3.9%	-0.64

ANALYSIS BY TODAY'S STARTING PRICE

Price	Prop	Win	Runs	Wins%	£
Odds On	3%	1	2	50.0%	-0.14
Ev-2/1	6%	2	6	33.3%	-0.02
9/4-4/1	15%	5	20	25.0%	0.08
9/2-6/1	18%	6	42	14.3%	-0.14
13/2-10/1	24%	8	79	10.1%	-0.13
11/1-16/1	12%	4	122	3.3%	-0.49
18/1-33/1	18%	6	191	3.1%	-0.26
40/1+	6%	2	268	0.7%	-0.37

ANALYSIS BY STARTING PRICE LAST TIME

Price	Prop	Win	Runs	Wins%	£
Odds On	12%	4	35	11.4%	0.77
Ev-2/1	12%	4	66	6.1%	-0.23
9/4-4/1	32%	11	156	7.1%	-0.39
9/2-6/1	12%	4	67	6.0%	0.46
13/2-10/1	12%	4	117	3.4%	0.16
11/1-16/1	3%	1	81	1.2%	-0.92
18/1-33/1	9%	3	78	3.8%	-0.60
40/1+	0%	0	54	0.0%	-1.00
Unraced	9%	3	76	3.9%	-0.64

ANALYSIS BY DISTANCE BEATEN LAST TIME

Lengths	Prop	Win	Runs	Wins%	£
..-10	0%	0	0	0.0%	0.00
-10..0	38%	13	148	8.8%	0.20
0.1..2	29%	10	134	7.5%	-0.36
2.1..5	15%	5	115	4.3%	-0.61
5.1..10	6%	2	160	1.3%	-0.56
10.1..20	3%	1	82	1.2%	0.23
20.0..30	0%	0	12	0.0%	-1.00
30.1+	0%	0	3	0.0%	-1.00
Not Compl	0%	0	0	0.0%	0.00
Unraced	9%	3	76	3.9%	-0.64

ANALYSIS BY RUN NUMBER

Run No	Prop	Win	Runs	Wins%	£
FTO	9%	3	76	3.9%	-0.64
2nd Run	6%	2	58	3.4%	-0.80
3rd Run	24%	8	107	7.5%	1.23
4th+ Run	62%	21	489	4.3%	-0.53

ANALYSIS BY POSITION LAST TIME

Pos LT	Prop	Win	Runs	Wins%	£
Won	38%	13	149	8.7%	0.19
2nd or 3rd	29%	10	182	5.5%	-0.25
Unplaced	24%	8	323	2.5%	-0.49
Not Compl	9%	3	76	3.9%	-0.64

OTHER FACTORS (WINS-RUNS, £)

Course Winner:	0-19	-£1.00
Distance Winner:	17-255	-£0.35
Going Winner:	4-105	-£0.55
Beaten Favourite:	6-76	-£0.38
BHA Top Rated:	1-24	-£0.88
Up in class:	17-443	-£0.15
Same class:	6-106	-£0.52
Down in class:	8-105	-£0.51
7-Day Winners:	1-12	-£0.38
Colts and Geldings:	21-436	-£0.34
Fillies:	8-191	-£0.05
Absolute Favourites:	9-31	£0.12

TRAINERS (WINS-RUNS, £)

R Hannon 5-81 £0.68; J H M Gosden 2-10 £2.90; T D Easterby 2-15 £1.67; W J Haggas 2-12 £0.89; S Kirk 2-11 £0.41.

Conditions Stakes

2-Y.O Races: Conditions Stakes – good or faster going

ANALYSIS BY BHA RATING

Rating	Prop	Win	Runs	Wins%	£
120..139	0%	0	0	0.0%	0.00
110..119	0%	0	0	0.0%	0.00
100..109	3%	10	27	37.0%	0.06
90..99	7%	22	144	15.3%	-0.42
70..89	13%	42	350	12.0%	-0.14
50..69	0%	1	40	2.5%	-0.77
..49	0%	0	4	0.0%	-1.00
Unrated	77%	247	1839	13.4%	-0.15

ANALYSIS BY WEIGHT CARRIED

Weight	Prop	Win	Runs	Wins%	£
10-01+	0%	0	0	0.0%	0.00
9-8..10-00	0%	1	8	12.5%	0.00
9-0..9-07	44%	141	698	20.2%	-0.10
8-8..8-13	45%	145	1171	12.4%	-0.20
8-0..8-07	11%	35	491	7.1%	-0.16
..7-13	0%	0	36	0.0%	-1.00

ANALYSIS BY DAYS SINCE LAST RUN

Days	Prop	Win	Runs	Wins%	£
1..7	8%	26	144	18.1%	-0.16
8..14	27%	87	523	16.6%	0.04
15..28	36%	115	812	14.2%	-0.30
29..60	17%	54	429	12.6%	-0.37
61..100	2%	8	73	11.0%	0.58
101+	0%	1	16	6.3%	-0.91
Unraced	10%	31	407	7.6%	-0.12

ANALYSIS BY TODAY'S STARTING PRICE

Price	Prop	Win	Runs	Wins%	£
Odds On	20%	65	99	65.7%	0.02
Ev-2/1	25%	80	207	38.6%	-0.05
9/4-4/1	22%	72	392	18.4%	-0.27
9/2-6/1	9%	29	219	13.2%	-0.17
13/2-10/1	14%	44	341	12.9%	0.16
11/1-16/1	4%	14	324	4.3%	-0.35
18/1-33/1	4%	14	392	3.6%	-0.18
40/1+	1%	4	430	0.9%	-0.33

ANALYSIS BY STARTING PRICE LAST TIME

Price	Prop	Win	Runs	Wins%	£
Odds On	8%	26	105	24.8%	0.37
Ev-2/1	12%	39	201	19.4%	-0.24
9/4-4/1	19%	61	377	16.2%	-0.33
9/2-6/1	13%	43	219	19.6%	0.15
13/2-10/1	14%	45	352	12.8%	-0.08
11/1-16/1	12%	38	294	12.9%	-0.33
18/1-33/1	8%	26	265	9.8%	-0.18
40/1+	4%	13	184	7.1%	-0.55
Unraced	10%	31	407	7.6%	-0.12

ANALYSIS BY DISTANCE BEATEN LAST TIME

Lengths	Prop	Win	Runs	Wins%	£
..-10	0%	0	2	0.0%	-1.00
-10..0	47%	150	686	21.9%	-0.10
0.1..2	17%	55	294	18.7%	-0.15
2.1..5	16%	51	334	15.3%	-0.09
5.1..10	7%	24	374	6.4%	-0.43
10.1..20	3%	10	240	4.2%	-0.04
20.0..30	0%	0	51	0.0%	-1.00
30.1+	0%	1	16	6.3%	-0.56
Not Compl	0%	0	0	0.0%	0.00
Unraced	10%	31	407	7.6%	-0.12

ANALYSIS BY RUN NUMBER

Run No	Prop	Win	Runs	Wins%	£
FTO	10%	31	407	7.6%	-0.12
2nd Run	33%	107	529	20.2%	-0.16
3rd Run	22%	72	487	14.8%	0.12
4th+ Run	35%	112	981	11.4%	-0.35

ANALYSIS BY POSITION LAST TIME

Pos LT	Prop	Win	Runs	Wins%	£
Won	47%	150	688	21.8%	-0.10
2nd or 3rd	21%	67	415	16.1%	-0.13
Unplaced	23%	74	894	8.3%	-0.28
Not Compl	10%	31	407	7.6%	-0.12

OTHER FACTORS (WINS-RUNS, £)

Course Winner:	18-101	-£0.48
Distance Winner:	145-778	-£0.14
Going Winner:	75-416	-£0.27
Beaten Favourite:	24-149	-£0.33
BHA Top Rated:	25-105	-£0.33
Up in class:	126-1060	-£0.21
Same class:	74-466	-£0.13
Down in class:	91-471	-£0.19
7-Day Winners:	13-42	£0.26
Colts and Geldings:	223-1525	-£0.17
Fillies:	57-523	-£0.16
Absolute Favourites:	143-305	£0.00

TRAINERS (WINS-RUNS, £)

G M Moore 2-12 £5.42; R M Beckett 4-29 £1.68; A P Jarvis 1-16 £2.19; R Hannon 41-214 £0.16; A M Balding 8-34 £0.95; J H M Gosden 6-23 £1.40; G G Margarson 2-10 £2.20; M P Tregoning 5-18 £1.19; P D Evans 12-42 £0.50; W J Haggas 6-17 £1.10; B J Meehan 11-71 £0.14; T P Tate 1-13 £0.62; D Nicholls 2-13 £0.54; Mrs A Duffield 5-15 £0.30; A Bailey 2-12 £0.33; E A L Dunlop 5-17 £0.20; C G Cox 2-10 £0.25; E J O'Neill 7-29 £0.06; P W Chapple-Hyam 4-14 £0.09; J Noseda 6-19 £0.03.

Race Profiles

2-Y.O Races: Conditions Stakes – good to soft or softer going

ANALYSIS BY BHA RATING

Rating	Prop	Win	Runs	Wins%	£
120..139	0%	0	0	0.0%	0.00
110..119	0%	0	0	0.0%	0.00
100..109	3%	3	16	18.8%	-0.48
90..99	10%	12	60	20.0%	0.19
70..89	18%	21	155	13.5%	-0.28
50..69	0%	0	23	0.0%	-1.00
..49	0%	0	5	0.0%	-1.00
Unrated	69%	79	589	13.4%	-0.24

ANALYSIS BY WEIGHT CARRIED

Weight	Prop	Win	Runs	Wins%	£
10-01+	0%	0	0	0.0%	0.00
9-8..10-00	0%	0	3	0.0%	-1.00
9-0..9-07	44%	51	228	22.4%	0.03
8-8..8-13	45%	52	401	13.0%	-0.19
8-0..8-07	10%	12	207	5.8%	-0.62
..7-13	0%	0	9	0.0%	-1.00

ANALYSIS BY DAYS SINCE LAST RUN

Days	Prop	Win	Runs	Wins%	£
1..7	7%	8	60	13.3%	-0.50
8..14	27%	31	186	16.7%	-0.25
15..28	33%	38	275	13.8%	-0.36
29..60	21%	24	145	16.6%	-0.04
61..100	3%	4	26	15.4%	-0.18
101+	0%	0	6	0.0%	-1.00
Unraced	9%	10	150	6.7%	-0.11

ANALYSIS BY TODAY'S STARTING PRICE

Price	Prop	Win	Runs	Wins%	£
Odds On	17%	20	42	47.6%	-0.24
Ev-2/1	18%	21	72	29.2%	-0.26
9/4-4/1	28%	32	127	25.2%	0.01
9/2-6/1	17%	19	84	22.6%	0.43
13/2-10/1	12%	14	124	11.3%	0.01
11/1-16/1	4%	5	117	4.3%	-0.42
18/1-33/1	3%	3	143	2.1%	-0.56
40/1+	1%	1	139	0.7%	-0.63

ANALYSIS BY STARTING PRICE LAST TIME

Price	Prop	Win	Runs	Wins%	£
Odds On	10%	12	42	28.6%	0.10
Ev-2/1	17%	20	58	34.5%	0.20
9/4-4/1	20%	23	146	15.8%	-0.13
9/2-6/1	10%	12	72	16.7%	-0.32
13/2-10/1	16%	18	121	14.9%	-0.23
11/1-16/1	5%	6	85	7.1%	-0.73
18/1-33/1	9%	10	97	10.3%	-0.16
40/1+	3%	4	77	5.2%	-0.76
Unraced	9%	10	150	6.7%	-0.11

ANALYSIS BY DISTANCE BEATEN LAST TIME

Lengths	Prop	Win	Runs	Wins%	£
..-10	0%	0	1	0.0%	-1.00
-10..0	38%	44	209	21.1%	-0.13
0.1..2	19%	22	111	19.8%	0.00
2.1..5	17%	20	126	15.9%	-0.36
5.1..10	14%	16	136	11.8%	-0.29
10.1..20	2%	2	80	2.5%	-0.81
20.0..30	1%	1	24	4.2%	-0.13
30.1+	0%	0	11	0.0%	-1.00
Not Compl	0%	0	0	0.0%	0.00
Unraced	9%	10	150	6.7%	-0.11

ANALYSIS BY RUN NUMBER

Run No	Prop	Win	Runs	Wins%	£
FTO	9%	10	150	6.7%	-0.11
2nd Run	23%	27	149	18.1%	-0.31
3rd Run	24%	28	173	16.2%	-0.45
4th+ Run	43%	50	376	13.3%	-0.18

ANALYSIS BY POSITION LAST TIME

Pos LT	Prop	Win	Runs	Wins%	£
Won	38%	44	211	20.9%	-0.14
2nd or 3rd	30%	34	168	20.2%	0.03
Unplaced	23%	27	318	8.5%	-0.52
Not Compl	9%	10	151	6.6%	-0.12

OTHER FACTORS (WINS-RUNS, £)

Course Winner:	6-33	-£0.36
Distance Winner:	49-283	-£0.22
Going Winner:	12-58	£0.01
Beaten Favourite:	12-50	£0.18
BHA Top Rated:	12-58	-£0.37
Up in class:	53-492	-£0.33
Same class:	23-146	-£0.29
Down in class:	29-160	-£0.12
7-Day Winners:	4-15	-£0.39
Colts and Geldings:	82-565	-£0.20
Fillies:	26-234	-£0.34
Absolute Favourites:	40-111	-£0.20

TRAINERS (WINS-RUNS, £)

B J Meehan 4-24 £0.92; T D Easterby 2-20 £0.55; Mrs L Stubbs 2-10 £0.50; R A Fahey 3-14 £0.05; K A Ryan 5-34 £0.02; B Smart 6-20 £0.03.

Conditions Stakes

2-Y.O Races: Conditions Stakes – 5 to 6 furlong races

ANALYSIS BY BHA RATING

Rating	Prop	Win	Runs	Wins%	£
120..139	0%	0	0	0.0%	0.00
110..119	0%	0	0	0.0%	0.00
100..109	3%	8	25	32.0%	-0.07
90..99	6%	18	129	14.0%	-0.33
70..89	10%	30	328	9.1%	-0.26
50..69	0%	1	51	2.0%	-0.82
..49	0%	0	5	0.0%	-1.00
Unrated	81%	250	1876	13.3%	-0.15

ANALYSIS BY WEIGHT CARRIED

Weight	Prop	Win	Runs	Wins%	£
10-01+	0%	0	0	0.0%	0.00
9-8..10-00	0%	1	9	11.1%	-0.11
9-0..9-07	40%	124	570	21.8%	-0.07
8-8..8-13	47%	144	1184	12.2%	-0.19
8-0..8-07	12%	38	608	6.3%	-0.27
..7-13	0%	0	43	0.0%	-1.00

ANALYSIS BY DAYS SINCE LAST RUN

Days	Prop	Win	Runs	Wins%	£
1..7	9%	29	181	16.0%	-0.25
8..14	28%	86	551	15.6%	-0.08
15..28	33%	100	758	13.2%	-0.32
29..60	17%	51	412	12.4%	-0.30
61..100	3%	10	66	15.2%	1.01
101+	0%	1	17	5.9%	-0.92
Unraced	10%	30	429	7.0%	-0.15

ANALYSIS BY TODAY'S STARTING PRICE

Price	Prop	Win	Runs	Wins%	£
Odds On	16%	50	90	55.6%	-0.11
Ev-2/1	24%	74	196	37.8%	-0.05
9/4-4/1	22%	69	360	19.2%	-0.24
9/2-6/1	12%	36	224	16.1%	0.02
13/2-10/1	15%	47	367	12.8%	0.14
11/1-16/1	5%	14	336	4.2%	-0.39
18/1-33/1	4%	13	412	3.2%	-0.31
40/1+	1%	4	429	0.9%	-0.37

ANALYSIS BY STARTING PRICE LAST TIME

Price	Prop	Win	Runs	Wins%	£
Odds On	6%	19	92	20.7%	0.38
Ev-2/1	14%	44	194	22.7%	-0.22
9/4-4/1	20%	62	415	14.9%	-0.27
9/2-6/1	10%	32	210	15.2%	-0.25
13/2-10/1	16%	48	355	13.5%	0.02
11/1-16/1	11%	34	272	12.5%	-0.33
18/1-33/1	8%	25	260	9.6%	-0.13
40/1+	4%	13	187	7.0%	-0.62
Unraced	10%	30	429	7.0%	-0.15

ANALYSIS BY DISTANCE BEATEN LAST TIME

Lengths	Prop	Win	Runs	Wins%	£
..-10	0%	0	2	0.0%	-1.00
-10..0	44%	135	652	20.7%	-0.09
0.1..2	18%	55	309	17.8%	-0.11
2.1..5	15%	47	330	14.2%	-0.15
5.1..10	9%	29	397	7.3%	-0.51
10.1..20	3%	10	228	4.4%	0.01
20.0..30	0%	0	50	0.0%	-1.00
30.1+	0%	1	17	5.9%	-0.59
Not Compl	0%	0	0	0.0%	0.00
Unraced	10%	30	429	7.0%	-0.15

ANALYSIS BY RUN NUMBER

Run No	Prop	Win	Runs	Wins%	£
FTO	10%	30	429	7.0%	-0.15
2nd Run	30%	92	464	19.8%	-0.11
3rd Run	23%	72	465	15.5%	0.02
4th+ Run	37%	113	1056	10.7%	-0.34

ANALYSIS BY POSITION LAST TIME

Pos LT	Prop	Win	Runs	Wins%	£
Won	44%	135	655	20.6%	-0.09
2nd or 3rd	21%	66	431	15.3%	-0.22
Unplaced	25%	76	899	8.5%	-0.28
Not Compl	10%	30	429	7.0%	-0.15

OTHER FACTORS (WINS-RUNS, £)

Course Winner:	19-100	-£0.40
Distance Winner:	161-906	-£0.14
Going Winner:	64-356	-£0.13
Beaten Favourite:	23-145	-£0.26
BHA Top Rated:	18-82	-£0.48
Up in class:	128-1113	-£0.27
Same class:	67-410	-£0.01
Down in class:	82-462	-£0.22
7-Day Winners:	13-48	£0.03
Colts and Geldings:	200-1467	-£0.21
Fillies:	66-630	-£0.15
Absolute Favourites:	122-290	-£0.05

TRAINERS (WINS-RUNS, £)

G M Moore 1-13 £4.15; A P Jarvis 1-12 £3.25; R Hannon 41-212 £0.17; B J Meehan 12-68 £0.41; A M Balding 6-23 £1.03; G G Margarson 2-11 £1.91; J G Portman 3-16 £1.23; M W Easterby 3-15 £1.30; J R Jenkins 2-12 £1.43; W J Haggas 6-19 £0.89; T D Easterby 5-46 £0.36; P D Evans 14-54 £0.27; Mrs L Stubbs 4-19 £0.42; Mrs A Duffield 5-15 £0.49; J Noseda 5-17 £0.34; P W Chapple-Hyam 5-13 £0.36; B Smart 13-43 £0.08; J A Osborne 7-19 £0.16; A Bailey 2-14 £0.14; E A L Dunlop 4-15 £0.11.

Race Profiles

2-Y.O Races: Conditions Stakes – 7 to 8 furlong races

ANALYSIS BY BHA RATING

Rating	Prop	Win	Runs	Wins%	£
120..139	0%	0	0	0.0%	0.00
110..119	0%	0	0	0.0%	0.00
100..109	4%	5	18	27.8%	-0.23
90..99	12%	15	71	21.1%	-0.18
70..89	22%	27	152	17.8%	0.02
50..69	0%	0	10	0.0%	-1.00
..49	0%	0	3	0.0%	-1.00
Unrated	61%	75	543	13.8%	-0.23

ANALYSIS BY WEIGHT CARRIED

Weight	Prop	Win	Runs	Wins%	£
10-01+	0%	0	0	0.0%	0.00
9-8..10-00	0%	0	2	0.0%	-1.00
9-0..9-07	52%	63	333	18.9%	-0.06
8-8..8-13	41%	50	374	13.4%	-0.23
8-0..8-07	7%	9	86	10.5%	-0.47
..7-13	0%	0	2	0.0%	-1.00

ANALYSIS BY DAYS SINCE LAST RUN

Days	Prop	Win	Runs	Wins%	£
1..7	4%	5	23	21.7%	-0.34
8..14	25%	31	154	20.1%	0.12
15..28	40%	49	311	15.8%	-0.29
29..60	20%	24	146	16.4%	-0.26
61..100	2%	2	30	6.7%	-0.87
101+	0%	0	5	0.0%	-1.00
Unraced	9%	11	128	8.6%	-0.03

ANALYSIS BY TODAY'S STARTING PRICE

Price	Prop	Win	Runs	Wins%	£
Odds On	26%	32	48	66.7%	0.00
Ev-2/1	20%	25	76	32.9%	-0.20
9/4-4/1	27%	33	150	22.0%	-0.12
9/2-6/1	10%	12	75	16.0%	-0.01
13/2-10/1	8%	10	93	10.8%	-0.02
11/1-16/1	4%	5	101	5.0%	-0.26
18/1-33/1	3%	4	118	3.4%	-0.18
40/1+	1%	1	136	0.7%	-0.51

ANALYSIS BY STARTING PRICE LAST TIME

Price	Prop	Win	Runs	Wins%	£
Odds On	16%	19	50	38.0%	0.27
Ev-2/1	11%	13	60	21.7%	0.13
9/4-4/1	16%	20	100	20.0%	-0.32
9/2-6/1	17%	21	77	27.3%	0.77
13/2-10/1	11%	14	110	12.7%	-0.51
11/1-16/1	8%	10	102	9.8%	-0.62
18/1-33/1	8%	10	98	10.2%	-0.38
40/1+	3%	4	72	5.6%	-0.58
Unraced	9%	11	128	8.6%	-0.03

ANALYSIS BY DISTANCE BEATEN LAST TIME

Lengths	Prop	Win	Runs	Wins%	£
..-10	0%	0	1	0.0%	-1.00
-10..0	43%	53	222	23.9%	-0.13
0.1..2	17%	21	89	23.6%	-0.09
2.1..5	20%	24	126	19.0%	-0.18
5.1..10	8%	10	107	9.3%	-0.01
10.1..20	2%	2	89	2.2%	-0.82
20.0..30	1%	1	25	4.0%	-0.16
30.1+	0%	0	10	0.0%	-1.00
Not Compl	0%	0	0	0.0%	0.00
Unraced	9%	11	128	8.6%	-0.03

ANALYSIS BY RUN NUMBER

Run No	Prop	Win	Runs	Wins%	£
FTO	9%	11	128	8.6%	-0.03
2nd Run	32%	39	207	18.8%	-0.40
3rd Run	20%	25	184	13.6%	-0.14
4th+ Run	39%	47	278	16.9%	-0.15

ANALYSIS BY POSITION LAST TIME

Pos LT	Prop	Win	Runs	Wins%	£
Won	43%	53	223	23.8%	-0.13
2nd or 3rd	28%	34	147	23.1%	0.33
Unplaced	20%	24	298	8.1%	-0.56
Not Compl	9%	11	129	8.5%	-0.03

OTHER FACTORS (WINS-RUNS, £)

Course Winner:	4-31	-£0.61
Distance Winner:	33-154	-£0.28
Going Winner:	21-111	-£0.55
Beaten Favourite:	13-53	-£0.03
BHA Top Rated:	17-73	-£0.17
Up in class:	44-305	-£0.13
Same class:	30-198	-£0.48
Down in class:	37-166	-£0.08
7-Day Winners:	4-9	£0.37
Colts and Geldings:	98-592	-£0.08
Fillies:	16-117	-£0.54
Absolute Favourites:	56-118	-£0.08

TRAINERS (WINS-RUNS, £)

R M Beckett 2-10 £5.95; J H M Gosden 5-18 £1.79; M P Tregoning 3-13 £1.48; M Johnston 18-52 £0.33; B J Meehan 3-27 £0.17; A M Balding 2-16 £0.23; B W Hills 4-20 £0.07.

Conditions Stakes

2-Y.O Races: Conditions Stakes – 9+ furlong races

ANALYSIS BY BHA RATING

Rating	Prop	Win	Runs	Wins%	£
120..139	0%	0	0	0.0%	0.00
110..119	0%	0	0	0.0%	0.00
100..109	0%	0	0	0.0%	0.00
90..99	13%	1	4	25.0%	1.50
70..89	75%	6	25	24.0%	-0.34
50..69	0%	0	2	0.0%	-1.00
..49	0%	0	1	0.0%	-1.00
Unrated	13%	1	9	11.1%	-0.80

ANALYSIS BY WEIGHT CARRIED

Weight	Prop	Win	Runs	Wins%	£
10-01+	0%	0	0	0.0%	0.00
9-8..10-00	0%	0	0	0.0%	0.00
9-0..9-07	63%	5	23	21.7%	-0.12
8-8..8-13	38%	3	14	21.4%	-0.42
8-0..8-07	0%	0	4	0.0%	-1.00
..7-13	0%	0	0	0.0%	0.00

ANALYSIS BY DAYS SINCE LAST RUN

Days	Prop	Win	Runs	Wins%	£
1..7	0%	0	0	0.0%	0.00
8..14	13%	1	4	25.0%	-0.50
15..28	50%	4	18	22.2%	-0.31
29..60	38%	3	16	18.8%	-0.14
61..100	0%	0	3	0.0%	-1.00
101+	0%	0	0	0.0%	0.00
Unraced	0%	0	0	0.0%	0.00

ANALYSIS BY TODAY'S STARTING PRICE

Price	Prop	Win	Runs	Wins%	£
Odds On	38%	3	3	100.0%	0.75
Ev-2/1	25%	2	7	28.6%	-0.43
9/4-4/1	25%	2	9	22.2%	0.00
9/2-6/1	0%	0	4	0.0%	-1.00
13/2-10/1	13%	1	5	20.0%	1.00
11/1-16/1	0%	0	4	0.0%	-1.00
18/1-33/1	0%	0	5	0.0%	-1.00
40/1+	0%	0	4	0.0%	-1.00

ANALYSIS BY STARTING PRICE LAST TIME

Price	Prop	Win	Runs	Wins%	£
Odds On	0%	0	5	0.0%	-1.00
Ev-2/1	25%	2	5	40.0%	-0.23
9/4-4/1	25%	2	8	25.0%	-0.21
9/2-6/1	25%	2	4	50.0%	0.53
13/2-10/1	13%	1	8	12.5%	-0.75
11/1-16/1	0%	0	5	0.0%	-1.00
18/1-33/1	13%	1	4	25.0%	1.50
40/1+	0%	0	2	0.0%	-1.00
Unraced	0%	0	0	0.0%	0.00

ANALYSIS BY DISTANCE BEATEN LAST TIME

Lengths	Prop	Win	Runs	Wins%	£
..-10	0%	0	0	0.0%	0.00
-10..0	75%	6	21	28.6%	-0.35
0.1..2	13%	1	7	14.3%	-0.36
2.1..5	0%	0	4	0.0%	-1.00
5.1..10	13%	1	6	16.7%	0.67
10.1..20	0%	0	3	0.0%	-1.00
20.0..30	0%	0	0	0.0%	0.00
30.1+	0%	0	0	0.0%	0.00
Not Compl	0%	0	0	0.0%	0.00
Unraced	0%	0	0	0.0%	0.00

ANALYSIS BY RUN NUMBER

Run No	Prop	Win	Runs	Wins%	£
FTO	0%	0	0	0.0%	0.00
2nd Run	38%	3	7	42.9%	0.13
3rd Run	38%	3	11	27.3%	-0.47
4th+ Run	25%	2	23	8.7%	-0.37

ANALYSIS BY POSITION LAST TIME

Pos LT	Prop	Win	Runs	Wins%	£
Won	75%	6	21	28.6%	-0.35
2nd or 3rd	13%	1	5	20.0%	-0.10
Unplaced	13%	1	15	6.7%	-0.33
Not Compl	0%	0	0	0.0%	0.00

OTHER FACTORS (WINS-RUNS, £)

Course Winner:	1-3	-£0.40
Distance Winner:	0-1	-£1.00
Going Winner:	2-7	-£0.51
Beaten Favourite:	0-1	-£1.00
BHA Top Rated:	2-8	-£0.52
Up in class:	7-34	-£0.46
Same class:	0-4	-£1.00
Down in class:	1-3	£2.33
Colts and Geldings:	7-31	-£0.23
Fillies:	1-10	-£0.55
Absolute Favourites:	5-8	£0.16

JUVENILE RACES

Race Profiles

2-Y.0 Races: Maiden Races

ANALYSIS BY BHA RATING

Rating	Prop	Win	Runs	Wins%	£
120..139	0%	0	0	0.0%	0.00
110..119	0%	0	0	0.0%	0.00
100..109	0%	0	1	0.0%	-1.00
90..99	0%	7	20	35.0%	-0.20
70..89	7%	181	792	22.9%	-0.14
50..69	1%	33	635	5.2%	-0.41
..49	0%	0	201	0.0%	-1.00
Unrated	92%	2398	26125	9.2%	-0.29

ANALYSIS BY WEIGHT CARRIED

Weight	Prop	Win	Runs	Wins%	£
10-01+	0%	0	0	0.0%	0.00
9-8..10-00	0%	0	0	0.0%	0.00
9-0..9-07	65%	1699	16310	10.4%	-0.31
8-8..8-13	27%	711	8404	8.5%	-0.25
8-0..8-07	8%	205	2890	7.1%	-0.29
..7-13	0%	4	170	2.4%	-0.86

ANALYSIS BY DAYS SINCE LAST RUN

Days	Prop	Win	Runs	Wins%	£
1..7	3%	78	786	9.9%	-0.46
8..14	21%	551	4486	12.3%	-0.36
15..28	32%	830	6626	12.5%	-0.26
29..60	13%	334	3252	10.3%	-0.20
61..100	2%	59	704	8.4%	-0.28
101+	1%	16	216	7.4%	-0.45
Unraced	29%	751	11704	6.4%	-0.30

ANALYSIS BY TODAY'S STARTING PRICE

Price	Prop	Win	Runs	Wins%	£
Odds On	13%	349	621	56.2%	-0.09
Ev-2/1	19%	507	1375	36.9%	-0.05
9/4-4/1	26%	685	3068	22.3%	-0.08
9/2-6/1	13%	329	2221	14.8%	-0.08
13/2-10/1	13%	343	3756	9.1%	-0.17
11/1-16/1	8%	203	4077	5.0%	-0.27
18/1-33/1	6%	152	5867	2.6%	-0.33
40/1+	2%	51	6789	0.8%	-0.58

ANALYSIS BY STARTING PRICE LAST TIME

Price	Prop	Win	Runs	Wins%	£
Odds On	2%	56	172	32.6%	0.01
Ev-2/1	6%	159	540	29.4%	-0.06
9/4-4/1	11%	300	1458	20.6%	-0.21
9/2-6/1	10%	257	1254	20.5%	0.03
13/2-10/1	13%	336	2264	14.8%	-0.30
11/1-16/1	12%	319	2658	12.0%	-0.22
18/1-33/1	11%	286	3894	7.3%	-0.36
40/1+	6%	155	3830	4.0%	-0.43
Unraced	29%	751	11704	6.4%	-0.30

ANALYSIS BY DISTANCE BEATEN LAST TIME

Lengths	Prop	Win	Runs	Wins%	£
..-10	0%	0	0	0.0%	0.00
-10..0	0%	0	2	0.0%	-1.00
0.1..2	22%	586	2155	27.2%	-0.14
2.1..5	23%	599	3215	18.6%	-0.16
5.1..10	18%	467	4621	10.1%	-0.26
10.1..20	7%	184	4448	4.1%	-0.38
20.0..30	1%	28	1112	2.5%	-0.43
30.1+	0%	4	517	0.8%	-0.93
Not Compl	0%	0	0	0.0%	0.00
Unraced	29%	751	11704	6.4%	-0.30

ANALYSIS BY RUN NUMBER

Run No	Prop	Win	Runs	Wins%	£
FTO	29%	751	11704	6.4%	-0.30
2nd Run	37%	965	8258	11.7%	-0.23
3rd Run	21%	541	5164	10.5%	-0.38
4th+ Run	14%	362	2648	13.7%	-0.32

ANALYSIS BY POSITION LAST TIME

Pos LT	Prop	Win	Runs	Wins%	£
Won	0%	0	0	0.0%	0.00
2nd or 3rd	34%	899	3686	24.4%	-0.17
Unplaced	37%	969	12342	7.9%	-0.32
Not Compl	29%	751	11746	6.4%	-0.31

OTHER FACTORS (WINS-RUNS, £)

Beaten Favourite:	231-918	-£0.18
BHA Top Rated:	143-661	-£0.19
Up in class:	346-3866	-£0.37
Same class:	810-7184	-£0.29
Down in class:	712-5020	-£0.22
Colts and Geldings:	1639-15967	-£0.30
Fillies:	427-5552	-£0.31
Absolute Favourites:	950-2444	-£0.05

TRAINERS (WINS-RUNS, £)

R M Beckett 44-259 £0.64; K R Burke 39-275 £0.36; J L Spearing 8-87 £1.12; W R Muir 16-199 £0.44; P Winkworth 17-148 £0.55; D Nicholls 20-143 £0.57; G A Swinbank 20-166 £0.45; Mrs G S Rees 2-45 £1.39; D J Coakley 5-39 £1.43; H Morrison 12-159 £0.35; J Hetherton 1-15 £3.47; Miss J R Tooth 1-15 £3.47; J H M Gosden 69-376 £0.13; W M Brisbourne 2-72 £0.64; R Ingram 3-29 £1.56; Mrs L Stubbs 11-85 £0.53; A M Balding 33-294 £0.15; J S Wainwright 3-52 £0.83; M Dods 13-144 £0.29.

Maiden Races

2-Y.O Races: Maiden Races – 2 to 7 runners

ANALYSIS BY BHA RATING

Rating	Prop	Win	Runs	Wins%	£
120..139	0%	0	0	0.0%	0.00
110..119	0%	0	0	0.0%	0.00
100..109	0%	0	0	0.0%	0.00
90..99	0%	1	2	50.0%	0.38
70..89	8%	39	111	35.1%	-0.14
50..69	1%	5	65	7.7%	-0.23
..49	0%	0	16	0.0%	-1.00
Unrated	91%	437	2696	16.2%	-0.15

ANALYSIS BY WEIGHT CARRIED

Weight	Prop	Win	Runs	Wins%	£
10-01+	0%	0	0	0.0%	0.00
9-8..10-00	0%	0	0	0.0%	0.00
9-0..9-07	62%	297	1577	18.8%	-0.11
8-8..8-13	30%	144	947	15.2%	-0.17
8-0..8-07	8%	39	340	11.5%	-0.24
..7-13	0%	2	26	7.7%	-0.72

ANALYSIS BY DAYS SINCE LAST RUN

Days	Prop	Win	Runs	Wins%	£
1..7	6%	27	121	22.3%	0.37
8..14	27%	130	628	20.7%	-0.32
15..28	30%	147	748	19.7%	-0.07
29..60	13%	62	344	18.0%	-0.20
61..100	1%	4	58	6.9%	-0.15
101+	0%	2	13	15.4%	-0.11
Unraced	23%	110	978	11.2%	-0.16

ANALYSIS BY TODAY'S STARTING PRICE

Price	Prop	Win	Runs	Wins%	£
Odds On	30%	144	219	65.8%	0.01
Ev-2/1	23%	112	326	34.4%	-0.14
9/4-4/1	21%	100	475	21.1%	-0.16
9/2-6/1	9%	41	304	13.5%	-0.18
13/2-10/1	10%	50	395	12.7%	0.15
11/1-16/1	4%	18	376	4.8%	-0.27
18/1-33/1	3%	13	438	3.0%	-0.19
40/1+	1%	4	357	1.1%	-0.39

ANALYSIS BY STARTING PRICE LAST TIME

Price	Prop	Win	Runs	Wins%	£
Odds On	2%	8	22	36.4%	-0.10
Ev-2/1	7%	33	71	46.5%	0.11
9/4-4/1	13%	63	232	27.2%	-0.36
9/2-6/1	13%	63	198	31.8%	0.25
13/2-10/1	13%	63	298	21.1%	-0.29
11/1-16/1	14%	66	316	20.9%	-0.23
18/1-33/1	9%	45	301	11.5%	-0.22
40/1+	6%	31	384	8.1%	-0.04
Unraced	23%	110	978	11.2%	-0.16

ANALYSIS BY DISTANCE BEATEN LAST TIME

Lengths	Prop	Win	Runs	Wins%	£
..-10	0%	0	0	0.0%	0.00
-10..0	0%	0	0	0.0%	0.00
0.1..2	27%	131	365	35.9%	-0.22
2.1..5	24%	118	404	29.2%	-0.09
5.1..10	18%	87	554	15.7%	0.08
10.1..20	6%	30	438	6.8%	-0.22
20.0..30	1%	3	94	3.2%	-0.79
30.1+	1%	3	57	5.3%	-0.68
Not Compl	0%	0	0	0.0%	0.00
Unraced	23%	110	978	11.2%	-0.16

ANALYSIS BY RUN NUMBER

Run No	Prop	Win	Runs	Wins%	£
FTO	23%	110	978	11.2%	-0.16
2nd Run	37%	176	894	19.7%	-0.18
3rd Run	22%	104	605	17.2%	-0.11
4th+ Run	19%	92	413	22.3%	-0.13

ANALYSIS BY POSITION LAST TIME

Pos LT	Prop	Win	Runs	Wins%	£
Won	0%	0	0	0.0%	0.00
2nd or 3rd	42%	201	596	33.7%	-0.14
Unplaced	35%	171	1305	13.1%	-0.15
Not Compl	23%	110	989	11.1%	-0.17

OTHER FACTORS (WINS-RUNS, £)

Beaten Favourite:	48-127	-£0.04
BHA Top Rated:	32-83	-£0.08
Up in class:	62-443	-£0.12
Same class:	144-826	-£0.27
Down in class:	166-643	-£0.01
Colts and Geldings:	316-1760	-£0.15
Fillies:	100-727	-£0.15
Absolute Favourites:	224-451	-£0.06

TRAINERS (WINS-RUNS, £)

P T Midgley 3-20 £3.83; J G Portman 3-10 £4.50; E J O'Neill 7-24 £1.69; A P Jarvis 3-14 £2.25; M Brittain 2-16 £1.69; M Johnston 53-179 £0.13; D Nicholls 4-17 £1.26; A B Haynes 1-13 £1.62; P Winkworth 4-21 £0.94; T D Barron 7-20 £0.86; R A Fahey 16-67 £0.23; M G Quinlan 5-17 £0.80; B W Hills 18-43 £0.29; J L Spearing 4-14 £0.79; W J Haggas 7-15 £0.62; R M Beckett 5-25 £0.37; T P Tate 5-12 £0.70; P F I Cole 8-25 £0.31; M P Tregoning 4-11 £0.63; Saeed Bin Suroor 15-41 £0.15.

Race Profiles

2-Y.O Races: Maiden Races – 8 to 14 runners

ANALYSIS BY BHA RATING

Rating	Prop	Win	Runs	Wins%	£
120..139	0%	0	0	0.0%	0.00
110..119	0%	0	0	0.0%	0.00
100..109	0%	0	1	0.0%	-1.00
90..99	0%	6	16	37.5%	-0.18
70..89	6%	115	546	21.1%	-0.19
50..69	1%	25	481	5.2%	-0.42
..49	0%	0	159	0.0%	-1.00
Unrated	92%	1653	18203	9.1%	-0.28

ANALYSIS BY WEIGHT CARRIED

Weight	Prop	Win	Runs	Wins%	£
10-01+	0%	0	0	0.0%	0.00
9-8..10-00	0%	0	0	0.0%	0.00
9-0..9-07	66%	1181	11392	10.4%	-0.28
8-8..8-13	27%	478	5864	8.2%	-0.26
8-0..8-07	8%	138	2039	6.8%	-0.35
..7-13	0%	2	111	1.8%	-0.86

ANALYSIS BY DAYS SINCE LAST RUN

Days	Prop	Win	Runs	Wins%	£
1..7	2%	44	544	8.1%	-0.60
8..14	21%	373	3134	11.9%	-0.30
15..28	33%	596	4742	12.6%	-0.24
29..60	12%	218	2333	9.3%	-0.25
61..100	2%	43	505	8.5%	-0.26
101+	1%	13	159	8.2%	-0.36
Unraced	28%	512	7989	6.4%	-0.29

ANALYSIS BY TODAY'S STARTING PRICE

Price	Prop	Win	Runs	Wins%	£
Odds On	10%	179	361	49.6%	-0.17
Ev-2/1	19%	342	916	37.3%	-0.04
9/4-4/1	28%	500	2219	22.5%	-0.07
9/2-6/1	13%	233	1577	14.8%	-0.09
13/2-10/1	14%	244	2738	8.9%	-0.19
11/1-16/1	9%	154	2910	5.3%	-0.23
18/1-33/1	6%	113	4100	2.8%	-0.31
40/1+	2%	34	4585	0.7%	-0.58

ANALYSIS BY STARTING PRICE LAST TIME

Price	Prop	Win	Runs	Wins%	£
Odds On	2%	35	118	29.7%	-0.15
Ev-2/1	6%	108	399	27.1%	-0.07
9/4-4/1	11%	195	990	19.7%	-0.21
9/2-6/1	10%	173	866	20.0%	0.09
13/2-10/1	13%	239	1618	14.8%	-0.24
11/1-16/1	12%	217	1906	11.4%	-0.17
18/1-33/1	12%	216	2804	7.7%	-0.36
40/1+	6%	104	2716	3.8%	-0.47
Unraced	28%	512	7989	6.4%	-0.29

ANALYSIS BY DISTANCE BEATEN LAST TIME

Lengths	Prop	Win	Runs	Wins%	£
..-10	0%	0	0	0.0%	0.00
-10..0	0%	0	1	0.0%	-1.00
0.1..2	21%	378	1465	25.8%	-0.12
2.1..5	23%	417	2316	18.0%	-0.16
5.1..10	19%	335	3288	10.2%	-0.26
10.1..20	7%	134	3163	4.2%	-0.34
20.0..30	1%	22	825	2.7%	-0.45
30.1+	0%	1	359	0.3%	-0.95
Not Compl	0%	0	0	0.0%	0.00
Unraced	28%	512	7989	6.4%	-0.29

ANALYSIS BY RUN NUMBER

Run No	Prop	Win	Runs	Wins%	£
FTO	28%	512	7989	6.4%	-0.29
2nd Run	38%	685	5837	11.7%	-0.18
3rd Run	21%	369	3687	10.0%	-0.38
4th+ Run	13%	233	1893	12.3%	-0.40

ANALYSIS BY POSITION LAST TIME

Pos LT	Prop	Win	Runs	Wins%	£
Won	0%	0	0	0.0%	0.00
2nd or 3rd	33%	595	2554	23.3%	-0.16
Unplaced	38%	692	8838	7.8%	-0.31
Not Compl	28%	512	8014	6.4%	-0.30

OTHER FACTORS (WINS-RUNS, £)

Beaten Favourite:	148-650	-£0.27
BHA Top Rated:	89-478	-£0.32
Up in class:	246-2681	-£0.37
Same class:	577-5166	-£0.24
Down in class:	464-3570	-£0.26
Colts and Geldings:	1127-11158	-£0.27
Fillies:	282-3979	-£0.37
Absolute Favourites:	615-1677	-£0.06

TRAINERS (WINS-RUNS, £)

J L Spearing 4-56 £1.85; G A Swinbank 16-130 £0.72; A M Balding 26-200 £0.41; M Dods 11-99 £0.82; R M Beckett 31-177 £0.42; Mrs G S Rees 2-36 £1.99; K R Burke 26-191 £0.34; D Nicholls 15-111 £0.56; Mrs L Stubbs 9-63 £0.94; W R Muir 11-133 £0.45; J S Wainwright 3-39 £1.44; Miss J R Tooth 1-12 £4.58; J Hetherton 1-14 £3.79; J H M Gosden 45-218 £0.23; H Morrison 6-99 £0.43; M Mullineaux 1-12 £3.25; R A Fahey 40-318 £0.10; P D Evans 13-158 £0.21; D R Lanigan 4-26 £1.24; D J Coakley 4-24 £1.23.

Maiden Races

2-Y.O Races: Maiden Races – 15 runners or more

ANALYSIS BY BHA RATING

Rating	Prop	Win	Runs	Wins%	£
120..139	0%	0	0	0.0%	0.00
110..119	0%	0	0	0.0%	0.00
100..109	0%	0	0	0.0%	0.00
90..99	0%	0	2	0.0%	-1.00
70..89	8%	27	135	20.0%	0.03
50..69	1%	3	89	3.4%	-0.48
..49	0%	0	26	0.0%	-1.00
Unrated	91%	308	5226	5.9%	-0.42

ANALYSIS BY WEIGHT CARRIED

Weight	Prop	Win	Runs	Wins%	£
10-01+	0%	0	0	0.0%	0.00
9-8..10-00	0%	0	0	0.0%	0.00
9-0..9-07	65%	221	3341	6.6%	-0.52
8-8..8-13	26%	89	1593	5.6%	-0.27
8-0..8-07	8%	28	511	5.5%	-0.11
..7-13	0%	0	33	0.0%	-1.00

ANALYSIS BY DAYS SINCE LAST RUN

Days	Prop	Win	Runs	Wins%	£
1..7	2%	7	121	5.8%	-0.68
8..14	14%	48	724	6.6%	-0.66
15..28	26%	87	1136	7.7%	-0.47
29..60	16%	54	575	9.4%	0.00
61..100	4%	12	141	8.5%	-0.43
101+	0%	1	44	2.3%	-0.89
Unraced	38%	129	2737	4.7%	-0.39

ANALYSIS BY TODAY'S STARTING PRICE

Price	Prop	Win	Runs	Wins%	£
Odds On	8%	26	41	63.4%	0.11
Ev-2/1	16%	53	133	39.8%	0.03
9/4-4/1	25%	85	374	22.7%	-0.03
9/2-6/1	16%	55	340	16.2%	0.02
13/2-10/1	14%	49	623	7.9%	-0.28
11/1-16/1	9%	31	791	3.9%	-0.42
18/1-33/1	8%	26	1329	2.0%	-0.47
40/1+	4%	13	1847	0.7%	-0.61

ANALYSIS BY STARTING PRICE LAST TIME

Price	Prop	Win	Runs	Wins%	£
Odds On	4%	13	32	40.6%	0.67
Ev-2/1	5%	18	70	25.7%	-0.16
9/4-4/1	12%	42	236	17.8%	-0.09
9/2-6/1	6%	21	190	11.1%	-0.48
13/2-10/1	10%	34	348	9.8%	-0.59
11/1-16/1	11%	36	436	8.3%	-0.48
18/1-33/1	7%	25	699	3.6%	-0.43
40/1+	6%	20	730	2.7%	-0.51
Unraced	38%	129	2737	4.7%	-0.39

ANALYSIS BY DISTANCE BEATEN LAST TIME

Lengths	Prop	Win	Runs	Wins%	£
..-10	0%	0	0	0.0%	0.00
-10..0	0%	0	1	0.0%	-1.00
0.1..2	23%	77	325	23.7%	-0.14
2.1..5	19%	64	495	12.9%	-0.22
5.1..10	13%	45	779	5.8%	-0.52
10.1..20	6%	20	847	2.4%	-0.59
20.0..30	1%	3	193	1.6%	-0.18
30.1+	0%	0	101	0.0%	-1.00
Not Compl	0%	0	0	0.0%	0.00
Unraced	38%	129	2737	4.7%	-0.39

ANALYSIS BY RUN NUMBER

Run No	Prop	Win	Runs	Wins%	£
FTO	38%	129	2737	4.7%	-0.39
2nd Run	31%	104	1527	6.8%	-0.44
3rd Run	20%	68	872	7.8%	-0.54
4th+ Run	11%	37	342	10.8%	-0.14

ANALYSIS BY POSITION LAST TIME

Pos LT	Prop	Win	Runs	Wins%	£
Won	0%	0	0	0.0%	0.00
2nd or 3rd	30%	103	536	19.2%	-0.29
Unplaced	31%	106	2199	4.8%	-0.47
Not Compl	38%	129	2743	4.7%	-0.39

OTHER FACTORS (WINS-RUNS, £)

Beaten Favourite:	35-141	£0.10
BHA Top Rated:	22-100	£0.36
Up in class:	38-742	-£0.54
Same class:	89-1192	-£0.52
Down in class:	82-807	-£0.21
Colts and Geldings:	196-3049	-£0.50
Fillies:	45-846	-£0.16
Absolute Favourites:	111-316	-£0.00

TRAINERS (WINS-RUNS, £)

W M Brisbourne 1-11 £8.18; R M Beckett 8-57 £1.46; J R Weymes 3-16 £2.88; W R Muir 3-43 £1.06; I A Wood 1-24 £1.79; P Winkworth 3-24 £1.56; D K Ivory 4-31 £1.06; E F Vaughan 4-19 £1.51; D J Coakley 1-13 £2.15; K R Burke 2-24 £1.17; W J Knight 1-23 £1.22; H Candy 5-30 £0.84; T P Tate 2-23 £0.67; E S McMahon 3-22 £0.46; D W Barker 1-12 £0.58; Saeed Bin Suroor 21-75 £0.09; H R A Cecil 10-41 £0.13; J H M Gosden 16-130 £0.04; M Johnston 11-87 £0.05; M H Tompkins 2-64 £0.06.

Race Profiles

2-Y.O Races: Maiden Races – good or faster going

ANALYSIS BY BHA RATING

Rating	Prop	Win	Runs	Wins%	£
120..139	0%	0	0	0.0%	0.00
110..119	0%	0	0	0.0%	0.00
100..109	0%	0	1	0.0%	-1.00
90..99	0%	6	14	42.9%	-0.08
70..89	6%	119	511	23.3%	-0.13
50..69	1%	16	406	3.9%	-0.51
..49	0%	0	131	0.0%	-1.00
Unrated	92%	1725	18488	9.3%	-0.29

ANALYSIS BY WEIGHT CARRIED

Weight	Prop	Win	Runs	Wins%	£
10-01+	0%	0	0	0.0%	0.00
9-8..10-00	0%	0	0	0.0%	0.00
9-0..9-07	65%	1210	11467	10.6%	-0.31
8-8..8-13	27%	508	5823	8.7%	-0.25
8-0..8-07	8%	145	2141	6.8%	-0.31
..7-13	0%	3	120	2.5%	-0.88

ANALYSIS BY DAYS SINCE LAST RUN

Days	Prop	Win	Runs	Wins%	£
1..7	3%	62	567	10.9%	-0.50
8..14	21%	395	3210	12.3%	-0.37
15..28	32%	602	4659	12.9%	-0.28
29..60	12%	233	2258	10.3%	-0.21
61..100	2%	34	464	7.3%	-0.20
101+	1%	13	124	10.5%	-0.14
Unraced	28%	527	8269	6.4%	-0.29

ANALYSIS BY TODAY'S STARTING PRICE

Price	Prop	Win	Runs	Wins%	£
Odds On	15%	271	471	57.5%	-0.07
Ev-2/1	20%	375	990	37.9%	-0.03
9/4-4/1	25%	471	2167	21.7%	-0.11
9/2-6/1	12%	233	1547	15.1%	-0.06
13/2-10/1	13%	238	2593	9.2%	-0.17
11/1-16/1	7%	137	2807	4.9%	-0.29
18/1-33/1	5%	102	4117	2.5%	-0.36
40/1+	2%	39	4859	0.8%	-0.54

ANALYSIS BY STARTING PRICE LAST TIME

Price	Prop	Win	Runs	Wins%	£
Odds On	2%	45	131	34.4%	0.03
Ev-2/1	7%	123	403	30.5%	-0.07
9/4-4/1	12%	231	1088	21.2%	-0.20
9/2-6/1	10%	178	893	19.9%	-0.07
13/2-10/1	12%	232	1600	14.5%	-0.33
11/1-16/1	13%	237	1901	12.5%	-0.17
18/1-33/1	10%	183	2669	6.9%	-0.39
40/1+	6%	110	2597	4.2%	-0.45
Unraced	28%	527	8269	6.4%	-0.29

ANALYSIS BY DISTANCE BEATEN LAST TIME

Lengths	Prop	Win	Runs	Wins%	£
..-10	0%	0	0	0.0%	0.00
-10..0	0%	0	1	0.0%	-1.00
0.1..2	24%	440	1577	27.9%	-0.16
2.1..5	23%	427	2334	18.3%	-0.18
5.1..10	18%	328	3228	10.2%	-0.29
10.1..20	7%	123	3065	4.0%	-0.39
20.0..30	1%	18	736	2.4%	-0.38
30.1+	0%	3	341	0.9%	-0.95
Not Compl	0%	0	0	0.0%	0.00
Unraced	28%	527	8269	6.4%	-0.29

ANALYSIS BY RUN NUMBER

Run No	Prop	Win	Runs	Wins%	£
FTO	28%	527	8269	6.4%	-0.29
2nd Run	38%	701	5795	12.1%	-0.22
3rd Run	20%	375	3619	10.4%	-0.41
4th+ Run	14%	263	1868	14.1%	-0.34

ANALYSIS BY POSITION LAST TIME

Pos LT	Prop	Win	Runs	Wins%	£
Won	0%	0	0	0.0%	0.00
2nd or 3rd	36%	667	2664	25.0%	-0.18
Unplaced	36%	672	8586	7.8%	-0.33
Not Compl	28%	527	8301	6.3%	-0.29

OTHER FACTORS (WINS-RUNS, £)

Beaten Favourite:	188-691	-£0.14
BHA Top Rated:	93-415	-£0.21
Up in class:	243-2768	-£0.37
Same class:	582-4972	-£0.31
Down in class:	514-3542	-£0.22
Colts and Geldings:	1171-11170	-£0.29
Fillies:	291-3787	-£0.36
Absolute Favourites:	707-1749	-£0.03

TRAINERS (WINS-RUNS, £)

R M Beckett 29-178 £0.69; M Johnston 149-685 £0.17; J L Spearing 5-58 £2.03; H Morrison 9-106 £0.82; W H Cowell 12-108 £0.41; Mrs G S Rees 2-28 £2.84; W M Brisbourne 2-53 £1.23; D J Coakley 5-32 £1.96; D Nicholls 14-106 £0.56; J Hetherton 1-12 £4.58; W R Muir 12-147 £0.37; J S Wainwright 3-41 £1.32; R Ingram 3-22 £2.38; A M Balding 23-217 £0.22; P Winkworth 12-108 £0.41; J H M Gosden 49-267 £0.16; Jedd O'Keeffe 5-50 £0.80; J R Weymes 4-92 £0.40; R M H Cowell 4-12 £2.97; J R Boyle 3-37 £0.79; Rae Guest 3-41 £0.69.

Maiden Races

2-Y.O Races: Maiden Races – good to soft or softer going

ANALYSIS BY BHA RATING

Rating	Prop	Win	Runs	Wins%	£
120..139	0%	0	0	0.0%	0.00
110..119	0%	0	0	0.0%	0.00
100..109	0%	0	0	0.0%	0.00
90..99	0%	1	6	16.7%	-0.50
70..89	8%	62	281	22.1%	-0.17
50..69	2%	17	229	7.4%	-0.22
..49	0%	0	70	0.0%	-1.00
Unrated	89%	673	7637	8.8%	-0.30

ANALYSIS BY WEIGHT CARRIED

Weight	Prop	Win	Runs	Wins%	£
10-01+	0%	0	0	0.0%	0.00
9-8..10-00	0%	0	0	0.0%	0.00
9-0..9-07	65%	489	4843	10.1%	-0.31
8-8..8-13	27%	203	2581	7.9%	-0.27
8-0..8-07	8%	60	749	8.0%	-0.25
..7-13	0%	1	50	2.0%	-0.82

ANALYSIS BY DAYS SINCE LAST RUN

Days	Prop	Win	Runs	Wins%	£
1..7	2%	16	219	7.3%	-0.37
8..14	21%	156	1276	12.2%	-0.33
15..28	30%	228	1967	11.6%	-0.21
29..60	13%	101	994	10.2%	-0.16
61..100	3%	25	240	10.4%	-0.45
101+	0%	3	92	3.3%	-0.87
Unraced	30%	224	3435	6.5%	-0.34

ANALYSIS BY TODAY'S STARTING PRICE

Price	Prop	Win	Runs	Wins%	£
Odds On	10%	78	150	52.0%	-0.13
Ev-2/1	18%	132	385	34.3%	-0.11
9/4-4/1	28%	214	901	23.8%	-0.02
9/2-6/1	13%	96	674	14.2%	-0.12
13/2-10/1	14%	105	1163	9.0%	-0.18
11/1-16/1	9%	66	1270	5.2%	-0.24
18/1-33/1	7%	50	1750	2.9%	-0.27
40/1+	2%	12	1930	0.6%	-0.68

ANALYSIS BY STARTING PRICE LAST TIME

Price	Prop	Win	Runs	Wins%	£
Odds On	1%	11	41	26.8%	-0.05
Ev-2/1	5%	36	137	26.3%	-0.03
9/4-4/1	9%	69	370	18.6%	-0.26
9/2-6/1	10%	79	361	21.9%	0.26
13/2-10/1	14%	104	664	15.7%	-0.22
11/1-16/1	11%	82	757	10.8%	-0.35
18/1-33/1	14%	103	1225	8.4%	-0.30
40/1+	6%	45	1233	3.6%	-0.39
Unraced	30%	224	3435	6.5%	-0.34

ANALYSIS BY DISTANCE BEATEN LAST TIME

Lengths	Prop	Win	Runs	Wins%	£
..-10	0%	0	0	0.0%	0.00
-10..0	0%	0	1	0.0%	-1.00
0.1..2	19%	146	578	25.3%	-0.10
2.1..5	23%	172	881	19.5%	-0.11
5.1..10	18%	139	1393	10.0%	-0.20
10.1..20	8%	61	1383	4.4%	-0.35
20.0..30	1%	10	376	2.7%	-0.53
30.1+	0%	1	176	0.6%	-0.90
Not Compl	0%	0	0	0.0%	0.00
Unraced	30%	224	3435	6.5%	-0.34

ANALYSIS BY RUN NUMBER

Run No	Prop	Win	Runs	Wins%	£
FTO	30%	224	3435	6.5%	-0.34
2nd Run	35%	264	2463	10.7%	-0.25
3rd Run	22%	166	1545	10.7%	-0.29
4th+ Run	13%	99	780	12.7%	-0.27

ANALYSIS BY POSITION LAST TIME

Pos LT	Prop	Win	Runs	Wins%	£
Won	0%	0	0	0.0%	0.00
2nd or 3rd	31%	232	1022	22.7%	-0.14
Unplaced	39%	297	3756	7.9%	-0.30
Not Compl	30%	224	3445	6.5%	-0.34

OTHER FACTORS (WINS-RUNS, £)

Beaten Favourite:	43-227	-£0.32
BHA Top Rated:	50-246	-£0.16
Up in class:	103-1098	-£0.37
Same class:	228-2212	-£0.25
Down in class:	198-1478	-£0.21
Colts and Geldings:	468-4797	-£0.33
Fillies:	136-1765	-£0.20
Absolute Favourites:	243-695	-£0.11

TRAINERS (WINS-RUNS, £)

P T Midgley 4-41 £1.99; K R Burke 10-80 £0.99; G A Swinbank 6-57 £1.28; R A Fahey 26-127 £0.56; M Dods 6-50 £1.29; I A Wood 2-29 £2.03; R M Beckett 15-81 £0.54; Mrs L Stubbs 5-27 £1.56; P Winkworth 5-40 £0.95; Sir Michael Stoute 28-120 £0.28; W R Muir 4-52 £0.64; J G Portman 3-32 £0.91; C E Brittain 9-48 £0.51; D K Ivory 2-17 £1.38; D Nicholls 6-37 £0.61; SPARR 1-13 £1.62; B Ellison 2-16 £0.97; A B Haynes 3-25 £0.62; W S Kittow 2-14 £0.79; T P Tate 8-47 £0.23.

Race Profiles

2-Y.O Races: Maiden Races – 5 to 6 furlong races

ANALYSIS BY BHA RATING

Rating	Prop	Win	Runs	Wins%	£
120..139	0%	0	0	0.0%	0.00
110..119	0%	0	0	0.0%	0.00
100..109	0%	0	1	0.0%	-1.00
90..99	0%	3	12	25.0%	-0.38
70..89	6%	98	412	23.8%	-0.18
50..69	1%	20	370	5.4%	-0.29
..49	0%	0	88	0.0%	-1.00
Unrated	92%	1489	15449	9.6%	-0.25

ANALYSIS BY WEIGHT CARRIED

Weight	Prop	Win	Runs	Wins%	£
10-01+	0%	0	0	0.0%	0.00
9-8..10-00	0%	0	0	0.0%	0.00
9-0..9-07	59%	954	8543	11.2%	-0.23
8-8..8-13	30%	489	5511	8.9%	-0.26
8-0..8-07	10%	164	2146	7.6%	-0.28
..7-13	0%	3	132	2.3%	-0.84

ANALYSIS BY DAYS SINCE LAST RUN

Days	Prop	Win	Runs	Wins%	£
1..7	4%	59	558	10.6%	-0.38
8..14	22%	357	2723	13.1%	-0.31
15..28	29%	472	3590	13.1%	-0.21
29..60	11%	175	1672	10.5%	-0.19
61..100	2%	35	369	9.5%	-0.21
101+	1%	10	125	8.0%	-0.52
Unraced	31%	502	7295	6.9%	-0.26

ANALYSIS BY TODAY'S STARTING PRICE

Price	Prop	Win	Runs	Wins%	£
Odds On	13%	210	381	55.1%	-0.11
Ev-2/1	19%	305	838	36.4%	-0.07
9/4-4/1	27%	436	1931	22.6%	-0.07
9/2-6/1	13%	204	1402	14.6%	-0.10
13/2-10/1	13%	202	2247	9.0%	-0.19
11/1-16/1	8%	125	2481	5.0%	-0.27
18/1-33/1	6%	95	3395	2.8%	-0.27
40/1+	2%	33	3657	0.9%	-0.48

ANALYSIS BY STARTING PRICE LAST TIME

Price	Prop	Win	Runs	Wins%	£
Odds On	2%	31	107	29.0%	-0.10
Ev-2/1	5%	85	340	25.0%	-0.21
9/4-4/1	12%	191	896	21.3%	-0.25
9/2-6/1	10%	163	765	21.3%	0.09
13/2-10/1	12%	195	1325	14.7%	-0.30
11/1-16/1	11%	185	1520	12.2%	-0.18
18/1-33/1	11%	171	2098	8.2%	-0.28
40/1+	5%	87	1986	4.4%	-0.39
Unraced	31%	502	7295	6.9%	-0.26

ANALYSIS BY DISTANCE BEATEN LAST TIME

Lengths	Prop	Win	Runs	Wins%	£
..-10	0%	0	0	0.0%	0.00
-10..0	0%	0	2	0.0%	-1.00
0.1..2	22%	356	1309	27.2%	-0.12
2.1..5	23%	366	1955	18.7%	-0.16
5.1..10	16%	263	2631	10.0%	-0.22
10.1..20	7%	109	2350	4.6%	-0.27
20.0..30	1%	13	532	2.4%	-0.55
30.1+	0%	1	258	0.4%	-0.98
Not Compl	0%	0	0	0.0%	0.00
Unraced	31%	502	7295	6.9%	-0.26

ANALYSIS BY RUN NUMBER

Run No	Prop	Win	Runs	Wins%	£
FTO	31%	502	7295	6.9%	-0.26
2nd Run	37%	591	4584	12.9%	-0.16
3rd Run	19%	301	2830	10.6%	-0.35
4th+ Run	13%	216	1623	13.3%	-0.33

ANALYSIS BY POSITION LAST TIME

Pos LT	Prop	Win	Runs	Wins%	£
Won	0%	0	0	0.0%	0.00
2nd or 3rd	34%	547	2232	24.5%	-0.16
Unplaced	35%	561	6781	8.3%	-0.28
Not Compl	31%	502	7319	6.9%	-0.26

OTHER FACTORS (WINS-RUNS, £)

Beaten Favourite:	136-577	-£0.28
BHA Top Rated:	72-341	-£0.24
Up in class:	222-2152	-£0.26
Same class:	463-4065	-£0.26
Down in class:	423-2820	-£0.23
Colts and Geldings:	941-8614	-£0.20
Fillies:	312-3883	-£0.38
Absolute Favourites:	577-1497	-£0.06

TRAINERS (WINS-RUNS, £)

J L Spearing 8-75 £1.46; D Nicholls 19-114 £0.89; W R Muir 10-116 £0.84; K R Burke 36-222 £0.40; G A Swinbank 15-110 £0.81; W M Brisbourne 2-43 £1.74; A M Balding 13-138 £0.50; P Winkworth 13-109 £0.62; H Morrison 8-79 £0.82; R A Fahey 48-330 £0.19; E J O'Neill 17-80 £0.75; Mrs L Stubbs 10-70 £0.79; R Ingram 3-23 £2.23; J S Wainwright 2-34 £1.50; J G Portman 12-98 £0.51; D J Coakley 4-23 £1.98; M Mullineaux 1-11 £3.64; J R Weymes 3-77 £0.51; Jedd O'Keeffe 4-46 £0.80; J H M Gosden 25-111 £0.32.

Maiden Races

2-Y.O Races: Maiden Races – 7 to 8 furlong races

ANALYSIS BY BHA RATING

Rating	Prop	Win	Runs	Wins%	£
120..139	0%	0	0	0.0%	0.00
110..119	0%	0	0	0.0%	0.00
100..109	0%	0	0	0.0%	0.00
90..99	0%	4	8	50.0%	0.06
70..89	8%	77	338	22.8%	-0.06
50..69	1%	13	243	5.3%	-0.53
..49	0%	0	106	0.0%	-1.00
Unrated	90%	889	10474	8.5%	-0.36

ANALYSIS BY WEIGHT CARRIED

Weight	Prop	Win	Runs	Wins%	£
10-01+	0%	0	0	0.0%	0.00
9-8..10-00	0%	0	0	0.0%	0.00
9-0..9-07	74%	724	7551	9.6%	-0.39
8-8..8-13	22%	217	2843	7.6%	-0.26
8-0..8-07	4%	41	737	5.6%	-0.33
..7-13	0%	1	38	2.6%	-0.96

ANALYSIS BY DAYS SINCE LAST RUN

Days	Prop	Win	Runs	Wins%	£
1..7	2%	17	216	7.9%	-0.69
8..14	19%	184	1698	10.8%	-0.45
15..28	36%	349	2926	11.9%	-0.32
29..60	16%	156	1542	10.1%	-0.21
61..100	2%	22	324	6.8%	-0.38
101+	1%	6	90	6.7%	-0.35
Unraced	25%	249	4373	5.7%	-0.38

ANALYSIS BY TODAY'S STARTING PRICE

Price	Prop	Win	Runs	Wins%	£
Odds On	14%	136	236	57.6%	-0.05
Ev-2/1	20%	193	518	37.3%	-0.04
9/4-4/1	25%	244	1105	22.1%	-0.10
9/2-6/1	12%	122	796	15.3%	-0.05
13/2-10/1	14%	138	1478	9.3%	-0.15
11/1-16/1	8%	77	1560	4.9%	-0.28
18/1-33/1	6%	55	2435	2.3%	-0.44
40/1+	2%	18	3041	0.6%	-0.68

ANALYSIS BY STARTING PRICE LAST TIME

Price	Prop	Win	Runs	Wins%	£
Odds On	3%	25	64	39.1%	0.21
Ev-2/1	7%	73	196	37.2%	0.22
9/4-4/1	11%	104	539	19.3%	-0.15
9/2-6/1	9%	91	469	19.4%	-0.10
13/2-10/1	14%	140	908	15.4%	-0.28
11/1-16/1	13%	124	1097	11.3%	-0.30
18/1-33/1	11%	113	1741	6.5%	-0.45
40/1+	7%	64	1782	3.6%	-0.50
Unraced	25%	249	4373	5.7%	-0.38

ANALYSIS BY DISTANCE BEATEN LAST TIME

Lengths	Prop	Win	Runs	Wins%	£
..-10	0%	0	0	0.0%	0.00
-10..0	0%	0	0	0.0%	0.00
0.1..2	22%	220	812	27.1%	-0.17
2.1..5	23%	227	1206	18.8%	-0.12
5.1..10	20%	200	1945	10.3%	-0.31
10.1..20	7%	71	2030	3.5%	-0.51
20.0..30	1%	14	556	2.5%	-0.31
30.1+	0%	2	247	0.8%	-0.91
Not Compl	0%	0	0	0.0%	0.00
Unraced	25%	249	4373	5.7%	-0.38

ANALYSIS BY RUN NUMBER

Run No	Prop	Win	Runs	Wins%	£
FTO	25%	249	4373	5.7%	-0.38
2nd Run	37%	364	3598	10.1%	-0.32
3rd Run	23%	230	2249	10.2%	-0.41
4th+ Run	14%	140	949	14.8%	-0.28

ANALYSIS BY POSITION LAST TIME

Pos LT	Prop	Win	Runs	Wins%	£
Won	0%	0	0	0.0%	0.00
2nd or 3rd	34%	339	1388	24.4%	-0.19
Unplaced	40%	395	5390	7.3%	-0.38
Not Compl	25%	249	4391	5.7%	-0.38

OTHER FACTORS (WINS-RUNS, £)

Beaten Favourite:	94-332	£0.00
BHA Top Rated:	67-298	-£0.12
Up in class:	118-1635	-£0.50
Same class:	334-3010	-£0.34
Down in class:	282-2151	-£0.22
Colts and Geldings:	677-7127	-£0.42
Fillies:	110-1622	-£0.16
Absolute Favourites:	360-923	-£0.06

TRAINERS (WINS-RUNS, £)

R M Beckett 17-80 £1.83; M Johnston 101-510 £0.19; Mrs G S Rees 1-13 £6.77; Rae Guest 3-22 £2.17; J A R Toller 1-12 £3.25; I A Wood 2-31 £1.25; M Dods 3-40 £0.84; Mrs P N Dutfield 1-14 £1.93; G M Moore 5-25 £1.02; J H M Gosden 43-256 £0.08; H R A Cecil 26-129 £0.15; W R Swinburn 7-73 £0.23; R F Johnson Houghton 1-10 £1.60; P Winkworth 4-38 £0.42; C R Egerton 3-16 £0.91; Saeed Bin Suroor 57-222 £0.05; G Wragg 2-27 £0.41; J D Bethell 2-26 £0.42; D J Coakley 1-16 £0.63; K R Burke 3-53 £0.16.

Race Profiles

2-Y.O Races: Maiden Races – 9+ furlong races

JUVENILE RACES

ANALYSIS BY BHA RATING

Rating	Prop	Win	Runs	Wins%	£
120..139	0%	0	0	0.0%	0.00
110..119	0%	0	0	0.0%	0.00
100..109	0%	0	0	0.0%	0.00
90..99	0%	0	0	0.0%	0.00
70..89	23%	6	42	14.3%	-0.49
50..69	0%	0	22	0.0%	-1.00
..49	0%	0	7	0.0%	-1.00
Unrated	77%	20	202	9.9%	-0.30

ANALYSIS BY WEIGHT CARRIED

Weight	Prop	Win	Runs	Wins%	£
10-01+	0%	0	0	0.0%	0.00
9-8..10-00	0%	0	0	0.0%	0.00
9-0..9-07	81%	21	216	9.7%	-0.62
8-8..8-13	19%	5	50	10.0%	0.61
8-0..8-07	0%	0	7	0.0%	-1.00
..7-13	0%	0	0	0.0%	0.00

ANALYSIS BY DAYS SINCE LAST RUN

Days	Prop	Win	Runs	Wins%	£
1..7	8%	2	12	16.7%	-0.35
8..14	38%	10	65	15.4%	-0.53
15..28	35%	9	110	8.2%	-0.24
29..60	12%	3	38	7.9%	-0.20
61..100	8%	2	11	18.2%	-0.05
101+	0%	0	1	0.0%	-1.00
Unraced	0%	0	36	0.0%	-1.00

ANALYSIS BY TODAY'S STARTING PRICE

Price	Prop	Win	Runs	Wins%	£
Odds On	12%	3	4	75.0%	0.25
Ev-2/1	35%	9	19	47.4%	0.19
9/4-4/1	19%	5	32	15.6%	-0.31
9/2-6/1	12%	3	23	13.0%	-0.22
13/2-10/1	12%	3	31	9.7%	-0.18
11/1-16/1	4%	1	36	2.8%	-0.58
18/1-33/1	8%	2	37	5.4%	0.49
40/1+	0%	0	91	0.0%	-1.00

ANALYSIS BY STARTING PRICE LAST TIME

Price	Prop	Win	Runs	Wins%	£
Odds On	0%	0	1	0.0%	-1.00
Ev-2/1	4%	1	4	25.0%	-0.34
9/4-4/1	19%	5	23	21.7%	-0.40
9/2-6/1	12%	3	20	15.0%	0.43
13/2-10/1	4%	1	31	3.2%	-0.94
11/1-16/1	38%	10	41	24.4%	0.02
18/1-33/1	8%	2	55	3.6%	-0.86
40/1+	15%	4	62	6.5%	0.08
Unraced	0%	0	36	0.0%	-1.00

ANALYSIS BY DISTANCE BEATEN LAST TIME

Lengths	Prop	Win	Runs	Wins%	£
..-10	0%	0	0	0.0%	0.00
-10..0	0%	0	0	0.0%	0.00
0.1..2	38%	10	34	29.4%	-0.12
2.1..5	23%	6	54	11.1%	-0.60
5.1..10	15%	4	45	8.9%	-0.39
10.1..20	15%	4	68	5.9%	-0.01
20.0..30	4%	1	24	4.2%	-0.63
30.1+	4%	1	12	8.3%	-0.33
Not Compl	0%	0	0	0.0%	0.00
Unraced	0%	0	36	0.0%	-1.00

ANALYSIS BY RUN NUMBER

Run No	Prop	Win	Runs	Wins%	£
FTO	0%	0	36	0.0%	-1.00
2nd Run	38%	10	76	13.2%	0.24
3rd Run	38%	10	85	11.8%	-0.44
4th+ Run	23%	6	76	7.9%	-0.72

ANALYSIS BY POSITION LAST TIME

Pos LT	Prop	Win	Runs	Wins%	£
Won	0%	0	0	0.0%	0.00
2nd or 3rd	50%	13	66	19.7%	-0.40
Unplaced	50%	13	171	7.6%	-0.28
Not Compl	0%	0	36	0.0%	-1.00

OTHER FACTORS (WINS-RUNS, £)

Beaten Favourite:	1-9	-£0.71
BHA Top Rated:	4-22	-£0.30
Up in class:	6-79	-£0.57
Same class:	13-109	-£0.22
Down in class:	7-49	-£0.11
Colts and Geldings:	21-226	-£0.64
Fillies:	5-47	£0.72
Absolute Favourites:	13-24	£0.36

Claiming Races

2-Y.O Races: Claiming Races

ANALYSIS BY BHA RATING

Rating	Prop	Win	Runs	Wins%	£
120..139	0%	0	0	0.0%	0.00
110..119	0%	0	0	0.0%	0.00
100..109	0%	0	0	0.0%	0.00
90..99	0%	0	0	0.0%	0.00
70..89	8%	6	28	21.4%	-0.24
50..69	21%	16	153	10.5%	-0.38
..49	0%	0	17	0.0%	-1.00
Unrated	72%	56	554	10.1%	-0.16

ANALYSIS BY WEIGHT CARRIED

Weight	Prop	Win	Runs	Wins%	£
10-01+	0%	0	0	0.0%	0.00
9-8..10-00	1%	1	2	50.0%	-0.16
9-0..9-07	18%	14	110	12.7%	-0.08
8-8..8-13	42%	33	258	12.8%	-0.38
8-0..8-07	33%	26	328	7.9%	-0.12
..7-13	5%	4	54	7.4%	-0.48

ANALYSIS BY DAYS SINCE LAST RUN

Days	Prop	Win	Runs	Wins%	£
1..7	17%	13	84	15.5%	0.06
8..14	26%	20	210	9.5%	-0.53
15..28	41%	32	246	13.0%	-0.28
29..60	8%	6	96	6.3%	-0.61
61..100	1%	1	18	5.6%	-0.28
101+	0%	0	6	0.0%	-1.00
Unraced	8%	6	92	6.5%	0.79

ANALYSIS BY TODAY'S STARTING PRICE

Price	Prop	Win	Runs	Wins%	£
Odds On	12%	9	12	75.0%	0.16
Ev-2/1	17%	13	42	31.0%	-0.17
9/4-4/1	21%	16	97	16.5%	-0.29
9/2-6/1	17%	13	76	17.1%	0.00
13/2-10/1	22%	17	129	13.2%	0.17
11/1-16/1	5%	4	110	3.6%	-0.45
18/1-33/1	6%	5	154	3.2%	-0.18
40/1+	1%	1	132	0.8%	-0.61

ANALYSIS BY STARTING PRICE LAST TIME

Price	Prop	Win	Runs	Wins%	£
Odds On	8%	6	8	75.0%	0.62
Ev-2/1	4%	3	23	13.0%	-0.78
9/4-4/1	13%	10	81	12.3%	-0.45
9/2-6/1	14%	11	56	19.6%	0.30
13/2-10/1	19%	15	93	16.1%	-0.22
11/1-16/1	18%	14	100	14.0%	0.13
18/1-33/1	8%	6	138	4.3%	-0.70
40/1+	9%	7	161	4.3%	-0.00
Unraced	8%	6	92	6.5%	0.79

ANALYSIS BY DISTANCE BEATEN LAST TIME

Lengths	Prop	Win	Runs	Wins%	£
..-10	0%	0	0	0.0%	0.00
-10..0	17%	13	44	29.5%	-0.07
0.1..2	19%	15	62	24.2%	0.59
2.1..5	12%	9	94	9.6%	-0.50
5.1..10	31%	24	176	13.6%	-0.11
10.1..20	14%	11	190	5.8%	-0.61
20.0..30	0%	0	58	0.0%	-1.00
30.1+	0%	0	36	0.0%	-1.00
Not Compl	0%	0	0	0.0%	0.00
Unraced	8%	6	92	6.5%	0.79

ANALYSIS BY RUN NUMBER

Run No	Prop	Win	Runs	Wins%	£
FTO	8%	6	92	6.5%	0.79
2nd Run	17%	13	112	11.6%	-0.17
3rd Run	13%	10	153	6.5%	-0.60
4th+ Run	63%	49	395	12.4%	-0.34

ANALYSIS BY POSITION LAST TIME

Pos LT	Prop	Win	Runs	Wins%	£
Won	17%	13	44	29.5%	-0.07
2nd or 3rd	24%	19	106	17.9%	-0.13
Unplaced	51%	40	506	7.9%	-0.44
Not Compl	8%	6	96	6.3%	0.72

OTHER FACTORS (WINS-RUNS, £)

Course Winner:	3-19	-£0.45
Distance Winner:	11-66	-£0.58
Going Winner:	6-33	-£0.08
Beaten Favourite:	2-31	-£0.90
BHA Top Rated:	8-25	£0.17
Up in class:	12-135	-£0.49
Same class:	38-266	-£0.16
Down in class:	22-259	-£0.52
7-Day Winners:	1-4	-£0.65
Colts and Geldings:	36-363	-£0.40
Fillies:	42-389	-£0.07
Absolute Favourites:	27-73	-£0.04

TRAINERS (WINS-RUNS, £)

M W Easterby 1-46 £0.11; P T Midgley 2-26 £0.17.

Race Profiles

2-Y.O Races: Claiming Races – 2 to 7 runners

ANALYSIS BY BHA RATING

Rating	Prop	Win	Runs	Wins%	£
120..139	0%	0	0	0.0%	0.00
110..119	0%	0	0	0.0%	0.00
100..109	0%	0	0	0.0%	0.00
90..99	0%	0	0	0.0%	0.00
70..89	7%	2	10	20.0%	-0.34
50..69	17%	5	24	20.8%	-0.03
..49	0%	0	2	0.0%	-1.00
Unrated	77%	23	148	15.5%	-0.13

ANALYSIS BY WEIGHT CARRIED

Weight	Prop	Win	Runs	Wins%	£
10-01+	0%	0	0	0.0%	0.00
9-8..10-00	3%	1	1	100.0%	0.67
9-0..9-07	17%	5	32	15.6%	-0.68
8-8..8-13	37%	11	53	20.8%	-0.23
8-0..8-07	37%	11	85	12.9%	0.01
..7-13	7%	2	13	15.4%	0.58

ANALYSIS BY DAYS SINCE LAST RUN

Days	Prop	Win	Runs	Wins%	£
1..7	17%	5	19	26.3%	0.22
8..14	23%	7	44	15.9%	-0.33
15..28	50%	15	75	20.0%	-0.15
29..60	0%	0	14	0.0%	-1.00
61..100	3%	1	5	20.0%	1.60
101+	0%	0	0	0.0%	0.00
Unraced	7%	2	27	7.4%	0.11

ANALYSIS BY TODAY'S STARTING PRICE

Price	Prop	Win	Runs	Wins%	£
Odds On	27%	8	10	80.0%	0.26
Ev-2/1	10%	3	21	14.3%	-0.61
9/4-4/1	27%	8	40	20.0%	-0.12
9/2-6/1	13%	4	20	20.0%	0.17
13/2-10/1	13%	4	29	13.8%	0.26
11/1-16/1	10%	3	27	11.1%	0.59
18/1-33/1	0%	0	26	0.0%	-1.00
40/1+	0%	0	11	0.0%	-1.00

ANALYSIS BY STARTING PRICE LAST TIME

Price	Prop	Win	Runs	Wins%	£
Odds On	10%	3	5	60.0%	0.17
Ev-2/1	10%	3	15	20.0%	-0.66
9/4-4/1	17%	5	20	25.0%	-0.30
9/2-6/1	10%	3	16	18.8%	0.03
13/2-10/1	13%	4	26	15.4%	-0.29
11/1-16/1	13%	4	19	21.1%	0.32
18/1-33/1	13%	4	25	16.0%	0.05
40/1+	7%	2	31	6.5%	-0.42
Unraced	7%	2	27	7.4%	0.11

ANALYSIS BY DISTANCE BEATEN LAST TIME

Lengths	Prop	Win	Runs	Wins%	£
..-10	0%	0	0	0.0%	0.00
-10..0	17%	5	16	31.3%	-0.35
0.1..2	10%	3	18	16.7%	-0.34
2.1..5	13%	4	21	19.0%	-0.43
5.1..10	30%	9	43	20.9%	0.03
10.1..20	23%	7	39	17.9%	0.30
20.0..30	0%	0	14	0.0%	-1.00
30.1+	0%	0	6	0.0%	-1.00
Not Compl	0%	0	0	0.0%	0.00
Unraced	7%	2	27	7.4%	0.11

ANALYSIS BY RUN NUMBER

Run No	Prop	Win	Runs	Wins%	£
FTO	7%	2	27	7.4%	0.11
2nd Run	20%	6	27	22.2%	0.44
3rd Run	13%	4	36	11.1%	-0.33
4th+ Run	60%	18	94	19.1%	-0.29

ANALYSIS BY POSITION LAST TIME

Pos LT	Prop	Win	Runs	Wins%	£
Won	17%	5	16	31.3%	-0.35
2nd or 3rd	20%	6	32	18.8%	-0.36
Unplaced	57%	17	105	16.2%	-0.07
Not Compl	7%	2	31	6.5%	-0.03

OTHER FACTORS (WINS-RUNS, £)

Course Winner:	2-5	£0.32
Distance Winner:	5-15	-£0.39
Going Winner:	2-9	-£0.10
Beaten Favourite:	2-13	-£0.75
BHA Top Rated:	3-7	£0.61
Up in class:	2-24	-£0.72
Same class:	18-72	£0.24
Down in class:	8-61	-£0.46
7-Day Winners:	1-2	-£0.30
Colts and Geldings:	11-75	-£0.45
Fillies:	19-109	£0.08
Absolute Favourites:	11-27	-£0.23

JUVENILE RACES

Claiming Races

2-Y.O Races: Claiming Races – 8 to 14 runners

ANALYSIS BY BHA RATING

Rating	Prop	Win	Runs	Wins%	£
120..139	0%	0	0	0.0%	0.00
110..119	0%	0	0	0.0%	0.00
100..109	0%	0	0	0.0%	0.00
90..99	0%	0	0	0.0%	0.00
70..89	5%	2	7	28.6%	-0.04
50..69	15%	6	65	9.2%	-0.35
..49	0%	0	11	0.0%	-1.00
Unrated	80%	32	349	9.2%	-0.06

ANALYSIS BY WEIGHT CARRIED

Weight	Prop	Win	Runs	Wins%	£
10-01+	0%	0	0	0.0%	0.00
9-8..10-00	0%	0	0	0.0%	0.00
9-0..9-07	20%	8	66	12.1%	0.31
8-8..8-13	40%	16	152	10.5%	-0.44
8-0..8-07	35%	14	187	7.5%	0.07
..7-13	5%	2	27	7.4%	-0.71

ANALYSIS BY DAYS SINCE LAST RUN

Days	Prop	Win	Runs	Wins%	£
1..7	15%	6	50	12.0%	0.08
8..14	33%	13	134	9.7%	-0.48
15..28	33%	13	131	9.9%	-0.32
29..60	10%	4	52	7.7%	-0.41
61..100	0%	0	4	0.0%	-1.00
101+	0%	0	1	0.0%	-1.00
Unraced	10%	4	60	6.7%	1.25

ANALYSIS BY TODAY'S STARTING PRICE

Price	Prop	Win	Runs	Wins%	£
Odds On	3%	1	2	50.0%	-0.36
Ev-2/1	23%	9	19	47.4%	0.28
9/4-4/1	15%	6	51	11.8%	-0.50
9/2-6/1	15%	6	44	13.6%	-0.22
13/2-10/1	28%	11	75	14.7%	0.31
11/1-16/1	3%	1	68	1.5%	-0.75
18/1-33/1	13%	5	97	5.2%	0.30
40/1+	3%	1	76	1.3%	-0.33

ANALYSIS BY STARTING PRICE LAST TIME

Price	Prop	Win	Runs	Wins%	£
Odds On	5%	2	2	100.0%	1.52
Ev-2/1	0%	0	8	0.0%	-1.00
9/4-4/1	13%	5	52	9.6%	-0.42
9/2-6/1	18%	7	31	22.6%	0.68
13/2-10/1	25%	10	48	20.8%	-0.00
11/1-16/1	18%	7	61	11.5%	0.16
18/1-33/1	5%	2	84	2.4%	-0.83
40/1+	8%	3	86	3.5%	-0.74
Unraced	10%	4	60	6.7%	1.25

ANALYSIS BY DISTANCE BEATEN LAST TIME

Lengths	Prop	Win	Runs	Wins%	£
..-10	0%	0	0	0.0%	0.00
-10..0	18%	7	26	26.9%	0.09
0.1..2	23%	9	37	24.3%	0.93
2.1..5	13%	5	53	9.4%	-0.34
5.1..10	33%	13	97	13.4%	0.02
10.1..20	5%	2	115	1.7%	-0.92
20.0..30	0%	0	27	0.0%	-1.00
30.1+	0%	0	17	0.0%	-1.00
Not Compl	0%	0	0	0.0%	0.00
Unraced	10%	4	60	6.7%	1.25

ANALYSIS BY RUN NUMBER

Run No	Prop	Win	Runs	Wins%	£
FTO	10%	4	60	6.7%	1.25
2nd Run	18%	7	65	10.8%	-0.17
3rd Run	13%	5	92	5.4%	-0.67
4th+ Run	60%	24	215	11.2%	-0.26

ANALYSIS BY POSITION LAST TIME

Pos LT	Prop	Win	Runs	Wins%	£
Won	18%	7	26	26.9%	0.09
2nd or 3rd	25%	10	60	16.7%	-0.06
Unplaced	48%	19	286	6.6%	-0.45
Not Compl	10%	4	60	6.7%	1.25

OTHER FACTORS (WINS-RUNS, £)

Course Winner:	1-11	-£0.66
Distance Winner:	4-43	-£0.74
Going Winner:	2-18	-£0.29
Beaten Favourite:	0-14	-£1.00
BHA Top Rated:	3-11	-£0.09
Up in class:	10-101	-£0.39
Same class:	16-141	-£0.18
Down in class:	10-130	-£0.50
7-Day Winners:	0-2	-£1.00
Colts and Geldings:	20-211	-£0.28
Fillies:	20-221	£0.03
Absolute Favourites:	12-38	-£0.13

TRAINERS (WINS-RUNS, £)

M W Easterby 1-28 £0.82; P T Midgley 1-18 £0.17; W G M Turner 3-14 £0.05.

JUVENILE RACES

Race Profiles

2-Y.O Races: Claiming Races – 15 runners or more

ANALYSIS BY BHA RATING

Rating	Prop	Win	Runs	Wins%	£
120..139	0%	0	0	0.0%	0.00
110..119	0%	0	0	0.0%	0.00
100..109	0%	0	0	0.0%	0.00
90..99	0%	0	0	0.0%	0.00
70..89	25%	2	11	18.2%	-0.26
50..69	63%	5	64	7.8%	-0.55
..49	0%	0	4	0.0%	-1.00
Unrated	13%	1	57	1.8%	-0.87

ANALYSIS BY WEIGHT CARRIED

Weight	Prop	Win	Runs	Wins%	£
10-01+	0%	0	0	0.0%	0.00
9-8..10-00	0%	0	1	0.0%	-1.00
9-0..9-07	13%	1	12	8.3%	-0.67
8-8..8-13	75%	6	53	11.3%	-0.33
8-0..8-07	13%	1	56	1.8%	-0.92
..7-13	0%	0	14	0.0%	-1.00

ANALYSIS BY DAYS SINCE LAST RUN

Days	Prop	Win	Runs	Wins%	£
1..7	25%	2	15	13.3%	-0.23
8..14	0%	0	32	0.0%	-1.00
15..28	50%	4	40	10.0%	-0.35
29..60	25%	2	30	6.7%	-0.78
61..100	0%	0	9	0.0%	-1.00
101+	0%	0	5	0.0%	-1.00
Unraced	0%	0	5	0.0%	-1.00

ANALYSIS BY TODAY'S STARTING PRICE

Price	Prop	Win	Runs	Wins%	£
Odds On	0%	0	0	0.0%	0.00
Ev-2/1	13%	1	2	50.0%	0.05
9/4-4/1	25%	2	6	33.3%	0.42
9/2-6/1	38%	3	12	25.0%	0.50
13/2-10/1	25%	2	25	8.0%	-0.38
11/1-16/1	0%	0	15	0.0%	-1.00
18/1-33/1	0%	0	31	0.0%	-1.00
40/1+	0%	0	45	0.0%	-1.00

ANALYSIS BY STARTING PRICE LAST TIME

Price	Prop	Win	Runs	Wins%	£
Odds On	13%	1	1	100.0%	1.10
Ev-2/1	0%	0	0	0.0%	0.00
9/4-4/1	0%	0	9	0.0%	-1.00
9/2-6/1	13%	1	9	11.1%	-0.50
13/2-10/1	13%	1	19	5.3%	-0.68
11/1-16/1	38%	3	20	15.0%	-0.13
18/1-33/1	0%	0	29	0.0%	-1.00
40/1+	25%	2	44	4.5%	-0.68
Unraced	0%	0	5	0.0%	-1.00

ANALYSIS BY DISTANCE BEATEN LAST TIME

Lengths	Prop	Win	Runs	Wins%	£
..-10	0%	0	0	0.0%	0.00
-10..0	13%	1	2	50.0%	0.05
0.1..2	38%	3	7	42.9%	1.14
2.1..5	0%	0	20	0.0%	-1.00
5.1..10	25%	2	36	5.6%	-0.63
10.1..20	25%	2	36	5.6%	-0.63
20.0..30	0%	0	17	0.0%	-1.00
30.1+	0%	0	13	0.0%	-1.00
Not Compl	0%	0	0	0.0%	0.00
Unraced	0%	0	5	0.0%	-1.00

ANALYSIS BY RUN NUMBER

Run No	Prop	Win	Runs	Wins%	£
FTO	0%	0	5	0.0%	-1.00
2nd Run	0%	0	20	0.0%	-1.00
3rd Run	13%	1	25	4.0%	-0.70
4th+ Run	88%	7	86	8.1%	-0.57

ANALYSIS BY POSITION LAST TIME

Pos LT	Prop	Win	Runs	Wins%	£
Won	13%	1	2	50.0%	0.05
2nd or 3rd	38%	3	14	21.4%	0.07
Unplaced	50%	4	115	3.5%	-0.77
Not Compl	0%	0	5	0.0%	-1.00

OTHER FACTORS (WINS-RUNS, £)

Course Winner:	0-3	-£1.00
Distance Winner:	2-8	-£0.05
Going Winner:	2-6	£0.58
Beaten Favourite:	0-4	-£1.00
BHA Top Rated:	2-7	£0.16
Up in class:	0-10	-£1.00
Same class:	4-53	-£0.68
Down in class:	4-68	-£0.60
Colts and Geldings:	5-77	-£0.66
Fillies:	3-59	-£0.69
Absolute Favourites:	4-8	£1.01

Claiming Races

2-Y.O Races: Claiming Races – good or faster going

ANALYSIS BY BHA RATING

Rating	Prop	Win	Runs	Wins%	£
120..139	0%	0	0	0.0%	0.00
110..119	0%	0	0	0.0%	0.00
100..109	0%	0	0	0.0%	0.00
90..99	0%	0	0	0.0%	0.00
70..89	7%	4	20	20.0%	-0.28
50..69	17%	10	101	9.9%	-0.38
..49	0%	0	16	0.0%	-1.00
Unrated	77%	46	456	10.1%	-0.12

ANALYSIS BY WEIGHT CARRIED

Weight	Prop	Win	Runs	Wins%	£
10-01+	0%	0	0	0.0%	0.00
9-8..10-00	2%	1	2	50.0%	-0.16
9-0..9-07	18%	11	91	12.1%	-0.01
8-8..8-13	40%	24	203	11.8%	-0.42
8-0..8-07	37%	22	256	8.6%	0.01
..7-13	3%	2	41	4.9%	-0.76

ANALYSIS BY DAYS SINCE LAST RUN

Days	Prop	Win	Runs	Wins%	£
1..7	17%	10	69	14.5%	-0.01
8..14	27%	16	171	9.4%	-0.52
15..28	42%	25	187	13.4%	-0.20
29..60	7%	4	76	5.3%	-0.67
61..100	0%	0	13	0.0%	-1.00
101+	0%	0	5	0.0%	-1.00
Unraced	8%	5	72	6.9%	1.08

ANALYSIS BY TODAY'S STARTING PRICE

Price	Prop	Win	Runs	Wins%	£
Odds On	13%	8	10	80.0%	0.21
Ev-2/1	13%	8	31	25.8%	-0.31
9/4-4/1	20%	12	72	16.7%	-0.31
9/2-6/1	15%	9	57	15.8%	-0.06
13/2-10/1	25%	15	104	14.4%	0.26
11/1-16/1	3%	2	80	2.5%	-0.60
18/1-33/1	8%	5	128	3.9%	-0.02
40/1+	2%	1	111	0.9%	-0.54

ANALYSIS BY STARTING PRICE LAST TIME

Price	Prop	Win	Runs	Wins%	£
Odds On	7%	4	6	66.7%	0.34
Ev-2/1	3%	2	15	13.3%	-0.78
9/4-4/1	12%	7	61	11.5%	-0.48
9/2-6/1	12%	7	43	16.3%	0.31
13/2-10/1	22%	13	76	17.1%	-0.19
11/1-16/1	18%	11	77	14.3%	0.21
18/1-33/1	0%	5	114	4.4%	-0.73
40/1+	10%	6	129	4.7%	-0.68
Unraced	8%	5	72	6.9%	1.08

ANALYSIS BY DISTANCE BEATEN LAST TIME

Lengths	Prop	Win	Runs	Wins%	£
..-10	0%	0	0	0.0%	0.00
-10..0	15%	9	32	28.1%	-0.02
0.1..2	18%	11	49	22.4%	0.57
2.1..5	13%	8	75	10.7%	-0.41
5.1..10	35%	21	141	14.9%	-0.01
10.1..20	10%	6	152	3.9%	-0.77
20.0..30	0%	0	43	0.0%	-1.00
30.1+	0%	0	29	0.0%	-1.00
Not Compl	0%	0	0	0.0%	0.00
Unraced	8%	5	72	6.9%	1.08

ANALYSIS BY RUN NUMBER

Run No	Prop	Win	Runs	Wins%	£
FTO	8%	5	72	6.9%	1.08
2nd Run	20%	12	97	12.4%	-0.14
3rd Run	12%	7	125	5.6%	-0.68
4th+ Run	60%	36	299	12.0%	-0.32

ANALYSIS BY POSITION LAST TIME

Pos LT	Prop	Win	Runs	Wins%	£
Won	15%	9	32	28.1%	-0.02
2nd or 3rd	23%	14	80	17.5%	-0.15
Unplaced	53%	32	406	7.9%	-0.44
Not Compl	8%	5	75	6.7%	1.00

OTHER FACTORS (WINS-RUNS, £)

Course Winner:	2-13	-£0.59
Distance Winner:	7-49	-£0.68
Going Winner:	5-31	-£0.20
Beaten Favourite:	2-24	-£0.86
BHA Top Rated:	5-16	£0.08
Up in class:	9-105	-£0.46
Same class:	29-210	-£0.18
Down in class:	17-206	-£0.53
7-Day Winners:	1-3	-£0.53
Colts and Geldings:	28-285	-£0.37
Fillies:	32-308	-£0.04
Absolute Favourites:	20-56	-£0.12

TRAINERS (WINS-RUNS, £)

M W Easterby 1-38 £0.34; P T Midgley 1-20 £0.05; K A Ryan 4-21 £0.04; W G M Turner 4-21 £0.01.

JUVENILE RACES

47

Race Profiles

2-Y.O Races: Claiming Races – good to soft or softer going

JUVENILE RACES

ANALYSIS BY BHA RATING

Rating	Prop	Win	Runs	Wins%	£
120..139	0%	0	0	0.0%	0.00
110..119	0%	0	0	0.0%	0.00
100..109	0%	0	0	0.0%	0.00
90..99	0%	0	0	0.0%	0.00
70..89	11%	2	8	25.0%	-0.11
50..69	33%	6	52	11.5%	-0.39
..49	0%	0	1	0.0%	-1.00
Unrated	56%	10	98	10.2%	-0.32

ANALYSIS BY WEIGHT CARRIED

Weight	Prop	Win	Runs	Wins%	£
10-01+	0%	0	0	0.0%	0.00
9-8..10-00	0%	0	0	0.0%	0.00
9-0..9-07	17%	3	19	15.8%	-0.43
8-8..8-13	50%	9	55	16.4%	-0.20
8-0..8-07	22%	4	72	5.6%	-0.55
..7-13	11%	2	13	15.4%	0.42

ANALYSIS BY DAYS SINCE LAST RUN

Days	Prop	Win	Runs	Wins%	£
1..7	17%	3	15	20.0%	0.37
8..14	22%	4	39	10.3%	-0.57
15..28	39%	7	59	11.9%	-0.53
29..60	11%	2	20	10.0%	-0.39
61..100	6%	1	5	20.0%	1.60
101+	0%	0	1	0.0%	-1.00
Unraced	6%	1	20	5.0%	-0.25

ANALYSIS BY TODAY'S STARTING PRICE

Price	Prop	Win	Runs	Wins%	£
Odds On	6%	1	2	50.0%	-0.10
Ev-2/1	28%	5	11	45.5%	0.21
9/4-4/1	22%	4	25	16.0%	-0.20
9/2-6/1	22%	4	19	21.1%	0.18
13/2-10/1	11%	2	25	8.0%	-0.22
11/1-16/1	11%	2	30	6.7%	-0.07
18/1-33/1	0%	0	26	0.0%	-1.00
40/1+	0%	0	21	0.0%	-1.00

ANALYSIS BY STARTING PRICE LAST TIME

Price	Prop	Win	Runs	Wins%	£
Odds On	11%	2	2	100.0%	1.49
Ev-2/1	6%	1	8	12.5%	-0.78
9/4-4/1	17%	3	20	15.0%	-0.37
9/2-6/1	22%	4	13	30.8%	0.29
13/2-10/1	11%	2	17	11.8%	-0.35
11/1-16/1	17%	3	23	13.0%	-0.11
18/1-33/1	6%	1	24	4.2%	-0.60
40/1+	6%	1	32	3.1%	-0.59
Unraced	6%	1	20	5.0%	-0.25

ANALYSIS BY DISTANCE BEATEN LAST TIME

Lengths	Prop	Win	Runs	Wins%	£
..-10	0%	0	0	0.0%	0.00
-10..0	22%	4	12	33.3%	-0.22
0.1..2	22%	4	13	30.8%	0.65
2.1..5	6%	1	19	5.3%	-0.84
5.1..10	17%	3	35	8.6%	-0.49
10.1..20	28%	5	38	13.2%	0.01
20.0..30	0%	0	15	0.0%	-1.00
30.1+	0%	0	7	0.0%	-1.00
Not Compl	0%	0	0	0.0%	0.00
Unraced	6%	1	20	5.0%	-0.25

ANALYSIS BY RUN NUMBER

Run No	Prop	Win	Runs	Wins%	£
FTO	6%	1	20	5.0%	-0.25
2nd Run	6%	1	15	6.7%	-0.37
3rd Run	17%	3	28	10.7%	-0.25
4th+ Run	72%	13	96	13.5%	-0.38

ANALYSIS BY POSITION LAST TIME

Pos LT	Prop	Win	Runs	Wins%	£
Won	22%	4	12	33.3%	-0.22
2nd or 3rd	28%	5	26	19.2%	-0.07
Unplaced	44%	8	100	8.0%	-0.43
Not Compl	6%	1	21	4.8%	-0.29

OTHER FACTORS (WINS-RUNS, £)

Course Winner:	1-6	-£0.17
Distance Winner:	4-17	-£0.29
Going Winner:	1-2	£1.75
Beaten Favourite:	0-7	-£1.00
BHA Top Rated:	3-9	£0.34
Up in class:	3-30	-£0.61
Same class:	9-56	-£0.11
Down in class:	5-53	-£0.46
7-Day Winners:	0-1	-£1.00
Colts and Geldings:	8-78	-£0.49
Fillies:	10-81	-£0.19
Absolute Favourites:	7-17	£0.22

Claiming Races

2-Y.O Races: Claiming Races – 5 to 6 furlong races

ANALYSIS BY BHA RATING

Rating	Prop	Win	Runs	Wins%	£
120..139	0%	0	0	0.0%	0.00
110..119	0%	0	0	0.0%	0.00
100..109	0%	0	0	0.0%	0.00
90..99	0%	0	0	0.0%	0.00
70..89	5%	3	14	21.4%	-0.38
50..69	15%	8	64	12.5%	-0.16
..49	0%	0	2	0.0%	-1.00
Unrated	80%	44	381	11.5%	-0.03

ANALYSIS BY WEIGHT CARRIED

Weight	Prop	Win	Runs	Wins%	£
10-01+	0%	0	0	0.0%	0.00
9-8..10-00	2%	1	1	100.0%	0.67
9-0..9-07	16%	9	71	12.7%	0.04
8-8..8-13	38%	21	162	13.0%	-0.47
8-0..8-07	38%	21	196	10.7%	0.30
..7-13	5%	3	31	9.7%	-0.51

ANALYSIS BY DAYS SINCE LAST RUN

Days	Prop	Win	Runs	Wins%	£
1..7	15%	8	50	16.0%	0.30
8..14	22%	12	116	10.3%	-0.58
15..28	45%	25	160	15.6%	-0.18
29..60	7%	4	43	9.3%	-0.47
61..100	0%	0	6	0.0%	-1.00
101+	0%	0	2	0.0%	-1.00
Unraced	11%	6	84	7.1%	0.96

ANALYSIS BY TODAY'S STARTING PRICE

Price	Prop	Win	Runs	Wins%	£
Odds On	15%	8	10	80.0%	0.26
Ev-2/1	18%	10	30	33.3%	-0.12
9/4-4/1	20%	11	73	15.1%	-0.35
9/2-6/1	16%	9	53	17.0%	-0.03
13/2-10/1	15%	8	78	10.3%	-0.10
11/1-16/1	5%	3	68	4.4%	-0.31
18/1-33/1	9%	5	93	5.4%	0.35
40/1+	2%	1	56	1.8%	-0.09

ANALYSIS BY STARTING PRICE LAST TIME

Price	Prop	Win	Runs	Wins%	£
Odds On	11%	6	8	75.0%	0.62
Ev-2/1	5%	3	21	14.3%	-0.76
9/4-4/1	15%	8	55	14.5%	-0.36
9/2-6/1	13%	7	33	21.2%	0.38
13/2-10/1	18%	10	59	16.9%	-0.15
11/1-16/1	13%	7	51	13.7%	0.34
18/1-33/1	9%	5	79	6.3%	-0.60
40/1+	5%	3	71	4.2%	-0.75
Unraced	11%	6	84	7.1%	0.96

ANALYSIS BY DISTANCE BEATEN LAST TIME

Lengths	Prop	Win	Runs	Wins%	£
..-10	0%	0	0	0.0%	0.00
-10..0	20%	11	33	33.3%	-0.01
0.1..2	15%	8	45	17.8%	0.19
2.1..5	11%	6	59	10.2%	-0.44
5.1..10	31%	17	96	17.7%	0.15
10.1..20	13%	7	107	6.5%	-0.64
20.0..30	0%	0	25	0.0%	-1.00
30.1+	0%	0	12	0.0%	-1.00
Not Compl	0%	0	0	0.0%	0.00
Unraced	11%	6	84	7.1%	0.96

ANALYSIS BY RUN NUMBER

Run No	Prop	Win	Runs	Wins%	£
FTO	11%	6	84	7.1%	0.96
2nd Run	20%	11	72	15.3%	-0.00
3rd Run	13%	7	105	6.7%	-0.65
4th+ Run	56%	31	200	15.5%	-0.21

ANALYSIS BY POSITION LAST TIME

Pos LT	Prop	Win	Runs	Wins%	£
Won	20%	11	33	33.3%	-0.01
2nd or 3rd	22%	12	78	15.4%	-0.40
Unplaced	47%	26	263	9.9%	-0.29
Not Compl	11%	6	87	6.9%	0.90

OTHER FACTORS (WINS-RUNS, £)

Course Winner:	3-12	-£0.14
Distance Winner:	10-47	-£0.46
Going Winner:	5-24	£0.10
Beaten Favourite:	2-24	-£0.87
BHA Top Rated:	4-13	£0.12
Up in class:	7-69	-£0.53
Same class:	25-155	-£0.07
Down in class:	17-153	-£0.41
7-Day Winners:	1-4	-£0.65
Colts and Geldings:	22-206	-£0.34
Fillies:	33-255	£0.16
Absolute Favourites:	21-51	£0.02

TRAINERS (WINS-RUNS, £)
M W Easterby 1-31 £0.65; P T Midgley 2-18 £0.69.

Race Profiles

2-Y.O Races: Claiming Races – 7 to 8 furlong races

ANALYSIS BY BHA RATING

Rating	Prop	Win	Runs	Wins%	£
120..139	0%	0	0	0.0%	0.00
110..119	0%	0	0	0.0%	0.00
100..109	0%	0	0	0.0%	0.00
90..99	0%	0	0	0.0%	0.00
70..89	13%	3	14	21.4%	-0.09
50..69	35%	8	89	9.0%	-0.55
..49	0%	0	15	0.0%	-1.00
Unrated	52%	12	173	6.9%	-0.44

ANALYSIS BY WEIGHT CARRIED

Weight	Prop	Win	Runs	Wins%	£
10-01+	0%	0	0	0.0%	0.00
9-8..10-00	0%	0	1	0.0%	-1.00
9-0..9-07	22%	5	39	12.8%	-0.30
8-8..8-13	52%	12	96	12.5%	-0.22
8-0..8-07	22%	5	132	3.8%	-0.74
..7-13	4%	1	23	4.3%	-0.43

ANALYSIS BY DAYS SINCE LAST RUN

Days	Prop	Win	Runs	Wins%	£
1..7	22%	5	34	14.7%	-0.30
8..14	35%	8	94	8.5%	-0.46
15..28	30%	7	86	8.1%	-0.45
29..60	9%	2	53	3.8%	-0.73
61..100	4%	1	12	8.3%	0.08
101+	0%	0	4	0.0%	-1.00
Unraced	0%	0	8	0.0%	-1.00

ANALYSIS BY TODAY'S STARTING PRICE

Price	Prop	Win	Runs	Wins%	£
Odds On	4%	1	2	50.0%	-0.38
Ev-2/1	13%	3	12	25.0%	-0.31
9/4-4/1	22%	5	24	20.8%	-0.09
9/2-6/1	17%	4	23	17.4%	0.07
13/2-10/1	39%	9	51	17.6%	0.58
11/1-16/1	4%	1	42	2.4%	-0.69
18/1-33/1	0%	0	61	0.0%	-1.00
40/1+	0%	0	76	0.0%	-1.00

ANALYSIS BY STARTING PRICE LAST TIME

Price	Prop	Win	Runs	Wins%	£
Odds On	0%	0	0	0.0%	0.00
Ev-2/1	0%	0	2	0.0%	-1.00
9/4-4/1	9%	2	26	7.7%	-0.66
9/2-6/1	17%	4	23	17.4%	0.20
13/2-10/1	22%	5	34	14.7%	-0.35
11/1-16/1	30%	7	49	14.3%	-0.08
18/1-33/1	4%	1	59	1.7%	-0.85
40/1+	17%	4	90	4.4%	-0.59
Unraced	0%	0	8	0.0%	-1.00

ANALYSIS BY DISTANCE BEATEN LAST TIME

Lengths	Prop	Win	Runs	Wins%	£
..-10	0%	0	0	0.0%	0.00
-10..0	9%	2	11	18.2%	-0.25
0.1..2	30%	7	17	41.2%	1.65
2.1..5	13%	3	35	8.6%	-0.60
5.1..10	30%	7	80	8.8%	-0.41
10.1..20	17%	4	83	4.8%	-0.58
20.0..30	0%	0	33	0.0%	-1.00
30.1+	0%	0	24	0.0%	-1.00
Not Compl	0%	0	0	0.0%	0.00
Unraced	0%	0	8	0.0%	-1.00

ANALYSIS BY RUN NUMBER

Run No	Prop	Win	Runs	Wins%	£
FTO	0%	0	8	0.0%	-1.00
2nd Run	9%	2	40	5.0%	-0.47
3rd Run	13%	3	48	6.3%	-0.49
4th+ Run	78%	18	195	9.2%	-0.47

ANALYSIS BY POSITION LAST TIME

Pos LT	Prop	Win	Runs	Wins%	£
Won	9%	2	11	18.2%	-0.25
2nd or 3rd	30%	7	28	25.0%	0.61
Unplaced	61%	14	243	5.8%	-0.60
Not Compl	0%	0	9	0.0%	-1.00

OTHER FACTORS (WINS-RUNS, £)

Course Winner:	0-7	-£1.00
Distance Winner:	1-19	-£0.88
Going Winner:	1-9	-£0.56
Beaten Favourite:	0-7	-£1.00
BHA Top Rated:	4-12	£0.23
Up in class:	5-66	-£0.45
Same class:	13-111	-£0.29
Down in class:	5-106	-£0.67
Colts and Geldings:	14-157	-£0.47
Fillies:	9-134	-£0.51
Absolute Favourites:	6-22	-£0.18

Selling Races

2-Y.O Races: Selling Races

ANALYSIS BY BHA RATING

Rating	Prop	Win	Runs	Wins%	£
120..139	0%	0	0	0.0%	0.00
110..119	0%	0	0	0.0%	0.00
100..109	0%	0	0	0.0%	0.00
90..99	0%	0	0	0.0%	0.00
70..89	2%	5	13	38.5%	0.33
50..69	22%	45	343	13.1%	-0.18
..49	1%	3	72	4.2%	-0.52
Unrated	74%	153	1489	10.3%	-0.29

ANALYSIS BY WEIGHT CARRIED

Weight	Prop	Win	Runs	Wins%	£
10-01+	0%	0	0	0.0%	0.00
9-8..10-00	0%	0	0	0.0%	0.00
9-0..9-07	5%	11	99	11.1%	-0.72
8-8..8-13	44%	91	839	10.8%	-0.21
8-0..8-07	48%	99	930	10.6%	-0.29
..7-13	2%	5	49	10.2%	-0.20

ANALYSIS BY DAYS SINCE LAST RUN

Days	Prop	Win	Runs	Wins%	£
1..7	22%	45	301	15.0%	0.01
8..14	28%	58	520	11.2%	-0.30
15..28	26%	54	559	9.7%	-0.39
29..60	11%	23	255	9.0%	-0.45
61..100	2%	5	65	7.7%	0.40
101+	0%	0	14	0.0%	-1.00
Unraced	10%	21	203	10.3%	-0.24

ANALYSIS BY TODAY'S STARTING PRICE

Price	Prop	Win	Runs	Wins%	£
Odds On	9%	18	33	54.5%	-0.08
Ev-2/1	13%	26	78	33.3%	-0.14
9/4-4/1	35%	72	303	23.8%	-0.01
9/2-6/1	14%	29	221	13.1%	-0.19
13/2-10/1	16%	32	327	9.8%	-0.16
11/1-16/1	10%	20	285	7.0%	0.04
18/1-33/1	4%	8	376	2.1%	-0.49
40/1+	0%	1	294	0.3%	-0.83

ANALYSIS BY STARTING PRICE LAST TIME

Price	Prop	Win	Runs	Wins%	£
Odds On	3%	6	11	54.5%	0.58
Ev-2/1	1%	2	31	6.5%	-0.66
9/4-4/1	17%	35	177	19.8%	-0.17
9/2-6/1	13%	27	158	17.1%	-0.17
13/2-10/1	12%	25	251	10.0%	-0.36
11/1-16/1	14%	29	261	11.1%	-0.05
18/1-33/1	16%	33	370	8.9%	-0.16
40/1+	14%	28	455	6.2%	-0.54
Unraced	10%	21	203	10.3%	-0.24

ANALYSIS BY DISTANCE BEATEN LAST TIME

Lengths	Prop	Win	Runs	Wins%	£
..-10	0%	0	0	0.0%	0.00
-10..0	5%	10	59	16.9%	-0.25
0.1..2	10%	20	118	16.9%	-0.19
2.1..5	25%	52	273	19.0%	0.05
5.1..10	29%	59	489	12.1%	-0.14
10.1..20	16%	33	502	6.6%	-0.44
20.0..30	5%	10	180	5.6%	-0.50
30.1+	0%	1	93	1.1%	-0.82
Not Compl	0%	0	0	0.0%	0.00
Unraced	10%	21	203	10.3%	-0.24

ANALYSIS BY RUN NUMBER

Run No	Prop	Win	Runs	Wins%	£
FTO	10%	21	203	10.3%	-0.24
2nd Run	17%	36	351	10.3%	-0.19
3rd Run	14%	29	379	7.7%	-0.38
4th+ Run	58%	120	984	12.2%	-0.27

ANALYSIS BY POSITION LAST TIME

Pos LT	Prop	Win	Runs	Wins%	£
Won	5%	10	59	16.9%	-0.25
2nd or 3rd	21%	44	252	17.5%	-0.02
Unplaced	64%	131	1400	9.4%	-0.33
Not Compl	10%	21	206	10.2%	-0.25

OTHER FACTORS (WINS-RUNS, £)

Course Winner:	3-14	£0.04
Distance Winner:	17-108	-£0.38
Going Winner:	6-42	-£0.32
Beaten Favourite:	8-56	-£0.44
BHA Top Rated:	13-60	£0.02
Up in class:	24-290	-£0.35
Same class:	80-735	-£0.19
Down in class:	81-689	-£0.34
7-Day Winners:	5-22	-£0.10
Colts and Geldings:	78-766	-£0.27
Fillies:	125-1123	-£0.29
Absolute Favourites:	64-182	-£0.01

TRAINERS (WINS-RUNS, £)

M R Channon 23-94 £0.28; T D Easterby 3-30 £0.52; W M Brisbourne 4-29 £0.52; M Dods 3-16 £0.55; K A Ryan 8-46 £0.15; J G Portman 2-11 £0.55; D Nicholls 4-26 £0.16; K R Burke 7-34 £0.11; J G M O'Shea 2-15 £0.23; M G Quinlan 4-18 £0.13; R C Guest 3-16 £0.10; E J O'Neill 5-12 £0.03.

Race Profiles

2-Y.O Races: Selling Races – 2 to 7 runners

ANALYSIS BY BHA RATING

Rating	Prop	Win	Runs	Wins%	£
120..139	0%	0	0	0.0%	0.00
110..119	0%	0	0	0.0%	0.00
100..109	0%	0	0	0.0%	0.00
90..99	0%	0	0	0.0%	0.00
70..89	2%	1	3	33.3%	-0.25
50..69	13%	8	36	22.2%	0.30
..49	2%	1	7	14.3%	-0.66
Unrated	84%	54	323	16.7%	-0.05

ANALYSIS BY WEIGHT CARRIED

Weight	Prop	Win	Runs	Wins%	£
10-01+	0%	0	0	0.0%	0.00
9-8..10-00	0%	0	0	0.0%	0.00
9-0..9-07	8%	5	15	33.3%	-0.37
8-8..8-13	38%	24	129	18.6%	-0.05
8-0..8-07	53%	34	213	16.0%	0.03
..7-13	2%	1	12	8.3%	-0.58

ANALYSIS BY DAYS SINCE LAST RUN

Days	Prop	Win	Runs	Wins%	£
1..7	33%	21	79	26.6%	0.50
8..14	25%	16	95	16.8%	0.06
15..28	22%	14	96	14.6%	-0.28
29..60	5%	3	43	7.0%	-0.65
61..100	2%	1	6	16.7%	-0.17
101+	0%	0	1	0.0%	-1.00
Unraced	14%	9	49	18.4%	0.00

ANALYSIS BY TODAY'S STARTING PRICE

Price	Prop	Win	Runs	Wins%	£
Odds On	16%	10	20	50.0%	-0.17
Ev-2/1	13%	8	35	22.9%	-0.39
9/4-4/1	36%	23	98	23.5%	-0.03
9/2-6/1	14%	9	50	18.0%	0.11
13/2-10/1	14%	9	52	17.3%	0.49
11/1-16/1	5%	3	46	6.5%	-0.02
18/1-33/1	3%	2	51	3.9%	-0.08
40/1+	0%	0	17	0.0%	-1.00

ANALYSIS BY STARTING PRICE LAST TIME

Price	Prop	Win	Runs	Wins%	£
Odds On	3%	2	4	50.0%	0.20
Ev-2/1	2%	1	8	12.5%	-0.83
9/4-4/1	11%	7	40	17.5%	-0.34
9/2-6/1	9%	6	37	16.2%	-0.34
13/2-10/1	13%	8	51	15.7%	-0.27
11/1-16/1	14%	9	46	19.6%	0.68
18/1-33/1	17%	11	59	18.6%	0.06
40/1+	17%	11	75	14.7%	-0.00
Unraced	14%	9	49	18.4%	0.00

ANALYSIS BY DISTANCE BEATEN LAST TIME

Lengths	Prop	Win	Runs	Wins%	£
..-10	0%	0	0	0.0%	0.00
-10..0	6%	4	11	36.4%	0.53
0.1..2	8%	5	30	16.7%	0.04
2.1..5	30%	19	66	28.8%	0.41
5.1..10	27%	17	102	16.7%	-0.10
10.1..20	13%	8	73	11.0%	-0.30
20.0..30	3%	2	27	7.4%	-0.04
30.1+	0%	0	11	0.0%	-1.00
Not Compl	0%	0	0	0.0%	0.00
Unraced	14%	9	49	18.4%	0.00

ANALYSIS BY RUN NUMBER

Run No	Prop	Win	Runs	Wins%	£
FTO	14%	9	49	18.4%	0.00
2nd Run	27%	17	73	23.3%	0.43
3rd Run	8%	5	64	7.8%	-0.46
4th+ Run	52%	33	183	18.0%	-0.07

ANALYSIS BY POSITION LAST TIME

Pos LT	Prop	Win	Runs	Wins%	£
Won	6%	4	11	36.4%	0.53
2nd or 3rd	23%	15	67	22.4%	0.25
Unplaced	56%	36	242	14.9%	-0.14
Not Compl	14%	9	49	18.4%	0.00

OTHER FACTORS (WINS-RUNS, £)

Course Winner:	1-1	£1.25
Distance Winner:	6-23	-£0.01
Going Winner:	0-5	-£1.00
Beaten Favourite:	1-12	-£0.88
BHA Top Rated:	1-9	-£0.67
Up in class:	7-31	-£0.09
Same class:	27-152	£0.10
Down in class:	21-137	-£0.17
7-Day Winners:	3-7	£1.14
Colts and Geldings:	22-125	-£0.16
Fillies:	41-238	£0.05
Absolute Favourites:	17-56	-£0.34

TRAINERS (WINS-RUNS, £)

J S Moore 3-11 £0.32; M R Channon 4-21 £0.09.

Selling Races

2-Y.O Races: Selling Races – 8 to 14 runners

ANALYSIS BY BHA RATING
Rating	Prop	Win	Runs	Wins%	£
120..139	0%	0	0	0.0%	0.00
110..119	0%	0	0	0.0%	0.00
100..109	0%	0	0	0.0%	0.00
90..99	0%	0	0	0.0%	0.00
70..89	3%	4	10	40.0%	0.50
50..69	24%	31	234	13.2%	-0.14
..49	1%	1	57	1.8%	-0.74
Unrated	72%	91	1005	9.1%	-0.38

ANALYSIS BY WEIGHT CARRIED
Weight	Prop	Win	Runs	Wins%	£
10-01+	0%	0	0	0.0%	0.00
9-8..10-00	0%	0	0	0.0%	0.00
9-0..9-07	4%	5	65	7.7%	-0.77
8-8..8-13	46%	59	601	9.8%	-0.31
8-0..8-07	46%	59	607	9.7%	-0.35
..7-13	3%	4	33	12.1%	0.03

ANALYSIS BY DAYS SINCE LAST RUN
Days	Prop	Win	Runs	Wins%	£
1..7	17%	21	205	10.2%	-0.23
8..14	32%	41	358	11.5%	-0.29
15..28	25%	32	375	8.5%	-0.45
29..60	16%	20	175	11.4%	-0.29
61..100	2%	2	43	4.7%	-0.40
101+	0%	0	9	0.0%	-1.00
Unraced	9%	11	141	7.8%	-0.38

ANALYSIS BY TODAY'S STARTING PRICE
Price	Prop	Win	Runs	Wins%	£
Odds On	6%	8	13	61.5%	0.06
Ev-2/1	14%	18	42	42.9%	0.09
9/4-4/1	33%	42	183	23.0%	-0.05
9/2-6/1	15%	19	152	12.5%	-0.24
13/2-10/1	17%	21	241	8.7%	-0.25
11/1-16/1	10%	13	195	6.7%	-0.06
18/1-33/1	5%	6	264	2.3%	-0.45
40/1+	0%	0	216	0.0%	-1.00

ANALYSIS BY STARTING PRICE LAST TIME
Price	Prop	Win	Runs	Wins%	£
Odds On	3%	4	6	66.7%	1.10
Ev-2/1	1%	1	21	4.8%	-0.57
9/4-4/1	22%	28	124	22.6%	-0.03
9/2-6/1	13%	17	101	16.8%	-0.11
13/2-10/1	12%	15	176	8.5%	-0.43
11/1 16/1	13%	17	175	9.7%	-0.19
18/1-33/1	16%	20	250	7.8%	-0.26
40/1+	11%	14	306	4.6%	-0.65
Unraced	9%	11	141	7.8%	-0.38

ANALYSIS BY DISTANCE BEATEN LAST TIME
Lengths	Prop	Win	Runs	Wins%	£
..-10	0%	0	0	0.0%	0.00
-10..0	5%	6	43	14.0%	-0.36
0.1..2	10%	13	78	16.7%	-0.30
2.1..5	26%	33	184	17.9%	0.05
5.1..10	26%	33	320	10.3%	-0.36
10.1..20	17%	22	352	6.3%	-0.41
20.0..30	6%	8	128	6.3%	-0.50
30.1+	1%	1	60	1.7%	-0.72
Not Compl	0%	0	0	0.0%	0.00
Unraced	9%	11	141	7.8%	-0.38

ANALYSIS BY RUN NUMBER
Run No	Prop	Win	Runs	Wins%	£
FTO	9%	11	141	7.8%	-0.38
2nd Run	13%	17	244	7.0%	-0.49
3rd Run	17%	22	258	8.5%	-0.27
4th+ Run	61%	77	663	11.6%	-0.31

ANALYSIS BY POSITION LAST TIME
Pos LT	Prop	Win	Runs	Wins%	£
Won	5%	6	43	14.0%	-0.36
2nd or 3rd	20%	26	168	15.5%	-0.11
Unplaced	66%	84	952	8.8%	-0.38
Not Compl	9%	11	143	7.7%	-0.39

OTHER FACTORS (WINS-RUNS, £)
Course Winner:	2-12	£0.02
Distance Winner:	11-76	-£0.43
Going Winner:	5-30	-£0.20
Beaten Favourite:	7-41	-£0.27
BHA Top Rated:	11-41	£0.22
Up in class:	15-235	-£0.55
Same class:	47-488	-£0.26
Down in class:	54-442	-£0.31
7-Day Winners:	2-14	-£0.66
Colts and Geldings:	48-527	-£0.36
Fillies:	77-757	-£0.35
Absolute Favourites:	43-113	£0.13

TRAINERS (WINS-RUNS, £)
M R Channon 17-63 £0.40; T D Easterby 2-23 £0.74; K A Ryan 6-32 £0.43; W M Brisbourne 3-25 £0.54; T D Barron 2-10 £1.10; K R Burke 5-20 £0.49; M G Quinlan 3-11 £0.68; P Winkworth 1-10 £0.30; W G M Turner 10-74 £0.02.

JUVENILE RACES

Race Profiles

2-Y.O Races: Selling Races – 15 runners or more

ANALYSIS BY BHA RATING

Rating	Prop	Win	Runs	Wins%	£
120..139	0%	0	0	0.0%	0.00
110..119	0%	0	0	0.0%	0.00
100..109	0%	0	0	0.0%	0.00
90..99	0%	0	0	0.0%	0.00
70..89	0%	0	0	0.0%	0.00
50..69	40%	6	73	8.2%	-0.54
..49	7%	1	8	12.5%	1.13
Unrated	53%	8	161	5.0%	-0.25

ANALYSIS BY WEIGHT CARRIED

Weight	Prop	Win	Runs	Wins%	£
10-01+	0%	0	0	0.0%	0.00
9-8..10-00	0%	0	0	0.0%	0.00
9-0..9-07	7%	1	19	5.3%	-0.83
8-8..8-13	53%	8	109	7.3%	0.09
8-0..8-07	40%	6	110	5.5%	-0.55
..7-13	0%	0	4	0.0%	-1.00

ANALYSIS BY DAYS SINCE LAST RUN

Days	Prop	Win	Runs	Wins%	£
1..7	20%	3	17	17.6%	0.49
8..14	7%	1	67	1.5%	-0.90
15..28	53%	8	88	9.1%	-0.29
29..60	0%	0	37	0.0%	-1.00
61..100	13%	2	16	12.5%	2.75
101+	0%	0	4	0.0%	-1.00
Unraced	7%	1	13	7.7%	0.31

ANALYSIS BY TODAY'S STARTING PRICE

Price	Prop	Win	Runs	Wins%	£
Odds On	0%	0	0	0.0%	0.00
Ev-2/1	0%	0	1	0.0%	-1.00
9/4-4/1	47%	7	22	31.8%	0.40
9/2-6/1	7%	1	19	5.3%	-0.66
13/2-10/1	13%	2	34	5.9%	-0.50
11/1-16/1	27%	4	44	9.1%	0.50
18/1-33/1	0%	0	61	0.0%	-1.00
40/1+	7%	1	61	1.6%	-0.16

ANALYSIS BY STARTING PRICE LAST TIME

Price	Prop	Win	Runs	Wins%	£
Odds On	0%	0	1	0.0%	-1.00
Ev-2/1	0%	0	2	0.0%	-1.00
9/4-4/1	0%	0	13	0.0%	-1.00
9/2-6/1	27%	4	20	20.0%	-0.14
13/2-10/1	13%	2	24	8.3%	-0.10
11/1-16/1	20%	3	40	7.5%	-0.24
18/1-33/1	13%	2	55	3.6%	0.07
40/1+	20%	3	74	4.1%	-0.65
Unraced	7%	1	13	7.7%	0.31

ANALYSIS BY DISTANCE BEATEN LAST TIME

Lengths	Prop	Win	Runs	Wins%	£
..-10	0%	0	0	0.0%	0.00
-10..0	0%	0	5	0.0%	-1.00
0.1..2	13%	2	10	20.0%	-0.03
2.1..5	0%	0	23	0.0%	-1.00
5.1..10	60%	9	67	13.4%	0.87
10.1..20	20%	3	77	3.9%	-0.75
20.0..30	0%	0	25	0.0%	-1.00
30.1+	0%	0	22	0.0%	-1.00
Not Compl	0%	0	0	0.0%	0.00
Unraced	7%	1	13	7.7%	0.31

ANALYSIS BY RUN NUMBER

Run No	Prop	Win	Runs	Wins%	£
FTO	7%	1	13	7.7%	0.31
2nd Run	13%	2	34	5.9%	0.62
3rd Run	13%	2	57	3.5%	-0.80
4th+ Run	67%	10	138	7.2%	-0.36

ANALYSIS BY POSITION LAST TIME

Pos LT	Prop	Win	Runs	Wins%	£
Won	0%	0	5	0.0%	-1.00
2nd or 3rd	20%	3	17	17.6%	-0.19
Unplaced	73%	11	206	5.3%	-0.32
Not Compl	7%	1	14	7.1%	0.21

OTHER FACTORS (WINS-RUNS, £)

Course Winner:	0-1	-£1.00
Distance Winner:	0-9	-£1.00
Going Winner:	1-7	-£0.36
Beaten Favourite:	0-3	-£1.00
BHA Top Rated:	1-10	-£0.20
Up in class:	2-24	£1.26
Same class:	6-95	-£0.29
Down in class:	6-110	-£0.70
7-Day Winners:	0-1	-£1.00
Colts and Geldings:	8-114	£0.03
Fillies:	7-128	-£0.58
Absolute Favourites:	4-13	£0.25

Selling Races

2-Y.O Races: Selling Races – good or faster going

ANALYSIS BY BHA RATING

Rating	Prop	Win	Runs	Wins%	£
120..139	0%	0	0	0.0%	0.00
110..119	0%	0	0	0.0%	0.00
100..109	0%	0	0	0.0%	0.00
90..99	0%	0	0	0.0%	0.00
70..89	3%	4	10	40.0%	0.52
50..69	20%	32	242	13.2%	-0.17
..49	1%	1	51	2.0%	-0.71
Unrated	76%	120	1146	10.5%	-0.27

ANALYSIS BY WEIGHT CARRIED

Weight	Prop	Win	Runs	Wins%	£
10-01+	0%	0	0	0.0%	0.00
9-8..10-00	0%	0	0	0.0%	0.00
9-0..9-07	4%	7	74	9.5%	-0.81
8-8..8-13	46%	73	609	12.0%	-0.09
8-0..8-07	46%	73	730	10.0%	-0.36
..7-13	3%	4	36	11.1%	-0.03

ANALYSIS BY DAYS SINCE LAST RUN

Days	Prop	Win	Runs	Wins%	£
1..7	21%	33	243	13.6%	-0.12
8..14	27%	42	396	10.6%	-0.33
15..28	29%	45	443	10.2%	-0.37
29..60	11%	18	173	10.4%	-0.35
61..100	3%	4	49	8.2%	0.76
101+	0%	0	6	0.0%	-1.00
Unraced	10%	15	139	10.8%	-0.21

ANALYSIS BY TODAY'S STARTING PRICE

Price	Prop	Win	Runs	Wins%	£
Odds On	11%	17	30	56.7%	-0.05
Ev-2/1	11%	18	66	27.3%	-0.29
9/4-4/1	33%	52	220	23.6%	-0.01
9/2-6/1	15%	23	164	14.0%	-0.14
13/2-10/1	15%	24	240	10.0%	-0.13
11/1-16/1	10%	16	200	8.0%	0.16
18/1-33/1	4%	6	294	2.0%	-0.52
40/1+	1%	1	235	0.4%	-0.78

ANALYSIS BY STARTING PRICE LAST TIME

Price	Prop	Win	Runs	Wins%	£
Odds On	3%	4	8	50.0%	0.11
Ev-2/1	1%	2	26	7.7%	-0.60
9/4-4/1	14%	22	129	17.1%	-0.34
9/2-6/1	15%	23	126	18.3%	-0.10
13/2-10/1	12%	19	188	10.1%	-0.29
11/1 16/1	13%	20	189	10.6%	-0.23
18/1-33/1	17%	27	295	9.2%	-0.04
40/1+	16%	25	349	7.2%	-0.49
Unraced	10%	15	139	10.8%	-0.21

ANALYSIS BY DISTANCE BEATEN LAST TIME

Lengths	Prop	Win	Runs	Wins%	£
..-10	0%	0	0	0.0%	0.00
-10..0	3%	5	41	12.2%	-0.43
0.1..2	10%	15	101	14.9%	-0.33
2.1..5	24%	38	203	18.7%	0.05
5.1..10	29%	46	369	12.5%	-0.10
10.1..20	18%	28	386	7.3%	-0.40
20.0..30	6%	10	142	7.0%	-0.36
30.1+	0%	0	68	0.0%	-1.00
Not Compl	0%	0	0	0.0%	0.00
Unraced	10%	15	139	10.8%	-0.21

ANALYSIS BY RUN NUMBER

Run No	Prop	Win	Runs	Wins%	£
FTO	10%	15	139	10.8%	-0.21
2nd Run	19%	30	265	11.3%	-0.14
3rd Run	15%	24	285	8.4%	-0.32
4th+ Run	56%	88	760	11.6%	-0.29

ANALYSIS BY POSITION LAST TIME

Pos LT	Prop	Win	Runs	Wins%	£
Won	3%	5	41	12.2%	-0.43
2nd or 3rd	19%	30	187	16.0%	-0.09
Unplaced	68%	107	1079	9.9%	-0.29
Not Compl	10%	15	142	10.6%	-0.22

OTHER FACTORS (WINS-RUNS, £)

Course Winner:	2-10	£0.13
Distance Winner:	12-86	-£0.45
Going Winner:	4-32	-£0.36
Beaten Favourite:	6-47	-£0.45
BHA Top Rated:	7-43	-£0.19
Up in class:	18-217	-£0.32
Same class:	57-573	-£0.29
Down in class:	67-520	-£0.23
7-Day Winners:	3-16	-£0.20
Colts and Geldings:	64-563	-£0.15
Fillies:	90-858	-£0.35
Absolute Favourites:	48-137	-£0.03

TRAINERS (WINS-RUNS, £)

M R Channon 20-70 £0.49; W M Brisbourne 3-18 £1.14; M Dods 3-13 £0.90; J G Portman 2-10 £0.70; J G M O'Shea 2-12 £0.54; M G Quinlan 4-15 £0.36; K R Burke 4-25 £0.20; R C Guest 3-14 £0.26; A B Haynes 2-14 £0.18; E J O'Neill 5-10 £0.24; D Nicholls 2-18 £0.13; P S McEntee 2-18 £0.08.

Race Profiles

2-Y.O Races: Selling Races – good to soft or softer going

ANALYSIS BY BHA RATING

Rating	Prop	Win	Runs	Wins%	£
120..139	0%	0	0	0.0%	0.00
110..119	0%	0	0	0.0%	0.00
100..109	0%	0	0	0.0%	0.00
90..99	0%	0	0	0.0%	0.00
70..89	2%	1	3	33.3%	-0.33
50..69	27%	13	101	12.9%	-0.20
..49	4%	2	21	9.5%	-0.08
Unrated	67%	33	343	9.6%	-0.36

ANALYSIS BY WEIGHT CARRIED

Weight	Prop	Win	Runs	Wins%	£
10-01+	0%	0	0	0.0%	0.00
9-8..10-00	0%	0	0	0.0%	0.00
9-0..9-07	8%	4	25	16.0%	-0.45
8-8..8-13	37%	18	230	7.8%	-0.55
8-0..8-07	53%	26	200	13.0%	-0.01
..7-13	2%	1	13	7.7%	-0.69

ANALYSIS BY DAYS SINCE LAST RUN

Days	Prop	Win	Runs	Wins%	£
1..7	24%	12	58	20.7%	0.54
8..14	33%	16	124	12.9%	-0.21
15..28	18%	9	116	7.8%	-0.50
29..60	10%	5	82	6.1%	-0.68
61..100	2%	1	16	6.3%	-0.69
101+	0%	0	8	0.0%	-1.00
Unraced	12%	6	64	9.4%	-0.32

ANALYSIS BY TODAY'S STARTING PRICE

Price	Prop	Win	Runs	Wins%	£
Odds On	2%	1	3	33.3%	-0.36
Ev-2/1	16%	8	12	66.7%	0.71
9/4-4/1	41%	20	83	24.1%	-0.01
9/2-6/1	12%	6	57	10.5%	-0.35
13/2-10/1	16%	8	87	9.2%	-0.22
11/1-16/1	8%	4	85	4.7%	-0.27
18/1-33/1	4%	2	82	2.4%	-0.40
40/1+	0%	0	59	0.0%	-1.00

ANALYSIS BY STARTING PRICE LAST TIME

Price	Prop	Win	Runs	Wins%	£
Odds On	4%	2	3	66.7%	1.83
Ev-2/1	0%	0	5	0.0%	-1.00
9/4-4/1	27%	13	48	27.1%	0.27
9/2-6/1	8%	4	32	12.5%	-0.44
13/2-10/1	12%	6	63	9.5%	-0.57
11/1-16/1	18%	9	72	12.5%	0.43
18/1-33/1	12%	6	75	8.0%	-0.64
40/1+	6%	3	106	2.8%	-0.70
Unraced	12%	6	64	9.4%	-0.32

ANALYSIS BY DISTANCE BEATEN LAST TIME

Lengths	Prop	Win	Runs	Wins%	£
..-10	0%	0	0	0.0%	0.00
-10..0	10%	5	18	27.8%	0.17
0.1..2	10%	5	17	29.4%	0.62
2.1..5	29%	14	70	20.0%	0.04
5.1..10	27%	13	120	10.8%	-0.24
10.1..20	10%	5	116	4.3%	-0.59
20.0..30	0%	0	38	0.0%	-1.00
30.1+	2%	1	25	4.0%	-0.32
Not Compl	0%	0	0	0.0%	0.00
Unraced	12%	6	64	9.4%	-0.32

ANALYSIS BY RUN NUMBER

Run No	Prop	Win	Runs	Wins%	£
FTO	12%	6	64	9.4%	-0.32
2nd Run	12%	6	86	7.0%	-0.34
3rd Run	10%	5	94	5.3%	-0.57
4th+ Run	65%	32	224	14.3%	-0.20

ANALYSIS BY POSITION LAST TIME

Pos LT	Prop	Win	Runs	Wins%	£
Won	10%	5	18	27.8%	0.17
2nd or 3rd	29%	14	65	21.5%	0.16
Unplaced	49%	24	321	7.5%	-0.44
Not Compl	12%	6	64	9.4%	-0.32

OTHER FACTORS (WINS-RUNS, £)

Course Winner:	1-4	-£0.19
Distance Winner:	5-22	-£0.15
Going Winner:	2-10	-£0.20
Beaten Favourite:	2-9	-£0.43
BHA Top Rated:	6-17	£0.53
Up in class:	6-73	-£0.43
Same class:	23-162	£0.14
Down in class:	14-169	-£0.70
7-Day Winners:	2-6	£0.17
Colts and Geldings:	14-203	-£0.60
Fillies:	35-265	-£0.10
Absolute Favourites:	16-45	£0.06

TRAINERS (WINS-RUNS, £)

K A Ryan 3-12 £1.44; N Tinkler 1-14 £0.21.

Selling Races

2-Y.O Races: Selling Races – 5 to 6 furlong races

ANALYSIS BY BHA RATING
Rating	Prop	Win	Runs	Wins%	£
120..139	0%	0	0	0.0%	0.00
110..119	0%	0	0	0.0%	0.00
100..109	0%	0	0	0.0%	0.00
90..99	0%	0	0	0.0%	0.00
70..89	3%	4	11	36.4%	0.30
50..69	15%	23	159	14.5%	-0.18
..49	2%	3	49	6.1%	-0.30
Unrated	80%	123	1130	10.9%	-0.23

ANALYSIS BY WEIGHT CARRIED
Weight	Prop	Win	Runs	Wins%	£
10-01+	0%	0	0	0.0%	0.00
9-8..10-00	0%	0	0	0.0%	0.00
9-0..9-07	6%	9	89	10.1%	-0.78
8-8..8-13	44%	67	568	11.8%	-0.12
8-0..8-07	48%	73	658	11.1%	-0.23
..7-13	3%	4	34	11.8%	-0.09

ANALYSIS BY DAYS SINCE LAST RUN
Days	Prop	Win	Runs	Wins%	£
1..7	25%	38	227	16.7%	0.16
8..14	24%	37	351	10.5%	-0.28
15..28	25%	39	391	10.0%	-0.39
29..60	12%	18	160	11.3%	-0.35
61..100	2%	3	40	7.5%	0.52
101+	0%	0	4	0.0%	-1.00
Unraced	12%	18	176	10.2%	-0.25

ANALYSIS BY TODAY'S STARTING PRICE
Price	Prop	Win	Runs	Wins%	£
Odds On	11%	17	29	58.6%	-0.02
Ev-2/1	10%	16	58	27.6%	-0.33
9/4-4/1	37%	56	234	23.9%	0.01
9/2-6/1	12%	18	150	12.0%	-0.25
13/2-10/1	16%	24	226	10.6%	-0.08
11/1-16/1	9%	14	194	7.2%	0.08
18/1-33/1	5%	7	265	2.6%	-0.36
40/1+	1%	1	193	0.5%	-0.74

ANALYSIS BY STARTING PRICE LAST TIME
Price	Prop	Win	Runs	Wins%	£
Odds On	4%	6	11	54.5%	0.58
Ev-2/1	1%	2	27	7.4%	-0.61
9/4-4/1	17%	26	137	19.0%	-0.25
9/2-6/1	11%	17	114	14.9%	-0.28
13/2-10/1	12%	19	176	10.8%	-0.26
11/1-16/1	13%	20	176	11.4%	-0.07
18/1-33/1	14%	22	232	9.5%	-0.00
40/1+	15%	23	300	7.7%	-0.39
Unraced	12%	18	176	10.2%	-0.25

ANALYSIS BY DISTANCE BEATEN LAST TIME
Lengths	Prop	Win	Runs	Wins%	£
..-10	0%	0	0	0.0%	0.00
-10..0	5%	8	43	18.6%	-0.16
0.1..2	10%	15	89	16.9%	-0.36
2.1..5	24%	36	199	18.1%	-0.07
5.1..10	30%	46	344	13.4%	0.04
10.1..20	16%	25	330	7.6%	-0.29
20.0..30	3%	5	110	4.5%	-0.56
30.1+	0%	0	58	0.0%	-1.00
Not Compl	0%	0	0	0.0%	0.00
Unraced	12%	18	176	10.2%	-0.25

ANALYSIS BY RUN NUMBER
Run No	Prop	Win	Runs	Wins%	£
FTO	12%	18	176	10.2%	-0.25
2nd Run	20%	31	260	11.9%	0.01
3rd Run	14%	22	270	8.1%	-0.31
4th+ Run	54%	82	643	12.8%	-0.27

ANALYSIS BY POSITION LAST TIME
Pos LT	Prop	Win	Runs	Wins%	£
Won	5%	8	43	18.6%	-0.16
2nd or 3rd	18%	27	177	15.3%	-0.18
Unplaced	65%	100	950	10.5%	-0.22
Not Compl	12%	18	179	10.1%	-0.27

OTHER FACTORS (WINS-RUNS, £)
Course Winner:	2-10	£0.13
Distance Winner:	15-89	-£0.35
Going Winner:	4-31	-£0.34
Beaten Favourite:	8-46	-£0.32
BHA Top Rated:	7-32	-£0.01
Up in class:	18-209	-£0.35
Same class:	56-492	-£0.11
Down in class:	61-472	-£0.26
7-Day Winners:	4-20	-£0.16
Colts and Geldings:	56-503	-£0.18
Fillies:	94-818	-£0.26
Absolute Favourites:	50-138	-£0.03

TRAINERS (WINS-RUNS, £)
W M Brisbourne 3-22 £0.75; M Dods 3-10 £1.48; N Tinkler 3-32 £0.28; T D Easterby 2-20 £0.43; D Nicholls 3-18 £0.38; K R Burke 7-32 £0.18; R C Guest 3-14 £0.26; M R Channon 13-61 £0.04; P Winkworth 1-11 £0.18; T D Barron 2-19 £0.11; P S McEntee 2-19 £0.03.

Race Profiles

2-Y.O Races: Selling Races – 7 to 8 furlong races

ANALYSIS BY BHA RATING

Rating	Prop	Win	Runs	Wins%	£
120..139	0%	0	0	0.0%	0.00
110..119	0%	0	0	0.0%	0.00
100..109	0%	0	0	0.0%	0.00
90..99	0%	0	0	0.0%	0.00
70..89	2%	1	2	50.0%	0.50
50..69	42%	22	184	12.0%	-0.18
..49	0%	0	23	0.0%	-1.00
Unrated	57%	30	359	8.4%	-0.50

ANALYSIS BY WEIGHT CARRIED

Weight	Prop	Win	Runs	Wins%	£
10-01+	0%	0	0	0.0%	0.00
9-8..10-00	0%	0	0	0.0%	0.00
9-0..9-07	4%	2	10	20.0%	-0.20
8-8..8-13	45%	24	271	8.9%	-0.41
8-0..8-07	49%	26	272	9.6%	-0.42
..7-13	2%	1	15	6.7%	-0.47

ANALYSIS BY DAYS SINCE LAST RUN

Days	Prop	Win	Runs	Wins%	£
1..7	13%	7	74	9.5%	-0.47
8..14	40%	21	169	12.4%	-0.35
15..28	28%	15	168	8.9%	-0.42
29..60	9%	5	95	5.3%	-0.63
61..100	4%	2	25	8.0%	0.20
101+	0%	0	10	0.0%	-1.00
Unraced	6%	3	27	11.1%	-0.18

ANALYSIS BY TODAY'S STARTING PRICE

Price	Prop	Win	Runs	Wins%	£
Odds On	2%	1	4	25.0%	-0.52
Ev-2/1	19%	10	20	50.0%	0.41
9/4-4/1	30%	16	69	23.2%	-0.06
9/2-6/1	21%	11	71	15.5%	-0.08
13/2-10/1	15%	8	101	7.9%	-0.33
11/1-16/1	11%	6	91	6.6%	-0.05
18/1-33/1	2%	1	111	0.9%	-0.81
40/1+	0%	0	101	0.0%	-1.00

ANALYSIS BY STARTING PRICE LAST TIME

Price	Prop	Win	Runs	Wins%	£
Odds On	0%	0	0	0.0%	0.00
Ev-2/1	0%	0	4	0.0%	-1.00
9/4-4/1	17%	9	40	22.5%	0.10
9/2-6/1	19%	10	44	22.7%	0.12
13/2-10/1	11%	6	75	8.0%	-0.61
11/1-16/1	17%	9	85	10.6%	0.00
18/1-33/1	21%	11	138	8.0%	-0.42
40/1+	9%	5	155	3.2%	-0.84
Unraced	6%	3	27	11.1%	-0.18

ANALYSIS BY DISTANCE BEATEN LAST TIME

Lengths	Prop	Win	Runs	Wins%	£
..-10	0%	0	0	0.0%	0.00
-10..0	4%	2	16	12.5%	-0.47
0.1..2	9%	5	29	17.2%	0.30
2.1..5	30%	16	74	21.6%	0.35
5.1..10	25%	13	145	9.0%	-0.56
10.1..20	15%	8	172	4.7%	-0.75
20.0..30	9%	5	70	7.1%	-0.40
30.1+	2%	1	35	2.9%	-0.51
Not Compl	0%	0	0	0.0%	0.00
Unraced	6%	3	27	11.1%	-0.18

ANALYSIS BY RUN NUMBER

Run No	Prop	Win	Runs	Wins%	£
FTO	6%	3	27	11.1%	-0.18
2nd Run	9%	5	91	5.5%	-0.77
3rd Run	13%	7	109	6.4%	-0.56
4th+ Run	72%	38	341	11.1%	-0.28

ANALYSIS BY POSITION LAST TIME

Pos LT	Prop	Win	Runs	Wins%	£
Won	4%	2	16	12.5%	-0.47
2nd or 3rd	32%	17	75	22.7%	0.36
Unplaced	58%	31	450	6.9%	-0.55
Not Compl	6%	3	27	11.1%	-0.18

OTHER FACTORS (WINS-RUNS, £)

Course Winner:	1-4	-£0.19
Distance Winner:	2-19	-£0.54
Going Winner:	2-11	-£0.27
Beaten Favourite:	0-10	-£1.00
BHA Top Rated:	6-28	£0.05
Up in class:	6-81	-£0.34
Same class:	24-243	-£0.37
Down in class:	20-217	-£0.52
7-Day Winners:	1-2	£0.50
Colts and Geldings:	22-263	-£0.45
Fillies:	31-305	-£0.38
Absolute Favourites:	14-44	£0.06

TRAINERS (WINS-RUNS, £)

M R Channon 10-33 £0.71; K A Ryan 4-16 £1.02; P T Midgley 1-10 £1.10; T D Easterby 1-10 £0.70.

Handicaps

2-Y.O Races: Handicaps

ANALYSIS BY BHA RATING

Rating	Prop	Win	Runs	Wins%	£
120..139	0%	0	0	0.0%	0.00
110..119	0%	0	0	0.0%	0.00
100..109	0%	0	2	0.0%	-1.00
90..99	1%	9	93	9.7%	-0.42
70..89	67%	405	3637	11.1%	-0.17
50..69	31%	190	2616	7.3%	-0.22
..49	0%	0	48	0.0%	-1.00
Unrated	0%	0	1	0.0%	-1.00

ANALYSIS BY WEIGHT CARRIED

Weight	Prop	Win	Runs	Wins%	£
10-01+	0%	0	1	0.0%	-1.00
9-8..10-00	1%	7	37	18.9%	-0.16
9-0..9-07	49%	297	2521	11.8%	-0.15
8-8..8-13	26%	158	1708	9.3%	-0.21
8-0..8-07	17%	102	1448	7.0%	-0.21
..7-13	7%	40	682	5.9%	-0.38

ANALYSIS BY DAYS SINCE LAST RUN

Days	Prop	Win	Runs	Wins%	£
1..7	10%	61	505	12.1%	-0.18
8..14	27%	165	1546	10.7%	-0.20
15..28	40%	239	2661	9.0%	-0.21
29..60	20%	123	1381	8.9%	-0.18
61..100	2%	15	252	6.0%	-0.48
101+	0%	1	52	1.9%	0.29
Unraced	0%	0	0	0.0%	0.00

ANALYSIS BY TODAY'S STARTING PRICE

Price	Prop	Win	Runs	Wins%	£
Odds On	2%	13	23	56.5%	-0.03
Ev-2/1	9%	53	172	30.8%	-0.19
9/4-4/1	25%	151	743	20.3%	-0.15
9/2-6/1	20%	123	766	16.1%	-0.01
13/2-10/1	23%	139	1493	9.3%	-0.16
11/1-16/1	15%	88	1447	6.1%	-0.11
18/1-33/1	6%	35	1244	2.8%	-0.29
40/1+	0%	2	509	0.4%	-0.79

ANALYSIS BY STARTING PRICE LAST TIME

Price	Prop	Win	Runs	Wins%	£
Odds On	4%	26	141	18.4%	-0.07
Ev-2/1	8%	51	389	13.1%	-0.22
9/4-4/1	22%	131	1060	12.4%	-0.16
9/2-6/1	12%	75	731	10.3%	-0.18
13/2-10/1	19%	116	1278	9.1%	-0.17
11/1-16/1	17%	104	1140	9.1%	-0.19
18/1-33/1	11%	60	1022	6.7%	-0.29
40/1+	5%	33	636	5.2%	-0.29
Unraced	0%	0	0	0.0%	0.00

ANALYSIS BY DISTANCE BEATEN LAST TIME

Lengths	Prop	Win	Runs	Wins%	£
..-10	0%	0	4	0.0%	-1.00
-10..0	27%	161	1177	13.7%	-0.23
0.1..2	18%	107	935	11.4%	-0.19
2.1..5	22%	133	1385	9.6%	-0.19
5.1..10	21%	127	1613	7.9%	-0.18
10.1..20	11%	65	1022	6.4%	-0.18
20.0..30	1%	9	184	4.9%	-0.47
30.1+	0%	2	77	2.6%	-0.44
Not Compl	0%	0	0	0.0%	0.00
Unraced	0%	0	0	0.0%	0.00

ANALYSIS BY RUN NUMBER

Run No	Prop	Win	Runs	Wins%	£
FTO	0%	0	0	0.0%	0.00
2nd Run	1%	5	41	12.2%	-0.36
3rd Run	8%	50	402	12.4%	-0.37
4th+ Run	91%	549	5954	9.2%	-0.19

ANALYSIS BY POSITION LAST TIME

Pos LT	Prop	Win	Runs	Wins%	£
Won	27%	161	1182	13.6%	-0.23
2nd or 3rd	28%	167	1444	11.6%	-0.17
Unplaced	46%	275	3766	7.3%	-0.21
Not Compl	0%	1	5	20.0%	2.40

OTHER FACTORS (WINS-RUNS, £)

Course Winner:	39-273	-£0.08
Distance Winner:	209-1797	-£0.21
Going Winner:	104-942	-£0.32
Beaten Favourite:	38-370	-£0.34
Up in class:	228-2585	-£0.25
Same class:	181-2028	-£0.23
Down in class:	195-1784	-£0.10
7-Day Winners:	16-82	-£0.03
Colts and Geldings:	388-3763	-£0.17
Fillies:	179-2197	-£0.27
Absolute Favourites:	136-536	-£0.11

TRAINERS (WINS-RUNS, £)

J R Best 7-38 £1.26; D Nicholls 9-29 £1.56; P F I Cole 7-51 £0.71; H J L Dunlop 2-15 £2.00; P A Blockley 3-18 £1.50; T P Tate 4-29 £0.83; M J Polglase 1-13 £1.62; P C Haslam 3-52 £0.39; W J Haggas 11-43 £0.44; Tom Dascombe 6-38 £0.45; T G Mills 2-11 £1.55; M Blanshard 4-32 £0.49; M D I Usher 5-37 £0.43; D J Coakley 1-11 £1.36; E S McMahon 10-47 £0.32; Miss Amy Weaver 1-12 £1.17; Miss V Haigh 2-24 £0.57; D R C Elsworth 3-26 £0.49; C F Wall 3-13 £0.96; A King 2-16 £0.72.

Race Profiles

2-Y.O Races: Handicaps – 2 to 7 runners

ANALYSIS BY BHA RATING

Rating	Prop	Win	Runs	Wins%	£
120..139	0%	0	0	0.0%	0.00
110..119	0%	0	0	0.0%	0.00
100..109	0%	0	1	0.0%	-1.00
90..99	4%	5	16	31.3%	0.23
70..89	68%	94	518	18.1%	-0.20
50..69	29%	40	287	13.9%	-0.07
..49	0%	0	2	0.0%	-1.00
Unrated	0%	0	0	0.0%	0.00

ANALYSIS BY WEIGHT CARRIED

Weight	Prop	Win	Runs	Wins%	£
10-01+	0%	0	0	0.0%	0.00
9-8..10-00	3%	4	11	36.4%	0.32
9-0..9-07	41%	57	300	19.0%	-0.22
8-8..8-13	25%	35	199	17.6%	-0.09
8-0..8-07	21%	29	196	14.8%	-0.09
..7-13	10%	14	118	11.9%	-0.22

ANALYSIS BY DAYS SINCE LAST RUN

Days	Prop	Win	Runs	Wins%	£
1..7	17%	23	102	22.5%	0.18
8..14	32%	45	239	18.8%	-0.23
15..28	31%	43	317	13.6%	-0.27
29..60	19%	26	137	19.0%	0.12
61..100	1%	2	26	7.7%	-0.60
101+	0%	0	3	0.0%	-1.00
Unraced	0%	0	0	0.0%	0.00

ANALYSIS BY TODAY'S STARTING PRICE

Price	Prop	Win	Runs	Wins%	£
Odds On	7%	10	14	71.4%	0.19
Ev-2/1	20%	28	86	32.6%	-0.17
9/4-4/1	40%	55	243	22.6%	-0.04
9/2-6/1	18%	25	138	18.1%	0.11
13/2-10/1	10%	14	164	8.5%	-0.24
11/1-16/1	4%	6	103	5.8%	-0.20
18/1-33/1	1%	1	61	1.6%	-0.66
40/1+	0%	0	15	0.0%	-1.00

ANALYSIS BY STARTING PRICE LAST TIME

Price	Prop	Win	Runs	Wins%	£
Odds On	5%	7	30	23.3%	-0.30
Ev-2/1	12%	16	66	24.2%	0.17
9/4-4/1	24%	34	159	21.4%	-0.11
9/2-6/1	9%	13	84	15.5%	-0.19
13/2-10/1	19%	26	157	16.6%	-0.09
11/1-16/1	16%	22	139	15.8%	-0.13
18/1-33/1	9%	13	121	10.7%	-0.39
40/1+	6%	8	68	11.8%	-0.18
Unraced	0%	0	0	0.0%	0.00

ANALYSIS BY DISTANCE BEATEN LAST TIME

Lengths	Prop	Win	Runs	Wins%	£
..-10	0%	0	0	0.0%	0.00
-10..0	29%	40	174	23.0%	-0.06
0.1..2	20%	28	134	20.9%	-0.08
2.1..5	22%	31	164	18.9%	-0.04
5.1..10	21%	29	202	14.4%	-0.04
10.1..20	6%	9	122	7.4%	-0.62
20.0..30	1%	2	19	10.5%	-0.16
30.1+	0%	0	9	0.0%	-1.00
Not Compl	0%	0	0	0.0%	0.00
Unraced	0%	0	0	0.0%	0.00

ANALYSIS BY RUN NUMBER

Run No	Prop	Win	Runs	Wins%	£
FTO	0%	0	0	0.0%	0.00
2nd Run	1%	1	1	100.0%	3.00
3rd Run	11%	15	67	22.4%	-0.04
4th+ Run	88%	123	756	16.3%	-0.16

ANALYSIS BY POSITION LAST TIME

Pos LT	Prop	Win	Runs	Wins%	£
Won	29%	40	174	23.0%	-0.06
2nd or 3rd	34%	47	218	21.6%	0.06
Unplaced	37%	52	432	12.0%	-0.29
Not Compl	0%	0	0	0.0%	0.00

OTHER FACTORS (WINS-RUNS, £)

Course Winner:	13-72	-£0.12
Distance Winner:	54-292	-£0.20
Going Winner:	38-161	£0.01
Beaten Favourite:	8-52	-£0.39
Up in class:	55-355	-£0.14
Same class:	43-239	-£0.13
Down in class:	41-230	-£0.18
7-Day Winners:	6-16	£0.82
Colts and Geldings:	85-458	-£0.14
Fillies:	48-326	-£0.17
Absolute Favourites:	41-125	-£0.20

TRAINERS (WINS-RUNS, £)

R Hannon 9-41 £0.34; K R Burke 6-20 £0.36; P T Midgley 2-10 £0.55; A Berry 1-17 £0.24; K A Ryan 6-31 £0.11; B Smart 3-16 £0.16.

Handicaps

2-Y.O Races: Handicaps – 8 to 14 runners

ANALYSIS BY BHA RATING

Rating	Prop	Win	Runs	Wins%	£
120..139	0%	0	0	0.0%	0.00
110..119	0%	0	0	0.0%	0.00
100..109	0%	0	0	0.0%	0.00
90..99	1%	3	58	5.2%	-0.77
70..89	68%	253	2291	11.0%	-0.13
50..69	31%	114	1628	7.0%	-0.22
..49	0%	0	28	0.0%	-1.00
Unrated	0%	0	1	0.0%	-1.00

ANALYSIS BY WEIGHT CARRIED

Weight	Prop	Win	Runs	Wins%	£
10-01+	0%	0	1	0.0%	-1.00
9-8..10-00	1%	2	21	9.5%	-0.55
9-0..9-07	51%	189	1540	12.3%	-0.10
8-8..8-13	26%	95	1040	9.1%	-0.21
8-0..8-07	16%	58	929	6.2%	-0.21
..7-13	7%	26	475	5.5%	-0.30

ANALYSIS BY DAYS SINCE LAST RUN

Days	Prop	Win	Runs	Wins%	£
1..7	8%	31	298	10.4%	-0.27
8..14	27%	101	982	10.3%	-0.17
15..28	41%	153	1686	9.1%	-0.19
29..60	20%	73	844	8.6%	-0.16
61..100	3%	11	163	6.7%	-0.38
101+	0%	1	33	3.0%	1.03
Unraced	0%	0	0	0.0%	0.00

ANALYSIS BY TODAY'S STARTING PRICE

Price	Prop	Win	Runs	Wins%	£
Odds On	1%	3	9	33.3%	-0.39
Ev-2/1	6%	23	82	28.0%	-0.24
9/4-4/1	22%	82	442	18.6%	-0.23
9/2-6/1	22%	80	519	15.4%	-0.05
13/2-10/1	28%	102	1021	10.0%	-0.10
11/1-16/1	16%	58	896	6.5%	-0.05
18/1-33/1	5%	20	735	2.7%	-0.32
40/1+	1%	2	302	0.7%	-0.64

ANALYSIS BY STARTING PRICE LAST TIME

Price	Prop	Win	Runs	Wins%	£
Odds On	4%	15	84	17.9%	0.07
Ev-2/1	8%	29	232	12.5%	-0.20
9/4-4/1	22%	83	692	12.0%	-0.17
9/2-6/1	13%	47	479	9.8%	-0.23
13/2-10/1	19%	70	802	8.7%	-0.17
11/1-16/1	17%	62	727	8.5%	-0.20
18/1-33/1	12%	44	614	7.2%	-0.18
40/1+	5%	20	376	5.3%	-0.19
Unraced	0%	0	0	0.0%	0.00

ANALYSIS BY DISTANCE BEATEN LAST TIME

Lengths	Prop	Win	Runs	Wins%	£
..-10	0%	0	2	0.0%	-1.00
-10..0	26%	98	720	13.6%	-0.20
0.1..2	17%	63	596	10.6%	-0.24
2.1..5	22%	82	880	9.3%	-0.23
5.1..10	20%	74	1011	7.3%	-0.19
10.1..20	12%	45	636	7.1%	0.02
20.0..30	2%	6	115	5.2%	-0.42
30.1+	1%	2	46	4.3%	-0.07
Not Compl	0%	0	0	0.0%	0.00
Unraced	0%	0	0	0.0%	0.00

ANALYSIS BY RUN NUMBER

Run No	Prop	Win	Runs	Wins%	£
FTO	0%	0	0	0.0%	0.00
2nd Run	1%	3	28	10.7%	-0.38
3rd Run	8%	28	239	11.7%	-0.41
4th+ Run	92%	339	3739	9.1%	-0.16

ANALYSIS BY POSITION LAST TIME

Pos LT	Prop	Win	Runs	Wins%	£
Won	26%	98	723	13.6%	-0.20
2nd or 3rd	26%	95	910	10.4%	-0.26
Unplaced	48%	176	2371	7.4%	-0.15
Not Compl	0%	1	2	50.0%	7.50

OTHER FACTORS (WINS-RUNS, £)

Course Winner:	22-160	£0.00
Distance Winner:	126-1111	-£0.18
Going Winner:	52-575	-£0.42
Beaten Favourite:	27-254	-£0.29
Up in class:	144-1680	-£0.24
Same class:	116-1253	-£0.16
Down in class:	110-1073	-£0.12
7-Day Winners:	10-51	-£0.01
Colts and Geldings:	239-2378	-£0.13
Fillies:	109-1381	-£0.25
Absolute Favourites:	75-326	-£0.13

TRAINERS (WINS-RUNS, £)

J R Best 5-25 £1.96; M R Channon 32-258 £0.19; P C Haslam 2-30 £1.33; H J L Dunlop 2-10 £3.50; T P Tate 3-18 £1.28; Miss V Haigh 2-15 £1.52; M D I Usher 4-27 £0.81; M Blanshard 3-24 £0.88; D R C Elsworth 2-19 £0.95; T G Mills 2-10 £1.80; J J Quinn 4-21 £0.74; R C Guest 3-22 £0.70; E S McMahon 7-31 £0.48; W J Haggas 6-27 £0.54; D Carroll 2-13 £1.08; M P Tregoning 4-11 £1.27; K R Burke 8-66 £0.17; Sir Michael Stoute 4-13 £0.87; E A L Dunlop 6-38 £0.29; E J Alston 1-12 £0.75.

Race Profiles

2-Y.O Races: Handicaps – 15 runners or more

ANALYSIS BY BHA RATING

Rating	Prop	Win	Runs	Wins%	£
120..139	0%	0	0	0.0%	0.00
110..119	0%	0	0	0.0%	0.00
100..109	0%	0	1	0.0%	-1.00
90..99	1%	1	19	5.3%	0.11
70..89	61%	58	828	7.0%	-0.29
50..69	38%	36	701	5.1%	-0.29
..49	0%	0	18	0.0%	-1.00
Unrated	0%	0	0	0.0%	0.00

ANALYSIS BY WEIGHT CARRIED

Weight	Prop	Win	Runs	Wins%	£
10-01+	0%	0	0	0.0%	0.00
9-8..10-00	1%	1	5	20.0%	0.40
9-0..9-07	54%	51	681	7.5%	-0.24
8-8..8-13	29%	28	469	6.0%	-0.27
8-0..8-07	16%	15	323	4.6%	-0.25
..7-13	0%	0	89	0.0%	-1.00

ANALYSIS BY DAYS SINCE LAST RUN

Days	Prop	Win	Runs	Wins%	£
1..7	7%	7	105	6.7%	-0.27
8..14	20%	19	325	5.8%	-0.29
15..28	45%	43	658	6.5%	-0.23
29..60	25%	24	400	6.0%	-0.31
61..100	2%	2	63	3.2%	-0.68
101+	0%	0	16	0.0%	-1.00
Unraced	0%	0	0	0.0%	0.00

ANALYSIS BY TODAY'S STARTING PRICE

Price	Prop	Win	Runs	Wins%	£
Odds On	0%	0	0	0.0%	0.00
Ev-2/1	2%	2	4	50.0%	0.35
9/4-4/1	15%	14	58	24.1%	0.06
9/2-6/1	19%	18	109	16.5%	0.07
13/2-10/1	24%	23	308	7.5%	-0.32
11/1-16/1	25%	24	448	5.4%	-0.22
18/1-33/1	15%	14	448	3.1%	-0.19
40/1+	0%	0	192	0.0%	-1.00

ANALYSIS BY STARTING PRICE LAST TIME

Price	Prop	Win	Runs	Wins%	£
Odds On	4%	4	27	14.8%	-0.25
Ev-2/1	6%	6	91	6.6%	-0.56
9/4-4/1	15%	14	209	6.7%	-0.19
9/2-6/1	16%	15	168	8.9%	-0.03
13/2-10/1	21%	20	319	6.3%	-0.23
11/1-16/1	21%	20	274	7.3%	-0.19
18/1-33/1	12%	11	287	3.8%	-0.48
40/1+	5%	5	192	2.6%	-0.52
Unraced	0%	0	0	0.0%	0.00

ANALYSIS BY DISTANCE BEATEN LAST TIME

Lengths	Prop	Win	Runs	Wins%	£
..-10	0%	0	2	0.0%	-1.00
-10..0	24%	23	283	8.1%	-0.40
0.1..2	17%	16	205	7.8%	-0.12
2.1..5	21%	20	341	5.9%	-0.18
5.1..10	25%	24	400	6.0%	-0.21
10.1..20	12%	11	264	4.2%	-0.45
20.0..30	1%	1	50	2.0%	-0.70
30.1+	0%	0	22	0.0%	-1.00
Not Compl	0%	0	0	0.0%	0.00
Unraced	0%	0	0	0.0%	0.00

ANALYSIS BY RUN NUMBER

Run No	Prop	Win	Runs	Wins%	£
FTO	0%	0	0	0.0%	0.00
2nd Run	1%	1	12	8.3%	-0.58
3rd Run	7%	7	96	7.3%	-0.48
4th+ Run	92%	87	1459	6.0%	-0.28

ANALYSIS BY POSITION LAST TIME

Pos LT	Prop	Win	Runs	Wins%	£
Won	24%	23	285	8.1%	-0.40
2nd or 3rd	26%	25	316	7.9%	-0.06
Unplaced	49%	47	963	4.9%	-0.34
Not Compl	0%	0	3	0.0%	-1.00

OTHER FACTORS (WINS-RUNS, £)

Course Winner:	4-41	-£0.30
Distance Winner:	29-394	-£0.32
Going Winner:	14-206	-£0.32
Beaten Favourite:	3-64	-£0.51
Up in class:	29-550	-£0.35
Same class:	22-536	-£0.46
Down in class:	44-481	-£0.04
7-Day Winners:	0-15	-£1.00
Colts and Geldings:	64-927	-£0.28
Fillies:	22-490	-£0.37
Absolute Favourites:	20-85	£0.11

TRAINERS (WINS-RUNS, £)

B Smart 3-23 £1.52; P F I Cole 2-14 £2.29; J Howard Johnson 2-12 £1.33; N A Callaghan 3-13 £1.19; C E Brittain 3-21 £0.67; J W Hills 2-13 £0.65; T D Easterby 2-45 £0.13; M G Quinlan 1-17 £0.24; B J Meehan 4-25 £0.03; K A Ryan 4-34 £0.01.

Handicaps

2-Y.O Races: Handicaps – good or faster going

ANALYSIS BY BHA RATING

Rating	Prop	Win	Runs	Wins%	£
120..139	0%	0	0	0.0%	0.00
110..119	0%	0	0	0.0%	0.00
100..109	0%	0	2	0.0%	-1.00
90..99	2%	7	72	9.7%	-0.32
70..89	70%	288	2485	11.6%	-0.18
50..69	28%	116	1737	6.7%	-0.26
..49	0%	0	28	0.0%	-1.00
Unrated	0%	0	0	0.0%	0.00

ANALYSIS BY WEIGHT CARRIED

Weight	Prop	Win	Runs	Wins%	£
10-01+	0%	0	1	0.0%	-1.00
9-8..10-00	1%	4	24	16.7%	-0.50
9-0..9-07	52%	212	1640	12.9%	-0.11
8-8..8-13	25%	102	1145	8.9%	-0.28
8-0..8-07	16%	67	1037	6.5%	-0.21
..7-13	6%	26	477	5.5%	-0.43

ANALYSIS BY DAYS SINCE LAST RUN

Days	Prop	Win	Runs	Wins%	£
1..7	8%	33	343	9.6%	-0.41
8..14	30%	122	1074	11.4%	-0.17
15..28	40%	163	1790	9.1%	-0.21
29..60	20%	81	916	8.8%	-0.22
61..100	3%	11	169	6.5%	-0.45
101+	0%	1	32	3.1%	1.09
Unraced	0%	0	0	0.0%	0.00

ANALYSIS BY TODAY'S STARTING PRICE

Price	Prop	Win	Runs	Wins%	£
Odds On	3%	12	19	63.2%	0.10
Ev-2/1	9%	37	119	31.1%	-0.18
9/4-4/1	27%	112	509	22.0%	-0.07
9/2-6/1	20%	84	519	16.2%	-0.00
13/2-10/1	21%	86	1017	8.5%	-0.23
11/1-16/1	14%	56	962	5.8%	-0.15
18/1-33/1	5%	22	838	2.6%	-0.32
40/1+	0%	2	341	0.6%	-0.68

ANALYSIS BY STARTING PRICE LAST TIME

Price	Prop	Win	Runs	Wins%	£
Odds On	5%	20	108	18.5%	-0.17
Ev-2/1	10%	43	282	15.2%	-0.10
9/4-4/1	22%	89	728	12.2%	-0.22
9/2-6/1	12%	50	513	9.7%	-0.25
13/2-10/1	19%	78	841	9.3%	-0.20
11/1-16/1	16%	66	753	8.8%	-0.24
18/1-33/1	10%	42	689	6.1%	-0.28
40/1+	6%	23	410	5.6%	-0.19
Unraced	0%	0	0	0.0%	0.00

ANALYSIS BY DISTANCE BEATEN LAST TIME

Lengths	Prop	Win	Runs	Wins%	£
..-10	0%	0	1	0.0%	-1.00
-10..0	28%	115	809	14.2%	-0.21
0.1..2	16%	67	635	10.6%	-0.26
2.1..5	23%	96	934	10.3%	-0.18
5.1..10	20%	82	1110	7.4%	-0.27
10.1..20	10%	40	664	6.0%	-0.17
20.0..30	2%	9	116	7.8%	-0.16
30.1+	0%	2	55	3.6%	-0.22
Not Compl	0%	0	0	0.0%	0.00
Unraced	0%	0	0	0.0%	0.00

ANALYSIS BY RUN NUMBER

Run No	Prop	Win	Runs	Wins%	£
FTO	0%	0	0	0.0%	0.00
2nd Run	0%	1	19	5.3%	-0.79
3rd Run	9%	39	285	13.7%	-0.37
4th+ Run	90%	371	4020	9.2%	-0.21

ANALYSIS BY POSITION LAST TIME

Pos LT	Prop	Win	Runs	Wins%	£
Won	28%	115	810	14.2%	-0.21
2nd or 3rd	26%	107	979	10.9%	-0.27
Unplaced	46%	188	2532	7.4%	-0.21
Not Compl	0%	1	3	33.3%	4.67

OTHER FACTORS (WINS-RUNS, £)

Course Winner:	29-184	-£0.10
Distance Winner:	142-1223	-£0.24
Going Winner:	93-790	-£0.29
Beaten Favourite:	32-268	-£0.24
Up in class:	151-1810	-£0.31
Same class:	119-1362	-£0.24
Down in class:	141-1152	-£0.04
7-Day Winners:	9-49	-£0.07
Colts and Geldings:	261-2483	-£0.17
Fillies:	118-1468	-£0.30
Absolute Favourites:	102-366	-£0.01

TRAINERS (WINS-RUNS, £)

J R Best 5-27 £1.51; P A Blockley 3-13 £2.46; P C Haslam 2-38 £0.84; H J L Dunlop 1-11 £2.73; D Nicholls 5-21 £1.21; K R Burke 12-70 £0.35; M J Polglase 1-10 £2.40; M Blanshard 4-25 £0.91; P F I Cole 5-41 £0.54; Miss V Haigh 2-17 £1.22; M P Tregoning 4-10 £1.50; Peter Grayson 2-18 £0.78; J G Given 5-32 £0.36; Saeed Bin Suroor 8-24 £0.47; R F Fisher 1-10 £1.10; W J Haggas 9-31 £0.31; E J Alston 1-12 £0.75; H R A Cecil 3-10 £0.90; J L Spearing 2-17 £0.53; P T Midgley 2-17 £0.47.

Race Profiles

2-Y.O Races: Handicaps – good to soft or softer going

ANALYSIS BY BHA RATING

Rating	Prop	Win	Runs	Wins%	£
120..139	0%	0	0	0.0%	0.00
110..119	0%	0	0	0.0%	0.00
100..109	0%	0	0	0.0%	0.00
90..99	1%	2	21	9.5%	-0.74
70..89	61%	117	1152	10.2%	-0.16
50..69	38%	74	879	8.4%	-0.15
..49	0%	0	20	0.0%	-1.00
Unrated	0%	0	1	0.0%	-1.00

ANALYSIS BY WEIGHT CARRIED

Weight	Prop	Win	Runs	Wins%	£
10-01+	0%	0	0	0.0%	0.00
9-8..10-00	2%	3	13	23.1%	0.46
9-0..9-07	44%	85	881	9.6%	-0.22
8-8..8-13	29%	56	563	9.9%	-0.08
8-0..8-07	18%	35	411	8.5%	-0.18
..7-13	7%	14	205	6.8%	-0.24

ANALYSIS BY DAYS SINCE LAST RUN

Days	Prop	Win	Runs	Wins%	£
1..7	15%	28	162	17.3%	0.30
8..14	22%	43	472	9.1%	-0.28
15..28	39%	76	871	8.7%	-0.21
29..60	22%	42	465	9.0%	-0.08
61..100	2%	4	83	4.8%	-0.53
101+	0%	0	20	0.0%	-1.00
Unraced	0%	0	0	0.0%	0.00

ANALYSIS BY TODAY'S STARTING PRICE

Price	Prop	Win	Runs	Wins%	£
Odds On	1%	1	4	25.0%	-0.68
Ev-2/1	8%	16	53	30.2%	-0.20
9/4-4/1	20%	39	234	16.7%	-0.31
9/2-6/1	20%	39	247	15.8%	-0.01
13/2-10/1	27%	53	476	11.1%	-0.01
11/1-16/1	17%	32	485	6.6%	-0.03
18/1-33/1	7%	13	406	3.2%	-0.21
40/1+	0%	0	168	0.0%	-1.00

ANALYSIS BY STARTING PRICE LAST TIME

Price	Prop	Win	Runs	Wins%	£
Odds On	3%	6	33	18.2%	0.27
Ev-2/1	4%	8	107	7.5%	-0.55
9/4-4/1	22%	42	332	12.7%	-0.05
9/2-6/1	13%	25	218	11.5%	-0.01
13/2-10/1	20%	38	437	8.7%	-0.11
11/1-16/1	20%	38	387	9.8%	-0.10
18/1-33/1	13%	26	333	7.8%	-0.31
40/1+	5%	10	226	4.4%	-0.45
Unraced	0%	0	0	0.0%	0.00

ANALYSIS BY DISTANCE BEATEN LAST TIME

Lengths	Prop	Win	Runs	Wins%	£
..-10	0%	0	3	0.0%	-1.00
-10..0	24%	46	368	12.5%	-0.26
0.1..2	21%	40	300	13.3%	-0.05
2.1..5	19%	37	451	8.2%	-0.23
5.1..10	23%	45	503	8.9%	0.04
10.1..20	13%	25	358	7.0%	-0.19
20.0..30	0%	0	68	0.0%	-1.00
30.1+	0%	0	22	0.0%	-1.00
Not Compl	0%	0	0	0.0%	0.00
Unraced	0%	0	0	0.0%	0.00

ANALYSIS BY RUN NUMBER

Run No	Prop	Win	Runs	Wins%	£
FTO	0%	0	0	0.0%	0.00
2nd Run	2%	4	22	18.2%	0.01
3rd Run	6%	11	117	9.4%	-0.37
4th+ Run	92%	178	1934	9.2%	-0.16

ANALYSIS BY POSITION LAST TIME

Pos LT	Prop	Win	Runs	Wins%	£
Won	24%	46	372	12.4%	-0.27
2nd or 3rd	31%	60	465	12.9%	0.04
Unplaced	45%	87	1234	7.1%	-0.23
Not Compl	0%	0	2	0.0%	-1.00

OTHER FACTORS (WINS-RUNS, £)

Course Winner:	10-89	-£0.03
Distance Winner:	67-574	-£0.15
Going Winner:	11-152	-£0.52
Beaten Favourite:	6-102	-£0.62
Up in class:	77-775	-£0.10
Same class:	62-666	-£0.21
Down in class:	54-632	-£0.22
7-Day Winners:	7-33	£0.04
Colts and Geldings:	127-1280	-£0.17
Fillies:	61-729	-£0.20
Absolute Favourites:	34-170	-£0.32

TRAINERS (WINS-RUNS, £)

M R Channon 16-112 £0.54; P D Evans 6-35 £0.71; A P Jarvis 2-12 £1.92; Tom Dascombe 3-13 £1.71; T P Tate 2-17 £1.24; J Howard Johnson 3-16 £1.25; J W Hills 3-10 £1.95; M D I Usher 3-20 £0.71; D R C Elsworth 1-12 £1.17; P F I Cole 2-10 £1.40; E S McMahon 4-17 £0.74; N A Callaghan 4-16 £0.78; B Smart 4-31 £0.34; W J Haggas 2-12 £0.79; S Kirk 4-17 £0.44; J R Best 2-11 £0.64; M L W Bell 3-24 £0.21; K A Ryan 7-64 £0.07; N P Littmoden 2-14 £0.34; P Winkworth 2-11 £0.39.

Handicaps

2-Y.O Races: Handicaps – 5 to 6 furlong races

ANALYSIS BY BHA RATING
Rating	Prop	Win	Runs	Wins%	£
120..139	0%	0	0	0.0%	0.00
110..119	0%	0	0	0.0%	0.00
100..109	0%	0	2	0.0%	-1.00
90..99	3%	9	57	15.8%	-0.05
70..89	67%	232	1972	11.8%	-0.16
50..69	30%	103	1356	7.6%	-0.24
..49	0%	0	37	0.0%	-1.00
Unrated	0%	0	1	0.0%	-1.00

ANALYSIS BY WEIGHT CARRIED
Weight	Prop	Win	Runs	Wins%	£
10-01+	0%	0	1	0.0%	-1.00
9-8..10-00	1%	4	22	18.2%	-0.10
9-0..9-07	48%	166	1297	12.8%	-0.13
8-8..8-13	25%	86	903	9.5%	-0.21
8-0..8-07	17%	59	789	7.5%	-0.24
..7-13	8%	29	413	7.0%	-0.31

ANALYSIS BY DAYS SINCE LAST RUN
Days	Prop	Win	Runs	Wins%	£
1..7	13%	46	327	14.1%	-0.13
8..14	29%	100	875	11.4%	-0.18
15..28	38%	129	1359	9.5%	-0.17
29..60	18%	63	709	8.9%	-0.19
61..100	2%	6	124	4.8%	-0.69
101+	0%	0	31	0.0%	-1.00
Unraced	0%	0	0	0.0%	0.00

ANALYSIS BY TODAY'S STARTING PRICE
Price	Prop	Win	Runs	Wins%	£
Odds On	2%	6	14	42.9%	-0.27
Ev-2/1	9%	32	107	29.9%	-0.22
9/4-4/1	28%	96	453	21.2%	-0.11
9/2-6/1	22%	77	421	18.3%	0.12
13/2-10/1	21%	71	809	8.8%	-0.22
11/1-16/1	12%	41	778	5.3%	-0.23
18/1-33/1	6%	21	601	3.5%	-0.09
40/1+	0%	0	242	0.0%	-1.00

ANALYSIS BY STARTING PRICE LAST TIME
Price	Prop	Win	Runs	Wins%	£
Odds On	4%	14	86	16.3%	-0.15
Ev-2/1	10%	35	213	16.4%	-0.01
9/4-4/1	24%	81	601	13.5%	-0.12
9/2-6/1	12%	42	395	10.6%	-0.13
13/2-10/1	17%	59	678	8.7%	-0.28
11/1-16/1	17%	59	575	10.3%	-0.18
18/1-33/1	10%	33	542	6.1%	-0.28
40/1+	6%	21	335	0.3%	0.32
Unraced	0%	0	0	0.0%	0.00

ANALYSIS BY DISTANCE BEATEN LAST TIME
Lengths	Prop	Win	Runs	Wins%	£
..-10	0%	0	1	0.0%	-1.00
-10..0	27%	93	647	14.4%	-0.19
0.1..2	19%	67	515	13.0%	-0.15
2.1..5	21%	72	728	9.9%	-0.20
5.1..10	22%	74	861	8.6%	-0.13
10.1..20	9%	30	552	5.4%	-0.37
20.0..30	2%	6	90	6.7%	-0.39
30.1+	1%	2	31	6.5%	0.39
Not Compl	0%	0	0	0.0%	0.00
Unraced	0%	0	0	0.0%	0.00

ANALYSIS BY RUN NUMBER
Run No	Prop	Win	Runs	Wins%	£
FTO	0%	0	0	0.0%	0.00
2nd Run	1%	3	15	20.0%	-0.05
3rd Run	7%	24	225	10.7%	-0.42
4th+ Run	92%	317	3185	10.0%	-0.18

ANALYSIS BY POSITION LAST TIME
Pos LT	Prop	Win	Runs	Wins%	£
Won	27%	93	648	14.4%	-0.19
2nd or 3rd	30%	102	767	13.3%	-0.06
Unplaced	43%	148	2005	7.4%	-0.26
Not Compl	0%	1	5	20.0%	2.40

OTHER FACTORS (WINS-RUNS, £)
Course Winner:	30-169	£0.08
Distance Winner:	148-1275	-£0.22
Going Winner:	61-576	-£0.34
Beaten Favourite:	21-184	-£0.27
Up in class:	140-1375	-£0.17
Same class:	92-1069	-£0.34
Down in class:	112-981	-£0.08
7-Day Winners:	11-50	£0.23
Colts and Geldings:	206-1826	-£0.17
Fillies:	121-1374	-£0.26
Absolute Favourites:	79-307	-£0.09

TRAINERS (WINS-RUNS, £)
D Nicholls 9-23 £2.22; P F I Cole 4-13 £3.92; P A Blockley 3-13 £2.46; M D I Usher 5-29 £0.82; E S McMahon 10-39 £0.59; M Blanshard 4-30 £0.59; J R Best 4-18 £0.88; J Howard Johnson 3-21 £0.71; Miss V Haigh 2-23 £0.64; E A L Dunlop 3-21 £0.68; J A Osborne 4-22 £0.64; J L Spearing 3-22 £0.55; Peter Grayson 2-21 £0.52; J D Bethell 1-17 £0.53; E J Alston 1-14 £0.50; R C Guest 3-25 £0.24; K R Burke 12-74 £0.08; P T Midgley 3-27 £0.20; R Charlton 4-13 £0.37; P Winkworth 2-25 £0.16.

Race Profiles

2-Y.0 Races: Handicaps – 7 to 8 furlong races

ANALYSIS BY BHA RATING

Rating	Prop	Win	Runs	Wins%	£
120..139	0%	0	0	0.0%	0.00
110..119	0%	0	0	0.0%	0.00
100..109	0%	0	0	0.0%	0.00
90..99	0%	0	36	0.0%	-1.00
70..89	66%	167	1632	10.2%	-0.20
50..69	34%	85	1194	7.1%	-0.22
..49	0%	0	11	0.0%	-1.00
Unrated	0%	0	0	0.0%	0.00

ANALYSIS BY WEIGHT CARRIED

Weight	Prop	Win	Runs	Wins%	£
10-01+	0%	0	0	0.0%	0.00
9-8..10-00	1%	3	15	20.0%	-0.26
9-0..9-07	50%	125	1186	10.5%	-0.18
8-8..8-13	29%	72	776	9.3%	-0.19
8-0..8-07	16%	41	634	6.5%	-0.24
..7-13	4%	11	262	4.2%	-0.46

ANALYSIS BY DAYS SINCE LAST RUN

Days	Prop	Win	Runs	Wins%	£
1..7	6%	15	165	9.1%	-0.21
8..14	25%	62	645	9.6%	-0.23
15..28	43%	108	1262	8.6%	-0.24
29..60	23%	59	656	9.0%	-0.15
61..100	3%	8	125	6.4%	-0.30
101+	0%	0	20	0.0%	-1.00
Unraced	0%	0	0	0.0%	0.00

ANALYSIS BY TODAY'S STARTING PRICE

Price	Prop	Win	Runs	Wins%	£
Odds On	2%	6	7	85.7%	0.49
Ev-2/1	8%	20	63	31.7%	-0.16
9/4-4/1	22%	55	286	19.2%	-0.19
9/2-6/1	17%	43	333	12.9%	-0.18
13/2-10/1	27%	67	666	10.1%	-0.08
11/1-16/1	18%	46	643	7.2%	0.05
18/1-33/1	6%	14	621	2.3%	-0.45
40/1+	0%	1	254	0.4%	-0.84

ANALYSIS BY STARTING PRICE LAST TIME

Price	Prop	Win	Runs	Wins%	£
Odds On	4%	11	54	20.4%	-0.04
Ev-2/1	6%	16	175	9.1%	-0.48
9/4-4/1	19%	49	450	10.9%	-0.21
9/2-6/1	13%	33	320	10.3%	-0.21
13/2-10/1	22%	56	582	9.6%	-0.04
11/1-16/1	17%	42	545	7.7%	-0.20
18/1-33/1	13%	34	460	7.4%	-0.28
40/1+	4%	11	287	3.8%	-0.44
Unraced	0%	0	0	0.0%	0.00

ANALYSIS BY DISTANCE BEATEN LAST TIME

Lengths	Prop	Win	Runs	Wins%	£
..-10	0%	0	3	0.0%	-1.00
-10..0	26%	66	520	12.7%	-0.28
0.1..2	15%	38	410	9.3%	-0.25
2.1..5	24%	61	634	9.6%	-0.15
5.1..10	20%	50	725	6.9%	-0.24
10.1..20	13%	34	446	7.6%	-0.05
20.0..30	1%	3	92	3.3%	-0.53
30.1+	0%	0	43	0.0%	-1.00
Not Compl	0%	0	0	0.0%	0.00
Unraced	0%	0	0	0.0%	0.00

ANALYSIS BY RUN NUMBER

Run No	Prop	Win	Runs	Wins%	£
FTO	0%	0	0	0.0%	0.00
2nd Run	1%	2	26	7.7%	-0.54
3rd Run	10%	26	177	14.7%	-0.30
4th+ Run	89%	224	2670	8.4%	-0.21

ANALYSIS BY POSITION LAST TIME

Pos LT	Prop	Win	Runs	Wins%	£
Won	26%	66	524	12.6%	-0.29
2nd or 3rd	25%	62	654	9.5%	-0.29
Unplaced	49%	124	1695	7.3%	-0.18
Not Compl	0%	0	0	0.0%	0.00

OTHER FACTORS (WINS-RUNS, £)

Course Winner:	9-104	-£0.33
Distance Winner:	61-522	-£0.20
Going Winner:	42-357	-£0.31
Beaten Favourite:	16-182	-£0.43
Up in class:	87-1169	-£0.32
Same class:	87-925	-£0.16
Down in class:	78-779	-£0.14
7-Day Winners:	5-30	-£0.39
Colts and Geldings:	176-1870	-£0.20
Fillies:	56-791	-£0.27
Absolute Favourites:	55-221	-£0.13

TRAINERS (WINS-RUNS, £)

T P Tate 4-20 £1.65; J R Best 3-20 £1.60; H J L Dunlop 1-11 £2.73; K A Ryan 7-54 £0.44; D R C Elsworth 2-15 £1.47; A P Jarvis 2-16 £1.19; Tom Dascombe 3-20 £0.93; A King 2-13 £1.12; W J Haggas 7-26 £0.54; P D Evans 4-29 £0.47; Jedd O'Keeffe 2-12 £1.00; W R Swinburn 2-10 £1.20; N A Callaghan 5-25 £0.46; B Smart 2-30 £0.37; Saeed Bin Suroor 6-18 £0.55; M J Wallace 3-14 £0.68; M R Channon 22-216 £0.04; M H Tompkins 4-32 £0.23; R M Beckett 3-22 £0.34; D M Simcock 2-12 £0.46.

Handicaps

2-Y.O Races: Handicaps – 9+ furlong races

ANALYSIS BY BHA RATING

Rating	Prop	Win	Runs	Wins%	£
120..139	0%	0	0	0.0%	0.00
110..119	0%	0	0	0.0%	0.00
100..109	0%	0	0	0.0%	0.00
90..99	0%	0	0	0.0%	0.00
70..89	75%	6	33	18.2%	0.13
50..69	25%	2	66	3.0%	0.12
..49	0%	0	0	0.0%	0.00
Unrated	0%	0	0	0.0%	0.00

ANALYSIS BY WEIGHT CARRIED

Weight	Prop	Win	Runs	Wins%	£
10-01+	0%	0	0	0.0%	0.00
9-8..10-00	0%	0	0	0.0%	0.00
9-0..9-07	75%	6	38	15.8%	-0.02
8-8..8-13	0%	0	29	0.0%	-1.00
8-0..8-07	25%	2	25	8.0%	1.96
..7-13	0%	0	7	0.0%	-1.00

ANALYSIS BY DAYS SINCE LAST RUN

Days	Prop	Win	Runs	Wins%	£
1..7	0%	0	13	0.0%	-1.00
8..14	38%	3	26	11.5%	-0.19
15..28	25%	2	40	5.0%	-0.64
29..60	13%	1	16	6.3%	-0.84
61..100	13%	1	3	33.3%	1.00
101+	13%	1	1	100.0%	66.00
Unraced	0%	0	0	0.0%	0.00

ANALYSIS BY TODAY'S STARTING PRICE

Price	Prop	Win	Runs	Wins%	£
Odds On	13%	1	2	50.0%	-0.19
Ev-2/1	13%	1	2	50.0%	0.31
9/4-4/1	0%	0	4	0.0%	-1.00
9/2-6/1	38%	3	12	25.0%	0.63
13/2-10/1	13%	1	18	5.6%	-0.58
11/1-16/1	13%	1	26	3.8%	-0.50
18/1-33/1	0%	0	22	0.0%	-1.00
40/1+	13%	1	13	7.7%	4.15

ANALYSIS BY STARTING PRICE LAST TIME

Price	Prop	Win	Runs	Wins%	£
Odds On	13%	1	1	100.0%	5.50
Ev-2/1	0%	0	1	0.0%	-1.00
9/4-4/1	13%	1	9	11.1%	-0.71
9/2-6/1	0%	0	16	0.0%	-1.00
13/2-10/1	13%	1	18	5.6%	-0.28
11/1-16/1	38%	3	20	15.0%	-0.19
18/1-33/1	13%	1	20	5.0%	-0.70
40/1+	13%	1	14	7.1%	3.79
Unraced	0%	0	0	0.0%	0.00

ANALYSIS BY DISTANCE BEATEN LAST TIME

Lengths	Prop	Win	Runs	Wins%	£
..-10	0%	0	0	0.0%	0.00
-10..0	25%	2	10	20.0%	-0.04
0.1..2	25%	2	10	20.0%	-0.19
2.1..5	0%	0	23	0.0%	-1.00
5.1..10	38%	3	27	11.1%	-0.02
10.1..20	13%	1	24	4.2%	1.79
20.0..30	0%	0	2	0.0%	-1.00
30.1+	0%	0	3	0.0%	-1.00
Not Compl	0%	0	0	0.0%	0.00
Unraced	0%	0	0	0.0%	0.00

ANALYSIS BY RUN NUMBER

Run No	Prop	Win	Runs	Wins%	£
FTO	0%	0	0	0.0%	0.00
2nd Run	0%	0	0	0.0%	0.00
3rd Run	0%	0	0	0.0%	0.00
4th+ Run	100%	8	99	8.1%	0.12

ANALYSIS BY POSITION LAST TIME

Pos LT	Prop	Win	Runs	Wins%	£
Won	25%	2	10	20.0%	-0.04
2nd or 3rd	38%	3	23	13.0%	-0.39
Unplaced	38%	3	66	4.5%	0.33
Not Compl	0%	0	0	0.0%	0.00

OTHER FACTORS (WINS-RUNS, £)

Going Winner:	1-9	-£0.22
Beaten Favourite:	1-4	£0.63
Up in class:	1-41	-£0.84
Same class:	2-34	£1.15
Down in class:	5-24	£0.32
7-Day Winners:	0-2	-£1.00
Colts and Geldings:	6-67	£0.46
Fillies:	2-32	-£0.58
Absolute Favourites:	2-8	-£0.47

JUVENILE RACES

Race Profiles

3-Y.O Races: Group 1 Races

ANALYSIS BY BHA RATING

Rating	Prop	Win	Runs	Wins%	£
120..139	9%	3	12	25.0%	0.13
110..119	40%	14	110	12.7%	-0.06
100..109	9%	3	136	2.2%	-0.84
90..99	3%	1	38	2.6%	-0.11
70..89	3%	1	15	6.7%	0.40
50..69	0%	0	0	0.0%	0.00
..49	0%	0	0	0.0%	0.00
Unrated	37%	13	150	8.7%	-0.53

ANALYSIS BY WEIGHT CARRIED

Weight	Prop	Win	Runs	Wins%	£
10-01+	0%	0	0	0.0%	0.00
9-8..10-00	0%	0	0	0.0%	0.00
9-0..9-07	100%	35	458	7.6%	-0.42
8-8..8-13	0%	0	3	0.0%	-1.00
8-0..8-07	0%	0	0	0.0%	0.00
..7-13	0%	0	0	0.0%	0.00

ANALYSIS BY DAYS SINCE LAST RUN

Days	Prop	Win	Runs	Wins%	£
1..7	0%	0	3	0.0%	-1.00
8..14	6%	2	30	6.7%	-0.60
15..28	46%	16	223	7.2%	-0.46
29..60	17%	6	79	7.6%	-0.57
61..100	3%	1	19	5.3%	-0.90
101+	29%	10	93	10.8%	0.03
Unraced	0%	0	14	0.0%	-1.00

ANALYSIS BY TODAY'S STARTING PRICE

Price	Prop	Win	Runs	Wins%	£
Odds On	9%	3	4	75.0%	0.33
Ev-2/1	20%	7	12	58.3%	0.51
9/4-4/1	20%	7	39	17.9%	-0.33
9/2-6/1	14%	5	36	13.9%	-0.13
13/2-10/1	20%	7	87	8.0%	-0.29
11/1-16/1	9%	3	71	4.2%	-0.44
18/1-33/1	9%	3	92	3.3%	-0.12
40/1+	0%	0	120	0.0%	-1.00

ANALYSIS BY STARTING PRICE LAST TIME

Price	Prop	Win	Runs	Wins%	£
Odds On	20%	7	39	17.9%	0.26
Ev-2/1	29%	10	75	13.3%	0.16
9/4-4/1	20%	7	96	7.3%	-0.59
9/2-6/1	6%	2	54	3.7%	-0.85
13/2-10/1	14%	5	87	5.7%	-0.35
11/1-16/1	6%	2	50	4.0%	-0.64
18/1-33/1	6%	2	29	6.9%	-0.83
40/1+	0%	0	17	0.0%	-1.00
Unraced	0%	0	14	0.0%	-1.00

ANALYSIS BY DISTANCE BEATEN LAST TIME

Lengths	Prop	Win	Runs	Wins%	£
..-10	0%	0	0	0.0%	0.00
-10..0	66%	23	169	13.6%	-0.22
0.1..2	17%	6	107	5.6%	-0.28
2.1..5	9%	3	91	3.3%	-0.63
5.1..10	6%	2	42	4.8%	-0.64
10.1..20	0%	0	22	0.0%	-1.00
20.0..30	3%	1	10	10.0%	-0.30
30.1+	0%	0	6	0.0%	-1.00
Not Compl	0%	0	0	0.0%	0.00
Unraced	0%	0	14	0.0%	-1.00

ANALYSIS BY RUN NUMBER

Run No	Prop	Win	Runs	Wins%	£
FTO	0%	0	14	0.0%	-1.00
2nd Run	0%	0	8	0.0%	-1.00
3rd Run	14%	5	50	10.0%	0.40
4th+ Run	86%	30	389	7.7%	-0.50

ANALYSIS BY POSITION LAST TIME

Pos LT	Prop	Win	Runs	Wins%	£
Won	66%	23	169	13.6%	-0.22
2nd or 3rd	23%	8	135	5.9%	-0.22
Unplaced	11%	4	143	2.8%	-0.81
Not Compl	0%	0	14	0.0%	-1.00

OTHER FACTORS (WINS-RUNS, £)

Course Winner:	6-73	-£0.27
Distance Winner:	8-87	-£0.56
Going Winner:	14-187	-£0.55
Beaten Favourite:	3-49	-£0.69
BHA Top Rated:	7-35	-£0.20
Up in class:	21-322	-£0.37
Same class:	14-125	-£0.50
7-Day Winners:	0-2	-£1.00
Colts and Geldings:	14-176	-£0.57
Fillies:	0-1	-£1.00
Absolute Favourites:	14-32	£0.18

TRAINERS (WINS-RUNS, £)

B W Hills 3-21 £0.40.

Group 1 Races

3-Y.O Races: Group 1 Races – 2 to 7 runners

ANALYSIS BY BHA RATING

Rating	Prop	Win	Runs	Wins%	£
120..139	0%	0	0	0.0%	0.00
110..119	0%	0	2	0.0%	-1.00
100..109	0%	0	3	0.0%	-1.00
90..99	0%	0	0	0.0%	0.00
70..89	0%	0	0	0.0%	0.00
50..69	0%	0	0	0.0%	0.00
..49	0%	0	0	0.0%	0.00
Unrated	100%	1	1	100.0%	0.91

ANALYSIS BY WEIGHT CARRIED

Weight	Prop	Win	Runs	Wins%	£
10-01+	0%	0	0	0.0%	0.00
9-8..10-00	0%	0	0	0.0%	0.00
9-0..9-07	100%	1	6	16.7%	-0.68
8-8..8-13	0%	0	0	0.0%	0.00
8-0..8-07	0%	0	0	0.0%	0.00
..7-13	0%	0	0	0.0%	0.00

ANALYSIS BY DAYS SINCE LAST RUN

Days	Prop	Win	Runs	Wins%	£
1..7	0%	0	0	0.0%	0.00
8..14	0%	0	1	0.0%	-1.00
15..28	0%	0	4	0.0%	-1.00
29..60	0%	0	0	0.0%	0.00
61..100	100%	1	1	100.0%	0.91
101+	0%	0	0	0.0%	0.00
Unraced	0%	0	0	0.0%	0.00

ANALYSIS BY TODAY'S STARTING PRICE

Price	Prop	Win	Runs	Wins%	£
Odds On	100%	1	1	100.0%	0.91
Ev-2/1	0%	0	0	0.0%	0.00
9/4-4/1	0%	0	2	0.0%	-1.00
9/2-6/1	0%	0	0	0.0%	0.00
13/2-10/1	0%	0	0	0.0%	0.00
11/1-16/1	0%	0	1	0.0%	-1.00
18/1-33/1	0%	0	2	0.0%	-1.00
40/1+	0%	0	0	0.0%	0.00

ANALYSIS BY STARTING PRICE LAST TIME

Price	Prop	Win	Runs	Wins%	£
Odds On	0%	0	0	0.0%	0.00
Ev-2/1	0%	0	1	0.0%	-1.00
9/4-4/1	0%	0	1	0.0%	-1.00
9/2-6/1	0%	0	3	0.0%	-1.00
13/2-10/1	0%	0	0	0.0%	0.00
11/1-16/1	0%	0	0	0.0%	0.00
18/1-33/1	100%	1	1	100.0%	0.91
40/1+	0%	0	0	0.0%	0.00
Unraced	0%	0	0	0.0%	0.00

ANALYSIS BY DISTANCE BEATEN LAST TIME

Lengths	Prop	Win	Runs	Wins%	£
..-10	0%	0	0	0.0%	0.00
-10..0	0%	0	2	0.0%	-1.00
0.1..2	100%	1	3	33.3%	-0.36
2.1..5	0%	0	1	0.0%	-1.00
5.1..10	0%	0	0	0.0%	0.00
10.1..20	0%	0	0	0.0%	0.00
20.0..30	0%	0	0	0.0%	0.00
30.1+	0%	0	0	0.0%	0.00
Not Compl	0%	0	0	0.0%	0.00
Unraced	0%	0	0	0.0%	0.00

ANALYSIS BY RUN NUMBER

Run No	Prop	Win	Runs	Wins%	£
FTO	0%	0	0	0.0%	0.00
2nd Run	0%	0	0	0.0%	0.00
3rd Run	0%	0	0	0.0%	0.00
4th+ Run	100%	1	6	16.7%	-0.68

ANALYSIS BY POSITION LAST TIME

Pos LT	Prop	Win	Runs	Wins%	£
Won	0%	0	2	0.0%	-1.00
2nd or 3rd	100%	1	3	33.3%	-0.36
Unplaced	0%	0	1	0.0%	-1.00
Not Compl	0%	0	0	0.0%	0.00

OTHER FACTORS (WINS-RUNS, £)

Going Winner:	0-1	-£1.00
Beaten Favourite:	0-1	-£1.00
BHA Top Rated:	0-1	-£1.00
Up in class:	0-5	-£1.00
Same class:	1-1	£0.91
Colts and Geldings:	1-6	-£0.68
Absolute Favourites:	1-1	£0.91

Race Profiles

3-Y.O Races: Group 1 Races – 8 to 14 runners

ANALYSIS BY BHA RATING

Rating	Prop	Win	Runs	Wins%	£
120..139	9%	2	8	25.0%	-0.19
110..119	45%	10	65	15.4%	-0.10
100..109	14%	3	73	4.1%	-0.70
90..99	0%	0	13	0.0%	-1.00
70..89	5%	1	7	14.3%	2.00
50..69	0%	0	0	0.0%	0.00
..49	0%	0	0	0.0%	0.00
Unrated	27%	6	78	7.7%	-0.69

ANALYSIS BY WEIGHT CARRIED

Weight	Prop	Win	Runs	Wins%	£
10-01+	0%	0	0	0.0%	0.00
9-8..10-00	0%	0	0	0.0%	0.00
9-0..9-07	100%	22	241	9.1%	-0.45
8-8..8-13	0%	0	3	0.0%	-1.00
8-0..8-07	0%	0	0	0.0%	0.00
..7-13	0%	0	0	0.0%	0.00

ANALYSIS BY DAYS SINCE LAST RUN

Days	Prop	Win	Runs	Wins%	£
1..7	0%	0	2	0.0%	-1.00
8..14	5%	1	18	5.6%	-0.67
15..28	55%	12	110	10.9%	-0.42
29..60	23%	5	51	9.8%	-0.47
61..100	0%	0	16	0.0%	-1.00
101+	18%	4	39	10.3%	-0.10
Unraced	0%	0	8	0.0%	-1.00

ANALYSIS BY TODAY'S STARTING PRICE

Price	Prop	Win	Runs	Wins%	£
Odds On	9%	2	3	66.7%	0.13
Ev-2/1	23%	5	7	71.4%	0.95
9/4-4/1	27%	6	29	20.7%	-0.22
9/2-6/1	9%	2	19	10.5%	-0.39
13/2-10/1	23%	5	54	9.3%	-0.16
11/1-16/1	5%	1	38	2.6%	-0.61
18/1-33/1	5%	1	46	2.2%	-0.54
40/1+	0%	0	48	0.0%	-1.00

ANALYSIS BY STARTING PRICE LAST TIME

Price	Prop	Win	Runs	Wins%	£
Odds On	23%	5	21	23.8%	0.88
Ev-2/1	27%	6	39	15.4%	-0.33
9/4-4/1	14%	3	47	6.4%	-0.71
9/2-6/1	9%	2	30	6.7%	-0.73
13/2-10/1	14%	3	42	7.1%	-0.43
11/1-16/1	9%	2	27	7.4%	-0.33
18/1-33/1	5%	1	16	6.3%	-0.81
40/1+	0%	0	14	0.0%	-1.00
Unraced	0%	0	8	0.0%	-1.00

ANALYSIS BY DISTANCE BEATEN LAST TIME

Lengths	Prop	Win	Runs	Wins%	£
..-10	0%	0	0	0.0%	0.00
-10..0	77%	17	85	20.0%	0.10
0.1..2	9%	2	52	3.8%	-0.83
2.1..5	5%	1	50	2.0%	-0.70
5.1..10	9%	2	27	7.4%	-0.44
10.1..20	0%	0	13	0.0%	-1.00
20.0..30	0%	0	5	0.0%	-1.00
30.1+	0%	0	4	0.0%	-1.00
Not Compl	0%	0	0	0.0%	0.00
Unraced	0%	0	8	0.0%	-1.00

ANALYSIS BY RUN NUMBER

Run No	Prop	Win	Runs	Wins%	£
FTO	0%	0	8	0.0%	-1.00
2nd Run	0%	0	3	0.0%	-1.00
3rd Run	9%	2	21	9.5%	0.18
4th+ Run	91%	20	212	9.4%	-0.49

ANALYSIS BY POSITION LAST TIME

Pos LT	Prop	Win	Runs	Wins%	£
Won	77%	17	85	20.0%	0.10
2nd or 3rd	9%	2	72	2.8%	-0.75
Unplaced	14%	3	79	3.8%	-0.74
Not Compl	0%	0	8	0.0%	-1.00

OTHER FACTORS (WINS-RUNS, £)

Course Winner:	3-27	-£0.20
Distance Winner:	5-45	-£0.55
Going Winner:	10-92	-£0.54
Beaten Favourite:	2-26	-£0.64
BHA Top Rated:	6-21	£0.01
Up in class:	13-147	-£0.35
Same class:	9-89	-£0.59
7-Day Winners:	0-1	-£1.00
Colts and Geldings:	9-92	-£0.66
Fillies:	0-1	-£1.00
Absolute Favourites:	10-20	£0.38

TRAINERS (WINS-RUNS, £)

B W Hills 3-14 £1.11; Saeed Bin Suroor 2-12 £0.48.

Group 1 Races

3-Y.O Races: Group 1 Races – 15 runners or more

ANALYSIS BY BHA RATING

Rating	Prop	Win	Runs	Wins%	£
120..139	8%	1	4	25.0%	0.75
110..119	33%	4	43	9.3%	0.03
100..109	0%	0	60	0.0%	-1.00
90..99	8%	1	25	4.0%	0.36
70..89	0%	0	8	0.0%	-1.00
50..69	0%	0	0	0.0%	0.00
..49	0%	0	0	0.0%	0.00
Unrated	50%	6	71	8.5%	-0.37

ANALYSIS BY WEIGHT CARRIED

Weight	Prop	Win	Runs	Wins%	£
10-01+	0%	0	0	0.0%	0.00
9-8..10-00	0%	0	0	0.0%	0.00
9-0..9-07	100%	12	211	5.7%	-0.39
8-8..8-13	0%	0	0	0.0%	0.00
8-0..8-07	0%	0	0	0.0%	0.00
..7-13	0%	0	0	0.0%	0.00

ANALYSIS BY DAYS SINCE LAST RUN

Days	Prop	Win	Runs	Wins%	£
1..7	0%	0	1	0.0%	-1.00
8..14	8%	1	11	9.1%	-0.45
15..28	33%	4	109	3.7%	-0.48
29..60	8%	1	28	3.6%	-0.75
61..100	0%	0	2	0.0%	-1.00
101+	50%	6	54	11.1%	0.12
Unraced	0%	0	6	0.0%	-1.00

ANALYSIS BY TODAY'S STARTING PRICE

Price	Prop	Win	Runs	Wins%	£
Odds On	0%	0	0	0.0%	0.00
Ev-2/1	17%	2	5	40.0%	-0.10
9/4-4/1	8%	1	8	12.5%	-0.53
9/2-6/1	25%	3	17	17.6%	0.18
13/2-10/1	17%	2	33	6.1%	-0.50
11/1-16/1	17%	2	32	6.3%	-0.22
18/1-33/1	17%	2	44	4.5%	0.36
40/1+	0%	0	72	0.0%	-1.00

ANALYSIS BY STARTING PRICE LAST TIME

Price	Prop	Win	Runs	Wins%	£
Odds On	17%	2	18	11.1%	-0.46
Ev-2/1	33%	4	35	11.4%	0.74
9/4-4/1	33%	4	48	8.3%	-0.46
9/2-6/1	0%	0	21	0.0%	-1.00
13/2-10/1	17%	2	45	4.4%	-0.27
11/1-16/1	0%	0	23	0.0%	-1.00
18/1-33/1	0%	0	12	0.0%	-1.00
40/1+	0%	0	3	0.0%	-1.00
Unraced	0%	0	6	0.0%	-1.00

ANALYSIS BY DISTANCE BEATEN LAST TIME

Lengths	Prop	Win	Runs	Wins%	£
..-10	0%	0	0	0.0%	0.00
-10..0	50%	6	82	7.3%	-0.54
0.1..2	25%	3	52	5.8%	0.27
2.1..5	17%	2	40	5.0%	-0.52
5.1..10	0%	0	15	0.0%	-1.00
10.1..20	0%	0	9	0.0%	-1.00
20.0..30	8%	1	5	20.0%	0.40
30.1+	0%	0	2	0.0%	-1.00
Not Compl	0%	0	0	0.0%	0.00
Unraced	0%	0	6	0.0%	-1.00

ANALYSIS BY RUN NUMBER

Run No	Prop	Win	Runs	Wins%	£
FTO	0%	0	6	0.0%	-1.00
2nd Run	0%	0	5	0.0%	-1.00
3rd Run	25%	3	29	10.3%	0.56
4th+ Run	75%	9	171	5.3%	-0.51

ANALYSIS BY POSITION LAST TIME

Pos LT	Prop	Win	Runs	Wins%	£
Won	50%	6	82	7.3%	-0.54
2nd or 3rd	42%	5	60	8.3%	0.42
Unplaced	8%	1	63	1.6%	-0.89
Not Compl	0%	0	6	0.0%	-1.00

OTHER FACTORS (WINS-RUNS, £)

Course Winner:	3-46	-£0.30
Distance Winner:	3-42	-£0.57
Going Winner:	4-94	-£0.55
Beaten Favourite:	1-22	-£0.73
BHA Top Rated:	1-13	-£0.46
Up in class:	8-170	-£0.38
Same class:	4-35	-£0.32
7-Day Winners:	0-1	-£1.00
Colts and Geldings:	4-78	-£0.45
Absolute Favourites:	3-11	-£0.25

Race Profiles

3-Y.O Races: Group 1 Races – good or faster going

ANALYSIS BY BHA RATING

Rating	Prop	Win	Runs	Wins%	£
120..139	10%	3	12	25.0%	0.13
110..119	40%	12	94	12.8%	-0.10
100..109	3%	1	120	0.8%	-0.97
90..99	3%	1	36	2.8%	-0.06
70..89	3%	1	15	6.7%	0.40
50..69	0%	0	0	0.0%	0.00
..49	0%	0	0	0.0%	0.00
Unrated	40%	12	124	9.7%	-0.45

ANALYSIS BY WEIGHT CARRIED

Weight	Prop	Win	Runs	Wins%	£
10-01+	0%	0	0	0.0%	0.00
9-8..10-00	0%	0	0	0.0%	0.00
9-0..9-07	100%	30	400	7.5%	-0.44
8-8..8-13	0%	0	1	0.0%	-1.00
8-0..8-07	0%	0	0	0.0%	0.00
..7-13	0%	0	0	0.0%	0.00

ANALYSIS BY DAYS SINCE LAST RUN

Days	Prop	Win	Runs	Wins%	£
1..7	0%	0	2	0.0%	-1.00
8..14	7%	2	28	7.1%	-0.57
15..28	47%	14	198	7.1%	-0.49
29..60	13%	4	74	5.4%	-0.78
61..100	0%	0	7	0.0%	-1.00
101+	33%	10	81	12.3%	0.18
Unraced	0%	0	11	0.0%	-1.00

ANALYSIS BY TODAY'S STARTING PRICE

Price	Prop	Win	Runs	Wins%	£
Odds On	7%	2	3	66.7%	0.13
Ev-2/1	23%	7	12	58.3%	0.51
9/4-4/1	23%	7	30	23.3%	-0.13
9/2-6/1	17%	5	34	14.7%	-0.07
13/2-10/1	10%	3	73	4.1%	-0.65
11/1-16/1	10%	3	60	5.0%	-0.33
18/1-33/1	10%	3	80	3.8%	0.01
40/1+	0%	0	109	0.0%	-1.00

ANALYSIS BY STARTING PRICE LAST TIME

Price	Prop	Win	Runs	Wins%	£
Odds On	20%	6	33	18.2%	0.22
Ev-2/1	30%	9	68	13.2%	0.17
9/4-4/1	23%	7	86	8.1%	-0.54
9/2-6/1	7%	2	45	4.4%	-0.82
13/2-10/1	10%	3	77	3.9%	-0.52
11/1-16/1	7%	2	44	4.5%	-0.59
18/1-33/1	3%	1	25	4.0%	-0.88
40/1+	0%	0	12	0.0%	-1.00
Unraced	0%	0	11	0.0%	-1.00

ANALYSIS BY DISTANCE BEATEN LAST TIME

Lengths	Prop	Win	Runs	Wins%	£
..-10	0%	0	0	0.0%	0.00
-10..0	67%	20	146	13.7%	-0.29
0.1..2	17%	5	97	5.2%	-0.23
2.1..5	10%	3	80	3.8%	-0.57
5.1..10	3%	1	35	2.9%	-0.83
10.1..20	0%	0	20	0.0%	-1.00
20.0..30	3%	1	7	14.3%	0.00
30.1+	0%	0	5	0.0%	-1.00
Not Compl	0%	0	0	0.0%	0.00
Unraced	0%	0	11	0.0%	-1.00

ANALYSIS BY RUN NUMBER

Run No	Prop	Win	Runs	Wins%	£
FTO	0%	0	11	0.0%	-1.00
2nd Run	0%	0	7	0.0%	-1.00
3rd Run	17%	5	42	11.9%	0.67
4th+ Run	83%	25	341	7.3%	-0.54

ANALYSIS BY POSITION LAST TIME

Pos LT	Prop	Win	Runs	Wins%	£
Won	67%	20	146	13.7%	-0.29
2nd or 3rd	23%	7	118	5.9%	-0.13
Unplaced	10%	3	126	2.4%	-0.85
Not Compl	0%	0	11	0.0%	-1.00

OTHER FACTORS (WINS-RUNS, £)

Course Winner:	4-65	-£0.48
Distance Winner:	7-80	-£0.65
Going Winner:	13-174	-£0.56
Beaten Favourite:	3-45	-£0.66
BHA Top Rated:	7-30	-£0.06
Up in class:	18-288	-£0.39
Same class:	12-102	-£0.50
7-Day Winners:	0-2	-£1.00
Colts and Geldings:	13-170	-£0.56
Fillies:	0-1	-£1.00
Absolute Favourites:	13-28	£0.28

TRAINERS (WINS-RUNS, £)

B W Hills 3-18 £0.64.

Group 1 Races

3-Y.O Races: Group 1 Races – good to soft or softer going

ANALYSIS BY BHA RATING

Rating	Prop	Win	Runs	Wins%	£
120..139	0%	0	0	0.0%	0.00
110..119	40%	2	16	12.5%	0.13
100..109	40%	2	16	12.5%	0.16
90..99	0%	0	2	0.0%	-1.00
70..89	0%	0	0	0.0%	0.00
50..69	0%	0	0	0.0%	0.00
..49	0%	0	0	0.0%	0.00
Unrated	20%	1	26	3.8%	-0.93

ANALYSIS BY WEIGHT CARRIED

Weight	Prop	Win	Runs	Wins%	£
10-01+	0%	0	0	0.0%	0.00
9-8..10-00	0%	0	0	0.0%	0.00
9-0..9-07	100%	5	58	8.6%	-0.34
8-8..8-13	0%	0	2	0.0%	-1.00
8-0..8-07	0%	0	0	0.0%	0.00
..7-13	0%	0	0	0.0%	0.00

ANALYSIS BY DAYS SINCE LAST RUN

Days	Prop	Win	Runs	Wins%	£
1..7	0%	0	1	0.0%	-1.00
8..14	0%	0	2	0.0%	-1.00
15..28	40%	2	25	8.0%	-0.26
29..60	40%	2	5	40.0%	2.60
61..100	20%	1	12	8.3%	-0.84
101+	0%	0	12	0.0%	-1.00
Unraced	0%	0	3	0.0%	-1.00

ANALYSIS BY TODAY'S STARTING PRICE

Price	Prop	Win	Runs	Wins%	£
Odds On	20%	1	1	100.0%	0.91
Ev-2/1	0%	0	0	0.0%	0.00
9/4-4/1	0%	0	9	0.0%	-1.00
9/2-6/1	0%	0	2	0.0%	-1.00
13/2-10/1	80%	4	14	28.6%	1.61
11/1-16/1	0%	0	11	0.0%	-1.00
18/1-33/1	0%	0	12	0.0%	-1.00
40/1+	0%	0	11	0.0%	-1.00

ANALYSIS BY STARTING PRICE LAST TIME

Price	Prop	Win	Runs	Wins%	£
Odds On	20%	1	6	16.7%	0.50
Ev-2/1	20%	1	7	14.3%	0.07
9/4-4/1	0%	0	10	0.0%	-1.00
9/2-6/1	0%	0	9	0.0%	-1.00
13/2-10/1	40%	2	10	20.0%	1.00
11/1-16/1	0%	0	6	0.0%	-1.00
18/1-33/1	20%	1	4	25.0%	-0.52
40/1+	0%	0	5	0.0%	-1.00
Unraced	0%	0	3	0.0%	-1.00

ANALYSIS BY DISTANCE BEATEN LAST TIME

Lengths	Prop	Win	Runs	Wins%	£
...-10	0%	0	0	0.0%	0.00
-10..0	60%	3	23	13.0%	0.20
0.1..2	20%	1	10	10.0%	-0.81
2.1..5	0%	0	11	0.0%	-1.00
5.1..10	20%	1	7	14.3%	0.29
10.1..20	0%	0	2	0.0%	-1.00
20.0..30	0%	0	3	0.0%	-1.00
30.1+	0%	0	1	0.0%	-1.00
Not Compl	0%	0	0	0.0%	0.00
Unraced	0%	0	3	0.0%	-1.00

ANALYSIS BY RUN NUMBER

Run No	Prop	Win	Runs	Wins%	£
FTO	0%	0	3	0.0%	-1.00
2nd Run	0%	0	1	0.0%	-1.00
3rd Run	0%	0	8	0.0%	-1.00
4th+ Run	100%	5	48	10.4%	-0.20

ANALYSIS BY POSITION LAST TIME

Pos LT	Prop	Win	Runs	Wins%	£
Won	60%	3	23	13.0%	0.20
2nd or 3rd	20%	1	17	5.9%	-0.89
Unplaced	20%	1	17	5.9%	-0.47
Not Compl	0%	0	3	0.0%	-1.00

OTHER FACTORS (WINS-RUNS, £)

Course Winner:	2-8	£1.50
Distance Winner:	1-7	£0.57
Going Winner:	1-13	-£0.31
Beaten Favourite:	0-4	-£1.00
BHA Top Rated:	0-5	-£1.00
Up in class:	3-34	-£0.19
Same class:	2-23	-£0.53
Colts and Geldings:	1-6	-£0.68
Absolute Favourites:	1-4	-£0.52

THREE-YEAR-OLD RACES

Race Profiles

3-Y.O Races: Group 1 Races – 7 to 9 furlong races

ANALYSIS BY BHA RATING

Rating	Prop	Win	Runs	Wins%	£
120..139	5%	1	6	16.7%	-0.54
110..119	35%	7	71	9.9%	-0.12
100..109	5%	1	85	1.2%	-0.87
90..99	0%	0	22	0.0%	-1.00
70..89	5%	1	9	11.1%	1.33
50..69	0%	0	0	0.0%	0.00
..49	0%	0	0	0.0%	0.00
Unrated	50%	10	81	12.3%	-0.27

ANALYSIS BY WEIGHT CARRIED

Weight	Prop	Win	Runs	Wins%	£
10-01+	0%	0	0	0.0%	0.00
9-8..10-00	0%	0	0	0.0%	0.00
9-0..9-07	100%	20	274	7.3%	-0.43
8-8..8-13	0%	0	0	0.0%	0.00
8-0..8-07	0%	0	0	0.0%	0.00
..7-13	0%	0	0	0.0%	0.00

ANALYSIS BY DAYS SINCE LAST RUN

Days	Prop	Win	Runs	Wins%	£
1..7	0%	0	0	0.0%	0.00
8..14	5%	1	16	6.3%	-0.63
15..28	30%	6	108	5.6%	-0.67
29..60	15%	3	42	7.1%	-0.55
61..100	0%	0	8	0.0%	-1.00
101+	50%	10	89	11.2%	0.08
Unraced	0%	0	11	0.0%	-1.00

ANALYSIS BY TODAY'S STARTING PRICE

Price	Prop	Win	Runs	Wins%	£
Odds On	10%	2	3	66.7%	0.13
Ev-2/1	25%	5	8	62.5%	0.69
9/4-4/1	5%	1	18	5.6%	-0.79
9/2-6/1	15%	3	18	16.7%	0.03
13/2-10/1	25%	5	53	9.4%	-0.14
11/1-16/1	10%	2	47	4.3%	-0.47
18/1-33/1	10%	2	49	4.1%	-0.04
40/1+	0%	0	78	0.0%	-1.00

ANALYSIS BY STARTING PRICE LAST TIME

Price	Prop	Win	Runs	Wins%	£
Odds On	15%	3	20	15.0%	0.55
Ev-2/1	25%	5	35	14.3%	-0.05
9/4-4/1	20%	4	67	6.0%	-0.63
9/2-6/1	10%	2	27	7.4%	-0.69
13/2-10/1	20%	4	58	6.9%	-0.09
11/1-16/1	5%	1	28	3.6%	-0.89
18/1-33/1	5%	1	20	5.0%	-0.85
40/1+	0%	0	8	0.0%	-1.00
Unraced	0%	0	11	0.0%	-1.00

ANALYSIS BY DISTANCE BEATEN LAST TIME

Lengths	Prop	Win	Runs	Wins%	£
..-10	0%	0	0	0.0%	0.00
-10..0	70%	14	91	15.4%	0.00
0.1..2	10%	2	67	3.0%	-0.53
2.1..5	5%	1	53	1.9%	-0.77
5.1..10	10%	2	23	8.7%	-0.35
10.1..20	0%	0	17	0.0%	-1.00
20.0..30	5%	1	8	12.5%	-0.13
30.1+	0%	0	4	0.0%	-1.00
Not Compl	0%	0	0	0.0%	0.00
Unraced	0%	0	11	0.0%	-1.00

ANALYSIS BY RUN NUMBER

Run No	Prop	Win	Runs	Wins%	£
FTO	0%	0	11	0.0%	-1.00
2nd Run	0%	0	4	0.0%	-1.00
3rd Run	15%	3	27	11.1%	0.19
4th+ Run	85%	17	232	7.3%	-0.46

ANALYSIS BY POSITION LAST TIME

Pos LT	Prop	Win	Runs	Wins%	£
Won	70%	14	91	15.4%	0.00
2nd or 3rd	10%	2	74	2.7%	-0.49
Unplaced	20%	4	98	4.1%	-0.72
Not Compl	0%	0	11	0.0%	-1.00

OTHER FACTORS (WINS-RUNS, £)

Course Winner:	6-69	-£0.22
Distance Winner:	8-69	-£0.44
Going Winner:	10-123	-£0.45
Beaten Favourite:	1-28	-£0.79
BHA Top Rated:	4-22	-£0.35
Up in class:	10-173	-£0.35
Same class:	10-90	-£0.52
Colts and Geldings:	8-102	-£0.47
Absolute Favourites:	8-18	£0.15

TRAINERS (WINS-RUNS, £)
B W Hills 3-14 £1.11; A P O'Brien 7-38 £0.25.

Group 1 Races

3-Y.O Races: Group 1 Races – 10 to 14 furlong races

ANALYSIS BY BHA RATING

Rating	Prop	Win	Runs	Wins%	£
120..139	18%	2	6	33.3%	0.79
110..119	36%	4	25	16.0%	-0.52
100..109	18%	2	40	5.0%	-0.72
90..99	9%	1	15	6.7%	1.27
70..89	0%	0	6	0.0%	-1.00
50..69	0%	0	0	0.0%	0.00
..49	0%	0	0	0.0%	0.00
Unrated	18%	2	57	3.5%	-0.84

ANALYSIS BY WEIGHT CARRIED

Weight	Prop	Win	Runs	Wins%	£
10-01+	0%	0	0	0.0%	0.00
9-8..10-00	0%	0	0	0.0%	0.00
9-0..9-07	100%	11	148	7.4%	-0.48
8-8..8-13	0%	0	1	0.0%	-1.00
8-0..8-07	0%	0	0	0.0%	0.00
..7-13	0%	0	0	0.0%	0.00

ANALYSIS BY DAYS SINCE LAST RUN

Days	Prop	Win	Runs	Wins%	£
1..7	0%	0	2	0.0%	-1.00
8..14	9%	1	13	7.7%	-0.54
15..28	73%	8	96	8.3%	-0.32
29..60	18%	2	31	6.5%	-0.80
61..100	0%	0	1	0.0%	-1.00
101+	0%	0	3	0.0%	-1.00
Unraced	0%	0	3	0.0%	-1.00

ANALYSIS BY TODAY'S STARTING PRICE

Price	Prop	Win	Runs	Wins%	£
Odds On	0%	0	0	0.0%	0.00
Ev-2/1	18%	2	3	66.7%	0.54
9/4-4/1	45%	5	13	38.5%	0.38
9/2-6/1	18%	2	17	11.8%	-0.24
13/2-10/1	9%	1	27	3.7%	-0.72
11/1-16/1	0%	0	17	0.0%	-1.00
18/1-33/1	9%	1	38	2.6%	-0.11
40/1+	0%	0	34	0.0%	-1.00

ANALYSIS BY STARTING PRICE LAST TIME

Price	Prop	Win	Runs	Wins%	£
Odds On	27%	3	17	17.6%	-0.46
Ev-2/1	45%	5	35	14.3%	0.54
9/4-4/1	18%	2	23	8.7%	-0.55
9/2-6/1	0%	0	18	0.0%	-1.00
13/2-10/1	9%	1	25	4.0%	-0.85
11/1-16/1	0%	0	17	0.0%	-1.00
18/1-33/1	0%	0	6	0.0%	-1.00
40/1+	0%	0	5	0.0%	-1.00
Unraced	0%	0	3	0.0%	-1.00

ANALYSIS BY DISTANCE BEATEN LAST TIME

Lengths	Prop	Win	Runs	Wins%	£
..-10	0%	0	0	0.0%	0.00
-10..0	64%	7	68	10.3%	-0.60
0.1..2	27%	3	28	10.7%	0.54
2.1..5	9%	1	30	3.3%	-0.77
5.1..10	0%	0	14	0.0%	-1.00
10.1..20	0%	0	4	0.0%	-1.00
20.0..30	0%	0	1	0.0%	-1.00
30.1+	0%	0	1	0.0%	-1.00
Not Compl	0%	0	0	0.0%	0.00
Unraced	0%	0	3	0.0%	-1.00

ANALYSIS BY RUN NUMBER

Run No	Prop	Win	Runs	Wins%	£
FTO	0%	0	3	0.0%	-1.00
2nd Run	0%	0	3	0.0%	-1.00
3rd Run	18%	2	22	9.1%	0.72
4th+ Run	82%	9	121	7.4%	-0.67

ANALYSIS BY POSITION LAST TIME

Pos LT	Prop	Win	Runs	Wins%	£
Won	64%	7	68	10.3%	-0.60
2nd or 3rd	36%	4	45	8.9%	0.12
Unplaced	0%	0	33	0.0%	-1.00
Not Compl	0%	0	3	0.0%	-1.00

OTHER FACTORS (WINS-RUNS, £)

Course Winner:	0-3	-£1.00
Distance Winner:	0-18	-£1.00
Going Winner:	3-53	-£0.76
Beaten Favourite:	2-16	-£0.42
BHA Top Rated:	2-10	-£0.06
Up in class:	8-119	-£0.49
Same class:	3-27	-£0.38
7-Day Winners:	0-1	-£1.00
Colts and Geldings:	4-58	-£0.73
Fillies:	0-1	-£1.00
Absolute Favourites:	5-10	£0.51

THREE-YEAR-OLD RACES

Race Profiles

3-Y.O Races: Group 1 Races – 15+ furlong races

ANALYSIS BY BHA RATING

Rating	Prop	Win	Runs	Wins%	£
120..139	0%	0	0	0.0%	0.00
110..119	75%	3	14	21.4%	1.04
100..109	0%	0	11	0.0%	-1.00
90..99	0%	0	1	0.0%	-1.00
70..89	0%	0	0	0.0%	0.00
50..69	0%	0	0	0.0%	0.00
..49	0%	0	0	0.0%	0.00
Unrated	25%	1	12	8.3%	-0.84

ANALYSIS BY WEIGHT CARRIED

Weight	Prop	Win	Runs	Wins%	£
10-01+	0%	0	0	0.0%	0.00
9-8..10-00	0%	0	0	0.0%	0.00
9-0..9-07	100%	4	36	11.1%	-0.16
8-8..8-13	0%	0	2	0.0%	-1.00
8-0..8-07	0%	0	0	0.0%	0.00
..7-13	0%	0	0	0.0%	0.00

ANALYSIS BY DAYS SINCE LAST RUN

Days	Prop	Win	Runs	Wins%	£
1..7	0%	0	1	0.0%	-1.00
8..14	0%	0	1	0.0%	-1.00
15..28	50%	2	19	10.5%	0.03
29..60	25%	1	6	16.7%	0.50
61..100	25%	1	10	10.0%	-0.81
101+	0%	0	1	0.0%	-1.00
Unraced	0%	0	0	0.0%	0.00

ANALYSIS BY TODAY'S STARTING PRICE

Price	Prop	Win	Runs	Wins%	£
Odds On	25%	1	1	100.0%	0.91
Ev-2/1	0%	0	1	0.0%	-1.00
9/4-4/1	25%	1	8	12.5%	-0.44
9/2-6/1	0%	0	1	0.0%	-1.00
13/2-10/1	25%	1	7	14.3%	0.29
11/1-16/1	25%	1	7	14.3%	1.14
18/1-33/1	0%	0	5	0.0%	-1.00
40/1+	0%	0	8	0.0%	-1.00

ANALYSIS BY STARTING PRICE LAST TIME

Price	Prop	Win	Runs	Wins%	£
Odds On	25%	1	2	50.0%	3.50
Ev-2/1	0%	0	5	0.0%	-1.00
9/4-4/1	25%	1	6	16.7%	-0.25
9/2-6/1	0%	0	9	0.0%	-1.00
13/2-10/1	0%	0	4	0.0%	-1.00
11/1-16/1	25%	1	5	20.0%	2.00
18/1-33/1	25%	1	3	33.3%	-0.36
40/1+	0%	0	4	0.0%	-1.00
Unraced	0%	0	0	0.0%	0.00

ANALYSIS BY DISTANCE BEATEN LAST TIME

Lengths	Prop	Win	Runs	Wins%	£
..-10	0%	0	0	0.0%	0.00
-10..0	50%	2	10	20.0%	0.35
0.1..2	25%	1	12	8.3%	-0.84
2.1..5	25%	1	8	12.5%	0.88
5.1..10	0%	0	5	0.0%	-1.00
10.1..20	0%	0	1	0.0%	-1.00
20.0..30	0%	0	1	0.0%	-1.00
30.1+	0%	0	1	0.0%	-1.00
Not Compl	0%	0	0	0.0%	0.00
Unraced	0%	0	0	0.0%	0.00

ANALYSIS BY RUN NUMBER

Run No	Prop	Win	Runs	Wins%	£
FTO	0%	0	0	0.0%	0.00
2nd Run	0%	0	1	0.0%	-1.00
3rd Run	0%	0	1	0.0%	-1.00
4th+ Run	100%	4	36	11.1%	-0.16

ANALYSIS BY POSITION LAST TIME

Pos LT	Prop	Win	Runs	Wins%	£
Won	50%	2	10	20.0%	0.35
2nd or 3rd	50%	2	16	12.5%	0.06
Unplaced	0%	0	12	0.0%	-1.00
Not Compl	0%	0	0	0.0%	0.00

OTHER FACTORS (WINS-RUNS, £)

Course Winner:	0-1	-£1.00
Going Winner:	1-11	-£0.59
Beaten Favourite:	0-5	-£1.00
BHA Top Rated:	1-3	£0.50
Up in class:	3-30	-£0.05
Same class:	1-8	-£0.76
7-Day Winners:	0-1	-£1.00
Colts and Geldings:	2-16	-£0.60
Absolute Favourites:	1-4	-£0.52

Group 2 & 3 Races

3-Y.O Races: Group 2 & 3 Races

ANALYSIS BY BHA RATING

Rating	Prop	Win	Runs	Wins%	£
120..139	0%	0	4	0.0%	-1.00
110..119	19%	15	77	19.5%	-0.20
100..109	31%	25	213	11.7%	-0.06
90..99	21%	17	184	9.2%	-0.42
70..89	5%	4	100	4.0%	-0.13
50..69	0%	0	3	0.0%	-1.00
..49	0%	0	0	0.0%	0.00
Unrated	25%	20	140	14.3%	-0.21

ANALYSIS BY WEIGHT CARRIED

Weight	Prop	Win	Runs	Wins%	£
10-01+	0%	0	0	0.0%	0.00
9-8..10-00	0%	0	0	0.0%	0.00
9-0..9-07	44%	36	309	11.7%	-0.28
8-8..8-13	56%	45	411	10.9%	-0.17
8-0..8-07	0%	0	1	0.0%	-1.00
..7-13	0%	0	0	0.0%	0.00

ANALYSIS BY DAYS SINCE LAST RUN

Days	Prop	Win	Runs	Wins%	£
1..7	0%	0	10	0.0%	-1.00
8..14	10%	8	90	8.9%	-0.62
15..28	23%	19	212	9.0%	-0.30
29..60	22%	18	138	13.0%	0.16
61..100	1%	1	25	4.0%	-0.85
101+	41%	33	234	14.1%	-0.11
Unraced	2%	2	12	16.7%	-0.26

ANALYSIS BY TODAY'S STARTING PRICE

Price	Prop	Win	Runs	Wins%	£
Odds On	9%	7	12	58.3%	-0.01
Ev-2/1	22%	18	48	37.5%	-0.04
9/4-4/1	22%	18	93	19.4%	-0.16
9/2-6/1	16%	13	89	14.6%	-0.10
13/2-10/1	16%	13	137	9.5%	-0.16
11/1-16/1	7%	6	142	4.2%	-0.45
18/1-33/1	7%	6	118	5.1%	0.32
40/1+	0%	0	82	0.0%	-1.00

ANALYSIS BY STARTING PRICE LAST TIME

Price	Prop	Win	Runs	Wins%	£
Odds On	12%	10	65	15.4%	0.29
Ev-2/1	17%	14	91	15.4%	-0.25
9/4-4/1	23%	19	148	12.8%	-0.05
9/2-6/1	11%	9	71	12.7%	0.13
13/2-10/1	10%	8	140	5.7%	-0.57
11/1-16/1	7%	6	90	6.7%	-0.68
18/1-33/1	12%	10	70	14.3%	0.15
40/1+	4%	3	34	8.8%	-0.62
Unraced	2%	2	12	16.7%	-0.26

ANALYSIS BY DISTANCE BEATEN LAST TIME

Lengths	Prop	Win	Runs	Wins%	£
..-10	0%	0	4	0.0%	-1.00
-10..0	43%	35	279	12.5%	-0.18
0.1..2	21%	17	115	14.8%	0.19
2.1..5	17%	14	126	11.1%	-0.14
5.1..10	6%	5	105	4.8%	-0.79
10.1..20	7%	6	56	10.7%	-0.18
20.0..30	2%	2	12	16.7%	0.08
30.1+	0%	0	12	0.0%	-1.00
Not Compl	0%	0	0	0.0%	0.00
Unraced	2%	2	12	16.7%	-0.26

ANALYSIS BY RUN NUMBER

Run No	Prop	Win	Runs	Wins%	£
FTO	2%	2	12	16.7%	-0.26
2nd Run	6%	5	51	9.8%	-0.57
3rd Run	23%	19	120	15.8%	0.10
4th+ Run	68%	55	538	10.2%	-0.25

ANALYSIS BY POSITION LAST TIME

Pos LT	Prop	Win	Runs	Wins%	£
Won	43%	35	283	12.4%	-0.19
2nd or 3rd	27%	22	178	12.4%	0.02
Unplaced	27%	22	248	8.9%	-0.42
Not Compl	2%	2	12	16.7%	-0.26

OTHER FACTORS (WINS-RUNS, £)

Course Winner:	12-63	-£0.16
Distance Winner:	22-177	-£0.14
Going Winner:	28-226	-£0.20
Beaten Favourite:	10-55	-£0.16
BHA Top Rated:	19-74	£0.07
Up in class:	43-483	-£0.27
Same class:	8-69	-£0.11
Down in class:	28-157	-£0.10
7-Day Winners:	0-3	-£1.00
Colts and Geldings:	61-502	-£0.19
Fillies:	2-37	-£0.83
Absolute Favourites:	28-78	-£0.09

TRAINERS (WINS-RUNS, £)

J L Dunlop 4-18 £1.24; M R Channon 3-32 £0.44; A P O'Brien 10-54 £0.23; P W Chapple-Hyam 3-30 £0.31; B W Hills 4-44 £0.07; J H M Gosden 7-41 £0.04; M L W Bell 3-11 £0.14; M P Tregoning 1-12 £0.08.

THREE-YEAR-OLD RACES

Race Profiles

3-Y.O Races: Group 2 & 3 Races – 2 to 7 runners

ANALYSIS BY BHA RATING

Rating	Prop	Win	Runs	Wins%	£
120..139	0%	0	2	0.0%	-1.00
110..119	28%	8	26	30.8%	-0.30
100..109	14%	4	47	8.5%	0.10
90..99	24%	7	40	17.5%	-0.16
70..89	3%	1	14	7.1%	0.86
50..69	0%	0	2	0.0%	-1.00
..49	0%	0	0	0.0%	0.00
Unrated	31%	9	36	25.0%	0.30

ANALYSIS BY WEIGHT CARRIED

Weight	Prop	Win	Runs	Wins%	£
10-01+	0%	0	0	0.0%	0.00
9-8..10-00	0%	0	0	0.0%	0.00
9-0..9-07	45%	13	59	22.0%	0.16
8-8..8-13	55%	16	108	14.8%	0.00
8-0..8-07	0%	0	0	0.0%	0.00
..7-13	0%	0	0	0.0%	0.00

ANALYSIS BY DAYS SINCE LAST RUN

Days	Prop	Win	Runs	Wins%	£
1..7	0%	0	3	0.0%	-1.00
8..14	3%	1	22	4.5%	-0.77
15..28	34%	10	57	17.5%	0.73
29..60	17%	5	23	21.7%	0.18
61..100	0%	0	5	0.0%	-1.00
101+	41%	12	53	22.6%	-0.20
Unraced	3%	1	4	25.0%	-0.28

ANALYSIS BY TODAY'S STARTING PRICE

Price	Prop	Win	Runs	Wins%	£
Odds On	21%	6	10	60.0%	0.01
Ev-2/1	24%	7	23	30.4%	-0.23
9/4-4/1	24%	7	30	23.3%	0.04
9/2-6/1	14%	4	24	16.7%	0.04
13/2-10/1	3%	1	32	3.1%	-0.66
11/1-16/1	7%	2	27	7.4%	-0.04
18/1-33/1	7%	2	13	15.4%	3.23
40/1+	0%	0	8	0.0%	-1.00

ANALYSIS BY STARTING PRICE LAST TIME

Price	Prop	Win	Runs	Wins%	£
Odds On	17%	5	20	25.0%	0.51
Ev-2/1	14%	4	20	20.0%	-0.48
9/4-4/1	24%	7	31	22.6%	0.85
9/2-6/1	17%	5	20	25.0%	1.08
13/2-10/1	7%	2	29	6.9%	-0.85
11/1-16/1	10%	3	25	12.0%	-0.42
18/1-33/1	7%	2	11	18.2%	0.36
40/1+	0%	0	7	0.0%	-1.00
Unraced	3%	1	4	25.0%	-0.28

ANALYSIS BY DISTANCE BEATEN LAST TIME

Lengths	Prop	Win	Runs	Wins%	£
..-10	0%	0	0	0.0%	0.00
-10..0	34%	10	70	14.3%	-0.44
0.1..2	28%	8	33	24.2%	0.94
2.1..5	17%	5	23	21.7%	0.78
5.1..10	10%	3	21	14.3%	-0.45
10.1..20	3%	1	10	10.0%	0.30
20.0..30	3%	1	4	25.0%	0.25
30.1+	0%	0	2	0.0%	-1.00
Not Compl	0%	0	0	0.0%	0.00
Unraced	3%	1	4	25.0%	-0.28

ANALYSIS BY RUN NUMBER

Run No	Prop	Win	Runs	Wins%	£
FTO	3%	1	4	25.0%	-0.28
2nd Run	7%	2	11	18.2%	-0.21
3rd Run	31%	9	39	23.1%	0.26
4th+ Run	59%	17	113	15.0%	0.02

ANALYSIS BY POSITION LAST TIME

Pos LT	Prop	Win	Runs	Wins%	£
Won	34%	10	70	14.3%	-0.44
2nd or 3rd	31%	9	46	19.6%	0.47
Unplaced	31%	9	47	19.1%	0.42
Not Compl	3%	1	4	25.0%	-0.28

OTHER FACTORS (WINS-RUNS, £)

Course Winner:	2-8	-£0.25
Distance Winner:	3-34	-£0.35
Going Winner:	8-51	-£0.52
Beaten Favourite:	6-10	£1.11
BHA Top Rated:	8-26	-£0.17
Up in class:	13-108	-£0.15
Same class:	4-15	£1.67
Down in class:	11-40	£0.04
7-Day Winners:	0-2	-£1.00
Colts and Geldings:	25-144	£0.12
Absolute Favourites:	12-28	-£0.10

TRAINERS (WINS-RUNS, £)

B W Hills 2-14 £1.04; J H M Gosden 2-10 £0.85; Sir Michael Stoute 5-19 £0.39.

Group 2 & 3 Races

3-Y.O Races: Group 2 & 3 Races – 8 to 14 runners

ANALYSIS BY BHA RATING

Rating	Prop	Win	Runs	Wins%	£
120..139	0%	0	2	0.0%	-1.00
110..119	11%	5	40	12.5%	-0.44
100..109	41%	19	130	14.6%	0.02
90..99	20%	9	120	7.5%	-0.46
70..89	7%	3	73	4.1%	-0.17
50..69	0%	0	1	0.0%	-1.00
..49	0%	0	0	0.0%	0.00
Unrated	22%	10	89	11.2%	-0.36

ANALYSIS BY WEIGHT CARRIED

Weight	Prop	Win	Runs	Wins%	£
10-01+	0%	0	0	0.0%	0.00
9-8..10-00	0%	0	0	0.0%	0.00
9-0..9-07	39%	18	179	10.1%	-0.38
8-8..8-13	61%	28	276	10.1%	-0.18
8-0..8-07	0%	0	0	0.0%	0.00
..7-13	0%	0	0	0.0%	0.00

ANALYSIS BY DAYS SINCE LAST RUN

Days	Prop	Win	Runs	Wins%	£
1..7	0%	0	6	0.0%	-1.00
8..14	15%	7	61	11.5%	-0.52
15..28	13%	6	110	5.5%	-0.76
29..60	24%	11	95	11.6%	0.18
61..100	2%	1	14	7.1%	-0.73
101+	43%	20	164	12.2%	-0.03
Unraced	2%	1	5	20.0%	0.20

ANALYSIS BY TODAY'S STARTING PRICE

Price	Prop	Win	Runs	Wins%	£
Odds On	2%	1	2	50.0%	-0.10
Ev-2/1	24%	11	24	45.8%	0.18
9/4-4/1	24%	11	60	18.3%	-0.22
9/2-6/1	17%	8	57	14.0%	-0.15
13/2-10/1	17%	8	86	9.3%	-0.16
11/1-16/1	7%	3	96	3.1%	-0.59
18/1-33/1	9%	4	77	5.2%	0.31
40/1+	0%	0	53	0.0%	-1.00

ANALYSIS BY STARTING PRICE LAST TIME

Price	Prop	Win	Runs	Wins%	£
Odds On	11%	5	40	12.5%	0.34
Ev-2/1	20%	9	64	14.1%	-0.22
9/4-4/1	22%	10	91	11.0%	-0.26
9/2-6/1	9%	4	44	9.1%	-0.13
13/2-10/1	13%	6	93	6.5%	-0.39
11/1-16/1	4%	2	48	4.2%	-0.85
18/1-33/1	13%	6	50	12.0%	-0.11
40/1+	7%	3	20	15.0%	-0.35
Unraced	2%	1	5	20.0%	0.20

ANALYSIS BY DISTANCE BEATEN LAST TIME

Lengths	Prop	Win	Runs	Wins%	£
..-10	0%	0	4	0.0%	-1.00
-10..0	46%	21	178	11.8%	-0.10
0.1..2	20%	9	67	13.4%	0.08
2.1..5	20%	9	81	11.1%	-0.16
5.1..10	4%	2	70	2.9%	-0.85
10.1..20	9%	4	35	11.4%	-0.43
20.0..30	0%	0	7	0.0%	-1.00
30.1+	0%	0	8	0.0%	-1.00
Not Compl	0%	0	0	0.0%	0.00
Unraced	2%	1	5	20.0%	0.20

ANALYSIS BY RUN NUMBER

Run No	Prop	Win	Runs	Wins%	£
FTO	2%	1	5	20.0%	0.20
2nd Run	7%	3	36	8.3%	-0.64
3rd Run	20%	9	76	11.8%	-0.01
4th+ Run	72%	33	338	9.8%	-0.28

ANALYSIS BY POSITION LAST TIME

Pos LT	Prop	Win	Runs	Wins%	£
Won	46%	21	182	11.5%	-0.12
2nd or 3rd	28%	13	107	12.1%	0.07
Unplaced	24%	11	161	6.8%	-0.65
Not Compl	2%	1	5	20.0%	0.20

OTHER FACTORS (WINS-RUNS, £)

Course Winner:	9-48	-£0.17
Distance Winner:	15-100	-£0.06
Going Winner:	17-137	-£0.06
Beaten Favourite:	4-40	-£0.38
BHA Top Rated:	10-42	£0.18
Up in class:	27-313	-£0.24
Same class:	4-44	-£0.51
Down in class:	14-93	-£0.24
7-Day Winners:	0-1	-£1.00
Colts and Geldings:	31-284	-£0.29
Fillies:	2-28	-£0.78
Absolute Favourites:	16-44	£0.05

TRAINERS (WINS-RUNS, £)

J L Dunlop 3-13 £1.67; M R Channon 2-20 £0.95; A P O'Brien 4-33 £0.38; M Johnston 4-20 £0.30; H R A Cecil 2-10 £0.33.

Race Profiles

3-Y.O Races: Group 2 & 3 Races – 15 runners or more

ANALYSIS BY BHA RATING

Rating	Prop	Win	Runs	Wins%	£
120..139	0%	0	0	0.0%	0.00
110..119	33%	2	11	18.2%	0.91
100..109	33%	2	36	5.6%	-0.57
90..99	17%	1	24	4.2%	-0.69
70..89	0%	0	13	0.0%	-1.00
50..69	0%	0	0	0.0%	0.00
..49	0%	0	0	0.0%	0.00
Unrated	17%	1	15	6.7%	-0.47

ANALYSIS BY WEIGHT CARRIED

Weight	Prop	Win	Runs	Wins%	£
10-01+	0%	0	0	0.0%	0.00
9-8..10-00	0%	0	0	0.0%	0.00
9-0..9-07	83%	5	71	7.0%	-0.38
8-8..8-13	17%	1	27	3.7%	-0.70
8-0..8-07	0%	0	1	0.0%	-1.00
..7-13	0%	0	0	0.0%	0.00

ANALYSIS BY DAYS SINCE LAST RUN

Days	Prop	Win	Runs	Wins%	£
1..7	0%	0	1	0.0%	-1.00
8..14	0%	0	7	0.0%	-1.00
15..28	50%	3	45	6.7%	-0.46
29..60	33%	2	20	10.0%	0.03
61..100	0%	0	6	0.0%	-1.00
101+	17%	1	17	5.9%	-0.59
Unraced	0%	0	3	0.0%	-1.00

ANALYSIS BY TODAY'S STARTING PRICE

Price	Prop	Win	Runs	Wins%	£
Odds On	0%	0	0	0.0%	0.00
Ev-2/1	0%	0	1	0.0%	-1.00
9/4-4/1	0%	0	3	0.0%	-1.00
9/2-6/1	17%	1	8	12.5%	-0.13
13/2-10/1	67%	4	19	21.1%	0.68
11/1-16/1	17%	1	19	5.3%	-0.32
18/1-33/1	0%	0	28	0.0%	-1.00
40/1+	0%	0	21	0.0%	-1.00

ANALYSIS BY STARTING PRICE LAST TIME

Price	Prop	Win	Runs	Wins%	£
Odds On	0%	0	5	0.0%	-1.00
Ev-2/1	17%	1	7	14.3%	0.07
9/4-4/1	33%	2	26	7.7%	-0.37
9/2-6/1	0%	0	7	0.0%	-1.00
13/2-10/1	0%	0	18	0.0%	-1.00
11/1-16/1	17%	1	17	5.9%	-0.59
18/1-33/1	33%	2	9	22.2%	1.33
40/1+	0%	0	7	0.0%	-1.00
Unraced	0%	0	3	0.0%	-1.00

ANALYSIS BY DISTANCE BEATEN LAST TIME

Lengths	Prop	Win	Runs	Wins%	£
..-10	0%	0	0	0.0%	0.00
-10..0	67%	4	31	12.9%	0.00
0.1..2	0%	0	15	0.0%	-1.00
2.1..5	0%	0	22	0.0%	-1.00
5.1..10	0%	0	14	0.0%	-1.00
10.1..20	17%	1	11	9.1%	0.18
20.0..30	17%	1	1	100.0%	7.00
30.1+	0%	0	2	0.0%	-1.00
Not Compl	0%	0	0	0.0%	0.00
Unraced	0%	0	3	0.0%	-1.00

ANALYSIS BY RUN NUMBER

Run No	Prop	Win	Runs	Wins%	£
FTO	0%	0	3	0.0%	-1.00
2nd Run	0%	0	4	0.0%	-1.00
3rd Run	17%	1	5	20.0%	0.50
4th+ Run	83%	5	87	5.7%	-0.49

ANALYSIS BY POSITION LAST TIME

Pos LT	Prop	Win	Runs	Wins%	£
Won	67%	4	31	12.9%	0.00
2nd or 3rd	0%	0	25	0.0%	-1.00
Unplaced	33%	2	40	5.0%	-0.47
Not Compl	0%	0	3	0.0%	-1.00

OTHER FACTORS (WINS-RUNS, £)

Course Winner:	1-7	£0.00
Distance Winner:	4-43	-£0.16
Going Winner:	3-38	-£0.25
Beaten Favourite:	0-5	-£1.00
BHA Top Rated:	1-6	£0.33
Up in class:	3-62	-£0.61
Same class:	0-10	-£1.00
Down in class:	3-24	£0.17
Colts and Geldings:	5-74	-£0.39
Fillies:	0-9	-£1.00
Absolute Favourites:	0-6	-£1.00

Group 2 & 3 Races

3-Y.O Races: Group 2 & 3 Races – good or faster going

ANALYSIS BY BHA RATING
Rating	Prop	Win	Runs	Wins%	£
120..139	0%	0	4	0.0%	-1.00
110..119	20%	12	58	20.7%	-0.07
100..109	28%	17	163	10.4%	-0.16
90..99	23%	14	139	10.1%	-0.37
70..89	7%	4	74	5.4%	0.17
50..69	0%	0	3	0.0%	-1.00
..49	0%	0	0	0.0%	0.00
Unrated	22%	13	100	13.0%	-0.26

ANALYSIS BY WEIGHT CARRIED
Weight	Prop	Win	Runs	Wins%	£
10-01+	0%	0	0	0.0%	0.00
9-8..10-00	0%	0	0	0.0%	0.00
9-0..9-07	45%	27	218	12.4%	-0.15
8-8..8-13	55%	33	322	10.2%	-0.21
8-0..8-07	0%	0	1	0.0%	-1.00
..7-13	0%	0	0	0.0%	0.00

ANALYSIS BY DAYS SINCE LAST RUN
Days	Prop	Win	Runs	Wins%	£
1..7	0%	0	7	0.0%	-1.00
8..14	5%	3	64	4.7%	-0.81
15..28	28%	17	167	10.2%	-0.18
29..60	23%	14	115	12.2%	0.04
61..100	2%	1	18	5.6%	-0.79
101+	38%	23	161	14.3%	-0.02
Unraced	3%	2	9	22.2%	-0.01

ANALYSIS BY TODAY'S STARTING PRICE
Price	Prop	Win	Runs	Wins%	£
Odds On	10%	6	9	66.7%	0.11
Ev-2/1	22%	13	38	34.2%	-0.12
9/4-4/1	22%	13	61	21.3%	-0.07
9/2-6/1	15%	9	66	13.6%	-0.17
13/2-10/1	17%	10	109	9.2%	-0.17
11/1-16/1	5%	3	108	2.8%	-0.64
18/1-33/1	10%	6	92	6.5%	0.70
40/1+	0%	0	58	0.0%	-1.00

ANALYSIS BY STARTING PRICE LAST TIME
Price	Prop	Win	Runs	Wins%	£
Odds On	12%	7	50	14.0%	0.49
Ev-2/1	18%	11	67	16.4%	-0.18
9/4-4/1	20%	12	106	11.3%	-0.12
9/2-6/1	13%	8	60	13.3%	0.24
13/2-10/1	10%	6	112	5.4%	-0.58
11/1-16/1	8%	5	61	8.2%	-0.64
18/1-33/1	12%	7	51	13.7%	0.13
40/1+	3%	2	25	0.0%	-0.74
Unraced	3%	2	9	22.2%	-0.01

ANALYSIS BY DISTANCE BEATEN LAST TIME
Lengths	Prop	Win	Runs	Wins%	£
..-10	0%	0	4	0.0%	-1.00
-10..0	38%	23	208	11.1%	-0.18
0.1..2	22%	13	84	15.5%	0.25
2.1..5	20%	12	101	11.9%	-0.01
5.1..10	7%	4	79	5.1%	-0.78
10.1..20	8%	5	39	12.8%	-0.16
20.0..30	2%	1	9	11.1%	-0.44
30.1+	0%	0	8	0.0%	-1.00
Not Compl	0%	0	0	0.0%	0.00
Unraced	3%	2	9	22.2%	-0.01

ANALYSIS BY RUN NUMBER
Run No	Prop	Win	Runs	Wins%	£
FTO	3%	2	9	22.2%	-0.01
2nd Run	5%	3	37	8.1%	-0.64
3rd Run	22%	13	92	14.1%	0.07
4th+ Run	70%	42	403	10.4%	-0.21

ANALYSIS BY POSITION LAST TIME
Pos LT	Prop	Win	Runs	Wins%	£
Won	38%	23	212	10.8%	-0.20
2nd or 3rd	27%	16	136	11.8%	0.04
Unplaced	32%	19	184	10.3%	-0.35
Not Compl	3%	2	9	22.2%	-0.01

OTHER FACTORS (WINS-RUNS, £)
Course Winner:	9-47	-£0.24
Distance Winner:	13-130	-£0.21
Going Winner:	21-183	-£0.17
Beaten Favourite:	8-36	£0.08
BHA Top Rated:	14-53	£0.13
Up in class:	31-372	-£0.25
Same class:	7-47	£0.17
Down in class:	20-113	-£0.14
7-Day Winners:	0-2	-£1.00
Colts and Geldings:	45-377	-£0.19
Fillies:	1-23	-£0.92
Absolute Favourites:	21-59	-£0.09

TRAINERS (WINS-RUNS, £)
J L Dunlop 3-16 £1.31; P W Chapple-Hyam 2-24 £0.56; B W Hills 4-37 £0.27; A P O'Brien 7-43 £0.22; Sir Michael Stoute 11-42 £0.11; M R Channon 1-22 £0.18; Saeed Bin Suroor 3-18 £0.06; H R A Cecil 3-15 £0.01.

Race Profiles

3-Y.O Races: Group 2 & 3 Races – good to soft or softer going

ANALYSIS BY BHA RATING

Rating	Prop	Win	Runs	Wins%	£
120..139	0%	0	0	0.0%	0.00
110..119	14%	3	19	15.8%	-0.58
100..109	38%	8	50	16.0%	0.24
90..99	14%	3	45	6.7%	-0.59
70..89	0%	0	26	0.0%	-1.00
50..69	0%	0	0	0.0%	0.00
..49	0%	0	0	0.0%	0.00
Unrated	33%	7	40	17.5%	-0.07

ANALYSIS BY WEIGHT CARRIED

Weight	Prop	Win	Runs	Wins%	£
10-01+	0%	0	0	0.0%	0.00
9-8..10-00	0%	0	0	0.0%	0.00
9-0..9-07	43%	9	91	9.9%	-0.57
8-8..8-13	57%	12	89	13.5%	-0.03
8-0..8-07	0%	0	0	0.0%	0.00
..7-13	0%	0	0	0.0%	0.00

ANALYSIS BY DAYS SINCE LAST RUN

Days	Prop	Win	Runs	Wins%	£
1..7	0%	0	3	0.0%	-1.00
8..14	24%	5	26	19.2%	-0.15
15..28	10%	2	45	4.4%	-0.73
29..60	19%	4	23	17.4%	0.78
61..100	0%	0	7	0.0%	-1.00
101+	48%	10	73	13.7%	-0.30
Unraced	0%	0	3	0.0%	-1.00

ANALYSIS BY TODAY'S STARTING PRICE

Price	Prop	Win	Runs	Wins%	£
Odds On	5%	1	3	33.3%	-0.36
Ev-2/1	24%	5	10	50.0%	0.27
9/4-4/1	24%	5	32	15.6%	-0.34
9/2-6/1	19%	4	23	17.4%	0.13
13/2-10/1	14%	3	28	10.7%	-0.11
11/1-16/1	14%	3	34	8.8%	0.15
18/1-33/1	0%	0	26	0.0%	-1.00
40/1+	0%	0	24	0.0%	-1.00

ANALYSIS BY STARTING PRICE LAST TIME

Price	Prop	Win	Runs	Wins%	£
Odds On	14%	3	15	20.0%	-0.36
Ev-2/1	14%	3	24	12.5%	-0.46
9/4-4/1	33%	7	42	16.7%	0.14
9/2-6/1	5%	1	11	9.1%	-0.50
13/2-10/1	10%	2	28	7.1%	-0.52
11/1-16/1	5%	1	29	3.4%	-0.76
18/1-33/1	14%	3	19	15.8%	0.21
40/1+	5%	1	9	11.1%	-0.28
Unraced	0%	0	3	0.0%	-1.00

ANALYSIS BY DISTANCE BEATEN LAST TIME

Lengths	Prop	Win	Runs	Wins%	£
..-10	0%	0	0	0.0%	0.00
-10..0	57%	12	71	16.9%	-0.16
0.1..2	19%	4	31	12.9%	0.02
2.1..5	10%	2	25	8.0%	-0.63
5.1..10	5%	1	26	3.8%	-0.83
10.1..20	5%	1	17	5.9%	-0.24
20.0..30	5%	1	3	33.3%	1.67
30.1+	0%	0	4	0.0%	-1.00
Not Compl	0%	0	0	0.0%	0.00
Unraced	0%	0	3	0.0%	-1.00

ANALYSIS BY RUN NUMBER

Run No	Prop	Win	Runs	Wins%	£
FTO	0%	0	3	0.0%	-1.00
2nd Run	10%	2	14	14.3%	-0.39
3rd Run	29%	6	28	21.4%	0.20
4th+ Run	62%	13	135	9.6%	-0.38

ANALYSIS BY POSITION LAST TIME

Pos LT	Prop	Win	Runs	Wins%	£
Won	57%	12	71	16.9%	-0.16
2nd or 3rd	29%	6	42	14.3%	-0.03
Unplaced	14%	3	64	4.7%	-0.60
Not Compl	0%	0	3	0.0%	-1.00

OTHER FACTORS (WINS-RUNS, £)

Course Winner:	3-16	£0.08
Distance Winner:	9-47	£0.05
Going Winner:	7-43	-£0.33
Beaten Favourite:	2-19	-£0.62
BHA Top Rated:	5-21	-£0.08
Up in class:	12-111	-£0.32
Same class:	1-22	-£0.70
Down in class:	8-44	-£0.01
7-Day Winners:	0-1	-£1.00
Colts and Geldings:	16-125	-£0.19
Fillies:	1-14	-£0.68
Absolute Favourites:	7-19	-£0.06

TRAINERS (WINS-RUNS, £)

M R Channon 2-10 £1.00; A P O'Brien 3-11 £0.24.

Group 2 & 3 Races

3-Y.O Races: Group 2 & 3 Races – 7 to 9 furlong races

ANALYSIS BY BHA RATING

Rating	Prop	Win	Runs	Wins%	£
120..139	0%	0	2	0.0%	-1.00
110..119	32%	8	39	20.5%	0.11
100..109	36%	9	86	10.5%	-0.39
90..99	8%	2	74	2.7%	-0.85
70..89	8%	2	40	5.0%	-0.14
50..69	0%	0	0	0.0%	0.00
..49	0%	0	0	0.0%	0.00
Unrated	16%	4	41	9.8%	-0.45

ANALYSIS BY WEIGHT CARRIED

Weight	Prop	Win	Runs	Wins%	£
10-01+	0%	0	0	0.0%	0.00
9-8..10-00	0%	0	0	0.0%	0.00
9-0..9-07	60%	15	159	9.4%	-0.33
8-8..8-13	40%	10	122	8.2%	-0.53
8-0..8-07	0%	0	1	0.0%	-1.00
..7-13	0%	0	0	0.0%	0.00

ANALYSIS BY DAYS SINCE LAST RUN

Days	Prop	Win	Runs	Wins%	£
1..7	0%	0	5	0.0%	-1.00
8..14	8%	2	17	11.8%	-0.70
15..28	12%	3	60	5.0%	-0.63
29..60	12%	3	23	13.0%	0.20
61..100	0%	0	10	0.0%	-1.00
101+	68%	17	161	10.6%	-0.32
Unraced	0%	0	6	0.0%	-1.00

ANALYSIS BY TODAY'S STARTING PRICE

Price	Prop	Win	Runs	Wins%	£
Odds On	8%	2	4	50.0%	-0.13
Ev-2/1	20%	5	12	41.7%	0.03
9/4-4/1	20%	5	20	25.0%	-0.01
9/2-6/1	16%	4	27	14.8%	-0.07
13/2-10/1	24%	6	54	11.1%	-0.06
11/1-16/1	8%	2	57	3.5%	-0.54
18/1-33/1	4%	1	64	1.6%	-0.59
40/1+	0%	0	44	0.0%	-1.00

ANALYSIS BY STARTING PRICE LAST TIME

Price	Prop	Win	Runs	Wins%	£
Odds On	12%	3	24	12.5%	0.57
Ev-2/1	12%	3	24	12.5%	-0.33
9/4-4/1	28%	7	61	11.5%	-0.46
9/2-6/1	12%	3	23	13.0%	-0.38
13/2-10/1	8%	2	66	3.0%	-0.91
11/1-16/1	8%	2	37	5.4%	-0.74
18/1-33/1	20%	5	28	17.9%	0.67
40/1+	0%	0	13	0.0%	-1.00
Unraced	0%	0	6	0.0%	-1.00

ANALYSIS BY DISTANCE BEATEN LAST TIME

Lengths	Prop	Win	Runs	Wins%	£
..-10	0%	0	0	0.0%	0.00
-10..0	56%	14	106	13.2%	-0.02
0.1..2	16%	4	45	8.9%	-0.64
2.1..5	16%	4	53	7.5%	-0.63
5.1..10	8%	2	47	4.3%	-0.77
10.1..20	4%	1	21	4.8%	-0.38
20.0..30	0%	0	1	0.0%	-1.00
30.1+	0%	0	3	0.0%	-1.00
Not Compl	0%	0	0	0.0%	0.00
Unraced	0%	0	6	0.0%	-1.00

ANALYSIS BY RUN NUMBER

Run No	Prop	Win	Runs	Wins%	£
FTO	0%	0	6	0.0%	-1.00
2nd Run	4%	1	22	4.5%	-0.80
3rd Run	28%	7	36	19.4%	0.53
4th+ Run	68%	17	218	7.8%	-0.52

ANALYSIS BY POSITION LAST TIME

Pos LT	Prop	Win	Runs	Wins%	£
Won	56%	14	106	13.2%	-0.02
2nd or 3rd	20%	5	68	7.4%	-0.73
Unplaced	24%	6	102	5.9%	-0.60
Not Compl	0%	0	6	0.0%	-1.00

OTHER FACTORS (WINS-RUNS, £)

Course Winner:	12-51	£0.04
Distance Winner:	15-109	-£0.23
Going Winner:	15-110	£0.03
Beaten Favourite:	1-22	-£0.89
BHA Top Rated:	6-23	£0.34
Up in class:	12-170	-£0.49
Same class:	1-26	-£0.79
Down in class:	12-80	-£0.11
7-Day Winners:	0-1	-£1.00
Colts and Geldings:	15-152	-£0.43
Fillies:	2-30	-£0.79
Absolute Favourites:	9-25	-£0.06

TRAINERS (WINS-RUNS, £)

M R Channon 2-17 £0.94; J H M Gosden 2-10 £0.30; B W Hills 3-20 £0.05.

Race Profiles

3-Y.O Races: Group 2 & 3 Races – 10 to 14 furlong races

ANALYSIS BY BHA RATING

Rating	Prop	Win	Runs	Wins%	£
120..139	0%	0	2	0.0%	-1.00
110..119	14%	7	38	18.4%	-0.51
100..109	27%	14	117	12.0%	0.19
90..99	25%	13	95	13.7%	-0.13
70..89	4%	2	35	5.7%	0.49
50..69	0%	0	3	0.0%	-1.00
..49	0%	0	0	0.0%	0.00
Unrated	29%	15	87	17.2%	-0.07

ANALYSIS BY WEIGHT CARRIED

Weight	Prop	Win	Runs	Wins%	£
10-01+	0%	0	0	0.0%	0.00
9-8..10-00	0%	0	0	0.0%	0.00
9-0..9-07	33%	17	104	16.3%	-0.10
8-8..8-13	67%	34	273	12.5%	0.02
8-0..8-07	0%	0	0	0.0%	0.00
..7-13	0%	0	0	0.0%	0.00

ANALYSIS BY DAYS SINCE LAST RUN

Days	Prop	Win	Runs	Wins%	£
1..7	0%	0	5	0.0%	-1.00
8..14	10%	5	63	7.9%	-0.61
15..28	27%	14	128	10.9%	-0.09
29..60	25%	13	90	14.4%	0.33
61..100	2%	1	14	7.1%	-0.73
101+	31%	16	72	22.2%	0.39
Unraced	4%	2	5	40.0%	0.78

ANALYSIS BY TODAY'S STARTING PRICE

Price	Prop	Win	Runs	Wins%	£
Odds On	10%	5	8	62.5%	0.05
Ev-2/1	24%	12	35	34.3%	-0.11
9/4-4/1	22%	11	66	16.7%	-0.27
9/2-6/1	18%	9	56	16.1%	-0.01
13/2-10/1	10%	5	71	7.0%	-0.32
11/1-16/1	8%	4	69	5.8%	-0.25
18/1-33/1	10%	5	44	11.4%	1.95
40/1+	0%	0	28	0.0%	-1.00

ANALYSIS BY STARTING PRICE LAST TIME

Price	Prop	Win	Runs	Wins%	£
Odds On	14%	7	34	20.6%	0.36
Ev-2/1	20%	10	53	18.9%	-0.06
9/4-4/1	22%	11	75	14.7%	0.37
9/2-6/1	12%	6	42	14.3%	0.57
13/2-10/1	12%	6	66	9.1%	-0.17
11/1-16/1	6%	3	50	6.0%	-0.72
18/1-33/1	6%	3	36	8.3%	-0.50
40/1+	6%	3	16	18.8%	-0.19
Unraced	4%	2	5	40.0%	0.78

ANALYSIS BY DISTANCE BEATEN LAST TIME

Lengths	Prop	Win	Runs	Wins%	£
..-10	0%	0	3	0.0%	-1.00
-10..0	37%	19	147	12.9%	-0.19
0.1..2	24%	12	62	19.4%	0.86
2.1..5	18%	9	62	14.5%	0.31
5.1..10	6%	3	52	5.8%	-0.78
10.1..20	10%	5	32	15.6%	0.03
20.0..30	2%	1	8	12.5%	-0.38
30.1+	0%	0	6	0.0%	-1.00
Not Compl	0%	0	0	0.0%	0.00
Unraced	4%	2	5	40.0%	0.78

ANALYSIS BY RUN NUMBER

Run No	Prop	Win	Runs	Wins%	£
FTO	4%	2	5	40.0%	0.78
2nd Run	8%	4	26	15.4%	-0.34
3rd Run	24%	12	80	15.0%	-0.04
4th+ Run	65%	33	266	12.4%	0.02

ANALYSIS BY POSITION LAST TIME

Pos LT	Prop	Win	Runs	Wins%	£
Won	37%	19	150	12.7%	-0.21
2nd or 3rd	29%	15	95	15.8%	0.58
Unplaced	29%	15	127	11.8%	-0.25
Not Compl	4%	2	5	40.0%	0.78

OTHER FACTORS (WINS-RUNS, £)

Course Winner:	0-11	-£1.00
Distance Winner:	7-67	£0.03
Going Winner:	11-100	-£0.44
Beaten Favourite:	9-26	£0.67
BHA Top Rated:	11-46	-£0.11
Up in class:	28-261	-£0.04
Same class:	6-39	£0.31
Down in class:	15-72	-£0.14
7-Day Winners:	0-2	-£1.00
Colts and Geldings:	41-294	-£0.01
Fillies:	0-1	-£1.00
Absolute Favourites:	18-48	-£0.06

TRAINERS (WINS-RUNS, £)

P W Chapple-Hyam 2-12 £1.58; A P O'Brien 9-42 £0.39; Saeed Bin Suroor 3-13 £0.46; B W Hills 1-23 £0.13; J H M Gosden 5-29 £0.02.

Group 2 & 3 Races

3-Y.O Races: Group 2 & 3 Races – 15+ furlong races

ANALYSIS BY BHA RATING

Rating	Prop	Win	Runs	Wins%	£
120..139	0%	0	0	0.0%	0.00
110..119	0%	0	0	0.0%	0.00
100..109	40%	2	10	20.0%	-0.25
90..99	40%	2	15	13.3%	-0.13
70..89	0%	0	25	0.0%	-1.00
50..69	0%	0	0	0.0%	0.00
..49	0%	0	0	0.0%	0.00
Unrated	20%	1	12	8.3%	-0.33

ANALYSIS BY WEIGHT CARRIED

Weight	Prop	Win	Runs	Wins%	£
10-01+	0%	0	0	0.0%	0.00
9-8..10-00	0%	0	0	0.0%	0.00
9-0..9-07	80%	4	46	8.7%	-0.49
8-8..8-13	20%	1	16	6.3%	-0.69
8-0..8-07	0%	0	0	0.0%	0.00
..7-13	0%	0	0	0.0%	0.00

ANALYSIS BY DAYS SINCE LAST RUN

Days	Prop	Win	Runs	Wins%	£
1..7	0%	0	0	0.0%	0.00
8..14	20%	1	10	10.0%	-0.50
15..28	40%	2	24	8.3%	-0.56
29..60	40%	2	25	8.0%	-0.48
61..100	0%	0	1	0.0%	-1.00
101+	0%	0	1	0.0%	-1.00
Unraced	0%	0	1	0.0%	-1.00

ANALYSIS BY TODAY'S STARTING PRICE

Price	Prop	Win	Runs	Wins%	£
Odds On	0%	0	0	0.0%	0.00
Ev-2/1	20%	1	1	100.0%	1.50
9/4-4/1	40%	2	7	28.6%	0.43
9/2-6/1	0%	0	6	0.0%	-1.00
13/2-10/1	40%	2	12	16.7%	0.33
11/1-16/1	0%	0	16	0.0%	-1.00
18/1-33/1	0%	0	10	0.0%	-1.00
40/1+	0%	0	10	0.0%	-1.00

ANALYSIS BY STARTING PRICE LAST TIME

Price	Prop	Win	Runs	Wins%	£
Odds On	0%	0	7	0.0%	-1.00
Ev-2/1	20%	1	14	7.1%	-0.82
9/4-4/1	20%	1	12	8.3%	-0.58
9/2-6/1	0%	0	6	0.0%	-1.00
13/2-10/1	0%	0	8	0.0%	-1.00
11/1-16/1	20%	1	3	33.3%	0.67
18/1-33/1	40%	2	6	33.3%	1.67
40/1+	0%	0	5	0.0%	-1.00
Unraced	0%	0	1	0.0%	-1.00

ANALYSIS BY DISTANCE BEATEN LAST TIME

Lengths	Prop	Win	Runs	Wins%	£
..-10	0%	0	1	0.0%	-1.00
-10..0	40%	2	26	7.7%	-0.71
0.1..2	20%	1	8	12.5%	-0.38
2.1..5	20%	1	11	9.1%	-0.27
5.1..10	0%	0	6	0.0%	-1.00
10.1..20	0%	0	3	0.0%	-1.00
20.0..30	20%	1	3	33.3%	1.67
30.1+	0%	0	3	0.0%	-1.00
Not Compl	0%	0	0	0.0%	0.00
Unraced	0%	0	1	0.0%	-1.00

ANALYSIS BY RUN NUMBER

Run No	Prop	Win	Runs	Wins%	£
FTO	0%	0	1	0.0%	-1.00
2nd Run	0%	0	3	0.0%	-1.00
3rd Run	0%	0	4	0.0%	-1.00
4th+ Run	100%	5	54	9.3%	-0.47

ANALYSIS BY POSITION LAST TIME

Pos LT	Prop	Win	Runs	Wins%	£
Won	40%	2	27	7.4%	-0.72
2nd or 3rd	40%	2	15	13.3%	-0.13
Unplaced	20%	1	19	5.3%	-0.58
Not Compl	0%	0	1	0.0%	-1.00

OTHER FACTORS (WINS-RUNS, £)

Course Winner:	0-1	-£1.00
Distance Winner:	0-1	-£1.00
Going Winner:	2-16	-£0.19
Beaten Favourite:	0-7	-£1.00
BHA Top Rated:	2-5	£0.50
Up in class:	3-52	-£0.70
Same class:	1-4	£0.25
Down in class:	1-5	£0.60
Colts and Geldings:	5-56	-£0.49
Fillies:	0-6	-£1.00
Absolute Favourites:	1-5	-£0.50

Race Profiles

3-Y.O Races: Listed Races

ANALYSIS BY BHA RATING

Rating	Prop	Win	Runs	Wins%	£
120..139	0%	0	1	0.0%	-1.00
110..119	10%	12	37	32.4%	0.37
100..109	43%	54	293	18.4%	-0.15
90..99	30%	38	305	12.5%	-0.18
70..89	10%	13	199	6.5%	-0.42
50..69	0%	0	5	0.0%	-1.00
..49	0%	0	1	0.0%	-1.00
Unrated	7%	9	102	8.8%	-0.40

ANALYSIS BY WEIGHT CARRIED

Weight	Prop	Win	Runs	Wins%	£
10-01+	0%	0	0	0.0%	0.00
9-8..10-00	0%	0	0	0.0%	0.00
9-0..9-07	40%	50	301	16.6%	-0.08
8-8..8-13	60%	75	617	12.2%	-0.28
8-0..8-07	1%	1	25	4.0%	-0.64
..7-13	0%	0	0	0.0%	0.00

ANALYSIS BY DAYS SINCE LAST RUN

Days	Prop	Win	Runs	Wins%	£
1..7	3%	4	26	15.4%	0.63
8..14	11%	14	137	10.2%	-0.49
15..28	44%	55	361	15.2%	-0.22
29..60	22%	28	196	14.3%	-0.18
61..100	1%	1	21	4.8%	-0.91
101+	19%	24	190	12.6%	-0.10
Unraced	0%	0	12	0.0%	-1.00

ANALYSIS BY TODAY'S STARTING PRICE

Price	Prop	Win	Runs	Wins%	£
Odds On	14%	18	25	72.0%	0.19
Ev-2/1	24%	30	83	36.1%	-0.04
9/4-4/1	24%	30	137	21.9%	-0.10
9/2-6/1	14%	18	135	13.3%	-0.19
13/2-10/1	16%	20	191	10.5%	-0.04
11/1-16/1	4%	5	146	3.4%	-0.49
18/1-33/1	4%	5	161	3.1%	-0.20
40/1+	0%	0	65	0.0%	-1.00

ANALYSIS BY STARTING PRICE LAST TIME

Price	Prop	Win	Runs	Wins%	£
Odds On	4%	5	56	8.9%	-0.78
Ev-2/1	12%	15	87	17.2%	-0.28
9/4-4/1	21%	27	152	17.8%	-0.32
9/2-6/1	15%	19	127	15.0%	-0.22
13/2-10/1	23%	29	180	16.1%	0.18
11/1-16/1	11%	14	138	10.1%	-0.38
18/1-33/1	8%	10	126	7.9%	-0.32
40/1+	6%	7	65	10.8%	0.03
Unraced	0%	0	12	0.0%	-1.00

ANALYSIS BY DISTANCE BEATEN LAST TIME

Lengths	Prop	Win	Runs	Wins%	£
..-10	1%	1	2	50.0%	0.10
-10..0	30%	38	253	15.0%	-0.30
0.1..2	23%	29	156	18.6%	-0.30
2.1..5	20%	25	200	12.5%	-0.23
5.1..10	16%	20	183	10.9%	-0.17
10.1..20	7%	9	91	9.9%	-0.22
20.0..30	3%	4	24	16.7%	1.67
30.1+	0%	0	22	0.0%	-1.00
Not Compl	0%	0	0	0.0%	0.00
Unraced	0%	0	12	0.0%	-1.00

ANALYSIS BY RUN NUMBER

Run No	Prop	Win	Runs	Wins%	£
FTO	0%	0	12	0.0%	-1.00
2nd Run	10%	12	62	19.4%	0.09
3rd Run	15%	19	120	15.8%	-0.18
4th+ Run	75%	95	749	12.7%	-0.25

ANALYSIS BY POSITION LAST TIME

Pos LT	Prop	Win	Runs	Wins%	£
Won	31%	39	254	15.4%	-0.30
2nd or 3rd	36%	45	242	18.6%	-0.07
Unplaced	33%	42	434	9.7%	-0.25
Not Compl	0%	0	13	0.0%	-1.00

OTHER FACTORS (WINS-RUNS, £)

Course Winner:	18-99	-£0.29
Distance Winner:	40-298	-£0.23
Going Winner:	42-283	-£0.14
Beaten Favourite:	10-57	-£0.27
BHA Top Rated:	30-110	-£0.20
Up in class:	53-464	-£0.37
Same class:	33-252	-£0.23
Down in class:	40-215	£0.12
7-Day Winners:	0-5	-£1.00
Colts and Geldings:	76-496	-£0.17
Fillies:	7-110	-£0.46
Absolute Favourites:	47-112	£0.04

TRAINERS (WINS-RUNS, £)

D R C Elsworth 6-22 £1.38; M Johnston 9-27 £0.73; L M Cumani 5-12 £1.10; H R A Cecil 9-27 £0.38; R M Beckett 1-12 £0.75; A M Balding 1-12 £0.42; M R Channon 6-50 £0.04; A P O'Brien 3-16 £0.08.

Listed Races

3-Y.O Races: Listed Races – 2 to 7 runners

ANALYSIS BY BHA RATING

Rating	Prop	Win	Runs	Wins%	£
120..139	0%	0	0	0.0%	0.00
110..119	10%	7	16	43.8%	0.40
100..109	48%	32	117	27.4%	0.04
90..99	25%	17	117	14.5%	-0.28
70..89	10%	7	79	8.9%	-0.00
50..69	0%	0	2	0.0%	-1.00
..49	0%	0	0	0.0%	0.00
Unrated	6%	4	53	7.5%	-0.65

ANALYSIS BY WEIGHT CARRIED

Weight	Prop	Win	Runs	Wins%	£
10-01+	0%	0	0	0.0%	0.00
9-8..10-00	0%	0	0	0.0%	0.00
9-0..9-07	37%	25	117	21.4%	0.01
8-8..8-13	61%	41	254	16.1%	-0.22
8-0..8-07	1%	1	13	7.7%	-0.31
..7-13	0%	0	0	0.0%	0.00

ANALYSIS BY DAYS SINCE LAST RUN

Days	Prop	Win	Runs	Wins%	£
1..7	1%	1	7	14.3%	0.29
8..14	13%	9	63	14.3%	-0.38
15..28	45%	30	159	18.9%	-0.24
29..60	19%	13	62	21.0%	-0.09
61..100	1%	1	7	14.3%	-0.73
101+	19%	13	79	16.5%	0.23
Unraced	0%	0	7	0.0%	-1.00

ANALYSIS BY TODAY'S STARTING PRICE

Price	Prop	Win	Runs	Wins%	£
Odds On	19%	13	18	72.2%	0.17
Ev-2/1	30%	20	60	33.3%	-0.09
9/4-4/1	22%	15	59	25.4%	0.06
9/2-6/1	9%	6	69	8.7%	-0.47
13/2-10/1	15%	10	71	14.1%	0.27
11/1-16/1	1%	1	42	2.4%	-0.69
18/1-33/1	3%	2	51	3.9%	-0.08
40/1+	0%	0	14	0.0%	-1.00

ANALYSIS BY STARTING PRICE LAST TIME

Price	Prop	Win	Runs	Wins%	£
Odds On	3%	2	19	10.5%	-0.65
Ev-2/1	12%	8	31	25.8%	0.09
9/4-4/1	21%	14	56	25.0%	-0.19
9/2-6/1	19%	13	65	20.0%	0.06
13/2-10/1	19%	13	82	15.9%	-0.05
11/1-16/1	13%	9	56	16.1%	0.01
18/1-33/1	7%	5	42	11.9%	0.37
40/1+	4%	3	26	11.5%	-0.63
Unraced	0%	0	7	0.0%	-1.00

ANALYSIS BY DISTANCE BEATEN LAST TIME

Lengths	Prop	Win	Runs	Wins%	£
..-10	1%	1	2	50.0%	0.10
-10..0	34%	23	109	21.1%	-0.07
0.1..2	25%	17	65	26.2%	-0.09
2.1..5	15%	10	86	11.6%	-0.35
5.1..10	13%	9	70	12.9%	-0.32
10.1..20	9%	6	35	17.1%	0.33
20.0..30	1%	1	7	14.3%	0.86
30.1+	0%	0	3	0.0%	-1.00
Not Compl	0%	0	0	0.0%	0.00
Unraced	0%	0	7	0.0%	-1.00

ANALYSIS BY RUN NUMBER

Run No	Prop	Win	Runs	Wins%	£
FTO	0%	0	7	0.0%	-1.00
2nd Run	13%	9	36	25.0%	0.29
3rd Run	10%	7	53	13.2%	-0.42
4th+ Run	76%	51	288	17.7%	-0.14

ANALYSIS BY POSITION LAST TIME

Pos LT	Prop	Win	Runs	Wins%	£
Won	36%	24	111	21.6%	-0.07
2nd or 3rd	36%	24	103	23.3%	-0.08
Unplaced	28%	19	163	11.7%	-0.22
Not Compl	0%	0	7	0.0%	-1.00

OTHER FACTORS (WINS-RUNS, £)

Course Winner:	11-51	-£0.37
Distance Winner:	19-106	-£0.35
Going Winner:	22-105	£0.25
Beaten Favourite:	5-20	£0.18
BHA Top Rated:	20-55	-£0.06
Up in class:	31-203	-£0.29
Same class:	13-71	£0.16
Down in class:	23-103	-£0.04
7-Day Winners:	0-1	-£1.00
Colts and Geldings:	43-223	-£0.25
Fillies:	3-33	-£0.44
Absolute Favourites:	24-60	-£0.17

TRAINERS (WINS-RUNS, £)

H R A Cecil 5-12 £0.81; M R Channon 5-19 £0.37; J H M Gosden 3-18 £0.04.

THREE-YEAR-OLD RACES

Race Profiles

3-Y.O Races: Listed Races – 8 to 14 runners

ANALYSIS BY BHA RATING

Rating	Prop	Win	Runs	Wins%	£
120..139	0%	0	1	0.0%	-1.00
110..119	9%	5	20	25.0%	0.42
100..109	39%	22	164	13.4%	-0.22
90..99	33%	19	176	10.8%	-0.29
70..89	11%	6	120	5.0%	-0.69
50..69	0%	0	3	0.0%	-1.00
..49	0%	0	1	0.0%	-1.00
Unrated	9%	5	44	11.4%	-0.04

ANALYSIS BY WEIGHT CARRIED

Weight	Prop	Win	Runs	Wins%	£
10-01+	0%	0	0	0.0%	0.00
9-8..10-00	0%	0	0	0.0%	0.00
9-0..9-07	42%	24	168	14.3%	-0.11
8-8..8-13	58%	33	349	9.5%	-0.39
8-0..8-07	0%	0	12	0.0%	-1.00
..7-13	0%	0	0	0.0%	0.00

ANALYSIS BY DAYS SINCE LAST RUN

Days	Prop	Win	Runs	Wins%	£
1..7	5%	3	19	15.8%	0.76
8..14	9%	5	71	7.0%	-0.57
15..28	42%	24	188	12.8%	-0.32
29..60	25%	14	122	11.5%	-0.20
61..100	0%	0	13	0.0%	-1.00
101+	19%	11	111	9.9%	-0.34
Unraced	0%	0	5	0.0%	-1.00

ANALYSIS BY TODAY'S STARTING PRICE

Price	Prop	Win	Runs	Wins%	£
Odds On	9%	5	7	71.4%	0.27
Ev-2/1	18%	10	23	43.5%	0.10
9/4-4/1	26%	15	75	20.0%	-0.19
9/2-6/1	21%	12	66	18.2%	0.11
13/2-10/1	16%	9	112	8.0%	-0.23
11/1-16/1	7%	4	96	4.2%	-0.36
18/1-33/1	4%	2	103	1.9%	-0.54
40/1+	0%	0	47	0.0%	-1.00

ANALYSIS BY STARTING PRICE LAST TIME

Price	Prop	Win	Runs	Wins%	£
Odds On	5%	3	32	9.4%	-0.82
Ev-2/1	12%	7	52	13.5%	-0.44
9/4-4/1	21%	12	90	13.3%	-0.44
9/2-6/1	11%	6	57	10.5%	-0.48
13/2-10/1	28%	16	94	17.0%	0.44
11/1-16/1	9%	5	81	6.2%	-0.64
18/1-33/1	9%	5	82	6.1%	-0.27
40/1+	5%	3	36	8.3%	-0.35
Unraced	0%	0	5	0.0%	-1.00

ANALYSIS BY DISTANCE BEATEN LAST TIME

Lengths	Prop	Win	Runs	Wins%	£
..-10	0%	0	0	0.0%	0.00
-10..0	25%	14	132	10.6%	-0.49
0.1..2	21%	12	88	13.6%	-0.43
2.1..5	26%	15	109	13.8%	-0.09
5.1..10	19%	11	110	10.0%	-0.06
10.1..20	5%	3	56	5.4%	-0.56
20.0..30	4%	2	12	16.7%	0.42
30.1+	0%	0	17	0.0%	-1.00
Not Compl	0%	0	0	0.0%	0.00
Unraced	0%	0	5	0.0%	-1.00

ANALYSIS BY RUN NUMBER

Run No	Prop	Win	Runs	Wins%	£
FTO	0%	0	5	0.0%	-1.00
2nd Run	5%	3	24	12.5%	-0.13
3rd Run	21%	12	63	19.0%	0.07
4th+ Run	74%	42	437	9.6%	-0.37

ANALYSIS BY POSITION LAST TIME

Pos LT	Prop	Win	Runs	Wins%	£
Won	25%	14	131	10.7%	-0.48
2nd or 3rd	37%	21	133	15.8%	-0.03
Unplaced	39%	22	259	8.5%	-0.36
Not Compl	0%	0	6	0.0%	-1.00

OTHER FACTORS (WINS-RUNS, £)

Course Winner:	7-48	-£0.21
Distance Winner:	19-177	-£0.32
Going Winner:	19-166	-£0.37
Beaten Favourite:	5-35	-£0.49
BHA Top Rated:	10-53	-£0.31
Up in class:	21-250	-£0.43
Same class:	20-173	-£0.36
Down in class:	16-101	£0.07
7-Day Winners:	0-4	-£1.00
Colts and Geldings:	31-243	-£0.16
Fillies:	4-77	-£0.47
Absolute Favourites:	23-50	£0.33

TRAINERS (WINS-RUNS, £)

M Johnston 6-14 £1.51; H R A Cecil 4-14 £0.12.

Listed Races

3-Y.O Races: Listed Races – 15 runners or more

ANALYSIS BY BHA RATING

Rating	Prop	Win	Runs	Wins%	£
120..139	0%	0	0	0.0%	0.00
110..119	0%	0	1	0.0%	-1.00
100..109	0%	0	12	0.0%	-1.00
90..99	100%	2	12	16.7%	2.46
70..89	0%	0	0	0.0%	0.00
50..69	0%	0	0	0.0%	0.00
..49	0%	0	0	0.0%	0.00
Unrated	0%	0	5	0.0%	-1.00

ANALYSIS BY WEIGHT CARRIED

Weight	Prop	Win	Runs	Wins%	£
10-01+	0%	0	0	0.0%	0.00
9-8..10-00	0%	0	0	0.0%	0.00
9-0..9-07	50%	1	16	6.3%	-0.53
8-8..8-13	50%	1	14	7.1%	1.43
8-0..8-07	0%	0	0	0.0%	0.00
..7-13	0%	0	0	0.0%	0.00

ANALYSIS BY DAYS SINCE LAST RUN

Days	Prop	Win	Runs	Wins%	£
1..7	0%	0	0	0.0%	0.00
8..14	0%	0	3	0.0%	-1.00
15..28	50%	1	14	7.1%	1.43
29..60	50%	1	12	8.3%	-0.38
61..100	0%	0	1	0.0%	-1.00
101+	0%	0	0	0.0%	0.00
Unraced	0%	0	0	0.0%	0.00

ANALYSIS BY TODAY'S STARTING PRICE

Price	Prop	Win	Runs	Wins%	£
Odds On	0%	0	0	0.0%	0.00
Ev-2/1	0%	0	0	0.0%	0.00
9/4-4/1	0%	0	3	0.0%	-1.00
9/2-6/1	0%	0	0	0.0%	0.00
13/2-10/1	50%	1	8	12.5%	-0.06
11/1-16/1	0%	0	8	0.0%	-1.00
18/1-33/1	50%	1	7	14.3%	3.86
40/1+	0%	0	4	0.0%	-1.00

ANALYSIS BY STARTING PRICE LAST TIME

Price	Prop	Win	Runs	Wins%	£
Odds On	0%	0	5	0.0%	-1.00
Ev-2/1	0%	0	4	0.0%	-1.00
9/4-4/1	50%	1	6	16.7%	0.25
9/2-6/1	0%	0	5	0.0%	-1.00
13/2-10/1	0%	0	4	0.0%	-1.00
11/1-16/1	0%	0	1	0.0%	-1.00
18/1-33/1	0%	0	2	0.0%	-1.00
40/1+	50%	1	3	33.3%	10.33
Unraced	0%	0	0	0.0%	0.00

ANALYSIS BY DISTANCE BEATEN LAST TIME

Lengths	Prop	Win	Runs	Wins%	£
..-10	0%	0	0	0.0%	0.00
-10..0	50%	1	12	8.3%	-0.38
0.1..2	0%	0	3	0.0%	-1.00
2.1..5	0%	0	5	0.0%	-1.00
5.1..10	0%	0	3	0.0%	-1.00
10.1..20	0%	0	0	0.0%	0.00
20.0..30	50%	1	5	20.0%	5.80
30.1+	0%	0	2	0.0%	-1.00
Not Compl	0%	0	0	0.0%	0.00
Unraced	0%	0	0	0.0%	0.00

ANALYSIS BY RUN NUMBER

Run No	Prop	Win	Runs	Wins%	£
FTO	0%	0	0	0.0%	0.00
2nd Run	0%	0	2	0.0%	-1.00
3rd Run	0%	0	4	0.0%	-1.00
4th+ Run	100%	2	24	8.3%	0.73

ANALYSIS BY POSITION LAST TIME

Pos LT	Prop	Win	Runs	Wins%	£
Won	50%	1	12	8.3%	-0.38
2nd or 3rd	0%	0	6	0.0%	-1.00
Unplaced	50%	1	12	8.3%	1.83
Not Compl	0%	0	0	0.0%	0.00

OTHER FACTORS (WINS-RUNS, £)

Distance Winner:	2-15	£1.77
Going Winner:	1-12	-£0.38
Beaten Favourite:	0-2	-£1.00
BHA Top Rated:	0-2	-£1.00
Up in class:	1-11	-£0.32
Same class:	0-8	-£1.00
Down in class:	1-11	£2.09
Colts and Geldings:	2-30	£0.38
Absolute Favourites:	0-2	-£1.00

THREE-YEAR-OLD RACES

Race Profiles

3-Y.O Races: Listed Races – good or faster going

ANALYSIS BY BHA RATING

Rating	Prop	Win	Runs	Wins%	£
120..139	0%	0	1	0.0%	-1.00
110..119	10%	10	28	35.7%	0.54
100..109	40%	40	238	16.8%	-0.29
90..99	35%	35	243	14.4%	-0.02
70..89	11%	11	160	6.9%	-0.44
50..69	0%	0	2	0.0%	-1.00
..49	0%	0	1	0.0%	-1.00
Unrated	4%	4	83	4.8%	-0.63

ANALYSIS BY WEIGHT CARRIED

Weight	Prop	Win	Runs	Wins%	£
10-01+	0%	0	0	0.0%	0.00
9-8..10-00	0%	0	0	0.0%	0.00
9-0..9-07	41%	41	268	15.3%	-0.14
8-8..8-13	58%	58	477	12.2%	-0.31
8-0..8-07	1%	1	11	9.1%	-0.18
..7-13	0%	0	0	0.0%	0.00

ANALYSIS BY DAYS SINCE LAST RUN

Days	Prop	Win	Runs	Wins%	£
1..7	4%	4	19	21.1%	1.24
8..14	9%	9	112	8.0%	-0.60
15..28	47%	47	296	15.9%	-0.19
29..60	21%	21	151	13.9%	-0.24
61..100	1%	1	20	5.0%	-0.90
101+	18%	18	147	12.2%	-0.15
Unraced	0%	0	11	0.0%	-1.00

ANALYSIS BY TODAY'S STARTING PRICE

Price	Prop	Win	Runs	Wins%	£
Odds On	14%	14	20	70.0%	0.22
Ev-2/1	24%	24	67	35.8%	-0.06
9/4-4/1	25%	25	109	22.9%	-0.07
9/2-6/1	13%	13	104	12.5%	-0.24
13/2-10/1	18%	18	148	12.2%	0.12
11/1-16/1	2%	2	116	1.7%	-0.75
18/1-33/1	4%	4	133	3.0%	-0.20
40/1+	0%	0	59	0.0%	-1.00

ANALYSIS BY STARTING PRICE LAST TIME

Price	Prop	Win	Runs	Wins%	£
Odds On	4%	4	48	8.3%	-0.80
Ev-2/1	12%	12	72	16.7%	-0.39
9/4-4/1	22%	22	132	16.7%	-0.31
9/2-6/1	15%	15	103	14.6%	-0.39
13/2-10/1	23%	23	137	16.8%	0.16
11/1-16/1	11%	11	112	9.8%	-0.31
18/1-33/1	7%	7	97	7.2%	-0.38
40/1+	6%	6	44	13.6%	0.49
Unraced	0%	0	11	0.0%	-1.00

ANALYSIS BY DISTANCE BEATEN LAST TIME

Lengths	Prop	Win	Runs	Wins%	£
..-10	1%	1	2	50.0%	0.10
-10..0	32%	32	207	15.5%	-0.33
0.1..2	20%	20	122	16.4%	-0.44
2.1..5	21%	21	161	13.0%	-0.19
5.1..10	17%	17	143	11.9%	-0.07
10.1..20	6%	6	70	8.6%	-0.34
20.0..30	3%	3	20	15.0%	1.55
30.1+	0%	0	20	0.0%	-1.00
Not Compl	0%	0	0	0.0%	0.00
Unraced	0%	0	11	0.0%	-1.00

ANALYSIS BY RUN NUMBER

Run No	Prop	Win	Runs	Wins%	£
FTO	0%	0	11	0.0%	-1.00
2nd Run	7%	7	54	13.0%	-0.38
3rd Run	18%	18	101	17.8%	-0.06
4th+ Run	75%	75	590	12.7%	-0.25

ANALYSIS BY POSITION LAST TIME

Pos LT	Prop	Win	Runs	Wins%	£
Won	33%	33	208	15.9%	-0.32
2nd or 3rd	32%	32	191	16.8%	-0.21
Unplaced	35%	35	345	10.1%	-0.20
Not Compl	0%	0	12	0.0%	-1.00

OTHER FACTORS (WINS-RUNS, £)

Course Winner:	17-83	-£0.24
Distance Winner:	30-230	-£0.21
Going Winner:	37-255	-£0.20
Beaten Favourite:	7-46	-£0.50
BHA Top Rated:	23-84	-£0.11
Up in class:	41-380	-£0.40
Same class:	28-205	-£0.28
Down in class:	31-160	£0.20
7-Day Winners:	0-2	-£1.00
Colts and Geldings:	59-400	-£0.23
Fillies:	6-77	-£0.30
Absolute Favourites:	37-89	£0.04

TRAINERS (WINS-RUNS, £)

D R C Elsworth 6-20 £1.62; M Johnston 9-25 £0.87; L M Cumani 5-12 £1.10; H R A Cecil 9-25 £0.49; M R Channon 5-37 £0.06; A P O'Brien 3-16 £0.08; W J Haggas 3-13 £0.02.

Listed Races

3-Y.O Races: Listed Races – good to soft or softer going

ANALYSIS BY BHA RATING

Rating	Prop	Win	Runs	Wins%	£
120..139	0%	0	0	0.0%	0.00
110..119	8%	2	9	22.2%	-0.14
100..109	54%	14	55	25.5%	0.48
90..99	12%	3	62	4.8%	-0.80
70..89	8%	2	39	5.1%	-0.31
50..69	0%	0	3	0.0%	-1.00
..49	0%	0	0	0.0%	0.00
Unrated	19%	5	19	26.3%	0.60

ANALYSIS BY WEIGHT CARRIED

Weight	Prop	Win	Runs	Wins%	£
10-01+	0%	0	0	0.0%	0.00
9-8..10-00	0%	0	0	0.0%	0.00
9-0..9-07	35%	9	33	27.3%	0.40
8-8..8-13	65%	17	140	12.1%	-0.19
8-0..8-07	0%	0	14	0.0%	-1.00
..7-13	0%	0	0	0.0%	0.00

ANALYSIS BY DAYS SINCE LAST RUN

Days	Prop	Win	Runs	Wins%	£
1..7	0%	0	7	0.0%	-1.00
8..14	19%	5	25	20.0%	-0.03
15..28	31%	8	65	12.3%	-0.34
29..60	27%	7	45	15.6%	0.03
61..100	0%	0	1	0.0%	-1.00
101+	23%	6	43	14.0%	0.05
Unraced	0%	0	1	0.0%	-1.00

ANALYSIS BY TODAY'S STARTING PRICE

Price	Prop	Win	Runs	Wins%	£
Odds On	15%	4	5	80.0%	0.08
Ev-2/1	23%	6	16	37.5%	0.06
9/4-4/1	19%	5	28	17.9%	-0.23
9/2-6/1	19%	5	31	16.1%	-0.02
13/2-10/1	8%	2	43	4.7%	-0.57
11/1-16/1	12%	3	30	10.0%	0.50
18/1-33/1	4%	1	28	3.6%	-0.25
40/1+	0%	0	6	0.0%	-1.00

ANALYSIS BY STARTING PRICE LAST TIME

Price	Prop	Win	Runs	Wins%	£
Odds On	4%	1	8	12.5%	-0.64
Ev-2/1	12%	3	15	20.0%	0.23
9/4-4/1	19%	5	20	25.0%	-0.36
9/2-6/1	15%	4	24	16.7%	0.48
13/2-10/1	23%	6	43	14.0%	0.26
11/1-16/1	12%	3	26	11.5%	-0.69
18/1-33/1	12%	3	29	10.3%	-0.12
40/1+	4%	1	21	4.8%	-0.93
Unraced	0%	0	1	0.0%	-1.00

ANALYSIS BY DISTANCE BEATEN LAST TIME

Lengths	Prop	Win	Runs	Wins%	£
..-10	0%	0	0	0.0%	0.00
-10..0	23%	6	46	13.0%	-0.19
0.1..2	35%	9	34	26.5%	0.20
2.1..5	15%	4	39	10.3%	-0.37
5.1..10	12%	3	40	7.5%	-0.55
10.1..20	12%	3	21	14.3%	0.19
20.0..30	4%	1	4	25.0%	2.25
30.1+	0%	0	2	0.0%	-1.00
Not Compl	0%	0	0	0.0%	0.00
Unraced	0%	0	1	0.0%	-1.00

ANALYSIS BY RUN NUMBER

Run No	Prop	Win	Runs	Wins%	£
FTO	0%	0	1	0.0%	-1.00
2nd Run	19%	5	8	62.5%	3.28
3rd Run	4%	1	19	5.3%	-0.82
4th+ Run	77%	20	159	12.6%	-0.24

ANALYSIS BY POSITION LAST TIME

Pos LT	Prop	Win	Runs	Wins%	£
Won	23%	6	46	13.0%	-0.19
2nd or 3rd	50%	13	51	25.5%	0.42
Unplaced	27%	7	89	7.9%	-0.45
Not Compl	0%	0	1	0.0%	-1.00

OTHER FACTORS (WINS-RUNS, £)

Course Winner: 1-16 -£0.59
Distance Winner: 10-68 -£0.28
Going Winner: 5-28 £0.46
Beaten Favourite: 3-11 £0.68
BHA Top Rated: 7-26 -£0.47
Up in class: 12-84 -£0.23
Same class: 5-47 -£0.03
Down in class: 9-55 -£0.12
7-Day Winners: 0-3 -£1.00
Colts and Geldings: 17-96 £0.08
Fillies: 1-33 -£0.83
Absolute Favourites: 10-23 £0.05

TRAINERS (WINS-RUNS, £)

R Hannon 3-12 £1.25; Saeed Bin Suroor 2-10 £0.04.

Race Profiles

3-Y.O Races: Listed Races – 5 to 6 furlong races

ANALYSIS BY BHA RATING

Rating	Prop	Win	Runs	Wins%	£
120..139	0%	0	0	0.0%	0.00
110..119	30%	6	11	54.5%	0.45
100..109	55%	11	68	16.2%	-0.27
90..99	15%	3	53	5.7%	-0.65
70..89	0%	0	15	0.0%	-1.00
50..69	0%	0	2	0.0%	-1.00
..49	0%	0	0	0.0%	0.00
Unrated	0%	0	8	0.0%	-1.00

ANALYSIS BY WEIGHT CARRIED

Weight	Prop	Win	Runs	Wins%	£
10-01+	0%	0	0	0.0%	0.00
9-8..10-00	0%	0	0	0.0%	0.00
9-0..9-07	60%	12	60	20.0%	-0.23
8-8..8-13	40%	8	83	9.6%	-0.55
8-0..8-07	0%	0	14	0.0%	-1.00
..7-13	0%	0	0	0.0%	0.00

ANALYSIS BY DAYS SINCE LAST RUN

Days	Prop	Win	Runs	Wins%	£
1..7	5%	1	9	11.1%	0.22
8..14	20%	4	30	13.3%	-0.52
15..28	35%	7	55	12.7%	-0.46
29..60	25%	5	28	17.9%	-0.62
61..100	0%	0	1	0.0%	-1.00
101+	15%	3	34	8.8%	-0.46
Unraced	0%	0	0	0.0%	0.00

ANALYSIS BY TODAY'S STARTING PRICE

Price	Prop	Win	Runs	Wins%	£
Odds On	25%	5	5	100.0%	0.67
Ev-2/1	35%	7	12	58.3%	0.60
9/4-4/1	15%	3	21	14.3%	-0.37
9/2-6/1	10%	2	22	9.1%	-0.45
13/2-10/1	15%	3	32	9.4%	-0.03
11/1-16/1	0%	0	28	0.0%	-1.00
18/1-33/1	0%	0	27	0.0%	-1.00
40/1+	0%	0	10	0.0%	-1.00

ANALYSIS BY STARTING PRICE LAST TIME

Price	Prop	Win	Runs	Wins%	£
Odds On	10%	2	11	18.2%	-0.68
Ev-2/1	5%	1	11	9.1%	-0.50
9/4-4/1	20%	4	27	14.8%	-0.59
9/2-6/1	35%	7	26	26.9%	0.38
13/2-10/1	10%	2	34	5.9%	-0.77
11/1-16/1	10%	2	19	10.5%	-0.64
18/1-33/1	5%	1	21	4.8%	-0.48
40/1+	5%	1	8	12.5%	-0.70
Unraced	0%	0	0	0.0%	0.00

ANALYSIS BY DISTANCE BEATEN LAST TIME

Lengths	Prop	Win	Runs	Wins%	£
..-10	0%	0	0	0.0%	0.00
-10..0	35%	7	34	20.6%	-0.32
0.1..2	25%	5	31	16.1%	-0.31
2.1..5	25%	5	39	12.8%	-0.46
5.1..10	5%	1	29	3.4%	-0.62
10.1..20	10%	2	19	10.5%	-0.61
20.0..30	0%	0	2	0.0%	-1.00
30.1+	0%	0	3	0.0%	-1.00
Not Compl	0%	0	0	0.0%	0.00
Unraced	0%	0	0	0.0%	0.00

ANALYSIS BY RUN NUMBER

Run No	Prop	Win	Runs	Wins%	£
FTO	0%	0	0	0.0%	0.00
2nd Run	0%	0	1	0.0%	-1.00
3rd Run	10%	2	6	33.3%	1.42
4th+ Run	90%	18	150	12.0%	-0.54

ANALYSIS BY POSITION LAST TIME

Pos LT	Prop	Win	Runs	Wins%	£
Won	35%	7	34	20.6%	-0.32
2nd or 3rd	45%	9	48	18.8%	-0.17
Unplaced	20%	4	75	5.3%	-0.72
Not Compl	0%	0	0	0.0%	0.00

OTHER FACTORS (WINS-RUNS, £)

Course Winner:	3-16	-£0.38
Distance Winner:	16-110	-£0.38
Going Winner:	10-65	-£0.38
Beaten Favourite:	0-12	-£1.00
BHA Top Rated:	7-19	£0.27
Up in class:	8-69	-£0.58
Same class:	6-60	-£0.40
Down in class:	6-28	-£0.34
7-Day Winners:	0-3	-£1.00
Colts and Geldings:	18-112	-£0.38
Fillies:	2-45	-£0.69
Absolute Favourites:	11-18	£0.53

Listed Races

3-Y.O Races: Listed Races – 7 to 9 furlong races

ANALYSIS BY BHA RATING

Rating	Prop	Win	Runs	Wins%	£
120..139	0%	0	1	0.0%	-1.00
110..119	7%	3	17	17.6%	0.46
100..109	49%	20	113	17.7%	-0.01
90..99	29%	12	108	11.1%	-0.21
70..89	7%	3	64	4.7%	-0.75
50..69	0%	0	2	0.0%	-1.00
..49	0%	0	0	0.0%	0.00
Unrated	7%	3	20	15.0%	0.15

ANALYSIS BY WEIGHT CARRIED

Weight	Prop	Win	Runs	Wins%	£
10-01+	0%	0	0	0.0%	0.00
9-8..10-00	0%	0	0	0.0%	0.00
9-0..9-07	34%	14	70	20.0%	0.18
8-8..8-13	66%	27	246	11.0%	-0.28
8-0..8-07	0%	0	9	0.0%	-1.00
..7-13	0%	0	0	0.0%	0.00

ANALYSIS BY DAYS SINCE LAST RUN

Days	Prop	Win	Runs	Wins%	£
1..7	5%	2	11	18.2%	1.05
8..14	15%	6	43	14.0%	-0.29
15..28	27%	11	104	10.6%	-0.47
29..60	29%	12	84	14.3%	-0.08
61..100	0%	0	10	0.0%	-1.00
101+	24%	10	72	13.9%	0.04
Unraced	0%	0	1	0.0%	-1.00

ANALYSIS BY TODAY'S STARTING PRICE

Price	Prop	Win	Runs	Wins%	£
Odds On	7%	3	7	42.9%	-0.26
Ev-2/1	15%	6	23	26.1%	-0.31
9/4-4/1	27%	11	45	24.4%	0.05
9/2-6/1	27%	11	61	18.0%	0.08
13/2-10/1	15%	6	68	8.8%	-0.19
11/1-16/1	7%	3	44	6.8%	0.02
18/1-33/1	2%	1	59	1.7%	-0.56
40/1+	0%	0	18	0.0%	-1.00

ANALYSIS BY STARTING PRICE LAST TIME

Price	Prop	Win	Runs	Wins%	£
Odds On	2%	1	16	6.3%	-0.86
Ev-2/1	12%	5	28	17.9%	-0.05
9/4-4/1	17%	7	46	15.2%	-0.34
9/2-6/1	10%	4	38	10.5%	-0.52
13/2-10/1	34%	14	64	21.9%	0.81
11/1-16/1	7%	3	56	5.4%	-0.67
18/1-33/1	12%	5	51	9.8%	-0.25
40/1+	5%	2	25	8.0%	-0.58
Unraced	0%	0	1	0.0%	-1.00

ANALYSIS BY DISTANCE BEATEN LAST TIME

Lengths	Prop	Win	Runs	Wins%	£
..-10	0%	0	0	0.0%	0.00
-10..0	22%	9	77	11.7%	-0.39
0.1..2	20%	8	51	15.7%	-0.24
2.1..5	27%	11	66	16.7%	0.24
5.1..10	22%	9	73	12.3%	-0.09
10.1..20	5%	2	40	5.0%	-0.80
20.0..30	5%	2	9	22.2%	1.00
30.1+	0%	0	8	0.0%	-1.00
Not Compl	0%	0	0	0.0%	0.00
Unraced	0%	0	1	0.0%	-1.00

ANALYSIS BY RUN NUMBER

Run No	Prop	Win	Runs	Wins%	£
FTO	0%	0	1	0.0%	-1.00
2nd Run	5%	2	11	18.2%	-0.09
3rd Run	12%	5	34	14.7%	-0.46
4th+ Run	83%	34	279	12.2%	-0.17

ANALYSIS BY POSITION LAST TIME

Pos LT	Prop	Win	Runs	Wins%	£
Won	22%	9	77	11.7%	-0.39
2nd or 3rd	39%	16	75	21.3%	0.43
Unplaced	39%	16	172	9.3%	-0.38
Not Compl	0%	0	1	0.0%	-1.00

OTHER FACTORS (WINS-RUNS, £)

Course Winner:	4-28	-£0.28
Distance Winner:	13-121	-£0.29
Going Winner:	15-94	-£0.02
Beaten Favourite:	3-23	-£0.20
BHA Top Rated:	7-37	-£0.36
Up in class:	14-149	-£0.33
Same class:	11-88	-£0.22
Down in class:	16-87	£0.06
7-Day Winners:	0-1	-£1.00
Colts and Geldings:	26-170	£0.08
Fillies:	1-33	-£0.83
Absolute Favourites:	9-36	-£0.36

TRAINERS (WINS-RUNS, £)

M R Channon 2-15 £1.60; R Hannon 4-19 £0.65; B W Hills 4-12 £0.18; Saeed Bin Suroor 3-17 £0.01.

Race Profiles

3-Y.O Races: Listed Races – 10 to 14 furlong races

ANALYSIS BY BHA RATING

Rating	Prop	Win	Runs	Wins%	£
120..139	0%	0	0	0.0%	0.00
110..119	5%	3	9	33.3%	0.11
100..109	34%	22	111	19.8%	-0.21
90..99	36%	23	143	16.1%	0.03
70..89	16%	10	118	8.5%	-0.15
50..69	0%	0	1	0.0%	-1.00
..49	0%	0	1	0.0%	-1.00
Unrated	9%	6	74	8.1%	-0.49

ANALYSIS BY WEIGHT CARRIED

Weight	Prop	Win	Runs	Wins%	£
10-01+	0%	0	0	0.0%	0.00
9-8..10-00	0%	0	0	0.0%	0.00
9-0..9-07	38%	24	171	14.0%	-0.14
8-8..8-13	61%	39	285	13.7%	-0.20
8-0..8-07	2%	1	1	100.0%	8.00
..7-13	0%	0	0	0.0%	0.00

ANALYSIS BY DAYS SINCE LAST RUN

Days	Prop	Win	Runs	Wins%	£
1..7	2%	1	6	16.7%	0.50
8..14	6%	4	64	6.3%	-0.62
15..28	56%	36	198	18.2%	-0.01
29..60	17%	11	84	13.1%	-0.12
61..100	2%	1	10	10.0%	-0.81
101+	17%	11	84	13.1%	-0.09
Unraced	0%	0	11	0.0%	-1.00

ANALYSIS BY TODAY'S STARTING PRICE

Price	Prop	Win	Runs	Wins%	£
Odds On	14%	9	12	75.0%	0.25
Ev-2/1	27%	17	48	35.4%	-0.07
9/4-4/1	25%	16	71	22.5%	-0.12
9/2-6/1	8%	5	51	9.8%	-0.38
13/2-10/1	17%	11	91	12.1%	0.08
11/1-16/1	3%	2	73	2.7%	-0.60
18/1-33/1	6%	4	74	5.4%	0.38
40/1+	0%	0	37	0.0%	-1.00

ANALYSIS BY STARTING PRICE LAST TIME

Price	Prop	Win	Runs	Wins%	£
Odds On	3%	2	29	6.9%	-0.77
Ev-2/1	14%	9	48	18.8%	-0.36
9/4-4/1	25%	16	79	20.3%	-0.21
9/2-6/1	13%	8	62	12.9%	-0.28
13/2-10/1	20%	13	82	15.9%	0.09
11/1-16/1	13%	8	61	13.1%	-0.03
18/1-33/1	6%	4	54	7.4%	-0.32
40/1+	6%	4	31	12.9%	0.74
Unraced	0%	0	11	0.0%	-1.00

ANALYSIS BY DISTANCE BEATEN LAST TIME

Lengths	Prop	Win	Runs	Wins%	£
..-10	2%	1	2	50.0%	0.10
-10..0	34%	22	140	15.7%	-0.24
0.1..2	23%	15	73	20.5%	-0.35
2.1..5	14%	9	95	9.5%	-0.46
5.1..10	16%	10	81	12.3%	-0.09
10.1..20	8%	5	31	16.1%	0.79
20.0..30	3%	2	13	15.4%	2.54
30.1+	0%	0	11	0.0%	-1.00
Not Compl	0%	0	0	0.0%	0.00
Unraced	0%	0	11	0.0%	-1.00

ANALYSIS BY RUN NUMBER

Run No	Prop	Win	Runs	Wins%	£
FTO	0%	0	11	0.0%	-1.00
2nd Run	16%	10	50	20.0%	0.15
3rd Run	19%	12	80	15.0%	-0.18
4th+ Run	66%	42	316	13.3%	-0.18

ANALYSIS BY POSITION LAST TIME

Pos LT	Prop	Win	Runs	Wins%	£
Won	36%	23	141	16.3%	-0.23
2nd or 3rd	30%	19	118	16.1%	-0.36
Unplaced	34%	22	186	11.8%	0.07
Not Compl	0%	0	12	0.0%	-1.00

OTHER FACTORS (WINS-RUNS, £)

Course Winner:	11-55	-£0.28
Distance Winner:	11-67	£0.14
Going Winner:	17-122	-£0.02
Beaten Favourite:	7-22	£0.05
BHA Top Rated:	15-53	-£0.26
Up in class:	31-244	-£0.33
Same class:	16-104	-£0.14
Down in class:	17-98	£0.32
7-Day Winners:	0-1	-£1.00
Colts and Geldings:	31-211	-£0.26
Fillies:	4-31	£0.28
Absolute Favourites:	26-57	£0.14

TRAINERS (WINS-RUNS, £)

D R C Elsworth 5-13 £2.88; L M Cumani 5-11 £1.29; A P O'Brien 3-13 £0.33; H R A Cecil 7-20 £0.11; J H M Gosden 4-24 £0.01.

Listed Races

3-Y.O Races: Listed Races – 15+ furlong races

ANALYSIS BY BHA RATING

Rating	Prop	Win	Runs	Wins%	£
120..139	0%	0	0	0.0%	0.00
110..119	0%	0	0	0.0%	0.00
100..109	100%	1	1	100.0%	0.29
90..99	0%	0	1	0.0%	-1.00
70..89	0%	0	2	0.0%	-1.00
50..69	0%	0	0	0.0%	0.00
..49	0%	0	0	0.0%	0.00
Unrated	0%	0	0	0.0%	0.00

ANALYSIS BY WEIGHT CARRIED

Weight	Prop	Win	Runs	Wins%	£
10-01+	0%	0	0	0.0%	0.00
9-8..10-00	0%	0	0	0.0%	0.00
9-0..9-07	0%	0	0	0.0%	0.00
8-8..8-13	100%	1	3	33.3%	-0.57
8-0..8-07	0%	0	1	0.0%	-1.00
..7-13	0%	0	0	0.0%	0.00

ANALYSIS BY DAYS SINCE LAST RUN

Days	Prop	Win	Runs	Wins%	£
1..7	0%	0	0	0.0%	0.00
8..14	0%	0	0	0.0%	0.00
15..28	100%	1	4	25.0%	-0.68
29..60	0%	0	0	0.0%	0.00
61..100	0%	0	0	0.0%	0.00
101+	0%	0	0	0.0%	0.00
Unraced	0%	0	0	0.0%	0.00

ANALYSIS BY TODAY'S STARTING PRICE

Price	Prop	Win	Runs	Wins%	£
Odds On	100%	1	1	100.0%	0.29
Ev-2/1	0%	0	0	0.0%	0.00
9/4-4/1	0%	0	0	0.0%	0.00
9/2-6/1	0%	0	1	0.0%	-1.00
13/2-10/1	0%	0	0	0.0%	0.00
11/1-16/1	0%	0	1	0.0%	-1.00
18/1-33/1	0%	0	1	0.0%	-1.00
40/1+	0%	0	0	0.0%	0.00

ANALYSIS BY STARTING PRICE LAST TIME

Price	Prop	Win	Runs	Wins%	£
Odds On	0%	0	0	0.0%	0.00
Ev-2/1	0%	0	0	0.0%	0.00
9/4-4/1	0%	0	0	0.0%	0.00
9/2-6/1	0%	0	1	0.0%	-1.00
13/2-10/1	0%	0	U	0.0%	0.00
11/1-16/1	100%	1	2	50.0%	-0.36
18/1-33/1	0%	0	0	0.0%	0.00
40/1+	0%	0	1	0.0%	-1.00
Unraced	0%	0	0	0.0%	0.00

ANALYSIS BY DISTANCE BEATEN LAST TIME

Lengths	Prop	Win	Runs	Wins%	£
..-10	0%	0	0	0.0%	0.00
-10..0	0%	0	2	0.0%	-1.00
0.1..2	100%	1	1	100.0%	0.29
2.1..5	0%	0	0	0.0%	0.00
5.1..10	0%	0	0	0.0%	0.00
10.1..20	0%	0	1	0.0%	-1.00
20.0..30	0%	0	0	0.0%	0.00
30.1+	0%	0	0	0.0%	0.00
Not Compl	0%	0	0	0.0%	0.00
Unraced	0%	0	0	0.0%	0.00

ANALYSIS BY RUN NUMBER

Run No	Prop	Win	Runs	Wins%	£
FTO	0%	0	0	0.0%	0.00
2nd Run	0%	0	0	0.0%	0.00
3rd Run	0%	0	0	0.0%	0.00
4th+ Run	100%	1	4	25.0%	-0.68

ANALYSIS BY POSITION LAST TIME

Pos LT	Prop	Win	Runs	Wins%	£
Won	0%	0	2	0.0%	-1.00
2nd or 3rd	100%	1	1	100.0%	0.29
Unplaced	0%	0	1	0.0%	-1.00
Not Compl	0%	0	0	0.0%	0.00

OTHER FACTORS (WINS-RUNS, £)

Going Winner:	0-2	-£1.00
BHA Top Rated:	1-1	£0.29
Up in class:	0-2	-£1.00
Down in class:	1-2	-£0.36
Colts and Geldings:	1-3	-£0.57
Fillies:	0-1	-£1.00
Absolute Favourites:	1-1	£0.29

Race Profiles

3-Y.O Races: Conditions Stakes

ANALYSIS BY BHA RATING
Rating	Prop	Win	Runs	Wins%	£
120..139	0%	0	0	0.0%	0.00
110..119	4%	4	8	50.0%	-0.10
100..109	29%	27	106	25.5%	-0.06
90..99	28%	26	160	16.3%	-0.03
70..89	25%	23	125	18.4%	0.10
50..69	0%	0	9	0.0%	-1.00
..49	0%	0	2	0.0%	-1.00
Unrated	13%	12	153	7.8%	-0.27

ANALYSIS BY WEIGHT CARRIED
Weight	Prop	Win	Runs	Wins%	£
10-01+	0%	0	0	0.0%	0.00
9-8..10-00	0%	0	1	0.0%	-1.00
9-0..9-07	42%	39	244	16.0%	-0.20
8-8..8-13	47%	43	257	16.7%	0.07
8-0..8-07	11%	10	60	16.7%	-0.30
..7-13	0%	0	1	0.0%	-1.00

ANALYSIS BY DAYS SINCE LAST RUN
Days	Prop	Win	Runs	Wins%	£
1..7	1%	1	14	7.1%	-0.84
8..14	7%	6	59	10.2%	-0.72
15..28	29%	27	121	22.3%	0.00
29..60	13%	12	60	20.0%	0.02
61..100	2%	2	15	13.3%	-0.76
101+	39%	36	192	18.8%	0.11
Unraced	9%	8	102	7.8%	-0.09

ANALYSIS BY TODAY'S STARTING PRICE
Price	Prop	Win	Runs	Wins%	£
Odds On	21%	19	34	55.9%	-0.08
Ev-2/1	27%	25	59	42.4%	0.03
9/4-4/1	24%	22	118	18.6%	-0.23
9/2-6/1	12%	11	63	17.5%	0.09
13/2-10/1	7%	6	81	7.4%	-0.30
11/1-16/1	4%	4	75	5.3%	-0.23
18/1-33/1	3%	3	71	4.2%	-0.11
40/1+	2%	2	62	3.2%	0.32

ANALYSIS BY STARTING PRICE LAST TIME
Price	Prop	Win	Runs	Wins%	£
Odds On	3%	3	20	15.0%	-0.69
Ev-2/1	12%	11	38	28.9%	0.92
9/4-4/1	23%	21	71	29.6%	-0.01
9/2-6/1	13%	12	57	21.1%	-0.08
13/2-10/1	13%	12	83	14.5%	-0.33
11/1-16/1	14%	13	75	17.3%	0.11
18/1-33/1	8%	7	76	9.2%	-0.49
40/1+	5%	5	41	12.2%	-0.05
Unraced	9%	8	102	7.8%	-0.09

ANALYSIS BY DISTANCE BEATEN LAST TIME
Lengths	Prop	Win	Runs	Wins%	£
..-10	0%	0	1	0.0%	-1.00
-10..0	27%	25	110	22.7%	0.30
0.1..2	13%	12	57	21.1%	-0.32
2.1..5	21%	19	97	19.6%	-0.10
5.1..10	20%	18	97	18.6%	-0.30
10.1..20	5%	5	52	9.6%	-0.15
20.0..30	5%	5	30	16.7%	0.24
30.1+	0%	0	17	0.0%	-1.00
Not Compl	0%	0	0	0.0%	0.00
Unraced	9%	8	102	7.8%	-0.09

ANALYSIS BY RUN NUMBER
Run No	Prop	Win	Runs	Wins%	£
FTO	9%	8	102	7.8%	-0.09
2nd Run	9%	8	51	15.7%	0.05
3rd Run	13%	12	49	24.5%	0.90
4th+ Run	70%	64	361	17.7%	-0.25

ANALYSIS BY POSITION LAST TIME
Pos LT	Prop	Win	Runs	Wins%	£
Won	27%	25	111	22.5%	0.29
2nd or 3rd	22%	20	94	21.3%	-0.17
Unplaced	42%	39	256	15.2%	-0.23
Not Compl	9%	8	102	7.8%	-0.09

OTHER FACTORS (WINS-RUNS, £)
Course Winner:	12-51	£0.59
Distance Winner:	28-151	-£0.33
Going Winner:	27-124	-£0.08
Beaten Favourite:	6-24	-£0.36
BHA Top Rated:	16-75	-£0.53
Up in class:	25-162	-£0.03
Same class:	12-68	-£0.22
Down in class:	47-231	-£0.09
Colts and Geldings:	63-400	-£0.22
Fillies:	16-92	£0.60
Absolute Favourites:	41-87	£0.01

TRAINERS (WINS-RUNS, £)
E A L Dunlop 3-12 £1.77; H R A Cecil 6-16 £1.06; R Hannon 5-30 £0.47; B W Hills 3-22 £0.50; J Noseda 4-12 £0.10.

Conditions Stakes

3-Y.O Races: Conditions Stakes – 2 to 7 runners

ANALYSIS BY BHA RATING
Rating	Prop	Win	Runs	Wins%	£
120..139	0%	0	0	0.0%	0.00
110..119	5%	4	6	66.7%	0.20
100..109	30%	22	83	26.5%	-0.19
90..99	34%	25	126	19.8%	0.21
70..89	27%	20	106	18.9%	0.12
50..69	0%	0	8	0.0%	-1.00
..49	0%	0	1	0.0%	-1.00
Unrated	4%	3	54	5.6%	-0.82

ANALYSIS BY WEIGHT CARRIED
Weight	Prop	Win	Runs	Wins%	£
10-01+	0%	0	0	0.0%	0.00
9-8..10-00	0%	0	0	0.0%	0.00
9-0..9-07	39%	29	137	21.2%	-0.18
8-8..8-13	47%	35	195	17.9%	0.03
8-0..8-07	14%	10	51	19.6%	-0.18
..7-13	0%	0	1	0.0%	-1.00

ANALYSIS BY DAYS SINCE LAST RUN
Days	Prop	Win	Runs	Wins%	£
1..7	1%	1	7	14.3%	-0.68
8..14	8%	6	52	11.5%	-0.68
15..28	32%	24	102	23.5%	0.07
29..60	14%	10	45	22.2%	0.02
61..100	3%	2	14	14.3%	-0.75
101+	42%	31	151	20.5%	0.17
Unraced	0%	0	13	0.0%	-1.00

ANALYSIS BY TODAY'S STARTING PRICE
Price	Prop	Win	Runs	Wins%	£
Odds On	24%	18	31	58.1%	-0.05
Ev-2/1	31%	23	50	46.0%	0.11
9/4-4/1	23%	17	94	18.1%	-0.24
9/2-6/1	11%	8	54	14.8%	-0.08
13/2-10/1	3%	2	48	4.2%	-0.60
11/1-16/1	3%	2	35	5.7%	-0.26
18/1-33/1	4%	3	35	8.6%	0.80
40/1+	1%	1	37	2.7%	0.11

ANALYSIS BY STARTING PRICE LAST TIME
Price	Prop	Win	Runs	Wins%	£
Odds On	4%	3	14	21.4%	-0.56
Ev-2/1	14%	10	30	33.3%	1.16
9/4-4/1	27%	20	62	32.3%	0.09
9/2-6/1	12%	9	42	21.4%	-0.13
13/2-10/1	14%	10	71	14.1%	-0.45
11/1-16/1	10%	12	57	21.1%	0.40
18/1-33/1	8%	6	62	9.7%	-0.56
40/1+	5%	4	33	12.1%	0.01
Unraced	0%	0	13	0.0%	-1.00

ANALYSIS BY DISTANCE BEATEN LAST TIME
Lengths	Prop	Win	Runs	Wins%	£
..-10	0%	0	1	0.0%	-1.00
-10..0	28%	21	90	23.3%	0.29
0.1..2	15%	11	44	25.0%	-0.18
2.1..5	20%	15	77	19.5%	-0.27
5.1..10	23%	17	80	21.3%	-0.19
10.1..20	7%	5	41	12.2%	0.08
20.0..30	7%	5	23	21.7%	0.62
30.1+	0%	0	15	0.0%	-1.00
Not Compl	0%	0	0	0.0%	0.00
Unraced	0%	0	13	0.0%	-1.00

ANALYSIS BY RUN NUMBER
Run No	Prop	Win	Runs	Wins%	£
FTO	0%	0	13	0.0%	-1.00
2nd Run	8%	6	44	13.6%	-0.13
3rd Run	16%	12	42	28.6%	1.21
4th+ Run	76%	56	285	19.6%	-0.22

ANALYSIS BY POSITION LAST TIME
Pos LT	Prop	Win	Runs	Wins%	£
Won	28%	21	91	23.1%	0.27
2nd or 3rd	23%	17	74	23.0%	-0.18
Unplaced	49%	36	206	17.5%	-0.13
Not Compl	0%	0	13	0.0%	-1.00

OTHER FACTORS (WINS-RUNS, £)
Course Winner:	9-40	£0.42
Distance Winner:	24-116	-£0.31
Going Winner:	22-96	-£0.13
Beaten Favourite:	6-20	-£0.24
BHA Top Rated:	16-68	-£0.48
Up in class:	22-134	-£0.01
Same class:	10-47	-£0.20
Down in class:	42-190	-£0.03
Colts and Geldings:	51-266	-£0.19
Fillies:	12-64	£0.52
Absolute Favourites:	37-71	£0.10

TRAINERS (WINS-RUNS, £)
R Hannon 5-20 £1.20; H R A Cecil 3-11 £0.28.

Race Profiles

3-Y.O Races: Conditions Stakes – 8 to 14 runners

ANALYSIS BY BHA RATING

Rating	Prop	Win	Runs	Wins%	£
120..139	0%	0	0	0.0%	0.00
110..119	0%	0	2	0.0%	-1.00
100..109	29%	5	22	22.7%	0.47
90..99	6%	1	30	3.3%	-0.88
70..89	18%	3	13	23.1%	0.45
50..69	0%	0	1	0.0%	-1.00
..49	0%	0	1	0.0%	-1.00
Unrated	47%	8	92	8.7%	0.01

ANALYSIS BY WEIGHT CARRIED

Weight	Prop	Win	Runs	Wins%	£
10-01+	0%	0	0	0.0%	0.00
9-8..10-00	0%	0	1	0.0%	-1.00
9-0..9-07	53%	9	93	9.7%	-0.21
8-8..8-13	47%	8	58	13.8%	0.28
8-0..8-07	0%	0	9	0.0%	-1.00
..7-13	0%	0	0	0.0%	0.00

ANALYSIS BY DAYS SINCE LAST RUN

Days	Prop	Win	Runs	Wins%	£
1..7	0%	0	6	0.0%	-1.00
8..14	0%	0	5	0.0%	-1.00
15..28	18%	3	15	20.0%	-0.23
29..60	12%	2	13	15.4%	0.18
61..100	0%	0	1	0.0%	-1.00
101+	24%	4	32	12.5%	-0.13
Unraced	47%	8	89	9.0%	0.04

ANALYSIS BY TODAY'S STARTING PRICE

Price	Prop	Win	Runs	Wins%	£
Odds On	6%	1	3	33.3%	-0.42
Ev-2/1	12%	2	9	22.2%	-0.46
9/4-4/1	29%	5	22	22.7%	-0.10
9/2-6/1	18%	3	9	33.3%	1.11
13/2-10/1	18%	3	31	9.7%	-0.06
11/1-16/1	12%	2	37	5.4%	-0.14
18/1-33/1	0%	0	31	0.0%	-1.00
40/1+	6%	1	19	5.3%	1.16

ANALYSIS BY STARTING PRICE LAST TIME

Price	Prop	Win	Runs	Wins%	£
Odds On	0%	0	3	0.0%	-1.00
Ev-2/1	6%	1	5	20.0%	0.60
9/4-4/1	6%	1	7	14.3%	-0.54
9/2-6/1	12%	2	12	16.7%	-0.43
13/2-10/1	12%	2	9	22.2%	0.83
11/1-16/1	6%	1	16	6.3%	-0.78
18/1-33/1	6%	1	12	8.3%	-0.08
40/1+	6%	1	8	12.5%	-0.31
Unraced	47%	8	89	9.0%	0.04

ANALYSIS BY DISTANCE BEATEN LAST TIME

Lengths	Prop	Win	Runs	Wins%	£
..-10	0%	0	0	0.0%	0.00
-10..0	18%	3	15	20.0%	0.20
0.1..2	6%	1	9	11.1%	-0.72
2.1..5	24%	4	15	26.7%	1.06
5.1..10	6%	1	14	7.1%	-0.77
10.1..20	0%	0	10	0.0%	-1.00
20.0..30	0%	0	7	0.0%	-1.00
30.1+	0%	0	2	0.0%	-1.00
Not Compl	0%	0	0	0.0%	0.00
Unraced	47%	8	89	9.0%	0.04

ANALYSIS BY RUN NUMBER

Run No	Prop	Win	Runs	Wins%	£
FTO	47%	8	89	9.0%	0.04
2nd Run	6%	1	4	25.0%	0.63
3rd Run	0%	0	4	0.0%	-1.00
4th+ Run	47%	8	64	12.5%	-0.25

ANALYSIS BY POSITION LAST TIME

Pos LT	Prop	Win	Runs	Wins%	£
Won	18%	3	15	20.0%	0.20
2nd or 3rd	18%	3	15	20.0%	0.19
Unplaced	18%	3	42	7.1%	-0.55
Not Compl	47%	8	89	9.0%	0.04

OTHER FACTORS (WINS-RUNS, £)

Course Winner:	2-9	£0.72
Distance Winner:	4-33	-£0.38
Going Winner:	4-24	-£0.11
Beaten Favourite:	0-1	-£1.00
BHA Top Rated:	0-7	-£1.00
Up in class:	2-17	-£0.15
Same class:	2-15	£0.02
Down in class:	5-40	-£0.38
Colts and Geldings:	11-120	-£0.28
Fillies:	4-24	£1.08
Absolute Favourites:	4-15	-£0.31

TRAINERS (WINS-RUNS, £)

B W Hills 1-12 £0.25.

Conditions Stakes

3-Y.O Races: Conditions Stakes – good or faster going

ANALYSIS BY BHA RATING

Rating	Prop	Win	Runs	Wins%	£
120..139	0%	0	0	0.0%	0.00
110..119	3%	2	4	50.0%	-0.19
100..109	32%	19	74	25.7%	0.01
90..99	17%	10	104	9.6%	-0.47
70..89	30%	18	79	22.8%	0.27
50..69	0%	0	4	0.0%	-1.00
..49	0%	0	1	0.0%	-1.00
Unrated	18%	11	128	8.6%	-0.14

ANALYSIS BY WEIGHT CARRIED

Weight	Prop	Win	Runs	Wins%	£
10-01+	0%	0	0	0.0%	0.00
9-8..10-00	0%	0	1	0.0%	-1.00
9-0..9-07	48%	29	193	15.0%	-0.14
8-8..8-13	45%	27	167	16.2%	-0.07
8-0..8-07	7%	4	32	12.5%	-0.35
..7-13	0%	0	1	0.0%	-1.00

ANALYSIS BY DAYS SINCE LAST RUN

Days	Prop	Win	Runs	Wins%	£
1..7	2%	1	13	7.7%	-0.83
8..14	3%	2	32	6.3%	-0.74
15..28	32%	19	86	22.1%	0.13
29..60	13%	8	38	21.1%	0.28
61..100	2%	1	9	11.1%	-0.80
101+	35%	21	118	17.8%	-0.22
Unraced	13%	8	98	8.2%	-0.05

ANALYSIS BY TODAY'S STARTING PRICE

Price	Prop	Win	Runs	Wins%	£
Odds On	20%	12	22	54.5%	-0.12
Ev-2/1	25%	15	32	46.9%	0.13
9/4-4/1	23%	14	85	16.5%	-0.29
9/2-6/1	12%	7	37	18.9%	0.19
13/2-10/1	10%	6	60	10.0%	-0.05
11/1-16/1	5%	3	57	5.3%	-0.21
18/1-33/1	3%	2	58	3.4%	-0.31
40/1+	2%	1	43	2.3%	-0.05

ANALYSIS BY STARTING PRICE LAST TIME

Price	Prop	Win	Runs	Wins%	£
Odds On	5%	3	16	18.8%	-0.61
Ev-2/1	12%	7	25	28.0%	0.04
9/4-4/1	15%	9	35	25.7%	-0.15
9/2-6/1	15%	9	39	23.1%	0.15
13/2-10/1	12%	7	55	12.7%	-0.41
11/1-16/1	12%	7	47	14.9%	-0.12
18/1-33/1	8%	5	47	10.6%	-0.35
40/1+	8%	5	32	15.6%	0.21
Unraced	13%	8	98	8.2%	-0.05

ANALYSIS BY DISTANCE BEATEN LAST TIME

Lengths	Prop	Win	Runs	Wins%	£
..-10	0%	0	0	0.0%	0.00
-10..0	27%	16	67	23.9%	-0.07
0.1..2	13%	8	41	19.5%	-0.40
2.1..5	17%	10	57	17.5%	-0.23
5.1..10	13%	8	59	13.6%	-0.37
10.1..20	8%	5	39	12.8%	0.14
20.0..30	8%	5	25	20.0%	0.49
30.1+	0%	0	8	0.0%	-1.00
Not Compl	0%	0	0	0.0%	0.00
Unraced	13%	8	98	8.2%	-0.05

ANALYSIS BY RUN NUMBER

Run No	Prop	Win	Runs	Wins%	£
FTO	13%	8	98	8.2%	-0.05
2nd Run	10%	6	32	18.8%	-0.16
3rd Run	10%	6	29	20.7%	0.25
4th+ Run	67%	40	235	17.0%	-0.21

ANALYSIS BY POSITION LAST TIME

Pos LT	Prop	Win	Runs	Wins%	£
Won	27%	16	67	23.9%	-0.07
2nd or 3rd	18%	11	64	17.2%	-0.36
Unplaced	42%	25	165	15.2%	-0.11
Not Compl	13%	8	98	8.2%	-0.05

OTHER FACTORS (WINS-RUNS, £)

Course Winner:	10-34	£1.29
Distance Winner:	18-106	-£0.33
Going Winner:	19-88	£0.02
Beaten Favourite:	4-18	-£0.35
BHA Top Rated:	9-45	-£0.55
Up in class:	14-92	-£0.38
Same class:	8-49	-£0.13
Down in class:	30-155	-£0.03
Colts and Geldings:	43-290	-£0.26
Fillies:	10-62	£0.53
Absolute Favourites:	28-57	£0.09

TRAINERS (WINS-RUNS, £)

R Hannon 5-23 £0.91; H R A Cecil 5-10 £1.75; J Noseda 4-11 £0.20.

Race Profiles

3-Y.O Races: Conditions Stakes – good to soft or softer going

ANALYSIS BY BHA RATING

Rating	Prop	Win	Runs	Wins%	£
120..139	0%	0	0	0.0%	0.00
110..119	6%	2	4	50.0%	-0.01
100..109	25%	8	32	25.0%	-0.21
90..99	50%	16	56	28.6%	0.80
70..89	16%	5	46	10.9%	-0.20
50..69	0%	0	5	0.0%	-1.00
..49	0%	0	1	0.0%	-1.00
Unrated	3%	1	25	4.0%	-0.93

ANALYSIS BY WEIGHT CARRIED

Weight	Prop	Win	Runs	Wins%	£
10-01+	0%	0	0	0.0%	0.00
9-8..10-00	0%	0	0	0.0%	0.00
9-0..9-07	31%	10	51	19.6%	-0.44
8-8..8-13	50%	16	90	17.8%	0.32
8-0..8-07	19%	6	28	21.4%	-0.24
..7-13	0%	0	0	0.0%	0.00

ANALYSIS BY DAYS SINCE LAST RUN

Days	Prop	Win	Runs	Wins%	£
1..7	0%	0	1	0.0%	-1.00
8..14	13%	4	27	14.8%	-0.69
15..28	25%	8	35	22.9%	-0.32
29..60	13%	4	22	18.2%	-0.44
61..100	3%	1	6	16.7%	-0.71
101+	47%	15	74	20.3%	0.65
Unraced	0%	0	4	0.0%	-1.00

ANALYSIS BY TODAY'S STARTING PRICE

Price	Prop	Win	Runs	Wins%	£
Odds On	22%	7	12	58.3%	-0.02
Ev-2/1	31%	10	27	37.0%	-0.10
9/4-4/1	25%	8	33	24.2%	-0.06
9/2-6/1	13%	4	26	15.4%	-0.06
13/2-10/1	0%	0	21	0.0%	-1.00
11/1-16/1	3%	1	18	5.6%	-0.28
18/1-33/1	3%	1	13	7.7%	0.77
40/1+	3%	1	19	5.3%	1.16

ANALYSIS BY STARTING PRICE LAST TIME

Price	Prop	Win	Runs	Wins%	£
Odds On	0%	0	4	0.0%	-1.00
Ev-2/1	13%	4	13	30.8%	2.60
9/4-4/1	38%	12	36	33.3%	0.14
9/2-6/1	9%	3	18	16.7%	-0.56
13/2-10/1	16%	5	28	17.9%	-0.17
11/1-16/1	19%	6	28	21.4%	0.50
18/1-33/1	6%	2	29	6.9%	-0.73
40/1+	0%	0	9	0.0%	-1.00
Unraced	0%	0	4	0.0%	-1.00

ANALYSIS BY DISTANCE BEATEN LAST TIME

Lengths	Prop	Win	Runs	Wins%	£
..-10	0%	0	1	0.0%	-1.00
-10..0	28%	9	43	20.9%	0.87
0.1..2	13%	4	16	25.0%	-0.12
2.1..5	28%	9	40	22.5%	0.09
5.1..10	31%	10	38	26.3%	-0.19
10.1..20	0%	0	13	0.0%	-1.00
20.0..30	0%	0	5	0.0%	-1.00
30.1+	0%	0	9	0.0%	-1.00
Not Compl	0%	0	0	0.0%	0.00
Unraced	0%	0	4	0.0%	-1.00

ANALYSIS BY RUN NUMBER

Run No	Prop	Win	Runs	Wins%	£
FTO	0%	0	4	0.0%	-1.00
2nd Run	6%	2	19	10.5%	0.41
3rd Run	19%	6	20	30.0%	1.84
4th+ Run	75%	24	126	19.0%	-0.32

ANALYSIS BY POSITION LAST TIME

Pos LT	Prop	Win	Runs	Wins%	£
Won	28%	9	44	20.5%	0.83
2nd or 3rd	28%	9	30	30.0%	0.24
Unplaced	44%	14	91	15.4%	-0.44
Not Compl	0%	0	4	0.0%	-1.00

OTHER FACTORS (WINS-RUNS, £)

Course Winner:	2-17	-£0.79
Distance Winner:	10-45	-£0.33
Going Winner:	8-36	-£0.32
Beaten Favourite:	2-6	-£0.41
BHA Top Rated:	7-30	-£0.50
Up in class:	11-70	£0.42
Same class:	4-19	-£0.45
Down in class:	17-76	-£0.23
Colts and Geldings:	20-110	-£0.13
Fillies:	6-30	£0.75
Absolute Favourites:	13-30	-£0.14

Conditions Stakes

3-Y.O Races: Conditions Stakes – 5 to 6 furlong races

ANALYSIS BY BHA RATING

Rating	Prop	Win	Runs	Wins%	£
120..139	0%	0	0	0.0%	0.00
110..119	6%	1	1	100.0%	0.83
100..109	29%	5	22	22.7%	-0.13
90..99	29%	5	42	11.9%	-0.62
70..89	29%	5	30	16.7%	0.74
50..69	0%	0	1	0.0%	-1.00
..49	0%	0	1	0.0%	-1.00
Unrated	6%	1	10	10.0%	-0.73

ANALYSIS BY WEIGHT CARRIED

Weight	Prop	Win	Runs	Wins%	£
10-01+	0%	0	0	0.0%	0.00
9-8..10-00	0%	0	0	0.0%	0.00
9-0..9-07	29%	5	39	12.8%	-0.18
8-8..8-13	53%	9	47	19.1%	0.03
8-0..8-07	18%	3	21	14.3%	-0.45
..7-13	0%	0	0	0.0%	0.00

ANALYSIS BY DAYS SINCE LAST RUN

Days	Prop	Win	Runs	Wins%	£
1..7	6%	1	5	20.0%	-0.55
8..14	12%	2	12	16.7%	-0.66
15..28	29%	5	22	22.7%	-0.46
29..60	12%	2	12	16.7%	0.88
61..100	0%	0	1	0.0%	-1.00
101+	41%	7	51	13.7%	0.00
Unraced	0%	0	4	0.0%	-1.00

ANALYSIS BY TODAY'S STARTING PRICE

Price	Prop	Win	Runs	Wins%	£
Odds On	24%	4	6	66.7%	0.16
Ev-2/1	35%	6	12	50.0%	0.15
9/4-4/1	18%	3	23	13.0%	-0.54
9/2-6/1	6%	1	12	8.3%	-0.46
13/2-10/1	6%	1	12	8.3%	-0.17
11/1-16/1	0%	0	11	0.0%	-1.00
18/1-33/1	12%	2	19	10.5%	1.32
40/1+	0%	0	12	0.0%	-1.00

ANALYSIS BY STARTING PRICE LAST TIME

Price	Prop	Win	Runs	Wins%	£
Odds On	6%	1	3	33.3%	-0.39
Ev-2/1	6%	1	5	20.0%	-0.70
9/4-4/1	24%	4	16	25.0%	-0.32
9/2-6/1	18%	3	14	21.4%	-0.50
13/2-10/1	6%	1	18	5.6%	-0.44
11/1-16/1	29%	5	21	23.8%	0.75
18/1-33/1	6%	1	18	5.6%	-0.85
40/1+	6%	1	8	12.5%	1.63
Unraced	0%	0	4	0.0%	-1.00

ANALYSIS BY DISTANCE BEATEN LAST TIME

Lengths	Prop	Win	Runs	Wins%	£
..-10	0%	0	0	0.0%	0.00
-10..0	29%	5	15	33.3%	1.16
0.1..2	12%	2	13	15.4%	-0.67
2.1..5	29%	5	30	16.7%	-0.25
5.1..10	18%	3	26	11.5%	-0.63
10.1..20	6%	1	9	11.1%	1.33
20.0..30	6%	1	6	16.7%	-0.70
30.1+	0%	0	4	0.0%	-1.00
Not Compl	0%	0	0	0.0%	0.00
Unraced	0%	0	4	0.0%	-1.00

ANALYSIS BY RUN NUMBER

Run No	Prop	Win	Runs	Wins%	£
FTO	0%	0	4	0.0%	-1.00
2nd Run	6%	1	5	20.0%	3.60
3rd Run	6%	1	7	14.3%	-0.70
4th+ Run	88%	15	91	16.5%	-0.27

ANALYSIS BY POSITION LAST TIME

Pos LT	Prop	Win	Runs	Wins%	£
Won	29%	5	15	33.3%	1.16
2nd or 3rd	29%	5	24	20.8%	-0.32
Unplaced	41%	7	64	10.9%	-0.33
Not Compl	0%	0	4	0.0%	-1.00

OTHER FACTORS (WINS-RUNS, £)

Course Winner:	2-13	£1.38
Distance Winner:	10-64	-£0.43
Going Winner:	5-26	-£0.32
Beaten Favourite:	1-5	-£0.63
BHA Top Rated:	1-13	-£0.85
Up in class:	2-23	£0.09
Same class:	1-18	-£0.88
Down in class:	14-62	£0.04
Colts and Geldings:	10-70	-£0.65
Fillies:	6-33	£0.98
Absolute Favourites:	10-16	£0.36

Race Profiles

3-Y.O Races: Conditions Stakes – 7 to 9 furlong races

ANALYSIS BY BHA RATING

Rating	Prop	Win	Runs	Wins%	£
120..139	0%	0	0	0.0%	0.00
110..119	4%	2	4	50.0%	-0.22*
100..109	32%	17	65	26.2%	-0.00
90..99	26%	14	79	17.7%	0.35
70..89	21%	11	61	18.0%	0.04
50..69	0%	0	5	0.0%	-1.00
..49	0%	0	1	0.0%	-1.00
Unrated	17%	9	124	7.3%	-0.21

ANALYSIS BY WEIGHT CARRIED

Weight	Prop	Win	Runs	Wins%	£
10-01+	0%	0	0	0.0%	0.00
9-8..10-00	0%	0	1	0.0%	-1.00
9-0..9-07	38%	20	141	14.2%	-0.14
8-8..8-13	53%	28	163	17.2%	0.17
8-0..8-07	9%	5	33	15.2%	-0.26
..7-13	0%	0	1	0.0%	-1.00

ANALYSIS BY DAYS SINCE LAST RUN

Days	Prop	Win	Runs	Wins%	£
1..7	0%	0	7	0.0%	-1.00
8..14	8%	4	36	11.1%	-0.65
15..28	30%	16	69	23.2%	0.32
29..60	11%	6	35	17.1%	-0.21
61..100	4%	2	11	18.2%	-0.68
101+	32%	17	88	19.3%	0.23
Unraced	15%	8	93	8.6%	-0.00

ANALYSIS BY TODAY'S STARTING PRICE

Price	Prop	Win	Runs	Wins%	£
Odds On	19%	10	18	55.6%	-0.11
Ev-2/1	21%	11	33	33.3%	-0.17
9/4-4/1	26%	14	69	20.3%	-0.13
9/2-6/1	17%	9	32	28.1%	0.77
13/2-10/1	6%	3	58	5.2%	-0.48
11/1-16/1	6%	3	53	5.7%	-0.15
18/1-33/1	2%	1	40	2.5%	-0.52
40/1+	4%	2	36	5.6%	1.28

ANALYSIS BY STARTING PRICE LAST TIME

Price	Prop	Win	Runs	Wins%	£
Odds On	0%	0	8	0.0%	-1.00
Ev-2/1	9%	5	16	31.3%	2.31
9/4-4/1	15%	8	35	22.9%	-0.10
9/2-6/1	15%	8	34	23.5%	0.08
13/2-10/1	15%	8	46	17.4%	-0.36
11/1-16/1	13%	7	43	16.3%	0.03
18/1-33/1	11%	6	37	16.2%	-0.04
40/1+	6%	3	27	11.1%	-0.53
Unraced	15%	8	93	8.6%	-0.00

ANALYSIS BY DISTANCE BEATEN LAST TIME

Lengths	Prop	Win	Runs	Wins%	£
..-10	0%	0	0	0.0%	0.00
-10..0	17%	9	57	15.8%	0.26
0.1..2	13%	7	29	24.1%	-0.20
2.1..5	21%	11	50	22.0%	-0.05
5.1..10	21%	11	52	21.2%	-0.10
10.1..20	8%	4	32	12.5%	-0.27
20.0..30	6%	3	18	16.7%	0.69
30.1+	0%	0	8	0.0%	-1.00
Not Compl	0%	0	0	0.0%	0.00
Unraced	15%	8	93	8.6%	-0.00

ANALYSIS BY RUN NUMBER

Run No	Prop	Win	Runs	Wins%	£
FTO	15%	8	93	8.6%	-0.00
2nd Run	8%	4	31	12.9%	-0.41
3rd Run	15%	8	32	25.0%	1.53
4th+ Run	62%	33	183	18.0%	-0.21

ANALYSIS BY POSITION LAST TIME

Pos LT	Prop	Win	Runs	Wins%	£
Won	17%	9	57	15.8%	0.26
2nd or 3rd	21%	11	51	21.6%	-0.07
Unplaced	47%	25	138	18.1%	-0.11
Not Compl	15%	8	93	8.6%	-0.00

OTHER FACTORS (WINS-RUNS, £)

Course Winner:	7-27	£0.37
Distance Winner:	13-69	-£0.27
Going Winner:	14-66	-£0.03
Beaten Favourite:	4-12	-£0.11
BHA Top Rated:	11-42	-£0.48
Up in class:	9-84	-£0.17
Same class:	8-35	£0.25
Down in class:	28-127	£0.02
Colts and Geldings:	35-228	£0.01
Fillies:	6-44	£0.25
Absolute Favourites:	21-51	-£0.12

TRAINERS (WINS-RUNS, £)

E A L Dunlop 2-11 £1.73; H R A Cecil 4-10 £0.94; B W Hills 2-16 £0.25; R Hannon 3-19 £0.11.

Conditions Stakes

3-Y.O Races: Conditions Stakes – 10 to 14 furlong races

ANALYSIS BY BHA RATING

Rating	Prop	Win	Runs	Wins%	£
120..139	0%	0	0	0.0%	0.00
110..119	5%	1	3	33.3%	-0.25
100..109	23%	5	19	26.3%	-0.16
90..99	32%	7	39	17.9%	-0.15
70..89	32%	7	34	20.6%	-0.37
50..69	0%	0	3	0.0%	-1.00
..49	0%	0	0	0.0%	0.00
Unrated	9%	2	19	10.5%	-0.44

ANALYSIS BY WEIGHT CARRIED

Weight	Prop	Win	Runs	Wins%	£
10-01+	0%	0	0	0.0%	0.00
9-8..10-00	0%	0	0	0.0%	0.00
9-0..9-07	64%	14	64	21.9%	-0.35
8-8..8-13	27%	6	47	12.8%	-0.24
8-0..8-07	9%	2	6	33.3%	0.00
..7-13	0%	0	0	0.0%	0.00

ANALYSIS BY DAYS SINCE LAST RUN

Days	Prop	Win	Runs	Wins%	£
1..7	0%	0	2	0.0%	-1.00
8..14	0%	0	11	0.0%	-1.00
15..28	27%	6	30	20.0%	-0.39
29..60	18%	4	13	30.8%	-0.15
61..100	0%	0	3	0.0%	-1.00
101+	55%	12	53	22.6%	0.03
Unraced	0%	0	5	0.0%	-1.00

ANALYSIS BY TODAY'S STARTING PRICE

Price	Prop	Win	Runs	Wins%	£
Odds On	23%	5	10	50.0%	-0.18
Ev-2/1	36%	8	14	57.1%	0.39
9/4-4/1	23%	5	26	19.2%	-0.21
9/2-6/1	5%	1	19	5.3%	-0.71
13/2-10/1	9%	2	11	18.2%	0.55
11/1-16/1	5%	1	11	9.1%	0.18
18/1-33/1	0%	0	12	0.0%	-1.00
40/1+	0%	0	14	0.0%	-1.00

ANALYSIS BY STARTING PRICE LAST TIME

Price	Prop	Win	Runs	Wins%	£
Odds On	9%	2	9	22.2%	-0.51
Ev-2/1	23%	5	17	29.4%	0.08
9/4-4/1	41%	9	20	45.0%	0.42
9/2-6/1	5%	1	9	11.1%	0.00
13/2-10/1	14%	3	19	15.8%	-0.13
11/1-16/1	5%	1	11	9.1%	-0.81
18/1-33/1	0%	0	21	0.0%	-1.00
40/1+	5%	1	6	16.7%	-0.17
Unraced	0%	0	5	0.0%	-1.00

ANALYSIS BY DISTANCE BEATEN LAST TIME

Lengths	Prop	Win	Runs	Wins%	£
..-10	0%	0	1	0.0%	-1.00
-10..0	50%	11	38	28.9%	0.01
0.1..2	14%	3	15	20.0%	-0.25
2.1..5	14%	3	17	17.6%	0.02
5.1..10	18%	4	19	21.1%	-0.39
10.1..20	0%	0	11	0.0%	-1.00
20.0..30	5%	1	6	16.7%	-0.17
30.1+	0%	0	5	0.0%	-1.00
Not Compl	0%	0	0	0.0%	0.00
Unraced	0%	0	5	0.0%	-1.00

ANALYSIS BY RUN NUMBER

Run No	Prop	Win	Runs	Wins%	£
FTO	0%	0	5	0.0%	-1.00
2nd Run	14%	3	15	20.0%	-0.16
3rd Run	14%	3	10	30.0%	0.01
4th+ Run	73%	16	87	18.4%	-0.30

ANALYSIS BY POSITION LAST TIME

Pos LT	Prop	Win	Runs	Wins%	£
Won	50%	11	39	28.2%	-0.01
2nd or 3rd	18%	4	19	21.1%	-0.24
Unplaced	32%	7	54	13.0%	-0.43
Not Compl	0%	0	5	0.0%	-1.00

OTHER FACTORS (WINS-RUNS, £)

Course Winner:	3-11	£0.22
Distance Winner:	5-18	-£0.23
Going Winner:	8-32	£0.01
Beaten Favourite:	1-7	-£0.61
BHA Top Rated:	4-20	-£0.42
Up in class:	14-55	£0.13
Same class:	3-15	-£0.55
Down in class:	5-42	-£0.64
Colts and Geldings:	18-102	-£0.44
Fillies:	4-15	£0.80
Absolute Favourites:	10-20	£0.08

Race Profiles

3-Y.O Races: Maiden Races

ANALYSIS BY BHA RATING

Rating	Prop	Win	Runs	Wins%	£
120..139	0%	0	0	0.0%	0.00
110..119	0%	0	1	0.0%	-1.00
100..109	1%	6	11	54.5%	-0.03
90..99	1%	9	26	34.6%	-0.28
70..89	24%	155	710	21.8%	-0.13
50..69	6%	39	451	8.6%	-0.20
..49	1%	4	204	2.0%	-0.30
Unrated	67%	423	5265	8.0%	-0.36

ANALYSIS BY WEIGHT CARRIED

Weight	Prop	Win	Runs	Wins%	£
10-01+	0%	0	0	0.0%	0.00
9-8..10-00	0%	0	0	0.0%	0.00
9-0..9-07	77%	488	4371	11.2%	-0.29
8-8..8-13	22%	137	2061	6.6%	-0.41
8-0..8-07	2%	11	238	4.6%	-0.22
..7-13	0%	0	0	0.0%	0.00

ANALYSIS BY DAYS SINCE LAST RUN

Days	Prop	Win	Runs	Wins%	£
1..7	3%	16	191	8.4%	0.37
8..14	17%	109	847	12.9%	-0.17
15..28	23%	148	1472	10.1%	-0.39
29..60	11%	71	675	10.5%	-0.38
61..100	2%	10	180	5.6%	-0.68
101+	31%	196	1695	11.6%	-0.29
Unraced	14%	86	1610	5.3%	-0.39

ANALYSIS BY TODAY'S STARTING PRICE

Price	Prop	Win	Runs	Wins%	£
Odds On	17%	106	188	56.4%	-0.08
Ev-2/1	22%	143	360	39.7%	-0.01
9/4-4/1	26%	165	717	23.0%	-0.06
9/2-6/1	10%	66	490	13.5%	-0.18
13/2-10/1	12%	75	803	9.3%	-0.15
11/1-16/1	6%	40	924	4.3%	-0.34
18/1-33/1	5%	29	1236	2.3%	-0.35
40/1+	2%	12	1952	0.6%	-0.58

ANALYSIS BY STARTING PRICE LAST TIME

Price	Prop	Win	Runs	Wins%	£
Odds On	3%	20	79	25.3%	-0.15
Ev-2/1	10%	64	226	28.3%	-0.11
9/4-4/1	16%	103	543	19.0%	-0.17
9/2-6/1	12%	74	389	19.0%	-0.22
13/2-10/1	14%	91	677	13.4%	-0.19
11/1-16/1	13%	81	818	9.9%	-0.32
18/1-33/1	10%	65	1050	6.2%	-0.47
40/1+	8%	52	1278	4.1%	-0.33
Unraced	14%	86	1610	5.3%	-0.39

ANALYSIS BY DISTANCE BEATEN LAST TIME

Lengths	Prop	Win	Runs	Wins%	£
..-10	0%	0	0	0.0%	0.00
-10..0	0%	1	1	100.0%	3.00
0.1..2	27%	169	695	24.3%	-0.18
2.1..5	26%	167	896	18.6%	-0.14
5.1..10	21%	131	1285	10.2%	-0.31
10.1..20	9%	60	1403	4.3%	-0.56
20.0..30	2%	13	451	2.9%	-0.31
30.1+	1%	9	329	2.7%	0.13
Not Compl	0%	0	0	0.0%	0.00
Unraced	14%	86	1610	5.3%	-0.39

ANALYSIS BY RUN NUMBER

Run No	Prop	Win	Runs	Wins%	£
FTO	14%	86	1610	5.3%	-0.39
2nd Run	29%	184	1847	10.0%	-0.24
3rd Run	23%	149	1768	8.4%	-0.45
4th+ Run	34%	217	1445	15.0%	-0.19

ANALYSIS BY POSITION LAST TIME

Pos LT	Prop	Win	Runs	Wins%	£
Won	0%	0	0	0.0%	0.00
2nd or 3rd	44%	279	1209	23.1%	-0.17
Unplaced	42%	270	3840	7.0%	-0.34
Not Compl	14%	87	1621	5.4%	-0.39

OTHER FACTORS (WINS-RUNS, £)

Distance Winner:	0-1	-£1.00
Beaten Favourite:	96-370	-£0.16
BHA Top Rated:	118-461	-£0.18
Up in class:	65-960	-£0.52
Same class:	316-3055	-£0.29
Down in class:	169-1045	-£0.14
Colts and Geldings:	406-3623	-£0.28
Fillies:	103-1652	-£0.45
Absolute Favourites:	263-600	£0.01

TRAINERS (WINS-RUNS, £)

J L Spearing 2-14 £9.86; P J Makin 5-29 £3.60; G L Moore 1-28 £2.61; C G Cox 6-59 £1.14; H R A Cecil 25-128 £0.48; T D Barron 6-24 £2.53; R M Beckett 4-51 £1.12; W M Brisbourne 1-14 £3.79; M Botti 3-14 £2.77; M A Jarvis 40-155 £0.24; D W Barker 2-17 £2.19; N Bycroft 2-10 £3.70; M G Quinlan 4-20 £1.78; P W Chapple-Hyam 20-88 £0.40; P D Evans 2-18 £1.14; G A Huffer 3-14 £0.78; G A Butler 4-40 £0.26; P A Blockley 2-29 £0.34; C R Egerton 2-15 £0.58; A King 4-23 £0.34.

Maiden Races

3-Y.O Races: Maiden Races – 2 to 7 runners

ANALYSIS BY BHA RATING

Rating	Prop	Win	Runs	Wins%	£
120..139	0%	0	0	0.0%	0.00
110..119	0%	0	1	0.0%	-1.00
100..109	3%	4	5	80.0%	0.20
90..99	1%	1	4	25.0%	-0.65
70..89	35%	42	138	30.4%	-0.08
50..69	11%	13	78	16.7%	0.18
..49	1%	1	34	2.9%	-0.79
Unrated	50%	60	471	12.7%	-0.33

ANALYSIS BY WEIGHT CARRIED

Weight	Prop	Win	Runs	Wins%	£
10-01+	0%	0	0	0.0%	0.00
9-8..10-00	0%	0	0	0.0%	0.00
9-0..9-07	73%	88	466	18.9%	-0.24
8-8..8-13	26%	31	227	13.7%	-0.18
8-0..8-07	2%	2	38	5.3%	-0.72
..7-13	0%	0	0	0.0%	0.00

ANALYSIS BY DAYS SINCE LAST RUN

Days	Prop	Win	Runs	Wins%	£
1..7	7%	9	24	37.5%	0.76
8..14	21%	25	110	22.7%	-0.04
15..28	26%	32	206	15.5%	-0.53
29..60	13%	16	93	17.2%	-0.32
61..100	2%	3	29	10.3%	-0.45
101+	19%	23	154	14.9%	-0.39
Unraced	11%	13	115	11.3%	0.16

ANALYSIS BY TODAY'S STARTING PRICE

Price	Prop	Win	Runs	Wins%	£
Odds On	29%	35	55	63.6%	-0.03
Ev-2/1	22%	27	81	33.3%	-0.19
9/4-4/1	25%	30	125	24.0%	-0.03
9/2-6/1	9%	11	65	16.9%	0.05
13/2-10/1	11%	13	103	12.6%	0.12
11/1-16/1	2%	3	86	3.5%	-0.45
18/1-33/1	1%	1	114	0.9%	-0.70
40/1+	1%	1	102	1.0%	-0.60

ANALYSIS BY STARTING PRICE LAST TIME

Price	Prop	Win	Runs	Wins%	£
Odds On	2%	3	9	33.3%	-0.54
Ev-2/1	11%	13	34	38.2%	-0.05
9/4-4/1	25%	30	86	34.9%	0.11
9/2-6/1	9%	11	60	18.3%	-0.47
13/2-10/1	12%	14	82	17.1%	-0.48
11/1-16/1	14%	17	97	17.5%	-0.12
18/1-33/1	9%	11	105	10.5%	-0.55
40/1+	7%	9	143	6.3%	-0.45
Unraced	11%	13	115	11.3%	0.16

ANALYSIS BY DISTANCE BEATEN LAST TIME

Lengths	Prop	Win	Runs	Wins%	£
..-10	0%	0	0	0.0%	0.00
-10..0	0%	0	0	0.0%	0.00
0.1..2	33%	40	120	33.3%	-0.06
2.1..5	19%	23	108	21.3%	-0.32
5.1..10	19%	23	138	16.7%	-0.30
10.1..20	12%	15	150	10.0%	-0.49
20.0..30	4%	5	63	7.9%	-0.22
30.1+	2%	2	37	5.4%	-0.75
Not Compl	0%	0	0	0.0%	0.00
Unraced	11%	13	115	11.3%	0.16

ANALYSIS BY RUN NUMBER

Run No	Prop	Win	Runs	Wins%	£
FTO	11%	13	115	11.3%	0.16
2nd Run	20%	24	167	14.4%	-0.50
3rd Run	18%	22	181	12.2%	-0.49
4th+ Run	51%	62	268	23.1%	-0.10

ANALYSIS BY POSITION LAST TIME

Pos LT	Prop	Win	Runs	Wins%	£
Won	0%	0	0	0.0%	0.00
2nd or 3rd	50%	61	204	29.9%	-0.14
Unplaced	38%	46	410	11.2%	-0.41
Not Compl	12%	14	117	12.0%	0.15

OTHER FACTORS (WINS-RUNS, £)

Beaten Favourite:	22-49	£0.11
BHA Top Rated:	33-89	-£0.05
Up in class:	16-130	-£0.53
Same class:	63-354	-£0.38
Down in class:	29-132	£0.03
Colts and Geldings:	80-428	-£0.22
Fillies:	26-212	-£0.29
Absolute Favourites:	60-115	£0.02

TRAINERS (WINS-RUNS, £)

M A Jarvis 10-16 £1.25; Mrs A J Perrett 4-11 £0.86; M P Tregoning 5-15 £0.48; J H M Gosden 5-21 £0.28; B W Hills 8-27 £0.13; L M Cumani 2-11 £0.02.

Race Profiles

3-Y.O Races: Maiden Races – 8 to 14 runners

ANALYSIS BY BHA RATING

Rating	Prop	Win	Runs	Wins%	£
120..139	0%	0	0	0.0%	0.00
110..119	0%	0	0	0.0%	0.00
100..109	0%	2	6	33.3%	-0.23
90..99	1%	6	18	33.3%	-0.30
70..89	22%	97	485	20.0%	-0.16
50..69	5%	24	306	7.8%	-0.16
..49	1%	3	148	2.0%	-0.09
Unrated	70%	310	3801	8.2%	-0.33

ANALYSIS BY WEIGHT CARRIED

Weight	Prop	Win	Runs	Wins%	£
10-01+	0%	0	0	0.0%	0.00
9-8..10-00	0%	0	0	0.0%	0.00
9-0..9-07	78%	343	3167	10.8%	-0.29
8-8..8-13	21%	91	1442	6.3%	-0.36
8-0..8-07	2%	8	157	5.1%	0.08
..7-13	0%	0	0	0.0%	0.00

ANALYSIS BY DAYS SINCE LAST RUN

Days	Prop	Win	Runs	Wins%	£
1..7	1%	5	135	3.7%	0.36
8..14	17%	77	606	12.7%	-0.06
15..28	22%	97	1041	9.3%	-0.42
29..60	11%	50	489	10.2%	-0.32
61..100	1%	6	121	5.0%	-0.72
101+	33%	144	1240	11.6%	-0.29
Unraced	14%	63	1134	5.6%	-0.34

ANALYSIS BY TODAY'S STARTING PRICE

Price	Prop	Win	Runs	Wins%	£
Odds On	14%	64	118	54.2%	-0.10
Ev-2/1	22%	99	247	40.1%	-0.01
9/4-4/1	27%	119	512	23.2%	-0.05
9/2-6/1	10%	42	356	11.8%	-0.29
13/2-10/1	12%	53	588	9.0%	-0.18
11/1-16/1	8%	34	683	5.0%	-0.25
18/1-33/1	5%	21	873	2.4%	-0.34
40/1+	2%	10	1389	0.7%	-0.51

ANALYSIS BY STARTING PRICE LAST TIME

Price	Prop	Win	Runs	Wins%	£
Odds On	3%	14	57	24.6%	-0.15
Ev-2/1	10%	45	161	28.0%	-0.08
9/4-4/1	14%	60	383	15.7%	-0.23
9/2-6/1	12%	53	269	19.7%	-0.10
13/2-10/1	16%	70	489	14.3%	-0.14
11/1-16/1	12%	53	582	9.1%	-0.33
18/1-33/1	10%	45	776	5.8%	-0.59
40/1+	9%	39	915	4.3%	-0.19
Unraced	14%	63	1134	5.6%	-0.34

ANALYSIS BY DISTANCE BEATEN LAST TIME

Lengths	Prop	Win	Runs	Wins%	£
..-10	0%	0	0	0.0%	0.00
-10..0	0%	1	1	100.0%	3.00
0.1..2	24%	107	475	22.5%	-0.26
2.1..5	28%	122	647	18.9%	-0.12
5.1..10	21%	94	951	9.9%	-0.28
10.1..20	10%	43	989	4.3%	-0.46
20.0..30	2%	7	325	2.2%	-0.30
30.1+	1%	5	244	2.0%	-0.06
Not Compl	0%	0	0	0.0%	0.00
Unraced	14%	63	1134	5.6%	-0.34

ANALYSIS BY RUN NUMBER

Run No	Prop	Win	Runs	Wins%	£
FTO	14%	63	1134	5.6%	-0.34
2nd Run	31%	137	1362	10.1%	-0.24
3rd Run	24%	108	1280	8.4%	-0.42
4th+ Run	30%	134	990	13.5%	-0.17

ANALYSIS BY POSITION LAST TIME

Pos LT	Prop	Win	Runs	Wins%	£
Won	0%	0	0	0.0%	0.00
2nd or 3rd	41%	182	830	21.9%	-0.21
Unplaced	45%	197	2797	7.0%	-0.30
Not Compl	14%	63	1139	5.5%	-0.35

OTHER FACTORS (WINS-RUNS, £)

Distance Winner:	0-1	-£1.00
Beaten Favourite:	65-262	-£0.16
BHA Top Rated:	71-317	-£0.23
Up in class:	43-679	-£0.45
Same class:	214-2180	-£0.26
Down in class:	122-773	-£0.21
Colts and Geldings:	280-2582	-£0.28
Fillies:	68-1167	-£0.40
Absolute Favourites:	170-414	-£0.05

TRAINERS (WINS-RUNS, £)

G L Moore 1-17 £4.94; R M Beckett 3-35 £2.03; H R A Cecil 19-98 £0.66; T D Barron 6-20 £3.24; W M Brisbourne 1-13 £4.15; D W Barker 2-15 £2.62; P W Chapple-Hyam 16-68 £0.54; M G Quinlan 1-10 £2.40; M L W Bell 5-51 £0.39; M A Jarvis 25-118 £0.14; C R Egerton 2-10 £1.36; M Dods 4-34 £0.36; M H Tompkins 1-39 £0.31; G A Huffer 3-13 £0.91; J A R Toller 2-22 £0.36; D Nicholls 2-29 £0.27; P J Makin 3-16 £0.47; Saeed Bin Suroor 12-34 £0.19; Rae Guest 2-14 £0.39; W J Knight 2-14 £0.36.

Maiden Races

3-Y.O Races: Maiden Races – 15 runners or more

ANALYSIS BY BHA RATING

Rating	Prop	Win	Runs	Wins%	£
120..139	0%	0	0	0.0%	0.00
110..119	0%	0	0	0.0%	0.00
100..109	0%	0	0	0.0%	0.00
90..99	3%	2	4	50.0%	0.16
70..89	22%	16	87	18.4%	-0.02
50..69	3%	2	67	3.0%	-0.79
..49	0%	0	22	0.0%	-1.00
Unrated	73%	53	993	5.3%	-0.48

ANALYSIS BY WEIGHT CARRIED

Weight	Prop	Win	Runs	Wins%	£
10-01+	0%	0	0	0.0%	0.00
9-8..10-00	0%	0	0	0.0%	0.00
9-0..9-07	78%	57	738	7.7%	-0.33
8-8..8-13	21%	15	392	3.8%	-0.70
8-0..8-07	1%	1	43	2.3%	-0.85
..7-13	0%	0	0	0.0%	0.00

ANALYSIS BY DAYS SINCE LAST RUN

Days	Prop	Win	Runs	Wins%	£
1..7	3%	2	32	6.3%	0.16
8..14	10%	7	131	5.3%	-0.79
15..28	26%	19	225	8.4%	-0.11
29..60	7%	5	93	5.4%	-0.77
61..100	1%	1	30	3.3%	-0.73
101+	40%	29	301	9.6%	-0.26
Unraced	14%	10	361	2.8%	-0.72

ANALYSIS BY TODAY'S STARTING PRICE

Price	Prop	Win	Runs	Wins%	£
Odds On	10%	7	15	46.7%	-0.18
Ev-2/1	23%	17	32	53.1%	0.37
9/4-4/1	22%	16	80	20.0%	-0.22
9/2-6/1	18%	13	69	18.8%	0.15
13/2-10/1	12%	9	112	8.0%	-0.27
11/1-16/1	4%	3	155	1.9%	-0.70
18/1-33/1	10%	7	249	2.8%	-0.23
40/1+	1%	1	461	0.2%	-0.78

ANALYSIS BY STARTING PRICE LAST TIME

Price	Prop	Win	Runs	Wins%	£
Odds On	4%	3	13	23.1%	0.10
Ev-2/1	8%	6	31	19.4%	-0.38
9/4-4/1	18%	13	74	17.6%	-0.22
9/2-6/1	14%	10	60	16.7%	-0.47
13/2-10/1	10%	7	106	6.6%	-0.20
11/1-16/1	15%	11	139	7.9%	-0.43
18/1-33/1	12%	9	169	5.3%	0.09
40/1+	5%	4	220	1.8%	-0.79
Unraced	14%	10	361	2.8%	-0.72

ANALYSIS BY DISTANCE BEATEN LAST TIME

Lengths	Prop	Win	Runs	Wins%	£
..-10	0%	0	0	0.0%	0.00
-10..0	0%	0	0	0.0%	0.00
0.1..2	30%	22	100	22.0%	0.07
2.1..5	30%	22	141	15.6%	-0.10
5.1..10	19%	14	196	7.1%	-0.45
10.1..20	3%	2	264	0.8%	-0.97
20.0..30	1%	1	63	1.6%	-0.46
30.1+	3%	2	48	4.2%	1.81
Not Compl	0%	0	0	0.0%	0.00
Unraced	14%	10	361	2.8%	-0.72

ANALYSIS BY RUN NUMBER

Run No	Prop	Win	Runs	Wins%	£
FTO	14%	10	361	2.8%	-0.72
2nd Run	32%	23	318	7.2%	-0.14
3rd Run	26%	19	307	6.2%	-0.56
4th+ Run	29%	21	187	11.2%	-0.42

ANALYSIS BY POSITION LAST TIME

Pos LT	Prop	Win	Runs	Wins%	£
Won	0%	0	0	0.0%	0.00
2nd or 3rd	49%	36	175	20.6%	-0.05
Unplaced	37%	27	633	4.3%	-0.44
Not Compl	14%	10	365	2.7%	-0.72

OTHER FACTORS (WINS-RUNS, £)

Beaten Favourite:	9-59	-£0.41
BHA Top Rated:	14-55	-£0.10
Up in class:	6-151	-£0.80
Same class:	39-521	-£0.36
Down in class:	18-140	£0.11
Colts and Geldings:	46-613	-£0.31
Fillies:	9-273	-£0.77
Absolute Favourites:	33-71	£0.33

TRAINERS (WINS-RUNS, £)

C G Cox 3-14 £4.21; D R C Elsworth 3-20 £0.58; G A Butler 3-10 £1.15; H Candy 2-14 £0.68; G Wragg 3-17 £0.47; J Noseda 3-24 £0.11; J H M Gosden 4-38 £0.05; H R A Cecil 2-12 £0.13; Saeed Bin Suroor 4-13 £0.10; M A Jarvis 5-21 £0.05; E A L Dunlop 3-17 £0.06.

Race Profiles

3-Y.O Races: Maiden Races – good or faster going

ANALYSIS BY BHA RATING					
Rating	Prop	Win	Runs	Wins%	£
120..139	0%	0	0	0.0%	0.00
110..119	0%	0	1	0.0%	-1.00
100..109	1%	4	6	66.7%	0.30
90..99	1%	6	18	33.3%	-0.33
70..89	25%	113	529	21.4%	-0.10
50..69	6%	28	328	8.5%	-0.20
..49	1%	3	162	1.9%	-0.17
Unrated	66%	304	3763	8.1%	-0.32

ANALYSIS BY WEIGHT CARRIED					
Weight	Prop	Win	Runs	Wins%	£
10-01+	0%	0	0	0.0%	0.00
9-8..10-00	0%	0	0	0.0%	0.00
9-0..9-07	77%	354	3149	11.2%	-0.23
8-8..8-13	21%	96	1475	6.5%	-0.42
8-0..8-07	2%	8	185	4.3%	-0.06
..7-13	0%	0	0	0.0%	0.00

ANALYSIS BY DAYS SINCE LAST RUN					
Days	Prop	Win	Runs	Wins%	£
1..7	2%	10	137	7.3%	0.65
8..14	16%	74	616	12.0%	-0.25
15..28	24%	112	1080	10.4%	-0.36
29..60	12%	53	508	10.4%	-0.34
61..100	1%	6	126	4.8%	-0.76
101+	32%	147	1213	12.1%	-0.19
Unraced	12%	56	1129	5.0%	-0.37

ANALYSIS BY TODAY'S STARTING PRICE					
Price	Prop	Win	Runs	Wins%	£
Odds On	18%	81	143	56.6%	-0.08
Ev-2/1	22%	102	259	39.4%	-0.02
9/4-4/1	25%	114	505	22.6%	-0.08
9/2-6/1	10%	44	334	13.2%	-0.20
13/2-10/1	11%	49	574	8.5%	-0.22
11/1-16/1	7%	34	657	5.2%	-0.21
18/1-33/1	5%	23	916	2.5%	-0.31
40/1+	2%	11	1421	0.8%	-0.49

ANALYSIS BY STARTING PRICE LAST TIME					
Price	Prop	Win	Runs	Wins%	£
Odds On	3%	13	54	24.1%	-0.40
Ev-2/1	10%	44	171	25.7%	-0.20
9/4-4/1	18%	82	408	20.1%	-0.06
9/2-6/1	11%	51	264	19.3%	-0.32
13/2-10/1	15%	69	505	13.7%	-0.14
11/1-16/1	12%	54	608	8.9%	-0.28
18/1-33/1	11%	49	773	6.3%	-0.40
40/1+	9%	40	897	4.5%	-0.26
Unraced	12%	56	1129	5.0%	-0.37

ANALYSIS BY DISTANCE BEATEN LAST TIME					
Lengths	Prop	Win	Runs	Wins%	£
..-10	0%	0	0	0.0%	0.00
-10..0	0%	1	1	100.0%	3.00
0.1..2	27%	123	517	23.8%	-0.22
2.1..5	27%	123	655	18.8%	-0.12
5.1..10	19%	89	937	9.5%	-0.32
10.1..20	10%	48	1011	4.7%	-0.45
20.0..30	2%	9	332	2.7%	-0.44
30.1+	2%	9	227	4.0%	0.64
Not Compl	0%	0	0	0.0%	0.00
Unrated	12%	56	1129	5.0%	-0.37

ANALYSIS BY RUN NUMBER					
Run No	Prop	Win	Runs	Wins%	£
FTO	12%	56	1129	5.0%	-0.37
2nd Run	31%	141	1312	10.7%	-0.14
3rd Run	23%	104	1289	8.1%	-0.46
4th+ Run	34%	157	1079	14.6%	-0.16

ANALYSIS BY POSITION LAST TIME					
Pos LT	Prop	Win	Runs	Wins%	£
Won	0%	0	0	0.0%	0.00
2nd or 3rd	43%	199	870	22.9%	-0.19
Unplaced	44%	202	2801	7.2%	-0.28
Not Compl	12%	57	1138	5.0%	-0.37

OTHER FACTORS (WINS-RUNS, £)
Distance Winner:	0-1	-£1.00
Beaten Favourite:	69-273	-£0.20
BHA Top Rated:	80-329	-£0.19
Up in class:	46-691	-£0.48
Same class:	219-2197	-£0.28
Down in class:	137-792	£0.00
Colts and Geldings:	286-2531	-£0.20
Fillies:	75-1198	-£0.49
Absolute Favourites:	194-436	£0.01

TRAINERS (WINS-RUNS, £)

J L Spearing 2-12 £11.70; P J Makin 5-23 £4.80; C G Cox 5-44 £1.77; G L Moore 1-24 £3.21; H R A Cecil 19-96 £0.58; W M Brisbourne 1-13 £4.15; T D Barron 4-13 £4.03; P W Chapple-Hyam 13-59 £0.72; D W Barker 2-14 £2.88; M Botti 2-13 £2.92; P D Evans 2-13 £1.96; G A Butler 4-32 £0.58; M H Tompkins 2-38 £0.49; H Candy 4-34 £0.43; P A Blockley 1-21 £0.62; G A Huffer 2-10 £1.20; W J Haggas 13-64 £0.14; M G Quinlan 3-14 £0.55; A King 2-16 £0.47; J A R Toller 3-26 £0.24.

Maiden Races

3-Y.O Races: Maiden Races – good to soft or softer going

ANALYSIS BY BHA RATING

Rating	Prop	Win	Runs	Wins%	£
120..139	0%	0	0	0.0%	0.00
110..119	0%	0	0	0.0%	0.00
100..109	1%	2	5	40.0%	-0.43
90..99	2%	3	8	37.5%	-0.18
70..89	24%	42	181	23.2%	-0.22
50..69	6%	11	123	8.9%	-0.18
..49	1%	1	42	2.4%	-0.83
Unrated	67%	119	1502	7.9%	-0.46

ANALYSIS BY WEIGHT CARRIED

Weight	Prop	Win	Runs	Wins%	£
10-01+	0%	0	0	0.0%	0.00
9-8..10-00	0%	0	0	0.0%	0.00
9-0..9-07	75%	134	1222	11.0%	-0.43
8-8..8-13	23%	41	586	7.0%	-0.37
8-0..8-07	2%	3	53	5.7%	-0.75
..7-13	0%	0	0	0.0%	0.00

ANALYSIS BY DAYS SINCE LAST RUN

Days	Prop	Win	Runs	Wins%	£
1..7	3%	6	54	11.1%	-0.33
8..14	20%	35	231	15.2%	0.05
15..28	20%	36	392	9.2%	-0.47
29..60	10%	18	167	10.8%	-0.52
61..100	2%	4	54	7.4%	-0.48
101+	28%	49	482	10.2%	-0.56
Unraced	17%	30	481	6.2%	-0.44

ANALYSIS BY TODAY'S STARTING PRICE

Price	Prop	Win	Runs	Wins%	£
Odds On	14%	25	45	55.6%	-0.09
Ev-2/1	23%	41	101	40.6%	0.01
9/4-4/1	29%	51	212	24.1%	-0.01
9/2-6/1	12%	22	156	14.1%	-0.14
13/2-10/1	15%	26	229	11.4%	0.03
11/1-16/1	3%	6	267	2.2%	-0.68
18/1-33/1	3%	6	320	1.9%	-0.48
40/1+	1%	1	531	0.2%	-0.81

ANALYSIS BY STARTING PRICE LAST TIME

Price	Prop	Win	Runs	Wins%	£
Odds On	4%	7	25	28.0%	0.38
Ev-2/1	11%	20	55	36.4%	0.17
9/4-4/1	12%	21	135	15.6%	-0.51
9/2-6/1	13%	23	125	18.4%	0.00
13/2-10/1	12%	22	172	12.8%	-0.34
11/1-16/1	15%	27	210	12.9%	-0.45
18/1-33/1	9%	16	277	5.8%	-0.67
40/1+	7%	12	381	3.1%	-0.49
Unraced	17%	30	481	6.2%	-0.44

ANALYSIS BY DISTANCE BEATEN LAST TIME

Lengths	Prop	Win	Runs	Wins%	£
..-10	0%	0	0	0.0%	0.00
-10..0	0%	0	0	0.0%	0.00
0.1..2	26%	46	178	25.8%	-0.07
2.1..5	25%	44	241	18.3%	-0.20
5.1..10	24%	42	348	12.1%	-0.25
10.1..20	7%	12	392	3.1%	-0.84
20.0..30	2%	4	119	3.4%	0.04
30.1+	0%	0	102	0.0%	-1.00
Not Compl	0%	0	0	0.0%	0.00
Unraced	17%	30	481	6.2%	-0.44

ANALYSIS BY RUN NUMBER

Run No	Prop	Win	Runs	Wins%	£
FTO	17%	30	481	6.2%	-0.44
2nd Run	24%	43	535	8.0%	-0.50
3rd Run	25%	45	479	9.4%	-0.43
4th+ Run	34%	60	366	16.4%	-0.28

ANALYSIS BY POSITION LAST TIME

Pos LT	Prop	Win	Runs	Wins%	£
Won	0%	0	0	0.0%	0.00
2nd or 3rd	45%	80	339	23.6%	-0.14
Unplaced	38%	68	1039	6.5%	-0.51
Not Compl	17%	30	483	6.2%	-0.44

OTHER FACTORS (WINS-RUNS, £)

Beaten Favourite:	27-97	-£0.04
BHA Top Rated:	38-132	-£0.16
Up in class:	19-269	-£0.61
Same class:	97-858	-£0.30
Down in class:	32-253	-£0.59
Colts and Geldings:	120-1092	-£0.45
Fillies:	28-454	-£0.34
Absolute Favourites:	69-164	£0.00

TRAINERS (WINS-RUNS, £)

R M Beckett 1-10 £9.10; M A Jarvis 18-45 £1.07; D Nicholls 1-10 £2.40; J Noseda 5-20 £0.91; M L W Bell 2-24 £0.49; T D Barron 2-11 £0.76; Saeed Bin Suroor 6-16 £0.44; J H M Gosden 14-72 £0.08; H R A Cecil 6-32 £0.17; L M Cumani 5-21 £0.25; G Wragg 4-22 £0.23; W Jarvis 3-19 £0.13; M Dods 2-10 £0.23.

Race Profiles

3-Y.O Races: Maiden Races – 5 to 6 furlong races

ANALYSIS BY BHA RATING

Rating	Prop	Win	Runs	Wins%	£
120..139	0%	0	0	0.0%	0.00
110..119	0%	0	0	0.0%	0.00
100..109	0%	0	0	0.0%	0.00
90..99	2%	2	3	66.7%	0.88
70..89	23%	19	92	20.7%	-0.14
50..69	12%	10	126	7.9%	-0.56
..49	5%	4	57	7.0%	1.49
Unrated	57%	46	544	8.5%	-0.15

ANALYSIS BY WEIGHT CARRIED

Weight	Prop	Win	Runs	Wins%	£
10-01+	0%	0	0	0.0%	0.00
9-8..10-00	0%	0	0	0.0%	0.00
9-0..9-07	69%	56	469	11.9%	-0.01
8-8..8-13	26%	21	298	7.0%	-0.28
8-0..8-07	5%	4	55	7.3%	0.17
..7-13	0%	0	0	0.0%	0.00

ANALYSIS BY DAYS SINCE LAST RUN

Days	Prop	Win	Runs	Wins%	£
1..7	6%	5	45	11.1%	1.66
8..14	23%	19	127	15.0%	-0.11
15..28	19%	15	175	8.6%	0.32
29..60	10%	8	74	10.8%	-0.47
61..100	1%	1	28	3.6%	-0.85
101+	30%	24	228	10.5%	-0.38
Unraced	11%	9	145	6.2%	-0.32

ANALYSIS BY TODAY'S STARTING PRICE

Price	Prop	Win	Runs	Wins%	£
Odds On	12%	10	26	38.5%	-0.35
Ev-2/1	17%	14	42	33.3%	-0.17
9/4-4/1	33%	27	97	27.8%	0.19
9/2-6/1	9%	7	53	13.2%	-0.19
13/2-10/1	15%	12	115	10.4%	-0.03
11/1-16/1	5%	4	113	3.5%	-0.50
18/1-33/1	4%	3	146	2.1%	-0.50
40/1+	5%	4	230	1.7%	0.28

ANALYSIS BY STARTING PRICE LAST TIME

Price	Prop	Win	Runs	Wins%	£
Odds On	1%	1	9	11.1%	-0.71
Ev-2/1	11%	9	31	29.0%	-0.07
9/4-4/1	12%	10	78	12.8%	-0.61
9/2-6/1	15%	12	51	23.5%	0.09
13/2-10/1	14%	11	87	12.6%	-0.07
11/1-16/1	9%	7	99	7.1%	-0.62
18/1-33/1	14%	11	137	8.0%	0.26
40/1+	14%	11	185	5.9%	0.29
Unraced	11%	9	145	6.2%	-0.32

ANALYSIS BY DISTANCE BEATEN LAST TIME

Lengths	Prop	Win	Runs	Wins%	£
..-10	0%	0	0	0.0%	0.00
-10..0	0%	0	0	0.0%	0.00
0.1..2	23%	19	87	21.8%	-0.21
2.1..5	23%	19	116	16.4%	-0.18
5.1..10	21%	17	190	8.9%	-0.51
10.1..20	16%	13	193	6.7%	-0.08
20.0..30	2%	2	59	3.4%	-0.85
30.1+	2%	2	32	6.3%	5.31
Not Compl	0%	0	0	0.0%	0.00
Unraced	11%	9	145	6.2%	-0.32

ANALYSIS BY RUN NUMBER

Run No	Prop	Win	Runs	Wins%	£
FTO	11%	9	145	6.2%	-0.32
2nd Run	25%	20	171	11.7%	0.52
3rd Run	21%	17	222	7.7%	-0.53
4th+ Run	43%	35	284	12.3%	-0.01

ANALYSIS BY POSITION LAST TIME

Pos LT	Prop	Win	Runs	Wins%	£
Won	0%	0	0	0.0%	0.00
2nd or 3rd	35%	28	146	19.2%	-0.27
Unplaced	54%	44	530	8.3%	0.02
Not Compl	11%	9	146	6.2%	-0.32

OTHER FACTORS (WINS-RUNS, £)

Beaten Favourite:	14-59	-£0.24
BHA Top Rated:	15-68	-£0.13
Up in class:	9-130	£0.06
Same class:	40-400	-£0.17
Down in class:	23-147	£0.21
Colts and Geldings:	51-422	£0.00
Fillies:	17-271	-£0.62
Absolute Favourites:	26-77	-£0.21

TRAINERS (WINS-RUNS, £)

P J Makin 2-10 £9.55; R A Fahey 2-11 £0.41; M Dods 1-13 £0.31; T D Barron 3-13 £0.26; L M Cumani 2-10 £0.26; E S McMahon 2-10 £0.20.

Maiden Races

3-Y.O Races: Maiden Races – 7 to 9 furlong races

ANALYSIS BY BHA RATING

Rating	Prop	Win	Runs	Wins%	£
120..139	0%	0	0	0.0%	0.00
110..119	0%	0	0	0.0%	0.00
100..109	0%	1	4	25.0%	-0.74
90..99	1%	2	11	18.2%	-0.50
70..89	25%	80	358	22.3%	-0.13
50..69	6%	19	220	8.6%	-0.09
..49	0%	0	105	0.0%	-1.00
Unrated	68%	221	2828	7.8%	-0.39

ANALYSIS BY WEIGHT CARRIED

Weight	Prop	Win	Runs	Wins%	£
10-01+	0%	0	0	0.0%	0.00
9-8..10-00	0%	0	0	0.0%	0.00
9-0..9-07	76%	247	2269	10.9%	-0.35
8-8..8-13	21%	69	1132	6.1%	-0.43
8-0..8-07	2%	7	127	5.5%	-0.04
..7-13	0%	0	0	0.0%	0.00

ANALYSIS BY DAYS SINCE LAST RUN

Days	Prop	Win	Runs	Wins%	£
1..7	2%	7	92	7.6%	-0.64
8..14	15%	50	410	12.2%	-0.21
15..28	23%	73	757	9.6%	-0.49
29..60	12%	38	369	10.3%	-0.27
61..100	1%	4	94	4.3%	-0.75
101+	33%	106	889	11.9%	-0.32
Unraced	14%	45	917	4.9%	-0.35

ANALYSIS BY TODAY'S STARTING PRICE

Price	Prop	Win	Runs	Wins%	£
Odds On	16%	52	93	55.9%	-0.09
Ev-2/1	24%	76	192	39.6%	-0.02
9/4-4/1	26%	83	337	24.6%	-0.02
9/2-6/1	9%	29	257	11.3%	-0.32
13/2-10/1	13%	41	415	9.9%	-0.09
11/1-16/1	7%	24	491	4.9%	-0.26
18/1-33/1	4%	12	682	1.8%	-0.47
40/1+	2%	6	1061	0.6%	-0.66

ANALYSIS BY STARTING PRICE LAST TIME

Price	Prop	Win	Runs	Wins%	£
Odds On	4%	13	46	28.3%	-0.18
Ev-2/1	10%	32	121	26.4%	-0.19
9/4-4/1	17%	55	283	19.4%	-0.11
9/2-6/1	12%	40	199	20.1%	-0.27
13/2-10/1	12%	39	342	11.4%	-0.34
11/1-16/1	12%	40	402	10.0%	-0.32
18/1-33/1	11%	36	566	6.4%	-0.57
40/1+	7%	23	652	3.5%	-0.43
Unraced	14%	45	917	4.9%	-0.35

ANALYSIS BY DISTANCE BEATEN LAST TIME

Lengths	Prop	Win	Runs	Wins%	£
..-10	0%	0	0	0.0%	0.00
-10..0	0%	1	1	100.0%	3.00
0.1..2	27%	86	337	25.5%	-0.20
2.1..5	31%	100	490	20.4%	-0.05
5.1..10	17%	54	671	8.0%	-0.50
10.1..20	8%	27	739	3.7%	-0.69
20.0..30	2%	7	210	3.3%	0.09
30.1+	1%	3	163	1.8%	-0.31
Not Compl	0%	0	0	0.0%	0.00
Unraced	14%	45	917	4.9%	-0.35

ANALYSIS BY RUN NUMBER

Run No	Prop	Win	Runs	Wins%	£
FTO	14%	45	917	4.9%	-0.35
2nd Run	29%	95	972	9.8%	-0.25
3rd Run	24%	79	926	8.5%	-0.58
4th+ Run	32%	104	713	14.6%	-0.26

ANALYSIS BY POSITION LAST TIME

Pos LT	Prop	Win	Runs	Wins%	£
Won	0%	0	0	0.0%	0.00
2nd or 3rd	48%	154	602	25.6%	-0.11
Unplaced	38%	124	2004	6.2%	-0.45
Not Compl	14%	45	922	4.9%	-0.35

OTHER FACTORS (WINS-RUNS, £)

Distance Winner:	0-1	-£1.00
Beaten Favourite:	49-196	-£0.17
BHA Top Rated:	55-227	-£0.23
Up in class:	29-480	-£0.63
Same class:	171-1623	-£0.32
Down in class:	78-508	-£0.30
Colts and Geldings:	195-1770	-£0.34
Fillies:	50-856	-£0.37
Absolute Favourites:	133-304	£0.02

TRAINERS (WINS-RUNS, £)

R M Beckett 2-35 £1.95; T D Barron 3-11 £5.22; D W Barker 2-12 £3.52; M A Jarvis 20-63 £0.64; M L W Bell 3-35 £0.71; H R A Cecil 9-46 £0.54; C G Cox 3-32 £0.47; W J Haggas 14-59 £0.24; J A R Toller 2-16 £0.88; C R Egerton 2-13 £0.82; P J Makin 3-18 £0.56; W J Knight 2-10 £0.91; D Nicholls 2-28 £0.32; P W Chapple-Hyam 9-42 £0.18; E A L Dunlop 7-50 £0.14; J A Osborne 2-15 £0.27; Mrs A Duffield 3-14 £0.09; I Semple 1-10 £0.10.

Race Profiles

3-Y.O Races: Maiden Races – 10 to 14 furlong races

ANALYSIS BY BHA RATING

Rating	Prop	Win	Runs	Wins%	£
120..139	0%	0	0	0.0%	0.00
110..119	0%	0	1	0.0%	-1.00
100..109	2%	5	7	71.4%	0.37
90..99	2%	5	12	41.7%	-0.37
70..89	24%	56	260	21.5%	-0.12
50..69	4%	10	105	9.5%	0.01
..49	0%	0	42	0.0%	-1.00
Unrated	67%	156	1893	8.2%	-0.38

ANALYSIS BY WEIGHT CARRIED

Weight	Prop	Win	Runs	Wins%	£
10-01+	0%	0	0	0.0%	0.00
9-8..10-00	0%	0	0	0.0%	0.00
9-0..9-07	80%	185	1633	11.3%	-0.28
8-8..8-13	20%	47	631	7.4%	-0.42
8-0..8-07	0%	0	56	0.0%	-1.00
..7-13	0%	0	0	0.0%	0.00

ANALYSIS BY DAYS SINCE LAST RUN

Days	Prop	Win	Runs	Wins%	£
1..7	2%	4	54	7.4%	1.02
8..14	17%	40	310	12.9%	-0.14
15..28	26%	60	540	11.1%	-0.48
29..60	11%	25	232	10.8%	-0.53
61..100	2%	5	58	8.6%	-0.47
101+	28%	66	578	11.4%	-0.22
Unraced	14%	32	548	5.8%	-0.48

ANALYSIS BY TODAY'S STARTING PRICE

Price	Prop	Win	Runs	Wins%	£
Odds On	19%	44	69	63.8%	0.02
Ev-2/1	23%	53	126	42.1%	0.05
9/4-4/1	24%	55	283	19.4%	-0.19
9/2-6/1	13%	30	180	16.7%	0.02
13/2-10/1	9%	22	273	8.1%	-0.29
11/1-16/1	5%	12	320	3.8%	-0.41
18/1-33/1	6%	14	408	3.4%	-0.10
40/1+	1%	2	661	0.3%	-0.75

ANALYSIS BY STARTING PRICE LAST TIME

Price	Prop	Win	Runs	Wins%	£
Odds On	3%	6	24	25.0%	0.11
Ev-2/1	10%	23	74	31.1%	-0.01
9/4-4/1	16%	38	182	20.9%	-0.08
9/2-6/1	9%	22	139	15.8%	-0.25
13/2-10/1	18%	41	248	16.5%	-0.03
11/1-16/1	15%	34	317	10.7%	-0.23
18/1-33/1	8%	18	347	5.2%	-0.60
40/1+	8%	18	441	4.1%	-0.43
Unraced	14%	32	548	5.8%	-0.48

ANALYSIS BY DISTANCE BEATEN LAST TIME

Lengths	Prop	Win	Runs	Wins%	£
..-10	0%	0	0	0.0%	0.00
-10..0	0%	0	0	0.0%	0.00
0.1..2	28%	64	271	23.6%	-0.14
2.1..5	21%	48	290	16.6%	-0.28
5.1..10	26%	60	424	14.2%	0.09
10.1..20	9%	20	471	4.2%	-0.55
20.0..30	2%	4	182	2.2%	-0.60
30.1+	2%	4	134	3.0%	-0.56
Not Compl	0%	0	0	0.0%	0.00
Unraced	14%	32	548	5.8%	-0.48

ANALYSIS BY RUN NUMBER

Run No	Prop	Win	Runs	Wins%	£
FTO	14%	32	548	5.8%	-0.48
2nd Run	30%	69	704	9.8%	-0.42
3rd Run	23%	53	620	8.5%	-0.23
4th+ Run	34%	78	448	17.4%	-0.19

ANALYSIS BY POSITION LAST TIME

Pos LT	Prop	Win	Runs	Wins%	£
Won	0%	0	0	0.0%	0.00
2nd or 3rd	42%	97	461	21.0%	-0.23
Unplaced	44%	102	1306	7.8%	-0.32
Not Compl	14%	33	553	6.0%	-0.48

OTHER FACTORS (WINS-RUNS, £)

Beaten Favourite:	33-115	-£0.10
BHA Top Rated:	48-166	-£0.14
Up in class:	27-350	-£0.58
Same class:	105-1032	-£0.29
Down in class:	68-390	-£0.06
Colts and Geldings:	160-1431	-£0.29
Fillies:	36-525	-£0.49
Absolute Favourites:	104-219	£0.08

TRAINERS (WINS-RUNS, £)

G L Moore 1-12 £7.42; H R A Cecil 16-80 £0.48; D R C Elsworth 8-40 £0.77; P W Chapple-Hyam 8-38 £0.70; G A Butler 2-16 £1.38; P D Evans 1-12 £1.83; C G Cox 2-18 £1.11; B J Meehan 4-55 £0.34; J H M Gosden 18-97 £0.17; A King 4-18 £0.71; H Candy 2-20 £0.26; Saeed Bin Suroor 11-29 £0.09; M A Jarvis 19-87 £0.00.

Claiming Races

3-Y.O Races: Claiming Races

ANALYSIS BY BHA RATING

Rating	Prop	Win	Runs	Wins%	£
120..139	0%	0	0	0.0%	0.00
110..119	0%	0	0	0.0%	0.00
100..109	0%	0	0	0.0%	0.00
90..99	3%	3	3	100.0%	1.22
70..89	19%	21	150	14.0%	-0.43
50..69	64%	72	544	13.2%	-0.16
..49	11%	12	313	3.8%	-0.49
Unrated	4%	5	96	5.2%	-0.44

ANALYSIS BY WEIGHT CARRIED

Weight	Prop	Win	Runs	Wins%	£
10-01+	0%	0	0	0.0%	0.00
9-8..10-00	3%	3	20	15.0%	-0.53
9-0..9-07	27%	30	223	13.5%	-0.21
8-8..8-13	32%	36	325	11.1%	-0.37
8-0..8-07	32%	36	443	8.1%	-0.32
..7-13	7%	8	96	8.3%	-0.26

ANALYSIS BY DAYS SINCE LAST RUN

Days	Prop	Win	Runs	Wins%	£
1..7	12%	14	115	12.2%	-0.33
8..14	33%	37	282	13.1%	-0.14
15..28	37%	42	380	11.1%	-0.28
29..60	7%	8	183	4.4%	-0.69
61..100	4%	4	46	8.7%	-0.16
101+	4%	5	82	6.1%	-0.54
Unraced	3%	3	19	15.8%	1.03

ANALYSIS BY TODAY'S STARTING PRICE

Price	Prop	Win	Runs	Wins%	£
Odds On	7%	8	15	53.3%	-0.08
Ev-2/1	21%	24	59	40.7%	0.04
9/4-4/1	26%	29	163	17.8%	-0.24
9/2-6/1	12%	14	100	14.0%	-0.13
13/2-10/1	19%	22	170	12.9%	0.15
11/1-16/1	10%	11	183	6.0%	-0.07
18/1-33/1	4%	5	216	2.3%	-0.48
40/1+	0%	0	201	0.0%	-1.00

ANALYSIS BY STARTING PRICE LAST TIME

Price	Prop	Win	Runs	Wins%	£
Odds On	1%	1	6	16.7%	-0.17
Ev-2/1	6%	7	27	25.9%	-0.16
9/4-4/1	16%	18	100	18.0%	-0.23
9/2-6/1	16%	18	91	19.8%	0.38
13/2-10/1	20%	23	179	12.8%	-0.13
11/1-16/1	18%	20	213	9.4%	-0.42
18/1-33/1	19%	21	273	7.7%	-0.31
40/1+	2%	2	199	1.0%	-0.85
Unraced	3%	3	19	15.8%	1.03

ANALYSIS BY DISTANCE BEATEN LAST TIME

Lengths	Prop	Win	Runs	Wins%	£
..-10	0%	0	0	0.0%	0.00
-10..0	6%	7	40	17.5%	-0.31
0.1..2	9%	10	79	12.7%	-0.38
2.1..5	22%	25	168	14.9%	-0.36
5.1..10	27%	30	270	11.1%	-0.15
10.1..20	19%	21	315	6.7%	-0.56
20.0..30	10%	11	108	10.2%	0.06
30.1+	5%	6	108	5.6%	-0.46
Not Compl	0%	0	0	0.0%	0.00
Unraced	3%	3	19	15.8%	1.03

ANALYSIS BY RUN NUMBER

Run No	Prop	Win	Runs	Wins%	£
FTO	3%	3	19	15.8%	1.03
2nd Run	1%	1	32	3.1%	-0.69
3rd Run	1%	1	40	2.5%	-0.73
4th+ Run	96%	108	1016	10.6%	-0.31

ANALYSIS BY POSITION LAST TIME

Pos LT	Prop	Win	Runs	Wins%	£
Won	6%	7	41	17.1%	-0.33
2nd or 3rd	19%	21	152	13.8%	-0.32
Unplaced	73%	82	890	9.2%	-0.33
Not Compl	3%	3	24	12.5%	0.60

OTHER FACTORS (WINS-RUNS, £)

Course Winner:	7-34	-£0.13
Distance Winner:	31-178	-£0.13
Going Winner:	14-80	£0.04
Beaten Favourite:	14-54	£0.06
BHA Top Rated:	31-108	£0.19
Up in class:	28-320	-£0.37
Same class:	46-500	-£0.39
Down in class:	36-268	-£0.18
7-Day Winners:	1-5	-£0.56
Colts and Geldings:	66-641	-£0.35
Fillies:	47-466	-£0.25
Absolute Favourites:	36-107	£0.13

TRAINERS (WINS-RUNS, £)

I A Wood 3-13 £2.04; B R Millman 1-11 £1.64; P D Evans 5-19 £0.87; P T Midgley 2-10 £1.50; M R Channon 4-16 £0.72; P F I Cole 2-16 £0.50; A Berry 2-23 £0.04.

Race Profiles

3-Y.O Races: Claiming Races – 2 to 7 runners

ANALYSIS BY BHA RATING

Rating	Prop	Win	Runs	Wins%	£
120..139	0%	0	0	0.0%	0.00
110..119	0%	0	0	0.0%	0.00
100..109	0%	0	0	0.0%	0.00
90..99	8%	2	2	100.0%	0.84
70..89	25%	6	28	21.4%	-0.33
50..69	50%	12	75	16.0%	-0.37
..49	13%	3	27	11.1%	0.11
Unrated	4%	1	14	7.1%	-0.81

ANALYSIS BY WEIGHT CARRIED

Weight	Prop	Win	Runs	Wins%	£
10-01+	0%	0	0	0.0%	0.00
9-8..10-00	4%	1	3	33.3%	-0.44
9-0..9-07	33%	8	31	25.8%	-0.34
8-8..8-13	17%	4	36	11.1%	-0.57
8-0..8-07	38%	9	63	14.3%	-0.10
..7-13	8%	2	13	15.4%	-0.38

ANALYSIS BY DAYS SINCE LAST RUN

Days	Prop	Win	Runs	Wins%	£
1..7	13%	3	23	13.0%	-0.59
8..14	33%	8	33	24.2%	0.26
15..28	29%	7	46	15.2%	-0.46
29..60	13%	3	29	10.3%	-0.33
61..100	8%	2	6	33.3%	-0.22
101+	4%	1	9	11.1%	-0.74
Unraced	0%	0	0	0.0%	0.00

ANALYSIS BY TODAY'S STARTING PRICE

Price	Prop	Win	Runs	Wins%	£
Odds On	21%	5	8	62.5%	0.07
Ev-2/1	33%	8	19	42.1%	0.08
9/4-4/1	21%	5	30	16.7%	-0.24
9/2-6/1	17%	4	14	28.6%	0.75
13/2-10/1	4%	1	17	5.9%	-0.47
11/1-16/1	4%	1	24	4.2%	-0.29
18/1-33/1	0%	0	23	0.0%	-1.00
40/1+	0%	0	11	0.0%	-1.00

ANALYSIS BY STARTING PRICE LAST TIME

Price	Prop	Win	Runs	Wins%	£
Odds On	4%	1	3	33.3%	0.67
Ev-2/1	8%	2	5	40.0%	-0.02
9/4-4/1	17%	4	20	20.0%	-0.18
9/2-6/1	17%	4	15	26.7%	0.26
13/2-10/1	21%	5	21	23.8%	0.45
11/1-16/1	13%	3	28	10.7%	-0.62
18/1-33/1	21%	5	35	14.3%	-0.53
40/1+	0%	0	19	0.0%	-1.00
Unraced	0%	0	0	0.0%	0.00

ANALYSIS BY DISTANCE BEATEN LAST TIME

Lengths	Prop	Win	Runs	Wins%	£
..-10	0%	0	0	0.0%	0.00
-10..0	8%	2	8	25.0%	0.07
0.1..2	8%	2	8	25.0%	-0.33
2.1..5	29%	7	29	24.1%	0.01
5.1..10	29%	7	33	21.2%	0.22
10.1..20	8%	2	46	4.3%	-0.83
20.0..30	13%	3	10	30.0%	-0.13
30.1+	4%	1	12	8.3%	-0.80
Not Compl	0%	0	0	0.0%	0.00
Unraced	0%	0	0	0.0%	0.00

ANALYSIS BY RUN NUMBER

Run No	Prop	Win	Runs	Wins%	£
FTO	0%	0	0	0.0%	0.00
2nd Run	0%	0	5	0.0%	-1.00
3rd Run	0%	0	5	0.0%	-1.00
4th+ Run	100%	24	136	17.6%	-0.25

ANALYSIS BY POSITION LAST TIME

Pos LT	Prop	Win	Runs	Wins%	£
Won	8%	2	9	22.2%	-0.05
2nd or 3rd	21%	5	17	29.4%	0.36
Unplaced	71%	17	120	14.2%	-0.41
Not Compl	0%	0	0	0.0%	0.00

OTHER FACTORS (WINS-RUNS, £)

Course Winner:	0-5	-£1.00
Distance Winner:	6-27	-£0.39
Going Winner:	5-17	£0.21
Beaten Favourite:	6-13	£1.14
BHA Top Rated:	8-23	-£0.03
Up in class:	8-45	-£0.18
Same class:	8-64	-£0.33
Down in class:	8-37	-£0.39
7-Day Winners:	0-1	-£1.00
Colts and Geldings:	16-86	-£0.23
Fillies:	8-60	-£0.40
Absolute Favourites:	12-24	£0.13

Claiming Races

3-Y.O Races: Claiming Races – 8 to 14 runners

ANALYSIS BY BHA RATING

Rating	Prop	Win	Runs	Wins%	£
120..139	0%	0	0	0.0%	0.00
110..119	0%	0	0	0.0%	0.00
100..109	0%	0	0	0.0%	0.00
90..99	1%	1	1	100.0%	2.00
70..89	18%	14	97	14.4%	-0.38
50..69	67%	52	377	13.8%	-0.08
..49	10%	8	241	3.3%	-0.55
Unrated	4%	3	70	4.3%	-0.41

ANALYSIS BY WEIGHT CARRIED

Weight	Prop	Win	Runs	Wins%	£
10-01+	0%	0	0	0.0%	0.00
9-8..10-00	3%	2	16	12.5%	-0.52
9-0..9-07	24%	19	162	11.7%	-0.23
8-8..8-13	37%	29	234	12.4%	-0.26
8-0..8-07	29%	23	301	7.6%	-0.30
..7-13	6%	5	74	6.8%	-0.43

ANALYSIS BY DAYS SINCE LAST RUN

Days	Prop	Win	Runs	Wins%	£
1..7	14%	11	77	14.3%	-0.12
8..14	32%	25	211	11.8%	-0.19
15..28	41%	32	269	11.9%	-0.21
29..60	5%	4	121	3.3%	-0.75
61..100	3%	2	35	5.7%	-0.03
101+	1%	1	56	1.8%	-0.90
Unraced	4%	3	18	16.7%	1.14

ANALYSIS BY TODAY'S STARTING PRICE

Price	Prop	Win	Runs	Wins%	£
Odds On	4%	3	7	42.9%	-0.24
Ev-2/1	18%	14	36	38.9%	-0.02
9/4-4/1	29%	23	123	18.7%	-0.22
9/2-6/1	9%	7	73	9.6%	-0.43
13/2-10/1	24%	19	126	15.1%	0.34
11/1-16/1	10%	8	125	6.4%	-0.04
18/1-33/1	5%	4	155	2.6%	-0.41
40/1+	0%	0	142	0.0%	-1.00

ANALYSIS BY STARTING PRICE LAST TIME

Price	Prop	Win	Runs	Wins%	£
Odds On	0%	0	2	0.0%	-1.00
Ev-2/1	6%	5	18	27.8%	-0.02
9/4-4/1	17%	13	69	18.8%	-0.21
9/2-6/1	15%	12	65	18.5%	0.06
13/2-10/1	17%	13	121	10.7%	-0.29
11/1-16/1	22%	17	150	11.3%	-0.25
18/1-33/1	17%	13	201	6.5%	-0.24
40/1+	3%	2	143	1.4%	-0.79
Unraced	4%	3	18	16.7%	1.14

ANALYSIS BY DISTANCE BEATEN LAST TIME

Lengths	Prop	Win	Runs	Wins%	£
..-10	0%	0	0	0.0%	0.00
-10..0	6%	5	28	17.9%	-0.32
0.1..2	10%	8	57	14.0%	-0.23
2.1..5	18%	14	110	12.7%	-0.61
5.1..10	23%	18	185	9.7%	-0.21
10.1..20	23%	18	222	8.1%	-0.44
20.0..30	10%	8	82	9.8%	0.29
30.1+	5%	4	85	4.7%	-0.55
Not Compl	0%	0	0	0.0%	0.00
Unraced	4%	3	18	16.7%	1.14

ANALYSIS BY RUN NUMBER

Run No	Prop	Win	Runs	Wins%	£
FTO	4%	3	18	16.7%	1.14
2nd Run	0%	0	25	0.0%	-1.00
3rd Run	1%	1	26	3.8%	-0.58
4th+ Run	95%	74	718	10.3%	-0.29

ANALYSIS BY POSITION LAST TIME

Pos LT	Prop	Win	Runs	Wins%	£
Won	6%	5	28	17.9%	-0.32
2nd or 3rd	19%	15	114	13.2%	-0.38
Unplaced	71%	55	625	8.8%	-0.31
Not Compl	4%	3	20	15.0%	0.93

OTHER FACTORS (WINS-RUNS, £)

Course Winner:	6-24	£0.11
Distance Winner:	23-120	-£0.06
Going Winner:	8-47	-£0.03
Beaten Favourite:	8-34	-£0.13
BHA Top Rated:	21-73	£0.37
Up in class:	16-229	-£0.46
Same class:	35-360	-£0.39
Down in class:	24-180	-£0.02
7-Day Winners:	1-3	-£0.27
Colts and Geldings:	44-452	-£0.35
Fillies:	34-335	-£0.21
Absolute Favourites:	22-74	-£0.19

TRAINERS (WINS-RUNS, £)

I A Wood 3-12 £2.29; M R Channon 3-12 £0.92; A Berry 2-18 £0.33; R Hannon 9-27 £0.22; P D Evans 4-13 £0.43; P F I Cole 1-11 £0.36.

Race Profiles

3-Y.O Races: Claiming Races – 15 runners or more

ANALYSIS BY BHA RATING

Rating	Prop	Win	Runs	Wins%	£
120..139	0%	0	0	0.0%	0.00
110..119	0%	0	0	0.0%	0.00
100..109	0%	0	0	0.0%	0.00
90..99	0%	0	0	0.0%	0.00
70..89	9%	1	25	4.0%	-0.72
50..69	73%	8	92	8.7%	-0.29
..49	9%	1	45	2.2%	-0.53
Unrated	9%	1	12	8.3%	-0.17

ANALYSIS BY WEIGHT CARRIED

Weight	Prop	Win	Runs	Wins%	£
10-01+	0%	0	0	0.0%	0.00
9-8..10-00	0%	0	1	0.0%	-1.00
9-0..9-07	27%	3	30	10.0%	0.05
8-8..8-13	27%	3	55	5.5%	-0.70
8-0..8-07	36%	4	79	5.1%	-0.56
..7-13	9%	1	9	11.1%	1.33

ANALYSIS BY DAYS SINCE LAST RUN

Days	Prop	Win	Runs	Wins%	£
1..7	0%	0	15	0.0%	-1.00
8..14	36%	4	38	10.5%	-0.19
15..28	27%	3	65	4.6%	-0.45
29..60	9%	1	33	3.0%	-0.79
61..100	0%	0	5	0.0%	-1.00
101+	27%	3	17	17.6%	0.76
Unraced	0%	0	1	0.0%	-1.00

ANALYSIS BY TODAY'S STARTING PRICE

Price	Prop	Win	Runs	Wins%	£
Odds On	0%	0	0	0.0%	0.00
Ev-2/1	18%	2	4	50.0%	0.44
9/4-4/1	9%	1	10	10.0%	-0.55
9/2-6/1	27%	3	13	23.1%	0.58
13/2-10/1	18%	2	27	7.4%	-0.33
11/1-16/1	18%	2	34	5.9%	0.00
18/1-33/1	9%	1	38	2.6%	-0.45
40/1+	0%	0	48	0.0%	-1.00

ANALYSIS BY STARTING PRICE LAST TIME

Price	Prop	Win	Runs	Wins%	£
Odds On	0%	0	1	0.0%	-1.00
Ev-2/1	0%	0	4	0.0%	-1.00
9/4-4/1	9%	1	11	9.1%	-0.41
9/2-6/1	18%	2	11	18.2%	2.45
13/2-10/1	45%	5	37	13.5%	0.07
11/1-16/1	0%	0	35	0.0%	-1.00
18/1-33/1	27%	3	37	8.1%	-0.47
40/1+	0%	0	37	0.0%	-1.00
Unraced	0%	0	1	0.0%	-1.00

ANALYSIS BY DISTANCE BEATEN LAST TIME

Lengths	Prop	Win	Runs	Wins%	£
..-10	0%	0	0	0.0%	0.00
-10..0	0%	0	4	0.0%	-1.00
0.1..2	0%	0	14	0.0%	-1.00
2.1..5	36%	4	29	13.8%	0.22
5.1..10	45%	5	52	9.6%	-0.17
10.1..20	9%	1	47	2.1%	-0.83
20.0..30	0%	0	16	0.0%	-1.00
30.1+	9%	1	11	9.1%	0.55
Not Compl	0%	0	0	0.0%	0.00
Unraced	0%	0	1	0.0%	-1.00

ANALYSIS BY RUN NUMBER

Run No	Prop	Win	Runs	Wins%	£
FTO	0%	0	1	0.0%	-1.00
2nd Run	9%	1	2	50.0%	4.00
3rd Run	0%	0	9	0.0%	-1.00
4th+ Run	91%	10	162	6.2%	-0.42

ANALYSIS BY POSITION LAST TIME

Pos LT	Prop	Win	Runs	Wins%	£
Won	0%	0	4	0.0%	-1.00
2nd or 3rd	9%	1	21	4.8%	-0.52
Unplaced	91%	10	145	6.9%	-0.35
Not Compl	0%	0	4	0.0%	-1.00

OTHER FACTORS (WINS-RUNS, £)

Course Winner:	1-5	-£0.40
Distance Winner:	2-31	-£0.19
Going Winner:	1-16	£0.06
Beaten Favourite:	0-7	-£1.00
BHA Top Rated:	2-12	-£0.52
Up in class:	4-46	-£0.08
Same class:	3-76	-£0.45
Down in class:	4-51	-£0.62
7-Day Winners:	0-1	-£1.00
Colts and Geldings:	6-103	-£0.46
Fillies:	5-71	-£0.32
Absolute Favourites:	2-9	-£0.36

Claiming Races

3-Y.O Races: Claiming Races – good or faster going

ANALYSIS BY BHA RATING

Rating	Prop	Win	Runs	Wins%	£
120..139	0%	0	0	0.0%	0.00
110..119	0%	0	0	0.0%	0.00
100..109	0%	0	0	0.0%	0.00
90..99	4%	3	3	100.0%	1.22
70..89	20%	16	112	14.3%	-0.38
50..69	61%	50	373	13.4%	-0.17
..49	11%	9	218	4.1%	-0.54
Unrated	5%	4	72	5.6%	-0.49

ANALYSIS BY WEIGHT CARRIED

Weight	Prop	Win	Runs	Wins%	£
10-01+	0%	0	0	0.0%	0.00
9-8..10-00	2%	2	15	13.3%	-0.52
9-0..9-07	23%	19	147	12.9%	-0.29
8-8..8-13	33%	27	238	11.3%	-0.36
8-0..8-07	34%	28	311	9.0%	-0.32
..7-13	7%	6	68	8.8%	-0.29

ANALYSIS BY DAYS SINCE LAST RUN

Days	Prop	Win	Runs	Wins%	£
1..7	11%	9	75	12.0%	-0.32
8..14	33%	27	206	13.1%	-0.24
15..28	38%	31	262	11.8%	-0.24
29..60	7%	6	134	4.5%	-0.66
61..100	4%	3	32	9.4%	-0.45
101+	5%	4	55	7.3%	-0.41
Unraced	2%	2	15	13.3%	0.43

ANALYSIS BY TODAY'S STARTING PRICE

Price	Prop	Win	Runs	Wins%	£
Odds On	7%	6	11	54.5%	-0.07
Ev-2/1	23%	19	48	39.6%	0.04
9/4-4/1	28%	23	117	19.7%	-0.17
9/2-6/1	9%	7	68	10.3%	-0.35
13/2-10/1	21%	17	120	14.2%	0.28
11/1-16/1	10%	8	124	6.5%	-0.03
18/1-33/1	2%	2	153	1.3%	-0.67
40/1+	0%	0	138	0.0%	-1.00

ANALYSIS BY STARTING PRICE LAST TIME

Price	Prop	Win	Runs	Wins%	£
Odds On	1%	1	3	33.3%	0.67
Ev-2/1	6%	5	19	26.3%	-0.07
9/4-4/1	15%	12	70	17.1%	-0.24
9/2-6/1	16%	13	65	20.0%	0.04
13/2-10/1	23%	19	124	15.3%	-0.01
11/1-16/1	17%	14	149	9.4%	-0.40
18/1-33/1	18%	15	187	8.0%	-0.26
40/1+	1%	1	147	0.7%	-0.94
Unraced	2%	2	15	13.3%	0.43

ANALYSIS BY DISTANCE BEATEN LAST TIME

Lengths	Prop	Win	Runs	Wins%	£
..-10	0%	0	0	0.0%	0.00
-10..0	7%	6	27	22.2%	-0.06
0.1..2	6%	5	52	9.6%	-0.57
2.1..5	21%	17	120	14.2%	-0.46
5.1..10	29%	24	193	12.4%	-0.10
10.1..20	20%	16	213	7.5%	-0.51
20.0..30	9%	7	80	8.8%	-0.24
30.1+	6%	5	79	6.3%	-0.34
Not Compl	0%	0	0	0.0%	0.00
Unraced	2%	2	15	13.3%	0.43

ANALYSIS BY RUN NUMBER

Run No	Prop	Win	Runs	Wins%	£
FTO	2%	2	15	13.3%	0.43
2nd Run	1%	1	24	4.2%	-0.58
3rd Run	1%	1	30	3.3%	-0.63
4th+ Run	95%	78	710	11.0%	-0.32

ANALYSIS BY POSITION LAST TIME

Pos LT	Prop	Win	Runs	Wins%	£
Won	7%	6	28	21.4%	-0.10
2nd or 3rd	18%	15	103	14.6%	-0.31
Unplaced	72%	59	629	9.4%	-0.35
Not Compl	2%	2	19	10.5%	0.13

OTHER FACTORS (WINS-RUNS, £)

Course Winner:	4-20	-£0.22
Distance Winner:	22-122	-£0.19
Going Winner:	12-64	-£0.00
Beaten Favourite:	8-36	£0.10
BHA Top Rated:	24-76	£0.38
Up in class:	18-183	-£0.39
Same class:	32-352	-£0.44
Down in class:	30-229	-£0.15
7-Day Winners:	1-3	-£0.27
Colts and Geldings:	45-460	-£0.43
Fillies:	37-319	-£0.18
Absolute Favourites:	27-79	-£0.10

TRAINERS (WINS-RUNS, £)

P D Evans 5-11 £2.23; I A Wood 2-11 £1.82; P F I Cole 2-11 £1.18; M R Channon 3-14 £0.64.

Race Profiles

3-Y.O Races: Claiming Races – good to soft or softer going

ANALYSIS BY BHA RATING

Rating	Prop	Win	Runs	Wins%	£
120..139	0%	0	0	0.0%	0.00
110..119	0%	0	0	0.0%	0.00
100..109	0%	0	0	0.0%	0.00
90..99	0%	0	0	0.0%	0.00
70..89	16%	5	38	13.2%	-0.57
50..69	71%	22	171	12.9%	-0.14
..49	10%	3	95	3.2%	-0.38
Unrated	3%	1	24	4.2%	-0.29

ANALYSIS BY WEIGHT CARRIED

Weight	Prop	Win	Runs	Wins%	£
10-01+	0%	0	0	0.0%	0.00
9-8..10-00	3%	1	5	20.0%	-0.56
9-0..9-07	35%	11	76	14.5%	-0.05
8-8..8-13	29%	9	87	10.3%	-0.39
8-0..8-07	26%	8	132	6.1%	-0.32
..7-13	6%	2	28	7.1%	-0.18

ANALYSIS BY DAYS SINCE LAST RUN

Days	Prop	Win	Runs	Wins%	£
1..7	16%	5	40	12.5%	-0.35
8..14	32%	10	76	13.2%	0.12
15..28	35%	11	118	9.3%	-0.38
29..60	6%	2	49	4.1%	-0.76
61..100	3%	1	14	7.1%	0.50
101+	3%	1	27	3.7%	-0.80
Unraced	3%	1	4	25.0%	3.25

ANALYSIS BY TODAY'S STARTING PRICE

Price	Prop	Win	Runs	Wins%	£
Odds On	6%	2	4	50.0%	-0.09
Ev-2/1	16%	5	11	45.5%	0.05
9/4-4/1	19%	6	46	13.0%	-0.42
9/2-6/1	23%	7	32	21.9%	0.33
13/2-10/1	16%	5	50	10.0%	-0.16
11/1-16/1	10%	3	59	5.1%	-0.14
18/1-33/1	10%	3	63	4.8%	0.00
40/1+	0%	0	63	0.0%	-1.00

ANALYSIS BY STARTING PRICE LAST TIME

Price	Prop	Win	Runs	Wins%	£
Odds On	0%	0	3	0.0%	-1.00
Ev-2/1	6%	2	8	25.0%	-0.39
9/4-4/1	19%	6	30	20.0%	-0.20
9/2-6/1	16%	5	26	19.2%	1.23
13/2-10/1	13%	4	55	7.3%	-0.41
11/1-16/1	19%	6	64	9.4%	-0.48
18/1-33/1	19%	6	86	7.0%	-0.42
40/1+	3%	1	52	1.9%	-0.60
Unraced	3%	1	4	25.0%	3.25

ANALYSIS BY DISTANCE BEATEN LAST TIME

Lengths	Prop	Win	Runs	Wins%	£
..-10	0%	0	0	0.0%	0.00
-10..0	3%	1	13	7.7%	-0.82
0.1..2	16%	5	27	18.5%	-0.01
2.1..5	26%	8	48	16.7%	-0.10
5.1..10	19%	6	77	7.8%	-0.28
10.1..20	16%	5	102	4.9%	-0.65
20.0..30	13%	4	28	14.3%	0.93
30.1+	3%	1	29	3.4%	-0.81
Not Compl	0%	0	0	0.0%	0.00
Unraced	3%	1	4	25.0%	3.25

ANALYSIS BY RUN NUMBER

Run No	Prop	Win	Runs	Wins%	£
FTO	3%	1	4	25.0%	3.25
2nd Run	0%	0	8	0.0%	-1.00
3rd Run	0%	0	10	0.0%	-1.00
4th+ Run	97%	30	306	9.8%	-0.27

ANALYSIS BY POSITION LAST TIME

Pos LT	Prop	Win	Runs	Wins%	£
Won	3%	1	13	7.7%	-0.82
2nd or 3rd	19%	6	49	12.2%	-0.34
Unplaced	74%	23	261	8.8%	-0.28
Not Compl	3%	1	5	20.0%	2.40

OTHER FACTORS (WINS-RUNS, £)

Course Winner:	3-14	£0.01
Distance Winner:	9-56	-£0.02
Going Winner:	2-16	£0.20
Beaten Favourite:	6-18	-£0.01
BHA Top Rated:	7-32	-£0.27
Up in class:	10-137	-£0.34
Same class:	14-148	-£0.26
Down in class:	6-39	-£0.39
7-Day Winners:	0-2	-£1.00
Colts and Geldings:	21-181	-£0.17
Fillies:	10-147	-£0.39
Absolute Favourites:	9-28	-£0.21

Claiming Races

3-Y.O Races: Claiming Races – 5 to 6 furlong races

ANALYSIS BY BHA RATING

Rating	Prop	Win	Runs	Wins%	£
120..139	0%	0	0	0.0%	0.00
110..119	0%	0	0	0.0%	0.00
100..109	0%	0	0	0.0%	0.00
90..99	0%	0	0	0.0%	0.00
70..89	20%	4	23	17.4%	-0.30
50..69	70%	14	103	13.6%	-0.33
..49	0%	0	44	0.0%	-1.00
Unrated	10%	2	21	9.5%	-0.26

ANALYSIS BY WEIGHT CARRIED

Weight	Prop	Win	Runs	Wins%	£
10-01+	0%	0	0	0.0%	0.00
9-8..10-00	0%	0	0	0.0%	0.00
9-0..9-07	25%	5	37	13.5%	-0.49
8-8..8-13	40%	8	54	14.8%	-0.36
8-0..8-07	35%	7	86	8.1%	-0.45
..7-13	0%	0	14	0.0%	-1.00

ANALYSIS BY DAYS SINCE LAST RUN

Days	Prop	Win	Runs	Wins%	£
1..7	25%	5	17	29.4%	0.02
8..14	30%	6	45	13.3%	-0.26
15..28	30%	6	71	8.5%	-0.59
29..60	5%	1	29	3.4%	-0.83
61..100	0%	0	2	0.0%	-1.00
101+	5%	1	25	4.0%	-0.88
Unraced	5%	1	2	50.0%	5.50

ANALYSIS BY TODAY'S STARTING PRICE

Price	Prop	Win	Runs	Wins%	£
Odds On	5%	1	3	33.3%	-0.42
Ev-2/1	30%	6	11	54.5%	0.51
9/4-4/1	40%	8	26	30.8%	0.33
9/2-6/1	15%	3	23	13.0%	-0.15
13/2-10/1	0%	0	29	0.0%	-1.00
11/1-16/1	10%	2	33	6.1%	-0.15
18/1-33/1	0%	0	32	0.0%	-1.00
40/1+	0%	0	34	0.0%	-1.00

ANALYSIS BY STARTING PRICE LAST TIME

Price	Prop	Win	Runs	Wins%	£
Odds On	0%	0	3	0.0%	-1.00
Ev-2/1	5%	1	3	33.3%	0.67
9/4-4/1	15%	3	17	17.6%	-0.19
9/2-6/1	15%	3	17	17.6%	-0.40
13/2-10/1	25%	5	29	17.2%	-0.37
11/1-16/1	15%	3	45	6.7%	-0.77
18/1-33/1	20%	4	43	9.3%	-0.31
40/1+	0%	0	32	0.0%	-1.00
Unraced	5%	1	2	50.0%	5.50

ANALYSIS BY DISTANCE BEATEN LAST TIME

Lengths	Prop	Win	Runs	Wins%	£
..-10	0%	0	0	0.0%	0.00
-10..0	5%	1	5	20.0%	-0.45
0.1..2	5%	1	12	8.3%	-0.71
2.1..5	35%	7	35	20.0%	-0.14
5.1..10	35%	7	63	11.1%	-0.60
10.1..20	5%	1	51	2.0%	-0.88
20.0..30	10%	2	10	20.0%	1.00
30.1+	0%	0	13	0.0%	-1.00
Not Compl	0%	0	0	0.0%	0.00
Unraced	5%	1	2	50.0%	5.50

ANALYSIS BY RUN NUMBER

Run No	Prop	Win	Runs	Wins%	£
FTO	5%	1	2	50.0%	5.50
2nd Run	0%	0	8	0.0%	-1.00
3rd Run	0%	0	9	0.0%	-1.00
4th+ Run	95%	19	172	11.0%	-0.49

ANALYSIS BY POSITION LAST TIME

Pos LT	Prop	Win	Runs	Wins%	£
Won	5%	1	5	20.0%	-0.45
2nd or 3rd	25%	5	26	19.2%	-0.24
Unplaced	65%	13	157	8.3%	-0.59
Not Compl	5%	1	3	33.3%	3.33

OTHER FACTORS (WINS-RUNS, £)

Course Winner:	2-5	£0.50
Distance Winner:	6-48	-£0.64
Going Winner:	1-18	-£0.75
Beaten Favourite:	1-8	-£0.38
BHA Top Rated:	7-16	£1.30
Up in class:	0-15	-£1.00
Same class:	6-102	-£0.77
Down in class:	13-72	-£0.11
Colts and Geldings:	12-102	-£0.49
Fillies:	8-89	-£0.45
Absolute Favourites:	9-20	£0.39

Race Profiles

3-Y.O Races: Claiming Races – 7 to 9 furlong races

ANALYSIS BY BHA RATING

Rating	Prop	Win	Runs	Wins%	£
120..139	0%	0	0	0.0%	0.00
110..119	0%	0	0	0.0%	0.00
100..109	0%	0	0	0.0%	0.00
90..99	5%	3	3	100.0%	1.22
70..89	23%	14	112	12.5%	-0.45
50..69	61%	37	281	13.2%	-0.19
..49	10%	6	184	3.3%	-0.60
Unrated	2%	1	46	2.2%	-0.78

ANALYSIS BY WEIGHT CARRIED

Weight	Prop	Win	Runs	Wins%	£
10-01+	0%	0	0	0.0%	0.00
9-8..10-00	5%	3	12	25.0%	-0.22
9-0..9-07	28%	17	125	13.6%	-0.11
8-8..8-13	31%	19	184	10.3%	-0.45
8-0..8-07	30%	18	248	7.3%	-0.55
..7-13	7%	4	57	7.0%	-0.18

ANALYSIS BY DAYS SINCE LAST RUN

Days	Prop	Win	Runs	Wins%	£
1..7	7%	4	66	6.1%	-0.57
8..14	43%	26	173	15.0%	-0.09
15..28	38%	23	196	11.7%	-0.26
29..60	7%	4	111	3.6%	-0.81
61..100	3%	2	34	5.9%	-0.57
101+	3%	2	36	5.6%	-0.57
Unraced	0%	0	10	0.0%	-1.00

ANALYSIS BY TODAY'S STARTING PRICE

Price	Prop	Win	Runs	Wins%	£
Odds On	8%	5	9	55.6%	-0.06
Ev-2/1	21%	13	30	43.3%	0.07
9/4-4/1	20%	12	80	15.0%	-0.37
9/2-6/1	16%	10	53	18.9%	0.16
13/2-10/1	25%	15	98	15.3%	0.33
11/1-16/1	8%	5	106	4.7%	-0.27
18/1-33/1	2%	1	122	0.8%	-0.83
40/1+	0%	0	128	0.0%	-1.00

ANALYSIS BY STARTING PRICE LAST TIME

Price	Prop	Win	Runs	Wins%	£
Odds On	2%	1	2	50.0%	1.50
Ev-2/1	8%	5	17	29.4%	-0.10
9/4-4/1	15%	9	50	18.0%	-0.14
9/2-6/1	20%	12	53	22.6%	0.87
13/2-10/1	15%	9	102	8.8%	-0.32
11/1-16/1	21%	13	121	10.7%	-0.46
18/1-33/1	18%	11	159	6.9%	-0.53
40/1+	2%	1	112	0.9%	-0.92
Unraced	0%	0	10	0.0%	-1.00

ANALYSIS BY DISTANCE BEATEN LAST TIME

Lengths	Prop	Win	Runs	Wins%	£
..-10	0%	0	0	0.0%	0.00
-10..0	8%	5	25	20.0%	-0.34
0.1..2	10%	6	49	12.2%	-0.29
2.1..5	21%	13	90	14.4%	-0.32
5.1..10	25%	15	145	10.3%	-0.21
10.1..20	25%	15	193	7.8%	-0.44
20.0..30	8%	5	59	8.5%	-0.43
30.1+	3%	2	55	3.6%	-0.77
Not Compl	0%	0	0	0.0%	0.00
Unraced	0%	0	10	0.0%	-1.00

ANALYSIS BY RUN NUMBER

Run No	Prop	Win	Runs	Wins%	£
FTO	0%	0	10	0.0%	-1.00
2nd Run	2%	1	17	5.9%	-0.41
3rd Run	0%	0	17	0.0%	-1.00
4th+ Run	98%	60	582	10.3%	-0.36

ANALYSIS BY POSITION LAST TIME

Pos LT	Prop	Win	Runs	Wins%	£
Won	8%	5	26	19.2%	-0.37
2nd or 3rd	20%	12	81	14.8%	-0.13
Unplaced	72%	44	506	8.7%	-0.42
Not Compl	0%	0	13	0.0%	-1.00

OTHER FACTORS (WINS-RUNS, £)

Course Winner:	4-21	-£0.13
Distance Winner:	21-107	£0.13
Going Winner:	11-55	£0.18
Beaten Favourite:	9-29	£0.39
BHA Top Rated:	17-62	-£0.08
Up in class:	22-239	-£0.34
Same class:	25-262	-£0.38
Down in class:	14-115	-£0.47
7-Day Winners:	1-3	-£0.27
Colts and Geldings:	37-374	-£0.40
Fillies:	24-252	-£0.38
Absolute Favourites:	20-58	-£0.17

TRAINERS (WINS-RUNS, £)

P F I Cole 2-12 £1.00; A Berry 2-19 £0.26; K A Ryan 2-12 £0.33.

Claiming Races

3-Y.O Races: Claiming Races – 10 to 14 furlong races

ANALYSIS BY BHA RATING

Rating	Prop	Win	Runs	Wins%	£
120..139	0%	0	0	0.0%	0.00
110..119	0%	0	0	0.0%	0.00
100..109	0%	0	0	0.0%	0.00
90..99	0%	0	0	0.0%	0.00
70..89	9%	3	15	20.0%	-0.48
50..69	66%	21	160	13.1%	0.01
..49	19%	6	85	7.1%	0.01
Unrated	6%	2	29	6.9%	-0.03

ANALYSIS BY WEIGHT CARRIED

Weight	Prop	Win	Runs	Wins%	£
10-01+	0%	0	0	0.0%	0.00
9-8..10-00	0%	0	8	0.0%	-1.00
9-0..9-07	25%	8	61	13.1%	-0.23
8-8..8-13	28%	9	87	10.3%	-0.19
8-0..8-07	34%	11	109	10.1%	0.30
..7-13	13%	4	25	16.0%	-0.04

ANALYSIS BY DAYS SINCE LAST RUN

Days	Prop	Win	Runs	Wins%	£
1..7	16%	5	32	15.6%	-0.03
8..14	16%	5	64	7.8%	-0.19
15..28	41%	13	113	11.5%	-0.11
29..60	9%	3	43	7.0%	-0.28
61..100	6%	2	10	20.0%	1.40
101+	6%	2	21	9.5%	-0.08
Unraced	6%	2	7	28.6%	2.64

ANALYSIS BY TODAY'S STARTING PRICE

Price	Prop	Win	Runs	Wins%	£
Odds On	6%	2	3	66.7%	0.21
Ev-2/1	16%	5	18	27.8%	-0.30
9/4-4/1	28%	9	57	15.8%	-0.33
9/2-6/1	3%	1	24	4.2%	-0.77
13/2-10/1	22%	7	43	16.3%	0.51
11/1-16/1	13%	4	44	9.1%	0.50
18/1-33/1	13%	4	62	6.5%	0.48
40/1+	0%	0	39	0.0%	-1.00

ANALYSIS BY STARTING PRICE LAST TIME

Price	Prop	Win	Runs	Wins%	£
Odds On	0%	0	1	0.0%	-1.00
Ev-2/1	3%	1	7	14.3%	-0.68
9/4-4/1	19%	6	33	18.2%	-0.37
9/2-6/1	9%	3	21	14.3%	-0.23
13/2-10/1	28%	9	48	18.8%	0.42
11/1-16/1	13%	4	47	8.5%	-0.02
18/1-33/1	19%	6	71	8.5%	0.17
40/1+	3%	1	55	1.8%	-0.62
Unraced	6%	2	7	28.6%	2.64

ANALYSIS BY DISTANCE BEATEN LAST TIME

Lengths	Prop	Win	Runs	Wins%	£
..-10	0%	0	0	0.0%	0.00
-10..0	3%	1	10	10.0%	-0.15
0.1..2	9%	3	18	16.7%	-0.39
2.1..5	16%	5	43	11.6%	-0.61
5.1..10	25%	8	62	12.9%	0.45
10.1..20	16%	5	71	7.0%	-0.65
20.0..30	13%	4	39	10.3%	0.56
30.1+	13%	4	40	10.0%	0.13
Not Compl	0%	0	0	0.0%	0.00
Unraced	6%	2	7	28.6%	2.64

ANALYSIS BY RUN NUMBER

Run No	Prop	Win	Runs	Wins%	£
FTO	6%	2	7	28.6%	2.64
2nd Run	0%	0	7	0.0%	-1.00
3rd Run	3%	1	14	7.1%	-0.21
4th+ Run	91%	29	262	11.1%	-0.06

ANALYSIS BY POSITION LAST TIME

Pos LT	Prop	Win	Runs	Wins%	£
Won	3%	1	10	10.0%	-0.15
2nd or 3rd	13%	4	45	8.9%	-0.71
Unplaced	78%	25	227	11.0%	0.04
Not Compl	6%	2	8	25.0%	2.19

OTHER FACTORS (WINS-RUNS, £)

Course Winner:	1-8	-£0.50
Distance Winner:	4-23	-£0.30
Going Winner:	2-7	£0.93
Beaten Favourite:	4-17	-£0.28
BHA Top Rated:	7-30	£0.15
Up in class:	6-66	-£0.33
Same class:	15-136	-£0.12
Down in class:	9-81	£0.16
7-Day Winners:	0-2	-£1.00
Colts and Geldings:	17-165	-£0.17
Fillies:	15-125	£0.17
Absolute Favourites:	7-29	-£0.41

Race Profiles

3-Y.O Races: Selling Races

ANALYSIS BY BHA RATING

Rating	Prop	Win	Runs	Wins%	£
120..139	0%	0	0	0.0%	0.00
110..119	0%	0	0	0.0%	0.00
100..109	0%	0	0	0.0%	0.00
90..99	2%	2	13	15.4%	-0.12
70..89	16%	20	88	22.7%	-0.25
50..69	54%	68	500	11.7%	-0.27
..49	21%	26	492	5.3%	-0.32
Unrated	8%	10	112	8.9%	0.29

ANALYSIS BY WEIGHT CARRIED

Weight	Prop	Win	Runs	Wins%	£
10-01+	0%	0	0	0.0%	0.00
9-8..10-00	1%	1	3	33.3%	-0.33
9-0..9-07	21%	26	213	12.2%	-0.34
8-8..8-13	46%	58	594	9.8%	-0.30
8-0..8-07	33%	41	468	8.8%	-0.09
..7-13	0%	0	9	0.0%	-1.00

ANALYSIS BY DAYS SINCE LAST RUN

Days	Prop	Win	Runs	Wins%	£
1..7	15%	19	157	12.1%	-0.44
8..14	31%	39	296	13.2%	0.18
15..28	29%	36	422	8.5%	-0.44
29..60	20%	25	237	10.5%	0.14
61..100	2%	2	49	4.1%	-0.86
101+	4%	5	112	4.5%	-0.69
Unraced	0%	0	14	0.0%	-1.00

ANALYSIS BY TODAY'S STARTING PRICE

Price	Prop	Win	Runs	Wins%	£
Odds On	1%	1	4	25.0%	-0.60
Ev-2/1	24%	30	61	49.2%	0.27
9/4-4/1	30%	38	180	21.1%	-0.15
9/2-6/1	13%	17	141	12.1%	-0.23
13/2-10/1	14%	18	238	7.6%	-0.35
11/1-16/1	12%	15	214	7.0%	-0.04
18/1-33/1	3%	4	229	1.7%	-0.53
40/1+	2%	3	220	1.4%	-0.20

ANALYSIS BY STARTING PRICE LAST TIME

Price	Prop	Win	Runs	Wins%	£
Odds On	2%	2	4	50.0%	0.15
Ev-2/1	5%	6	26	23.1%	-0.19
9/4-4/1	13%	17	74	23.0%	0.06
9/2-6/1	6%	7	92	7.6%	-0.53
13/2-10/1	22%	28	195	14.4%	-0.10
11/1-16/1	20%	25	234	10.7%	-0.22
18/1-33/1	24%	30	341	8.8%	-0.21
40/1+	9%	11	307	3.6%	-0.32
Unraced	0%	0	14	0.0%	-1.00

ANALYSIS BY DISTANCE BEATEN LAST TIME

Lengths	Prop	Win	Runs	Wins%	£
..-10	0%	0	0	0.0%	0.00
-10..0	6%	7	26	26.9%	0.08
0.1..2	11%	14	89	15.7%	-0.38
2.1..5	20%	25	186	13.4%	-0.21
5.1..10	29%	36	307	11.7%	-0.21
10.1..20	25%	32	377	8.5%	-0.16
20.0..30	5%	6	142	4.2%	-0.45
30.1+	5%	6	146	4.1%	-0.20
Not Compl	0%	0	0	0.0%	0.00
Unraced	0%	0	14	0.0%	-1.00

ANALYSIS BY RUN NUMBER

Run No	Prop	Win	Runs	Wins%	£
FTO	0%	0	14	0.0%	-1.00
2nd Run	2%	3	35	8.6%	-0.31
3rd Run	6%	7	55	12.7%	0.04
4th+ Run	92%	116	1183	9.8%	-0.24

ANALYSIS BY POSITION LAST TIME

Pos LT	Prop	Win	Runs	Wins%	£
Won	6%	7	26	26.9%	0.08
2nd or 3rd	13%	16	152	10.5%	-0.49
Unplaced	82%	103	1092	9.4%	-0.20
Not Compl	0%	0	17	0.0%	-1.00

OTHER FACTORS (WINS-RUNS, £)

Course Winner: 2-34 -£0.85
Distance Winner: 14-109 -£0.29
Going Winner: 7-75 -£0.62
Beaten Favourite: 10-49 -£0.13
BHA Top Rated: 28-130 £0.20
Up in class: 14-151 -£0.06
Same class: 69-770 -£0.25
Down in class: 43-352 -£0.26
7-Day Winners: 2-5 -£0.00
Colts and Geldings: 60-650 -£0.42
Fillies: 66-637 -£0.04
Absolute Favourites: 44-112 £0.17

TRAINERS (WINS-RUNS, £)

B Palling 2-17 £4.65; M D I Usher 1-10 £5.70; Mrs C A Dunnett 1-12 £2.42; M Quinn 4-13 £0.81; A B Haynes 4-23 £0.40; M H Tompkins 4-22 £0.39; Miss Gay Kelleway 3-12 £0.60; J M Bradley 1-14 £0.50; R A Harris 2-14 £0.32; B Smart 3-11 £0.35; R Hollinshead 3-15 £0.18.

Selling Races

3-Y.O Races: Selling Races – 2 to 7 runners

ANALYSIS BY BHA RATING

Rating	Prop	Win	Runs	Wins%	£
120..139	0%	0	0	0.0%	0.00
110..119	0%	0	0	0.0%	0.00
100..109	0%	0	0	0.0%	0.00
90..99	3%	1	7	14.3%	-0.66
70..89	34%	10	45	22.2%	-0.18
50..69	41%	12	72	16.7%	-0.48
..49	10%	3	49	6.1%	-0.64
Unrated	10%	3	10	30.0%	7.30

ANALYSIS BY WEIGHT CARRIED

Weight	Prop	Win	Runs	Wins%	£
10-01+	0%	0	0	0.0%	0.00
9-8..10-00	0%	0	0	0.0%	0.00
9-0..9-07	17%	5	34	14.7%	-0.48
8-8..8-13	59%	17	94	18.1%	-0.31
8-0..8-07	24%	7	54	13.0%	0.74
..7-13	0%	0	1	0.0%	-1.00

ANALYSIS BY DAYS SINCE LAST RUN

Days	Prop	Win	Runs	Wins%	£
1..7	17%	5	30	16.7%	-0.22
8..14	34%	10	46	21.7%	1.20
15..28	24%	7	52	13.5%	-0.47
29..60	10%	3	28	10.7%	-0.60
61..100	3%	1	4	25.0%	-0.41
101+	10%	3	23	13.0%	-0.53
Unraced	0%	0	0	0.0%	0.00

ANALYSIS BY TODAY'S STARTING PRICE

Price	Prop	Win	Runs	Wins%	£
Odds On	3%	1	2	50.0%	-0.19
Ev-2/1	38%	11	23	47.8%	0.22
9/4-4/1	45%	13	51	25.5%	-0.03
9/2-6/1	3%	1	21	4.8%	-0.71
13/2-10/1	0%	0	34	0.0%	-1.00
11/1-16/1	7%	2	22	9.1%	0.14
18/1-33/1	0%	0	22	0.0%	-1.00
40/1+	3%	1	8	12.5%	7.38

ANALYSIS BY STARTING PRICE LAST TIME

Price	Prop	Win	Runs	Wins%	£
Odds On	0%	0	0	0.0%	0.00
Ev-2/1	3%	1	2	50.0%	1.00
9/4-4/1	21%	6	21	28.6%	-0.12
9/2-6/1	3%	1	17	5.9%	-0.87
13/2-10/1	28%	8	36	22.2%	-0.31
11/1-16/1	14%	4	28	14.3%	-0.52
18/1-33/1	17%	5	41	12.2%	-0.31
40/1+	14%	4	38	10.5%	1.26
Unraced	0%	0	0	0.0%	0.00

ANALYSIS BY DISTANCE BEATEN LAST TIME

Lengths	Prop	Win	Runs	Wins%	£
..-10	0%	0	0	0.0%	0.00
-10..0	3%	1	7	14.3%	-0.54
0.1..2	17%	5	25	20.0%	-0.39
2.1..5	24%	7	27	25.9%	-0.22
5.1..10	17%	5	40	12.5%	-0.64
10.1..20	24%	7	55	12.7%	-0.51
20.0..30	7%	2	16	12.5%	0.00
30.1+	7%	2	13	15.4%	5.15
Not Compl	0%	0	0	0.0%	0.00
Unraced	0%	0	0	0.0%	0.00

ANALYSIS BY RUN NUMBER

Run No	Prop	Win	Runs	Wins%	£
FTO	0%	0	0	0.0%	0.00
2nd Run	0%	0	5	0.0%	-1.00
3rd Run	10%	3	6	50.0%	2.21
4th+ Run	90%	26	172	15.1%	-0.08

ANALYSIS BY POSITION LAST TIME

Pos LT	Prop	Win	Runs	Wins%	£
Won	3%	1	7	14.3%	-0.54
2nd or 3rd	14%	4	35	11.4%	-0.68
Unplaced	83%	24	141	17.0%	0.15
Not Compl	0%	0	0	0.0%	0.00

OTHER FACTORS (WINS-RUNS, £)

Course Winner:	1-8	-£0.70
Distance Winner:	3-24	-£0.65
Going Winner:	3-23	-£0.47
Beaten Favourite:	5-12	£0.40
BHA Top Rated:	11-35	£0.03
Up in class:	4-23	-£0.46
Same class:	12-102	-£0.01
Down in class:	13-58	£0.09
7-Day Winners:	0-1	-£1.00
Colts and Geldings:	15-111	-£0.55
Fillies:	14-72	£0.76
Absolute Favourites:	13-26	£0.28

Race Profiles

3-Y.O Races: Selling Races – 8 to 14 runners

ANALYSIS BY BHA RATING

Rating	Prop	Win	Runs	Wins%	£
120..139	0%	0	0	0.0%	0.00
110..119	0%	0	0	0.0%	0.00
100..109	0%	0	0	0.0%	0.00
90..99	1%	1	6	16.7%	0.50
70..89	11%	9	41	22.0%	-0.34
50..69	57%	47	407	11.5%	-0.26
..49	22%	18	319	5.6%	-0.23
Unrated	9%	7	87	8.0%	-0.29

ANALYSIS BY WEIGHT CARRIED

Weight	Prop	Win	Runs	Wins%	£
10-01+	0%	0	0	0.0%	0.00
9-8..10-00	1%	1	3	33.3%	-0.33
9-0..9-07	21%	17	128	13.3%	-0.26
8-8..8-13	41%	34	393	8.7%	-0.32
8-0..8-07	37%	30	331	9.1%	-0.16
..7-13	0%	0	6	0.0%	-1.00

ANALYSIS BY DAYS SINCE LAST RUN

Days	Prop	Win	Runs	Wins%	£
1..7	17%	14	97	14.4%	-0.34
8..14	28%	23	196	11.7%	0.01
15..28	33%	27	294	9.2%	-0.34
29..60	20%	16	155	10.3%	0.09
61..100	1%	1	37	2.7%	-0.88
101+	1%	1	70	1.4%	-0.83
Unraced	0%	0	12	0.0%	-1.00

ANALYSIS BY TODAY'S STARTING PRICE

Price	Prop	Win	Runs	Wins%	£
Odds On	0%	0	2	0.0%	-1.00
Ev-2/1	22%	18	35	51.4%	0.36
9/4-4/1	27%	22	117	18.8%	-0.23
9/2-6/1	15%	12	94	12.8%	-0.18
13/2-10/1	20%	16	169	9.5%	-0.18
11/1-16/1	12%	10	147	6.8%	-0.06
18/1-33/1	2%	2	157	1.3%	-0.72
40/1+	2%	2	140	1.4%	-0.23

ANALYSIS BY STARTING PRICE LAST TIME

Price	Prop	Win	Runs	Wins%	£
Odds On	2%	2	4	50.0%	0.15
Ev-2/1	6%	5	20	25.0%	-0.14
9/4-4/1	10%	8	44	18.2%	-0.01
9/2-6/1	7%	6	62	9.7%	-0.34
13/2-10/1	18%	15	126	11.9%	-0.28
11/1-16/1	24%	20	161	12.4%	0.01
18/1-33/1	23%	19	227	8.4%	-0.30
40/1+	9%	7	205	3.4%	-0.40
Unraced	0%	0	12	0.0%	-1.00

ANALYSIS BY DISTANCE BEATEN LAST TIME

Lengths	Prop	Win	Runs	Wins%	£
..-10	0%	0	0	0.0%	0.00
-10..0	7%	6	18	33.3%	0.37
0.1..2	10%	8	56	14.3%	-0.38
2.1..5	18%	15	117	12.8%	-0.09
5.1..10	34%	28	205	13.7%	-0.13
10.1..20	22%	18	247	7.3%	-0.17
20.0..30	4%	3	100	3.0%	-0.43
30.1+	5%	4	106	3.8%	-0.66
Not Compl	0%	0	0	0.0%	0.00
Unraced	0%	0	12	0.0%	-1.00

ANALYSIS BY RUN NUMBER

Run No	Prop	Win	Runs	Wins%	£
FTO	0%	0	12	0.0%	-1.00
2nd Run	4%	3	26	11.5%	-0.08
3rd Run	5%	4	41	9.8%	-0.08
4th+ Run	91%	75	782	9.6%	-0.26

ANALYSIS BY POSITION LAST TIME

Pos LT	Prop	Win	Runs	Wins%	£
Won	7%	6	18	33.3%	0.37
2nd or 3rd	13%	11	96	11.5%	-0.36
Unplaced	79%	65	732	8.9%	-0.24
Not Compl	0%	0	15	0.0%	-1.00

OTHER FACTORS (WINS-RUNS, £)

Course Winner:	1-18	-£0.84
Distance Winner:	8-64	-£0.39
Going Winner:	3-38	-£0.74
Beaten Favourite:	4-30	-£0.37
BHA Top Rated:	13-78	-£0.04
Up in class:	9-100	£0.24
Same class:	48-519	-£0.28
Down in class:	25-230	-£0.37
7-Day Winners:	2-3	£0.66
Colts and Geldings:	37-413	-£0.35
Fillies:	45-448	-£0.17
Absolute Favourites:	27-72	£0.14

TRAINERS (WINS-RUNS, £)

A B Haynes 4-16 £1.02; M Quinn 4-11 £1.14; M H Tompkins 3-18 £0.57; K R Burke 3-15 £0.47; Miss Gay Kelleway 2-10 £0.70; N Tinkler 1-11 £0.09.

Selling Races

3-Y.O Races: Selling Races – 15 runners or more

ANALYSIS BY BHA RATING

Rating	Prop	Win	Runs	Wins%	£
120..139	0%	0	0	0.0%	0.00
110..119	0%	0	0	0.0%	0.00
100..109	0%	0	0	0.0%	0.00
90..99	0%	0	0	0.0%	0.00
70..89	7%	1	2	50.0%	0.13
50..69	60%	9	101	8.9%	-0.15
..49	33%	5	124	4.0%	-0.40
Unrated	0%	0	15	0.0%	-1.00

ANALYSIS BY WEIGHT CARRIED

Weight	Prop	Win	Runs	Wins%	£
10-01+	0%	0	0	0.0%	0.00
9-8..10-00	0%	0	0	0.0%	0.00
9-0..9-07	27%	4	51	7.8%	-0.43
8-8..8-13	47%	7	107	6.5%	-0.25
8-0..8-07	27%	4	83	4.8%	-0.36
..7-13	0%	0	2	0.0%	-1.00

ANALYSIS BY DAYS SINCE LAST RUN

Days	Prop	Win	Runs	Wins%	£
1..7	0%	0	30	0.0%	-1.00
8..14	40%	6	54	11.1%	-0.11
15..28	13%	2	76	2.6%	-0.83
29..60	40%	6	54	11.1%	0.66
61..100	0%	0	8	0.0%	-1.00
101+	7%	1	19	5.3%	-0.37
Unraced	0%	0	2	0.0%	-1.00

ANALYSIS BY TODAY'S STARTING PRICE

Price	Prop	Win	Runs	Wins%	£
Odds On	0%	0	0	0.0%	0.00
Ev-2/1	7%	1	3	33.3%	-0.25
9/4-4/1	20%	3	12	25.0%	0.15
9/2-6/1	27%	4	26	15.4%	-0.04
13/2-10/1	13%	2	35	5.7%	-0.53
11/1-16/1	20%	3	45	6.7%	-0.07
18/1-33/1	13%	2	50	4.0%	0.26
40/1+	0%	0	72	0.0%	-1.00

ANALYSIS BY STARTING PRICE LAST TIME

Price	Prop	Win	Runs	Wins%	£
Odds On	0%	0	0	0.0%	0.00
Ev-2/1	0%	0	4	0.0%	-1.00
9/4-4/1	20%	3	9	33.3%	0.86
9/2-6/1	0%	0	13	0.0%	-1.00
13/2-10/1	33%	5	33	15.2%	0.81
11/1-16/1	7%	1	45	2.2%	-0.89
18/1-33/1	40%	6	73	8.2%	0.11
40/1+	0%	0	64	0.0%	-1.00
Unraced	0%	0	2	0.0%	-1.00

ANALYSIS BY DISTANCE BEATEN LAST TIME

Lengths	Prop	Win	Runs	Wins%	£
..-10	0%	0	0	0.0%	0.00
-10..0	0%	0	1	0.0%	-1.00
0.1..2	7%	1	8	12.5%	-0.38
2.1..5	20%	3	42	7.1%	-0.55
5.1..10	20%	3	62	4.8%	-0.22
10.1..20	47%	7	75	9.3%	0.13
20.0..30	7%	1	26	3.8%	-0.81
30.1+	0%	0	27	0.0%	-1.00
Not Compl	0%	0	0	0.0%	0.00
Unraced	0%	0	2	0.0%	-1.00

ANALYSIS BY RUN NUMBER

Run No	Prop	Win	Runs	Wins%	£
FTO	0%	0	2	0.0%	-1.00
2nd Run	0%	0	4	0.0%	-1.00
3rd Run	0%	0	8	0.0%	-1.00
4th+ Run	100%	15	229	6.6%	-0.29

ANALYSIS BY POSITION LAST TIME

Pos LT	Prop	Win	Runs	Wins%	£
Won	0%	0	1	0.0%	-1.00
2nd or 3rd	7%	1	21	4.8%	-0.76
Unplaced	93%	14	219	6.4%	-0.28
Not Compl	0%	0	2	0.0%	-1.00

OTHER FACTORS (WINS-RUNS, £)

Course Winner:	0-8	-£1.00
Distance Winner:	3-21	£0.40
Going Winner:	1-14	-£0.54
Beaten Favourite:	1-7	£0.00
BHA Top Rated:	4-17	£1.66
Up in class:	1-28	-£0.82
Same class:	9-149	-£0.30
Down in class:	5-64	-£0.17
7-Day Winners:	0-1	-£1.00
Colts and Geldings:	8-126	-£0.57
Fillies:	7-117	-£0.08
Absolute Favourites:	4-14	£0.14

Race Profiles

3-Y.O Races: Selling Races – good or faster going

ANALYSIS BY BHA RATING

Rating	Prop	Win	Runs	Wins%	£
120..139	0%	0	0	0.0%	0.00
110..119	0%	0	0	0.0%	0.00
100..109	0%	0	0	0.0%	0.00
90..99	2%	2	13	15.4%	-0.12
70..89	18%	17	78	21.8%	-0.30
50..69	52%	49	454	10.8%	-0.29
..49	19%	18	360	5.0%	-0.50
Unrated	9%	8	84	9.5%	0.57

ANALYSIS BY WEIGHT CARRIED

Weight	Prop	Win	Runs	Wins%	£
10-01+	0%	0	0	0.0%	0.00
9-8..10-00	1%	1	3	33.3%	-0.33
9-0..9-07	24%	23	175	13.1%	-0.25
8-8..8-13	41%	39	448	8.7%	-0.43
8-0..8-07	33%	31	359	8.6%	-0.12
..7-13	0%	0	6	0.0%	-1.00

ANALYSIS BY DAYS SINCE LAST RUN

Days	Prop	Win	Runs	Wins%	£
1..7	15%	14	123	11.4%	-0.53
8..14	31%	29	236	12.3%	-0.04
15..28	29%	27	328	8.2%	-0.46
29..60	21%	20	182	11.0%	0.16
61..100	1%	1	31	3.2%	-0.92
101+	3%	3	80	3.8%	-0.66
Unraced	0%	0	11	0.0%	-1.00

ANALYSIS BY TODAY'S STARTING PRICE

Price	Prop	Win	Runs	Wins%	£
Odds On	0%	0	1	0.0%	-1.00
Ev-2/1	24%	23	45	51.1%	0.33
9/4-4/1	29%	27	131	20.6%	-0.17
9/2-6/1	16%	15	113	13.3%	-0.16
13/2-10/1	14%	13	178	7.3%	-0.38
11/1-16/1	12%	11	172	6.4%	-0.11
18/1-33/1	4%	4	178	2.2%	-0.40
40/1+	1%	1	173	0.6%	-0.61

ANALYSIS BY STARTING PRICE LAST TIME

Price	Prop	Win	Runs	Wins%	£
Odds On	1%	1	3	33.3%	-0.17
Ev-2/1	5%	5	18	27.8%	-0.05
9/4-4/1	13%	12	57	21.1%	0.03
9/2-6/1	6%	6	73	8.2%	-0.44
13/2-10/1	21%	20	147	13.6%	-0.13
11/1-16/1	16%	15	186	8.1%	-0.42
18/1-33/1	28%	26	252	10.3%	-0.16
40/1+	10%	9	244	3.7%	-0.45
Unraced	0%	0	11	0.0%	-1.00

ANALYSIS BY DISTANCE BEATEN LAST TIME

Lengths	Prop	Win	Runs	Wins%	£
..-10	0%	0	0	0.0%	0.00
-10..0	6%	6	21	28.6%	0.23
0.1..2	12%	11	65	16.9%	-0.31
2.1..5	20%	19	148	12.8%	-0.26
5.1..10	32%	30	236	12.7%	-0.10
10.1..20	22%	21	294	7.1%	-0.38
20.0..30	2%	2	109	1.8%	-0.83
30.1+	5%	5	107	4.7%	0.00
Not Compl	0%	0	0	0.0%	0.00
Unraced	0%	0	11	0.0%	-1.00

ANALYSIS BY RUN NUMBER

Run No	Prop	Win	Runs	Wins%	£
FTO	0%	0	11	0.0%	-1.00
2nd Run	2%	2	26	7.7%	-0.27
3rd Run	6%	6	41	14.6%	0.20
4th+ Run	91%	86	913	9.4%	-0.31

ANALYSIS BY POSITION LAST TIME

Pos LT	Prop	Win	Runs	Wins%	£
Won	6%	6	21	28.6%	0.23
2nd or 3rd	12%	11	104	10.6%	-0.51
Unplaced	82%	77	853	9.0%	-0.27
Not Compl	0%	0	13	0.0%	-1.00

OTHER FACTORS (WINS-RUNS, £)

Course Winner:	2-31	-£0.83
Distance Winner:	11-94	-£0.41
Going Winner:	7-68	-£0.58
Beaten Favourite:	7-34	-£0.14
BHA Top Rated:	16-94	£0.12
Up in class:	11-112	-£0.45
Same class:	53-595	-£0.24
Down in class:	30-273	-£0.31
7-Day Winners:	1-4	-£0.28
Colts and Geldings:	48-503	-£0.44
Fillies:	46-488	-£0.14
Absolute Favourites:	32-81	£0.20

TRAINERS (WINS-RUNS, £)

B Palling 2-13 £6.38; A B Haynes 4-17 £0.90; M H Tompkins 3-15 £0.88; J M Bradley 1-14 £0.50; R A Harris 2-13 £0.42; B Smart 3-10 £0.49; K R Burke 3-19 £0.16; R Hollinshead 2-14 £0.07.

Selling Races

3-Y.O Races: Selling Races – good to soft or softer going

ANALYSIS BY BHA RATING

Rating	Prop	Win	Runs	Wins%	£
120..139	0%	0	0	0.0%	0.00
110..119	0%	0	0	0.0%	0.00
100..109	0%	0	0	0.0%	0.00
90..99	0%	0	0	0.0%	0.00
70..89	9%	3	10	30.0%	0.17
50..69	59%	19	126	15.1%	-0.19
..49	25%	8	132	6.1%	0.17
Unrated	6%	2	28	7.1%	-0.54

ANALYSIS BY WEIGHT CARRIED

Weight	Prop	Win	Runs	Wins%	£
10-01+	0%	0	0	0.0%	0.00
9-8..10-00	0%	0	0	0.0%	0.00
9-0..9-07	9%	3	38	7.9%	-0.73
8-8..8-13	59%	19	146	13.0%	0.10
8-0..8-07	31%	10	109	9.2%	0.02
..7-13	0%	0	3	0.0%	-1.00

ANALYSIS BY DAYS SINCE LAST RUN

Days	Prop	Win	Runs	Wins%	£
1..7	16%	5	34	14.7%	-0.13
8..14	31%	10	60	16.7%	1.04
15..28	28%	9	94	9.6%	-0.39
29..60	16%	5	55	9.1%	0.08
61..100	3%	1	18	5.6%	-0.75
101+	6%	2	32	6.3%	-0.76
Unraced	0%	0	3	0.0%	-1.00

ANALYSIS BY TODAY'S STARTING PRICE

Price	Prop	Win	Runs	Wins%	£
Odds On	3%	1	3	33.3%	-0.46
Ev-2/1	22%	7	16	43.8%	0.11
9/4-4/1	34%	11	49	22.4%	-0.11
9/2-6/1	6%	2	28	7.1%	-0.52
13/2-10/1	16%	5	60	8.3%	-0.26
11/1-16/1	13%	4	42	9.5%	0.24
18/1-33/1	0%	0	51	0.0%	-1.00
40/1+	6%	2	47	4.3%	1.30

ANALYSIS BY STARTING PRICE LAST TIME

Price	Prop	Win	Runs	Wins%	£
Odds On	3%	1	1	100.0%	1.10
Ev-2/1	3%	1	8	12.5%	-0.50
9/4-4/1	16%	5	17	29.4%	0.17
9/2-6/1	3%	1	19	5.3%	-0.88
13/2-10/1	25%	8	48	16.7%	-0.02
11/1-16/1	31%	10	48	20.8%	0.54
18/1-33/1	13%	4	89	4.5%	-0.36
40/1+	6%	2	63	3.2%	0.19
Unraced	0%	0	3	0.0%	-1.00

ANALYSIS BY DISTANCE BEATEN LAST TIME

Lengths	Prop	Win	Runs	Wins%	£
..-10	0%	0	0	0.0%	0.00
-10..0	3%	1	5	20.0%	-0.58
0.1..2	9%	3	24	12.5%	-0.59
2.1..5	19%	6	38	15.8%	-0.02
5.1..10	19%	6	71	8.5%	-0.59
10.1..20	34%	11	83	13.3%	0.61
20.0..30	13%	4	33	12.1%	0.83
30.1+	3%	1	39	2.6%	-0.77
Not Compl	0%	0	0	0.0%	0.00
Unraced	0%	0	3	0.0%	-1.00

ANALYSIS BY RUN NUMBER

Run No	Prop	Win	Runs	Wins%	£
FTO	0%	0	3	0.0%	-1.00
2nd Run	3%	1	9	11.1%	-0.44
3rd Run	3%	1	14	7.1%	-0.43
4th+ Run	94%	30	270	11.1%	-0.01

ANALYSIS BY POSITION LAST TIME

Pos LT	Prop	Win	Runs	Wins%	£
Won	3%	1	5	20.0%	-0.58
2nd or 3rd	16%	5	48	10.4%	-0.43
Unplaced	81%	26	239	10.9%	0.05
Not Compl	0%	0	4	0.0%	-1.00

OTHER FACTORS (WINS-RUNS, £)

Course Winner:	0-3	-£1.00
Distance Winner:	3-15	£0.45
Going Winner:	0-7	-£1.00
Beaten Favourite:	3-15	-£0.09
BHA Top Rated:	12-36	£0.43
Up in class:	3-39	£1.04
Same class:	16-175	-£0.25
Down in class:	13-79	-£0.10
7-Day Winners:	1-1	£1.10
Colts and Geldings:	12-147	-£0.37
Fillies:	20-149	£0.26
Absolute Favourites:	12-31	£0.11

Race Profiles

3-Y.O Races: Selling Races – 5 to 6 furlong races

ANALYSIS BY BHA RATING

Rating	Prop	Win	Runs	Wins%	£
120..139	0%	0	0	0.0%	0.00
110..119	0%	0	0	0.0%	0.00
100..109	0%	0	0	0.0%	0.00
90..99	12%	2	13	15.4%	-0.12
70..89	41%	7	29	24.1%	-0.13
50..69	17%	8	55	14.5%	-0.33
..49	0%	0	41	0.0%	-1.00
Unrated	0%	0	8	0.0%	-1.00

ANALYSIS BY WEIGHT CARRIED

Weight	Prop	Win	Runs	Wins%	£
10-01+	0%	0	0	0.0%	0.00
9-8..10-00	0%	0	0	0.0%	0.00
9-0..9-07	18%	3	30	10.0%	-0.60
8-8..8-13	65%	11	71	15.5%	-0.33
8-0..8-07	18%	3	43	7.0%	-0.67
..7-13	0%	0	2	0.0%	-1.00

ANALYSIS BY DAYS SINCE LAST RUN

Days	Prop	Win	Runs	Wins%	£
1..7	24%	4	22	18.2%	-0.50
8..14	35%	6	30	20.0%	-0.27
15..28	24%	4	50	8.0%	-0.40
29..60	12%	2	29	6.9%	-0.79
61..100	6%	1	3	33.3%	0.50
101+	0%	0	11	0.0%	-1.00
Unraced	0%	0	1	0.0%	-1.00

ANALYSIS BY TODAY'S STARTING PRICE

Price	Prop	Win	Runs	Wins%	£
Odds On	0%	0	0	0.0%	0.00
Ev-2/1	47%	8	13	61.5%	0.61
9/4-4/1	35%	6	27	22.2%	-0.16
9/2-6/1	6%	1	15	6.7%	-0.60
13/2-10/1	6%	1	26	3.8%	-0.65
11/1-16/1	6%	1	19	5.3%	-0.21
18/1-33/1	0%	0	21	0.0%	-1.00
40/1+	0%	0	25	0.0%	-1.00

ANALYSIS BY STARTING PRICE LAST TIME

Price	Prop	Win	Runs	Wins%	£
Odds On	0%	0	1	0.0%	-1.00
Ev-2/1	6%	1	4	25.0%	-0.28
9/4-4/1	24%	4	16	25.0%	-0.27
9/2-6/1	0%	0	12	0.0%	-1.00
13/2-10/1	24%	4	19	21.1%	-0.09
11/1-16/1	24%	4	27	14.8%	-0.03
18/1-33/1	18%	3	33	9.1%	-0.61
40/1+	6%	1	33	3.0%	-0.92
Unraced	0%	0	1	0.0%	-1.00

ANALYSIS BY DISTANCE BEATEN LAST TIME

Lengths	Prop	Win	Runs	Wins%	£
..-10	0%	0	0	0.0%	0.00
-10..0	12%	2	8	25.0%	-0.23
0.1..2	18%	3	15	20.0%	-0.01
2.1..5	24%	4	23	17.4%	-0.43
5.1..10	29%	5	41	12.2%	-0.34
10.1..20	18%	3	45	6.7%	-0.72
20.0..30	0%	0	8	0.0%	-1.00
30.1+	0%	0	5	0.0%	-1.00
Not Compl	0%	0	0	0.0%	0.00
Unraced	0%	0	1	0.0%	-1.00

ANALYSIS BY RUN NUMBER

Run No	Prop	Win	Runs	Wins%	£
FTO	0%	0	1	0.0%	-1.00
2nd Run	0%	0	3	0.0%	-1.00
3rd Run	6%	1	6	16.7%	-0.46
4th+ Run	94%	16	136	11.8%	-0.48

ANALYSIS BY POSITION LAST TIME

Pos LT	Prop	Win	Runs	Wins%	£
Won	12%	2	8	25.0%	-0.23
2nd or 3rd	12%	2	18	11.1%	-0.29
Unplaced	76%	13	119	10.9%	-0.54
Not Compl	0%	0	1	0.0%	-1.00

OTHER FACTORS (WINS-RUNS, £)

Course Winner:	2-10	-£0.47
Distance Winner:	6-41	-£0.59
Going Winner:	4-22	-£0.32
Beaten Favourite:	2-10	-£0.39
BHA Top Rated:	4-20	-£0.37
Up in class:	5-34	-£0.31
Same class:	5-72	-£0.66
Down in class:	7-39	-£0.35
7-Day Winners:	1-2	£0.44
Colts and Geldings:	8-73	-£0.45
Fillies:	9-73	-£0.54
Absolute Favourites:	10-15	£0.94

Selling Races

3-Y.O Races: Selling Races – 7 to 9 furlong races

ANALYSIS BY BHA RATING

Rating	Prop	Win	Runs	Wins%	£
120..139	0%	0	0	0.0%	0.00
110..119	0%	0	0	0.0%	0.00
100..109	0%	0	0	0.0%	0.00
90..99	0%	0	0	0.0%	0.00
70..89	17%	9	34	26.5%	-0.17
50..69	58%	31	300	10.3%	-0.30
..49	19%	10	216	4.6%	-0.27
Unrated	6%	3	46	6.5%	-0.48

ANALYSIS BY WEIGHT CARRIED

Weight	Prop	Win	Runs	Wins%	£
10-01+	0%	0	0	0.0%	0.00
9-8..10-00	0%	0	2	0.0%	-1.00
9-0..9-07	26%	14	98	14.3%	-0.09
8-8..8-13	43%	23	282	8.2%	-0.35
8-0..8-07	30%	16	214	7.5%	-0.31
..7-13	0%	0	2	0.0%	-1.00

ANALYSIS BY DAYS SINCE LAST RUN

Days	Prop	Win	Runs	Wins%	£
1..7	15%	8	71	11.3%	-0.60
8..14	23%	12	142	8.5%	-0.55
15..28	28%	15	199	7.5%	-0.48
29..60	25%	13	103	12.6%	0.84
61..100	0%	0	20	0.0%	-1.00
101+	9%	5	55	9.1%	-0.37
Unraced	0%	0	8	0.0%	-1.00

ANALYSIS BY TODAY'S STARTING PRICE

Price	Prop	Win	Runs	Wins%	£
Odds On	0%	0	1	0.0%	-1.00
Ev-2/1	25%	13	24	54.2%	0.43
9/4-4/1	26%	14	68	20.6%	-0.18
9/2-6/1	15%	8	63	12.7%	-0.20
13/2-10/1	15%	8	101	7.9%	-0.32
11/1-16/1	11%	6	102	5.9%	-0.16
18/1-33/1	6%	3	112	2.7%	-0.25
40/1+	2%	1	127	0.8%	-0.68

ANALYSIS BY STARTING PRICE LAST TIME

Price	Prop	Win	Runs	Wins%	£
Odds On	4%	2	2	100.0%	1.30
Ev-2/1	6%	3	14	21.4%	-0.27
9/4-4/1	17%	9	31	29.0%	0.63
9/2-6/1	2%	1	39	2.6%	-0.92
13/2-10/1	21%	11	94	11.7%	-0.04
11/1-16/1	17%	9	106	8.5%	-0.54
18/1-33/1	26%	14	160	8.8%	0.05
40/1+	8%	4	144	2.8%	-0.69
Unraced	0%	0	8	0.0%	-1.00

ANALYSIS BY DISTANCE BEATEN LAST TIME

Lengths	Prop	Win	Runs	Wins%	£
..-10	0%	0	0	0.0%	0.00
-10..0	6%	3	9	33.3%	-0.13
0.1..2	6%	3	37	8.1%	-0.71
2.1..5	21%	11	86	12.8%	-0.27
5.1..10	36%	19	162	11.7%	-0.10
10.1..20	26%	14	167	8.4%	-0.19
20.0..30	4%	2	63	3.2%	-0.27
30.1+	2%	1	66	1.5%	-0.80
Not Compl	0%	0	0	0.0%	0.00
Unraced	0%	0	8	0.0%	-1.00

ANALYSIS BY RUN NUMBER

Run No	Prop	Win	Runs	Wins%	£
FTO	0%	0	8	0.0%	-1.00
2nd Run	0%	0	17	0.0%	-1.00
3rd Run	6%	3	19	15.8%	0.26
4th+ Run	94%	50	554	9.0%	-0.28

ANALYSIS BY POSITION LAST TIME

Pos LT	Prop	Win	Runs	Wins%	£
Won	6%	3	9	33.3%	-0.13
2nd or 3rd	9%	5	68	7.4%	-0.70
Unplaced	85%	45	513	8.8%	-0.23
Not Compl	0%	0	8	0.0%	-1.00

OTHER FACTORS (WINS-RUNS, £)

Course Winner:	0-16	-£1.00
Distance Winner:	6-45	£0.23
Going Winner:	3-34	-£0.60
Beaten Favourite:	4-25	-£0.45
BHA Top Rated:	13-53	£0.64
Up in class:	4-50	-£0.29
Same class:	30-376	-£0.30
Down in class:	19-164	-£0.26
7-Day Winners:	1-2	£0.05
Colts and Geldings:	29-318	-£0.41
Fillies:	24-280	-£0.17
Absolute Favourites:	19-50	£0.18

TRAINERS (WINS-RUNS, £)

M Quinn 4-10 £1.35; J M Bradley 1-10 £1.10; W R Muir 1-12 £0.08.

Race Profiles

3-Y.O Races: Selling Races – 10 to 14 furlong races

ANALYSIS BY BHA RATING

Rating	Prop	Win	Runs	Wins%	£
120..139	0%	0	0	0.0%	0.00
110..119	0%	0	0	0.0%	0.00
100..109	0%	0	0	0.0%	0.00
90..99	0%	0	0	0.0%	0.00
70..89	7%	4	25	16.0%	-0.48
50..69	52%	29	225	12.9%	-0.21
..49	29%	16	235	6.8%	-0.24
Unrated	13%	7	58	12.1%	1.08

ANALYSIS BY WEIGHT CARRIED

Weight	Prop	Win	Runs	Wins%	£
10-01+	0%	0	0	0.0%	0.00
9-8..10-00	2%	1	1	100.0%	1.00
9-0..9-07	16%	9	85	10.6%	-0.52
8-8..8-13	43%	24	241	10.0%	-0.24
8-0..8-07	39%	22	211	10.4%	0.25
..7-13	0%	0	5	0.0%	-1.00

ANALYSIS BY DAYS SINCE LAST RUN

Days	Prop	Win	Runs	Wins%	£
1..7	13%	7	64	10.9%	-0.25
8..14	38%	21	124	16.9%	1.11
15..28	30%	17	173	9.8%	-0.42
29..60	18%	10	105	9.5%	-0.29
61..100	2%	1	26	3.8%	-0.91
101+	0%	0	46	0.0%	-1.00
Unraced	0%	0	5	0.0%	-1.00

ANALYSIS BY TODAY'S STARTING PRICE

Price	Prop	Win	Runs	Wins%	£
Odds On	2%	1	3	33.3%	-0.46
Ev-2/1	16%	9	24	37.5%	-0.06
9/4-4/1	32%	18	85	21.2%	-0.13
9/2-6/1	14%	8	63	12.7%	-0.18
13/2-10/1	16%	9	111	8.1%	-0.31
11/1-16/1	14%	8	93	8.6%	0.12
18/1-33/1	2%	1	96	1.0%	-0.76
40/1+	4%	2	68	2.9%	0.97

ANALYSIS BY STARTING PRICE LAST TIME

Price	Prop	Win	Runs	Wins%	£
Odds On	0%	0	1	0.0%	-1.00
Ev-2/1	4%	2	8	25.0%	0.00
9/4-4/1	7%	4	27	14.8%	-0.38
9/2-6/1	11%	6	41	14.6%	-0.02
13/2-10/1	23%	13	82	15.9%	-0.18
11/1-16/1	21%	12	101	11.9%	0.06
18/1-33/1	23%	13	148	8.8%	-0.41
40/1+	11%	6	130	4.6%	0.24
Unraced	0%	0	5	0.0%	-1.00

ANALYSIS BY DISTANCE BEATEN LAST TIME

Lengths	Prop	Win	Runs	Wins%	£
..-10	0%	0	0	0.0%	0.00
-10..0	4%	2	9	22.2%	0.56
0.1..2	14%	8	37	21.6%	-0.20
2.1..5	18%	10	77	13.0%	-0.09
5.1..10	21%	12	104	11.5%	-0.34
10.1..20	27%	15	165	9.1%	0.03
20.0..30	7%	4	71	5.6%	-0.55
30.1+	9%	5	75	6.7%	0.38
Not Compl	0%	0	0	0.0%	0.00
Unraced	0%	0	5	0.0%	-1.00

ANALYSIS BY RUN NUMBER

Run No	Prop	Win	Runs	Wins%	£
FTO	0%	0	5	0.0%	-1.00
2nd Run	5%	3	15	20.0%	0.60
3rd Run	5%	3	30	10.0%	-0.01
4th+ Run	89%	50	493	10.1%	-0.12

ANALYSIS BY POSITION LAST TIME

Pos LT	Prop	Win	Runs	Wins%	£
Won	4%	2	9	22.2%	0.56
2nd or 3rd	16%	9	66	13.6%	-0.32
Unplaced	80%	45	460	9.8%	-0.07
Not Compl	0%	0	8	0.0%	-1.00

OTHER FACTORS (WINS-RUNS, £)

Course Winner:	0-8	-£1.00
Distance Winner:	2-23	-£0.79
Going Winner:	0-19	-£1.00
Beaten Favourite:	4-14	£0.64
BHA Top Rated:	11-57	-£0.00
Up in class:	5-67	£0.23
Same class:	34-322	-£0.09
Down in class:	17-149	-£0.24
7-Day Winners:	0-1	-£1.00
Colts and Geldings:	23-259	-£0.44
Fillies:	33-284	£0.21
Absolute Favourites:	15-47	-£0.08

TRAINERS (WINS-RUNS, £)

A B Haynes 1-14 £0.64; M H Tompkins 3-15 £0.23.

Handicaps (Class 1..3)

3-Y.O Races: Handicaps (Class 1..3)

ANALYSIS BY BHA RATING

Rating	Prop	Win	Runs	Wins%	£
120..139	0%	0	0	0.0%	0.00
110..119	0%	0	4	0.0%	-1.00
100..109	2%	12	159	7.5%	-0.24
90..99	27%	141	1440	9.8%	-0.29
70..89	71%	371	3745	9.9%	-0.18
50..69	0%	0	16	0.0%	-1.00
..49	0%	0	0	0.0%	0.00
Unrated	0%	0	1	0.0%	-1.00

ANALYSIS BY WEIGHT CARRIED

Weight	Prop	Win	Runs	Wins%	£
10-01+	0%	0	0	0.0%	0.00
9-8..10-00	2%	8	97	8.2%	-0.64
9-0..9-07	46%	242	2056	11.8%	-0.20
8-8..8-13	33%	172	1827	9.4%	-0.24
8-0..8-07	19%	97	1259	7.7%	-0.16
..7-13	1%	5	126	4.0%	-0.10

ANALYSIS BY DAYS SINCE LAST RUN

Days	Prop	Win	Runs	Wins%	£
1..7	7%	36	286	12.6%	0.04
8..14	15%	80	1015	7.9%	-0.37
15..28	40%	212	2079	10.2%	-0.18
29..60	20%	106	1026	10.3%	-0.18
61..100	4%	21	191	11.0%	0.09
101+	13%	69	762	9.1%	-0.28
Unraced	0%	0	6	0.0%	-1.00

ANALYSIS BY TODAY'S STARTING PRICE

Price	Prop	Win	Runs	Wins%	£
Odds On	4%	21	30	70.0%	0.23
Ev-2/1	12%	63	176	35.8%	-0.07
9/4-4/1	27%	139	666	20.9%	-0.12
9/2-6/1	19%	102	631	16.2%	-0.01
13/2-10/1	20%	104	1215	8.6%	-0.21
11/1-16/1	11%	59	1225	4.8%	-0.31
18/1-33/1	6%	31	1030	3.0%	-0.26
40/1+	1%	5	392	1.3%	-0.32

ANALYSIS BY STARTING PRICE LAST TIME

Price	Prop	Win	Runs	Wins%	£
Odds On	7%	38	216	17.6%	-0.02
Ev-2/1	14%	73	468	15.6%	-0.17
9/4-4/1	22%	114	1008	11.3%	-0.29
9/2-6/1	15%	80	724	11.0%	-0.17
13/2-10/1	19%	101	1105	9.1%	-0.25
11/1-16/1	12%	61	891	6.8%	-0.27
18/1-33/1	8%	44	697	6.3%	-0.13
40/1+	2%	13	250	5.2%	-0.12
Unraced	0%	0	6	0.0%	-1.00

ANALYSIS BY DISTANCE BEATEN LAST TIME

Lengths	Prop	Win	Runs	Wins%	£
..-10	0%	2	14	14.3%	-0.75
-10..0	35%	184	1360	13.5%	-0.29
0.1..2	21%	111	903	12.3%	-0.17
2.1..5	18%	94	1045	9.0%	-0.28
5.1..10	17%	89	1139	7.8%	-0.09
10.1..20	5%	28	646	4.3%	-0.29
20.0..30	2%	12	154	7.8%	0.05
30.1+	1%	4	98	4.1%	0.16
Not Compl	0%	0	0	0.0%	0.00
Unraced	0%	0	6	0.0%	-1.00

ANALYSIS BY RUN NUMBER

Run No	Prop	Win	Runs	Wins%	£
FTO	0%	0	6	0.0%	-1.00
2nd Run	3%	15	62	24.2%	0.04
3rd Run	7%	39	224	17.4%	-0.06
4th+ Run	90%	470	5073	9.3%	-0.22

ANALYSIS BY POSITION LAST TIME

Pos LT	Prop	Win	Runs	Wins%	£
Won	35%	186	1375	13.5%	-0.30
2nd or 3rd	30%	155	1239	12.5%	-0.12
Unplaced	35%	183	2740	6.7%	-0.21
Not Compl	0%	0	11	0.0%	-1.00

OTHER FACTORS (WINS-RUNS, £)

Course Winner:	63-481	£0.04
Distance Winner:	283-2582	-£0.20
Going Winner:	187-1847	-£0.25
Beaten Favourite:	62-453	-£0.12
Up in class:	298-2869	-£0.21
Same class:	152-1629	-£0.24
Down in class:	74-841	-£0.14
7-Day Winners:	11-63	-£0.06
Colts and Geldings:	432-4291	-£0.21
Fillies:	75-852	-£0.20
Absolute Favourites:	148-473	-£0.00

TRAINERS (WINS-RUNS, £)

H Morrison 6-50 £0.99; B Ellison 3-13 £2.12; M H Tompkins 6-57 £0.47; Peter Grayson 2-12 £2.00; M L W Bell 11-79 £0.28; J G Portman 1-12 £1.83; P W Chapple-Hyam 8-53 £0.41; W Jarvis 4-25 £0.85; R M Whitaker 1-20 £1.05; R A Fahey 14-157 £0.12; J R Best 3-14 £1.33; D Nicholls 6-49 £0.34; M P Tregoning 2-44 £0.36; R M Beckett 3-28 £0.54; J Noseda 8-51 £0.21; W G M Turner 3-12 £0.83; H Candy 6-30 £0.33; E S McMahon 4-24 £0.25; J J Quinn 3-25 £0.22; G A Swinbank 6-33 £0.13.

Race Profiles

3-Y.O Races: Handicaps (Class 1..3) – 2 to 7 runners

ANALYSIS BY BHA RATING

Rating	Prop	Win	Runs	Wins%	£
120..139	0%	0	0	0.0%	0.00
110..119	0%	0	0	0.0%	0.00
100..109	1%	1	11	9.1%	-0.68
90..99	26%	34	137	24.8%	0.12
70..89	73%	97	630	15.4%	-0.12
50..69	0%	0	0	0.0%	-1.00
..49	0%	0	0	0.0%	0.00
Unrated	0%	0	0	0.0%	0.00

ANALYSIS BY WEIGHT CARRIED

Weight	Prop	Win	Runs	Wins%	£
10-01+	0%	0	0	0.0%	0.00
9-8..10-00	3%	4	13	30.8%	-0.39
9-0..9-07	55%	72	378	19.0%	-0.16
8-8..8-13	28%	37	242	15.3%	-0.13
8-0..8-07	14%	19	135	14.1%	0.32
..7-13	0%	0	18	0.0%	-1.00

ANALYSIS BY DAYS SINCE LAST RUN

Days	Prop	Win	Runs	Wins%	£
1..7	8%	11	48	22.9%	0.08
8..14	17%	23	175	13.1%	-0.20
15..28	30%	40	274	14.6%	-0.41
29..60	25%	33	161	20.5%	0.26
61..100	6%	8	28	28.6%	1.43
101+	13%	17	100	17.0%	-0.13
Unraced	0%	0	0	0.0%	0.00

ANALYSIS BY TODAY'S STARTING PRICE

Price	Prop	Win	Runs	Wins%	£
Odds On	14%	18	26	69.2%	0.20
Ev-2/1	25%	33	86	38.4%	-0.03
9/4-4/1	27%	35	186	18.8%	-0.24
9/2-6/1	13%	17	114	14.9%	-0.10
13/2-10/1	16%	21	194	10.8%	0.04
11/1-16/1	4%	5	111	4.5%	-0.37
18/1-33/1	2%	3	60	5.0%	0.35
40/1+	0%	0	9	0.0%	-1.00

ANALYSIS BY STARTING PRICE LAST TIME

Price	Prop	Win	Runs	Wins%	£
Odds On	9%	12	49	24.5%	-0.08
Ev-2/1	17%	23	67	34.3%	0.21
9/4-4/1	19%	25	164	15.2%	-0.21
9/2-6/1	16%	21	114	18.4%	-0.14
13/2-10/1	17%	22	148	14.9%	-0.26
11/1-16/1	13%	17	124	13.7%	0.07
18/1-33/1	7%	9	86	10.5%	-0.30
40/1+	2%	3	34	8.8%	0.65
Unraced	0%	0	0	0.0%	0.00

ANALYSIS BY DISTANCE BEATEN LAST TIME

Lengths	Prop	Win	Runs	Wins%	£
..-10	2%	2	5	40.0%	-0.29
-10..0	44%	58	238	24.4%	-0.08
0.1..2	20%	26	135	19.3%	-0.14
2.1..5	17%	22	141	15.6%	-0.13
5.1..10	13%	17	147	11.6%	0.12
10.1..20	3%	4	86	4.7%	-0.57
20.0..30	2%	2	14	14.3%	1.64
30.1+	1%	1	20	5.0%	-0.45
Not Compl	0%	0	0	0.0%	0.00
Unraced	0%	0	0	0.0%	0.00

ANALYSIS BY RUN NUMBER

Run No	Prop	Win	Runs	Wins%	£
FTO	0%	0	0	0.0%	0.00
2nd Run	4%	5	15	33.3%	0.13
3rd Run	11%	14	45	31.1%	0.24
4th+ Run	86%	113	726	15.6%	-0.12

ANALYSIS BY POSITION LAST TIME

Pos LT	Prop	Win	Runs	Wins%	£
Won	45%	60	243	24.7%	-0.09
2nd or 3rd	27%	36	185	19.5%	-0.01
Unplaced	27%	36	358	10.1%	-0.15
Not Compl	0%	0	0	0.0%	0.00

OTHER FACTORS (WINS-RUNS, £)

Course Winner:	11-65	-£0.48
Distance Winner:	71-336	£0.00
Going Winner:	51-241	£0.01
Beaten Favourite:	11-70	-£0.28
Up in class:	80-468	-£0.10
Same class:	42-199	£0.10
Down in class:	10-119	-£0.37
7-Day Winners:	3-9	-£0.00
Colts and Geldings:	106-618	-£0.06
Fillies:	23-150	-£0.15
Absolute Favourites:	55-129	£0.01

TRAINERS (WINS-RUNS, £)

M A Jarvis 10-25 £0.50; M Johnston 21-75 £0.12; J H M Gosden 6-19 £0.42; J Noseda 4-10 £0.73; M H Tompkins 3-19 £0.32; R Charlton 3-13 £0.21.

Handicaps (Class 1..3)

3-Y.O Races: Handicaps (Class 1..3) – 8 to 14 runners

ANALYSIS BY BHA RATING

Rating	Prop	Win	Runs	Wins%	£
120..139	0%	0	0	0.0%	0.00
110..119	0%	0	3	0.0%	-1.00
100..109	3%	8	74	10.8%	-0.39
90..99	23%	72	773	9.3%	-0.33
70..89	75%	240	2436	9.9%	-0.18
50..69	0%	0	8	0.0%	-1.00
..49	0%	0	0	0.0%	0.00
Unrated	0%	0	0	0.0%	0.00

ANALYSIS BY WEIGHT CARRIED

Weight	Prop	Win	Runs	Wins%	£
10-01+	0%	0	0	0.0%	0.00
9-8..10-00	1%	4	77	5.2%	-0.65
9-0..9-07	45%	145	1286	11.3%	-0.20
8-8..8-13	35%	111	1128	9.8%	-0.24
8-0..8-07	18%	59	739	8.0%	-0.12
..7-13	0%	1	64	1.6%	-0.87

ANALYSIS BY DAYS SINCE LAST RUN

Days	Prop	Win	Runs	Wins%	£
1..7	6%	19	172	11.0%	0.09
8..14	16%	51	627	8.1%	-0.38
15..28	43%	138	1242	11.1%	-0.14
29..60	18%	56	583	9.6%	-0.24
61..100	3%	11	113	9.7%	-0.08
101+	14%	45	552	8.2%	-0.31
Unraced	0%	0	5	0.0%	-1.00

ANALYSIS BY TODAY'S STARTING PRICE

Price	Prop	Win	Runs	Wins%	£
Odds On	1%	3	4	75.0%	0.37
Ev-2/1	9%	29	86	33.7%	-0.09
9/4-4/1	29%	92	440	20.9%	-0.10
9/2-6/1	22%	70	437	16.0%	-0.01
13/2-10/1	21%	66	771	8.6%	-0.23
11/1-16/1	13%	42	795	5.3%	-0.24
18/1-33/1	5%	16	578	2.8%	-0.35
40/1+	1%	2	183	1.1%	-0.50

ANALYSIS BY STARTING PRICE LAST TIME

Price	Prop	Win	Runs	Wins%	£
Odds On	7%	22	132	16.7%	0.07
Ev-2/1	12%	39	292	13.4%	-0.23
9/4-4/1	23%	74	613	12.1%	-0.24
9/2-6/1	15%	48	451	10.6%	-0.18
13/2-10/1	20%	64	671	9.5%	-0.21
11/1-16/1	12%	38	557	6.8%	-0.30
18/1-33/1	9%	28	431	6.5%	-0.12
40/1+	2%	7	142	4.9%	-0.52
Unraced	0%	0	5	0.0%	-1.00

ANALYSIS BY DISTANCE BEATEN LAST TIME

Lengths	Prop	Win	Runs	Wins%	£
..-10	0%	0	8	0.0%	-1.00
-10..0	32%	103	825	12.5%	-0.28
0.1..2	22%	70	561	12.5%	-0.20
2.1..5	19%	62	628	9.9%	-0.24
5.1..10	18%	56	711	7.9%	-0.09
10.1..20	7%	22	408	5.4%	-0.20
20.0..30	2%	6	93	6.5%	-0.34
30.1+	0%	1	55	1.8%	-0.82
Not Compl	0%	0	0	0.0%	0.00
Unraced	0%	0	5	0.0%	-1.00

ANALYSIS BY RUN NUMBER

Run No	Prop	Win	Runs	Wins%	£
FTO	0%	0	5	0.0%	-1.00
2nd Run	3%	10	37	27.0%	0.29
3rd Run	7%	22	164	13.4%	-0.19
4th+ Run	90%	288	3088	9.3%	-0.23

ANALYSIS BY POSITION LAST TIME

Pos LT	Prop	Win	Runs	Wins%	£
Won	32%	103	834	12.4%	-0.29
2nd or 3rd	31%	100	747	13.4%	-0.12
Unplaced	37%	117	1704	6.9%	-0.23
Not Compl	0%	0	9	0.0%	-1.00

OTHER FACTORS (WINS-RUNS, £)

Course Winner:	40-299	-£0.08
Distance Winner:	173-1588	-£0.19
Going Winner:	100-1110	-£0.35
Beaten Favourite:	44-285	-£0.01
Up in class:	181-1806	-£0.22
Same class:	84-929	-£0.24
Down in class:	55-554	-£0.17
7-Day Winners:	4-40	-£0.51
Colts and Geldings:	269-2651	-£0.21
Fillies:	44-566	-£0.24
Absolute Favourites:	76-280	-£0.07

TRAINERS (WINS-RUNS, £)

M H Tompkins 3-29 £1.03; M P Tregoning 2-31 £0.94; P W Chapple-Hyam 5-28 £0.98; W Jarvis 3-17 £1.20; R M Beckett 2-19 £0.95; L M Cumani 5-24 £0.50; P A Blockley 2-10 £1.20; H Candy 5-20 £0.59; M A Jarvis 22-100 £0.10; J Noseda 3-29 £0.34; E S McMahon 3-19 £0.29; A Berry 1-12 £0.42; J J Quinn 2-17 £0.26; W G M Turner 2-10 £0.40; C E Brittain 4-35 £0.09; W R Swinburn 4-24 £0.10; M L W Bell 7-44 £0.04; Sir Mark Prescott 3-16 £0.09; J W Hills 3-24 £0.03; C G Cox 6-33 £0.01.

Race Profiles

3-Y.O Races: Handicaps (Class 1..3) – 15 runners or more

ANALYSIS BY BHA RATING

Rating	Prop	Win	Runs	Wins%	£
120..139	0%	0	0	0.0%	0.00
110..119	0%	0	1	0.0%	-1.00
100..109	4%	3	74	4.1%	-0.03
90..99	49%	35	530	6.6%	-0.32
70..89	47%	34	679	5.0%	-0.23
50..69	0%	0	0	0.0%	0.00
..49	0%	0	0	0.0%	0.00
Unrated	0%	0	1	0.0%	-1.00

ANALYSIS BY WEIGHT CARRIED

Weight	Prop	Win	Runs	Wins%	£
10-01+	0%	0	0	0.0%	0.00
9-8..10-00	0%	0	7	0.0%	-1.00
9-0..9-07	35%	25	392	6.4%	-0.25
8-8..8-13	33%	24	457	5.3%	-0.28
8-0..8-07	26%	19	385	4.9%	-0.41
..7-13	6%	4	44	9.1%	1.39

ANALYSIS BY DAYS SINCE LAST RUN

Days	Prop	Win	Runs	Wins%	£
1..7	8%	6	66	9.1%	-0.13
8..14	8%	6	213	2.8%	-0.49
15..28	47%	34	563	6.0%	-0.15
29..60	24%	17	282	6.0%	-0.31
61..100	3%	2	50	4.0%	-0.27
101+	10%	7	110	6.4%	-0.25
Unraced	0%	0	1	0.0%	-1.00

ANALYSIS BY TODAY'S STARTING PRICE

Price	Prop	Win	Runs	Wins%	£
Odds On	0%	0	0	0.0%	0.00
Ev-2/1	1%	1	4	25.0%	-0.44
9/4-4/1	17%	12	40	30.0%	0.23
9/2-6/1	21%	15	80	18.8%	0.11
13/2-10/1	24%	17	250	6.8%	-0.34
11/1-16/1	17%	12	319	3.8%	-0.47
18/1-33/1	17%	12	392	3.1%	-0.22
40/1+	4%	3	200	1.5%	-0.13

ANALYSIS BY STARTING PRICE LAST TIME

Price	Prop	Win	Runs	Wins%	£
Odds On	6%	4	35	11.4%	-0.26
Ev-2/1	15%	11	109	10.1%	-0.25
9/4-4/1	21%	15	231	6.5%	-0.46
9/2-6/1	15%	11	159	6.9%	-0.14
13/2-10/1	21%	15	286	5.2%	-0.32
11/1-16/1	8%	6	210	2.9%	-0.40
18/1-33/1	10%	7	180	3.9%	-0.07
40/1+	4%	3	74	4.1%	0.30
Unraced	0%	0	1	0.0%	-1.00

ANALYSIS BY DISTANCE BEATEN LAST TIME

Lengths	Prop	Win	Runs	Wins%	£
..-10	0%	0	1	0.0%	-1.00
-10..0	32%	23	297	7.7%	-0.50
0.1..2	21%	15	207	7.2%	-0.14
2.1..5	14%	10	276	3.6%	-0.45
5.1..10	22%	16	281	5.7%	-0.19
10.1..20	3%	2	152	1.3%	-0.39
20.0..30	6%	4	47	8.5%	0.35
30.1+	3%	2	23	8.7%	3.04
Not Compl	0%	0	0	0.0%	0.00
Unraced	0%	0	1	0.0%	-1.00

ANALYSIS BY RUN NUMBER

Run No	Prop	Win	Runs	Wins%	£
FTO	0%	0	1	0.0%	-1.00
2nd Run	0%	0	10	0.0%	-1.00
3rd Run	4%	3	15	20.0%	0.43
4th+ Run	96%	69	1259	5.5%	-0.26

ANALYSIS BY POSITION LAST TIME

Pos LT	Prop	Win	Runs	Wins%	£
Won	32%	23	298	7.7%	-0.50
2nd or 3rd	26%	19	307	6.2%	-0.18
Unplaced	42%	30	678	4.4%	-0.18
Not Compl	0%	0	2	0.0%	-1.00

OTHER FACTORS (WINS-RUNS, £)

Course Winner: 12-117 £0.62
Distance Winner: 39-658 -£0.32
Going Winner: 36-496 -£0.14
Beaten Favourite: 7-98 -£0.32
Up in class: 37-595 -£0.27
Same class: 26-501 -£0.36
Down in class: 9-188 £0.09
7-Day Winners: 4-14 £1.20
Colts and Geldings: 57-1022 -£0.31
Fillies: 8-136 -£0.09
Absolute Favourites: 17-64 £0.25

TRAINERS (WINS-RUNS, £)

H Morrison 3-21 £2.82; R A Fahey 2-30 £1.93; M L W Bell 3-22 £1.07; D Nicholls 3-19 £1.12; R Charlton 2-20 £1.00; A M Balding 3-24 £0.71; D R C Elsworth 2-12 £1.33; J L Dunlop 3-23 £0.43; S Kirk 2-33 £0.30; K R Burke 1-19 £0.11; P W Chapple-Hyam 2-15 £0.08; Sir Michael Stoute 8-48 £0.01.

Handicaps (Class 1..3)

3-Y.O Races: Handicaps (Class 1..3) – good or faster going

ANALYSIS BY BHA RATING
Rating	Prop	Win	Runs	Wins%	£
120..139	0%	0	0	0.0%	0.00
110..119	0%	0	4	0.0%	-1.00
100..109	3%	12	143	8.4%	-0.15
90..99	27%	105	1128	9.3%	-0.33
70..89	70%	279	2873	9.7%	-0.18
50..69	0%	0	15	0.0%	-1.00
..49	0%	0	0	0.0%	0.00
Unrated	0%	0	1	0.0%	-1.00

ANALYSIS BY WEIGHT CARRIED
Weight	Prop	Win	Runs	Wins%	£
10-01+	0%	0	0	0.0%	0.00
9-8..10-00	1%	5	79	6.3%	-0.66
9-0..9-07	49%	195	1610	12.1%	-0.19
8-8..8-13	31%	124	1403	8.8%	-0.24
8-0..8-07	17%	69	972	7.1%	-0.25
..7-13	1%	3	100	3.0%	0.03

ANALYSIS BY DAYS SINCE LAST RUN
Days	Prop	Win	Runs	Wins%	£
1..7	6%	25	232	10.8%	-0.05
8..14	15%	60	795	7.5%	-0.35
15..28	42%	167	1626	10.3%	-0.20
29..60	20%	79	785	10.1%	-0.17
61..100	4%	15	144	10.4%	-0.03
101+	13%	50	577	8.7%	-0.31
Unraced	0%	0	5	0.0%	-1.00

ANALYSIS BY TODAY'S STARTING PRICE
Price	Prop	Win	Runs	Wins%	£
Odds On	4%	16	24	66.7%	0.17
Ev-2/1	11%	44	123	35.8%	-0.08
9/4-4/1	26%	104	503	20.7%	-0.12
9/2-6/1	21%	84	482	17.4%	0.06
13/2-10/1	19%	76	917	8.3%	-0.23
11/1-16/1	11%	45	962	4.7%	-0.33
18/1-33/1	6%	23	819	2.8%	-0.31
40/1+	1%	4	334	1.2%	-0.32

ANALYSIS BY STARTING PRICE LAST TIME
Price	Prop	Win	Runs	Wins%	£
Odds On	7%	29	157	18.5%	-0.03
Ev-2/1	13%	52	359	14.5%	-0.19
9/4-4/1	21%	82	783	10.5%	-0.34
9/2-6/1	18%	70	584	12.0%	-0.05
13/2-10/1	18%	72	845	8.5%	-0.28
11/1-16/1	12%	49	688	7.1%	-0.26
18/1-33/1	8%	30	536	5.6%	-0.28
40/1+	3%	12	207	5.8%	0.01
Unraced	0%	0	5	0.0%	-1.00

ANALYSIS BY DISTANCE BEATEN LAST TIME
Lengths	Prop	Win	Runs	Wins%	£
..-10	0%	1	7	14.3%	-0.71
-10..0	34%	135	1035	13.0%	-0.32
0.1..2	20%	81	702	11.5%	-0.25
2.1..5	19%	74	806	9.2%	-0.27
5.1..10	17%	69	908	7.6%	-0.09
10.1..20	5%	21	504	4.2%	-0.36
20.0..30	3%	11	118	9.3%	0.28
30.1+	1%	4	79	5.1%	0.44
Not Compl	0%	0	0	0.0%	0.00
Unraced	0%	0	5	0.0%	-1.00

ANALYSIS BY RUN NUMBER
Run No	Prop	Win	Runs	Wins%	£
FTO	0%	0	5	0.0%	-1.00
2nd Run	3%	12	50	24.0%	0.14
3rd Run	6%	25	160	15.6%	-0.30
4th+ Run	91%	359	3949	9.1%	-0.22

ANALYSIS BY POSITION LAST TIME
Pos LT	Prop	Win	Runs	Wins%	£
Won	34%	136	1043	13.0%	-0.33
2nd or 3rd	28%	111	956	11.6%	-0.19
Unplaced	38%	149	2156	6.9%	-0.19
Not Compl	0%	0	9	0.0%	-1.00

OTHER FACTORS (WINS-RUNS, £)
Course Winner:	46-351	-£0.03
Distance Winner:	216-2035	-£0.21
Going Winner:	162-1636	-£0.25
Beaten Favourite:	46-344	-£0.12
Up in class:	225-2197	-£0.22
Same class:	116-1305	-£0.28
Down in class:	55-657	-£0.14
7-Day Winners:	7-49	-£0.11
Colts and Geldings:	323-3295	-£0.23
Fillies:	58-661	-£0.19
Absolute Favourites:	110-356	£0.00

TRAINERS (WINS-RUNS, £)
H Morrison 5-42 £1.13; R M Whitaker 1-14 £1.93; Peter Grayson 2-10 £2.60; W Jarvis 4-22 £1.11; M L W Bell 8-54 £0.42; D Nicholls 5-41 £0.54; J Noseda 8-42 £0.47; J R Best 3-14 £1.33; J L Dunlop 11-72 £0.24; M P Tregoning 1-35 £0.46; R A Fahey 9-115 £0.13; G A Swinbank 6-25 £0.49; H Candy 5-26 £0.44; P A Blockley 2-14 £0.57; E S McMahon 4-23 £0.30; J J Quinn 2-19 £0.37; J G Given 4-33 £0.18; J A Osborne 3-18 £0.29; R Charlton 9-72 £0.07; L M Cumani 6-29 £0.17.

Race Profiles

3-Y.O Races: Handicaps (Class 1..3) – good to soft or softer going

ANALYSIS BY BHA RATING

Rating	Prop	Win	Runs	Wins%	£
120..139	0%	0	0	0.0%	0.00
110..119	0%	0	0	0.0%	0.00
100..109	0%	0	16	0.0%	-1.00
90..99	28%	36	312	11.5%	-0.13
70..89	72%	92	872	10.6%	-0.16
50..69	0%	0	1	0.0%	-1.00
..49	0%	0	0	0.0%	0.00
Unrated	0%	0	0	0.0%	0.00

ANALYSIS BY WEIGHT CARRIED

Weight	Prop	Win	Runs	Wins%	£
10-01+	0%	0	0	0.0%	0.00
9-8..10-00	2%	3	18	16.7%	-0.57
9-0..9-07	37%	47	446	10.5%	-0.26
8-8..8-13	38%	48	424	11.3%	-0.23
8-0..8-07	22%	28	287	9.8%	0.14
..7-13	2%	2	26	7.7%	-0.59

ANALYSIS BY DAYS SINCE LAST RUN

Days	Prop	Win	Runs	Wins%	£
1..7	9%	11	54	20.4%	0.39
8..14	16%	20	220	9.1%	-0.45
15..28	35%	45	453	9.9%	-0.11
29..60	21%	27	241	11.2%	-0.23
61..100	5%	6	47	12.8%	0.46
101+	15%	19	185	10.3%	-0.18
Unraced	0%	0	1	0.0%	-1.00

ANALYSIS BY TODAY'S STARTING PRICE

Price	Prop	Win	Runs	Wins%	£
Odds On	4%	5	6	83.3%	0.44
Ev-2/1	15%	19	53	35.8%	-0.06
9/4-4/1	27%	35	163	21.5%	-0.12
9/2-6/1	14%	18	149	12.1%	-0.25
13/2-10/1	22%	28	298	9.4%	-0.13
11/1-16/1	11%	14	263	5.3%	-0.24
18/1-33/1	6%	8	211	3.8%	-0.08
40/1+	1%	1	58	1.7%	-0.29

ANALYSIS BY STARTING PRICE LAST TIME

Price	Prop	Win	Runs	Wins%	£
Odds On	7%	9	59	15.3%	0.02
Ev-2/1	16%	21	109	19.3%	-0.10
9/4-4/1	25%	32	225	14.2%	-0.09
9/2-6/1	8%	10	140	7.1%	-0.67
13/2-10/1	23%	29	260	11.2%	-0.14
11/1-16/1	9%	12	203	5.9%	-0.31
18/1-33/1	11%	14	161	8.7%	0.38
40/1+	1%	1	43	2.3%	-0.77
Unraced	0%	0	1	0.0%	-1.00

ANALYSIS BY DISTANCE BEATEN LAST TIME

Lengths	Prop	Win	Runs	Wins%	£
..-10	1%	1	7	14.3%	-0.78
-10..0	38%	49	325	15.1%	-0.19
0.1..2	23%	30	201	14.9%	0.09
2.1..5	16%	20	239	8.4%	-0.33
5.1..10	16%	20	231	8.7%	-0.08
10.1..20	5%	7	142	4.9%	-0.05
20.0..30	1%	1	36	2.8%	-0.69
30.1+	0%	0	19	0.0%	-1.00
Not Compl	0%	0	0	0.0%	0.00
Unraced	0%	0	1	0.0%	-1.00

ANALYSIS BY RUN NUMBER

Run No	Prop	Win	Runs	Wins%	£
FTO	0%	0	1	0.0%	-1.00
2nd Run	2%	3	12	25.0%	-0.36
3rd Run	11%	14	64	21.9%	0.55
4th+ Run	87%	111	1124	9.9%	-0.20

ANALYSIS BY POSITION LAST TIME

Pos LT	Prop	Win	Runs	Wins%	£
Won	39%	50	332	15.1%	-0.20
2nd or 3rd	34%	44	283	15.5%	0.13
Unplaced	27%	34	584	5.8%	-0.28
Not Compl	0%	0	2	0.0%	-1.00

OTHER FACTORS (WINS-RUNS, £)

Course Winner:	17-130	£0.21
Distance Winner:	67-547	-£0.15
Going Winner:	25-211	-£0.19
Beaten Favourite:	16-109	-£0.12
Up in class:	73-672	-£0.21
Same class:	36-324	-£0.08
Down in class:	19-204	-£0.15
7-Day Winners:	4-14	£0.11
Colts and Geldings:	109-996	-£0.14
Fillies:	17-191	-£0.26
Absolute Favourites:	38-117	-£0.03

TRAINERS (WINS-RUNS, £)

M H Tompkins 5-18 £2.94; B W Hills 8-49 £0.82; P W Chapple-Hyam 5-13 £2.77; M Johnston 15-75 £0.18; S Kirk 1-14 £0.86; M A Jarvis 8-31 £0.31; C G Cox 3-11 £0.64; R A Fahey 5-42 £0.10.

Handicaps (Class 1..3)

3-Y.O Races: Handicaps (Class 1..3) – 5 to 6 furlong races

ANALYSIS BY BHA RATING

Rating	Prop	Win	Runs	Wins%	£
120..139	0%	0	0	0.0%	0.00
110..119	0%	0	0	0.0%	0.00
100..109	1%	1	40	2.5%	-0.70
90..99	33%	43	441	9.8%	-0.27
70..89	66%	86	958	9.0%	-0.22
50..69	0%	0	2	0.0%	-1.00
..49	0%	0	0	0.0%	0.00
Unrated	0%	0	1	0.0%	-1.00

ANALYSIS BY WEIGHT CARRIED

Weight	Prop	Win	Runs	Wins%	£
10-01+	0%	0	0	0.0%	0.00
9-8..10-00	1%	1	35	2.9%	-0.95
9-0..9-07	46%	60	507	11.8%	-0.14
8-8..8-13	29%	38	464	8.2%	-0.40
8-0..8-07	22%	29	401	7.2%	-0.16
..7-13	2%	2	35	5.7%	-0.16

ANALYSIS BY DAYS SINCE LAST RUN

Days	Prop	Win	Runs	Wins%	£
1..7	13%	17	112	15.2%	0.42
8..14	16%	21	326	6.4%	-0.60
15..28	40%	52	514	10.1%	-0.11
29..60	13%	17	228	7.5%	-0.42
61..100	2%	2	30	6.7%	-0.50
101+	16%	21	232	9.1%	-0.19
Unraced	0%	0	0	0.0%	0.00

ANALYSIS BY TODAY'S STARTING PRICE

Price	Prop	Win	Runs	Wins%	£
Odds On	3%	4	4	100.0%	0.88
Ev-2/1	9%	12	36	33.3%	0.20
9/4-4/1	25%	33	152	21.7%	-0.12
9/2-6/1	18%	23	159	14.5%	-0.13
13/2-10/1	24%	31	342	9.1%	-0.17
11/1-16/1	15%	19	330	5.8%	-0.14
18/1-33/1	5%	7	311	2.3%	-0.48
40/1+	1%	1	108	0.9%	-0.62

ANALYSIS BY STARTING PRICE LAST TIME

Price	Prop	Win	Runs	Wins%	£
Odds On	5%	6	29	20.7%	0.17
Ev-2/1	11%	14	98	14.3%	-0.19
9/4-4/1	22%	28	233	12.0%	-0.18
9/2-6/1	16%	21	197	10.7%	-0.16
13/2-10/1	23%	30	336	8.9%	-0.34
11/1-16/1	11%	14	233	6.0%	-0.42
18/1-33/1	10%	13	231	5.6%	-0.10
40/1+	3%	4	85	4.7%	-0.46
Unraced	0%	0	0	0.0%	0.00

ANALYSIS BY DISTANCE BEATEN LAST TIME

Lengths	Prop	Win	Runs	Wins%	£
..-10	0%	0	0	0.0%	0.00
-10..0	26%	34	284	12.0%	-0.35
0.1..2	25%	32	260	12.3%	-0.05
2.1..5	26%	34	316	10.8%	-0.17
5.1..10	15%	19	338	5.6%	-0.28
10.1..20	5%	6	187	3.2%	-0.49
20.0..30	3%	4	40	10.0%	-0.01
30.1+	1%	1	17	5.9%	-0.41
Not Compl	0%	0	0	0.0%	0.00
Unraced	0%	0	0	0.0%	0.00

ANALYSIS BY RUN NUMBER

Run No	Prop	Win	Runs	Wins%	£
FTO	0%	0	0	0.0%	0.00
2nd Run	1%	1	9	11.1%	-0.78
3rd Run	5%	6	38	15.8%	-0.22
4th+ Run	95%	123	1395	8.8%	-0.25

ANALYSIS BY POSITION LAST TIME

Pos LT	Prop	Win	Runs	Wins%	£
Won	26%	34	284	12.0%	-0.35
2nd or 3rd	32%	41	308	13.3%	0.04
Unplaced	42%	55	848	6.5%	-0.32
Not Compl	0%	0	2	0.0%	-1.00

OTHER FACTORS (WINS-RUNS, £)

Course Winner:	15-146	-£0.17
Distance Winner:	102-1073	-£0.19
Going Winner:	47-552	-£0.26
Beaten Favourite:	14-103	-£0.27
Up in class:	68-708	-£0.22
Same class:	37-471	-£0.34
Down in class:	25-263	-£0.17
7-Day Winners:	3-23	-£0.26
Colts and Geldings:	100-1105	-£0.31
Fillies:	30-337	-£0.06
Absolute Favourites:	36-111	£0.04

TRAINERS (WINS-RUNS, £)

P W Chapple-Hyam 4-10 £2.93; D Nicholls 6-38 £0.73; R M Whitaker 1-15 £1.73; Peter Grayson 2-12 £2.00; E S McMahon 4-15 £1.00; W J Haggas 3-17 £0.62; W G M Turner 3-87 £0.83; J J Quinn 3-24 £0.27; H Morrison 3-17 £0.37; A Berry 1-14 £0.21; R Charlton 4-18 £0.14.

Race Profiles

3-Y.O Races: Handicaps (Class 1..3) – 7 to 9 furlong races

ANALYSIS BY BHA RATING

Rating	Prop	Win	Runs	Wins%	£
120..139	0%	0	0	0.0%	0.00
110..119	0%	0	3	0.0%	-1.00
100..109	4%	9	90	10.0%	-0.17
90..99	23%	49	595	8.2%	-0.38
70..89	73%	156	1549	10.1%	-0.19
50..69	0%	0	5	0.0%	1.00
..49	0%	0	0	0.0%	0.00
Unrated	0%	0	0	0.0%	0.00

ANALYSIS BY WEIGHT CARRIED

Weight	Prop	Win	Runs	Wins%	£
10-01+	0%	0	0	0.0%	0.00
9-8..10-00	2%	5	39	12.8%	-0.31
9-0..9-07	43%	92	884	10.4%	-0.28
8-8..8-13	38%	81	789	10.3%	-0.16
8-0..8-07	16%	34	482	7.1%	-0.26
..7-13	1%	2	48	4.2%	-0.64

ANALYSIS BY DAYS SINCE LAST RUN

Days	Prop	Win	Runs	Wins%	£
1..7	6%	12	99	12.1%	0.07
8..14	13%	28	389	7.2%	-0.51
15..28	37%	79	867	9.1%	-0.33
29..60	24%	51	425	12.0%	-0.02
61..100	7%	14	100	14.0%	0.49
101+	14%	30	358	8.4%	-0.28
Unraced	0%	0	4	0.0%	-1.00

ANALYSIS BY TODAY'S STARTING PRICE

Price	Prop	Win	Runs	Wins%	£
Odds On	4%	8	11	72.7%	0.29
Ev-2/1	11%	23	70	32.9%	-0.13
9/4-4/1	29%	62	281	22.1%	-0.07
9/2-6/1	21%	45	260	17.3%	0.07
13/2-10/1	18%	38	467	8.1%	-0.25
11/1-16/1	12%	25	523	4.8%	-0.34
18/1-33/1	5%	11	445	2.5%	-0.38
40/1+	1%	2	185	1.1%	-0.42

ANALYSIS BY STARTING PRICE LAST TIME

Price	Prop	Win	Runs	Wins%	£
Odds On	7%	16	79	20.3%	0.15
Ev-2/1	16%	35	199	17.6%	-0.12
9/4-4/1	23%	49	427	11.5%	-0.28
9/2-6/1	15%	33	296	11.1%	-0.11
13/2-10/1	19%	40	431	9.3%	-0.18
11/1-16/1	11%	23	397	5.8%	-0.51
18/1-33/1	7%	15	293	5.1%	-0.23
40/1+	1%	3	116	2.6%	-0.23
Unraced	0%	0	4	0.0%	-1.00

ANALYSIS BY DISTANCE BEATEN LAST TIME

Lengths	Prop	Win	Runs	Wins%	£
..-10	0%	1	3	33.3%	-0.48
-10..0	36%	78	536	14.6%	-0.22
0.1..2	21%	46	367	12.5%	-0.14
2.1..5	15%	32	453	7.1%	-0.41
5.1..10	17%	36	477	7.5%	-0.33
10.1..20	7%	15	291	5.2%	-0.17
20.0..30	2%	5	66	7.6%	0.16
30.1+	0%	1	45	2.2%	0.49
Not Compl	0%	0	0	0.0%	0.00
Unraced	0%	0	4	0.0%	-1.00

ANALYSIS BY RUN NUMBER

Run No	Prop	Win	Runs	Wins%	£
FTO	0%	0	4	0.0%	-1.00
2nd Run	3%	7	30	23.3%	-0.04
3rd Run	9%	20	105	19.0%	0.26
4th+ Run	87%	187	2103	8.9%	-0.27

ANALYSIS BY POSITION LAST TIME

Pos LT	Prop	Win	Runs	Wins%	£
Won	37%	79	539	14.7%	-0.23
2nd or 3rd	30%	64	503	12.7%	-0.11
Unplaced	33%	71	1193	6.0%	-0.30
Not Compl	0%	0	7	0.0%	-1.00

OTHER FACTORS (WINS-RUNS, £)

Course Winner:	23-184	-£0.18
Distance Winner:	115-985	-£0.20
Going Winner:	79-765	-£0.24
Beaten Favourite:	28-191	-£0.00
Up in class:	123-1165	-£0.24
Same class:	64-668	-£0.26
Down in class:	27-405	-£0.22
7-Day Winners:	4-20	£0.23
Colts and Geldings:	176-1711	-£0.22
Fillies:	22-315	-£0.35
Absolute Favourites:	62-198	£0.06

TRAINERS (WINS-RUNS, £)

H Morrison 3-23 £2.32; B W Hills 21-121 £0.38; M H Tompkins 4-28 £1.50; J Noseda 6-23 £1.36; M L W Bell 6-43 £0.60; R M Beckett 1-13 £1.23; J L Dunlop 7-35 £0.38; W Jarvis 2-13 £0.95; R Charlton 5-36 £0.32; J W Hills 3-23 £0.21; C G Cox 4-22 £0.20; J R Fanshawe 4-11 £0.38; E J O'Neill 2-11 £0.23; W R Swinburn 3-20 £0.13; J G Given 1-13 £0.15.

Handicaps (Class 1..3)

3-Y.O Races: Handicaps (Class 1..3) – 10 to 14 furlong races

ANALYSIS BY BHA RATING

Rating	Prop	Win	Runs	Wins%	£
120..139	0%	0	0	0.0%	0.00
110..119	0%	0	1	0.0%	-1.00
100..109	1%	2	29	6.9%	0.17
90..99	27%	49	404	12.1%	-0.17
70..89	72%	128	1233	10.4%	-0.13
50..69	0%	0	8	0.0%	-1.00
..49	0%	0	0	0.0%	0.00
Unrated	0%	0	0	0.0%	0.00

ANALYSIS BY WEIGHT CARRIED

Weight	Prop	Win	Runs	Wins%	£
10-01+	0%	0	0	0.0%	0.00
9-8..10-00	1%	2	22	9.1%	-0.72
9-0..9-07	50%	89	662	13.4%	-0.15
8-8..8-13	30%	53	573	9.2%	-0.21
8-0..8-07	19%	34	375	9.1%	-0.04
..7-13	1%	1	43	2.3%	0.56

ANALYSIS BY DAYS SINCE LAST RUN

Days	Prop	Win	Runs	Wins%	£
1..7	4%	7	75	9.3%	-0.58
8..14	17%	31	299	10.4%	0.06
15..28	45%	80	694	11.5%	-0.05
29..60	21%	38	372	10.2%	-0.22
61..100	3%	5	61	8.2%	-0.26
101+	10%	18	172	10.5%	-0.41
Unraced	0%	0	2	0.0%	-1.00

ANALYSIS BY TODAY'S STARTING PRICE

Price	Prop	Win	Runs	Wins%	£
Odds On	5%	9	15	60.0%	0.00
Ev-2/1	16%	28	70	40.0%	0.05
9/4-4/1	25%	44	230	19.1%	-0.19
9/2-6/1	19%	34	211	16.1%	-0.02
13/2-10/1	19%	34	404	8.4%	-0.22
11/1-16/1	8%	15	372	4.0%	-0.43
18/1-33/1	7%	13	274	4.7%	0.16
40/1+	1%	2	99	2.0%	0.19

ANALYSIS BY STARTING PRICE LAST TIME

Price	Prop	Win	Runs	Wins%	£
Odds On	9%	16	107	15.0%	-0.18
Ev-2/1	13%	24	171	14.0%	-0.21
9/4-4/1	21%	37	346	10.7%	-0.36
9/2-6/1	14%	25	230	10.9%	-0.28
13/2-10/1	17%	31	336	9.2%	-0.23
11/1-16/1	13%	24	261	9.2%	0.23
18/1-33/1	9%	16	173	9.2%	0.00
40/1+	3%	6	49	12.2%	0.73
Unraced	0%	0	2	0.0%	-1.00

ANALYSIS BY DISTANCE BEATEN LAST TIME

Lengths	Prop	Win	Runs	Wins%	£
..-10	1%	1	11	9.1%	-0.82
-10..0	40%	72	539	13.4%	-0.33
0.1..2	18%	33	274	12.0%	-0.32
2.1..5	16%	28	276	10.1%	-0.18
5.1..10	19%	34	322	10.6%	0.48
10.1..20	3%	6	167	3.6%	-0.32
20.0..30	2%	3	48	6.3%	-0.05
30.1+	1%	2	36	5.6%	0.03
Not Compl	0%	0	0	0.0%	0.00
Unraced	0%	0	2	0.0%	-1.00

ANALYSIS BY RUN NUMBER

Run No	Prop	Win	Runs	Wins%	£
FTO	0%	0	2	0.0%	-1.00
2nd Run	4%	7	23	30.4%	0.46
3rd Run	7%	13	81	16.0%	-0.40
4th+ Run	89%	159	1569	10.1%	-0.13

ANALYSIS BY POSITION LAST TIME

Pos LT	Prop	Win	Runs	Wins%	£
Won	41%	73	551	13.2%	-0.34
2nd or 3rd	28%	50	425	11.8%	-0.23
Unplaced	31%	56	697	8.0%	0.08
Not Compl	0%	0	2	0.0%	-1.00

OTHER FACTORS (WINS-RUNS, £)

Course Winner:	25-151	£0.51
Distance Winner:	66-524	-£0.23
Going Winner:	61-528	-£0.24
Beaten Favourite:	20-158	-£0.15
Up in class:	107-992	-£0.18
Same class:	50-489	-£0.12
Down in class:	22-192	£0.06
7-Day Winners:	4-20	-£0.11
Colts and Geldings:	155-1470	-£0.12
Fillies:	23-199	-£0.23
Absolute Favourites:	50-163	-£0.10

TRAINERS (WINS-RUNS, £)

R A Fahey 5-41 £1.57; B J Meehan 4-24 £1.52; M P Tregoning 1-22 £1.32; S Kirk 2-22 £0.95; L M Cumani 6-27 £0.46; K A Ryan 1-15 £0.73; P F I Cole 3-16 £0.67; W R Muir 4-17 £0.45; C E Brittain 3-24 £0.27; M A Jarvis 14-54 £0.09; M Johnston 32-196 £0.02; G A Swinbank 4-13 £0.21; Sir Mark Prescott 3-15 £0.17; P W Chapple-Hyam 1-12 £0.08.

Race Profiles

3-Y.O Races: Handicaps (Class 4..7)

ANALYSIS BY BHA RATING

Rating	Prop	Win	Runs	Wins%	£
120..139	0%	0	0	0.0%	0.00
110..119	0%	0	0	0.0%	0.00
100..109	0%	0	0	0.0%	0.00
90..99	0%	1	4	25.0%	0.08
70..89	45%	1014	8509	11.9%	-0.17
50..69	52%	1164	13736	8.5%	-0.24
..49	3%	79	1536	5.1%	-0.37
Unrated	0%	0	0	0.0%	0.00

ANALYSIS BY WEIGHT CARRIED

Weight	Prop	Win	Runs	Wins%	£
10-01+	0%	0	2	0.0%	-1.00
9-8..10-00	4%	81	361	22.4%	-0.10
9-0..9-07	54%	1214	10403	11.7%	-0.20
8-8..8-13	29%	660	7655	8.6%	-0.20
8-0..8-07	12%	282	4751	5.9%	-0.27
..7-13	1%	21	613	3.4%	-0.52

ANALYSIS BY DAYS SINCE LAST RUN

Days	Prop	Win	Runs	Wins%	£
1..7	12%	272	2016	13.5%	-0.18
8..14	25%	554	5557	10.0%	-0.26
15..28	37%	844	8546	9.9%	-0.20
29..60	15%	342	4081	8.4%	-0.22
61..100	2%	51	831	6.1%	-0.44
101+	9%	193	2740	7.0%	-0.17
Unraced	0%	2	14	14.3%	0.04

ANALYSIS BY TODAY'S STARTING PRICE

Price	Prop	Win	Runs	Wins%	£
Odds On	3%	78	129	60.5%	0.03
Ev-2/1	12%	262	707	37.1%	-0.02
9/4-4/1	28%	622	2853	21.8%	-0.09
9/2-6/1	17%	391	2886	13.5%	-0.16
13/2-10/1	21%	475	5255	9.0%	-0.18
11/1-16/1	12%	275	5223	5.3%	-0.24
18/1-33/1	6%	141	4768	3.0%	-0.26
40/1+	1%	14	1964	0.7%	-0.55

ANALYSIS BY STARTING PRICE LAST TIME

Price	Prop	Win	Runs	Wins%	£
Odds On	3%	57	296	19.3%	-0.12
Ev-2/1	8%	184	957	19.2%	-0.13
9/4-4/1	18%	411	2968	13.8%	-0.21
9/2-6/1	15%	337	2787	12.1%	-0.16
13/2-10/1	22%	499	4885	10.2%	-0.21
11/1-16/1	17%	378	4727	8.0%	-0.18
18/1-33/1	13%	287	4609	6.2%	-0.23
40/1+	5%	103	2542	4.1%	-0.43
Unraced	0%	2	14	14.3%	0.04

ANALYSIS BY DISTANCE BEATEN LAST TIME

Lengths	Prop	Win	Runs	Wins%	£
..-10	0%	4	13	30.8%	-0.24
-10..0	21%	481	2785	17.3%	-0.16
0.1..2	20%	452	3052	14.8%	-0.12
2.1..5	22%	507	4626	11.0%	-0.19
5.1..10	20%	460	6046	7.6%	-0.23
10.1..20	11%	252	5043	5.0%	-0.29
20.0..30	3%	59	1309	4.5%	-0.33
30.1+	2%	41	897	4.6%	-0.28
Not Compl	0%	0	0	0.0%	0.00
Unraced	0%	2	14	14.3%	0.04

ANALYSIS BY RUN NUMBER

Run No	Prop	Win	Runs	Wins%	£
FTO	0%	2	14	14.3%	0.04
2nd Run	1%	25	119	21.0%	0.08
3rd Run	3%	59	399	14.8%	-0.13
4th+ Run	96%	2172	23253	9.3%	-0.22

ANALYSIS BY POSITION LAST TIME

Pos LT	Prop	Win	Runs	Wins%	£
Won	22%	487	2798	17.4%	-0.16
2nd or 3rd	29%	651	4614	14.1%	-0.16
Unplaced	49%	1116	16322	6.8%	-0.25
Not Compl	0%	4	51	7.8%	-0.07

OTHER FACTORS (WINS-RUNS, £)

Course Winner: 142-1081 -£0.26
Distance Winner: 769-5834 -£0.14
Going Winner: 381-3096 -£0.24
Beaten Favourite: 204-1329 -£0.18
Up in class: 475-5084 -£0.25
Same class: 1255-12683 -£0.19
Down in class: 526-6004 -£0.27
7-Day Winners: 99-310 £0.06
Colts and Geldings: 1474-14485 -£0.20
Fillies: 601-7372 -£0.27
Absolute Favourites: 602-2011 -£0.04

TRAINERS (WINS-RUNS, £)

T D Walford 10-33 £2.67; E J Creighton 2-18 £4.22; B G Powell 9-82 £0.91; J Pearce 4-72 £0.94; T T Clement 3-15 £4.23; J L Dunlop 50-362 £0.17; Miss J Feilden 6-55 £1.04; M D I Usher 10-101 £0.55; Sir Mark Prescott 67-170 £0.32; Garry Moss 3-18 £2.19; Mrs G S Rees 5-55 £0.70; C F Wall 23-106 £0.35; Rae Guest 16-80 £0.44; J M P Eustace 9-92 £0.37; J Balding 4-38 £0.80; E S McMahon 15-97 £0.31; Pat Eddery 9-74 £0.41; A Dickman 14-65 £0.43; P D Cundell 3-24 £1.17; John Berry 5-31 £0.86.

Handicaps (Class 4..7)

3-Y.O Races: Handicaps (Class 4..7) – 2 to 7 runners

ANALYSIS BY BHA RATING

Rating	Prop	Win	Runs	Wins%	£
120..139	0%	0	0	0.0%	0.00
110..119	0%	0	0	0.0%	0.00
100..109	0%	0	0	0.0%	0.00
90..99	0%	1	1	100.0%	3.33
70..89	64%	291	1549	18.8%	-0.11
50..69	35%	161	1211	13.3%	-0.21
..49	0%	2	54	3.7%	-0.64
Unrated	0%	0	0	0.0%	0.00

ANALYSIS BY WEIGHT CARRIED

Weight	Prop	Win	Runs	Wins%	£
10-01+	0%	0	1	0.0%	-1.00
9-8..10-00	5%	21	68	30.9%	0.11
9-0..9-07	63%	287	1406	20.4%	-0.12
8-8..8-13	22%	102	767	13.3%	-0.16
8-0..8-07	9%	41	497	8.2%	-0.29
..7-13	1%	4	76	5.3%	-0.38

ANALYSIS BY DAYS SINCE LAST RUN

Days	Prop	Win	Runs	Wins%	£
1..7	13%	61	308	19.8%	-0.13
8..14	26%	120	682	17.6%	-0.12
15..28	37%	169	1068	15.8%	-0.17
29..60	15%	67	431	15.5%	-0.22
61..100	2%	8	104	7.7%	-0.37
101+	7%	30	220	13.6%	-0.13
Unraced	0%	0	2	0.0%	-1.00

ANALYSIS BY TODAY'S STARTING PRICE

Price	Prop	Win	Runs	Wins%	£
Odds On	10%	44	70	62.9%	0.07
Ev-2/1	22%	98	270	36.3%	-0.05
9/4-4/1	40%	180	765	23.5%	-0.06
9/2-6/1	11%	51	422	12.1%	-0.25
13/2-10/1	10%	47	584	8.0%	-0.27
11/1-16/1	6%	27	400	6.8%	-0.08
18/1-33/1	2%	8	268	3.0%	-0.30
40/1+	0%	0	36	0.0%	-1.00

ANALYSIS BY STARTING PRICE LAST TIME

Price	Prop	Win	Runs	Wins%	£
Odds On	4%	17	64	26.6%	-0.25
Ev-2/1	10%	46	175	26.3%	-0.07
9/4-4/1	24%	111	482	23.0%	-0.05
9/2-6/1	13%	61	362	16.9%	-0.18
13/2-10/1	25%	113	631	17.9%	0.05
11/1-16/1	14%	63	513	12.3%	-0.19
18/1-33/1	7%	32	424	7.5%	-0.50
40/1+	3%	12	162	7.4%	-0.39
Unraced	0%	0	2	0.0%	-1.00

ANALYSIS BY DISTANCE BEATEN LAST TIME

Lengths	Prop	Win	Runs	Wins%	£
..-10	0%	2	4	50.0%	0.28
-10..0	25%	112	475	23.6%	-0.14
0.1..2	24%	111	447	24.8%	-0.04
2.1..5	22%	102	598	17.1%	-0.10
5.1..10	19%	85	655	13.0%	-0.15
10.1..20	8%	35	446	7.8%	-0.27
20.0..30	1%	3	102	2.9%	-0.60
30.1+	1%	5	86	5.8%	-0.42
Not Compl	0%	0	0	0.0%	0.00
Unraced	0%	0	2	0.0%	-1.00

ANALYSIS BY RUN NUMBER

Run No	Prop	Win	Runs	Wins%	£
FTO	0%	0	2	0.0%	-1.00
2nd Run	1%	6	23	26.1%	0.05
3rd Run	3%	15	57	26.3%	-0.10
4th+ Run	95%	434	2733	15.9%	-0.17

ANALYSIS BY POSITION LAST TIME

Pos LT	Prop	Win	Runs	Wins%	£
Won	25%	115	478	24.1%	-0.13
2nd or 3rd	36%	163	687	23.7%	-0.05
Unplaced	39%	176	1643	10.7%	-0.22
Not Compl	0%	1	7	14.3%	0.00

OTHER FACTORS (WINS-RUNS, £)

Course Winner:	50-217	£0.03
Distance Winner:	197-981	-£0.13
Going Winner:	109-554	-£0.19
Beaten Favourite:	46-191	-£0.03
Up in class:	110-821	-£0.22
Same class:	243-1436	-£0.14
Down in class:	102-556	-£0.14
7-Day Winners:	20-66	-£0.17
Colts and Geldings:	291-1777	-£0.22
Fillies:	132-832	-£0.01
Absolute Favourites:	159-420	-£0.03

TRAINERS (WINS-RUNS, £)

J L Dunlop 14-40 £1.37; Mrs A J Perrett 10-39 £0.69; P J Makin 8-13 £1.84; M Johnston 30-114 £0.16; Jedd O'Keeffe 3-12 £1.46; Rae Guest 5-12 £1.28; M W Easterby 5-20 £0.76; E J O'Neill 4-13 £1.10; B W Hills 12-42 £0.30; Mrs A Duffield 4-19 £0.57; J Akehurst 2-11 £0.86; J W Hills 2-11 £0.84; W R Muir 8-36 £0.25; J M P Eustace 2-11 £0.77; C G Cox 6-17 £0.47; P D Evans 6-22 £0.34; P F I Cole 6-28 £0.27; Miss L A Perratt 1-14 £0.50; B R Millman 8-35 £0.17; M S Saunders 3-11 £0.50.

Race Profiles

3-Y.O Races: Handicaps (Class 4..7) – 8 to 14 runners

ANALYSIS BY BHA RATING

Rating	Prop	Win	Runs	Wins%	£
120..139	0%	0	0	0.0%	0.00
110..119	0%	0	0	0.0%	0.00
100..109	0%	0	0	0.0%	0.00
90..99	0%	0	2	0.0%	-1.00
70..89	43%	632	5657	11.2%	-0.16
50..69	53%	784	8065	8.7%	0.26
..49	4%	60	1035	5.8%	-0.28
Unrated	0%	0	0	0.0%	0.00

ANALYSIS BY WEIGHT CARRIED

Weight	Prop	Win	Runs	Wins%	£
10-01+	0%	0	1	0.0%	-1.00
9-8..10-00	4%	55	240	22.9%	-0.06
9-0..9-07	52%	768	6841	11.2%	-0.20
8-8..8-13	29%	434	4906	8.8%	-0.24
8-0..8-07	14%	203	3256	6.2%	-0.24
..7-13	1%	16	415	3.9%	-0.46

ANALYSIS BY DAYS SINCE LAST RUN

Days	Prop	Win	Runs	Wins%	£
1..7	12%	173	1330	13.0%	-0.21
8..14	24%	350	3694	9.5%	-0.29
15..28	38%	566	5666	10.0%	-0.17
29..60	15%	226	2715	8.3%	-0.24
61..100	2%	36	546	6.6%	-0.41
101+	8%	124	1699	7.3%	-0.18
Unraced	0%	1	9	11.1%	-0.50

ANALYSIS BY TODAY'S STARTING PRICE

Price	Prop	Win	Runs	Wins%	£
Odds On	2%	32	55	58.2%	-0.01
Ev-2/1	10%	149	400	37.3%	-0.01
9/4-4/1	27%	397	1852	21.4%	-0.10
9/2-6/1	19%	279	2047	13.6%	-0.16
13/2-10/1	23%	343	3654	9.4%	-0.15
11/1-16/1	12%	180	3504	5.1%	-0.26
18/1-33/1	6%	90	2948	3.1%	-0.24
40/1+	0%	6	1199	0.5%	-0.71

ANALYSIS BY STARTING PRICE LAST TIME

Price	Prop	Win	Runs	Wins%	£
Odds On	2%	34	189	18.0%	-0.20
Ev-2/1	8%	122	647	18.9%	-0.12
9/4-4/1	18%	263	1982	13.3%	-0.20
9/2-6/1	15%	228	1878	12.1%	-0.15
13/2-10/1	21%	312	3223	9.7%	-0.24
11/1-16/1	17%	255	3153	8.1%	-0.24
18/1-33/1	13%	188	2942	6.4%	-0.21
40/1+	5%	73	1636	4.5%	-0.36
Unraced	0%	1	9	11.1%	-0.50

ANALYSIS BY DISTANCE BEATEN LAST TIME

Lengths	Prop	Win	Runs	Wins%	£
..-10	0%	2	8	25.0%	-0.40
-10..0	22%	324	1843	17.6%	-0.12
0.1..2	18%	267	2001	13.3%	-0.21
2.1..5	23%	335	3101	10.8%	-0.19
5.1..10	21%	310	4006	7.7%	-0.19
10.1..20	11%	165	3253	5.1%	-0.34
20.0..30	3%	43	848	5.1%	-0.34
30.1+	2%	29	590	4.9%	-0.19
Not Compl	0%	0	0	0.0%	0.00
Unraced	0%	1	9	11.1%	-0.50

ANALYSIS BY RUN NUMBER

Run No	Prop	Win	Runs	Wins%	£
FTO	0%	1	9	11.1%	-0.50
2nd Run	1%	14	74	18.9%	-0.03
3rd Run	2%	35	274	12.8%	-0.22
4th+ Run	97%	1426	15302	9.3%	-0.23

ANALYSIS BY POSITION LAST TIME

Pos LT	Prop	Win	Runs	Wins%	£
Won	22%	327	1853	17.6%	-0.12
2nd or 3rd	27%	399	3055	13.1%	-0.19
Unplaced	51%	748	10717	7.0%	-0.25
Not Compl	0%	2	34	5.9%	-0.10

OTHER FACTORS (WINS-RUNS, £)

Course Winner:	87-718	-£0.25
Distance Winner:	496-3898	-£0.12
Going Winner:	242-2064	-£0.21
Beaten Favourite:	136-886	-£0.16
Up in class:	318-3466	-£0.27
Same class:	832-8372	-£0.18
Down in class:	325-3812	-£0.28
7-Day Winners:	74-195	£0.30
Colts and Geldings:	965-9473	-£0.19
Fillies:	380-4785	-£0.30
Absolute Favourites:	386-1290	£0.01

TRAINERS (WINS-RUNS, £)

E J Creighton 2-10 £8.40; M D I Usher 6-53 £1.39; T T Clement 3-11 £6.13; T D Walford 6-19 £2.71; Sir Mark Prescott 45-112 £0.36; B G Powell 5-48 £0.73; J R Best 6-89 £0.36; J M P Eustace 6-55 £0.55; D Haydn Jones 5-39 £0.76; C R Egerton 2-24 £1.04; E F Vaughan 4-31 £0.81; John Berry 3-21 £1.19; Rae Guest 10-60 £0.40; B R Millman 18-139 £0.16; N Bycroft 3-30 £0.70; Paul Green 1-30 £0.70; P W D'Arcy 4-42 £0.49; J Ryan 2-15 £1.33; M L W Bell 33-195 £0.10; M S Saunders 3-24 £0.79.

Handicaps (Class 4..7)

3-Y.O Races: Handicaps (Class 4..7) – 15 runners or more

ANALYSIS BY BHA RATING

Rating	Prop	Win	Runs	Wins%	£
120..139	0%	0	0	0.0%	0.00
110..119	0%	0	0	0.0%	0.00
100..109	0%	0	0	0.0%	0.00
90..99	0%	0	1	0.0%	-1.00
70..89	28%	91	1303	7.0%	-0.29
50..69	67%	219	3560	6.2%	-0.19
..49	5%	17	447	3.8%	-0.55
Unrated	0%	0	0	0.0%	0.00

ANALYSIS BY WEIGHT CARRIED

Weight	Prop	Win	Runs	Wins%	£
10-01+	0%	0	0	0.0%	0.00
9-8..10-00	2%	5	53	9.4%	-0.53
9-0..9-07	49%	159	2156	7.4%	-0.25
8-8..8-13	38%	124	1982	6.3%	-0.12
8-0..8-07	12%	38	998	3.8%	-0.37
..7-13	0%	1	122	0.8%	-0.83

ANALYSIS BY DAYS SINCE LAST RUN

Days	Prop	Win	Runs	Wins%	£
1..7	12%	38	378	10.1%	-0.11
8..14	26%	84	1181	7.1%	-0.26
15..28	33%	109	1812	6.0%	-0.30
29..60	15%	49	935	5.2%	-0.18
61..100	2%	7	181	3.9%	-0.56
101+	12%	39	821	4.8%	-0.17
Unraced	0%	1	3	33.3%	2.33

ANALYSIS BY TODAY'S STARTING PRICE

Price	Prop	Win	Runs	Wins%	£
Odds On	1%	2	4	50.0%	-0.13
Ev-2/1	5%	15	37	40.5%	0.09
9/4-4/1	14%	45	236	19.1%	-0.20
9/2-6/1	19%	61	417	14.6%	-0.06
13/2-10/1	26%	85	1017	8.4%	-0.22
11/1-16/1	21%	68	1319	5.2%	-0.25
18/1-33/1	13%	43	1552	2.8%	-0.30
40/1+	2%	8	729	1.1%	-0.28

ANALYSIS BY STARTING PRICE LAST TIME

Price	Prop	Win	Runs	Wins%	£
Odds On	2%	6	43	14.0%	0.38
Ev-2/1	5%	16	135	11.9%	-0.28
9/4-4/1	11%	37	504	7.3%	-0.38
9/2-6/1	15%	48	547	8.8%	-0.16
13/2-10/1	23%	74	1031	7.2%	-0.31
11/1-16/1	18%	60	1061	5.7%	-0.02
18/1-33/1	20%	67	1243	5.4%	-0.18
40/1+	6%	18	744	2.4%	-0.60
Unraced	0%	1	3	33.3%	2.33

ANALYSIS BY DISTANCE BEATEN LAST TIME

Lengths	Prop	Win	Runs	Wins%	£
..-10	0%	0	1	0.0%	-1.00
-10..0	14%	45	467	9.6%	-0.31
0.1..2	23%	74	604	12.3%	0.12
2.1..5	21%	70	927	7.6%	-0.27
5.1..10	20%	65	1385	4.7%	-0.39
10.1..20	16%	52	1344	3.9%	-0.18
20.0..30	4%	13	359	3.6%	-0.25
30.1+	2%	7	221	3.2%	-0.48
Not Compl	0%	0	0	0.0%	0.00
Unraced	0%	1	3	33.3%	2.33

ANALYSIS BY RUN NUMBER

Run No	Prop	Win	Runs	Wins%	£
FTO	0%	1	3	33.3%	2.33
2nd Run	2%	5	22	22.7%	0.50
3rd Run	3%	9	68	13.2%	0.23
4th+ Run	95%	312	5218	6.0%	-0.25

ANALYSIS BY POSITION LAST TIME

Pos LT	Prop	Win	Runs	Wins%	£
Won	14%	45	467	9.6%	-0.31
2nd or 3rd	27%	89	872	10.2%	-0.15
Unplaced	59%	192	3962	4.8%	-0.26
Not Compl	0%	1	10	10.0%	0.00

OTHER FACTORS (WINS-RUNS, £)

Course Winner:	5-146	-£0.79
Distance Winner:	76-955	-£0.21
Going Winner:	30-478	-£0.47
Beaten Favourite:	22-252	-£0.38
Up in class:	47-797	-£0.20
Same class:	180-2875	-£0.24
Down in class:	99-1636	-£0.27
7-Day Winners:	5-49	-£0.57
Colts and Geldings:	218-3235	-£0.21
Fillies:	89-1755	-£0.29
Absolute Favourites:	57-301	-£0.27

TRAINERS (WINS-RUNS, £)

J Pearce 2-20 £4.65; B G Powell 4-26 £1.85; A Berry 4-32 £1.44; J Balding 2-15 £2.87; I A Wood 4-49 £0.85; T D Walford 4-10 £4.05; J H M Gosden 7-33 £1.12; M Dods 6-44 £0.83; D R C Elsworth 3-16 £1.66; Miss J Feilden 1-16 £1.56; S Dow 1-10 £2.40; E S McMahon 3-24 £0.98; C F Wall 4-22 £1.05; A Dickman 2-14 £1.39; W J Haggas 7-39 £0.50; B J Meehan 3-44 £0.41; R A Harris 4-27 £0.63; Sir Mark Prescott 8-25 £0.66; J R Boyle 1-14 £0.80; E J O'Neill 1-13 £0.02

Race Profiles

3-Y.O Races: Handicaps (Class 4..7) – good or faster going

ANALYSIS BY BHA RATING

Rating	Prop	Win	Runs	Wins%	£
120..139	0%	0	0	0.0%	0.00
110..119	0%	0	0	0.0%	0.00
100..109	0%	0	0	0.0%	0.00
90..99	0%	1	1	100.0%	3.33
70..89	45%	765	6371	12.0%	-0.17
50..69	51%	868	10281	8.4%	-0.25
..49	3%	58	1219	4.8%	-0.46
Unrated	0%	0	0	0.0%	0.00

ANALYSIS BY WEIGHT CARRIED

Weight	Prop	Win	Runs	Wins%	£
10-01+	0%	0	1	0.0%	-1.00
9-8..10-00	4%	62	296	20.9%	-0.17
9-0..9-07	56%	940	7966	11.8%	-0.19
8-8..8-13	28%	478	5622	8.5%	-0.19
8-0..8-07	12%	201	3532	5.7%	-0.36
..7-13	1%	11	455	2.4%	-0.58

ANALYSIS BY DAYS SINCE LAST RUN

Days	Prop	Win	Runs	Wins%	£
1..7	12%	199	1486	13.4%	-0.18
8..14	25%	422	4245	9.9%	-0.26
15..28	37%	632	6509	9.7%	-0.22
29..60	15%	260	3076	8.5%	-0.26
61..100	2%	42	615	6.8%	-0.32
101+	8%	135	1929	7.0%	-0.19
Unraced	0%	2	12	16.7%	0.21

ANALYSIS BY TODAY'S STARTING PRICE

Price	Prop	Win	Runs	Wins%	£
Odds On	3%	57	99	57.6%	-0.02
Ev-2/1	12%	197	530	37.2%	-0.02
9/4-4/1	28%	473	2121	22.3%	-0.07
9/2-6/1	17%	295	2164	13.6%	-0.15
13/2-10/1	21%	363	3943	9.2%	-0.16
11/1-16/1	11%	191	3899	4.9%	-0.29
18/1-33/1	6%	106	3597	2.9%	-0.27
40/1+	1%	10	1519	0.7%	-0.62

ANALYSIS BY STARTING PRICE LAST TIME

Price	Prop	Win	Runs	Wins%	£
Odds On	2%	41	219	18.7%	-0.19
Ev-2/1	9%	148	729	20.3%	-0.08
9/4-4/1	19%	323	2263	14.3%	-0.20
9/2-6/1	14%	236	2074	11.4%	-0.22
13/2-10/1	22%	370	3662	10.1%	-0.21
11/1-16/1	16%	270	3545	7.6%	-0.26
18/1-33/1	13%	225	3462	6.5%	-0.21
40/1+	5%	77	1906	4.0%	-0.41
Unraced	0%	2	12	16.7%	0.21

ANALYSIS BY DISTANCE BEATEN LAST TIME

Lengths	Prop	Win	Runs	Wins%	£
..-10	0%	2	5	40.0%	-0.17
-10..0	21%	349	2077	16.8%	-0.20
0.1..2	20%	344	2314	14.9%	-0.11
2.1..5	23%	383	3488	11.0%	-0.21
5.1..10	20%	345	4499	7.7%	-0.23
10.1..20	11%	188	3805	4.9%	-0.33
20.0..30	3%	48	989	4.9%	-0.30
30.1+	2%	31	683	4.5%	-0.29
Not Compl	0%	0	0	0.0%	0.00
Unraced	0%	2	12	16.7%	0.21

ANALYSIS BY RUN NUMBER

Run No	Prop	Win	Runs	Wins%	£
FTO	0%	2	12	16.7%	0.21
2nd Run	1%	16	86	18.6%	-0.03
3rd Run	3%	43	287	15.0%	-0.05
4th+ Run	96%	1631	17487	9.3%	-0.24

ANALYSIS BY POSITION LAST TIME

Pos LT	Prop	Win	Runs	Wins%	£
Won	21%	352	2081	16.9%	-0.20
2nd or 3rd	30%	508	3510	14.5%	-0.13
Unplaced	49%	830	12244	6.8%	-0.27
Not Compl	0%	2	37	5.4%	-0.61

OTHER FACTORS (WINS-RUNS, £)

Course Winner:105-809-£0.27
Distance Winner: 568-4341 -£0.15
Going Winner: 336-2639 -£0.22
Beaten Favourite: 168-1012 -£0.12
Up in class: 350-3826 -£0.31
Same class: 936-9504 -£0.20
Down in class: 404-4530 -£0.24
7-Day Winners: 71-216 £0.01
Colts and Geldings: 1111-10885 -£0.22
Fillies: 448-5586 -£0.27
Absolute Favourites: 448-1507 -£0.06

TRAINERS (WINS-RUNS, £)

B G Powell 9-67 £1.34; T D Walford 8-25 £3.20; E J Creighton 2-17 £4.53; J Pearce 3-58 £1.20; Miss J Feilden 6-46 £1.43; J M P Eustace 9-66 £0.91; J G Given 22-187 £0.29; J L Dunlop 38-267 £0.19; Sir Mark Prescott 51-120 £0.37; J Balding 4-27 £1.54; D R C Elsworth 14-83 £0.48; P D Cundell 3-17 £2.06; C F Wall 16-74 £0.47; Garry Moss 2-12 £2.71; Rae Guest 13-60 £0.50; Mrs G S Rees 4-44 £0.65; E S McMahon 9-67 £0.39; D Haydn Jones 4-40 £0.58; E F Vaughan 5-44 £0.52; M D I Usher 5-62 £0.35.

Handicaps (Class 4..7)

3-Y.O Races: Handicaps (Class 4..7) – good to soft or softer going

ANALYSIS BY BHA RATING
Rating	Prop	Win	Runs	Wins%	£
120..139	0%	0	0	0.0%	0.00
110..119	0%	0	0	0.0%	0.00
100..109	0%	0	0	0.0%	0.00
90..99	0%	0	3	0.0%	-1.00
70..89	44%	249	2138	11.6%	-0.17
50..69	52%	296	3455	8.6%	-0.21
..49	4%	21	317	6.6%	0.00
Unrated	0%	0	0	0.0%	0.00

ANALYSIS BY WEIGHT CARRIED
Weight	Prop	Win	Runs	Wins%	£
10-01+	0%	0	1	0.0%	-1.00
9-8..10-00	3%	19	65	29.2%	0.24
9-0..9-07	48%	274	2437	11.2%	-0.24
8-8..8-13	32%	182	2033	9.0%	-0.22
8-0..8-07	14%	81	1219	6.6%	-0.01
..7-13	2%	10	158	6.3%	-0.36

ANALYSIS BY DAYS SINCE LAST RUN
Days	Prop	Win	Runs	Wins%	£
1..7	13%	73	530	13.8%	-0.17
8..14	23%	132	1312	10.1%	-0.26
15..28	37%	212	2037	10.4%	-0.13
29..60	14%	82	1005	8.2%	-0.10
61..100	2%	9	216	4.2%	-0.78
101+	10%	58	811	7.2%	-0.13
Unraced	0%	0	2	0.0%	-1.00

ANALYSIS BY TODAY'S STARTING PRICE
Price	Prop	Win	Runs	Wins%	£
Odds On	4%	21	30	70.0%	0.22
Ev-2/1	11%	65	177	36.7%	-0.02
9/4-4/1	26%	149	732	20.4%	-0.15
9/2-6/1	17%	96	722	13.3%	-0.18
13/2-10/1	20%	112	1312	8.5%	-0.24
11/1-16/1	15%	84	1324	6.3%	-0.09
18/1-33/1	6%	35	1171	3.0%	-0.24
40/1+	1%	4	445	0.9%	-0.32

ANALYSIS BY STARTING PRICE LAST TIME
Price	Prop	Win	Runs	Wins%	£
Odds On	3%	16	77	20.8%	0.05
Ev-2/1	6%	36	228	15.8%	-0.30
9/4-4/1	16%	88	705	12.5%	-0.22
9/2-6/1	18%	101	713	14.2%	0.03
13/2-10/1	23%	129	1223	10.5%	-0.23
11/1-16/1	19%	108	1182	9.1%	0.05
18/1-33/1	11%	62	1147	5.4%	-0.30
40/1+	5%	26	636	4.1%	-0.50
Unraced	0%	0	2	0.0%	-1.00

ANALYSIS BY DISTANCE BEATEN LAST TIME
Lengths	Prop	Win	Runs	Wins%	£
..-10	0%	2	8	25.0%	-0.28
-10..0	23%	132	708	18.6%	-0.05
0.1..2	19%	108	738	14.6%	-0.15
2.1..5	22%	124	1138	10.9%	-0.13
5.1..10	20%	115	1547	7.4%	-0.25
10.1..20	11%	64	1238	5.2%	-0.16
20.0..30	2%	11	320	3.4%	-0.46
30.1+	2%	10	214	4.7%	-0.27
Not Compl	0%	0	0	0.0%	0.00
Unraced	0%	0	2	0.0%	-1.00

ANALYSIS BY RUN NUMBER
Run No	Prop	Win	Runs	Wins%	£
FTO	0%	0	2	0.0%	-1.00
2nd Run	2%	9	33	27.3%	0.37
3rd Run	3%	16	112	14.3%	-0.33
4th+ Run	96%	541	5766	9.4%	-0.18

ANALYSIS BY POSITION LAST TIME
Pos LT	Prop	Win	Runs	Wins%	£
Won	24%	135	717	18.8%	-0.04
2nd or 3rd	25%	143	1104	13.0%	-0.24
Unplaced	51%	286	4078	7.0%	-0.20
Not Compl	0%	2	14	14.3%	1.36

OTHER FACTORS (WINS-RUNS, £)
Course Winner:	37-272	-£0.24
Distance Winner:	201-1493	-£0.09
Going Winner:	45-457	-£0.39
Beaten Favourite:	36-317	-£0.39
Up in class:	125-1258	-£0.08
Same class:	319-3179	-£0.16
Down in class:	122-1474	-£0.33
7-Day Winners:	28-94	£0.18
Colts and Geldings:	363-3600	-£0.14
Fillies:	153-1786	-£0.25
Absolute Favourites:	154-504	-£0.00

TRAINERS (WINS-RUNS, £)
B J Meehan 6-49 £0.96; Paul Green 1-15 £2.40; A Dickman 5-17 £2.03; M D I Usher 5-39 £0.87; Pat Eddery 4-21 £1.62; J R Best 5-27 £1.11; B Ellison 4-20 £1.45; A B Haynes 3-13 £2.19; M S Saunders 3-11 £2.36; H Morrison 10-62 £0.36; C R Egerton 1-13 £1.62; Sir Michael Stoute 10-29 £0.71; H Candy 2-18 £1.11; M Blanshard 5-38 £0.49; M H Tompkins 6-70 £0.24; R Johnson 3-14 £1.13; M Brittain 2-29 £0.41; M G Quinlan 3-34 £0.35; J A Geake 4-34 £0.34; J L Spearing 4-29 £0.40.

Race Profiles

3-Y.O Races: Handicaps (Class 4..7) – 5 to 6 furlong races

THREE-YEAR-OLD RACES

ANALYSIS BY BHA RATING

Rating	Prop	Win	Runs	Wins%	£
120..139	0%	0	0	0.0%	0.00
110..119	0%	0	0	0.0%	0.00
100..109	0%	0	0	0.0%	0.00
90..99	0%	0	2	0.0%	-1.00
70..89	42%	273	2279	12.0%	-0.16
50..69	55%	357	3790	9.4%	-0.17
..49	4%	23	513	4.5%	-0.30
Unrated	0%	0	0	0.0%	0.00

ANALYSIS BY WEIGHT CARRIED

Weight	Prop	Win	Runs	Wins%	£
10-01+	0%	0	0	0.0%	0.00
9-8..10-00	3%	21	101	20.8%	-0.07
9-0..9-07	50%	325	2666	12.2%	-0.24
8-8..8-13	31%	200	2120	9.4%	-0.11
8-0..8-07	15%	100	1471	6.8%	-0.14
..7-13	1%	7	226	3.1%	-0.40

ANALYSIS BY DAYS SINCE LAST RUN

Days	Prop	Win	Runs	Wins%	£
1..7	16%	106	843	12.6%	-0.16
8..14	26%	169	1692	10.0%	-0.25
15..28	38%	247	2212	11.2%	-0.10
29..60	11%	73	923	7.9%	-0.17
61..100	1%	9	211	4.3%	-0.58
101+	7%	47	698	6.7%	-0.16
Unraced	0%	2	5	40.0%	1.90

ANALYSIS BY TODAY'S STARTING PRICE

Price	Prop	Win	Runs	Wins%	£
Odds On	4%	26	33	78.8%	0.36
Ev-2/1	10%	66	178	37.1%	-0.02
9/4-4/1	29%	190	877	21.7%	-0.10
9/2-6/1	17%	108	884	12.2%	-0.25
13/2-10/1	22%	143	1525	9.4%	-0.16
11/1-16/1	12%	76	1410	5.4%	-0.22
18/1-33/1	6%	37	1212	3.1%	-0.21
40/1+	1%	7	465	1.5%	-0.14

ANALYSIS BY STARTING PRICE LAST TIME

Price	Prop	Win	Runs	Wins%	£
Odds On	1%	9	71	12.7%	-0.03
Ev-2/1	8%	52	249	20.9%	-0.09
9/4-4/1	19%	121	846	14.3%	-0.18
9/2-6/1	17%	113	824	13.7%	-0.05
13/2-10/1	23%	150	1360	11.0%	-0.22
11/1-16/1	15%	97	1339	7.2%	-0.28
18/1-33/1	12%	79	1281	6.2%	-0.17
40/1+	5%	30	609	4.9%	-0.12
Unraced	0%	2	5	40.0%	1.90

ANALYSIS BY DISTANCE BEATEN LAST TIME

Lengths	Prop	Win	Runs	Wins%	£
..-10	0%	0	1	0.0%	-1.00
-10..0	19%	123	750	16.4%	-0.11
0.1..2	20%	132	962	13.7%	-0.29
2.1..5	27%	178	1496	11.9%	-0.14
5.1..10	22%	142	1750	8.1%	-0.15
10.1..20	9%	58	1248	4.6%	-0.29
20.0..30	1%	6	248	2.4%	-0.40
30.1+	2%	12	124	9.7%	0.96
Not Compl	0%	0	0	0.0%	0.00
Unraced	0%	2	5	40.0%	1.90

ANALYSIS BY RUN NUMBER

Run No	Prop	Win	Runs	Wins%	£
FTO	0%	2	5	40.0%	1.90
2nd Run	1%	6	28	21.4%	0.44
3rd Run	2%	16	78	20.5%	0.44
4th+ Run	96%	629	6473	9.7%	-0.19

ANALYSIS BY POSITION LAST TIME

Pos LT	Prop	Win	Runs	Wins%	£
Won	19%	123	752	16.4%	-0.11
2nd or 3rd	29%	187	1264	14.8%	-0.19
Unplaced	52%	340	4554	7.5%	-0.19
Not Compl	0%	3	14	21.4%	1.89

OTHER FACTORS (WINS-RUNS, £)

Course Winner:	58-430	-£0.10
Distance Winner:	346-2932	-£0.20
Going Winner:	130-1150	-£0.34
Beaten Favourite:	58-375	-£0.21
Up in class:	125-1345	-£0.25
Same class:	365-3528	-£0.11
Down in class:	161-1706	-£0.26
7-Day Winners:	31-115	-£0.10
Colts and Geldings:	377-3556	-£0.16
Fillies:	226-2479	-£0.20
Absolute Favourites:	174-579	-£0.02

TRAINERS (WINS-RUNS, £)

B J Meehan 12-53 £1.77; E J Creighton 2-15 £5.27; J G Given 9-61 £0.81; M S Saunders 6-24 £1.48; B P J Baugh 4-26 £1.33; J Balding 4-34 £1.01; W M Brisbourne 3-22 £1.55; A Dickman 11-45 £0.74; Paul Green 2-34 £0.88; E S McMahon 10-49 £0.56; I A Wood 2-45 £0.60; P W D'Arcy 2-13 £1.90; E A L Dunlop 2-12 £1.75; J Akehurst 5-20 £1.00; M L W Bell 8-42 £0.48; Rae Guest 10-39 £0.48; P D Evans 7-70 £0.26; M Brittain 3-49 £0.37; M W Easterby 7-57 £0.22; M D I Usher 6-37 £0.34.

Handicaps (Class 4..7)

3-Y.O Races: Handicaps (Class 4..7) – 7 to 9 furlong races

ANALYSIS BY BHA RATING

Rating	Prop	Win	Runs	Wins%	£
120..139	0%	0	0	0.0%	0.00
110..119	0%	0	0	0.0%	0.00
100..109	0%	0	0	0.0%	0.00
90..99	0%	1	1	100.0%	3.33
70..89	49%	390	3414	11.4%	-0.17
50..69	48%	381	5171	7.4%	-0.23
..49	3%	26	459	5.7%	-0.49
Unrated	0%	0	0	0.0%	0.00

ANALYSIS BY WEIGHT CARRIED

Weight	Prop	Win	Runs	Wins%	£
10-01+	0%	0	0	0.0%	0.00
9-8..10-00	4%	30	127	23.6%	-0.08
9-0..9-07	56%	448	4064	11.0%	-0.16
8-8..8-13	28%	225	2953	7.6%	-0.24
8-0..8-07	11%	85	1705	5.0%	-0.31
..7-13	1%	10	196	5.1%	-0.49

ANALYSIS BY DAYS SINCE LAST RUN

Days	Prop	Win	Runs	Wins%	£
1..7	10%	81	671	12.1%	-0.20
8..14	25%	196	2043	9.6%	-0.25
15..28	36%	287	3188	9.0%	-0.23
29..60	16%	130	1598	8.1%	-0.15
61..100	3%	23	325	7.1%	-0.36
101+	10%	81	1217	6.7%	-0.18
Unraced	0%	0	3	0.0%	-1.00

ANALYSIS BY TODAY'S STARTING PRICE

Price	Prop	Win	Runs	Wins%	£
Odds On	2%	19	42	45.2%	-0.22
Ev-2/1	10%	83	229	36.2%	-0.04
9/4-4/1	26%	205	948	21.6%	-0.10
9/2-6/1	18%	144	1007	14.3%	-0.11
13/2-10/1	21%	169	1920	8.8%	-0.19
11/1-16/1	13%	106	2083	5.1%	-0.26
18/1-33/1	8%	67	2022	3.3%	-0.19
40/1+	1%	5	794	0.6%	-0.59

ANALYSIS BY STARTING PRICE LAST TIME

Price	Prop	Win	Runs	Wins%	£
Odds On	3%	27	112	24.1%	0.02
Ev-2/1	7%	59	331	17.8%	-0.12
9/4-4/1	15%	123	1053	11.7%	-0.26
9/2-6/1	14%	113	998	11.3%	-0.13
13/2-10/1	21%	171	1921	8.9%	-0.29
11/1-16/1	19%	155	1888	8.2%	-0.08
18/1-33/1	14%	115	1788	6.4%	-0.21
40/1+	4%	35	951	3.7%	-0.47
Unraced	0%	0	3	0.0%	-1.00

ANALYSIS BY DISTANCE BEATEN LAST TIME

Lengths	Prop	Win	Runs	Wins%	£
..-10	1%	4	7	57.1%	0.42
-10..0	23%	182	1036	17.6%	-0.13
0.1..2	18%	146	1091	13.4%	-0.14
2.1..5	20%	159	1682	9.5%	-0.24
5.1..10	20%	161	2368	6.8%	-0.27
10.1..20	13%	100	1995	5.0%	-0.18
20.0..30	4%	33	514	6.4%	-0.18
30.1+	2%	13	349	3.7%	-0.56
Not Compl	0%	0	0	0.0%	0.00
Unraced	0%	0	3	0.0%	-1.00

ANALYSIS BY RUN NUMBER

Run No	Prop	Win	Runs	Wins%	£
FTO	0%	0	3	0.0%	-1.00
2nd Run	2%	12	60	20.0%	-0.12
3rd Run	3%	27	186	14.5%	-0.16
4th+ Run	95%	759	8796	8.6%	-0.22

ANALYSIS BY POSITION LAST TIME

Pos LT	Prop	Win	Runs	Wins%	£
Won	23%	187	1043	17.9%	-0.12
2nd or 3rd	25%	197	1604	12.3%	-0.23
Unplaced	52%	413	6382	6.5%	-0.23
Not Compl	0%	1	16	6.3%	-0.56

OTHER FACTORS (WINS-RUNS, £)

Course Winner:	46-388	-£0.38
Distance Winner:	254-1884	-£0.07
Going Winner:	125-1118	-£0.22
Beaten Favourite:	66-502	-£0.15
Up in class:	161-1839	-£0.20
Same class:	434-4798	-£0.24
Down in class:	203-2405	-£0.19
7-Day Winners:	30-105	£0.14
Colts and Geldings:	547-5587	-£0.16
Fillies:	169-2578	-£0.34
Absolute Favourites:	199-708	-£0.08

TRAINERS (WINS-RUNS, £)

Miss J Feilden 5-28 £2.71; Mrs G S Rees 5-32 £1.92; M D I Usher 4-47 £1.28; B G Powell 5-43 £1.16; J L Dunlop 10-95 £0.52; R Hannon 33-257 £0.17; C F Wall 15-58 £0.72; T D Walford 6-19 £2.16; B R Millman 16-109 £0.37; G L Moore 6-44 £0.73; M G Quinlan 5-36 £0.88; A Berry 3-42 £0.74; B Ellison 5-35 £0.79; R Johnson 4-15 £1.58; A B Haynes 4-29 £0.79; J A Osborne 10-51 £0.43; P A Blockley 5-44 £0.49; S Dow 1-13 £1.62; J A Geake 5-40 £0.39; John Derry 4-20 £0.74.

Race Profiles

3-Y.O Races: Handicaps (Class 4..7) – 10 to 14 furlong races

THREE-YEAR-OLD RACES

ANALYSIS BY BHA RATING

Rating	Prop	Win	Runs	Wins%	£
120..139	0%	0	0	0.0%	0.00
110..119	0%	0	0	0.0%	0.00
100..109	0%	0	0	0.0%	0.00
90..99	0%	0	1	0.0%	-1.00
70..89	45%	343	2749	12.5%	-0.17
50..69	52%	402	4505	8.9%	0.29
..49	3%	25	476	5.3%	-0.35
Unrated	0%	0	0	0.0%	0.00

ANALYSIS BY WEIGHT CARRIED

Weight	Prop	Win	Runs	Wins%	£
10-01+	0%	0	2	0.0%	-1.00
9-8..10-00	4%	28	122	23.0%	-0.11
9-0..9-07	55%	424	3523	12.0%	-0.22
8-8..8-13	29%	224	2457	9.1%	-0.22
8-0..8-07	12%	91	1455	6.3%	-0.34
..7-13	0%	3	172	1.7%	-0.73

ANALYSIS BY DAYS SINCE LAST RUN

Days	Prop	Win	Runs	Wins%	£
1..7	10%	79	477	16.6%	-0.21
8..14	24%	182	1705	10.7%	-0.26
15..28	38%	296	2997	9.9%	-0.22
29..60	17%	131	1464	8.9%	-0.32
61..100	2%	18	277	6.5%	-0.41
101+	8%	64	807	7.9%	-0.17
Unraced	0%	0	4	0.0%	-1.00

ANALYSIS BY TODAY'S STARTING PRICE

Price	Prop	Win	Runs	Wins%	£
Odds On	4%	32	53	60.4%	0.02
Ev-2/1	14%	109	286	38.1%	0.00
9/4-4/1	28%	213	977	21.8%	-0.09
9/2-6/1	18%	136	955	14.2%	-0.12
13/2-10/1	20%	155	1733	8.9%	-0.19
11/1-16/1	11%	86	1639	5.2%	-0.25
18/1-33/1	5%	37	1442	2.6%	-0.36
40/1+	0%	2	646	0.3%	-0.76

ANALYSIS BY STARTING PRICE LAST TIME

Price	Prop	Win	Runs	Wins%	£
Odds On	3%	20	109	18.3%	-0.35
Ev-2/1	9%	68	356	19.1%	-0.18
9/4-4/1	21%	159	1025	15.5%	-0.18
9/2-6/1	14%	105	921	11.4%	-0.29
13/2-10/1	22%	173	1538	11.2%	-0.10
11/1-16/1	16%	123	1428	8.6%	-0.19
18/1-33/1	11%	88	1443	6.1%	-0.29
40/1+	4%	34	907	3.7%	-0.60
Unraced	0%	0	4	0.0%	-1.00

ANALYSIS BY DISTANCE BEATEN LAST TIME

Lengths	Prop	Win	Runs	Wins%	£
..-10	0%	0	5	0.0%	-1.00
-10..0	22%	173	966	17.9%	-0.21
0.1..2	21%	162	947	17.1%	0.05
2.1..5	21%	161	1390	11.6%	-0.21
5.1..10	19%	149	1831	8.1%	-0.26
10.1..20	12%	91	1683	5.4%	-0.37
20.0..30	2%	19	514	3.7%	-0.44
30.1+	2%	15	391	3.8%	-0.41
Not Compl	0%	0	0	0.0%	0.00
Unraced	0%	0	4	0.0%	-1.00

ANALYSIS BY RUN NUMBER

Run No	Prop	Win	Runs	Wins%	£
FTO	0%	0	4	0.0%	-1.00
2nd Run	1%	7	31	22.6%	0.16
3rd Run	2%	16	133	12.0%	-0.40
4th+ Run	97%	747	7563	9.9%	-0.25

ANALYSIS BY POSITION LAST TIME

Pos LT	Prop	Win	Runs	Wins%	£
Won	23%	174	970	17.9%	-0.21
2nd or 3rd	32%	248	1646	15.1%	-0.08
Unplaced	45%	348	5096	6.8%	-0.31
Not Compl	0%	0	19	0.0%	-1.00

OTHER FACTORS (WINS-RUNS, £)

Course Winner:	38-253	-£0.34
Distance Winner:	165-1003	-£0.07
Going Winner:	117-791	-£0.15
Beaten Favourite:	73-432	-£0.23
Up in class:	187-1816	-£0.28
Same class:	430-4142	-£0.20
Down in class:	153-1769	-£0.35
7-Day Winners:	38-90	£0.18
Colts and Geldings:	525-5086	-£0.26
Fillies:	194-2146	-£0.24
Absolute Favourites:	219-694	-£0.03

TRAINERS (WINS-RUNS, £)

J Pearce 1-33 £2.06; D R C Elsworth 12-65 £0.71; Sir Mark Prescott 49-122 £0.38; J L Dunlop 38-233 £0.17; Pat Eddery 5-27 £1.43; T D Walford 3-12 £3.17; Mrs A J Perrett 29-174 £0.20; J M P Eustace 5-38 £0.74; B G Powell 3-32 £0.78; R A Fahey 20-111 £0.22; C R Egerton 2-26 £0.88; P J Makin 5-17 £1.31; W R Swinburn 10-60 £0.37; J H M Gosden 16-100 £0.22; D Haydn Jones 2-13 £1.46; G Wragg 2-18 £0.89; Saeed Bin Suroor 7-18 £0.81; Sir Michael Stoute 16-77 £0.18; B Palling 2-11 £1.18; W R Muir 7-67 £0.19.

Handicaps (Class 4..7)

3-Y.O Races: Handicaps (Class 4..7) – 15+ furlong races

ANALYSIS BY BHA RATING

Rating	Prop	Win	Runs	Wins%	£
120..139	0%	0	0	0.0%	0.00
110..119	0%	0	0	0.0%	0.00
100..109	0%	0	0	0.0%	0.00
90..99	0%	0	0	0.0%	0.00
70..89	22%	8	67	11.9%	-0.37
50..69	65%	24	270	8.9%	-0.43
..49	14%	5	88	5.7%	-0.26
Unrated	0%	0	0	0.0%	0.00

ANALYSIS BY WEIGHT CARRIED

Weight	Prop	Win	Runs	Wins%	£
10-01+	0%	0	0	0.0%	0.00
9-8..10-00	5%	2	11	18.2%	-0.38
9-0..9-07	46%	17	150	11.3%	-0.32
8-8..8-13	30%	11	125	8.8%	-0.42
8-0..8-07	16%	6	120	5.0%	-0.41
..7-13	3%	1	19	5.3%	-0.58

ANALYSIS BY DAYS SINCE LAST RUN

Days	Prop	Win	Runs	Wins%	£
1..7	16%	6	25	24.0%	0.66
8..14	19%	7	117	6.0%	-0.54
15..28	38%	14	149	9.4%	-0.33
29..60	22%	8	96	8.3%	-0.44
61..100	3%	1	18	5.6%	-0.81
101+	3%	1	18	5.6%	-0.56
Unraced	0%	0	2	0.0%	-1.00

ANALYSIS BY TODAY'S STARTING PRICE

Price	Prop	Win	Runs	Wins%	£
Odds On	3%	1	1	100.0%	0.57
Ev-2/1	11%	4	14	28.6%	-0.26
9/4-4/1	38%	14	51	27.5%	0.14
9/2-6/1	8%	3	40	7.5%	-0.55
13/2-10/1	22%	8	77	10.4%	-0.08
11/1-16/1	19%	7	91	7.7%	0.12
18/1-33/1	0%	0	92	0.0%	-1.00
40/1+	0%	0	59	0.0%	-1.00

ANALYSIS BY STARTING PRICE LAST TIME

Price	Prop	Win	Runs	Wins%	£
Odds On	3%	1	4	25.0%	-0.06
Ev-2/1	14%	5	21	23.8%	-0.18
9/4-4/1	22%	8	44	18.2%	-0.04
9/2-6/1	16%	6	44	13.6%	-0.15
13/2-10/1	14%	5	66	7.6%	-0.48
11/1-16/1	8%	3	72	4.2%	-0.72
18/1-33/1	14%	5	97	5.2%	-0.47
40/1+	11%	4	75	5.3%	-0.29
Unraced	0%	0	2	0.0%	-1.00

ANALYSIS BY DISTANCE BEATEN LAST TIME

Lengths	Prop	Win	Runs	Wins%	£
..-10	0%	0	0	0.0%	0.00
-10..0	8%	3	33	9.1%	-0.68
0.1..2	32%	12	52	23.1%	0.14
2.1..5	24%	9	58	15.5%	0.20
5.1..10	22%	8	97	8.2%	-0.32
10.1..20	8%	3	117	2.6%	-0.78
20.0..30	3%	1	33	3.0%	-0.64
30.1+	3%	1	33	3.0%	-0.48
Not Compl	0%	0	0	0.0%	0.00
Unraced	0%	0	2	0.0%	-1.00

ANALYSIS BY RUN NUMBER

Run No	Prop	Win	Runs	Wins%	£
FTO	0%	0	2	0.0%	-1.00
2nd Run	0%	0	0	0.0%	0.00
3rd Run	0%	0	2	0.0%	-1.00
4th+ Run	100%	37	421	8.8%	-0.38

ANALYSIS BY POSITION LAST TIME

Pos LT	Prop	Win	Runs	Wins%	£
Won	8%	3	33	9.1%	-0.68
2nd or 3rd	51%	19	100	19.0%	0.01
Unplaced	41%	15	290	5.2%	-0.49
Not Compl	0%	0	2	0.0%	-1.00

OTHER FACTORS (WINS-RUNS, £)

Course Winner:	0-10	-£1.00
Distance Winner:	4-15	-£0.19
Going Winner:	9-37	£0.03
Beaten Favourite:	7-20	£0.56
Up in class:	2-84	-£0.90
Same class:	26-215	-£0.13
Down in class:	9-124	-£0.47
Colts and Geldings:	25-256	-£0.35
Fillies:	12-169	-£0.45
Absolute Favourites:	10-30	£0.13

TRAINERS (WINS-RUNS, £)

Mrs A J Perrett 3-12 £0.07.

Race Profiles

All Age Races: Group 1 Races

ANALYSIS BY AGE

Age	Prop	Win	Runs	Wins%	£
2yo	1%	1	6	16.7%	1.17
3yo	32%	31	243	12.8%	0.23
4yo	33%	32	339	9.4%	-0.40
5yo	20%	19	201	9.5%	-0.46
6yo	10%	10	103	9.7%	-0.09
7yo	3%	3	59	5.1%	-0.07
8yo	1%	1	16	6.3%	-0.84
9yo	0%	0	6	0.0%	-1.00
10yo	0%	0	4	0.0%	-1.00
11yo+	0%	0	0	0.0%	0.00

ANALYSIS BY BHA RATING

Rating	Prop	Win	Runs	Wins%	£
120..139	15%	15	84	17.9%	-0.41
110..119	35%	34	438	7.8%	-0.15
100..109	6%	6	202	3.0%	-0.64
90..99	1%	1	16	6.3%	2.19
70..89	0%	0	5	0.0%	-1.00
50..69	0%	0	0	0.0%	0.00
..49	0%	0	0	0.0%	0.00
Unrated	42%	41	232	17.7%	-0.17

ANALYSIS BY WEIGHT CARRIED

Weight	Prop	Win	Runs	Wins%	£
10-01+	0%	0	0	0.0%	0.00
9-8..10-00	4%	4	66	6.1%	-0.44
9-0..9-07	60%	58	664	8.7%	-0.44
8-8..8-13	35%	34	229	14.8%	0.40
8-0..8-07	1%	1	15	6.7%	-0.13
..7-13	0%	0	3	0.0%	-1.00

ANALYSIS BY DAYS SINCE LAST RUN

Days	Prop	Win	Runs	Wins%	£
1..7	3%	3	33	9.1%	1.27
8..14	1%	1	63	1.6%	-0.94
15..28	44%	43	369	11.7%	-0.03
29..60	27%	26	272	9.6%	-0.48
61..100	8%	8	74	10.8%	-0.23
101+	9%	9	102	8.8%	-0.45
Unraced	7%	7	64	10.9%	-0.23

ANALYSIS BY TODAY'S STARTING PRICE

Price	Prop	Win	Runs	Wins%	£
Odds On	11%	11	17	64.7%	0.01
Ev - 2/1	20%	19	55	34.5%	-0.14
9/4 - 4/1	19%	18	99	18.2%	-0.24
9/2 - 6/1	15%	15	94	16.0%	-0.02
13/2-10/1	18%	17	154	11.0%	-0.01
11/1-16/1	10%	10	179	5.6%	-0.20
18/1-33/1	6%	6	194	3.1%	-0.17
40/1+	1%	1	185	0.5%	-0.72

ANALYSIS BY STARTING PRICE LAST TIME

Price	Prop	Win	Runs	Wins%	£
Odds On	18%	17	56	30.4%	0.07
Ev - 2/1	15%	15	102	14.7%	-0.23
9/4 - 4/1	19%	18	183	9.8%	-0.28
9/2 - 6/1	14%	14	125	11.2%	-0.43
13/2-10/1	18%	17	209	8.1%	-0.15
11/1-16/1	4%	4	125	3.2%	-0.60
18/1-33/1	4%	4	80	5.0%	-0.09
40/1+	1%	1	33	3.0%	0.55
Unraced	7%	7	64	10.9%	-0.23

ANALYSIS BY DISTANCE BEATEN LAST TIME

Lengths	Prop	Win	Runs	Wins%	£
..-10	0%	0	0	0.0%	0.00
-10..0	33%	32	243	13.2%	-0.38
0.1..2	29%	28	226	12.4%	-0.03
2.1..5	15%	15	203	7.4%	-0.01
5.1..10	8%	8	148	5.4%	-0.68
10.1..20	4%	4	66	6.1%	-0.16
20.0..30	0%	0	13	0.0%	-1.00
30.1+	3%	3	14	21.4%	0.36
Not Compl	0%	0	0	0.0%	0.00
Unraced	7%	7	64	10.9%	-0.23

ANALYSIS BY RUN NUMBER

Run No	Prop	Win	Runs	Wins%	£
FTO	7%	7	64	10.9%	-0.23
2nd Run	6%	6	44	13.6%	-0.13
3rd Run	5%	5	27	18.5%	0.03
4th+ Run	81%	79	842	9.4%	-0.26

ANALYSIS BY POSITION LAST TIME

Pos LT	Prop	Win	Runs	Wins%	£
Won	33%	32	243	13.2%	-0.38
2nd or 3rd	31%	30	273	11.0%	-0.18
Unplaced	29%	28	396	7.1%	-0.20
Not Compl	7%	7	65	10.8%	-0.25

OTHER FACTORS (WINS-RUNS, £)

Course Winner:	23-279	-£0.25
Distance Winner:	61-583	-£0.21
Going Winner:	57-538	-£0.32
Beaten Favourite:	12-109	-£0.35
BHA Top Rated:	12-96	£0.02
Up in class:	34-536	-£0.40
Same class:	56-377	-£0.02
7-Day Winners:	0-6	-£1.00
Colts and Geldings:	70-731	-£0.30
Fillies:	8-93	-£0.36
Absolute Favourites:	36-96	-£0.09

TRAINERS (WINS-RUNS, £)

C E Brittain 1-20 £1.55; H Morrison 2-10 £1.85; B J Meehan 2-14 £1.09; M L W Bell 2-15 £1.00; E A L Dunlop 3-12 £0.63; J Noseda 4-28 £0.21; H R A Cecil 2-18 £0.19; D Nicholls 1-14 £0.07.

Group 1 Races

All Age Races: Group 1 Races – 2 to 7 runners

ANALYSIS BY AGE

Age	Prop	Win	Runs	Wins%	£
2yo	0%	0	0	0.0%	0.00
3yo	43%	12	55	21.8%	0.81
4yo	25%	7	62	11.3%	-0.38
5yo	29%	8	46	17.4%	-0.18
6yo	4%	1	12	8.3%	-0.29
7yo	0%	0	4	0.0%	-1.00
8yo	0%	0	1	0.0%	-1.00
9yo	0%	0	0	0.0%	0.00
10yo	0%	0	0	0.0%	0.00
11yo+	0%	0	0	0.0%	0.00

ANALYSIS BY BHA RATING

Rating	Prop	Win	Runs	Wins%	£
120..139	21%	6	30	20.0%	-0.42
110..119	25%	7	59	11.9%	-0.20
100..109	4%	1	30	3.3%	-0.57
90..99	4%	1	3	33.3%	16.00
70..89	0%	0	1	0.0%	-1.00
50..69	0%	0	0	0.0%	0.00
..49	0%	0	0	0.0%	0.00
Unrated	46%	13	57	22.8%	-0.02

ANALYSIS BY WEIGHT CARRIED

Weight	Prop	Win	Runs	Wins%	£
10-01+	0%	0	0	0.0%	0.00
9-8 ..10-00	0%	0	0	0.0%	0.00
9-0..9-07	54%	15	121	12.4%	-0.37
8-8..8-13	46%	13	56	23.2%	0.94
8-0..8-07	0%	0	3	0.0%	-1.00
..7-13	0%	0	0	0.0%	0.00

ANALYSIS BY DAYS SINCE LAST RUN

Days	Prop	Win	Runs	Wins%	£
1..7	0%	0	1	0.0%	-1.00
8..14	0%	0	7	0.0%	-1.00
15..28	36%	10	65	15.4%	0.61
29..60	46%	13	57	22.8%	0.01
61..100	14%	4	19	21.1%	-0.12
101+	0%	0	19	0.0%	-1.00
Unraced	4%	1	12	8.3%	-0.54

ANALYSIS BY TODAY'S STARTING PRICE

Price	Prop	Win	Runs	Wins%	£
Odds On	25%	7	10	70.0%	0.07
Ev - 2/1	21%	6	20	30.0%	-0.28
9/4 - 4/1	7%	2	29	6.9%	-0.71
9/2 - 6/1	18%	5	23	21.7%	0.35
13/2-10/1	18%	5	24	20.8%	0.79
11/1-16/1	7%	2	27	7.4%	-0.04
18/1-33/1	0%	0	20	0.0%	-1.00
40/1+	4%	1	27	3.7%	0.89

ANALYSIS BY STARTING PRICE LAST TIME

Price	Prop	Win	Runs	Wins%	£
Odds On	29%	8	18	44.4%	0.12
Ev - 2/1	25%	7	27	25.9%	-0.22
9/4 - 4/1	11%	3	36	8.3%	-0.47
9/2 - 6/1	14%	4	24	16.7%	0.06
13/2-10/1	11%	3	33	9.1%	-0.12
11/1-16/1	4%	1	16	6.3%	-0.19
18/1-33/1	0%	0	8	0.0%	-1.00
40/1+	4%	1	6	16.7%	7.50
Unraced	4%	1	12	8.3%	-0.54

ANALYSIS BY DISTANCE BEATEN LAST TIME

Lengths	Prop	Win	Runs	Wins%	£
..-10	0%	0	0	0.0%	0.00
-10..0	39%	11	55	20.0%	-0.45
0.1..2	29%	8	49	16.3%	0.13
2.1..5	14%	4	32	12.5%	1.15
5.1..10	4%	1	21	4.8%	-0.71
10.1..20	7%	2	7	28.6%	0.64
20.0..30	0%	0	1	0.0%	-1.00
30.1+	4%	1	3	33.3%	1.50
Not Compl	0%	0	0	0.0%	0.00
Unraced	4%	1	12	8.3%	-0.54

ANALYSIS BY RUN NUMBER

Run No	Prop	Win	Runs	Wins%	£
FTO	4%	1	12	8.3%	-0.54
2nd Run	4%	1	8	12.5%	-0.78
3rd Run	11%	3	8	37.5%	0.15
4th+ Run	82%	23	152	15.1%	0.11

ANALYSIS BY POSITION LAST TIME

Pos LT	Prop	Win	Runs	Wins%	£
Won	39%	11	55	20.0%	-0.45
2nd or 3rd	39%	11	62	17.7%	0.24
Unplaced	18%	5	51	9.8%	0.41
Not Compl	4%	1	12	8.3%	-0.54

OTHER FACTORS (WINS-RUNS, £)

Course Winner:	6-54	£0.38
Distance Winner:	19-105	£0.15
Going Winner:	16-104	-£0.23
Beaten Favourite:	5-21	£0.02
BHA Top Rated:	5-30	-£0.26
Up in class:	8-79	-£0.41
Same class:	19-89	£0.49
7-Day Winners:	0-1	-£1.00
Colts and Geldings:	18-112	-£0.21
Fillies:	1-10	-£0.10
Absolute Favourites:	13-28	-£0.11

TRAINERS (WINS-RUNS, £)

A P O'Brien 9-32 £0.36; J H M Gosden 2-10 £0.05.

Race Profiles

All Age Races: Group 1 Races – 8 to 14 runners

ANALYSIS BY AGE

Age	Prop	Win	Runs	Wins%	£
2yo	0%	0	4	0.0%	-1.00
3yo	26%	14	135	10.4%	-0.16
4yo	43%	23	213	10.8%	-0.37
5yo	19%	10	117	8.5%	-0.43
6yo	9%	5	46	10.9%	-0.39
7yo	2%	1	25	4.0%	0.90
8yo	2%	1	9	11.1%	-0.72
9yo	0%	0	3	0.0%	-1.00
10yo	0%	0	1	0.0%	-1.00
11yo+	0%	0	0	0.0%	0.00

ANALYSIS BY BHA RATING

Rating	Prop	Win	Runs	Wins%	£
120..139	17%	9	48	18.8%	-0.32
110..119	35%	19	267	7.1%	-0.38
100..109	6%	3	103	2.9%	-0.56
90..99	0%	0	9	0.0%	-1.00
70..89	0%	0	4	0.0%	-1.00
50..69	0%	0	0	0.0%	0.00
..49	0%	0	0	0.0%	0.00
Unrated	43%	23	122	18.9%	-0.13

ANALYSIS BY WEIGHT CARRIED

Weight	Prop	Win	Runs	Wins%	£
10-01+	0%	0	0	0.0%	0.00
9-8..10-00	4%	2	24	8.3%	-0.21
9-0..9-07	67%	36	391	9.2%	-0.48
8-8..8-13	30%	16	125	12.8%	0.02
8-0..8-07	0%	0	10	0.0%	-1.00
..7-13	0%	0	3	0.0%	-1.00

ANALYSIS BY DAYS SINCE LAST RUN

Days	Prop	Win	Runs	Wins%	£
1..7	0%	0	9	0.0%	-1.00
8..14	2%	1	45	2.2%	-0.92
15..28	48%	26	206	12.6%	-0.17
29..60	20%	11	150	7.3%	-0.71
61..100	7%	4	34	11.8%	0.18
101+	15%	8	70	11.4%	-0.24
Unraced	7%	4	39	10.3%	-0.10

ANALYSIS BY TODAY'S STARTING PRICE

Price	Prop	Win	Runs	Wins%	£
Odds On	7%	4	7	57.1%	-0.07
Ev - 2/1	22%	12	31	38.7%	-0.02
9/4 - 4/1	26%	14	57	24.6%	0.02
9/2 - 6/1	15%	8	52	15.4%	-0.06
13/2-10/1	15%	8	93	8.6%	-0.24
11/1-16/1	11%	6	107	5.6%	-0.16
18/1-33/1	4%	2	108	1.9%	-0.59
40/1+	0%	0	98	0.0%	-1.00

ANALYSIS BY STARTING PRICE LAST TIME

Price	Prop	Win	Runs	Wins%	£
Odds On	15%	8	33	24.2%	-0.09
Ev - 2/1	11%	6	60	10.0%	-0.56
9/4 - 4/1	24%	13	102	12.7%	-0.12
9/2 - 6/1	17%	9	71	12.7%	-0.48
13/2-10/1	19%	10	111	9.0%	-0.20
11/1 16/1	6%	3	71	4.2%	-0.49
18/1-33/1	2%	1	49	2.0%	-0.91
40/1+	0%	0	17	0.0%	-1.00
Unraced	7%	4	39	10.3%	-0.10

ANALYSIS BY DISTANCE BEATEN LAST TIME

Lengths	Prop	Win	Runs	Wins%	£
..-10	0%	0	0	0.0%	0.00
-10..0	31%	17	142	12.0%	-0.51
0.1..2	30%	16	117	13.7%	0.05
2.1..5	13%	7	117	6.0%	-0.60
5.1..10	13%	7	85	8.2%	-0.52
10.1..20	2%	1	35	2.9%	-0.40
20.0..30	0%	0	9	0.0%	-1.00
30.1+	4%	2	9	22.2%	0.28
Not Compl	0%	0	0	0.0%	0.00
Unraced	7%	4	39	10.3%	-0.10

ANALYSIS BY RUN NUMBER

Run No	Prop	Win	Runs	Wins%	£
FTO	7%	4	39	10.3%	-0.10
2nd Run	7%	4	25	16.0%	0.36
3rd Run	2%	1	12	8.3%	-0.54
4th+ Run	83%	45	477	9.4%	-0.43

ANALYSIS BY POSITION LAST TIME

Pos LT	Prop	Win	Runs	Wins%	£
Won	31%	17	142	12.0%	-0.51
2nd or 3rd	28%	15	149	10.1%	-0.29
Unplaced	33%	18	222	8.1%	-0.38
Not Compl	7%	4	40	10.0%	-0.12

OTHER FACTORS (WINS-RUNS, £)

Course Winner:	13-147	-£0.41
Distance Winner:	33-302	-£0.35
Going Winner:	35-294	-£0.29
Beaten Favourite:	5-58	-£0.49
BHA Top Rated:	5-49	-£0.46
Up in class:	17-287	-£0.49
Same class:	33-227	-£0.27
7-Day Winners:	0-1	-£1.00
Colts and Geldings:	39-401	-£0.43
Fillies:	5-57	-£0.33
Absolute Favourites:	20-54	-£0.04

TRAINERS (WINS-RUNS, £)

H R A Cecil 2-16 £0.34; J Noseda 2-15 £0.13.

Group 1 Races

All Age Races: Group 1 Races – 15 runners or more

ANALYSIS BY AGE

Age	Prop	Win	Runs	Wins%	£
2yo	7%	1	2	50.0%	5.50
3yo	33%	5	53	9.4%	0.60
4yo	13%	2	64	3.1%	-0.52
5yo	7%	1	38	2.6%	-0.90
6yo	27%	4	45	8.9%	0.28
7yo	13%	2	30	6.7%	-0.43
8yo	0%	0	6	0.0%	-1.00
9yo	0%	0	3	0.0%	-1.00
10yo	0%	0	3	0.0%	-1.00
11yo+	0%	0	0	0.0%	0.00

ANALYSIS BY BHA RATING

Rating	Prop	Win	Runs	Wins%	£
120..139	0%	0	6	0.0%	-1.00
110..119	53%	8	112	7.1%	0.44
100..109	13%	2	69	2.9%	-0.78
90..99	0%	0	4	0.0%	-1.00
70..89	0%	0	0	0.0%	0.00
50..69	0%	0	0	0.0%	0.00
..49	0%	0	0	0.0%	0.00
Unrated	33%	5	53	9.4%	-0.42

ANALYSIS BY WEIGHT CARRIED

Weight	Prop	Win	Runs	Wins%	£
10-01+	0%	0	0	0.0%	0.00
9-8 ..10-00	13%	2	42	4.8%	-0.57
9-0..9-07	47%	7	152	4.6%	-0.40
8-8..8-13	33%	5	48	10.4%	0.77
8-0..8-07	7%	1	2	50.0%	5.50
..7-13	0%	0	0	0.0%	0.00

ANALYSIS BY DAYS SINCE LAST RUN

Days	Prop	Win	Runs	Wins%	£
1..7	20%	3	23	13.0%	2.26
8..14	0%	0	11	0.0%	-1.00
15..28	47%	7	98	7.1%	-0.18
29..60	13%	2	65	3.1%	-0.37
61..100	0%	0	21	0.0%	-1.00
101+	7%	1	13	7.7%	-0.79
Unraced	13%	2	13	15.4%	-0.37

ANALYSIS BY TODAY'S STARTING PRICE

Price	Prop	Win	Runs	Wins%	£
Odds On	0%	0	0	0.0%	0.00
Ev - 2/1	7%	1	4	25.0%	-0.31
9/4 - 4/1	13%	2	13	15.4%	-0.37
9/2 - 6/1	13%	2	19	10.5%	-0.34
13/2-10/1	27%	4	37	10.8%	0.05
11/1-16/1	13%	2	45	4.4%	-0.38
18/1-33/1	27%	4	66	6.1%	0.77
40/1+	0%	0	60	0.0%	-1.00

ANALYSIS BY STARTING PRICE LAST TIME

Price	Prop	Win	Runs	Wins%	£
Odds On	7%	1	5	20.0%	1.00
Ev - 2/1	13%	2	15	13.3%	1.10
9/4 - 4/1	13%	2	45	4.4%	-0.49
9/2 - 6/1	7%	1	30	3.3%	-0.73
13/2-10/1	27%	4	65	6.2%	-0.10
11/1-16/1	0%	0	38	0.0%	-1.00
18/1-33/1	20%	3	23	13.0%	1.96
40/1+	0%	0	10	0.0%	-1.00
Unraced	13%	2	13	15.4%	-0.37

ANALYSIS BY DISTANCE BEATEN LAST TIME

Lengths	Prop	Win	Runs	Wins%	£
..-10	0%	0	0	0.0%	0.00
-10..0	27%	4	46	8.7%	0.10
0.1..2	27%	4	60	6.7%	-0.32
2.1..5	27%	4	54	7.4%	0.57
5.1..10	0%	0	42	0.0%	-1.00
10.1..20	7%	1	24	4.2%	-0.04
20.0..30	0%	0	3	0.0%	-1.00
30.1+	0%	0	2	0.0%	-1.00
Not Compl	0%	0	0	0.0%	0.00
Unraced	13%	2	13	15.4%	-0.37

ANALYSIS BY RUN NUMBER

Run No	Prop	Win	Runs	Wins%	£
FTO	13%	2	13	15.4%	-0.37
2nd Run	7%	1	11	9.1%	-0.75
3rd Run	7%	1	7	14.3%	0.86
4th+ Run	73%	11	213	5.2%	-0.14

ANALYSIS BY POSITION LAST TIME

Pos LT	Prop	Win	Runs	Wins%	£
Won	27%	4	46	8.7%	0.10
2nd or 3rd	27%	4	62	6.5%	-0.34
Unplaced	33%	5	123	4.1%	-0.12
Not Compl	13%	2	13	15.4%	-0.37

OTHER FACTORS (WINS-RUNS, £)

Course Winner:	4-78	-£0.37
Distance Winner:	9-176	-£0.19
Going Winner:	6-140	-£0.44
Beaten Favourite:	2-30	-£0.33
BHA Top Rated:	2-17	£1.88
Up in class:	9-170	-£0.24
Same class:	4-61	£0.16
7-Day Winners:	0-4	-£1.00
Colts and Geldings:	13-218	-£0.11
Fillies:	2-26	-£0.52
Absolute Favourites:	3-14	-£0.21

Race Profiles

All Age Races: Group 1 Races – good or faster going

ANALYSIS BY AGE

Age	Prop	Win	Runs	Wins%	£
2yo	1%	1	5	20.0%	1.60
3yo	31%	22	163	13.5%	0.38
4yo	35%	25	255	9.8%	-0.44
5yo	17%	12	151	7.9%	-0.63
6yo	11%	8	73	11.0%	0.09
7yo	4%	3	49	6.1%	-0.60
8yo	1%	1	11	9.1%	-0.77
9yo	0%	0	5	0.0%	-1.00
10yo	0%	0	3	0.0%	-1.00
11yo+	0%	0	0	0.0%	0.00

ANALYSIS BY BHA RATING

Rating	Prop	Win	Runs	Wins%	£
120..139	18%	13	64	20.3%	-0.44
110..119	29%	21	315	6.7%	-0.22
100..109	6%	4	148	2.7%	-0.69
90..99	1%	1	13	7.7%	2.92
70..89	0%	0	3	0.0%	-1.00
50..69	0%	0	0	0.0%	0.00
..49	0%	0	0	0.0%	0.00
Unrated	46%	33	172	19.2%	-0.06

ANALYSIS BY WEIGHT CARRIED

Weight	Prop	Win	Runs	Wins%	£
10-01+	0%	0	0	0.0%	0.00
9-8..10-00	4%	3	53	5.7%	-0.42
9-0..9-07	63%	45	492	9.1%	-0.47
8-8..8-13	32%	23	161	14.3%	0.45
8-0..8-07	1%	1	7	14.3%	0.86
..7-13	0%	0	2	0.0%	-1.00

ANALYSIS BY DAYS SINCE LAST RUN

Days	Prop	Win	Runs	Wins%	£
1..7	4%	3	25	12.0%	2.00
8..14	0%	0	38	0.0%	-1.00
15..28	44%	32	280	11.4%	-0.11
29..60	26%	19	192	9.9%	-0.54
61..100	10%	7	48	14.6%	0.01
101+	8%	6	79	7.6%	-0.52
Unraced	7%	5	53	9.4%	-0.25

ANALYSIS BY TODAY'S STARTING PRICE

Price	Prop	Win	Runs	Wins%	£
Odds On	14%	10	14	71.4%	0.13
Ev - 2/1	22%	16	45	35.6%	-0.11
9/4 - 4/1	17%	12	66	18.2%	-0.26
9/2 - 6/1	15%	11	72	15.3%	-0.07
13/2-10/1	14%	10	105	9.5%	-0.16
11/1-16/1	11%	8	131	6.1%	-0.11
18/1-33/1	6%	4	140	2.9%	-0.20
40/1+	1%	1	142	0.7%	-0.64

ANALYSIS BY STARTING PRICE LAST TIME

Price	Prop	Win	Runs	Wins%	£
Odds On	19%	14	42	33.3%	0.10
Ev - 2/1	17%	12	74	16.2%	-0.44
9/4 - 4/1	19%	14	129	10.9%	-0.18
9/2 - 6/1	14%	10	89	11.2%	-0.45
13/2-10/1	17%	12	150	8.0%	-0.08
11/1-16/1	1%	1	89	1.1%	-0.81
18/1-33/1	4%	3	61	4.9%	-0.19
40/1+	1%	1	28	3.6%	0.82
Unraced	7%	5	53	9.4%	-0.25

ANALYSIS BY DISTANCE BEATEN LAST TIME

Lengths	Prop	Win	Runs	Wins%	£
..-10	0%	0	0	0.0%	0.00
-10..0	38%	27	181	14.9%	-0.40
0.1..2	26%	19	165	11.5%	-0.06
2.1..5	17%	12	144	8.3%	0.22
5.1..10	6%	4	101	4.0%	-0.84
10.1..20	4%	3	51	5.9%	-0.36
20.0..30	0%	0	9	0.0%	-1.00
30.1+	3%	2	11	18.2%	-0.09
Not Compl	0%	0	0	0.0%	0.00
Unraced	7%	5	53	9.4%	-0.25

ANALYSIS BY RUN NUMBER

Run No	Prop	Win	Runs	Wins%	£
FTO	7%	5	53	9.4%	-0.25
2nd Run	8%	6	35	17.1%	0.10
3rd Run	7%	5	23	21.7%	0.20
4th+ Run	78%	56	604	9.3%	-0.28

ANALYSIS BY POSITION LAST TIME

Pos LT	Prop	Win	Runs	Wins%	£
Won	38%	27	181	14.9%	-0.40
2nd or 3rd	24%	17	197	8.6%	-0.36
Unplaced	32%	23	283	8.1%	-0.07
Not Compl	7%	5	54	9.3%	-0.26

OTHER FACTORS (WINS-RUNS, £)

Course Winner:	17-198	-£0.25
Distance Winner:	43-411	-£0.24
Going Winner:	45-438	-£0.23
Beaten Favourite:	9-80	-£0.38
BHA Top Rated:	9-65	£0.18
Up in class:	24-382	-£0.41
Same class:	43-280	-£0.02
7-Day Winners:	0-4	-£1.00
Colts and Geldings:	55-545	-£0.31
Fillies:	3-60	-£0.50
Absolute Favourites:	30-72	-£0.02

TRAINERS (WINS-RUNS, £)

C E Brittain 1-13 £2.92; M L W Bell 1-11 £0.91; A P O'Brien 20-76 £0.12; J Noseda 2-18 £0.11; H R A Cecil 1-14 £0.07; R Channon 1-16 £0.06; A Fabre 4-11 £0.04.

Group 1 Races

All Age Races: Group 1 Races – good to soft or softer going

ANALYSIS BY AGE

Age	Prop	Win	Runs	Wins%	£
2yo	0%	0	1	0.0%	-1.00
3yo	36%	9	80	11.3%	-0.08
4yo	28%	7	84	8.3%	-0.28
5yo	28%	7	50	14.0%	0.06
6yo	8%	2	30	6.7%	-0.52
7yo	0%	0	10	0.0%	-1.00
8yo	0%	0	5	0.0%	-1.00
9yo	0%	0	1	0.0%	-1.00
10yo	0%	0	1	0.0%	-1.00
11yo+	0%	0	0	0.0%	0.00

ANALYSIS BY BHA RATING

Rating	Prop	Win	Runs	Wins%	£
120..139	8%	2	20	10.0%	-0.30
110..119	52%	13	123	10.6%	0.04
100..109	8%	2	54	3.7%	-0.48
90..99	0%	0	3	0.0%	-1.00
70..89	0%	0	2	0.0%	-1.00
50..69	0%	0	0	0.0%	0.00
..49	0%	0	0	0.0%	0.00
Unrated	32%	8	60	13.3%	-0.48

ANALYSIS BY WEIGHT CARRIED

Weight	Prop	Win	Runs	Wins%	£
10-01+	0%	0	0	0.0%	0.00
9-8 ..10-00	4%	1	13	7.7%	-0.54
9-0..9-07	52%	13	172	7.6%	-0.37
8-8..8-13	44%	11	68	16.2%	0.29
8-0..8-07	0%	0	8	0.0%	-1.00
..7-13	0%	0	1	0.0%	-1.00

ANALYSIS BY DAYS SINCE LAST RUN

Days	Prop	Win	Runs	Wins%	£
1..7	0%	0	8	0.0%	-1.00
8..14	4%	1	25	4.0%	-0.85
15..28	44%	11	89	12.4%	0.21
29..60	28%	7	80	8.8%	-0.32
61..100	4%	1	26	3.8%	-0.69
101+	12%	3	23	13.0%	-0.20
Unraced	8%	2	11	18.2%	-0.18

ANALYSIS BY TODAY'S STARTING PRICE

Price	Prop	Win	Runs	Wins%	£
Odds On	4%	1	3	33.3%	-0.52
Ev - 2/1	12%	3	10	30.0%	-0.25
9/4 - 4/1	24%	6	33	18.2%	-0.20
9/2 - 6/1	16%	4	22	18.2%	0.16
13/2-10/1	28%	7	49	14.3%	0.31
11/1-16/1	8%	2	48	4.2%	-0.42
18/1-33/1	8%	2	54	3.7%	-0.09
40/1+	0%	0	43	0.0%	-1.00

ANALYSIS BY STARTING PRICE LAST TIME

Price	Prop	Win	Runs	Wins%	£
Odds On	12%	3	14	21.4%	0.00
Ev - 2/1	12%	3	28	10.7%	0.33
9/4 - 4/1	16%	4	54	7.4%	-0.51
9/2 - 6/1	16%	4	36	11.1%	-0.41
13/2-10/1	20%	5	59	8.5%	-0.36
11/1-16/1	12%	3	36	8.3%	-0.10
18/1-33/1	4%	1	19	5.3%	0.21
40/1+	0%	0	5	0.0%	-1.00
Unraced	8%	2	11	18.2%	-0.18

ANALYSIS BY DISTANCE BEATEN LAST TIME

Lengths	Prop	Win	Runs	Wins%	£
..-10	0%	0	0	0.0%	0.00
-10..0	20%	5	62	8.1%	-0.34
0.1..2	36%	9	61	14.8%	0.04
2.1..5	12%	3	59	5.1%	-0.57
5.1..10	16%	4	47	8.5%	-0.35
10.1..20	4%	1	15	6.7%	0.53
20.0..30	0%	0	4	0.0%	-1.00
30.1+	4%	1	3	33.3%	2.00
Not Compl	0%	0	0	0.0%	0.00
Unraced	8%	2	11	18.2%	-0.18

ANALYSIS BY RUN NUMBER

Run No	Prop	Win	Runs	Wins%	£
FTO	8%	2	11	18.2%	-0.18
2nd Run	0%	0	9	0.0%	-1.00
3rd Run	0%	0	4	0.0%	-1.00
4th+ Run	92%	23	238	9.7%	-0.19

ANALYSIS BY POSITION LAST TIME

Pos LT	Prop	Win	Runs	Wins%	£
Won	20%	5	62	8.1%	-0.34
2nd or 3rd	52%	13	76	17.1%	0.28
Unplaced	20%	5	113	4.4%	-0.52
Not Compl	8%	2	11	18.2%	-0.18

OTHER FACTORS (WINS-RUNS, £)

Course Winner:	6-81	-£0.25
Distance Winner:	18-172	-£0.13
Going Winner:	12-100	-£0.28
Beaten Favourite:	3-29	-£0.25
BHA Top Rated:	3-31	-£0.32
Up in class:	10-154	-£0.37
Same class:	13-97	-£0.02
7-Day Winners:	0-2	-£1.00
Colts and Geldings:	15-186	-£0.27
Fillies:	5-33	-£0.11
Absolute Favourites:	6-24	-£0.28

TRAINERS (WINS-RUNS, £)

J Noseda 2-10 £0.40; Sir Michael Stoute 4-28 £0.07.

Race Profiles

All Age Races: Group 1 Races – 5 to 6 furlong races

ANALYSIS BY AGE

Age	Prop	Win	Runs	Wins%	£
2yo	5%	1	6	16.7%	1.17
3yo	27%	6	73	8.2%	0.41
4yo	18%	4	91	4.4%	-0.41
5yo	23%	5	56	8.9%	-0.43
6yo	18%	4	51	7.8%	0.33
7yo	9%	2	37	5.4%	-0.54
8yo	0%	0	8	0.0%	-1.00
9yo	0%	0	5	0.0%	-1.00
10yo	0%	0	4	0.0%	-1.00
11yo+	0%	0	0	0.0%	0.00

ANALYSIS BY BHA RATING

Rating	Prop	Win	Runs	Wins%	£
120..139	0%	0	12	0.0%	-1.00
110..119	55%	12	157	7.6%	0.20
100..109	18%	4	101	4.0%	-0.57
90..99	0%	0	6	0.0%	-1.00
70..89	0%	0	0	0.0%	0.00
50..69	0%	0	0	0.0%	0.00
..49	0%	0	0	0.0%	0.00
Unrated	27%	6	55	10.9%	-0.00

ANALYSIS BY WEIGHT CARRIED

Weight	Prop	Win	Runs	Wins%	£
10-01+	0%	0	0	0.0%	0.00
9-8 ..10-00	18%	4	66	6.1%	-0.44
9-0..9-07	50%	11	211	5.2%	-0.36
8-8..8-13	27%	6	48	12.5%	1.15
8-0..8-07	5%	1	3	33.3%	3.33
..7-13	0%	0	3	0.0%	-1.00

ANALYSIS BY DAYS SINCE LAST RUN

Days	Prop	Win	Runs	Wins%	£
1..7	14%	3	28	10.7%	1.68
8..14	5%	1	28	3.6%	-0.87
15..28	55%	12	140	8.6%	-0.04
29..60	9%	2	73	2.7%	-0.71
61..100	5%	1	29	3.4%	-0.28
101+	0%	0	19	0.0%	-1.00
Unraced	14%	3	14	21.4%	1.23

ANALYSIS BY TODAY'S STARTING PRICE

Price	Prop	Win	Runs	Wins%	£
Odds On	0%	0	0	0.0%	0.00
Ev - 2/1	0%	0	6	0.0%	-1.00
9/4 - 4/1	18%	4	22	18.2%	-0.30
9/2 - 6/1	14%	3	27	11.1%	-0.31
13/2-10/1	23%	5	51	9.8%	-0.04
11/1-16/1	23%	5	62	8.1%	0.11
18/1-33/1	23%	5	93	5.4%	0.45
40/1+	0%	0	70	0.0%	-1.00

ANALYSIS BY STARTING PRICE LAST TIME

Price	Prop	Win	Runs	Wins%	£
Odds On	5%	1	7	14.3%	0.43
Ev - 2/1	5%	1	18	5.6%	-0.69
9/4 - 4/1	14%	3	65	4.6%	-0.45
9/2 - 6/1	14%	3	43	7.0%	-0.65
13/2-10/1	32%	7	83	8.4%	0.28
11/1-16/1	5%	1	52	1.9%	-0.71
18/1-33/1	14%	3	39	7.7%	0.74
40/1+	0%	0	10	0.0%	-1.00
Unraced	14%	3	14	21.4%	1.23

ANALYSIS BY DISTANCE BEATEN LAST TIME

Lengths	Prop	Win	Runs	Wins%	£
..-10	0%	0	0	0.0%	0.00
-10..0	18%	4	67	6.0%	-0.58
0.1..2	27%	6	83	7.2%	-0.16
2.1..5	27%	6	78	7.7%	0.41
5.1..10	5%	1	61	1.6%	-0.94
10.1..20	9%	2	24	8.3%	0.83
20.0..30	0%	0	2	0.0%	-1.00
30.1+	0%	0	2	0.0%	-1.00
Not Compl	0%	0	0	0.0%	0.00
Unraced	14%	3	14	21.4%	1.23

ANALYSIS BY RUN NUMBER

Run No	Prop	Win	Runs	Wins%	£
FTO	14%	3	14	21.4%	1.23
2nd Run	0%	0	19	0.0%	-1.00
3rd Run	5%	1	10	10.0%	0.30
4th+ Run	82%	18	288	6.3%	-0.16

ANALYSIS BY POSITION LAST TIME

Pos LT	Prop	Win	Runs	Wins%	£
Won	18%	4	67	6.0%	-0.58
2nd or 3rd	27%	6	81	7.4%	-0.02
Unplaced	41%	9	169	5.3%	-0.12
Not Compl	14%	3	14	21.4%	1.23

OTHER FACTORS (WINS-RUNS, £)

Course Winner:	4-105	-£0.58
Distance Winner:	13-257	-£0.29
Going Winner:	11-185	-£0.29
Beaten Favourite:	2-35	-£0.43
BHA Top Rated:	2-23	£1.13
Up in class:	12-219	-£0.28
Same class:	7-98	£0.00
7-Day Winners:	0-4	-£1.00
Colts and Geldings:	19-294	-£0.11
Fillies:	3-37	-£0.31
Absolute Favourites:	4-21	-£0.26

TRAINERS (WINS-RUNS, £)

J Noseda 2-14 £0.64; D Nicholls 1-13 £0.15.

Group 1 Races

All Age Races: Group 1 Races – 7 to 9 furlong races

ANALYSIS BY AGE

Age	Prop	Win	Runs	Wins%	£
2yo	0%	0	0	0.0%	0.00
3yo	40%	12	69	17.4%	0.80
4yo	30%	9	97	9.3%	-0.33
5yo	23%	7	49	14.3%	-0.27
6yo	7%	2	22	9.1%	-0.49
7yo	0%	0	6	0.0%	-1.00
8yo	0%	0	2	0.0%	-1.00
9yo	0%	0	0	0.0%	0.00
10yo	0%	0	0	0.0%	0.00
11yo+	0%	0	0	0.0%	0.00

ANALYSIS BY BHA RATING

Rating	Prop	Win	Runs	Wins%	£
120..139	20%	6	21	28.6%	0.01
110..119	47%	14	122	11.5%	-0.19
100..109	7%	2	36	5.6%	-0.17
90..99	3%	1	5	20.0%	9.20
70..89	0%	0	2	0.0%	-1.00
50..69	0%	0	0	0.0%	0.00
..49	0%	0	0	0.0%	0.00
Unrated	23%	7	59	11.9%	-0.42

ANALYSIS BY WEIGHT CARRIED

Weight	Prop	Win	Runs	Wins%	£
10-01+	0%	0	0	0.0%	0.00
9-8..10-00	0%	0	0	0.0%	0.00
9-0..9-07	53%	16	170	9.4%	-0.43
8-8..8-13	47%	14	72	19.4%	0.92
8-0..8-07	0%	0	3	0.0%	-1.00
..7-13	0%	0	0	0.0%	0.00

ANALYSIS BY DAYS SINCE LAST RUN

Days	Prop	Win	Runs	Wins%	£
1..7	0%	0	4	0.0%	-1.00
8..14	0%	0	11	0.0%	-1.00
15..28	30%	9	85	10.6%	0.36
29..60	37%	11	70	15.7%	-0.22
61..100	13%	4	19	21.1%	0.32
101+	17%	5	40	12.5%	-0.06
Unraced	3%	1	16	6.3%	-0.83

ANALYSIS BY TODAY'S STARTING PRICE

Price	Prop	Win	Runs	Wins%	£
Odds On	7%	2	4	50.0%	-0.26
Ev - 2/1	17%	5	22	22.7%	-0.39
9/4 - 4/1	23%	7	33	21.2%	-0.07
9/2 - 6/1	20%	6	32	18.8%	0.17
13/2-10/1	20%	6	39	15.4%	0.36
11/1-16/1	10%	3	42	7.1%	0.12
18/1-33/1	0%	0	41	0.0%	-1.00
40/1+	3%	1	32	3.1%	0.59

ANALYSIS BY STARTING PRICE LAST TIME

Price	Prop	Win	Runs	Wins%	£
Odds On	10%	3	17	17.6%	-0.53
Ev - 2/1	7%	2	38	5.3%	-0.84
9/4 - 4/1	27%	8	46	17.4%	0.44
9/2 - 6/1	27%	8	37	21.6%	0.07
13/2-10/1	17%	5	43	11.6%	-0.26
11/1-16/1	7%	2	27	7.4%	0.11
18/1-33/1	0%	0	16	0.0%	-1.00
40/1+	3%	1	5	20.0%	9.20
Unraced	3%	1	16	6.3%	-0.83

ANALYSIS BY DISTANCE BEATEN LAST TIME

Lengths	Prop	Win	Runs	Wins%	£
..-10	0%	0	0	0.0%	0.00
-10..0	23%	7	67	10.4%	-0.62
0.1..2	37%	11	65	16.9%	0.41
2.1..5	13%	4	48	8.3%	0.41
5.1..10	10%	3	33	9.1%	-0.39
10.1..20	7%	2	12	16.7%	-0.04
20.0..30	0%	0	2	0.0%	-1.00
30.1+	7%	2	2	100.0%	7.25
Not Compl	0%	0	0	0.0%	0.00
Unraced	3%	1	16	6.3%	-0.83

ANALYSIS BY RUN NUMBER

Run No	Prop	Win	Runs	Wins%	£
FTO	3%	1	16	6.3%	-0.83
2nd Run	13%	4	10	40.0%	2.40
3rd Run	7%	2	6	33.3%	0.67
4th+ Run	77%	23	213	10.8%	-0.11

ANALYSIS BY POSITION LAST TIME

Pos LT	Prop	Win	Runs	Wins%	£
Won	23%	7	67	10.4%	-0.62
2nd or 3rd	33%	10	77	13.0%	-0.16
Unplaced	40%	12	85	14.1%	0.69
Not Compl	3%	1	16	6.3%	-0.83

OTHER FACTORS (WINS-RUNS, £)

Course Winner:	8-85	£0.10
Distance Winner:	19-149	-£0.04
Going Winner:	18-124	-£0.15
Beaten Favourite:	3-28	-£0.14
BHA Top Rated:	7-27	£0.49
Up in class:	11-125	-£0.32
Same class:	18-104	£0.42
7-Day Winners:	0-1	-£1.00
Colts and Geldings:	18-146	-£0.43
Fillies:	2-17	-£0.18
Absolute Favourites:	8-30	-£0.32

TRAINERS (WINS-RUNS, £)
Saeed Bin Suroor 4-19 £0.13; A P O'Brien 7-30 £0.02.

Race Profiles

All Age Races: Group 1 Races – 10 to 14 furlong races

ANALYSIS BY AGE

Age	Prop	Win	Runs	Wins%	£
2yo	0%	0	0	0.0%	0.00
3yo	33%	13	101	12.9%	-0.29
4yo	48%	19	136	14.0%	-0.37
5yo	15%	6	79	7.6%	-0.59
6yo	5%	2	16	12.5%	-0.34
7yo	0%	0	5	0.0%	-1.00
8yo	0%	0	2	0.0%	-1.00
9yo	0%	0	0	0.0%	0.00
10yo	0%	0	0	0.0%	0.00
11yo+	0%	0	0	0.0%	0.00

ANALYSIS BY BHA RATING

Rating	Prop	Win	Runs	Wins%	£
120..139	20%	8	49	16.3%	-0.47
110..119	20%	8	134	6.0%	-0.36
100..109	0%	0	48	0.0%	-1.00
90..99	0%	0	5	0.0%	-1.00
70..89	0%	0	2	0.0%	-1.00
50..69	0%	0	0	0.0%	0.00
..49	0%	0	0	0.0%	0.00
Unrated	60%	24	101	23.8%	-0.12

ANALYSIS BY WEIGHT CARRIED

Weight	Prop	Win	Runs	Wins%	£
10-01+	0%	0	0	0.0%	0.00
9-8..10-00	0%	0	0	0.0%	0.00
9-0..9-07	65%	26	226	11.5%	-0.47
8-8..8-13	35%	14	104	13.5%	-0.23
8-0..8-07	0%	0	9	0.0%	-1.00
..7-13	0%	0	0	0.0%	0.00

ANALYSIS BY DAYS SINCE LAST RUN

Days	Prop	Win	Runs	Wins%	£
1..7	0%	0	1	0.0%	-1.00
8..14	0%	0	20	0.0%	-1.00
15..28	53%	21	119	17.6%	-0.12
29..60	28%	11	109	10.1%	-0.43
61..100	8%	3	26	11.5%	-0.59
101+	5%	2	35	5.7%	-0.78
Unraced	8%	3	29	10.3%	-0.48

ANALYSIS BY TODAY'S STARTING PRICE

Price	Prop	Win	Runs	Wins%	£
Odds On	20%	8	12	66.7%	0.05
Ev - 2/1	28%	11	23	47.8%	0.15
9/4 - 4/1	18%	7	41	17.1%	-0.30
9/2 - 6/1	15%	6	31	19.4%	0.18
13/2-10/1	13%	5	59	8.5%	-0.28
11/1-16/1	5%	2	64	3.1%	-0.56
18/1-33/1	3%	1	44	2.3%	-0.41
40/1+	0%	0	65	0.0%	-1.00

ANALYSIS BY STARTING PRICE LAST TIME

Price	Prop	Win	Runs	Wins%	£
Odds On	25%	10	26	38.5%	0.37
Ev - 2/1	30%	12	44	27.3%	0.53
9/4 - 4/1	15%	6	61	9.8%	-0.64
9/2 - 6/1	8%	3	39	7.7%	-0.60
13/2-10/1	10%	4	69	5.8%	-0.48
11/1-16/1	3%	1	36	2.8%	-0.88
18/1-33/1	3%	1	19	5.3%	-0.76
40/1+	0%	0	16	0.0%	-1.00
Unraced	8%	3	29	10.3%	-0.48

ANALYSIS BY DISTANCE BEATEN LAST TIME

Lengths	Prop	Win	Runs	Wins%	£
..-10	0%	0	0	0.0%	0.00
-10..0	48%	19	93	20.4%	0.00
0.1..2	23%	9	72	12.5%	-0.36
2.1..5	13%	5	64	7.8%	-0.64
5.1..10	10%	4	46	8.7%	-0.50
10.1..20	0%	0	23	0.0%	-1.00
20.0..30	0%	0	6	0.0%	-1.00
30.1+	0%	0	6	0.0%	-1.00
Not Compl	0%	0	0	0.0%	0.00
Unraced	8%	3	29	10.3%	-0.48

ANALYSIS BY RUN NUMBER

Run No	Prop	Win	Runs	Wins%	£
FTO	8%	3	29	10.3%	-0.48
2nd Run	3%	1	11	9.1%	-0.84
3rd Run	5%	2	9	22.2%	-0.48
4th+ Run	85%	34	290	11.7%	-0.38

ANALYSIS BY POSITION LAST TIME

Pos LT	Prop	Win	Runs	Wins%	£
Won	48%	19	93	20.4%	0.00
2nd or 3rd	33%	13	101	12.9%	-0.24
Unplaced	13%	5	116	4.3%	-0.87
Not Compl	8%	3	29	10.3%	-0.48

OTHER FACTORS (WINS-RUNS, £)

Course Winner:	8-76	-£0.13
Distance Winner:	26-170	-£0.24
Going Winner:	24-193	-£0.41
Beaten Favourite:	6-38	-£0.35
BHA Top Rated:	3-42	-£0.80
Up in class:	8-144	-£0.49
Same class:	29-166	-£0.33
7-Day Winners:	0-1	-£1.00
Colts and Geldings:	28-234	-£0.37
Fillies:	3-34	-£0.41
Absolute Favourites:	20-40	£0.06

TRAINERS (WINS-RUNS, £)

B J Meehan 2-10 £1.93; H R A Cecil 2-14 £0.54.

Group 1 Races

All Age Races: Group 1 Races – 15+ furlong races

ANALYSIS BY AGE

Age	Prop	Win	Runs	Wins%	£
2yo	0%	0	0	0.0%	0.00
3yo	0%	0	0	0.0%	0.00
4yo	0%	0	15	0.0%	-1.00
5yo	20%	1	17	5.9%	-0.53
6yo	40%	2	14	14.3%	-0.69
7yo	20%	1	11	9.1%	-0.78
8yo	20%	1	4	25.0%	-0.38
9yo	0%	0	1	0.0%	-1.00
10yo	0%	0	0	0.0%	0.00
11yo+	0%	0	0	0.0%	0.00

ANALYSIS BY BHA RATING

Rating	Prop	Win	Runs	Wins%	£
120..139	20%	1	2	50.0%	0.25
110..119	0%	0	25	0.0%	-1.00
100..109	0%	0	17	0.0%	-1.00
90..99	0%	0	0	0.0%	0.00
70..89	0%	0	1	0.0%	-1.00
50..69	0%	0	0	0.0%	0.00
..49	0%	0	0	0.0%	0.00
Unrated	80%	4	17	23.5%	-0.13

ANALYSIS BY WEIGHT CARRIED

Weight	Prop	Win	Runs	Wins%	£
10-01+	0%	0	0	0.0%	0.00
9-8..10-00	0%	0	0	0.0%	0.00
9-0..9-07	100%	5	57	8.8%	-0.70
8-8..8-13	0%	0	5	0.0%	-1.00
8-0..8-07	0%	0	0	0.0%	0.00
..7-13	0%	0	0	0.0%	0.00

ANALYSIS BY DAYS SINCE LAST RUN

Days	Prop	Win	Runs	Wins%	£
1..7	0%	0	0	0.0%	0.00
8..14	0%	0	4	0.0%	-1.00
15..28	20%	1	25	4.0%	-0.94
29..60	40%	2	20	10.0%	-0.76
61..100	0%	0	0	0.0%	0.00
101+	40%	2	8	25.0%	0.34
Unraced	0%	0	5	0.0%	-1.00

ANALYSIS BY TODAY'S STARTING PRICE

Price	Prop	Win	Runs	Wins%	£
Odds On	20%	1	1	100.0%	0.62
Ev - 2/1	60%	3	4	75.0%	0.91
9/4 - 4/1	0%	0	3	0.0%	-1.00
9/2 - 6/1	0%	0	4	0.0%	-1.00
13/2-10/1	20%	1	5	20.0%	0.60
11/1-16/1	0%	0	11	0.0%	-1.00
18/1-33/1	0%	0	16	0.0%	-1.00
40/1+	0%	0	18	0.0%	-1.00

ANALYSIS BY STARTING PRICE LAST TIME

Price	Prop	Win	Runs	Wins%	£
Odds On	60%	3	6	50.0%	0.08
Ev - 2/1	0%	0	2	0.0%	-1.00
9/4 - 4/1	20%	1	11	9.1%	-0.27
9/2 - 6/1	0%	0	6	0.0%	-1.00
13/2-10/1	20%	1	14	7.1%	-0.80
11/1-16/1	0%	0	10	0.0%	-1.00
18/1-33/1	0%	0	6	0.0%	-1.00
40/1+	0%	0	2	0.0%	-1.00
Unraced	0%	0	5	0.0%	-1.00

ANALYSIS BY DISTANCE BEATEN LAST TIME

Lengths	Prop	Win	Runs	Wins%	£
..-10	0%	0	0	0.0%	0.00
-10..0	40%	2	16	12.5%	-0.75
0.1..2	40%	2	6	33.3%	0.79
2.1..5	0%	0	13	0.0%	-1.00
5.1..10	0%	0	8	0.0%	-1.00
10.1..20	0%	0	7	0.0%	-1.00
20.0..30	0%	0	3	0.0%	-1.00
30.1+	20%	1	4	25.0%	-0.38
Not Compl	0%	0	0	0.0%	0.00
Unraced	0%	0	5	0.0%	-1.00

ANALYSIS BY RUN NUMBER

Run No	Prop	Win	Runs	Wins%	£
FTO	0%	0	5	0.0%	-1.00
2nd Run	20%	1	4	25.0%	-0.31
3rd Run	0%	0	2	0.0%	-1.00
4th+ Run	80%	4	51	7.8%	-0.72

ANALYSIS BY POSITION LAST TIME

Pos LT	Prop	Win	Runs	Wins%	£
Won	40%	2	16	12.5%	-0.75
2nd or 3rd	20%	1	14	7.1%	-0.80
Unplaced	40%	2	26	7.7%	-0.60
Not Compl	0%	0	6	0.0%	-1.00

OTHER FACTORS (WINS-RUNS, £)

Course Winner:	3-13	-£0.50
Distance Winner:	3-7	-£0.07
Going Winner:	4-36	-£0.60
Beaten Favourite:	1-8	-£0.69
BHA Top Rated:	0-4	-£1.00
Up in class:	3-48	-£0.86
Same class:	2-9	£0.19
Colts and Geldings:	5-57	-£0.70
Fillies:	0-5	-£1.00
Absolute Favourites:	4-5	£0.85

Race Profiles

All Age Races: Group 2 & 3 Races

ANALYSIS BY AGE

Age	Prop	Win	Runs	Wins%	£
2yo	0%	0	0	0.0%	0.00
3yo	19%	57	549	10.4%	-0.14
4yo	39%	117	964	12.1%	-0.12
5yo	22%	67	584	11.5%	-0.30
6yo	9%	26	303	8.6%	-0.34
7yo	5%	14	170	8.2%	-0.29
8yo	5%	14	117	12.0%	0.31
9yo	1%	2	44	4.5%	-0.66
10yo	1%	2	17	11.8%	-0.38
11yo+	0%	0	6	0.0%	-1.00

ANALYSIS BY BHA RATING

Rating	Prop	Win	Runs	Wins%	£
120..139	4%	12	28	42.9%	0.24
110..119	41%	122	898	13.6%	-0.25
100..109	39%	117	1257	9.3%	-0.13
90..99	5%	15	279	5.4%	-0.30
70..89	1%	4	79	5.1%	-0.53
50..69	0%	0	6	0.0%	-1.00
..49	0%	0	1	0.0%	-1.00
Unrated	10%	29	206	14.1%	-0.08

ANALYSIS BY WEIGHT CARRIED

Weight	Prop	Win	Runs	Wins%	£
10-01+	0%	0	0	0.0%	0.00
9-8 ..10-00	3%	9	46	19.6%	-0.46
9-0..9-07	65%	193	1742	11.1%	-0.16
8-8..8-13	25%	75	766	9.8%	-0.32
8-0..8-07	7%	22	199	11.1%	0.05
..7-13	0%	0	1	0.0%	-1.00

ANALYSIS BY DAYS SINCE LAST RUN

Days	Prop	Win	Runs	Wins%	£
1..7	4%	12	103	11.7%	0.51
8..14	11%	32	384	8.3%	-0.13
15..28	33%	100	1018	9.8%	-0.37
29..60	23%	68	550	12.4%	-0.06
61..100	6%	17	129	13.2%	0.17
101+	21%	62	498	12.4%	-0.25
Unraced	3%	8	72	11.1%	-0.25

ANALYSIS BY TODAY'S STARTING PRICE

Price	Prop	Win	Runs	Wins%	£
Odds On	6%	19	42	45.2%	-0.28
Ev - 2/1	18%	54	147	36.7%	-0.06
9/4 - 4/1	25%	74	363	20.4%	-0.18
9/2 - 6/1	12%	37	281	13.2%	-0.19
13/2-10/1	21%	63	552	11.4%	0.02
11/1-16/1	12%	35	574	6.1%	-0.13
18/1-33/1	5%	15	510	2.9%	-0.27
40/1+	1%	2	285	0.7%	-0.64

ANALYSIS BY STARTING PRICE LAST TIME

Price	Prop	Win	Runs	Wins%	£
Odds On	6%	19	83	22.9%	0.04
Ev - 2/1	12%	35	217	16.1%	-0.19
9/4 - 4/1	22%	67	501	13.4%	-0.14
9/2 - 6/1	11%	34	352	9.7%	-0.33
13/2-10/1	20%	60	547	11.0%	-0.15
11/1-16/1	13%	40	448	8.9%	-0.34
18/1-33/1	9%	28	384	7.3%	-0.09
40/1+	3%	8	150	5.3%	-0.13
Unraced	3%	8	72	11.1%	-0.25

ANALYSIS BY DISTANCE BEATEN LAST TIME

Lengths	Prop	Win	Runs	Wins%	£
..-10	1%	2	6	33.3%	0.42
-10..0	27%	82	578	14.2%	-0.35
0.1..2	21%	64	541	11.8%	-0.19
2.1..5	18%	54	581	9.3%	-0.12
5.1..10	17%	51	516	9.9%	-0.16
10.1..20	8%	24	292	8.2%	-0.15
20.0..30	3%	9	99	9.1%	-0.06
30.1+	2%	5	69	7.2%	-0.08
Not Compl	0%	0	0	0.0%	0.00
Unraced	3%	8	72	11.1%	-0.25

ANALYSIS BY RUN NUMBER

Run No	Prop	Win	Runs	Wins%	£
FTO	3%	8	72	11.1%	-0.25
2nd Run	2%	7	37	18.9%	0.16
3rd Run	1%	4	40	10.0%	-0.45
4th+ Run	94%	280	2605	10.7%	-0.19

ANALYSIS BY POSITION LAST TIME

Pos LT	Prop	Win	Runs	Wins%	£
Won	28%	84	583	14.4%	-0.34
2nd or 3rd	30%	90	711	12.7%	0.01
Unplaced	39%	117	1382	8.5%	-0.22
Not Compl	3%	8	78	10.3%	-0.31

OTHER FACTORS (WINS-RUNS, £)

Course Winner:	84-743	-£0.24
Distance Winner:	192-1661	-£0.11
Going Winner:	186-1540	-£0.19
Beaten Favourite:	31-244	-£0.32
BHA Top Rated:	58-293	-£0.07
Up in class:	129-1553	-£0.29
Same class:	67-571	-£0.23
Down in class:	95-558	£0.12
7-Day Winners:	1-13	-£0.54
Colts and Geldings:	223-2042	-£0.21
Fillies:	21-208	£0.14
Absolute Favourites:	96-279	-£0.06

TRAINERS (WINS-RUNS, £)

Sir Michael Stoute 57-196 £0.39; J G Given 3-20 £1.85; B J Meehan 5-46 £0.63; M H Tompkins 4-37 £0.59; M P Tregoning 7-36 £0.54; B Smart 4-20 £0.93; W J Haggas 6-43 £0.33; M F de Kock 3-15 £0.80; Mrs A J Perrett 4-35 £0.33; T P Tate 2-17 £0.44; C F Wall 3-22 £0.22; J H M Gosden 16-69 £0.06; G A Butler 3-33 £0.08; D W Barker 2-21 £0.10; J J Quinn 2-10 £0.20; J A Osborne 2-12 £0.13; P R Chamings 1-11 £0.09; W R Muir 2-25 £0.04; J Noseda 12-58 £0.01.

Group 2 & 3 Races

All Age Races: Group 2 & 3 Races - 2 to 7 runners

ANALYSIS BY AGE

Age	Prop	Win	Runs	Wins%	£
2yo	0%	0	0	0.0%	0.00
3yo	11%	10	66	15.2%	-0.01
4yo	40%	35	196	17.9%	0.01
5yo	21%	18	111	16.2%	-0.29
6yo	11%	10	54	18.5%	0.02
7yo	6%	5	37	13.5%	0.11
8yo	8%	7	31	22.6%	1.68
9yo	1%	1	12	8.3%	-0.58
10yo	1%	1	1	100.0%	3.50
11yo+	0%	0	2	0.0%	-1.00

ANALYSIS BY BHA RATING

Rating	Prop	Win	Runs	Wins%	£
120..139	8%	7	15	46.7%	0.14
110..119	39%	34	205	16.6%	-0.25
100..109	45%	39	210	18.6%	0.50
90..99	3%	3	33	9.1%	-0.24
70..89	0%	0	15	0.0%	-1.00
50..69	0%	0	0	0.0%	0.00
..49	0%	0	0	0.0%	0.00
Unrated	5%	4	32	12.5%	-0.41

ANALYSIS BY WEIGHT CARRIED

Weight	Prop	Win	Runs	Wins%	£
10-01+	0%	0	0	0.0%	0.00
9-8..10-00	3%	3	12	25.0%	-0.28
9-0..9-07	68%	59	343	17.2%	0.10
8-8..8-13	22%	19	124	15.3%	-0.25
8-0..8-07	7%	6	31	19.4%	0.71
..7-13	0%	0	0	0.0%	0.00

ANALYSIS BY DAYS SINCE LAST RUN

Days	Prop	Win	Runs	Wins%	£
1..7	5%	4	17	23.5%	0.62
8..14	10%	9	70	12.9%	0.18
15..28	37%	32	194	16.5%	-0.16
29..60	16%	14	86	16.3%	0.11
61..100	8%	7	28	25.0%	1.40
101+	23%	20	105	19.0%	-0.12
Unraced	1%	1	10	10.0%	-0.81

ANALYSIS BY TODAY'S STARTING PRICE

Price	Prop	Win	Runs	Wins%	£
Odds On	15%	13	31	41.9%	-0.35
Ev - 2/1	20%	17	53	32.1%	-0.18
9/4 - 4/1	22%	19	109	17.4%	-0.30
9/2 - 6/1	10%	9	59	15.3%	-0.05
13/2-10/1	22%	19	101	18.8%	0.71
11/1-16/1	9%	8	77	10.4%	0.43
18/1-33/1	2%	2	49	4.1%	0.06
40/1+	0%	0	31	0.0%	-1.00

ANALYSIS BY STARTING PRICE LAST TIME

Price	Prop	Win	Runs	Wins%	£
Odds On	8%	7	21	33.3%	-0.11
Ev - 2/1	10%	9	46	19.6%	-0.18
9/4 - 4/1	21%	18	98	18.4%	-0.08
9/2 - 6/1	9%	8	57	14.0%	0.01
13/2-10/1	21%	18	100	18.0%	0.09
11/1-16/1	20%	17	89	19.1%	0.25
18/1-33/1	10%	9	64	14.1%	0.61
40/1+	0%	0	25	0.0%	-1.00
Unraced	1%	1	10	10.0%	-0.81

ANALYSIS BY DISTANCE BEATEN LAST TIME

Lengths	Prop	Win	Runs	Wins%	£
..-10	1%	1	2	50.0%	-0.25
-10..0	29%	25	116	21.6%	-0.25
0.1..2	23%	20	98	20.4%	0.04
2.1..5	21%	18	108	16.7%	0.15
5.1..10	14%	12	76	15.8%	0.45
10.1..20	7%	6	57	10.5%	-0.32
20.0..30	1%	1	22	4.5%	0.18
30.1+	3%	3	21	14.3%	0.88
Not Compl	0%	0	0	0.0%	0.00
Unraced	1%	1	10	10.0%	-0.81

ANALYSIS BY RUN NUMBER

Run No	Prop	Win	Runs	Wins%	£
FTO	1%	1	10	10.0%	-0.81
2nd Run	0%	0	4	0.0%	-1.00
3rd Run	0%	0	12	0.0%	-1.00
4th+ Run	99%	86	484	17.8%	0.09

ANALYSIS BY POSITION LAST TIME

Pos LT	Prop	Win	Runs	Wins%	£
Won	30%	26	118	22.0%	-0.25
2nd or 3rd	29%	25	136	18.4%	-0.06
Unplaced	40%	35	246	14.2%	0.27
Not Compl	1%	1	10	10.0%	-0.81

OTHER FACTORS (WINS-RUNS, £)

Course Winner:	24-151	-£0.14
Distance Winner:	55-282	£0.22
Going Winner:	60-286	£0.28
Beaten Favourite:	9-47	-£0.04
BHA Top Rated:	20-83	-£0.04
Up in class:	34-245	-£0.06
Same class:	22-119	£0.01
Down in class:	30-136	£0.31
7-Day Winners:	0-3	-£1.00
Colts and Geldings:	73-415	£0.07
Fillies:	4-39	-£0.24
Absolute Favourites:	29-84	-£0.26

TRAINERS (WINS-RUNS, £)

J H M Gosden 6-13 £1.29; M R Channon 3-17 £0.94; J L Dunlop 3-11 £1.16; J Noseda 4-10 £0.71; G Wragg 2-12 £0.46; B J Meehan 2-12 £0.06; Sir Michael Stoute 20-63 £0.00.

Race Profiles

All Age Races: Group 2 & 3 Races – 8 to 14 runners

ANALYSIS BY AGE

Age	Prop	Win	Runs	Wins%	£
2yo	0%	0	0	0.0%	0.00
3yo	22%	42	388	10.8%	-0.13
4yo	39%	73	661	11.0%	-0.15
5yo	22%	42	381	11.0%	-0.32
6yo	7%	14	192	7.3%	-0.37
7yo	4%	7	95	7.4%	-0.51
8yo	4%	7	65	10.8%	0.08
9yo	1%	1	21	4.8%	-0.52
10yo	1%	1	13	7.7%	-0.54
11yo+	0%	0	4	0.0%	-1.00

ANALYSIS BY BHA RATING

Rating	Prop	Win	Runs	Wins%	£
120..139	3%	5	13	38.5%	0.35
110..119	43%	80	563	14.2%	-0.21
100..109	38%	71	842	8.4%	-0.18
90..99	5%	10	208	4.8%	-0.33
70..89	2%	4	58	6.9%	-0.35
50..69	0%	0	6	0.0%	-1.00
..49	0%	0	1	0.0%	-1.00
Unrated	9%	17	129	13.2%	-0.33

ANALYSIS BY WEIGHT CARRIED

Weight	Prop	Win	Runs	Wins%	£
10-01+	0%	0	0	0.0%	0.00
9-8 ..10-00	3%	5	26	19.2%	-0.46
9-0..9-07	61%	115	1108	10.4%	-0.20
8-8..8-13	28%	53	526	10.1%	-0.25
8-0..8-07	7%	14	159	8.8%	-0.23
..7-13	0%	0	1	0.0%	-1.00

ANALYSIS BY DAYS SINCE LAST RUN

Days	Prop	Win	Runs	Wins%	£
1..7	4%	8	73	11.0%	0.75
8..14	12%	22	262	8.4%	-0.14
15..28	34%	63	654	9.6%	-0.36
29..60	24%	44	377	11.7%	-0.20
61..100	5%	9	83	10.8%	-0.05
101+	19%	36	324	11.1%	-0.33
Unraced	3%	5	47	10.6%	-0.15

ANALYSIS BY TODAY'S STARTING PRICE

Price	Prop	Win	Runs	Wins%	£
Odds On	3%	5	10	50.0%	-0.16
Ev - 2/1	20%	37	92	40.2%	0.03
9/4 - 4/1	28%	52	238	21.8%	-0.12
9/2 - 6/1	13%	25	193	13.0%	-0.20
13/2-10/1	19%	36	376	9.6%	-0.15
11/1-16/1	12%	22	388	5.7%	-0.18
18/1-33/1	4%	8	352	2.3%	-0.42
40/1+	1%	2	171	1.2%	-0.40

ANALYSIS BY STARTING PRICE LAST TIME

Price	Prop	Win	Runs	Wins%	£
Odds On	6%	11	50	22.0%	0.11
Ev - 2/1	12%	23	149	15.4%	-0.25
9/4 - 4/1	23%	43	329	13.1%	-0.22
9/2 - 6/1	13%	24	232	10.3%	-0.29
13/2-10/1	18%	33	354	9.3%	-0.33
11/1-16/1	11%	21	297	7.1%	-0.42
18/1-33/1	10%	19	254	7.5%	-0.04
40/1+	4%	8	108	7.4%	0.22
Unraced	3%	5	47	10.6%	-0.15

ANALYSIS BY DISTANCE BEATEN LAST TIME

Lengths	Prop	Win	Runs	Wins%	£
..-10	1%	1	4	25.0%	0.75
-10..0	27%	51	372	13.7%	-0.39
0.1..2	19%	36	352	10.2%	-0.32
2.1..5	18%	34	388	8.8%	-0.05
5.1..10	19%	36	354	10.2%	-0.17
10.1..20	9%	16	196	8.2%	-0.17
20.0..30	3%	6	66	9.1%	-0.24
30.1+	1%	2	41	4.9%	-0.41
Not Compl	0%	0	0	0.0%	0.00
Unraced	3%	5	47	10.6%	-0.15

ANALYSIS BY RUN NUMBER

Run No	Prop	Win	Runs	Wins%	£
FTO	3%	5	47	10.6%	-0.15
2nd Run	3%	6	30	20.0%	0.16
3rd Run	2%	4	22	18.2%	0.00
4th+ Run	92%	172	1721	10.0%	-0.24

ANALYSIS BY POSITION LAST TIME

Pos LT	Prop	Win	Runs	Wins%	£
Won	28%	52	375	13.9%	-0.37
2nd or 3rd	30%	56	480	11.7%	-0.28
Unplaced	40%	74	912	8.1%	-0.28
Not Compl	3%	5	53	9.4%	-0.25

OTHER FACTORS (WINS-RUNS, £)

Course Winner:	56-461	-£0.14
Distance Winner:	117-1049	-£0.15
Going Winner:	112-979	-£0.23
Beaten Favourite:	19-156	-£0.44
BHA Top Rated:	37-182	£0.03
Up in class:	85-1045	-£0.31
Same class:	39-374	-£0.32
Down in class:	58-354	£0.12
7-Day Winners:	1-10	-£0.40
Colts and Geldings:	130-1260	-£0.26
Fillies:	13-128	£0.32
Absolute Favourites:	61-172	£0.02

TRAINERS (WINS-RUNS, £)

Sir Michael Stoute 35-122 £0.57; J G Given 3-18 £2.17; B J Meehan 3-29 £1.15; M P Tregoning 4-21 £1.21; B Smart 3-10 £1.75; Mrs A J Perrett 2-22 £0.64; D W Barker 2-12 £0.92; W R Muir 2-18 £0.44; T P Tate 1-11 £0.55; J Noseda 8-36 £0.16; W J Haggas 3-25 £0.22; R Charlton 3-13 £0.38.

Group 2 & 3 Races

All Age Races: Group 2 & 3 Races – 15 runners or more

ANALYSIS BY AGE

Age	Prop	Win	Runs	Wins%	£
2yo	0%	0	0	0.0%	0.00
3yo	20%	5	95	5.3%	-0.27
4yo	36%	9	107	8.4%	-0.21
5yo	28%	7	92	7.6%	-0.23
6yo	8%	2	57	3.5%	-0.56
7yo	8%	2	38	5.3%	-0.11
8yo	0%	0	21	0.0%	-1.00
9yo	0%	0	11	0.0%	-1.00
10yo	0%	0	3	0.0%	-1.00
11yo+	0%	0	0	0.0%	0.00

ANALYSIS BY BHA RATING

Rating	Prop	Win	Runs	Wins%	£
120..139	0%	0	0	0.0%	0.00
110..119	32%	8	130	6.2%	-0.43
100..109	28%	7	205	3.4%	-0.55
90..99	8%	2	38	5.3%	-0.16
70..89	0%	0	6	0.0%	-1.00
50..69	0%	0	0	0.0%	0.00
..49	0%	0	0	0.0%	0.00
Unrated	32%	8	45	17.8%	0.86

ANALYSIS BY WEIGHT CARRIED

Weight	Prop	Win	Runs	Wins%	£
10-01+	0%	0	0	0.0%	0.00
9-8..10-00	4%	1	8	12.5%	-0.76
9-0..9-07	76%	19	291	6.5%	-0.27
8-8..8-13	12%	3	116	2.6%	-0.70
8-0..8-07	8%	2	9	22.2%	2.78
..7-13	0%	0	0	0.0%	0.00

ANALYSIS BY DAYS SINCE LAST RUN

Days	Prop	Win	Runs	Wins%	£
1..7	0%	0	13	0.0%	-1.00
8..14	4%	1	52	1.9%	-0.50
15..28	20%	5	170	2.9%	-0.66
29..60	40%	10	87	11.5%	0.36
61..100	4%	1	18	5.6%	-0.69
101+	24%	6	69	8.7%	-0.07
Unraced	8%	2	15	13.3%	-0.20

ANALYSIS BY TODAY'S STARTING PRICE

Price	Prop	Win	Runs	Wins%	£
Odds On	4%	1	1	100.0%	0.91
Ev - 2/1	0%	0	2	0.0%	-1.00
9/4 - 4/1	12%	3	16	18.8%	-0.22
9/2 - 6/1	12%	3	29	10.3%	-0.41
13/2-10/1	32%	8	75	10.7%	-0.07
11/1-16/1	20%	5	109	4.6%	-0.39
18/1-33/1	20%	5	109	4.6%	0.06
40/1+	0%	0	83	0.0%	-1.00

ANALYSIS BY STARTING PRICE LAST TIME

Price	Prop	Win	Runs	Wins%	£
Odds On	4%	1	12	8.3%	0.00
Ev - 2/1	12%	3	22	13.6%	0.25
9/4 - 4/1	24%	6	74	8.1%	0.11
9/2 - 6/1	8%	2	63	3.2%	-0.78
13/2-10/1	36%	9	93	9.7%	0.30
11/1-16/1	8%	2	62	3.2%	-0.77
18/1-33/1	0%	0	66	0.0%	-1.00
40/1+	0%	0	17	0.0%	-1.00
Unraced	8%	2	15	13.3%	-0.20

ANALYSIS BY DISTANCE BEATEN LAST TIME

Lengths	Prop	Win	Runs	Wins%	£
..-10	0%	0	0	0.0%	0.00
-10..0	24%	6	90	6.7%	-0.33
0.1..2	32%	8	91	8.8%	0.07
2.1..5	8%	2	85	2.4%	-0.75
5.1..10	12%	3	86	3.5%	-0.67
10.1..20	8%	2	39	5.1%	0.21
20.0..30	8%	2	11	18.2%	0.55
30.1+	0%	0	7	0.0%	-1.00
Not Compl	0%	0	0	0.0%	0.00
Unraced	8%	2	15	13.3%	-0.20

ANALYSIS BY RUN NUMBER

Run No	Prop	Win	Runs	Wins%	£
FTO	8%	2	15	13.3%	-0.20
2nd Run	4%	1	3	33.3%	1.67
3rd Run	0%	0	6	0.0%	-1.00
4th+ Run	88%	22	400	5.5%	-0.34

ANALYSIS BY POSITION LAST TIME

Pos LT	Prop	Win	Runs	Wins%	£
Won	24%	6	90	6.7%	-0.33
2nd or 3rd	36%	9	95	9.5%	0.11
Unplaced	32%	8	224	3.6%	-0.53
Not Compl	8%	2	15	13.3%	-0.20

OTHER FACTORS (WINS-RUNS, £)

Course Winner:	4-131	-£0.73
Distance Winner:	20-330	-£0.27
Going Winner:	14-275	-£0.52
Beaten Favourite:	3-41	-£0.20
BHA Top Rated:	1-28	-£0.84
Up in class:	10-263	-£0.41
Same class:	6-78	-£0.15
Down in class:	7-68	-£0.26
Colts and Geldings:	20-367	-£0.37
Fillies:	4-41	-£0.06
Absolute Favourites:	6-23	£0.10

TRAINERS (WINS-RUNS, £)

Saeed Bin Suroor 2-15 £1.27; L M Cumani 1-10 £1.10; B W Hills 2-19 £0.34; R A Fahey 1-11 £0.55; Sir Michael Stoute 2-11 £0.55.

Race Profiles

All Age Races: Group 2 & 3 Races – good or faster going

ANALYSIS BY AGE

Age	Prop	Win	Runs	Wins%	£
2yo	0%	0	0	0.0%	0.00
3yo	21%	43	377	11.4%	-0.05
4yo	38%	78	670	11.6%	-0.23
5yo	21%	43	390	11.0%	-0.35
6yo	8%	17	195	8.7%	-0.35
7yo	4%	9	114	7.9%	-0.39
8yo	6%	13	84	15.5%	0.58
9yo	1%	2	27	7.4%	-0.44
10yo	0%	0	9	0.0%	-1.00
11yo+	0%	0	5	0.0%	-1.00

ANALYSIS BY BHA RATING

Rating	Prop	Win	Runs	Wins%	£
120..139	5%	10	22	45.5%	0.31
110..119	44%	90	624	14.4%	-0.22
100..109	35%	72	832	8.7%	-0.20
90..99	4%	9	195	4.6%	-0.33
70..89	1%	3	52	5.8%	-0.53
50..69	0%	0	4	0.0%	-1.00
..49	0%	0	0	0.0%	0.00
Unrated	10%	21	142	14.8%	-0.01

ANALYSIS BY WEIGHT CARRIED

Weight	Prop	Win	Runs	Wins%	£
10-01+	0%	0	0	0.0%	0.00
9-8..10-00	3%	7	35	20.0%	-0.47
9-0..9-07	62%	127	1152	11.0%	-0.19
8-8..8-13	25%	52	546	9.5%	-0.38
8-0..8-07	9%	19	137	13.9%	0.36
..7-13	0%	0	1	0.0%	-1.00

ANALYSIS BY DAYS SINCE LAST RUN

Days	Prop	Win	Runs	Wins%	£
1..7	3%	6	73	8.2%	0.28
8..14	12%	25	259	9.7%	0.06
15..28	29%	60	688	8.7%	-0.47
29..60	22%	45	367	12.3%	-0.21
61..100	7%	14	86	16.3%	0.42
101+	23%	48	346	13.9%	-0.20
Unraced	3%	7	52	13.5%	0.00

ANALYSIS BY TODAY'S STARTING PRICE

Price	Prop	Win	Runs	Wins%	£
Odds On	7%	15	30	50.0%	-0.20
Ev - 2/1	20%	41	112	36.6%	-0.07
9/4 - 4/1	24%	50	243	20.6%	-0.18
9/2 - 6/1	13%	27	177	15.3%	-0.07
13/2-10/1	20%	41	361	11.4%	0.02
11/1-16/1	10%	20	397	5.0%	-0.28
18/1-33/1	4%	9	347	2.6%	-0.35
40/1+	1%	2	204	1.0%	-0.50

ANALYSIS BY STARTING PRICE LAST TIME

Price	Prop	Win	Runs	Wins%	£
Odds On	8%	16	60	26.7%	0.29
Ev - 2/1	12%	24	146	16.4%	-0.30
9/4 - 4/1	20%	42	320	13.1%	-0.12
9/2 - 6/1	11%	23	238	9.7%	-0.36
13/2-10/1	20%	42	379	11.1%	-0.17
11/1-16/1	14%	29	306	9.5%	-0.37
18/1-33/1	8%	16	267	6.0%	-0.26
40/1+	3%	6	103	5.8%	0.02
Unraced	3%	7	52	13.5%	0.00

ANALYSIS BY DISTANCE BEATEN LAST TIME

Lengths	Prop	Win	Runs	Wins%	£
..-10	1%	2	4	50.0%	1.13
-10..0	29%	60	396	15.2%	-0.37
0.1..2	21%	44	374	11.8%	-0.15
2.1..5	20%	41	400	10.3%	-0.01
5.1..10	13%	27	343	7.9%	-0.38
10.1..20	7%	15	183	8.2%	-0.31
20.0..30	3%	7	71	9.9%	0.14
30.1+	1%	2	48	4.2%	-0.39
Not Compl	0%	0	0	0.0%	0.00
Unraced	3%	7	52	13.5%	0.00

ANALYSIS BY RUN NUMBER

Run No	Prop	Win	Runs	Wins%	£
FTO	3%	7	52	13.5%	0.00
2nd Run	3%	6	30	20.0%	0.32
3rd Run	1%	3	28	10.7%	-0.48
4th+ Run	92%	189	1761	10.7%	-0.22

ANALYSIS BY POSITION LAST TIME

Pos LT	Prop	Win	Runs	Wins%	£
Won	30%	62	399	15.5%	-0.35
2nd or 3rd	30%	62	485	12.8%	0.11
Unplaced	36%	74	929	8.0%	-0.32
Not Compl	3%	7	58	12.1%	-0.10

OTHER FACTORS (WINS-RUNS, £)

Course Winner:	60-493	-£0.17
Distance Winner:	133-1116	-£0.12
Going Winner:	143-1202	-£0.21
Beaten Favourite:	21-164	-£0.38
BHA Top Rated:	44-183	£0.06
Up in class:	85-1062	-£0.31
Same class:	41-380	-£0.32
Down in class:	72-377	£0.14
7-Day Winners:	0-7	-£1.00
Colts and Geldings:	154-1367	-£0.20
Fillies:	10-132	-£0.13
Absolute Favourites:	71-195	-£0.03

TRAINERS (WINS-RUNS, £)

Sir Michael Stoute 41-144 £0.23; M P Tregoning 7-28 £0.98; B Smart 4-16 £1.41; B J Meehan 3-37 £0.56; Mrs A J Perrett 3-22 £0.89; T D Easterby 2-11 £0.86; G A Butler 3-28 £0.28; R Charlton 3-13 £0.38; J L Dunlop 5-36 £0.11; M F de Kock 2-11 £0.36; W J Haggas 4-33 £0.12; D W Barker 1-14 £0.21; J H M Gosden 10-46 £0.06; H R A Cecil 2-21 £0.05.

Group 2 & 3 Races

All Age Races: Group 2 & 3 Races – good to soft or softer going

ANALYSIS BY AGE

Age	Prop	Win	Runs	Wins%	£
2yo	0%	0	0	0.0%	0.00
3yo	15%	14	172	8.1%	-0.34
4yo	41%	39	294	13.3%	0.10
5yo	26%	24	194	12.4%	-0.20
6yo	10%	9	108	8.3%	-0.32
7yo	5%	5	56	8.9%	-0.08
8yo	1%	1	33	3.0%	-0.36
9yo	0%	0	17	0.0%	-1.00
10yo	2%	2	8	25.0%	0.31
11yo+	0%	0	1	0.0%	-1.00

ANALYSIS BY BHA RATING

Rating	Prop	Win	Runs	Wins%	£
120..139	2%	2	6	33.3%	-0.03
110..119	34%	32	274	11.7%	-0.33
100..109	48%	45	425	10.6%	0.02
90..99	6%	6	84	7.1%	-0.21
70..89	1%	1	27	3.7%	-0.52
50..69	0%	0	2	0.0%	-1.00
..49	0%	0	1	0.0%	-1.00
Unrated	9%	8	64	12.5%	-0.25

ANALYSIS BY WEIGHT CARRIED

Weight	Prop	Win	Runs	Wins%	£
10-01+	0%	0	0	0.0%	0.00
9-8 ..10-00	2%	2	11	18.2%	-0.43
9-0..9-07	70%	66	590	11.2%	-0.09
8-8..8-13	24%	23	220	10.5%	-0.17
8-0..8-07	3%	3	62	4.8%	-0.63
..7-13	0%	0	0	0.0%	0.00

ANALYSIS BY DAYS SINCE LAST RUN

Days	Prop	Win	Runs	Wins%	£
1..7	6%	6	30	20.0%	1.07
8..14	7%	7	125	5.6%	-0.52
15..28	43%	40	330	12.1%	-0.17
29..60	24%	23	183	12.6%	0.24
61..100	3%	3	43	7.0%	-0.33
101+	15%	14	152	9.2%	-0.36
Unraced	1%	1	20	5.0%	-0.90

ANALYSIS BY TODAY'S STARTING PRICE

Price	Prop	Win	Runs	Wins%	£
Odds On	4%	4	12	33.3%	-0.46
Ev - 2/1	14%	13	35	37.1%	0.00
9/4 - 4/1	26%	24	120	20.0%	-0.18
9/2 - 6/1	11%	10	104	9.6%	-0.40
13/2-10/1	23%	22	191	11.5%	0.01
11/1-16/1	16%	15	177	8.5%	0.19
18/1-33/1	6%	6	163	3.7%	-0.12
40/1+	0%	0	81	0.0%	-1.00

ANALYSIS BY STARTING PRICE LAST TIME

Price	Prop	Win	Runs	Wins%	£
Odds On	3%	3	23	13.0%	-0.61
Ev - 2/1	12%	11	71	15.5%	0.04
9/4 - 4/1	27%	25	181	13.8%	-0.19
9/2 - 6/1	12%	11	114	9.6%	-0.25
13/2-10/1	19%	18	168	10.7%	-0.10
11/1-16/1	12%	11	142	7.7%	-0.26
18/1-33/1	13%	12	117	10.3%	0.28
40/1+	2%	2	47	4.3%	-0.45
Unraced	1%	1	20	5.0%	-0.90

ANALYSIS BY DISTANCE BEATEN LAST TIME

Lengths	Prop	Win	Runs	Wins%	£
..-10	0%	0	2	0.0%	-1.00
-10..0	23%	22	182	12.1%	-0.31
0.1..2	21%	20	167	12.0%	-0.28
2.1..5	14%	13	181	7.2%	-0.36
5.1..10	26%	24	173	13.9%	0.26
10.1..20	10%	9	109	8.3%	0.12
20.0..30	2%	2	28	7.1%	-0.58
30.1+	3%	3	21	14.3%	0.62
Not Compl	0%	0	0	0.0%	0.00
Unraced	1%	1	20	5.0%	-0.90

ANALYSIS BY RUN NUMBER

Run No	Prop	Win	Runs	Wins%	£
FTO	1%	1	20	5.0%	-0.90
2nd Run	1%	1	7	14.3%	-0.57
3rd Run	1%	1	12	8.3%	-0.38
4th+ Run	97%	91	844	10.8%	-0.13

ANALYSIS BY POSITION LAST TIME

Pos LT	Prop	Win	Runs	Wins%	£
Won	23%	22	184	12.0%	-0.31
2nd or 3rd	30%	28	226	12.4%	-0.22
Unplaced	46%	43	453	9.5%	-0.02
Not Compl	1%	1	20	5.0%	-0.90

OTHER FACTORS (WINS-RUNS, £)

Course Winner:	24-250	-£0.38
Distance Winner:	59-545	-£0.10
Going Winner:	43-338	-£0.10
Beaten Favourite:	10-80	-£0.21
BHA Top Rated:	14-110	-£0.30
Up in class:	44-491	-£0.25
Same class:	26-191	-£0.04
Down in class:	23-181	£0.08
7-Day Winners:	1-6	£0.00
Colts and Geldings:	69-675	-£0.22
Fillies:	11-76	£0.61
Absolute Favourites:	25-84	-£0.11

TRAINERS (WINS-RUNS, £)

Sir Michael Stoute 16-52 £0.83; M H Tompkins 4-21 £1.81; L M Cumani 3-17 £0.94; T P Tate 2-10 £1.45; W J Haggas 2-10 £1.05; J Noseda 3-18 £0.17; Saeed Bin Suroor 7-48 £0.04; J H M Gosden 6-23 £0.06; M L W Bell 2-11 £0.05.

Race Profiles

All Age Races: Group 2 & 3 Races – 5 to 6 furlong races

ANALYSIS BY AGE

Age	Prop	Win	Runs	Wins%	£
2yo	0%	0	0	0.0%	0.00
3yo	26%	15	141	10.6%	0.18
4yo	28%	16	176	9.1%	-0.14
5yo	23%	13	148	8.8%	-0.17
6yo	9%	5	117	4.3%	-0.56
7yo	12%	7	75	9.3%	0.14
8yo	2%	1	38	2.6%	-0.91
9yo	0%	0	15	0.0%	-1.00
10yo	0%	0	7	0.0%	-1.00
11yo+	0%	0	0	0.0%	0.00

ANALYSIS BY BHA RATING

Rating	Prop	Win	Runs	Wins%	£
120..139	0%	0	1	0.0%	-1.00
110..119	26%	15	205	7.3%	-0.50
100..109	56%	32	377	8.5%	-0.13
90..99	4%	2	87	2.3%	-0.29
70..89	2%	1	9	11.1%	0.44
50..69	0%	0	0	0.0%	0.00
..49	0%	0	0	0.0%	0.00
Unrated	12%	7	38	18.4%	0.95

ANALYSIS BY WEIGHT CARRIED

Weight	Prop	Win	Runs	Wins%	£
10-01+	0%	0	0	0.0%	0.00
9-8..10-00	0%	0	18	0.0%	-1.00
9-0..9-07	67%	38	477	8.0%	-0.18
8-8..8-13	28%	16	209	7.7%	-0.29
8-0..8-07	5%	3	13	23.1%	2.27
..7-13	0%	0	0	0.0%	0.00

ANALYSIS BY DAYS SINCE LAST RUN

Days	Prop	Win	Runs	Wins%	£
1..7	7%	4	54	7.4%	-0.57
8..14	23%	13	143	9.1%	0.31
15..28	35%	20	271	7.4%	-0.33
29..60	16%	9	115	7.8%	-0.15
61..100	4%	2	25	8.0%	-0.14
101+	12%	7	94	7.4%	-0.40
Unraced	4%	2	15	13.3%	-0.20

ANALYSIS BY TODAY'S STARTING PRICE

Price	Prop	Win	Runs	Wins%	£
Odds On	0%	0	0	0.0%	0.00
Ev - 2/1	5%	3	13	23.1%	-0.39
9/4 - 4/1	23%	13	63	20.6%	-0.19
9/2 - 6/1	14%	8	66	12.1%	-0.27
13/2-10/1	26%	15	152	9.9%	-0.13
11/1-16/1	23%	13	171	7.6%	0.11
18/1-33/1	7%	4	148	2.7%	-0.33
40/1+	2%	1	104	1.0%	-0.51

ANALYSIS BY STARTING PRICE LAST TIME

Price	Prop	Win	Runs	Wins%	£
Odds On	0%	0	9	0.0%	-1.00
Ev - 2/1	7%	4	41	9.8%	-0.11
9/4 - 4/1	23%	13	121	10.7%	-0.28
9/2 - 6/1	14%	8	95	8.4%	-0.28
13/2-10/1	23%	13	140	9.3%	0.06
11/1-16/1	7%	4	127	3.1%	-0.74
18/1-33/1	19%	11	123	8.9%	0.06
40/1+	4%	2	46	4.3%	0.39
Unraced	4%	2	15	13.3%	-0.20

ANALYSIS BY DISTANCE BEATEN LAST TIME

Lengths	Prop	Win	Runs	Wins%	£
..-10	0%	0	0	0.0%	0.00
-10..0	19%	11	129	8.5%	-0.47
0.1..2	23%	13	165	7.9%	-0.25
2.1..5	23%	13	164	7.9%	0.21
5.1..10	18%	10	155	6.5%	-0.39
10.1..20	9%	5	73	6.8%	-0.17
20.0..30	5%	3	10	30.0%	1.25
30.1+	0%	0	6	0.0%	-1.00
Not Compl	0%	0	0	0.0%	0.00
Unraced	4%	2	15	13.3%	-0.20

ANALYSIS BY RUN NUMBER

Run No	Prop	Win	Runs	Wins%	£
FTO	4%	2	15	13.3%	-0.20
2nd Run	2%	1	3	33.3%	1.67
3rd Run	2%	1	3	33.3%	0.83
4th+ Run	93%	53	696	7.6%	-0.20

ANALYSIS BY POSITION LAST TIME

Pos LT	Prop	Win	Runs	Wins%	£
Won	19%	11	129	8.5%	-0.47
2nd or 3rd	28%	16	172	9.3%	0.29
Unplaced	49%	28	400	7.0%	-0.31
Not Compl	4%	2	16	12.5%	-0.25

OTHER FACTORS (WINS-RUNS, £)

Course Winner:	8-200	-£0.77
Distance Winner:	50-614	-£0.20
Going Winner:	34-468	-£0.72
Beaten Favourite:	6-66	-£0.34
BHA Top Rated:	11-63	-£0.02
Up in class:	30-436	-£0.15
Same class:	7-111	-£0.54
Down in class:	18-155	-£0.07
7-Day Winners:	1-5	£0.20
Colts and Geldings:	45-578	-£0.21
Fillies:	7-87	£0.02
Absolute Favourites:	12-53	-£0.20

TRAINERS (WINS-RUNS, £)

W J Haggas 4-27 £0.61; R A Fahey 3-16 £0.80; B Smart 3-16 £0.78; Saeed Bin Suroor 2-14 £0.25; D W Barker 2-21 £0.10; T D Easterby 2-19 £0.08; C F Wall 1-11 £0.09.

Group 2 & 3 Races

All Age Races: Group 2 & 3 Races – 7 to 9 furlong races

ANALYSIS BY AGE

Age	Prop	Win	Runs	Wins%	£
2yo	0%	0	0	0.0%	0.00
3yo	19%	19	221	8.6%	-0.46
4yo	40%	40	343	11.7%	-0.13
5yo	26%	26	179	14.5%	-0.16
6yo	7%	7	87	8.0%	-0.43
7yo	2%	2	28	7.1%	-0.55
8yo	5%	5	24	20.8%	1.73
9yo	0%	0	6	0.0%	-1.00
10yo	0%	0	2	0.0%	-1.00
11yo+	0%	0	0	0.0%	0.00

ANALYSIS BY BHA RATING

Rating	Prop	Win	Runs	Wins%	£
120..139	4%	4	9	44.4%	0.15
110..119	43%	43	292	14.7%	-0.08
100..109	40%	40	398	10.1%	-0.20
90..99	5%	5	87	5.7%	-0.46
70..89	0%	0	31	0.0%	-1.00
50..69	0%	0	0	0.0%	0.00
..49	0%	0	0	0.0%	0.00
Unrated	7%	7	73	9.6%	-0.32

ANALYSIS BY WEIGHT CARRIED

Weight	Prop	Win	Runs	Wins%	£
10-01+	0%	0	0	0.0%	0.00
9-8 ..10-00	4%	4	13	30.8%	-0.12
9-0..9-07	60%	59	527	11.2%	-0.13
8-8..8-13	35%	35	311	11.3%	-0.29
8-0..8-07	1%	1	39	2.6%	-0.86
..7-13	0%	0	0	0.0%	0.00

ANALYSIS BY DAYS SINCE LAST RUN

Days	Prop	Win	Runs	Wins%	£
1..7	4%	4	25	16.0%	2.20
8..14	9%	9	122	7.4%	-0.47
15..28	29%	29	334	8.7%	-0.43
29..60	26%	26	189	13.8%	-0.06
61..100	8%	8	37	21.6%	0.32
101+	22%	22	157	14.0%	-0.19
Unraced	1%	1	26	3.8%	-0.65

ANALYSIS BY TODAY'S STARTING PRICE

Price	Prop	Win	Runs	Wins%	£
Odds On	7%	7	15	46.7%	-0.24
Ev - 2/1	20%	20	55	36.4%	-0.04
9/4 - 4/1	22%	22	115	19.1%	-0.24
9/2 - 6/1	16%	16	91	17.6%	0.09
13/2-10/1	22%	22	186	11.8%	0.07
11/1-16/1	7%	7	182	3.8%	-0.45
18/1-33/1	4%	4	168	2.4%	-0.44
40/1+	1%	1	78	1.3%	-0.35

ANALYSIS BY STARTING PRICE LAST TIME

Price	Prop	Win	Runs	Wins%	£
Odds On	6%	6	31	19.4%	0.17
Ev - 2/1	16%	16	76	21.1%	0.02
9/4 - 4/1	19%	19	146	13.0%	0.05
9/2 - 6/1	16%	16	121	13.2%	-0.17
13/2-10/1	18%	18	172	10.5%	-0.29
11/1-16/1	14%	14	150	9.3%	-0.41
18/1-33/1	6%	6	127	4.7%	-0.49
40/1+	3%	3	41	7.3%	0.09
Unraced	1%	1	26	3.8%	-0.65

ANALYSIS BY DISTANCE BEATEN LAST TIME

Lengths	Prop	Win	Runs	Wins%	£
..-10	0%	0	0	0.0%	0.00
-10..0	28%	28	201	13.9%	-0.33
0.1..2	26%	26	171	15.2%	0.01
2.1..5	18%	18	208	8.7%	-0.26
5.1..10	16%	16	179	8.9%	-0.40
10.1..20	9%	9	74	12.2%	0.27
20.0..30	0%	0	23	0.0%	-1.00
30.1+	1%	1	8	12.5%	2.25
Not Compl	0%	0	0	0.0%	0.00
Unraced	1%	1	26	3.8%	-0.65

ANALYSIS BY RUN NUMBER

Run No	Prop	Win	Runs	Wins%	£
FTO	1%	1	26	3.8%	-0.65
2nd Run	2%	2	14	14.3%	0.39
3rd Run	2%	2	19	10.5%	-0.53
4th+ Run	95%	94	831	11.3%	-0.21

ANALYSIS BY POSITION LAST TIME

Pos LT	Prop	Win	Runs	Wins%	£
Won	28%	28	200	14.0%	-0.33
2nd or 3rd	35%	35	222	15.8%	0.23
Unplaced	35%	35	441	7.9%	-0.37
Not Compl	1%	1	27	3.7%	-0.67

OTHER FACTORS (WINS-RUNS, £)

Course Winner:	37-258	£0.05
Distance Winner:	66-515	£0.00
Going Winner:	62-487	-£0.02
Beaten Favourite:	10-81	-£0.25
BHA Top Rated:	15-93	-£0.37
Up in class:	49-516	-£0.28
Same class:	19-182	-£0.25
Down in class:	30-166	£0.06
7-Day Winners:	0-1	-£1.00
Colts and Geldings:	69-613	-£0.18
Fillies:	5-46	£0.20
Absolute Favourites:	32-92	-£0.06

TRAINERS (WINS-RUNS, £)

B J Meehan 2-19 £2.13; Sir Michael Stoute 18-67 £0.22; L M Cumani 2-14 £0.75; J H M Gosden 7-27 £0.02.

Race Profiles

All Age Races: Group 2 & 3 Races – 10 to 14 furlong races

ANALYSIS BY AGE

Age	Prop	Win	Runs	Wins%	£
2yo	0%	0	0	0.0%	0.00
3yo	17%	19	153	12.4%	-0.05
4yo	47%	52	360	14.4%	-0.02
5yo	21%	23	198	11.6%	-0.41
6yo	7%	8	60	13.3%	-0.20
7yo	2%	2	36	5.6%	-0.56
8yo	4%	4	29	13.8%	0.40
9yo	1%	1	12	8.3%	-0.17
10yo	1%	1	5	20.0%	-0.10
11yo+	0%	0	4	0.0%	-1.00

ANALYSIS BY BHA RATING

Rating	Prop	Win	Runs	Wins%	£
120..139	7%	8	18	44.4%	0.35
110..119	48%	53	327	16.2%	-0.28
100..109	29%	32	337	9.5%	0.09
90..99	6%	7	73	9.6%	-0.20
70..89	3%	3	30	10.0%	-0.18
50..69	0%	0	5	0.0%	-1.00
..49	0%	0	1	0.0%	-1.00
Unrated	6%	7	66	10.6%	-0.60

ANALYSIS BY WEIGHT CARRIED

Weight	Prop	Win	Runs	Wins%	£
10-01+	0%	0	0	0.0%	0.00
9-8 ..10-00	3%	3	9	33.3%	0.10
9-0..9-07	65%	71	522	13.6%	-0.12
8-8..8-13	20%	22	212	10.4%	-0.31
8-0..8-07	13%	14	114	12.3%	0.06
..7-13	0%	0	0	0.0%	0.00

ANALYSIS BY DAYS SINCE LAST RUN

Days	Prop	Win	Runs	Wins%	£
1..7	4%	4	22	18.2%	1.39
8..14	6%	7	98	7.1%	-0.38
15..28	35%	38	284	13.4%	-0.23
29..60	24%	26	178	14.6%	0.10
61..100	5%	5	49	10.2%	0.02
101+	24%	26	206	12.6%	-0.36
Unraced	4%	4	20	20.0%	0.42

ANALYSIS BY TODAY'S STARTING PRICE

Price	Prop	Win	Runs	Wins%	£
Odds On	8%	9	22	40.9%	-0.36
Ev - 2/1	21%	23	61	37.7%	-0.04
9/4 - 4/1	25%	28	139	20.1%	-0.18
9/2 - 6/1	8%	9	97	9.3%	-0.42
13/2-10/1	23%	25	169	14.8%	0.31
11/1-16/1	11%	12	164	7.3%	0.00
18/1-33/1	4%	4	131	3.1%	-0.18
40/1+	0%	0	74	0.0%	-1.00

ANALYSIS BY STARTING PRICE LAST TIME

Price	Prop	Win	Runs	Wins%	£
Odds On	11%	12	34	35.3%	0.43
Ev - 2/1	10%	11	80	13.8%	-0.37
9/4 - 4/1	25%	28	180	15.6%	-0.17
9/2 - 6/1	8%	9	102	8.8%	-0.35
13/2-10/1	18%	20	178	11.2%	-0.21
11/1-16/1	15%	16	128	12.5%	-0.09
18/1-33/1	6%	7	88	8.0%	0.28
40/1+	3%	3	47	6.4%	-0.52
Unraced	4%	4	20	20.0%	0.42

ANALYSIS BY DISTANCE BEATEN LAST TIME

Lengths	Prop	Win	Runs	Wins%	£
..-10	2%	2	4	50.0%	1.13
-10..0	29%	32	194	16.5%	-0.28
0.1..2	17%	19	154	12.3%	-0.34
2.1..5	19%	21	161	13.0%	-0.05
5.1..10	18%	20	143	14.0%	0.35
10.1..20	6%	7	108	6.5%	-0.61
20.0..30	4%	4	42	9.5%	0.40
30.1+	1%	1	31	3.2%	-0.68
Not Compl	0%	0	0	0.0%	0.00
Unraced	4%	4	20	20.0%	0.42

ANALYSIS BY RUN NUMBER

Run No	Prop	Win	Runs	Wins%	£
FTO	4%	4	20	20.0%	0.42
2nd Run	2%	2	16	12.5%	-0.39
3rd Run	1%	1	15	6.7%	-0.50
4th+ Run	94%	103	806	12.8%	-0.14

ANALYSIS BY POSITION LAST TIME

Pos LT	Prop	Win	Runs	Wins%	£
Won	31%	34	198	17.2%	-0.25
2nd or 3rd	29%	32	234	13.7%	-0.29
Unplaced	36%	40	401	10.0%	-0.02
Not Compl	4%	4	24	16.7%	0.18

OTHER FACTORS (WINS-RUNS, £)

Course Winner:	29-213	-£0.14
Distance Winner:	62-446	-£0.13
Going Winner:	72-432	£0.08
Beaten Favourite:	13-76	-£0.28
BHA Top Rated:	26-103	£0.12
Up in class:	42-433	-£0.28
Same class:	28-208	-£0.15
Down in class:	36-196	£0.13
7-Day Winners:	0-5	-£1.00
Colts and Geldings:	82-624	-£0.19
Fillies:	7-54	£0.33
Absolute Favourites:	37-103	-£0.08

TRAINERS (WINS-RUNS, £)

J G Given 2-12 £3.08; Sir Michael Stoute 30-97 £0.25; M P Tregoning 4-20 £1.12; G A Butler 1-14 £0.86; J H M Gosden 9-38 £0.20; M R Channon 3-26 £0.27; M A Jarvis 2-18 £0.14.

Group 2 & 3 Races

All Age Races: Group 2 & 3 Races – 15+ furlong races

ANALYSIS BY AGE

Age	Prop	Win	Runs	Wins%	£
2yo	0%	0	0	0.0%	0.00
3yo	12%	4	34	11.8%	0.20
4yo	27%	9	85	10.6%	-0.52
5yo	15%	5	59	8.5%	-0.68
6yo	18%	6	39	15.4%	0.33
7yo	9%	3	31	9.7%	-0.77
8yo	12%	4	26	15.4%	0.68
9yo	3%	1	11	9.1%	-0.55
10yo	3%	1	3	33.3%	1.00
11yo+	0%	0	2	0.0%	-1.00

ANALYSIS BY BHA RATING

Rating	Prop	Win	Runs	Wins%	£
120..139	0%	0	0	0.0%	0.00
110..119	33%	11	74	14.9%	-0.10
100..109	39%	13	145	9.0%	-0.45
90..99	3%	1	32	3.1%	-0.09
70..89	0%	0	9	0.0%	-1.00
50..69	0%	0	1	0.0%	-1.00
..49	0%	0	0	0.0%	0.00
Unrated	24%	8	29	27.6%	0.35

ANALYSIS BY WEIGHT CARRIED

Weight	Prop	Win	Runs	Wins%	£
10-01+	0%	0	0	0.0%	0.00
9-8 ..10-00	6%	2	6	33.3%	-0.43
9-0..9-07	76%	25	216	11.6%	-0.24
8-8..8-13	6%	2	34	5.9%	-0.78
8-0..8-07	12%	4	33	12.1%	0.23
..7-13	0%	0	1	0.0%	-1.00

ANALYSIS BY DAYS SINCE LAST RUN

Days	Prop	Win	Runs	Wins%	£
1..7	0%	0	2	0.0%	-1.00
8..14	9%	3	21	14.3%	0.07
15..28	39%	13	129	10.1%	-0.59
29..60	21%	7	68	10.3%	-0.33
61..100	6%	2	18	11.1%	0.73
101+	21%	7	41	17.1%	0.44
Unraced	3%	1	11	9.1%	-0.59

ANALYSIS BY TODAY'S STARTING PRICE

Price	Prop	Win	Runs	Wins%	£
Odds On	9%	3	5	60.0%	-0.03
Ev - 2/1	24%	8	18	44.4%	0.09
9/4 - 4/1	33%	11	46	23.9%	-0.03
9/2 - 6/1	12%	4	27	14.8%	-0.15
13/2-10/1	3%	1	45	2.2%	-0.80
11/1-16/1	9%	3	57	5.3%	-0.25
18/1-33/1	9%	3	63	4.8%	0.13
40/1+	0%	0	29	0.0%	-1.00

ANALYSIS BY STARTING PRICE LAST TIME

Price	Prop	Win	Runs	Wins%	£
Odds On	3%	1	9	11.1%	-0.84
Ev - 2/1	12%	4	20	20.0%	-0.39
9/4 - 4/1	21%	7	54	13.0%	-0.25
9/2 - 6/1	3%	1	34	2.9%	-0.94
13/2-10/1	27%	9	57	15.8%	-0.04
11/1-16/1	18%	6	43	14.0%	0.38
18/1-33/1	12%	4	46	8.7%	-0.13
40/1+	0%	0	16	0.0%	-1.00
Unraced	3%	1	11	9.1%	-0.59

ANALYSIS BY DISTANCE BEATEN LAST TIME

Lengths	Prop	Win	Runs	Wins%	£
..-10	0%	0	2	0.0%	-1.00
-10..0	33%	11	54	20.4%	-0.37
0.1..2	18%	6	51	11.8%	-0.23
2.1..5	6%	2	48	4.2%	-0.85
5.1..10	15%	5	39	12.8%	-0.01
10.1..20	9%	3	37	8.1%	0.39
20.0..30	6%	2	24	8.3%	-0.51
30.1+	9%	3	24	12.5%	0.15
Not Compl	0%	0	0	0.0%	0.00
Unraced	3%	1	11	9.1%	-0.59

ANALYSIS BY RUN NUMBER

Run No	Prop	Win	Runs	Wins%	£
FTO	3%	1	11	9.1%	-0.59
2nd Run	6%	2	4	50.0%	0.38
3rd Run	0%	0	3	0.0%	-1.00
4th+ Run	91%	30	272	11.0%	-0.25

ANALYSIS BY POSITION LAST TIME

Pos LT	Prop	Win	Runs	Wins%	£
Won	33%	11	56	19.6%	-0.39
2nd or 3rd	21%	7	83	8.4%	-0.37
Unplaced	42%	14	140	10.0%	-0.12
Not Compl	3%	1	11	9.1%	-0.59

OTHER FACTORS (WINS-RUNS, £)

Course Winner:	10-72	-£0.12
Distance Winner:	14-86	-£0.09
Going Winner:	18-153	-£0.47
Beaten Favourite:	2-21	-£0.70
BHA Top Rated:	6-34	£0.05
Up in class:	8-168	-£0.69
Same class:	13-70	£0.11
Down in class:	11-41	£0.98
7-Day Winners:	0-2	-£1.00
Colts and Geldings:	27-227	-£0.33
Fillies:	2-21	£0.05
Absolute Favourites:	15-31	£0.25

TRAINERS (WINS-RUNS, £)

Sir Michael Stoute 8-25 £1.46; Saeed Bin Suroor 3-12 £1.25; J L Dunlop 3-11 £0.82.

Race Profiles

All Age Races: Listed Races

ANALYSIS BY AGE

Age	Prop	Win	Runs	Wins%	£
2yo	0%	0	4	0.0%	-1.00
3yo	27%	96	939	10.2%	-0.16
4yo	37%	132	1041	12.7%	-0.12
5yo	19%	68	577	11.8%	-0.13
6yo	11%	38	304	12.5%	0.06
7yo	4%	16	180	8.9%	-0.37
8yo	2%	7	80	8.8%	-0.44
9yo	1%	2	34	5.9%	-0.37
10yo	0%	0	5	0.0%	-1.00
11yo+	0%	1	5	20.0%	0.60

ANALYSIS BY BHA RATING

Rating	Prop	Win	Runs	Wins%	£
120..139	1%	3	4	75.0%	0.46
110..119	20%	71	345	20.6%	-0.14
100..109	53%	189	1361	13.9%	-0.07
90..99	18%	64	820	7.8%	-0.31
70..89	6%	21	439	4.8%	0.11
50..69	0%	0	41	0.0%	-1.00
..49	0%	0	14	0.0%	-1.00
Unrated	3%	12	145	8.3%	-0.33

ANALYSIS BY WEIGHT CARRIED

Weight	Prop	Win	Runs	Wins%	£
10-01+	0%	0	1	0.0%	-1.00
9-8..10-00	4%	14	94	14.9%	0.08
9-0..9-07	56%	202	1660	12.2%	-0.10
8-8..8-13	32%	116	1104	10.5%	-0.20
8-0..8-07	8%	28	307	9.1%	-0.25
..7-13	0%	0	3	0.0%	-1.00

ANALYSIS BY DAYS SINCE LAST RUN

Days	Prop	Win	Runs	Wins%	£
1..7	5%	18	167	10.8%	-0.24
8..14	19%	68	571	11.9%	-0.13
15..28	31%	112	1036	10.8%	-0.10
29..60	19%	70	651	10.8%	-0.24
61..100	5%	19	155	12.3%	0.22
101+	19%	68	547	12.4%	-0.27
Unraced	1%	5	42	11.9%	0.67

ANALYSIS BY TODAY'S STARTING PRICE

Price	Prop	Win	Runs	Wins%	£
Odds On	7%	25	49	51.0%	-0.15
Ev - 2/1	16%	57	200	28.5%	-0.28
9/4 - 4/1	29%	105	458	22.9%	-0.06
9/2 - 6/1	15%	55	373	14.7%	-0.09
13/2-10/1	15%	55	606	9.1%	-0.16
11/1-16/1	12%	43	551	7.8%	0.15
18/1-33/1	4%	16	569	2.8%	-0.27
40/1+	1%	4	363	1.1%	-0.47

ANALYSIS BY STARTING PRICE LAST TIME

Price	Prop	Win	Runs	Wins%	£
Odds On	5%	17	69	24.6%	0.20
Ev - 2/1	11%	39	190	20.5%	0.16
9/4 - 4/1	17%	61	474	12.9%	-0.22
9/2 - 6/1	16%	58	424	13.7%	-0.06
13/2-10/1	21%	76	624	12.2%	-0.15
11/1-16/1	16%	58	607	9.6%	-0.18
18/1-33/1	9%	31	510	6.1%	-0.42
40/1+	4%	15	229	6.6%	0.08
Unraced	1%	5	42	11.9%	0.67

ANALYSIS BY DISTANCE BEATEN LAST TIME

Lengths	Prop	Win	Runs	Wins%	£
..-10	0%	0	4	0.0%	-1.00
-10..0	23%	83	489	17.0%	-0.09
0.1..2	20%	73	541	13.5%	-0.21
2.1..5	27%	97	769	12.6%	0.02
5.1..10	18%	64	699	9.2%	-0.16
10.1..20	7%	25	433	5.8%	-0.40
20.0..30	2%	7	95	7.4%	-0.57
30.1+	2%	6	97	6.2%	0.01
Not Compl	0%	0	0	0.0%	0.00
Unraced	1%	5	42	11.9%	0.67

ANALYSIS BY RUN NUMBER

Run No	Prop	Win	Runs	Wins%	£
FTO	1%	5	42	11.9%	0.67
2nd Run	1%	3	42	7.1%	-0.61
3rd Run	2%	8	65	12.3%	-0.49
4th+ Run	96%	344	3020	11.4%	-0.14

ANALYSIS BY POSITION LAST TIME

Pos LT	Prop	Win	Runs	Wins%	£
Won	23%	84	494	17.0%	-0.09
2nd or 3rd	28%	100	747	13.4%	-0.20
Unplaced	48%	171	1877	9.1%	-0.15
Not Compl	1%	5	51	9.8%	0.37

OTHER FACTORS (WINS-RUNS, £)

Course Winner:	71-643	-£0.36
Distance Winner:	250-2007	-£0.15
Going Winner:	194-1664	-£0.23
Beaten Favourite:	43-238	£0.01
BHA Top Rated:	67-335	-£0.21
Up in class:	117-1296	-£0.20
Same class:	106-980	-£0.12
Down in class:	132-851	-£0.12
7-Day Winners:	7-25	£0.38
Colts and Geldings:	214-1584	-£0.08
Fillies:	25-345	-£0.37
Absolute Favourites:	98-338	-£0.24

TRAINERS (WINS-RUNS, £)

G G Margarson 3-13 £5.08; R M Beckett 3-17 £2.18; W J Haggas 8-47 £0.69; R F Fisher 3-22 £1.45; K R Burke 5-23 £0.87; M Quinn 3-19 £1.03; R Hannon 15-115 £0.14; Sir Michael Stoute 31-106 £0.13; I Semple 3-20 £0.70; J M P Eustace 2-13 £1.00; M S Saunders 6-23 £0.56; C G Cox 6-27 £0.43; J R Fanshawe 7-50 £0.21; J Noseda 6-29 £0.34; H R A Cecil 8-35 £0.26; D R C Elsworth 8-55 £0.14; A Berry 4-19 £0.37; J A Geake 2-13 £0.54; P F I Cole 6-43 £0.13; G Wragg 5-46 £0.12.

Listed Races

All Age Races: Listed Races – 2 to 7 runners

ANALYSIS BY AGE

Age	Prop	Win	Runs	Wins%	£
2yo	0%	0	0	0.0%	0.00
3yo	15%	19	114	16.7%	-0.21
4yo	45%	57	277	20.6%	-0.01
5yo	20%	25	165	15.2%	-0.06
6yo	11%	14	90	15.6%	-0.05
7yo	6%	7	53	13.2%	-0.34
8yo	2%	3	18	16.7%	-0.57
9yo	1%	1	11	9.1%	-0.59
10yo	0%	0	2	0.0%	-1.00
11yo+	1%	1	2	50.0%	3.00

ANALYSIS BY BHA RATING

Rating	Prop	Win	Runs	Wins%	£
120..139	2%	2	2	100.0%	0.97
110..119	30%	38	142	26.8%	-0.13
100..109	48%	61	349	17.5%	-0.04
90..99	17%	21	135	15.6%	0.14
70..89	2%	3	60	5.0%	-0.37
50..69	0%	0	7	0.0%	-1.00
..49	0%	0	7	0.0%	-1.00
Unrated	2%	2	30	6.7%	-0.72

ANALYSIS BY WEIGHT CARRIED

Weight	Prop	Win	Runs	Wins%	£
10-01+	0%	0	0	0.0%	0.00
9-8 ..10-00	2%	3	18	16.7%	-0.14
9-0..9-07	64%	81	443	18.3%	-0.02
8-8..8-13	26%	33	197	16.8%	-0.22
8-0..8-07	8%	10	74	13.5%	-0.20
..7-13	0%	0	0	0.0%	0.00

ANALYSIS BY DAYS SINCE LAST RUN

Days	Prop	Win	Runs	Wins%	£
1..7	4%	5	34	14.7%	0.31
8..14	20%	25	139	18.0%	-0.24
15..28	31%	39	223	17.5%	-0.07
29..60	18%	23	150	15.3%	-0.09
61..100	2%	3	18	16.7%	0.61
101+	23%	29	159	18.2%	-0.26
Unraced	2%	3	9	33.3%	1.34

ANALYSIS BY TODAY'S STARTING PRICE

Price	Prop	Win	Runs	Wins%	£
Odds On	13%	17	33	51.5%	-0.18
Ev - 2/1	24%	30	96	31.3%	-0.21
9/4 - 4/1	33%	42	172	24.4%	0.01
9/2 - 6/1	11%	14	101	13.9%	-0.14
13/2-10/1	11%	14	129	10.9%	-0.01
11/1-16/1	6%	7	95	7.4%	0.03
18/1-33/1	2%	3	67	4.5%	0.10
40/1+	0%	0	39	0.0%	-1.00

ANALYSIS BY STARTING PRICE LAST TIME

Price	Prop	Win	Runs	Wins%	£
Odds On	6%	8	19	42.1%	0.09
Ev - 2/1	9%	12	58	20.7%	-0.17
9/4 - 4/1	21%	27	127	21.3%	0.07
9/2 - 6/1	17%	22	95	23.2%	0.05
13/2-10/1	21%	27	151	17.9%	-0.08
11/1-16/1	12%	15	125	12.0%	-0.22
18/1-33/1	6%	7	101	6.9%	-0.58
40/1+	5%	6	47	12.8%	0.23
Unraced	2%	3	9	33.3%	1.34

ANALYSIS BY DISTANCE BEATEN LAST TIME

Lengths	Prop	Win	Runs	Wins%	£
..-10	0%	0	1	0.0%	-1.00
-10..0	20%	26	120	21.7%	-0.18
0.1..2	22%	28	127	22.0%	-0.33
2.1..5	24%	31	167	18.6%	0.10
5.1..10	15%	19	143	13.3%	-0.15
10.1..20	9%	12	111	10.8%	-0.21
20.0..30	4%	5	27	18.5%	0.05
30.1+	2%	3	27	11.1%	0.40
Not Compl	0%	0	0	0.0%	0.00
Unraced	2%	3	9	33.3%	1.34

ANALYSIS BY RUN NUMBER

Run No	Prop	Win	Runs	Wins%	£
FTO	2%	3	9	33.3%	1.34
2nd Run	0%	0	15	0.0%	-1.00
3rd Run	3%	4	14	28.6%	-0.19
4th+ Run	94%	120	694	17.3%	-0.09

ANALYSIS BY POSITION LAST TIME

Pos LT	Prop	Win	Runs	Wins%	£
Won	20%	26	120	21.7%	-0.18
2nd or 3rd	28%	35	187	18.7%	-0.39
Unplaced	50%	63	414	15.2%	0.04
Not Compl	2%	3	11	27.3%	0.92

OTHER FACTORS (WINS-RUNS, £)

Course Winner:	24-156	-£0.24
Distance Winner:	85-433	-£0.06
Going Winner:	70-399	-£0.14
Beaten Favourite:	18-62	£0.11
BHA Top Rated:	29-109	-£0.21
Up in class:	41-273	-£0.16
Same class:	38-216	-£0.06
Down in class:	45-234	-£0.12
7-Day Winners:	2-4	£0.94
Colts and Geldings:	98-515	-£0.11
Fillies:	10-99	-£0.11
Absolute Favourites:	43-122	-£0.23

TRAINERS (WINS-RUNS, £)

R Hannon 4-29 £0.69; P F I Cole 4-14 £0.84; H R A Cecil 5-12 £0.77; L M Cumani 4-22 £0.33; D R C Elsworth 4-25 £0.17; B J Meehan 3-10 £0.38; M A Jarvis 4-12 £0.24; C E Brittain 2-12 £0.15; B W Hills 4-14 £0.10.

Race Profiles

All Age Races: Listed Races – 8 to 14 runners

ANALYSIS BY AGE

Age	Prop	Win	Runs	Wins%	£
2yo	0%	0	4	0.0%	-1.00
3yo	31%	66	693	9.5%	-0.18
4yo	33%	71	675	10.5%	-0.12
5yo	19%	41	362	11.3%	-0.10
6yo	10%	21	184	11.4%	0.11
7yo	4%	9	112	8.0%	-0.30
8yo	2%	4	58	6.9%	-0.35
9yo	0%	1	21	4.8%	-0.19
10yo	0%	0	3	0.0%	-1.00
11yo+	0%	0	3	0.0%	-1.00

ANALYSIS BY BHA RATING

Rating	Prop	Win	Runs	Wins%	£
120..139	0%	1	2	50.0%	-0.05
110..119	15%	31	185	16.8%	-0.12
100..109	55%	118	901	13.1%	-0.08
90..99	17%	36	585	6.2%	-0.44
70..89	8%	17	304	5.6%	0.36
50..69	0%	0	29	0.0%	-1.00
..49	0%	0	7	0.0%	-1.00
Unrated	5%	10	102	9.8%	-0.13

ANALYSIS BY WEIGHT CARRIED

Weight	Prop	Win	Runs	Wins%	£
10-01+	0%	0	1	0.0%	-1.00
9-8..10-00	5%	11	64	17.2%	0.34
9-0..9-07	53%	113	1059	10.7%	-0.07
8-8..8-13	33%	71	765	9.3%	-0.24
8-0..8-07	8%	18	223	8.1%	-0.24
..7-13	0%	0	3	0.0%	-1.00

ANALYSIS BY DAYS SINCE LAST RUN

Days	Prop	Win	Runs	Wins%	£
1..7	6%	12	121	9.9%	-0.45
8..14	20%	43	385	11.2%	0.01
15..28	31%	65	708	9.2%	-0.08
29..60	21%	44	433	10.2%	-0.29
61..100	6%	13	115	11.3%	0.10
101+	16%	34	323	10.5%	-0.28
Unraced	1%	2	30	6.7%	0.63

ANALYSIS BY TODAY'S STARTING PRICE

Price	Prop	Win	Runs	Wins%	£
Odds On	4%	8	15	53.3%	-0.02
Ev - 2/1	12%	26	100	26.0%	-0.33
9/4 - 4/1	29%	61	273	22.3%	-0.08
9/2 - 6/1	17%	37	247	15.0%	-0.08
13/2-10/1	17%	37	415	8.9%	-0.17
11/1-16/1	13%	28	393	7.1%	0.06
18/1-33/1	6%	12	417	2.9%	-0.26
40/1+	2%	4	255	1.6%	-0.24

ANALYSIS BY STARTING PRICE LAST TIME

Price	Prop	Win	Runs	Wins%	£
Odds On	4%	8	43	18.6%	0.16
Ev - 2/1	13%	27	119	22.7%	0.44
9/4 - 4/1	15%	32	309	10.4%	-0.30
9/2 - 6/1	14%	30	281	10.7%	-0.15
13/2-10/1	21%	45	403	11.2%	-0.13
11/1-16/1	20%	42	419	10.0%	-0.13
18/1-33/1	8%	18	348	5.2%	-0.45
40/1+	4%	9	163	5.5%	0.16
Unraced	1%	2	30	6.7%	0.63

ANALYSIS BY DISTANCE BEATEN LAST TIME

Lengths	Prop	Win	Runs	Wins%	£
..-10	0%	0	3	0.0%	-1.00
-10..0	25%	54	330	16.4%	-0.01
0.1..2	19%	41	370	11.1%	-0.16
2.1..5	28%	59	501	11.8%	0.01
5.1..10	19%	41	485	8.5%	-0.14
10.1..20	5%	11	274	4.0%	-0.46
20.0..30	1%	2	58	3.4%	-0.78
30.1+	1%	3	64	4.7%	-0.06
Not Compl	0%	0	0	0.0%	0.00
Unraced	1%	2	30	6.7%	0.63

ANALYSIS BY RUN NUMBER

Run No	Prop	Win	Runs	Wins%	£
FTO	1%	2	30	6.7%	0.63
2nd Run	1%	3	25	12.0%	-0.34
3rd Run	2%	4	45	8.9%	-0.52
4th+ Run	96%	204	2015	10.1%	-0.14

ANALYSIS BY POSITION LAST TIME

Pos LT	Prop	Win	Runs	Wins%	£
Won	26%	55	335	16.4%	-0.01
2nd or 3rd	29%	62	492	12.6%	-0.07
Unplaced	44%	94	1252	7.5%	-0.21
Not Compl	1%	2	36	5.6%	0.36

OTHER FACTORS (WINS-RUNS, £)

Course Winner:	43-421	-£0.38
Distance Winner:	150-1355	-£0.16
Going Winner:	114-1096	-£0.25
Beaten Favourite:	23-150	£0.03
BHA Top Rated:	36-206	-£0.19
Up in class:	68-883	-£0.23
Same class:	63-654	-£0.08
Down in class:	80-548	-£0.10
7-Day Winners:	5-21	£0.28
Colts and Geldings:	109-963	-£0.04
Fillies:	14-222	-£0.49
Absolute Favourites:	53-199	-£0.22

TRAINERS (WINS-RUNS, £)

R M Beckett 2-13 £2.62; W J Haggas 6-32 £1.06; Sir Michael Stoute 21-69 £0.33; M S Saunders 6-16 £1.24; I Semple 2-14 £1.07; J M P Eustace 2-11 £1.36; C G Cox 3-13 £1.00; M Quinn 2-15 £0.83; R F Fisher 2-18 £0.56; D R C Elsworth 4-25 £0.34; K R Burke 2-12 £0.71; J H M Gosden 7-45 £0.19; D M Simcock 1-13 £0.62; B W Hills 8-46 £0.15; J R Fanshawe 2-33 £0.17; Saeed Bin Suroor 16-101 £0.02; H R A Cecil 3-22 £0.03; M Johnston 4-22 £0.02.

Listed Races

All Age Races: Listed Races – 15 runners or more

ANALYSIS BY AGE
Age	Prop	Win	Runs	Wins%	£
2yo	0%	0	0	0.0%	0.00
3yo	55%	11	132	8.3%	-0.01
4yo	20%	4	89	4.5%	-0.52
5yo	10%	2	50	4.0%	-0.61
6yo	15%	3	30	10.0%	0.08
7yo	0%	0	15	0.0%	-1.00
8yo	0%	0	4	0.0%	-1.00
9yo	0%	0	2	0.0%	-1.00
10yo	0%	0	0	0.0%	0.00
11yo+	0%	0	0	0.0%	0.00

ANALYSIS BY BHA RATING
Rating	Prop	Win	Runs	Wins%	£
120..139	0%	0	0	0.0%	0.00
110..119	10%	2	18	11.1%	-0.48
100..109	50%	10	111	9.0%	-0.12
90..99	35%	7	100	7.0%	-0.15
70..89	5%	1	75	1.3%	-0.55
50..69	0%	0	5	0.0%	-1.00
..49	0%	0	0	0.0%	0.00
Unrated	0%	0	13	0.0%	-1.00

ANALYSIS BY WEIGHT CARRIED
Weight	Prop	Win	Runs	Wins%	£
10-01+	0%	0	0	0.0%	0.00
9-8 ..10-00	0%	0	12	0.0%	-1.00
9-0..9-07	40%	8	158	5.1%	-0.50
8-8..8-13	60%	12	142	8.5%	0.04
8-0..8-07	0%	0	10	0.0%	-1.00
..7-13	0%	0	0	0.0%	0.00

ANALYSIS BY DAYS SINCE LAST RUN
Days	Prop	Win	Runs	Wins%	£
1..7	5%	1	12	8.3%	0.25
8..14	0%	0	47	0.0%	-1.00
15..28	40%	8	105	7.6%	-0.27
29..60	15%	3	68	4.4%	-0.24
61..100	15%	3	22	13.6%	0.50
101+	25%	5	65	7.7%	-0.23
Unraced	0%	0	3	0.0%	-1.00

ANALYSIS BY TODAY'S STARTING PRICE
Price	Prop	Win	Runs	Wins%	£
Odds On	0%	0	1	0.0%	-1.00
Ev - 2/1	5%	1	4	25.0%	-0.41
9/4 - 4/1	10%	2	13	15.4%	-0.37
9/2 - 6/1	20%	4	25	16.0%	-0.02
13/2-10/1	20%	4	62	6.5%	-0.38
11/1-16/1	40%	8	63	12.7%	0.87
18/1-33/1	5%	1	85	1.2%	-0.60
40/1+	0%	0	69	0.0%	-1.00

ANALYSIS BY STARTING PRICE LAST TIME
Price	Prop	Win	Runs	Wins%	£
Odds On	5%	1	7	14.3%	0.71
Ev - 2/1	0%	0	13	0.0%	-1.00
9/4 - 4/1	10%	2	38	5.3%	-0.59
9/2 - 6/1	30%	6	48	12.5%	0.20
13/2-10/1	20%	4	70	5.7%	-0.37
11/1-16/1	5%	1	63	1.6%	-0.46
18/1-33/1	30%	6	61	9.8%	0.02
40/1+	0%	0	19	0.0%	-1.00
Unraced	0%	0	3	0.0%	-1.00

ANALYSIS BY DISTANCE BEATEN LAST TIME
Lengths	Prop	Win	Runs	Wins%	£
..-10	0%	0	0	0.0%	0.00
-10..0	15%	3	39	7.7%	-0.49
0.1..2	20%	4	44	9.1%	-0.23
2.1..5	35%	7	101	6.9%	-0.02
5.1..10	20%	4	71	5.6%	-0.30
10.1..20	10%	2	48	4.2%	-0.52
20.0..30	0%	0	10	0.0%	-1.00
30.1+	0%	0	6	0.0%	-1.00
Not Compl	0%	0	0	0.0%	0.00
Unraced	0%	0	3	0.0%	-1.00

ANALYSIS BY RUN NUMBER
Run No	Prop	Win	Runs	Wins%	£
FTO	0%	0	3	0.0%	-1.00
2nd Run	0%	0	2	0.0%	-1.00
3rd Run	0%	0	6	0.0%	-1.00
4th+ Run	100%	20	311	6.4%	-0.27

ANALYSIS BY POSITION LAST TIME
Pos LT	Prop	Win	Runs	Wins%	£
Won	15%	3	39	7.7%	-0.49
2nd or 3rd	15%	3	68	4.4%	-0.62
Unplaced	70%	14	211	6.6%	-0.15
Not Compl	0%	0	4	0.0%	-1.00

OTHER FACTORS (WINS-RUNS, £)
Course Winner:	4-66	-£0.52
Distance Winner:	15-219	-£0.31
Going Winner:	10-169	-£0.33
Beaten Favourite:	2-26	-£0.31
BHA Top Rated:	2-20	-£0.35
Up in class:	8-140	-£0.13
Same class:	5-110	-£0.50
Down in class:	7-69	-£0.29
Colts and Geldings:	7-106	-£0.25
Fillies:	1-24	-£0.38
Absolute Favourites:	2-17	-£0.60

TRAINERS (WINS-RUNS, £)
R Hannon 2-16 £1.00.

Race Profiles

All Age Races: Listed Races – good or faster going

ANALYSIS BY AGE

Age	Prop	Win	Runs	Wins%	£
2yo	0%	0	4	0.0%	-1.00
3yo	25%	64	631	10.1%	-0.30
4yo	40%	102	712	14.3%	-0.09
5yo	18%	45	415	10.8%	-0.23
6yo	9%	22	214	10.3%	-0.14
7yo	4%	11	130	8.5%	0.28
8yo	2%	5	53	9.4%	-0.22
9yo	1%	2	25	8.0%	-0.14
10yo	0%	0	4	0.0%	-1.00
11yo+	0%	1	1	100.0%	7.00

ANALYSIS BY BHA RATING

Rating	Prop	Win	Runs	Wins%	£
120..139	1%	2	3	66.7%	0.16
110..119	20%	51	252	20.2%	-0.18
100..109	55%	139	969	14.3%	-0.12
90..99	15%	39	570	6.8%	-0.33
70..89	5%	12	271	4.4%	-0.15
50..69	0%	0	25	0.0%	-1.00
..49	0%	0	7	0.0%	-1.00
Unrated	4%	9	92	9.8%	-0.06

ANALYSIS BY WEIGHT CARRIED

Weight	Prop	Win	Runs	Wins%	£
10-01+	0%	0	1	0.0%	-1.00
9-8 ..10-00	5%	12	80	15.0%	0.10
9-0..9-07	56%	142	1156	12.3%	-0.15
8-8..8-13	33%	82	732	11.2%	-0.19
8-0..8-07	6%	16	217	7.4%	-0.56
..7-13	0%	0	3	0.0%	-1.00

ANALYSIS BY DAYS SINCE LAST RUN

Days	Prop	Win	Runs	Wins%	£
1..7	4%	9	120	7.5%	-0.56
8..14	20%	51	399	12.8%	-0.04
15..28	33%	83	727	11.4%	-0.12
29..60	18%	45	459	9.8%	-0.43
61..100	5%	13	101	12.9%	0.11
101+	19%	48	356	13.5%	-0.22
Unraced	1%	3	27	11.1%	0.17

ANALYSIS BY TODAY'S STARTING PRICE

Price	Prop	Win	Runs	Wins%	£
Odds On	8%	21	37	56.8%	-0.04
Ev - 2/1	15%	39	135	28.9%	-0.26
9/4 - 4/1	29%	72	329	21.9%	-0.12
9/2 - 6/1	15%	39	245	15.9%	-0.01
13/2-10/1	15%	39	435	9.0%	-0.17
11/1-16/1	13%	32	385	8.3%	0.21
18/1-33/1	4%	9	391	2.3%	-0.46
40/1+	0%	1	232	0.4%	-0.78

ANALYSIS BY STARTING PRICE LAST TIME

Price	Prop	Win	Runs	Wins%	£
Odds On	4%	11	51	21.6%	0.05
Ev - 2/1	11%	28	125	22.4%	0.12
9/4 - 4/1	15%	38	333	11.4%	-0.39
9/2 - 6/1	19%	47	308	15.3%	0.09
13/2-10/1	22%	55	427	12.9%	-0.13
11/1-16/1	16%	40	406	9.9%	-0.23
18/1-33/1	8%	21	359	5.8%	-0.42
40/1+	4%	9	153	5.9%	-0.36
Unraced	1%	3	27	11.1%	0.17

ANALYSIS BY DISTANCE BEATEN LAST TIME

Lengths	Prop	Win	Runs	Wins%	£
..-10	0%	0	2	0.0%	-1.00
-10..0	21%	54	332	16.3%	-0.20
0.1..2	22%	55	375	14.7%	-0.29
2.1..5	27%	68	540	12.6%	0.06
5.1..10	18%	46	484	9.5%	-0.20
10.1..20	8%	19	294	6.5%	-0.42
20.0..30	1%	3	71	4.2%	-0.75
30.1+	2%	4	64	6.3%	-0.33
Not Compl	0%	0	0	0.0%	0.00
Unraced	1%	3	27	11.1%	0.17

ANALYSIS BY RUN NUMBER

Run No	Prop	Win	Runs	Wins%	£
FTO	1%	3	27	11.1%	0.17
2nd Run	0%	0	26	0.0%	-1.00
3rd Run	3%	8	50	16.0%	-0.34
4th+ Run	96%	241	2086	11.6%	-0.19

ANALYSIS BY POSITION LAST TIME

Pos LT	Prop	Win	Runs	Wins%	£
Won	22%	55	336	16.4%	-0.19
2nd or 3rd	30%	76	527	14.4%	-0.12
Unplaced	47%	118	1292	9.1%	-0.23
Not Compl	1%	3	34	8.8%	-0.07

OTHER FACTORS (WINS-RUNS, £)

Course Winner:	45-455	-£0.42
Distance Winner:	185-1418	-£0.12
Going Winner:	160-1324	-£0.19
Beaten Favourite:	24-158	-£0.14
BHA Top Rated:	48-221	-£0.14
Up in class:	83-886	-£0.23
Same class:	69-671	-£0.29
Down in class:	97-605	-£0.07
7-Day Winners:	2-14	-£0.53
Colts and Geldings:	153-1126	-£0.09
Fillies:	18-254	-£0.35
Absolute Favourites:	70-236	-£0.25

TRAINERS (WINS-RUNS, £)

Sir Michael Stoute 25-75 £0.35; W J Haggas 6-33 £0.71; P F I Cole 6-31 £0.57; C G Cox 6-24 £0.60; I Semple 2-17 £0.71; G Wragg 3-27 £0.40; R Hannon 12-82 £0.13; R F Fisher 2-19 £0.47; L M Cumani 9-55 £0.15; M S Saunders 4-16 £0.47; D M Simcock 1-14 £0.50; H R A Cecil 7-32 £0.12; D W Barker 3-20 £0.15; C F Wall 5-31 £0.08; D Nicholls 5-40 £0.03.

Listed Races

All Age Races: Listed Races – good to soft or softer going

ANALYSIS BY AGE

Age	Prop	Win	Runs	Wins%	£
2yo	0%	0	0	0.0%	0.00
3yo	30%	32	308	10.4%	0.14
4yo	28%	30	329	9.1%	-0.20
5yo	21%	23	162	14.2%	0.11
6yo	15%	16	90	17.8%	0.56
7yo	5%	5	50	10.0%	-0.62
8yo	2%	2	27	7.4%	-0.85
9yo	0%	0	9	0.0%	-1.00
10yo	0%	0	1	0.0%	-1.00
11yo+	0%	0	4	0.0%	-1.00

ANALYSIS BY BHA RATING

Rating	Prop	Win	Runs	Wins%	£
120..139	1%	1	1	100.0%	1.38
110..119	19%	20	93	21.5%	-0.03
100..109	46%	50	392	12.8%	0.05
90..99	23%	25	250	10.0%	-0.28
70..89	8%	9	168	5.4%	0.53
50..69	0%	0	16	0.0%	-1.00
..49	0%	0	7	0.0%	-1.00
Unrated	3%	3	53	5.7%	-0.79

ANALYSIS BY WEIGHT CARRIED

Weight	Prop	Win	Runs	Wins%	£
10-01+	0%	0	0	0.0%	0.00
9-8..10-00	2%	2	14	14.3%	-0.07
9-0..9-07	56%	60	504	11.9%	0.03
8-8..8-13	31%	34	372	9.1%	-0.22
8-0..8-07	11%	12	90	13.3%	0.49
..7-13	0%	0	0	0.0%	0.00

ANALYSIS BY DAYS SINCE LAST RUN

Days	Prop	Win	Runs	Wins%	£
1..7	8%	9	47	19.1%	0.55
8..14	16%	17	172	9.9%	-0.34
15..28	27%	29	309	9.4%	-0.05
29..60	23%	25	192	13.0%	0.24
61..100	6%	6	54	11.1%	0.42
101+	19%	20	191	10.5%	-0.36
Unraced	2%	2	15	13.3%	1.57

ANALYSIS BY TODAY'S STARTING PRICE

Price	Prop	Win	Runs	Wins%	£
Odds On	4%	4	12	33.3%	-0.48
Ev - 2/1	17%	18	65	27.7%	-0.30
9/4 - 4/1	31%	33	129	25.6%	0.11
9/2 - 6/1	15%	16	128	12.5%	-0.25
13/2-10/1	15%	16	171	9.4%	-0.13
11/1-16/1	10%	11	166	6.6%	0.00
18/1-33/1	6%	7	178	3.9%	0.16
40/1+	3%	3	131	2.3%	0.09

ANALYSIS BY STARTING PRICE LAST TIME

Price	Prop	Win	Runs	Wins%	£
Odds On	6%	6	18	33.3%	0.63
Ev - 2/1	10%	11	65	16.9%	0.23
9/4 - 4/1	21%	23	141	16.3%	0.16
9/2 - 6/1	10%	11	116	9.5%	-0.47
13/2-10/1	19%	21	197	10.7%	-0.19
11/1-16/1	17%	18	201	9.0%	-0.08
18/1-33/1	9%	10	151	6.6%	-0.42
40/1+	6%	6	76	7.9%	0.95
Unraced	2%	2	15	13.3%	1.57

ANALYSIS BY DISTANCE BEATEN LAST TIME

Lengths	Prop	Win	Runs	Wins%	£
..-10	0%	0	2	0.0%	-1.00
-10..0	27%	29	157	18.5%	0.13
0.1..2	17%	18	166	10.8%	-0.04
2.1..5	27%	29	229	12.7%	-0.06
5.1..10	17%	18	215	8.4%	-0.07
10.1..20	6%	6	139	4.3%	-0.38
20.0..30	4%	4	24	16.7%	-0.05
30.1+	2%	2	33	6.1%	0.67
Not Compl	0%	0	0	0.0%	0.00
Unraced	2%	2	15	13.3%	1.57

ANALYSIS BY RUN NUMBER

Run No	Prop	Win	Runs	Wins%	£
FTO	2%	2	15	13.3%	1.57
2nd Run	3%	3	16	18.8%	0.03
3rd Run	0%	0	15	0.0%	-1.00
4th+ Run	95%	103	934	11.0%	-0.04

ANALYSIS BY POSITION LAST TIME

Pos LT	Prop	Win	Runs	Wins%	£
Won	27%	29	158	18.4%	0.12
2nd or 3rd	22%	24	220	10.9%	-0.38
Unplaced	49%	53	585	9.1%	0.03
Not Compl	2%	2	17	11.8%	1.26

OTHER FACTORS (WINS-RUNS, £)

Course Winner:	26-188	-£0.23
Distance Winner:	65-589	-£0.24
Going Winner:	34-340	-£0.40
Beaten Favourite:	19-80	£0.31
BHA Top Rated:	19-114	-£0.33
Up in class:	34-410	-£0.15
Same class:	37-309	£0.23
Down in class:	35-246	-£0.24
7-Day Winners:	5-11	£1.55
Colts and Geldings:	61-458	-£0.05
Fillies:	7-91	-£0.45
Absolute Favourites:	28-102	-£0.24

TRAINERS (WINS-RUNS, £)

Saeed Bin Suroor 13-51 £0.70; K R Burke 3-12 £2.03; J R Fanshawe 5-27 £0.78; D R C Elsworth 3-14 £0.98; W J Haggas 2-14 £0.64; J H M Gosden 2-16 £0.38; R Hannon 3-33 £0.18; B W Hills 5-27 £0.15; R A Fahey 3-10 £0.29; M Johnston 4-24 £0.04.

Race Profiles

All Age Races: Listed Races – 5 to 6 furlong races

ANALYSIS BY AGE						ANALYSIS BY STARTING PRICE LAST TIME					
Age	Prop	Win	Runs	Wins%	£	Price	Prop	Win	Runs	Wins%	£
2yo	0%	0	4	0.0%	-1.00	Odds On	6%	6	14	42.9%	1.50
3yo	24%	24	294	8.2%	-0.08	Ev - 2/1	4%	4	39	10.3%	-0.36
4yo	28%	28	284	9.9%	-0.30	9/4 - 4/1	11%	11	135	8.1%	-0.47
5yo	21%	21	216	9.7%	-0.23	9/2 - 6/1	19%	19	146	13.0%	-0.16
6yo	16%	16	118	13.6%	-0.07	13/2-10/1	22%	22	229	9.6%	-0.12
7yo	7%	7	82	8.5%	-0.43	11/1-16/1	19%	19	220	8.6%	-0.38
8yo	3%	3	33	9.1%	-0.06	18/1-33/1	10%	10	183	5.5%	-0.53
9yo	0%	0	15	0.0%	-1.00	40/1+	6%	6	78	7.7%	0.66
10yo	0%	0	3	0.0%	-1.00	Unraced	2%	2	8	25.0%	1.07
11yo+	0%	0	3	0.0%	-1.00						

ANALYSIS BY BHA RATING						ANALYSIS BY DISTANCE BEATEN LAST TIME					
Rating	Prop	Win	Runs	Wins%	£	Lengths	Prop	Win	Runs	Wins%	£
120..139	1%	1	1	100.0%	0.57	..-10	0%	0	0	0.0%	0.00
110..119	10%	10	67	14.9%	-0.33	-10..0	23%	23	149	15.4%	-0.08
100..109	57%	56	428	13.1%	-0.04	0.1..2	18%	18	188	9.6%	-0.14
90..99	24%	24	320	7.5%	-0.25	2.1..5	33%	33	287	11.5%	-0.14
70..89	5%	5	167	3.0%	-0.42	5.1..10	18%	18	262	6.9%	-0.15
50..69	0%	0	17	0.0%	-1.00	10.1..20	5%	5	129	3.9%	-0.67
..49	0%	0	4	0.0%	-1.00	20.0..30	0%	0	17	0.0%	-1.00
Unrated	3%	3	48	6.3%	-0.36	30.1+	0%	0	12	0.0%	-1.00
						Not Compl	0%	0	0	0.0%	0.00
						Unraced	2%	2	8	25.0%	1.07

ANALYSIS BY WEIGHT CARRIED						ANALYSIS BY RUN NUMBER					
Weight	Prop	Win	Runs	Wins%	£	Run No	Prop	Win	Runs	Wins%	£
10-01+	0%	0	1	0.0%	-1.00	FTO	2%	2	8	25.0%	1.07
9-8 ..10-00	5%	5	55	9.1%	-0.51	2nd Run	0%	0	3	0.0%	-1.00
9-0..9-07	61%	60	581	10.3%	-0.23	3rd Run	0%	0	9	0.0%	-1.00
8-8..8-13	31%	31	323	9.6%	0.02	4th+ Run	98%	97	1032	9.4%	-0.22
8-0..8-07	3%	3	89	3.4%	-0.77						
..7-13	0%	0	3	0.0%	-1.00						

ANALYSIS BY DAYS SINCE LAST RUN						ANALYSIS BY POSITION LAST TIME					
Days	Prop	Win	Runs	Wins%	£	Pos LT	Prop	Win	Runs	Wins%	£
1..7	13%	13	80	16.3%	0.14	Won	23%	23	148	15.5%	-0.07
8..14	22%	22	231	9.5%	-0.12	2nd or 3rd	19%	19	205	9.3%	-0.40
15..28	28%	28	341	8.2%	-0.25	Unplaced	56%	55	688	8.0%	-0.20
29..60	15%	15	164	9.1%	-0.32	Not Compl	2%	2	11	18.2%	0.51
61..100	3%	3	32	9.4%	-0.16						
101+	16%	16	196	8.2%	-0.38	**OTHER FACTORS (WINS-RUNS, £)**					
Unraced	2%	2	8	25.0%	1.07	Course Winner:		28-268			-£0.36
						Distance Winner:		85-889			-£0.22

ANALYSIS BY TODAY'S STARTING PRICE					
Price	Prop	Win	Runs	Wins%	£
Odds On	1%	1	4	25.0%	-0.61
Ev - 2/1	7%	7	35	20.0%	-0.51
9/4 - 4/1	32%	32	130	24.6%	0.04
9/2 - 6/1	19%	19	130	14.6%	-0.10
13/2-10/1	20%	20	213	9.4%	-0.14
11/1-16/1	15%	15	189	7.9%	0.14
18/1-33/1	4%	4	222	1.8%	-0.53
40/1+	1%	1	129	0.8%	-0.60

OTHER FACTORS (WINS-RUNS, £) (continued)
Going Winner: 64-641 -£0.30
Beaten Favourite: 6-78 -£0.56
BHA Top Rated: 15-95 -£0.18
Up in class: 34-485 -£0.44
Same class: 29-303 £0.00
Down in class: 34-256 -£0.08
7-Day Winners: 5-14 £0.88
Colts and Geldings: 57-509 -£0.14
Fillies: 6-128 -£0.56
Absolute Favourites: 19-91 -£0.32

TRAINERS (WINS-RUNS, £)
R F Fisher 3-15 £2.60; W J Haggas 5-16 £1.49; M Quinn 3-19 £1.03; B W Hills 4-13 £1.31; M S Saunders 6-23 £0.56; R Hannon 10-55 £0.23; K R Burke 3-12 £0.90; A Berry 4-18 £0.44; J A Geake 2-12 £0.67; J R Fanshawe 3-15 £0.23; C F Wall 3-23 £0.08.

Listed Races

All Age Races: Listed Races – 7 to 9 furlong races

ANALYSIS BY AGE

Age	Prop	Win	Runs	Wins%	£
2yo	0%	0	0	0.0%	0.00
3yo	28%	29	276	10.5%	-0.36
4yo	36%	37	290	12.8%	-0.20
5yo	19%	20	135	14.8%	-0.28
6yo	11%	11	93	11.8%	-0.08
7yo	5%	5	51	9.8%	0.03
8yo	1%	1	19	5.3%	-0.66
9yo	1%	1	12	8.3%	0.42
10yo	0%	0	2	0.0%	-1.00
11yo+	0%	0	0	0.0%	0.00

ANALYSIS BY BHA RATING

Rating	Prop	Win	Runs	Wins%	£
120..139	1%	1	1	100.0%	1.38
110..119	22%	23	104	22.1%	-0.29
100..109	53%	55	408	13.5%	-0.19
90..99	15%	16	202	7.9%	-0.25
70..89	4%	4	112	3.6%	-0.36
50..69	0%	0	6	0.0%	-1.00
..49	0%	0	3	0.0%	-1.00
Unrated	5%	5	42	11.9%	-0.11

ANALYSIS BY WEIGHT CARRIED

Weight	Prop	Win	Runs	Wins%	£
10-01+	0%	0	0	0.0%	0.00
9-8 ..10-00	4%	4	17	23.5%	1.19
9-0..9-07	62%	64	439	14.6%	-0.02
8-8..8-13	30%	31	353	8.8%	-0.53
8-0..8-07	5%	5	69	7.2%	-0.51
..7-13	0%	0	0	0.0%	0.00

ANALYSIS BY DAYS SINCE LAST RUN

Days	Prop	Win	Runs	Wins%	£
1..7	3%	3	45	6.7%	-0.51
8..14	13%	14	141	9.9%	-0.32
15..28	25%	26	285	9.1%	-0.28
29..60	25%	26	182	14.3%	-0.19
61..100	8%	8	52	15.4%	0.49
101+	25%	26	163	16.0%	-0.29
Unraced	1%	1	10	10.0%	-0.55

ANALYSIS BY TODAY'S STARTING PRICE

Price	Prop	Win	Runs	Wins%	£
Odds On	9%	9	14	64.3%	0.06
Ev - 2/1	28%	29	71	40.8%	0.06
9/4 - 4/1	23%	24	137	17.5%	-0.29
9/2 - 6/1	13%	14	99	14.1%	-0.12
13/2-10/1	13%	13	150	8.7%	-0.18
11/1-16/1	10%	10	152	6.6%	0.01
18/1-33/1	5%	5	155	3.2%	-0.26
40/1+	0%	0	100	0.0%	-1.00

ANALYSIS BY STARTING PRICE LAST TIME

Price	Prop	Win	Runs	Wins%	£
Odds On	8%	8	25	32.0%	0.08
Ev - 2/1	13%	14	59	23.7%	-0.12
9/4 - 4/1	16%	17	137	12.4%	-0.40
9/2 - 6/1	18%	19	122	15.6%	-0.08
13/2-10/1	20%	21	144	14.6%	-0.03
11/1-16/1	12%	12	152	7.9%	-0.30
18/1-33/1	8%	8	155	5.2%	-0.34
40/1+	4%	4	74	5.4%	-0.47
Unraced	1%	1	10	10.0%	-0.55

ANALYSIS BY DISTANCE BEATEN LAST TIME

Lengths	Prop	Win	Runs	Wins%	£
..-10	0%	0	0	0.0%	0.00
-10..0	24%	25	137	18.2%	-0.13
0.1..2	23%	24	150	16.0%	-0.33
2.1..5	26%	27	209	12.9%	0.12
5.1..10	12%	12	188	6.4%	-0.51
10.1..20	8%	8	125	6.4%	-0.48
20.0..30	4%	4	37	10.8%	-0.45
30.1+	3%	3	22	13.6%	0.44
Not Compl	0%	0	0	0.0%	0.00
Unraced	1%	1	10	10.0%	-0.55

ANALYSIS BY RUN NUMBER

Run No	Prop	Win	Runs	Wins%	£
FTO	1%	1	10	10.0%	-0.55
2nd Run	1%	1	16	6.3%	-0.84
3rd Run	3%	3	18	16.7%	-0.24
4th+ Run	95%	99	834	11.9%	-0.23

ANALYSIS BY POSITION LAST TIME

Pos LT	Prop	Win	Runs	Wins%	£
Won	25%	26	138	18.8%	-0.10
2nd or 3rd	28%	29	196	14.8%	-0.39
Unplaced	46%	48	533	9.0%	-0.22
Not Compl	1%	1	11	9.1%	-0.59

OTHER FACTORS (WINS-RUNS, £)

Course Winner:	17-153	-£0.59
Distance Winner:	76-533	-£0.13
Going Winner:	65-461	-£0.07
Beaten Favourite:	17-71	-£0.12
BHA Top Rated:	23-98	-£0.32
Up in class:	34-350	-£0.20
Same class:	34-287	-£0.22
Down in class:	35-231	-£0.31
7-Day Winners:	1-5	-£0.20
Colts and Geldings:	65-471	-£0.16
Fillies:	5-75	-£0.49
Absolute Favourites:	37-96	-£0.07

TRAINERS (WINS-RUNS, £)

Sir Michael Stoute 16-36 £0.70; W J Haggas 3-17 £1.32; G Wragg 2-11 £1.63; P F I Cole 4-12 £1.48; L M Cumani 4-14 £0.86; I Semple 1-10 £1.10; C G Cox 4-14 £0.18; J Noseda 2-10 £0.13.

Race Profiles

All Age Races: Listed Races – 10 to 14 furlong races

ANALYSIS BY AGE
Age	Prop	Win	Runs	Wins%	£
2yo	0%	0	0	0.0%	0.00
3yo	29%	42	362	11.6%	-0.08
4yo	45%	65	442	14.7%	0.06
5yo	17%	25	210	11.9%	-0.26
6yo	5%	7	83	8.4%	0.12
7yo	2%	3	38	7.9%	0.74
8yo	1%	2	22	9.1%	-0.77
9yo	0%	0	5	0.0%	-1.00
10yo	0%	0	0	0.0%	0.00
11yo+	1%	1	2	50.0%	3.00

ANALYSIS BY BHA RATING
Rating	Prop	Win	Runs	Wins%	£
120..139	1%	1	2	50.0%	-0.05
110..119	26%	37	163	22.7%	0.07
100..109	50%	72	485	14.8%	-0.06
90..99	14%	21	279	7.5%	-0.44
70..89	7%	10	156	6.4%	0.64
50..69	0%	0	18	0.0%	-1.00
..49	0%	0	6	0.0%	-1.00
Unrated	3%	4	55	7.3%	-0.46

ANALYSIS BY WEIGHT CARRIED
Weight	Prop	Win	Runs	Wins%	£
10-01+	0%	0	0	0.0%	0.00
9-8..10-00	3%	5	22	22.7%	0.67
9-0..9-07	47%	68	583	11.7%	-0.16
8-8..8-13	37%	53	417	12.7%	-0.09
8-0..8-07	13%	19	142	13.4%	0.15
..7-13	0%	0	0	0.0%	0.00

ANALYSIS BY DAYS SINCE LAST RUN
Days	Prop	Win	Runs	Wins%	£
1..7	1%	2	41	4.9%	-0.69
8..14	21%	30	184	16.3%	0.01
15..28	37%	54	381	14.2%	0.05
29..60	17%	25	280	8.9%	-0.33
61..100	4%	6	69	8.7%	0.08
101+	18%	26	185	14.1%	-0.12
Unraced	1%	2	24	8.3%	1.04

ANALYSIS BY TODAY'S STARTING PRICE
Price	Prop	Win	Runs	Wins%	£
Odds On	10%	15	30	50.0%	-0.16
Ev - 2/1	14%	20	88	22.7%	-0.44
9/4 - 4/1	30%	44	172	25.6%	0.03
9/2 - 6/1	14%	20	130	15.4%	-0.07
13/2-10/1	14%	21	224	9.4%	-0.15
11/1-16/1	12%	17	205	8.3%	0.20
18/1-33/1	4%	6	185	3.2%	-0.08
40/1+	1%	2	130	1.5%	-0.29

ANALYSIS BY STARTING PRICE LAST TIME
Price	Prop	Win	Runs	Wins%	£
Odds On	2%	3	29	10.3%	-0.29
Ev - 2/1	13%	19	86	22.1%	0.54
9/4 - 4/1	22%	32	188	17.0%	0.07
9/2 - 6/1	13%	19	146	13.0%	-0.24
13/2-10/1	20%	29	234	12.4%	-0.31
11/1-16/1	17%	24	223	10.8%	-0.03
18/1-33/1	8%	12	162	7.4%	-0.38
40/1+	3%	5	72	6.9%	0.08
Unraced	1%	2	24	8.3%	1.04

ANALYSIS BY DISTANCE BEATEN LAST TIME
Lengths	Prop	Win	Runs	Wins%	£
..-10	0%	0	4	0.0%	-1.00
-10..0	21%	31	187	16.6%	-0.14
0.1..2	21%	30	191	15.7%	-0.15
2.1..5	23%	34	259	13.1%	-0.05
5.1..10	21%	31	237	13.1%	0.04
10.1..20	8%	12	166	7.2%	-0.09
20.0..30	2%	3	39	7.7%	-0.47
30.1+	1%	2	57	3.5%	-0.35
Not Compl	0%	0	0	0.0%	0.00
Unraced	1%	2	24	8.3%	1.04

ANALYSIS BY RUN NUMBER
Run No	Prop	Win	Runs	Wins%	£
FTO	1%	2	24	8.3%	1.04
2nd Run	1%	2	23	8.7%	-0.39
3rd Run	3%	5	38	13.2%	-0.49
4th+ Run	94%	136	1079	12.6%	-0.08

ANALYSIS BY POSITION LAST TIME
Pos LT	Prop	Win	Runs	Wins%	£
Won	21%	31	192	16.1%	-0.16
2nd or 3rd	34%	50	326	15.3%	-0.08
Unplaced	43%	62	617	10.0%	-0.09
Not Compl	1%	2	29	6.9%	0.69

OTHER FACTORS (WINS-RUNS, £)
Course Winner:	22-196	-£0.23
Distance Winner:	81-554	-£0.19
Going Winner:	60-515	-£0.30
Beaten Favourite:	19-84	£0.64
BHA Top Rated:	28-132	-£0.10
Up in class:	40-422	-£0.15
Same class:	41-374	-£0.16
Down in class:	62-344	£0.03
7-Day Winners:	1-6	-£0.28
Colts and Geldings:	81-537	-£0.08
Fillies:	13-134	-£0.18
Absolute Favourites:	41-140	-£0.28

TRAINERS (WINS-RUNS, £)
G G Margarson 3-12 £5.58; D R C Elsworth 7-32 £0.84; J R Fanshawe 1-14 £1.43; H R A Cecil 8-24 £0.83; J M P Eustace 2-10 £1.60; M Johnston 7-30 £0.34; J H M Gosden 6-36 £0.23; R A Fahey 3-10 £0.29; P F I Cole 2-17 £0.12; G A Swinbank 3-12 £0.09; M A Jarvis 5-17 £0.01.

Listed Races

All Age Races: Listed Races – 15+ furlong races

ANALYSIS BY AGE

Age	Prop	Win	Runs	Wins%	£
2yo	0%	0	0	0.0%	0.00
3yo	8%	1	7	14.3%	0.57
4yo	17%	2	25	8.0%	-0.60
5yo	17%	2	16	12.5%	4.00
6yo	33%	4	10	40.0%	2.50
7yo	8%	1	9	11.1%	-0.58
8yo	8%	1	6	16.7%	-0.56
9yo	8%	1	2	50.0%	1.25
10yo	0%	0	0	0.0%	0.00
11yo+	0%	0	0	0.0%	0.00

ANALYSIS BY BHA RATING

Rating	Prop	Win	Runs	Wins%	£
120..139	0%	0	0	0.0%	0.00
110..119	8%	1	11	9.1%	-0.76
100..109	50%	6	40	15.0%	0.64
90..99	25%	3	19	15.8%	-0.13
70..89	17%	2	4	50.0%	14.50
50..69	0%	0	0	0.0%	0.00
..49	0%	0	1	0.0%	-1.00
Unrated	0%	0	0	0.0%	0.00

ANALYSIS BY WEIGHT CARRIED

Weight	Prop	Win	Runs	Wins%	£
10-01+	0%	0	0	0.0%	0.00
9-8 ..10-00	0%	0	0	0.0%	0.00
9-0..9-07	83%	10	57	17.5%	1.27
8-8..8-13	8%	1	11	9.1%	-0.41
8-0..8-07	8%	1	7	14.3%	0.57
..7-13	0%	0	0	0.0%	0.00

ANALYSIS BY DAYS SINCE LAST RUN

Days	Prop	Win	Runs	Wins%	£
1..7	0%	0	1	0.0%	-1.00
8..14	17%	2	15	13.3%	-0.23
15..28	33%	4	29	13.8%	1.56
29..60	33%	4	25	16.0%	1.04
61..100	17%	2	2	100.0%	4.00
101+	0%	0	3	0.0%	-1.00
Unraced	0%	0	0	0.0%	0.00

ANALYSIS BY TODAY'S STARTING PRICE

Price	Prop	Win	Runs	Wins%	£
Odds On	0%	0	1	0.0%	-1.00
Ev - 2/1	8%	1	6	16.7%	-0.56
9/4 - 4/1	42%	5	19	26.3%	0.20
9/2 - 6/1	17%	2	14	14.3%	-0.04
13/2-10/1	8%	1	19	5.3%	-0.42
11/1-16/1	8%	1	5	20.0%	2.40
18/1-33/1	8%	1	7	14.3%	3.14
40/1+	8%	1	4	25.0%	11.75

ANALYSIS BY STARTING PRICE LAST TIME

Price	Prop	Win	Runs	Wins%	£
Odds On	0%	0	1	0.0%	-1.00
Ev - 2/1	17%	2	6	33.3%	0.71
9/4 - 4/1	8%	1	14	7.1%	-0.21
9/2 - 6/1	8%	1	10	10.0%	4.10
13/2-10/1	33%	4	17	23.5%	0.71
11/1-16/1	25%	3	12	25.0%	2.21
18/1-33/1	8%	1	10	10.0%	-0.30
40/1+	0%	0	5	0.0%	-1.00
Unraced	0%	0	0	0.0%	0.00

ANALYSIS BY DISTANCE BEATEN LAST TIME

Lengths	Prop	Win	Runs	Wins%	£
..-10	0%	0	0	0.0%	0.00
-10..0	33%	4	16	25.0%	0.67
0.1..2	8%	1	12	8.3%	-0.63
2.1..5	25%	3	14	21.4%	3.43
5.1..10	25%	3	12	25.0%	1.05
10.1..20	0%	0	13	0.0%	-1.00
20.0..30	0%	0	2	0.0%	-1.00
30.1+	8%	1	6	16.7%	3.83
Not Compl	0%	0	0	0.0%	0.00
Unraced	0%	0	0	0.0%	0.00

ANALYSIS BY RUN NUMBER

Run No	Prop	Win	Runs	Wins%	£
FTO	0%	0	0	0.0%	0.00
2nd Run	0%	0	0	0.0%	0.00
3rd Run	0%	0	0	0.0%	0.00
4th+ Run	100%	12	75	16.0%	0.96

ANALYSIS BY POSITION LAST TIME

Pos LT	Prop	Win	Runs	Wins%	£
Won	33%	4	16	25.0%	0.67
2nd or 3rd	17%	2	20	10.0%	1.77
Unplaced	50%	6	39	15.4%	0.66
Not Compl	0%	0	0	0.0%	0.00

OTHER FACTORS (WINS-RUNS, £)

Course Winner:	4-26	-£0.07
Distance Winner:	8-31	£2.17
Going Winner:	5-47	-£0.23
Beaten Favourite:	1-5	£0.30
BHA Top Rated:	1-10	-£0.74
Up in class:	9-39	£2.17
Same class:	2-16	£0.30
Down in class:	1-20	-£0.87
Colts and Geldings:	11-67	£1.03
Fillies:	1-8	£0.38
Absolute Favourites:	1-11	-£0.76

Race Profiles

All Age Races: Conditions Stakes

ANALYSIS BY AGE

Age	Prop	Win	Runs	Wins%	£
2yo	2%	4	17	23.5%	0.26
3yo	18%	40	279	14.3%	-0.26
4yo	31%	68	388	17.5%	0.05
5yo	22%	48	287	16.7%	-0.29
6yo	12%	26	177	14.7%	-0.35
7yo	6%	14	122	11.5%	0.31
8yo	4%	9	81	11.1%	-0.41
9yo	2%	4	44	9.1%	-0.58
10yo	1%	3	17	17.6%	-0.30
11yo+	0%	1	13	7.7%	-0.46

ANALYSIS BY BHA RATING

Rating	Prop	Win	Runs	Wins%	£
120..139	0%	0	1	0.0%	-1.00
110..119	12%	26	85	30.6%	-0.05
100..109	57%	124	581	21.3%	-0.11
90..99	19%	42	350	12.0%	-0.17
70..89	9%	19	203	9.4%	-0.05
50..69	0%	0	55	0.0%	-1.00
..49	0%	0	53	0.0%	-1.00
Unrated	3%	6	97	6.2%	-0.56

ANALYSIS BY WEIGHT CARRIED

Weight	Prop	Win	Runs	Wins%	£
10-01+	0%	0	0	0.0%	0.00
9-8..10-00	5%	10	54	18.5%	-0.20
9-0..9-07	36%	78	520	15.0%	-0.27
8-8..8-13	45%	97	586	16.6%	-0.12
8-0..8-07	14%	31	248	12.5%	-0.28
..7-13	0%	1	17	5.9%	-0.75

ANALYSIS BY DAYS SINCE LAST RUN

Days	Prop	Win	Runs	Wins%	£
1..7	9%	20	128	15.6%	-0.00
8..14	13%	29	249	11.6%	-0.45
15..28	27%	58	369	15.7%	-0.22
29..60	21%	46	252	18.3%	-0.10
61..100	1%	2	54	3.7%	-0.93
101+	28%	61	349	17.5%	-0.06
Unraced	0%	1	24	4.2%	-0.63

ANALYSIS BY TODAY'S STARTING PRICE

Price	Prop	Win	Runs	Wins%	£
Odds On	13%	29	57	50.9%	-0.11
Ev - 2/1	25%	54	147	36.7%	-0.08
9/4 - 4/1	34%	73	302	24.2%	-0.00
9/2 - 6/1	10%	21	173	12.1%	-0.26
13/2-10/1	12%	26	228	11.4%	0.01
11/1-16/1	4%	9	188	4.8%	-0.31
18/1-33/1	2%	4	144	2.8%	-0.43
40/1+	0%	1	186	0.5%	-0.64

ANALYSIS BY STARTING PRICE LAST TIME

Price	Prop	Win	Runs	Wins%	£
Odds On	2%	5	21	23.8%	-0.41
Ev - 2/1	6%	14	64	21.9%	-0.38
9/4 - 4/1	21%	45	173	26.0%	0.17
9/2 - 6/1	15%	32	149	21.5%	-0.19
13/2-10/1	20%	44	299	14.7%	-0.02
11/1-16/1	17%	36	267	13.5%	-0.37
18/1-33/1	16%	34	262	13.0%	-0.11
40/1+	3%	6	166	3.6%	-0.74
Unraced	0%	1	24	4.2%	-0.63

ANALYSIS BY DISTANCE BEATEN LAST TIME

Lengths	Prop	Win	Runs	Wins%	£
..-10	0%	0	0	0.0%	0.00
-10..0	12%	26	125	20.8%	-0.10
0.1..2	24%	52	212	24.5%	-0.16
2.1..5	21%	45	318	14.2%	-0.32
5.1..10	21%	45	349	12.9%	-0.25
10.1..20	13%	29	250	11.6%	-0.26
20.0..30	4%	8	67	11.9%	0.59
30.1+	5%	11	80	13.8%	-0.34
Not Compl	0%	0	0	0.0%	0.00
Unraced	0%	1	24	4.2%	-0.63

ANALYSIS BY RUN NUMBER

Run No	Prop	Win	Runs	Wins%	£
FTO	0%	1	24	4.2%	-0.63
2nd Run	3%	6	46	13.0%	-0.52
3rd Run	3%	6	36	16.7%	0.08
4th+ Run	94%	204	1319	15.5%	-0.20

ANALYSIS BY POSITION LAST TIME

Pos LT	Prop	Win	Runs	Wins%	£
Won	12%	26	125	20.8%	-0.10
2nd or 3rd	27%	58	273	21.2%	-0.17
Unplaced	60%	131	1000	13.1%	-0.23
Not Compl	1%	2	27	7.4%	-0.39

OTHER FACTORS (WINS-RUNS, £)

Course Winner:	49-268	-£0.13
Distance Winner:	143-875	-£0.21
Going Winner:	113-682	-£0.23
Beaten Favourite:	26-93	£0.05
BHA Top Rated:	56-191	-£0.08
Up in class:	23-292	-£0.38
Same class:	46-302	-£0.11
Down in class:	147-807	-£0.18
7-Day Winners:	3-6	£1.46
Colts and Geldings:	190-1190	-£0.24
Fillies:	14-154	£0.01
Absolute Favourites:	81-203	-£0.06

TRAINERS (WINS-RUNS, £)

J R Fanshawe 10-24 £1.88; Saeed Bin Suroor 42-108 £0.35; M R Channon 9-32 £0.57; R Hannon 10-55 £0.24; A M Balding 4-18 £0.69; M A Jarvis 8-36 £0.18; D W Barker 3-10 £0.60; B J Meehan 6-16 £0.34; W J Haggas 3-11 £0.48; J M Bradley 3-11 £0.39.

Conditions Stakes

All Age Races: Conditions Stakes – 2 to 7 runners

ANALYSIS BY AGE

Age	Prop	Win	Runs	Wins%	£
2yo	2%	3	10	30.0%	0.15
3yo	19%	31	185	16.8%	-0.20
4yo	33%	53	262	20.2%	0.26
5yo	21%	34	189	18.0%	-0.29
6yo	12%	19	106	17.9%	-0.21
7yo	6%	10	66	15.2%	-0.23
8yo	4%	7	42	16.7%	-0.21
9yo	1%	2	17	11.8%	-0.45
10yo	1%	1	9	11.1%	-0.79
11yo+	0%	0	4	0.0%	-1.00

ANALYSIS BY BHA RATING

Rating	Prop	Win	Runs	Wins%	£
120..139	0%	0	1	0.0%	-1.00
110..119	14%	23	64	35.9%	-0.01
100..109	56%	90	382	23.6%	-0.11
90..99	18%	29	211	13.7%	-0.02
70..89	8%	13	117	11.1%	0.31
50..69	0%	0	29	0.0%	-1.00
..49	0%	0	22	0.0%	-1.00
Unrated	3%	5	64	7.8%	-0.38

ANALYSIS BY WEIGHT CARRIED

Weight	Prop	Win	Runs	Wins%	£
10-01+	0%	0	0	0.0%	0.00
9-8..10-00	5%	8	35	22.9%	0.04
9-0..9-07	34%	55	315	17.5%	-0.19
8-8..8-13	46%	74	365	20.3%	0.06
8-0..8-07	14%	22	165	13.3%	-0.27
..7-13	1%	1	10	10.0%	-0.57

ANALYSIS BY DAYS SINCE LAST RUN

Days	Prop	Win	Runs	Wins%	£
1..7	6%	10	67	14.9%	0.04
8..14	13%	21	153	13.7%	-0.43
15..28	29%	47	231	20.3%	-0.03
29..60	19%	31	151	20.5%	-0.07
61..100	1%	2	36	5.6%	-0.89
101+	30%	48	234	20.5%	0.14
Unraced	1%	1	18	5.6%	-0.50

ANALYSIS BY TODAY'S STARTING PRICE

Price	Prop	Win	Runs	Wins%	£
Odds On	16%	26	52	50.0%	-0.13
Ev - 2/1	29%	47	126	37.3%	-0.07
9/4 - 4/1	33%	52	209	24.9%	0.02
9/2 - 6/1	6%	9	103	8.7%	-0.49
13/2-10/1	9%	14	122	11.5%	0.00
11/1-16/1	4%	7	106	6.6%	-0.03
18/1-33/1	3%	4	79	5.1%	0.04
40/1+	1%	1	93	1.1%	-0.28

ANALYSIS BY STARTING PRICE LAST TIME

Price	Prop	Win	Runs	Wins%	£
Odds On	3%	5	14	35.7%	-0.11
Ev - 2/1	8%	12	45	26.7%	-0.28
9/4 - 4/1	19%	31	102	30.4%	0.25
9/2 - 6/1	17%	27	106	25.5%	-0.05
13/2-10/1	18%	29	190	15.3%	0.11
11/1-16/1	17%	27	157	17.2%	-0.28
18/1-33/1	15%	24	160	15.0%	0.04
40/1+	3%	4	98	4.1%	-0.68
Unraced	1%	1	18	5.6%	-0.50

ANALYSIS BY DISTANCE BEATEN LAST TIME

Lengths	Prop	Win	Runs	Wins%	£
..-10	0%	0	0	0.0%	0.00
-10..0	13%	21	76	27.6%	0.01
0.1..2	23%	37	131	28.2%	-0.16
2.1..5	20%	32	199	16.1%	-0.20
5.1..10	22%	35	216	16.2%	-0.11
10.1..20	13%	21	155	13.5%	-0.13
20.0..30	4%	6	40	15.0%	1.34
30.1+	4%	7	55	12.7%	-0.53
Not Compl	0%	0	0	0.0%	0.00
Unraced	1%	1	18	5.6%	-0.50

ANALYSIS BY RUN NUMBER

Run No	Prop	Win	Runs	Wins%	£
FTO	1%	1	18	5.6%	-0.50
2nd Run	3%	5	25	20.0%	-0.34
3rd Run	3%	5	26	19.2%	0.42
4th+ Run	93%	149	821	18.1%	-0.10

ANALYSIS BY POSITION LAST TIME

Pos LT	Prop	Win	Runs	Wins%	£
Won	13%	21	76	27.6%	0.01
2nd or 3rd	23%	36	174	20.7%	-0.32
Unplaced	64%	102	620	16.5%	-0.03
Not Compl	1%	1	20	5.0%	-0.55

OTHER FACTORS (WINS-RUNS, £)

Course Winner:	32-164	-£0.12
Distance Winner:	105-555	-£0.14
Going Winner:	81-425	-£0.20
Beaten Favourite:	18-57	£0.01
BHA Top Rated:	43-136	-£0.11
Up in class:	18-154	-£0.08
Same class:	30-166	£0.07
Down in class:	111-552	-£0.14
7-Day Winners:	2-3	£1.75
Colts and Geldings:	140-733	-£0.14
Fillies:	10-101	£0.29
Absolute Favourites:	66-152	-£0.02

TRAINERS (WINS-RUNS, £)

Saeed Bin Suroor 35-80 £0.43; J R Fanshawe 8-19 £1.61; M R Channon 7-24 £0.73; A M Balding 3-14 £0.81; B J Meehan 5-10 £0.77; R A Fahey 5-16 £0.23; T P Tate 4-12 £0.05.

Race Profiles

All Age Races: Conditions Stakes – 8 to 14 runners

ANALYSIS BY AGE

Age	Prop	Win	Runs	Wins%	£
2yo	2%	1	7	14.3%	0.43
3yo	16%	9	94	9.6%	-0.38
4yo	25%	14	122	11.5%	-0.40
5yo	25%	14	93	15.1%	-0.26
6yo	13%	7	68	10.3%	-0.53
7yo	7%	4	55	7.3%	0.39
8yo	4%	2	38	5.3%	-0.62
9yo	4%	2	26	7.7%	-0.64
10yo	4%	2	8	25.0%	0.25
11yo+	2%	1	8	12.5%	-0.13

ANALYSIS BY BHA RATING

Rating	Prop	Win	Runs	Wins%	£
120..139	0%	0	0	0.0%	0.00
110..119	5%	3	21	14.3%	-0.17
100..109	61%	34	194	17.5%	-0.10
90..99	23%	13	137	9.5%	-0.38
70..89	11%	6	83	7.2%	-0.52
50..69	0%	0	24	0.0%	-1.00
..49	0%	0	31	0.0%	-1.00
Unrated	0%	0	29	0.0%	-1.00

ANALYSIS BY WEIGHT CARRIED

Weight	Prop	Win	Runs	Wins%	£
10-01+	0%	0	0	0.0%	0.00
9-8..10-00	4%	2	19	10.5%	-0.63
9-0..9-07	39%	22	189	11.6%	-0.35
8-8..8-13	41%	23	221	10.4%	-0.41
8-0..8-07	16%	9	83	10.8%	-0.32
..7-13	0%	0	7	0.0%	-1.00

ANALYSIS BY DAYS SINCE LAST RUN

Days	Prop	Win	Runs	Wins%	£
1..7	18%	10	59	16.9%	-0.02
8..14	14%	8	96	8.3%	-0.48
15..28	20%	11	132	8.3%	-0.53
29..60	25%	14	95	14.7%	-0.11
61..100	0%	0	18	0.0%	-1.00
101+	23%	13	113	11.5%	-0.46
Unraced	0%	0	6	0.0%	-1.00

ANALYSIS BY TODAY'S STARTING PRICE

Price	Prop	Win	Runs	Wins%	£
Odds On	5%	3	5	60.0%	0.05
Ev - 2/1	11%	6	20	30.0%	-0.25
9/4 - 4/1	38%	21	92	22.8%	-0.05
9/2 - 6/1	21%	12	69	17.4%	0.09
13/2-10/1	21%	12	104	11.5%	0.03
11/1-16/1	4%	2	80	2.5%	-0.68
18/1-33/1	0%	0	61	0.0%	-1.00
40/1+	0%	0	88	0.0%	-1.00

ANALYSIS BY STARTING PRICE LAST TIME

Price	Prop	Win	Runs	Wins%	£
Odds On	0%	0	7	0.0%	-1.00
Ev - 2/1	2%	1	17	5.9%	-0.74
9/4 - 4/1	25%	14	70	20.0%	0.06
9/2 - 6/1	9%	5	42	11.9%	-0.53
13/2-10/1	27%	15	106	14.2%	-0.22
11/1-16/1	16%	9	104	8.7%	-0.46
18/1-33/1	18%	10	99	10.1%	-0.32
40/1+	4%	2	68	2.9%	-0.83
Unraced	0%	0	6	0.0%	-1.00

ANALYSIS BY DISTANCE BEATEN LAST TIME

Lengths	Prop	Win	Runs	Wins%	£
..-10	0%	0	0	0.0%	0.00
-10..0	9%	5	47	10.6%	-0.23
0.1..2	27%	15	78	19.2%	-0.12
2.1..5	23%	13	113	11.5%	-0.49
5.1..10	16%	9	130	6.9%	-0.49
10.1..20	14%	8	93	8.6%	-0.47
20.0..30	4%	2	27	7.4%	-0.52
30.1+	7%	4	25	16.0%	0.06
Not Compl	0%	0	0	0.0%	0.00
Unraced	0%	0	6	0.0%	-1.00

ANALYSIS BY RUN NUMBER

Run No	Prop	Win	Runs	Wins%	£
FTO	0%	0	6	0.0%	-1.00
2nd Run	2%	1	21	4.8%	-0.74
3rd Run	2%	1	10	10.0%	-0.80
4th+ Run	96%	54	482	11.2%	-0.36

ANALYSIS BY POSITION LAST TIME

Pos LT	Prop	Win	Runs	Wins%	£
Won	9%	5	47	10.6%	-0.23
2nd or 3rd	39%	22	94	23.4%	0.14
Unplaced	50%	28	371	7.5%	-0.55
Not Compl	2%	1	7	14.3%	0.07

OTHER FACTORS (WINS-RUNS, £)

Course Winner:	17-101	-£0.11
Distance Winner:	38-318	-£0.32
Going Winner:	32-251	-£0.27
Beaten Favourite:	7-34	£0.12
BHA Top Rated:	13-54	£0.00
Up in class:	5-133	-£0.71
Same class:	16-129	-£0.29
Down in class:	35-251	-£0.26
7-Day Winners:	1-3	£1.17
Colts and Geldings:	49-441	-£0.39
Fillies:	4-53	-£0.52
Absolute Favourites:	14-50	-£0.23

TRAINERS (WINS-RUNS, £)

R Hannon 4-19 £1.00; M A Jarvis 3-12 £0.79; Saeed Bin Suroor 7-28 £0.11.

Conditions Stakes

All Age Races: Conditions Stakes – good or faster going

ANALYSIS BY AGE

Age	Prop	Win	Runs	Wins%	£
2yo	1%	2	9	22.2%	0.47
3yo	19%	29	198	14.6%	-0.17
4yo	35%	52	286	18.2%	-0.08
5yo	21%	32	203	15.8%	-0.33
6yo	9%	13	111	11.7%	-0.48
7yo	7%	11	83	13.3%	-0.18
8yo	5%	7	53	13.2%	-0.27
9yo	1%	2	32	6.3%	-0.59
10yo	1%	1	9	11.1%	-0.61
11yo+	1%	1	7	14.3%	0.00

ANALYSIS BY BHA RATING

Rating	Prop	Win	Runs	Wins%	£
120..139	0%	0	0	0.0%	0.00
110..119	14%	21	62	33.9%	0.15
100..109	59%	88	408	21.6%	-0.08
90..99	17%	25	244	10.2%	-0.22
70..89	8%	12	133	9.0%	-0.26
50..69	0%	0	35	0.0%	-1.00
..49	0%	0	36	0.0%	-1.00
Unrated	3%	4	73	5.5%	-0.61

ANALYSIS BY WEIGHT CARRIED

Weight	Prop	Win	Runs	Wins%	£
10-01+	0%	0	0	0.0%	0.00
9-8..10-00	3%	5	29	17.2%	-0.09
9-0..9-07	37%	55	363	15.2%	-0.25
8-8..8-13	43%	65	403	16.1%	-0.22
8-0..8-07	16%	24	186	12.9%	-0.21
..7-13	1%	1	10	10.0%	-0.57

ANALYSIS BY DAYS SINCE LAST RUN

Days	Prop	Win	Runs	Wins%	£
1..7	7%	10	83	12.0%	-0.18
8..14	15%	22	187	11.8%	-0.41
15..28	27%	41	257	16.0%	-0.16
29..60	20%	30	167	18.0%	-0.03
61..100	1%	2	38	5.3%	-0.90
101+	30%	45	240	18.8%	-0.15
Unraced	0%	0	19	0.0%	-1.00

ANALYSIS BY TODAY'S STARTING PRICE

Price	Prop	Win	Runs	Wins%	£
Odds On	12%	18	34	52.9%	-0.10
Ev - 2/1	25%	38	105	36.2%	-0.11
9/4 - 4/1	32%	48	209	23.0%	-0.05
9/2 - 6/1	11%	17	127	13.4%	-0.19
13/2-10/1	11%	17	165	10.3%	-0.09
11/1-16/1	6%	9	132	6.8%	-0.02
18/1-33/1	2%	3	91	3.3%	-0.33
40/1+	0%	0	128	0.0%	-1.00

ANALYSIS BY STARTING PRICE LAST TIME

Price	Prop	Win	Runs	Wins%	£
Odds On	2%	3	12	25.0%	-0.38
Ev - 2/1	7%	11	45	24.4%	-0.29
9/4 - 4/1	23%	35	126	27.8%	0.24
9/2 - 6/1	13%	19	99	19.2%	-0.28
13/2-10/1	21%	32	206	15.5%	-0.13
11/1-16/1	17%	25	189	13.2%	-0.36
18/1-33/1	15%	23	182	12.6%	-0.08
40/1+	1%	2	113	1.8%	-0.76
Unraced	0%	0	19	0.0%	-1.00

ANALYSIS BY DISTANCE BEATEN LAST TIME

Lengths	Prop	Win	Runs	Wins%	£
..-10	0%	0	0	0.0%	0.00
-10..0	10%	15	83	18.1%	-0.11
0.1..2	23%	35	135	25.9%	-0.11
2.1..5	22%	33	227	14.5%	-0.32
5.1..10	22%	33	247	13.4%	-0.15
10.1..20	15%	22	182	12.1%	-0.19
20.0..30	3%	5	44	11.4%	-0.36
30.1+	5%	7	54	13.0%	-0.42
Not Compl	0%	0	0	0.0%	0.00
Unraced	0%	0	19	0.0%	-1.00

ANALYSIS BY RUN NUMBER

Run No	Prop	Win	Runs	Wins%	£
FTO	0%	0	19	0.0%	-1.00
2nd Run	3%	4	34	11.8%	-0.52
3rd Run	3%	4	26	15.4%	0.22
4th+ Run	95%	142	912	15.6%	-0.21

ANALYSIS BY POSITION LAST TIME

Pos LT	Prop	Win	Runs	Wins%	£
Won	10%	15	83	18.1%	-0.11
2nd or 3rd	30%	45	195	23.1%	-0.06
Unplaced	60%	90	693	13.0%	-0.27
Not Compl	0%	0	20	0.0%	-1.00

OTHER FACTORS (WINS-RUNS, £)

Course Winner:	33-175	-£0.04
Distance Winner:	97-592	-£0.19
Going Winner:	88-543	-£0.21
Beaten Favourite:	18-58	£0.13
BHA Top Rated:	40-127	£0.03
Up in class:	13-190	-£0.60
Same class:	31-213	-£0.07
Down in class:	106-569	-£0.14
7-Day Winners:	2-5	£1.20
Colts and Geldings:	133-830	-£0.20
Fillies:	8-106	-£0.46
Absolute Favourites:	56-142	-£0.08

TRAINERS (WINS-RUNS, £)

Saeed Bin Suroor 28-74 £0.36; J R Fanshawe 5-18 £1.39; R Hannon 8-38 £0.55; M R Channon 5-21 £0.74; M A Jarvis 7-24 £0.60; A M Balding 2-11 £0.91; B J Meehan 6-14 £0.53; W J Haggas 3-10 £0.63.

Race Profiles

All Age Races: Conditions Stakes – good to soft or softer going

ANALYSIS BY AGE

Age	Prop	Win	Runs	Wins%	£
2yo	3%	2	8	25.0%	0.03
3yo	16%	11	81	13.6%	-0.49
4yo	24%	16	102	15.7%	0.41
5yo	24%	16	84	19.0%	-0.20
6yo	19%	13	66	19.7%	-0.13
7yo	4%	3	39	7.7%	-0.50
8yo	3%	2	28	7.1%	-0.67
9yo	3%	2	12	16.7%	-0.53
10yo	3%	2	8	25.0%	0.05
11yo+	0%	0	6	0.0%	-1.00

ANALYSIS BY BHA RATING

Rating	Prop	Win	Runs	Wins%	£
120..139	0%	0	1	0.0%	-1.00
110..119	7%	5	23	21.7%	-0.56
100..109	54%	36	173	20.8%	-0.20
90..99	25%	17	106	16.0%	-0.05
70..89	10%	7	70	10.0%	0.36
50..69	0%	0	20	0.0%	-1.00
..49	0%	0	17	0.0%	-1.00
Unrated	3%	2	24	8.3%	-0.44

ANALYSIS BY WEIGHT CARRIED

Weight	Prop	Win	Runs	Wins%	£
10-01+	0%	0	0	0.0%	0.00
9-8..10-00	7%	5	25	20.0%	-0.32
9-0..9-07	34%	23	157	14.6%	-0.30
8-8..8-13	48%	32	183	17.5%	0.10
8-0..8-07	10%	7	62	11.3%	-0.51
..7-13	0%	0	7	0.0%	-1.00

ANALYSIS BY DAYS SINCE LAST RUN

Days	Prop	Win	Runs	Wins%	£
1..7	15%	10	45	22.2%	0.33
8..14	10%	7	62	11.3%	-0.56
15..28	25%	17	112	15.2%	-0.36
29..60	24%	16	85	18.8%	-0.23
61..100	0%	0	16	0.0%	-1.00
101+	24%	16	109	14.7%	0.14
Unraced	1%	1	5	20.0%	0.80

ANALYSIS BY TODAY'S STARTING PRICE

Price	Prop	Win	Runs	Wins%	£
Odds On	16%	11	23	47.8%	-0.14
Ev - 2/1	24%	16	42	38.1%	-0.01
9/4 - 4/1	37%	25	93	26.9%	0.11
9/2 - 6/1	6%	4	46	8.7%	-0.43
13/2-10/1	13%	9	63	14.3%	0.26
11/1-16/1	0%	0	56	0.0%	-1.00
18/1-33/1	1%	1	53	1.9%	-0.60
40/1+	1%	1	58	1.7%	0.16

ANALYSIS BY STARTING PRICE LAST TIME

Price	Prop	Win	Runs	Wins%	£
Odds On	3%	2	9	22.2%	-0.45
Ev - 2/1	4%	3	19	15.8%	-0.61
9/4 - 4/1	15%	10	47	21.3%	-0.02
9/2 - 6/1	19%	13	50	26.0%	-0.03
13/2-10/1	18%	12	93	12.9%	0.22
11/1-16/1	16%	11	78	14.1%	0.40
18/1-33/1	16%	11	80	13.8%	-0.17
40/1+	6%	4	53	7.5%	-0.72
Unraced	1%	1	5	20.0%	0.80

ANALYSIS BY DISTANCE BEATEN LAST TIME

Lengths	Prop	Win	Runs	Wins%	£
..-10	0%	0	0	0.0%	0.00
-10..0	16%	11	42	26.2%	-0.06
0.1..2	25%	17	77	22.1%	-0.24
2.1..5	18%	12	91	13.2%	-0.31
5.1..10	18%	12	102	11.8%	-0.49
10.1..20	10%	7	68	10.3%	-0.46
20.0..30	4%	3	23	13.0%	2.40
30.1+	6%	4	26	15.4%	-0.18
Not Compl	0%	0	0	0.0%	0.00
Unraced	1%	1	5	20.0%	0.80

ANALYSIS BY RUN NUMBER

Run No	Prop	Win	Runs	Wins%	£
FTO	1%	1	5	20.0%	0.80
2nd Run	3%	2	12	16.7%	-0.52
3rd Run	3%	2	10	20.0%	-0.28
4th+ Run	93%	62	407	15.2%	-0.17

ANALYSIS BY POSITION LAST TIME

Pos LT	Prop	Win	Runs	Wins%	£
Won	16%	11	42	26.2%	-0.06
2nd or 3rd	19%	13	78	16.7%	-0.45
Unplaced	61%	41	307	13.4%	-0.16
Not Compl	3%	2	7	28.6%	1.36

OTHER FACTORS (WINS-RUNS, £)

Course Winner:	16-93	-£0.28
Distance Winner:	46-283	-£0.26
Going Winner:	25-139	-£0.31
Beaten Favourite:	8-35	-£0.06
BHA Top Rated:	16-64	-£0.32
Up in class:	10-102	£0.02
Same class:	15-89	-£0.20
Down in class:	41-238	-£0.27
7-Day Winners:	1-1	£2.75
Colts and Geldings:	57-360	-£0.33
Fillies:	6-48	£1.05
Absolute Favourites:	25-61	-£0.02

TRAINERS (WINS-RUNS, £)

Saeed Bin Suroor 14-34 £0.32; M R Channon 4-11 £0.23; R A Fahey 2-11 £0.17.

Conditions Stakes

All Age Races: Conditions Stakes – 5 to 6 furlong races

ANALYSIS BY AGE

Age	Prop	Win	Runs	Wins%	£
2yo	5%	4	17	23.5%	0.26
3yo	19%	14	113	12.4%	-0.28
4yo	20%	15	110	13.6%	-0.43
5yo	19%	14	94	14.9%	-0.36
6yo	12%	9	65	13.8%	-0.53
7yo	12%	9	55	16.4%	0.09
8yo	7%	5	40	12.5%	-0.20
9yo	3%	2	24	8.3%	-0.61
10yo	3%	2	10	20.0%	0.00
11yo+	0%	0	9	0.0%	-1.00

ANALYSIS BY BHA RATING

Rating	Prop	Win	Runs	Wins%	£
120..139	0%	0	0	0.0%	0.00
110..119	4%	3	18	16.7%	-0.34
100..109	58%	43	195	22.1%	-0.08
90..99	27%	20	156	12.8%	-0.12
70..89	11%	8	97	8.2%	-0.59
50..69	0%	0	22	0.0%	-1.00
..49	0%	0	29	0.0%	-1.00
Unrated	0%	0	20	0.0%	-1.00

ANALYSIS BY WEIGHT CARRIED

Weight	Prop	Win	Runs	Wins%	£
10-01+	0%	0	0	0.0%	0.00
9-8 ..10-00	4%	3	29	10.3%	-0.52
9-0..9-07	23%	17	138	12.3%	-0.42
8-8..8-13	49%	36	229	15.7%	-0.22
8-0..8-07	23%	17	134	12.7%	-0.31
..7-13	1%	1	7	14.3%	-0.38

ANALYSIS BY DAYS SINCE LAST RUN

Days	Prop	Win	Runs	Wins%	£
1..7	16%	12	69	17.4%	-0.14
8..14	24%	18	114	15.8%	-0.34
15..28	16%	12	128	9.4%	-0.61
29..60	18%	13	90	14.4%	-0.14
61..100	1%	1	17	5.9%	-0.87
101+	24%	18	117	15.4%	-0.12
Unraced	0%	0	2	0.0%	-1.00

ANALYSIS BY TODAY'S STARTING PRICE

Price	Prop	Win	Runs	Wins%	£
Odds On	12%	9	16	56.3%	-0.03
Ev - 2/1	15%	11	42	26.2%	-0.36
9/4 - 4/1	38%	28	112	25.0%	0.01
9/2 - 6/1	16%	12	67	17.9%	0.11
13/2-10/1	15%	11	92	12.0%	0.07
11/1-16/1	4%	3	71	4.2%	-0.42
18/1-33/1	0%	0	55	0.0%	-1.00
40/1+	0%	0	82	0.0%	-1.00

ANALYSIS BY STARTING PRICE LAST TIME

Price	Prop	Win	Runs	Wins%	£
Odds On	1%	1	3	33.3%	-0.27
Ev - 2/1	4%	3	21	14.3%	-0.61
9/4 - 4/1	20%	15	55	27.3%	0.51
9/2 - 6/1	14%	10	57	17.5%	-0.31
13/2-10/1	16%	12	120	10.0%	-0.51
11/1-16/1	23%	17	106	16.0%	-0.26
18/1-33/1	19%	14	103	13.6%	-0.16
40/1+	3%	2	70	2.9%	-0.84
Unraced	0%	0	2	0.0%	-1.00

ANALYSIS BY DISTANCE BEATEN LAST TIME

Lengths	Prop	Win	Runs	Wins%	£
..-10	0%	0	0	0.0%	0.00
-10..0	14%	10	46	21.7%	0.12
0.1..2	28%	21	92	22.8%	-0.23
2.1..5	27%	20	137	14.6%	-0.35
5.1..10	15%	11	146	7.5%	-0.55
10.1..20	12%	9	82	11.0%	-0.22
20.0..30	4%	3	23	13.0%	0.22
30.1+	0%	0	9	0.0%	-1.00
Not Compl	0%	0	0	0.0%	0.00
Unraced	0%	0	2	0.0%	-1.00

ANALYSIS BY RUN NUMBER

Run No	Prop	Win	Runs	Wins%	£
FTO	0%	0	2	0.0%	-1.00
2nd Run	1%	1	10	10.0%	-0.45
3rd Run	1%	1	8	12.5%	-0.59
4th+ Run	97%	72	517	13.9%	-0.30

ANALYSIS BY POSITION LAST TIME

Pos LT	Prop	Win	Runs	Wins%	£
Won	14%	10	46	21.7%	0.12
2nd or 3rd	30%	22	91	24.2%	-0.07
Unplaced	57%	42	397	10.6%	-0.42
Not Compl	0%	0	3	0.0%	-1.00

OTHER FACTORS (WINS-RUNS, £)

Course Winner:	23-120	£0.00
Distance Winner:	60-424	-£0.31
Going Winner:	41-300	-£0.36
Beaten Favourite:	10-37	£0.00
BHA Top Rated:	19-64	£0.09
Up in class:	8-127	-£0.64
Same class:	18-113	-£0.19
Down in class:	48-295	-£0.22
7-Day Winners:	2-4	£1.06
Colts and Geldings:	60-419	-£0.31
Fillies:	9-83	-£0.38
Absolute Favourites:	22-69	-£0.24

TRAINERS (WINS-RUNS, £)

R Hannon 7-29 £0.38; D W Barker 3-10 £0.60; J M Bradley 3-11 £0.39; Saeed Bin Suroor 5-14 £0.22; R A Fahey 5-14 £0.10.

Race Profiles

All Age Races: Conditions Stakes – 7 to 9 furlong races

ANALYSIS BY AGE

Age	Prop	Win	Runs	Wins%	£
2yo	0%	0	0	0.0%	0.00
3yo	18%	13	103	12.6%	-0.36
4yo	36%	26	150	17.3%	0.08
5yo	23%	17	77	22.1%	0.02
6yo	14%	10	50	20.0%	0.10
7yo	3%	2	38	5.3%	-0.85
8yo	3%	2	17	11.8%	-0.63
9yo	3%	2	12	16.7%	-0.22
10yo	1%	1	5	20.0%	-0.62
11yo+	0%	0	0	0.0%	0.00

ANALYSIS BY BHA RATING

Rating	Prop	Win	Runs	Wins%	£
120..139	0%	0	0	0.0%	0.00
110..119	18%	13	36	36.1%	0.14
100..109	56%	41	194	21.1%	-0.02
90..99	15%	11	108	10.2%	-0.23
70..89	8%	6	61	9.8%	-0.26
50..69	0%	0	12	0.0%	-1.00
..49	0%	0	10	0.0%	-1.00
Unrated	3%	2	31	6.5%	-0.16

ANALYSIS BY WEIGHT CARRIED

Weight	Prop	Win	Runs	Wins%	£
10-01+	0%	0	0	0.0%	0.00
9-8..10-00	5%	4	9	44.4%	0.53
9-0..9-07	34%	25	143	17.5%	-0.05
8-8..8-13	51%	37	227	16.3%	-0.17
8-0..8-07	10%	7	67	10.4%	-0.31
..7-13	0%	0	6	0.0%	-1.00

ANALYSIS BY DAYS SINCE LAST RUN

Days	Prop	Win	Runs	Wins%	£
1..7	4%	3	36	8.3%	-0.76
8..14	8%	6	85	7.1%	-0.54
15..28	32%	23	123	18.7%	0.11
29..60	26%	19	85	22.4%	0.27
61..100	0%	0	18	0.0%	-1.00
101+	29%	21	96	21.9%	-0.14
Unraced	1%	1	9	11.1%	0.00

ANALYSIS BY TODAY'S STARTING PRICE

Price	Prop	Win	Runs	Wins%	£
Odds On	12%	9	22	40.9%	-0.29
Ev - 2/1	27%	20	55	36.4%	-0.08
9/4 - 4/1	32%	23	90	25.6%	0.08
9/2 - 6/1	4%	3	53	5.7%	-0.68
13/2-10/1	15%	11	69	15.9%	0.33
11/1-16/1	7%	5	71	7.0%	0.03
18/1-33/1	3%	2	51	3.9%	-0.22
40/1+	0%	0	41	0.0%	-1.00

ANALYSIS BY STARTING PRICE LAST TIME

Price	Prop	Win	Runs	Wins%	£
Odds On	4%	3	11	27.3%	-0.36
Ev - 2/1	5%	4	21	19.0%	-0.34
9/4 - 4/1	21%	15	59	25.4%	0.04
9/2 - 6/1	15%	11	49	22.4%	-0.15
13/2-10/1	27%	20	95	21.1%	0.20
11/1-16/1	11%	8	79	10.1%	-0.48
18/1-33/1	12%	9	80	11.3%	-0.07
40/1+	3%	2	49	4.1%	-0.53
Unraced	1%	1	9	11.1%	0.00

ANALYSIS BY DISTANCE BEATEN LAST TIME

Lengths	Prop	Win	Runs	Wins%	£
..-10	0%	0	0	0.0%	0.00
-10..0	7%	5	42	11.9%	-0.53
0.1..2	26%	19	64	29.7%	0.10
2.1..5	22%	16	102	15.7%	-0.23
5.1..10	25%	18	107	16.8%	-0.06
10.1..20	12%	9	82	11.0%	-0.00
20.0..30	0%	0	18	0.0%	-1.00
30.1+	7%	5	28	17.9%	-0.12
Not Compl	0%	0	0	0.0%	0.00
Unraced	1%	1	9	11.1%	0.00

ANALYSIS BY RUN NUMBER

Run No	Prop	Win	Runs	Wins%	£
FTO	1%	1	9	11.1%	0.00
2nd Run	3%	2	13	15.4%	-0.46
3rd Run	3%	2	16	12.5%	0.19
4th+ Run	93%	68	414	16.4%	-0.15

ANALYSIS BY POSITION LAST TIME

Pos LT	Prop	Win	Runs	Wins%	£
Won	7%	5	42	11.9%	-0.53
2nd or 3rd	30%	22	90	24.4%	0.06
Unplaced	60%	44	309	14.2%	-0.18
Not Compl	3%	2	11	18.2%	0.50

OTHER FACTORS (WINS-RUNS, £)

Course Winner:	13-75	-£0.27
Distance Winner:	49-268	-£0.06
Going Winner:	37-207	-£0.13
Beaten Favourite:	8-25	£0.15
BHA Top Rated:	17-62	-£0.13
Up in class:	9-80	-£0.57
Same class:	13-94	-£0.05
Down in class:	50-269	-£0.06
7-Day Winners:	0-1	-£1.00
Colts and Geldings:	63-380	-£0.14
Fillies:	2-26	-£0.06
Absolute Favourites:	26-66	-£0.08

TRAINERS (WINS-RUNS, £)

A M Balding 3-12 £1.19; M A Jarvis 5-17 £0.68; R Hannon 3-20 £0.40; J R Fanshawe 5-12 £0.64; D Nicholls 2-11 £0.09.

Conditions Stakes

All Age Races: Conditions Stakes – 10 to 14 furlong races

ANALYSIS BY AGE

Age	Prop	Win	Runs	Wins%	£
2yo	0%	0	0	0.0%	0.00
3yo	17%	10	56	17.9%	-0.44
4yo	37%	22	106	20.8%	0.51
5yo	27%	16	99	16.2%	-0.46
6yo	12%	7	44	15.9%	-0.32
7yo	5%	3	20	15.0%	-0.08
8yo	3%	2	17	11.8%	-0.44
9yo	0%	0	1	0.0%	-1.00
10yo	0%	0	0	0.0%	0.00
11yo+	0%	0	1	0.0%	-1.00

ANALYSIS BY BHA RATING

Rating	Prop	Win	Runs	Wins%	£
120..139	0%	0	1	0.0%	-1.00
110..119	17%	10	29	34.5%	-0.03
100..109	60%	36	171	21.1%	-0.29
90..99	15%	9	68	13.2%	-0.10
70..89	3%	2	21	9.5%	2.71
50..69	0%	0	10	0.0%	-1.00
..49	0%	0	9	0.0%	-1.00
Unrated	5%	3	35	8.6%	-0.61

ANALYSIS BY WEIGHT CARRIED

Weight	Prop	Win	Runs	Wins%	£
10-01+	0%	0	0	0.0%	0.00
9-8..10-00	5%	3	15	20.0%	0.03
9-0..9-07	50%	30	165	18.2%	-0.22
8-8..8-13	38%	23	120	19.2%	0.21
8-0..8-07	7%	4	41	9.8%	-0.68
..7-13	0%	0	3	0.0%	-1.00

ANALYSIS BY DAYS SINCE LAST RUN

Days	Prop	Win	Runs	Wins%	£
1..7	3%	2	13	15.4%	0.92
8..14	8%	5	43	11.6%	-0.48
15..28	32%	19	88	21.6%	-0.12
29..60	18%	11	56	19.6%	-0.41
61..100	2%	1	14	7.1%	-0.88
101+	37%	22	119	18.5%	0.20
Unraced	0%	0	11	0.0%	-1.00

ANALYSIS BY TODAY'S STARTING PRICE

Price	Prop	Win	Runs	Wins%	£
Odds On	18%	11	18	61.1%	0.08
Ev - 2/1	32%	19	44	43.2%	0.07
9/4 - 4/1	35%	21	87	24.1%	0.01
9/2 - 6/1	5%	3	38	7.9%	-0.57
13/2-10/1	5%	3	54	5.6%	-0.47
11/1-16/1	2%	1	36	2.8%	-0.58
18/1-33/1	2%	1	28	3.6%	-0.25
40/1+	2%	1	39	2.6%	0.72

ANALYSIS BY STARTING PRICE LAST TIME

Price	Prop	Win	Runs	Wins%	£
Odds On	2%	1	6	16.7%	-0.46
Ev - 2/1	10%	6	19	31.6%	-0.23
9/4 - 4/1	23%	14	45	31.1%	0.21
9/2 - 6/1	13%	8	33	24.2%	-0.18
13/2-10/1	18%	11	64	17.2%	0.79
11/1-16/1	17%	10	66	15.2%	-0.58
18/1-33/1	13%	8	60	13.3%	-0.13
40/1+	3%	2	40	5.0%	-0.80
Unraced	0%	0	11	0.0%	-1.00

ANALYSIS BY DISTANCE BEATEN LAST TIME

Lengths	Prop	Win	Runs	Wins%	£
..-10	0%	0	0	0.0%	0.00
-10..0	13%	8	26	30.8%	-0.03
0.1..2	20%	12	45	26.7%	-0.17
2.1..5	15%	9	62	14.5%	-0.21
5.1..10	22%	13	74	17.6%	-0.18
10.1..20	17%	10	76	13.2%	-0.53
20.0..30	7%	4	20	20.0%	2.79
30.1+	7%	4	30	13.3%	-0.38
Not Compl	0%	0	0	0.0%	0.00
Unraced	0%	0	11	0.0%	-1.00

ANALYSIS BY RUN NUMBER

Run No	Prop	Win	Runs	Wins%	£
FTO	0%	0	11	0.0%	-1.00
2nd Run	5%	3	20	15.0%	-0.52
3rd Run	5%	3	10	30.0%	0.68
4th+ Run	90%	54	303	17.8%	-0.09

ANALYSIS BY POSITION LAST TIME

Pos LT	Prop	Win	Runs	Wins%	£
Won	13%	8	26	30.8%	-0.03
2nd or 3rd	23%	14	74	18.9%	-0.39
Unplaced	63%	38	233	16.3%	-0.00
Not Compl	0%	0	11	0.0%	-1.00

OTHER FACTORS (WINS-RUNS, £)

Course Winner:	12-58	-£0.09
Distance Winner:	34-172	-£0.14
Going Winner:	29-140	-£0.21
Beaten Favourite:	5-21	-£0.06
BHA Top Rated:	19-56	-£0.13
Up in class:	4-47	£0.63
Same class:	13-74	£0.03
Down in class:	43-212	-£0.29
Colts and Geldings:	57-309	-£0.28
Fillies:	3-35	£1.29
Absolute Favourites:	29-58	£0.14

TRAINERS (WINS-RUNS, £)

Saeed Bin Suroor 22-45 £0.73; M Johnston 4-14 £0.21; H R A Cecil 4-11 £0.00.

Race Profiles

All Age Races: Conditions Stakes – 15+ furlong races

ANALYSIS BY AGE

Age	Prop	Win	Runs	Wins%	£
2yo	0%	0	0	0.0%	0.00
3yo	30%	3	7	42.9%	2.79
4yo	50%	5	22	22.7%	-0.01
5yo	10%	1	17	5.9%	-0.35
6yo	0%	0	18	0.0%	-1.00
7yo	0%	0	9	0.0%	-1.00
8yo	0%	0	7	0.0%	-1.00
9yo	0%	0	7	0.0%	-1.00
10yo	0%	0	2	0.0%	-1.00
11yo+	10%	1	3	33.3%	1.33

ANALYSIS BY BHA RATING

Rating	Prop	Win	Runs	Wins%	£
120..139	0%	0	0	0.0%	0.00
110..119	0%	0	2	0.0%	-1.00
100..109	40%	4	21	19.0%	0.10
90..99	20%	2	18	11.1%	-0.46
70..89	30%	3	24	12.5%	0.28
50..69	0%	0	11	0.0%	-1.00
..49	0%	0	5	0.0%	-1.00
Unrated	10%	1	11	9.1%	-0.75

ANALYSIS BY WEIGHT CARRIED

Weight	Prop	Win	Runs	Wins%	£
10-01+	0%	0	0	0.0%	0.00
9-8..10-00	0%	0	1	0.0%	-1.00
9-0..9-07	60%	6	74	8.1%	-0.50
8-8..8-13	10%	1	10	10.0%	-0.73
8-0..8-07	30%	3	6	50.0%	3.42
..7-13	0%	0	1	0.0%	-1.00

ANALYSIS BY DAYS SINCE LAST RUN

Days	Prop	Win	Runs	Wins%	£
1..7	30%	3	10	30.0%	2.45
8..14	0%	0	7	0.0%	-1.00
15..28	40%	4	30	13.3%	-0.23
29..60	30%	3	21	14.3%	-0.58
61..100	0%	0	5	0.0%	-1.00
101+	0%	0	17	0.0%	-1.00
Unraced	0%	0	2	0.0%	-1.00

ANALYSIS BY TODAY'S STARTING PRICE

Price	Prop	Win	Runs	Wins%	£
Odds On	0%	0	1	0.0%	-1.00
Ev - 2/1	40%	4	6	66.7%	0.75
9/4 - 4/1	10%	1	13	7.7%	-0.75
9/2 - 6/1	30%	3	15	20.0%	0.37
13/2-10/1	10%	1	13	7.7%	-0.15
11/1-16/1	0%	0	10	0.0%	-1.00
18/1-33/1	10%	1	10	10.0%	1.10
40/1+	0%	0	24	0.0%	-1.00

ANALYSIS BY STARTING PRICE LAST TIME

Price	Prop	Win	Runs	Wins%	£
Odds On	0%	0	1	0.0%	-1.00
Ev - 2/1	10%	1	3	33.3%	-0.08
9/4 - 4/1	10%	1	14	7.1%	-0.80
9/2 - 6/1	30%	3	10	30.0%	0.25
13/2-10/1	10%	1	20	5.0%	-0.65
11/1-16/1	10%	1	16	6.3%	0.31
18/1-33/1	30%	3	19	15.8%	0.07
40/1+	0%	0	7	0.0%	-1.00
Unraced	0%	0	2	0.0%	-1.00

ANALYSIS BY DISTANCE BEATEN LAST TIME

Lengths	Prop	Win	Runs	Wins%	£
..-10	0%	0	0	0.0%	0.00
-10..0	30%	3	11	27.3%	0.52
0.1..2	0%	0	11	0.0%	-1.00
2.1..5	0%	0	17	0.0%	-1.00
5.1..10	30%	3	22	13.6%	0.58
10.1..20	10%	1	10	10.0%	-0.73
20.0..30	10%	1	6	16.7%	-0.54
30.1+	20%	2	13	15.4%	-0.29
Not Compl	0%	0	0	0.0%	0.00
Unraced	0%	0	2	0.0%	-1.00

ANALYSIS BY RUN NUMBER

Run No	Prop	Win	Runs	Wins%	£
FTO	0%	0	2	0.0%	-1.00
2nd Run	0%	0	3	0.0%	-1.00
3rd Run	0%	0	2	0.0%	-1.00
4th+ Run	100%	10	85	11.8%	-0.22

ANALYSIS BY POSITION LAST TIME

Pos LT	Prop	Win	Runs	Wins%	£
Won	30%	3	11	27.3%	0.52
2nd or 3rd	0%	0	18	0.0%	-1.00
Unplaced	70%	7	61	11.5%	-0.19
Not Compl	0%	0	2	0.0%	-1.00

OTHER FACTORS (WINS-RUNS, £)

Course Winner:	1-15	-£0.57
Distance Winner:	0-11	-£1.00
Going Winner:	6-35	£0.21
Beaten Favourite:	3-10	£0.00
BHA Top Rated:	1-9	-£0.69
Up in class:	2-38	-£0.36
Same class:	2-21	-£0.36
Down in class:	6-31	-£0.08
7-Day Winners:	1-1	£5.50
Colts and Geldings:	10-82	-£0.19
Fillies:	0-10	-£1.00
Absolute Favourites:	4-10	£0.05

Maiden Races

All Age Races: Maiden Races

ANALYSIS BY AGE

Age	Prop	Win	Runs	Wins%	£
2yo	0%	0	0	0.0%	0.00
3yo	92%	991	8356	11.9%	-0.33
4yo	7%	75	1704	4.4%	-0.53
5yo	1%	9	441	2.0%	-0.67
6yo	0%	3	159	1.9%	-0.57
7yo	0%	2	70	2.9%	-0.22
8yo	0%	0	18	0.0%	-1.00
9yo	0%	0	11	0.0%	-1.00
10yo	0%	0	2	0.0%	-1.00
11yo+	0%	0	5	0.0%	-1.00

ANALYSIS BY BHA RATING

Rating	Prop	Win	Runs	Wins%	£
120..139	0%	0	0	0.0%	0.00
110..119	0%	0	0	0.0%	0.00
100..109	1%	6	9	66.7%	1.01
90..99	1%	10	28	35.7%	-0.38
70..89	29%	316	1219	25.9%	-0.16
50..69	12%	130	1329	9.8%	-0.32
..49	2%	21	1129	1.9%	-0.58
Unrated	55%	597	7043	8.5%	-0.40

ANALYSIS BY WEIGHT CARRIED

Weight	Prop	Win	Runs	Wins%	£
10-01+	0%	0	0	0.0%	0.00
9-8..10-00	4%	45	1004	4.5%	-0.46
9-0..9-07	37%	395	3846	10.3%	-0.41
8-8..8-13	51%	553	4782	11.6%	-0.33
8-0..8-07	8%	86	1116	7.7%	-0.46
..7-13	0%	1	18	5.6%	3.50

ANALYSIS BY DAYS SINCE LAST RUN

Days	Prop	Win	Runs	Wins%	£
1..7	4%	39	462	8.4%	-0.53
8..14	18%	196	1757	11.2%	-0.38
15..28	32%	342	2656	12.9%	-0.30
29..60	15%	160	1541	10.4%	-0.38
61..100	4%	45	452	10.0%	-0.30
101+	19%	201	2035	9.9%	-0.43
Unraced	9%	97	1863	5.2%	-0.43

ANALYSIS BY TODAY'S STARTING PRICE

Price	Prop	Win	Runs	Wins%	£
Odds On	22%	235	381	61.7%	-0.03
Ev - 2/1	24%	261	683	38.2%	-0.03
9/4 - 4/1	24%	263	1182	22.3%	-0.10
9/2 - 6/1	9%	100	727	13.8%	-0.15
13/2-10/1	8%	89	1158	7.7%	-0.30
11/1-16/1	7%	74	1280	5.8%	-0.16
18/1-33/1	4%	43	1946	2.2%	-0.45
40/1+	1%	15	3409	0.4%	-0.72

ANALYSIS BY STARTING PRICE LAST TIME

Price	Prop	Win	Runs	Wins%	£
Odds On	5%	53	136	39.0%	0.03
Ev - 2/1	10%	106	351	30.2%	-0.15
9/4 - 4/1	19%	208	840	24.8%	-0.08
9/2 - 6/1	12%	126	632	19.9%	-0.09
13/2-10/1	15%	160	1150	13.9%	-0.24
11/1-16/1	13%	143	1333	10.7%	-0.39
18/1-33/1	12%	129	1915	6.7%	-0.41
40/1+	5%	58	2546	2.3%	-0.61
Unraced	9%	97	1863	5.2%	-0.43

ANALYSIS BY DISTANCE BEATEN LAST TIME

Lengths	Prop	Win	Runs	Wins%	£
..-10	0%	0	0	0.0%	0.00
-10..0	0%	1	3	33.3%	1.00
0.1..2	31%	330	1085	30.4%	-0.03
2.1..5	26%	278	1401	19.8%	-0.12
5.1..10	20%	219	2121	10.3%	-0.30
10.1..20	11%	121	2509	4.8%	-0.47
20.0..30	2%	19	957	2.0%	-0.72
30.1+	1%	15	827	1.8%	-0.74
Not Compl	0%	0	0	0.0%	0.00
Unraced	9%	97	1863	5.2%	-0.43

ANALYSIS BY RUN NUMBER

Run No	Prop	Win	Runs	Wins%	£
FTO	9%	97	1863	5.2%	-0.43
2nd Run	21%	222	2390	9.3%	-0.44
3rd Run	25%	268	2681	10.0%	-0.33
4th+ Run	46%	493	3832	12.9%	-0.36

ANALYSIS BY POSITION LAST TIME

Pos LT	Prop	Win	Runs	Wins%	£
Won	0%	0	1	0.0%	-1.00
2nd or 3rd	48%	522	1991	26.2%	-0.11
Unplaced	43%	460	6885	6.7%	-0.45
Not Compl	9%	98	1889	5.2%	-0.43

OTHER FACTORS (WINS-RUNS, £)

Course Winner:	1-1	£1.50
Distance Winner:	1-2	£0.25
Beaten Favourite:	181-559	-£0.07
BHA Top Rated:	221-842	-£0.12
Up in class:	92-1622	-£0.60
Same class:	608-5526	-£0.33
Down in class:	283-1755	-£0.28
Colts and Geldings:	650-5747	-£0.32
Fillies:	286-3597	-£0.48
Absolute Favourites:	462-1020	-£0.05

TRAINERS (WINS-RUNS, £)

A Bailey 3-17 £7.35; Miss J Feilden 1-15 £5.73; G M Moore 2-25 £3.16; D Nicholls 11-63 £1.18; T D Barron 14-71 £0.88; D Morris 1-11 £5.09; R M Whitaker 3-26 £2.03; P Winkworth 2-18 £2.92; R M Beckett 12-83 £0.58; J M Bradley 3-71 £0.59; J R Jenkins 4-29 £1.19; K A Morgan 1-18 £1.83; B Palling 1-23 £1.22; Dr J D Scargill 2-11 £2.55; D M Simcock 9-51 £0.52; A B Haynes 3-23 £1.04; K R Burke 8-54 £0.44; Miss A Stokell 1-17 £1.41; B W Hills 60-191 £0.12; JRGASK 2-14 £1.50.

Race Profiles

All Age Races: Maiden Races – 2 to 7 runners

ANALYSIS BY AGE

Age	Prop	Win	Runs	Wins%	£
2yo	0%	0	0	0.0%	0.00
3yo	93%	251	1299	19.3%	-0.19
4yo	7%	18	264	6.8%	-0.38
5yo	0%	0	53	0.0%	-1.00
6yo	0%	0	19	0.0%	-1.00
7yo	0%	1	11	9.1%	-0.70
8yo	0%	0	4	0.0%	-1.00
9yo	0%	0	2	0.0%	-1.00
10yo	0%	0	1	0.0%	-1.00
11yo+	0%	0	0	0.0%	0.00

ANALYSIS BY BHA RATING

Rating	Prop	Win	Runs	Wins%	£
120..139	0%	0	0	0.0%	0.00
110..119	0%	0	0	0.0%	0.00
100..109	0%	0	0	0.0%	0.00
90..99	1%	2	9	22.2%	-0.72
70..89	37%	99	283	35.0%	-0.07
50..69	14%	39	265	14.7%	-0.24
..49	1%	4	179	2.2%	-0.30
Unrated	47%	126	915	13.8%	-0.32

ANALYSIS BY WEIGHT CARRIED

Weight	Prop	Win	Runs	Wins%	£
10-01+	0%	0	0	0.0%	0.00
9-8..10-00	3%	7	154	4.5%	-0.72
9-0..9-07	36%	97	599	16.2%	-0.28
8-8..8-13	54%	145	705	20.6%	-0.04
8-0..8-07	8%	21	192	10.9%	-0.65
..7-13	0%	0	3	0.0%	-1.00

ANALYSIS BY DAYS SINCE LAST RUN

Days	Prop	Win	Runs	Wins%	£
1..7	4%	10	80	12.5%	-0.60
8..14	19%	52	309	16.8%	-0.11
15..28	34%	91	459	19.8%	-0.33
29..60	15%	41	244	16.8%	-0.10
61..100	6%	16	76	21.1%	0.63
101+	16%	43	248	17.3%	-0.37
Unraced	6%	17	237	7.2%	-0.57

ANALYSIS BY TODAY'S STARTING PRICE

Price	Prop	Win	Runs	Wins%	£
Odds On	35%	95	146	65.1%	0.01
Ev - 2/1	25%	67	180	37.2%	-0.05
9/4 - 4/1	21%	57	256	22.3%	-0.12
9/2 - 6/1	5%	14	115	12.2%	-0.27
13/2-10/1	7%	19	214	8.9%	-0.22
11/1-16/1	4%	12	178	6.7%	0.04
18/1-33/1	1%	4	242	1.7%	-0.57
40/1+	1%	2	322	0.6%	-0.58

ANALYSIS BY STARTING PRICE LAST TIME

Price	Prop	Win	Runs	Wins%	£
Odds On	7%	20	37	54.1%	0.32
Ev - 2/1	11%	30	73	41.1%	0.01
9/4 - 4/1	19%	50	176	28.4%	-0.19
9/2 - 6/1	10%	28	111	25.2%	-0.30
13/2-10/1	16%	42	193	21.8%	-0.26
11/1-16/1	13%	36	218	16.5%	-0.24
18/1-33/1	11%	30	272	11.0%	-0.38
40/1+	6%	17	336	5.1%	-0.13
Unraced	6%	17	237	7.2%	-0.57

ANALYSIS BY DISTANCE BEATEN LAST TIME

Lengths	Prop	Win	Runs	Wins%	£
..-10	0%	0	0	0.0%	0.00
-10..0	0%	0	1	0.0%	-1.00
0.1..2	33%	89	225	39.6%	-0.07
2.1..5	25%	67	277	24.2%	-0.15
5.1..10	21%	57	331	17.2%	-0.11
10.1..20	11%	31	334	9.3%	-0.11
20.0..30	3%	7	138	5.1%	-0.48
30.1+	1%	2	110	1.8%	-0.94
Not Compl	0%	0	0	0.0%	0.00
Unraced	6%	17	237	7.2%	-0.57

ANALYSIS BY RUN NUMBER

Run No	Prop	Win	Runs	Wins%	£
FTO	6%	17	237	7.2%	-0.57
2nd Run	22%	59	287	20.6%	-0.14
3rd Run	18%	49	374	13.1%	-0.25
4th+ Run	54%	145	755	19.2%	-0.22

ANALYSIS BY POSITION LAST TIME

Pos LT	Prop	Win	Runs	Wins%	£
Won	0%	0	0	0.0%	0.00
2nd or 3rd	48%	129	404	31.9%	-0.18
Unplaced	46%	124	1010	12.3%	-0.23
Not Compl	6%	17	239	7.1%	-0.57

OTHER FACTORS (WINS-RUNS, £)

Beaten Favourite:	56-124	£0.14
BHA Top Rated:	69-201	-£0.23
Up in class:	23-266	-£0.37
Same class:	152-843	-£0.25
Down in class:	78-307	£0.03
Colts and Geldings:	157-877	-£0.11
Fillies:	79-563	-£0.50
Absolute Favourites:	138-260	-£0.03

TRAINERS (WINS-RUNS, £)

A B Haynes 2-11 £1.73; I Semple 6-18 £0.71; J H M Gosden 13-38 £0.24; K R Burke 3-14 £0.63; Sir Michael Stoute 17-40 £0.21; M R Channon 5-30 £0.23; J Noseda 13-29 £0.20; B W Hills 14-34 £0.13; G A Swinbank 5-29 £0.13; Eve Johnson-Houghton 2-10 £0.30; Saeed Bin Suroor 12-22 £0.09; Rae Guest 2-14 £0.11; E A L Dunlop 5-10 £0.04; A M Balding 7-24 £0.01; P W Chapple-Hyam 5-16 £0.02.

Maiden Races

All Age Races: Maiden Races – 8 to 14 runners

ANALYSIS BY AGE
Age	Prop	Win	Runs	Wins%	£
2yo	0%	0	0	0.0%	0.00
3yo	91%	650	5907	11.0%	-0.38
4yo	7%	53	1207	4.4%	-0.50
5yo	1%	9	332	2.7%	-0.56
6yo	0%	3	116	2.6%	-0.41
7yo	0%	1	48	2.1%	0.06
8yo	0%	0	13	0.0%	-1.00
9yo	0%	0	9	0.0%	-1.00
10yo	0%	0	1	0.0%	-1.00
11yo+	0%	0	4	0.0%	-1.00

ANALYSIS BY BHA RATING
Rating	Prop	Win	Runs	Wins%	£
120..139	0%	0	0	0.0%	0.00
110..119	0%	0	0	0.0%	0.00
100..109	1%	6	9	66.7%	1.01
90..99	1%	5	14	35.7%	-0.37
70..89	28%	200	818	24.4%	-0.17
50..69	11%	82	926	8.9%	-0.37
..49	2%	14	806	1.7%	-0.66
Unrated	57%	409	5057	8.1%	-0.41

ANALYSIS BY WEIGHT CARRIED
Weight	Prop	Win	Runs	Wins%	£
10-01+	0%	0	0	0.0%	0.00
9-8 ..10-00	5%	37	720	5.1%	-0.31
9-0..9-07	36%	259	2691	9.6%	-0.43
8-8..8-13	50%	360	3425	10.5%	-0.40
8-0..8-07	8%	60	790	7.6%	-0.40
..7-13	0%	0	11	0.0%	-1.00

ANALYSIS BY DAYS SINCE LAST RUN
Days	Prop	Win	Runs	Wins%	£
1..7	4%	26	320	8.1%	-0.45
8..14	19%	135	1226	11.0%	-0.37
15..28	32%	226	1889	12.0%	-0.36
29..60	14%	103	1088	9.5%	-0.45
61..100	4%	27	318	8.5%	-0.45
101+	18%	131	1482	8.8%	-0.47
Unraced	9%	68	1314	5.2%	-0.37

ANALYSIS BY TODAY'S STARTING PRICE
Price	Prop	Win	Runs	Wins%	£
Odds On	19%	133	223	59.6%	-0.05
Ev - 2/1	25%	178	457	38.9%	-0.01
9/4 - 4/1	25%	179	813	22.0%	-0.10
9/2 - 6/1	10%	71	523	13.6%	-0.16
13/2-10/1	9%	61	790	7.7%	-0.27
11/1-16/1	7%	53	923	5.7%	-0.18
18/1-33/1	5%	33	1406	2.3%	-0.41
40/1+	1%	8	2502	0.3%	-0.78

ANALYSIS BY STARTING PRICE LAST TIME
Price	Prop	Win	Runs	Wins%	£
Odds On	4%	29	85	34.1%	-0.14
Ev - 2/1	9%	68	243	28.0%	-0.19
9/4 - 4/1	19%	139	564	24.6%	-0.03
9/2 - 6/1	12%	84	443	19.0%	-0.16
13/2-10/1	15%	105	837	12.5%	-0.23
11/1-16/1	14%	99	937	10.6%	-0.39
18/1-33/1	13%	91	1363	6.7%	-0.37
40/1+	5%	33	1851	1.8%	-0.76
Unraced	9%	68	1314	5.2%	-0.37

ANALYSIS BY DISTANCE BEATEN LAST TIME
Lengths	Prop	Win	Runs	Wins%	£
..-10	0%	0	0	0.0%	0.00
-10..0	0%	1	2	50.0%	2.00
0.1..2	31%	220	754	29.2%	0.02
2.1..5	26%	183	959	19.1%	-0.15
5.1..10	20%	142	1501	9.5%	-0.37
10.1..20	11%	81	1832	4.4%	-0.50
20.0..30	1%	10	686	1.5%	-0.85
30.1+	2%	11	589	1.9%	-0.74
Not Compl	0%	0	0	0.0%	0.00
Unraced	9%	68	1314	5.2%	-0.37

ANALYSIS BY RUN NUMBER
Run No	Prop	Win	Runs	Wins%	£
FTO	9%	68	1314	5.2%	-0.37
2nd Run	20%	143	1721	8.3%	-0.52
3rd Run	26%	189	1935	9.8%	-0.33
4th+ Run	44%	316	2667	11.8%	-0.40

ANALYSIS BY POSITION LAST TIME
Pos LT	Prop	Win	Runs	Wins%	£
Won	0%	0	1	0.0%	-1.00
2nd or 3rd	49%	351	1369	25.6%	-0.10
Unplaced	41%	296	4934	6.0%	-0.50
Not Compl	10%	69	1333	5.2%	-0.37

OTHER FACTORS (WINS-RUNS, £)
Course Winner:	1-1	£1.50
Distance Winner:	1-2	£0.25
Beaten Favourite:	111-369	-£0.11
BHA Top Rated:	139-562	-£0.04
Up in class:	61-1149	-£0.62
Same class:	406-3914	-£0.36
Down in class:	181-1260	-£0.37
Colts and Geldings:	429-4064	-£0.33
Fillies:	185-2489	-£0.53
Absolute Favourites:	293-672	-£0.06

TRAINERS (WINS-RUNS, £)
A Bailey 3-13 £9.92; G M Moore 1-19 £4.32; D Nicholls 10-48 £1.66; K A Morgan 1-14 £2.64; T D Barron 10-58 £0.60; Miss A Stokell 1-10 £3.10; D M Simcock 6-35 £0.86; R M Whitaker 2-15 £1.98; B Palling 1-22 £1.32; K R Burke 5-32 £0.73; W J Haggas 24-86 £0.27; B W Hills 43-137 £0.15; M S Saunders 1-15 £1.27; E J O'Neill 4-26 £0.68; M Johnston 39-209 £0.08; L Lungo 1-10 £1.60; Miss J A Camacho 1-10 £1.60; Miss Gay Kelleway 2-16 £0.90; Paul Green 1-10 £1.10; S Dow 1-15 £0.73.

Race Profiles

All Age Races: Maiden Races – 15 runners or more

ANALYSIS BY AGE

Age	Prop	Win	Runs	Wins%	£
2yo	0%	0	0	0.0%	0.00
3yo	96%	90	1150	7.8%	-0.24
4yo	4%	4	233	1.7%	-0.86
5yo	0%	0	56	0.0%	-1.00
6yo	0%	0	24	0.0%	-1.00
7yo	0%	0	11	0.0%	-1.00
8yo	0%	0	1	0.0%	-1.00
9yo	0%	0	0	0.0%	0.00
10yo	0%	0	0	0.0%	0.00
11yo+	0%	0	1	0.0%	-1.00

ANALYSIS BY BHA RATING

Rating	Prop	Win	Runs	Wins%	£
120..139	0%	0	0	0.0%	0.00
110..119	0%	0	0	0.0%	0.00
100..109	0%	0	0	0.0%	0.00
90..99	3%	3	5	60.0%	0.23
70..89	18%	17	118	14.4%	-0.32
50..69	10%	9	138	6.5%	-0.19
..49	3%	3	144	2.1%	-0.48
Unrated	66%	62	1071	5.8%	-0.41

ANALYSIS BY WEIGHT CARRIED

Weight	Prop	Win	Runs	Wins%	£
10-01+	0%	0	0	0.0%	0.00
9-8..10-00	1%	1	130	0.8%	-0.96
9-0..9-07	41%	39	556	7.0%	-0.48
8-8..8-13	51%	48	652	7.4%	-0.28
8-0..8-07	5%	5	134	3.7%	-0.57
..7-13	1%	1	4	25.0%	19.25

ANALYSIS BY DAYS SINCE LAST RUN

Days	Prop	Win	Runs	Wins%	£
1..7	3%	3	62	4.8%	-0.85
8..14	10%	9	222	4.1%	-0.80
15..28	27%	25	308	8.1%	0.12
29..60	17%	16	209	7.7%	-0.33
61..100	2%	2	58	3.4%	-0.72
101+	29%	27	305	8.9%	-0.30
Unraced	13%	12	312	3.8%	-0.57

ANALYSIS BY TODAY'S STARTING PRICE

Price	Prop	Win	Runs	Wins%	£
Odds On	7%	7	12	58.3%	-0.10
Ev - 2/1	17%	16	46	34.8%	-0.11
9/4 - 4/1	29%	27	113	23.9%	-0.05
9/2 - 6/1	16%	15	89	16.9%	0.06
13/2-10/1	10%	9	154	5.8%	-0.51
11/1-16/1	10%	9	179	5.0%	-0.22
18/1-33/1	6%	6	298	2.0%	-0.49
40/1+	5%	5	585	0.9%	-0.52

ANALYSIS BY STARTING PRICE LAST TIME

Price	Prop	Win	Runs	Wins%	£
Odds On	4%	4	14	28.6%	0.27
Ev - 2/1	9%	8	35	22.9%	-0.23
9/4 - 4/1	20%	19	100	19.0%	-0.15
9/2 - 6/1	15%	14	78	17.9%	0.57
13/2-10/1	14%	13	120	10.8%	-0.29
11/1-16/1	9%	8	178	4.5%	-0.59
18/1-33/1	9%	8	280	2.9%	-0.63
40/1+	9%	8	359	2.2%	-0.29
Unraced	13%	12	312	3.8%	-0.57

ANALYSIS BY DISTANCE BEATEN LAST TIME

Lengths	Prop	Win	Runs	Wins%	£
..-10	0%	0	0	0.0%	0.00
-10..0	0%	0	0	0.0%	0.00
0.1..2	22%	21	106	19.8%	-0.34
2.1..5	30%	28	165	17.0%	0.12
5.1..10	21%	20	289	6.9%	-0.15
10.1..20	10%	9	343	2.6%	-0.65
20.0..30	2%	2	133	1.5%	-0.28
30.1+	2%	2	128	1.6%	-0.60
Not Compl	0%	0	0	0.0%	0.00
Unraced	13%	12	312	3.8%	-0.57

ANALYSIS BY RUN NUMBER

Run No	Prop	Win	Runs	Wins%	£
FTO	13%	12	312	3.8%	-0.57
2nd Run	21%	20	382	5.2%	-0.30
3rd Run	32%	30	372	8.1%	-0.39
4th+ Run	34%	32	410	7.8%	-0.33

ANALYSIS BY POSITION LAST TIME

Pos LT	Prop	Win	Runs	Wins%	£
Won	0%	0	0	0.0%	0.00
2nd or 3rd	45%	42	218	19.3%	-0.05
Unplaced	43%	40	941	4.3%	-0.40
Not Compl	13%	12	317	3.8%	-0.58

OTHER FACTORS (WINS-RUNS, £)

Beaten Favourite:	14-66	-£0.25
BHA Top Rated:	13-79	-£0.35
Up in class:	8-207	-£0.78
Same class:	50-769	-£0.15
Down in class:	24-188	-£0.15
Colts and Geldings:	64-806	-£0.50
Fillies:	22-545	-£0.20
Absolute Favourites:	31-88	-£0.01

TRAINERS (WINS-RUNS, £)

J L Dunlop 4-21 £1.51; T D Barron 2-10 £2.80; T D Easterby 2-24 £0.92; M A Jarvis 9-25 £0.44; W J Haggas 2-19 £0.26; N Tinkler 1-11 £0.36; Saeed Bin Suroor 4-15 £0.26; J Noseda 3-18 £0.05.

Maiden Races

All Age Races: Maiden Races – good or faster going

ANALYSIS BY AGE

Age	Prop	Win	Runs	Wins%	£
2yo	0%	0	0	0.0%	0.00
3yo	92%	730	6079	12.0%	-0.34
4yo	7%	54	1223	4.4%	-0.52
5yo	1%	8	328	2.4%	-0.57
6yo	0%	3	114	2.6%	-0.40
7yo	0%	2	54	3.7%	0.00
8yo	0%	0	15	0.0%	-1.00
9yo	0%	0	7	0.0%	-1.00
10yo	0%	0	0	0.0%	0.00
11yo+	0%	0	4	0.0%	-1.00

ANALYSIS BY BHA RATING

Rating	Prop	Win	Runs	Wins%	£
120..139	0%	0	0	0.0%	0.00
110..119	0%	0	0	0.0%	0.00
100..109	1%	6	9	66.7%	1.01
90..99	1%	8	22	36.4%	-0.37
70..89	31%	245	921	26.6%	-0.17
50..69	11%	89	956	9.3%	-0.39
..49	2%	16	846	1.9%	-0.55
Unrated	54%	433	5062	8.6%	-0.39

ANALYSIS BY WEIGHT CARRIED

Weight	Prop	Win	Runs	Wins%	£
10-01+	0%	0	0	0.0%	0.00
9-8..10-00	4%	34	724	4.7%	-0.45
9-0..9-07	36%	287	2697	10.6%	-0.38
8-8..8-13	53%	424	3596	11.8%	-0.32
8-0..8-07	7%	52	798	6.5%	-0.56
..7-13	0%	0	9	0.0%	-1.00

ANALYSIS BY DAYS SINCE LAST RUN

Days	Prop	Win	Runs	Wins%	£
1..7	3%	27	346	7.8%	-0.60
8..14	17%	136	1239	11.0%	-0.43
15..28	34%	267	1999	13.4%	-0.26
29..60	14%	113	1094	10.3%	-0.35
61..100	4%	30	310	9.7%	-0.30
101+	18%	146	1507	9.7%	-0.48
Unraced	10%	78	1329	5.9%	-0.38

ANALYSIS BY TODAY'S STARTING PRICE

Price	Prop	Win	Runs	Wins%	£
Odds On	23%	182	294	61.9%	-0.03
Ev - 2/1	25%	196	520	37.7%	-0.03
9/4 - 4/1	25%	196	861	22.8%	-0.08
9/2 - 6/1	8%	65	506	12.8%	-0.22
13/2-10/1	8%	61	834	7.3%	-0.33
11/1-16/1	7%	54	905	6.0%	-0.13
18/1-33/1	4%	31	1378	2.2%	-0.44
40/1+	2%	12	2526	0.5%	-0.70

ANALYSIS BY STARTING PRICE LAST TIME

Price	Prop	Win	Runs	Wins%	£
Odds On	5%	38	100	38.0%	0.00
Ev - 2/1	9%	74	255	29.0%	-0.18
9/4 - 4/1	20%	159	641	24.8%	-0.11
9/2 - 6/1	13%	104	480	21.7%	0.01
13/2-10/1	14%	110	824	13.3%	-0.25
11/1-16/1	12%	99	950	10.4%	-0.41
18/1-33/1	12%	94	1369	6.9%	-0.42
40/1+	5%	41	1876	2.2%	-0.63
Unraced	10%	78	1329	5.9%	-0.38

ANALYSIS BY DISTANCE BEATEN LAST TIME

Lengths	Prop	Win	Runs	Wins%	£
..-10	0%	0	0	0.0%	0.00
-10..0	0%	1	2	50.0%	2.00
0.1..2	31%	245	810	30.2%	-0.02
2.1..5	25%	198	1027	19.3%	-0.16
5.1..10	20%	158	1549	10.2%	-0.32
10.1..20	11%	90	1814	5.0%	-0.45
20.0..30	2%	15	703	2.1%	-0.79
30.1+	2%	12	590	2.0%	-0.70
Not Compl	0%	0	0	0.0%	0.00
Unraced	10%	78	1329	5.9%	-0.38

ANALYSIS BY RUN NUMBER

Run No	Prop	Win	Runs	Wins%	£
FTO	10%	78	1329	5.9%	-0.38
2nd Run	21%	167	1726	9.7%	-0.40
3rd Run	22%	178	1923	9.3%	-0.38
4th+ Run	47%	374	2846	13.1%	-0.36

ANALYSIS BY POSITION LAST TIME

Pos LT	Prop	Win	Runs	Wins%	£
Won	0%	0	1	0.0%	-1.00
2nd or 3rd	48%	380	1454	26.1%	-0.11
Unplaced	42%	338	5022	6.7%	-0.46
Not Compl	10%	79	1347	5.9%	-0.38

OTHER FACTORS (WINS-RUNS, £)

Course Winner:	1-1	£1.50
Distance Winner:	1-2	£0.25
Beaten Favourite:	129-406	-£0.09
BHA Top Rated:	158-601	-£0.25
Up in class:	64-1189	-£0.65
Same class:	436-4009	-£0.33
Down in class:	219-1297	-£0.28
Colts and Geldings:	482-4121	-£0.30
Fillies:	206-2622	-£0.50
Absolute Favourites:	347-755	-£0.04

TRAINERS (WINS-RUNS, £)

A Bailey 3-13 £9.92; Miss J Feilden 1-13 £6.77; G M Moore 2-20 £4.19; R M Whitaker 3-20 £2.94; P Winkworth 2-13 £4.42; D Nicholls 9-46 £1.22; T D Barron 11-49 £1.13; J R Jenkins 4-18 £2.52; J M Bradley 2-55 £0.75; B Palling 1-17 £2.00; D M Simcock 8-36 £0.94; Miss A Stokell 1-16 £1.56; J R GASK 2-11 £2.18; W J Haggas 23-97 £0.24; A B Haynes 2-15 £1.27; E F Vaughan 2-23 £0.83; M S Saunders 1-15 £1.27; Miss J A Camacho 1-10 £1.60; B W Hills 47-151 £0.09; T P Tate 3-19 £0.70.

Race Profiles

All Age Races: Maiden Races – good to soft or softer going

ANALYSIS BY AGE

Age	Prop	Win	Runs	Wins%	£
2yo	0%	0	0	0.0%	0.00
3yo	92%	261	2277	11.5%	-0.31
4yo	7%	21	481	4.4%	-0.55
5yo	0%	1	113	0.9%	-0.95
6yo	0%	0	45	0.0%	-1.00
7yo	0%	0	16	0.0%	-1.00
8yo	0%	0	3	0.0%	-1.00
9yo	0%	0	4	0.0%	-1.00
10yo	0%	0	2	0.0%	-1.00
11yo+	0%	0	1	0.0%	-1.00

ANALYSIS BY BHA RATING

Rating	Prop	Win	Runs	Wins%	£
120..139	0%	0	0	0.0%	0.00
110..119	0%	0	0	0.0%	0.00
100..109	0%	0	0	0.0%	0.00
90..99	1%	2	6	33.3%	-0.39
70..89	25%	71	298	23.8%	-0.13
50..69	14%	41	373	11.0%	-0.15
..49	2%	5	283	1.8%	-0.67
Unrated	58%	164	1981	8.3%	-0.43

ANALYSIS BY WEIGHT CARRIED

Weight	Prop	Win	Runs	Wins%	£
10-01+	0%	0	0	0.0%	0.00
9-8..10-00	4%	11	280	3.9%	-0.47
9-0..9-07	38%	108	1149	9.4%	-0.49
8-8..8-13	46%	129	1186	10.9%	-0.38
8-0..8-07	12%	34	318	10.7%	-0.23
..7-13	0%	1	9	11.1%	8.00

ANALYSIS BY DAYS SINCE LAST RUN

Days	Prop	Win	Runs	Wins%	£
1..7	4%	12	116	10.3%	-0.32
8..14	21%	60	518	11.6%	-0.25
15..28	27%	75	657	11.4%	-0.43
29..60	17%	47	447	10.5%	-0.46
61..100	5%	15	142	10.6%	-0.29
101+	19%	55	528	10.4%	-0.28
Unraced	7%	19	534	3.6%	-0.56

ANALYSIS BY TODAY'S STARTING PRICE

Price	Prop	Win	Runs	Wins%	£
Odds On	19%	53	87	60.9%	-0.02
Ev - 2/1	23%	65	163	39.9%	0.00
9/4 - 4/1	24%	67	321	20.9%	-0.15
9/2 - 6/1	12%	35	221	15.8%	-0.01
13/2-10/1	10%	28	324	8.6%	-0.21
11/1-16/1	7%	20	375	5.3%	-0.21
18/1-33/1	4%	12	568	2.1%	-0.46
40/1+	1%	3	883	0.3%	-0.77

ANALYSIS BY STARTING PRICE LAST TIME

Price	Prop	Win	Runs	Wins%	£
Odds On	5%	15	36	41.7%	0.09
Ev - 2/1	11%	32	96	33.3%	-0.07
9/4 - 4/1	17%	49	199	24.6%	0.03
9/2 - 6/1	8%	22	152	14.5%	-0.41
13/2-10/1	18%	50	326	15.3%	-0.22
11/1-16/1	16%	44	383	11.5%	-0.33
18/1-33/1	12%	35	546	6.4%	-0.40
40/1+	6%	17	670	2.5%	-0.55
Unraced	7%	19	534	3.6%	-0.56

ANALYSIS BY DISTANCE BEATEN LAST TIME

Lengths	Prop	Win	Runs	Wins%	£
..-10	0%	0	0	0.0%	0.00
-10..0	0%	0	1	0.0%	-1.00
0.1..2	30%	85	275	30.9%	-0.06
2.1..5	28%	80	374	21.4%	0.01
5.1..10	22%	61	572	10.7%	-0.23
10.1..20	11%	31	695	4.5%	-0.53
20.0..30	1%	4	254	1.6%	-0.53
30.1+	1%	3	237	1.3%	-0.86
Not Compl	0%	0	0	0.0%	0.00
Unraced	7%	19	534	3.6%	-0.56

ANALYSIS BY RUN NUMBER

Run No	Prop	Win	Runs	Wins%	£
FTO	7%	19	534	3.6%	-0.56
2nd Run	19%	55	664	8.3%	-0.53
3rd Run	32%	90	758	11.9%	-0.20
4th+ Run	42%	119	986	12.1%	-0.35

ANALYSIS BY POSITION LAST TIME

Pos LT	Prop	Win	Runs	Wins%	£
Won	0%	0	0	0.0%	0.00
2nd or 3rd	50%	142	537	26.4%	-0.11
Unplaced	43%	122	1863	6.5%	-0.42
Not Compl	7%	19	542	3.5%	-0.57

OTHER FACTORS (WINS-RUNS, £)

Beaten Favourite:	52-153	-£0.01
BHA Top Rated:	63-241	£0.21
Up in class:	28-433	-£0.46
Same class:	172-1517	-£0.34
Down in class:	64-458	-£0.29
Colts and Geldings:	168-1626	-£0.36
Fillies:	80-975	-£0.41
Absolute Favourites:	115-265	-£0.06

TRAINERS (WINS-RUNS, £)

R M Beckett 5-26 £2.72; K R Burke 4-17 £2.09; D Nicholls 2-17 £1.09; M A Jarvis 11-40 £0.27; M P Tregoning 4-22 £0.47; P F I Cole 2-10 £1.00; J L Dunlop 14-47 £0.20; B W Hills 13-40 £0.24; R A Fahey 4-32 £0.28; A Berry 2-29 £0.28; E J O'Neill 2-11 £0.68; T D Barron 3-22 £0.33; M Dods 3-17 £0.26; Sir Michael Stoute 21-61 £0.07; B Smart 4-29 £0.11; K A Ryan 4-28 £0.08; M R Channon 4-19 £0.11; J M Bradley 1-16 £0.06; Rae Guest 2-22 £0.05.

Maiden Races

All Age Races: Maiden Races – 5 to 6 furlong races

ANALYSIS BY AGE
Age	Prop	Win	Runs	Wins%	£
2yo	0%	0	0	0.0%	0.00
3yo	92%	220	2005	11.0%	-0.18
4yo	7%	17	431	3.9%	-0.41
5yo	1%	2	78	2.6%	-0.65
6yo	0%	1	21	4.8%	0.62
7yo	0%	0	7	0.0%	-1.00
8yo	0%	0	1	0.0%	-1.00
9yo	0%	0	0	0.0%	0.00
10yo	0%	0	0	0.0%	0.00
11yo+	0%	0	1	0.0%	-1.00

ANALYSIS BY BHA RATING
Rating	Prop	Win	Runs	Wins%	£
120..139	0%	0	0	0.0%	0.00
110..119	0%	0	0	0.0%	0.00
100..109	0%	0	0	0.0%	0.00
90..99	1%	2	4	50.0%	-0.03
70..89	22%	53	207	25.6%	-0.20
50..69	23%	56	541	10.4%	-0.23
..49	5%	13	419	3.1%	-0.20
Unrated	48%	116	1371	8.5%	-0.24

ANALYSIS BY WEIGHT CARRIED
Weight	Prop	Win	Runs	Wins%	£
10-01+	0%	0	0	0.0%	0.00
9-8 ..10-00	2%	4	93	4.3%	-0.73
9-0..9-07	45%	108	1113	9.7%	-0.33
8-8..8-13	47%	113	1131	10.0%	-0.05
8-0..8-07	6%	15	204	7.4%	-0.44
..7-13	0%	0	3	0.0%	-1.00

ANALYSIS BY DAYS SINCE LAST RUN
Days	Prop	Win	Runs	Wins%	£
1..7	7%	16	155	10.3%	-0.13
8..14	21%	51	451	11.3%	-0.25
15..28	30%	71	629	11.3%	-0.01
29..60	12%	29	345	8.4%	-0.28
61..100	6%	14	110	12.7%	0.37
101+	17%	40	495	8.1%	-0.51
Unraced	8%	19	359	5.3%	-0.38

ANALYSIS BY TODAY'S STARTING PRICE
Price	Prop	Win	Runs	Wins%	£
Odds On	15%	35	59	59.3%	-0.08
Ev - 2/1	23%	56	145	38.6%	0.01
9/4 - 4/1	21%	51	294	17.3%	-0.29
9/2 - 6/1	11%	26	170	15.3%	-0.03
13/2-10/1	13%	30	323	9.3%	-0.12
11/1-16/1	7%	17	345	4.9%	-0.29
18/1-33/1	8%	18	509	3.5%	-0.11
40/1+	3%	7	699	1.0%	-0.41

ANALYSIS BY STARTING PRICE LAST TIME
Price	Prop	Win	Runs	Wins%	£
Odds On	3%	6	30	20.0%	-0.56
Ev - 2/1	9%	22	62	35.5%	0.03
9/4 - 4/1	20%	48	219	21.9%	-0.15
9/2 - 6/1	13%	30	143	21.0%	0.34
13/2-10/1	14%	33	303	10.9%	-0.15
11/1-16/1	13%	30	342	8.8%	-0.28
18/1-33/1	13%	31	506	6.1%	-0.42
40/1+	9%	21	580	3.6%	-0.16
Unraced	8%	19	359	5.3%	-0.38

ANALYSIS BY DISTANCE BEATEN LAST TIME
Lengths	Prop	Win	Runs	Wins%	£
..-10	0%	0	0	0.0%	0.00
-10..0	0%	0	0	0.0%	0.00
0.1..2	29%	70	281	24.9%	-0.04
2.1..5	27%	65	377	17.2%	0.07
5.1..10	19%	45	571	7.9%	-0.28
10.1..20	13%	31	628	4.9%	-0.18
20.0..30	2%	4	169	2.4%	-0.70
30.1+	3%	6	159	3.8%	-0.41
Not Compl	0%	0	0	0.0%	0.00
Unraced	8%	19	359	5.3%	-0.38

ANALYSIS BY RUN NUMBER
Run No	Prop	Win	Runs	Wins%	£
FTO	8%	19	359	5.3%	-0.38
2nd Run	16%	38	448	8.5%	-0.39
3rd Run	23%	54	532	10.2%	-0.05
4th+ Run	54%	129	1205	10.7%	-0.20

ANALYSIS BY POSITION LAST TIME
Pos LT	Prop	Win	Runs	Wins%	£
Won	0%	0	0	0.0%	0.00
2nd or 3rd	41%	99	430	23.0%	-0.05
Unplaced	51%	122	1750	7.0%	-0.24
Not Compl	8%	19	364	5.2%	-0.38

OTHER FACTORS (WINS-RUNS, £)
Beaten Favourite:	35-125	-£0.17
BHA Top Rated:	46-198	-£0.11
Up in class:	30-488	-£0.59
Same class:	145-1338	-£0.02
Down in class:	46-359	-£0.36
Colts and Geldings:	135-1309	-£0.19
Fillies:	86-1049	-£0.34
Absolute Favourites:	83-224	-£0.18

TRAINERS (WINS-RUNS, £)
J M Bradley 3-43 £1.63; D Nicholls 7-29 £1.41; R M Whitaker 2-15 £1.98; M S Saunders 1-12 £1.83; JRGASK 2-14 £1.50; W R Muir 3-11 £1.48; J A R Toller 4-17 £0.87; T D Easterby 10-78 £0.16; M Brittain 3-30 £0.37; L M Cumani 5-20 £0.51; A W Carroll 1-12 £0.75; R A Fahey 5-35 £0.20; T D Barron 6-36 £0.18; W S Kittow 2-15 £0.33; J R Best 2-11 £0.39; N Tinkler 2-18 £0.19; W J Haggas 9-31 £0.08; Eve JohnsonHoughton 2-11 £0.18; B W Hills 6-23 £0.08; R Charlton 3-12 £0.15.

Race Profiles

All Age Races: Maiden Races – 7 to 9 furlong races

ANALYSIS BY AGE

Age	Prop	Win	Runs	Wins%	£
2yo	0%	0	0	0.0%	0.00
3yo	93%	389	3385	11.5%	-0.44
4yo	6%	26	677	3.8%	-0.43
5yo	1%	4	161	2.5%	-0.70
6yo	0%	0	43	0.0%	-1.00
7yo	0%	1	19	5.3%	1.68
8yo	0%	0	2	0.0%	-1.00
9yo	0%	0	3	0.0%	-1.00
10yo	0%	0	0	0.0%	0.00
11yo+	0%	0	3	0.0%	-1.00

ANALYSIS BY BHA RATING

Rating	Prop	Win	Runs	Wins%	£
120..139	0%	0	0	0.0%	0.00
110..119	0%	0	0	0.0%	0.00
100..109	1%	3	4	75.0%	0.43
90..99	1%	3	8	37.5%	-0.48
70..89	29%	123	463	26.6%	-0.17
50..69	11%	47	459	10.2%	-0.25
..49	1%	5	437	1.1%	-0.85
Unrated	57%	239	2917	8.2%	-0.46

ANALYSIS BY WEIGHT CARRIED

Weight	Prop	Win	Runs	Wins%	£
10-01+	0%	0	0	0.0%	0.00
9-8..10-00	4%	16	362	4.4%	-0.16
9-0..9-07	42%	177	1654	10.7%	-0.44
8-8..8-13	50%	212	1932	11.0%	-0.44
8-0..8-07	4%	15	341	4.4%	-0.76
..7-13	0%	0	4	0.0%	-1.00

ANALYSIS BY DAYS SINCE LAST RUN

Days	Prop	Win	Runs	Wins%	£
1..7	3%	14	187	7.5%	-0.72
8..14	17%	71	652	10.9%	-0.52
15..28	32%	133	1012	13.1%	-0.39
29..60	16%	66	619	10.7%	-0.36
61..100	3%	14	166	8.4%	-0.49
101+	20%	82	873	9.4%	-0.52
Unraced	10%	40	784	5.1%	-0.37

ANALYSIS BY TODAY'S STARTING PRICE

Price	Prop	Win	Runs	Wins%	£
Odds On	21%	88	145	60.7%	-0.05
Ev - 2/1	26%	109	281	38.8%	-0.01
9/4 - 4/1	26%	108	450	24.0%	-0.03
9/2 - 6/1	8%	34	288	11.8%	-0.29
13/2-10/1	8%	35	413	8.5%	-0.23
11/1-16/1	7%	29	500	5.8%	-0.13
18/1-33/1	3%	13	792	1.6%	-0.58
40/1+	1%	4	1424	0.3%	-0.83

ANALYSIS BY STARTING PRICE LAST TIME

Price	Prop	Win	Runs	Wins%	£
Odds On	6%	24	53	45.3%	0.28
Ev - 2/1	10%	43	142	30.3%	-0.09
9/4 - 4/1	21%	90	328	27.4%	0.03
9/2 - 6/1	11%	46	251	18.3%	-0.28
13/2-10/1	13%	53	425	12.5%	-0.33
11/1-16/1	15%	64	527	12.1%	-0.36
18/1-33/1	10%	43	742	5.8%	-0.46
40/1+	4%	17	1041	1.6%	-0.86
Unraced	10%	40	784	5.1%	-0.37

ANALYSIS BY DISTANCE BEATEN LAST TIME

Lengths	Prop	Win	Runs	Wins%	£
..-10	0%	0	0	0.0%	0.00
-10..0	0%	0	2	0.0%	-1.00
0.1..2	30%	128	407	31.4%	-0.04
2.1..5	26%	111	539	20.6%	-0.11
5.1..10	21%	87	869	10.0%	-0.41
10.1..20	11%	45	991	4.5%	-0.59
20.0..30	1%	6	385	1.6%	-0.86
30.1+	1%	3	316	0.9%	-0.87
Not Compl	0%	0	0	0.0%	0.00
Unraced	10%	40	784	5.1%	-0.37

ANALYSIS BY RUN NUMBER

Run No	Prop	Win	Runs	Wins%	£
FTO	10%	40	784	5.1%	-0.37
2nd Run	21%	88	996	8.8%	-0.52
3rd Run	25%	104	1084	9.6%	-0.46
4th+ Run	45%	188	1429	13.2%	-0.42

ANALYSIS BY POSITION LAST TIME

Pos LT	Prop	Win	Runs	Wins%	£
Won	0%	0	1	0.0%	-1.00
2nd or 3rd	48%	201	745	27.0%	-0.13
Unplaced	43%	179	2752	6.5%	-0.55
Not Compl	10%	40	795	5.0%	-0.38

OTHER FACTORS (WINS-RUNS, £)

Course Winner:	1-1	£1.50
Distance Winner:	1-2	£0.25
Beaten Favourite:	76-213	£0.09
BHA Top Rated:	85-322	-£0.15
Up in class:	40-655	-£0.57
Same class:	225-2115	-£0.48
Down in class:	115-739	-£0.30
Colts and Geldings:	261-2322	-£0.36
Fillies:	104-1381	-£0.56
Absolute Favourites:	184-401	-£0.01

TRAINERS (WINS-RUNS, £)

T D Barron 8-33 £1.76; D Nicholls 4-28 £1.41; B Palling 1-13 £2.92; E F Vaughan 2-14 £2.00; K R Burke 7-33 £0.85; J L Dunlop 11-49 £0.52; E J O'Neill 4-18 £1.18; B W Hills 32-92 £0.16; J Noseda 16-51 £0.26; M P Tregoning 10-42 £0.28; M Dods 1-19 £0.37; A G Foster 1-11 £0.55; J S Goldie 1-17 £0.55; Sir Michael Stoute 25-68 £0.08; G A Butler 6-30 £0.11; P R Chamings 2-18 £0.11; W J Haggas 15-69 £0.02; M H Tompkins 6-21 £0.05.

Maiden Races

All Age Races: Maiden Races – 10 to 14 furlong races

ANALYSIS BY AGE

Age	Prop	Win	Runs	Wins%	£
2yo	0%	0	0	0.0%	0.00
3yo	91%	382	2966	12.9%	-0.31
4yo	8%	32	596	5.4%	-0.73
5yo	1%	3	202	1.5%	-0.65
6yo	0%	2	95	2.1%	-0.64
7yo	0%	1	44	2.3%	-0.93
8yo	0%	0	15	0.0%	-1.00
9yo	0%	0	8	0.0%	-1.00
10yo	0%	0	2	0.0%	-1.00
11yo+	0%	0	1	0.0%	-1.00

ANALYSIS BY BHA RATING

Rating	Prop	Win	Runs	Wins%	£
120..139	0%	0	0	0.0%	0.00
110..119	0%	0	0	0.0%	0.00
100..109	1%	3	5	60.0%	1.47
90..99	1%	5	16	31.3%	-0.41
70..89	33%	140	549	25.5%	-0.13
50..69	6%	27	329	8.2%	-0.59
..49	1%	3	273	1.1%	-0.70
Unrated	58%	242	2755	8.8%	-0.42

ANALYSIS BY WEIGHT CARRIED

Weight	Prop	Win	Runs	Wins%	£
10-01+	0%	0	0	0.0%	0.00
9-8..10-00	6%	25	549	4.6%	-0.62
9-0..9-07	26%	110	1079	10.2%	-0.45
8-8..8-13	54%	228	1719	13.3%	-0.40
8-0..8-07	13%	56	571	9.8%	-0.29
..7-13	0%	1	11	9.1%	6.36

ANALYSIS BY DAYS SINCE LAST RUN

Days	Prop	Win	Runs	Wins%	£
1..7	2%	9	120	7.5%	-0.75
8..14	18%	74	654	11.3%	-0.32
15..28	33%	138	1015	13.6%	-0.39
29..60	15%	65	577	11.3%	-0.46
61..100	4%	17	176	9.7%	-0.55
101+	19%	79	667	11.8%	-0.27
Unraced	9%	38	720	5.3%	-0.52

ANALYSIS BY TODAY'S STARTING PRICE

Price	Prop	Win	Runs	Wins%	£
Odds On	27%	112	177	63.3%	0.00
Ev - 2/1	23%	96	257	37.4%	-0.06
9/4 - 4/1	25%	104	438	23.7%	-0.04
9/2 - 6/1	10%	40	260	14.9%	-0.09
13/2-10/1	6%	24	422	5.7%	-0.49
11/1-16/1	7%	28	435	6.4%	-0.07
18/1-33/1	3%	12	645	1.9%	-0.55
40/1+	1%	4	1286	0.3%	-0.75

ANALYSIS BY STARTING PRICE LAST TIME

Price	Prop	Win	Runs	Wins%	£
Odds On	5%	23	53	43.4%	0.11
Ev - 2/1	10%	41	147	27.9%	-0.29
9/4 - 4/1	17%	70	293	23.9%	-0.14
9/2 - 6/1	12%	50	238	21.0%	-0.16
13/2-10/1	18%	74	422	17.5%	-0.22
11/1-16/1	12%	49	464	10.6%	-0.51
18/1-33/1	13%	55	667	8.2%	-0.35
40/1+	5%	20	925	2.2%	-0.61
Unraced	9%	38	720	5.3%	-0.52

ANALYSIS BY DISTANCE BEATEN LAST TIME

Lengths	Prop	Win	Runs	Wins%	£
..-10	0%	0	0	0.0%	0.00
-10..0	0%	1	1	100.0%	5.00
0.1..2	31%	132	397	33.2%	-0.01
2.1..5	24%	102	485	21.0%	-0.27
5.1..10	21%	87	681	12.8%	-0.16
10.1..20	11%	45	890	5.1%	-0.55
20.0..30	2%	9	403	2.2%	-0.59
30.1+	1%	6	352	1.7%	-0.78
Not Compl	0%	0	0	0.0%	0.00
Unraced	9%	38	720	5.3%	-0.52

ANALYSIS BY RUN NUMBER

Run No	Prop	Win	Runs	Wins%	£
FTO	9%	38	720	5.3%	-0.52
2nd Run	23%	96	946	10.1%	-0.38
3rd Run	26%	110	1065	10.3%	-0.34
4th+ Run	42%	176	1198	14.7%	-0.43

ANALYSIS BY POSITION LAST TIME

Pos LT	Prop	Win	Runs	Wins%	£
Won	0%	0	0	0.0%	0.00
2nd or 3rd	53%	222	816	27.2%	-0.14
Unplaced	38%	159	2383	6.7%	-0.47
Not Compl	9%	39	730	5.3%	-0.51

OTHER FACTORS (WINS-RUNS, £)

Beaten Favourite:	70-221	-£0.17
BHA Top Rated:	90-322	-£0.08
Up in class:	22-479	-£0.64
Same class:	238-2073	-£0.38
Down in class:	122-657	-£0.21
Colts and Geldings:	254-2116	-£0.35
Fillies:	96-1167	-£0.50
Absolute Favourites:	195-395	-£0.01

TRAINERS (WINS-RUNS, £)

R M Beckett 2-29 £1.98; D M Simcock 4-23 £1.64; W Jarvis 6-18 £1.35; T P Tate 2-13 £1.31; W J Haggas 5-26 £0.42; Rae Guest 2-14 £0.46; M P Tregoning 11-42 £0.20; B W Hills 22-76 £0.10; G Wragg 3-13 £0.44; C E Brittain 4-32 £0.16; J Noseda 10-41 £0.11; C A Cyzer 3-19 £0.23; G A Butler 3-16 £0.24; Saeed Bin Suroor 20-64 £0.06; B J Meehan 7-34 £0.04; M A Jarvis 23-87 £0.01.

Race Profiles

All Age Races: Claiming Races

ANALYSIS BY AGE

Age	Prop	Win	Runs	Wins%	£
2yo	0%	0	0	0.0%	0.00
3yo	16%	68	872	7.8%	-0.51
4yo	23%	99	1201	8.2%	-0.35
5yo	18%	77	699	11.0%	-0.02
6yo	13%	56	511	11.0%	-0.34
7yo	11%	47	394	11.9%	-0.18
8yo	11%	46	289	15.9%	-0.08
9yo	5%	20	183	10.9%	-0.45
10yo	3%	11	99	11.1%	-0.36
11yo+	3%	11	103	10.7%	-0.55

ANALYSIS BY BHA RATING

Rating	Prop	Win	Runs	Wins%	£
120..139	0%	0	0	0.0%	0.00
110..119	0%	0	0	0.0%	0.00
100..109	0%	1	5	20.0%	-0.60
90..99	3%	11	37	29.7%	0.12
70..89	42%	182	866	21.0%	-0.13
50..69	43%	187	1765	10.6%	-0.28
..49	12%	52	1471	3.5%	-0.36
Unrated	0%	2	203	1.0%	-0.96

ANALYSIS BY WEIGHT CARRIED

Weight	Prop	Win	Runs	Wins%	£
10-01+	1%	4	49	8.2%	0.05
9-8..10-00	24%	103	506	20.4%	-0.17
9-0..9-07	37%	162	1459	11.1%	-0.43
8-8..8-13	25%	108	1300	8.3%	-0.18
8-0..8-07	11%	50	902	5.5%	-0.33
..7-13	2%	8	135	5.9%	-0.62

ANALYSIS BY DAYS SINCE LAST RUN

Days	Prop	Win	Runs	Wins%	£
1..7	22%	97	669	14.5%	0.02
8..14	33%	143	1156	12.4%	-0.17
15..28	28%	121	1181	10.2%	-0.36
29..60	9%	41	684	6.0%	-0.57
61..100	3%	12	181	6.6%	-0.52
101+	5%	20	431	4.6%	-0.42
Unraced	0%	1	49	2.0%	-0.90

ANALYSIS BY TODAY'S STARTING PRICE

Price	Prop	Win	Runs	Wins%	£
Odds On	7%	31	50	62.0%	0.04
Ev - 2/1	21%	92	243	37.9%	-0.03
9/4 - 4/1	32%	140	599	23.4%	-0.06
9/2 - 6/1	14%	59	424	13.9%	-0.14
13/2-10/1	13%	58	655	8.9%	-0.20
11/1-16/1	7%	31	616	5.0%	-0.30
18/1-33/1	4%	17	797	2.1%	-0.46
40/1+	2%	7	967	0.7%	-0.56

ANALYSIS BY STARTING PRICE LAST TIME

Price	Prop	Win	Runs	Wins%	£
Odds On	2%	8	31	25.8%	-0.30
Ev - 2/1	8%	36	134	26.9%	-0.01
9/4 - 4/1	18%	77	383	20.1%	-0.15
9/2 - 6/1	13%	58	383	15.1%	-0.08
13/2-10/1	24%	105	797	13.2%	-0.16
11/1-16/1	19%	83	845	9.8%	-0.33
18/1-33/1	11%	50	932	5.4%	-0.33
40/1+	4%	17	797	2.1%	-0.59
Unraced	0%	1	49	2.0%	-0.90

ANALYSIS BY DISTANCE BEATEN LAST TIME

Lengths	Prop	Win	Runs	Wins%	£
..-10	0%	0	1	0.0%	-1.00
-10..0	16%	68	237	28.7%	0.05
0.1..2	15%	64	383	16.7%	-0.22
2.1..5	24%	104	782	13.3%	-0.24
5.1..10	19%	81	1019	7.9%	-0.39
10.1..20	19%	83	1117	7.4%	-0.44
20.0..30	5%	20	381	5.2%	0.19
30.1+	3%	14	382	3.7%	-0.54
Not Compl	0%	0	0	0.0%	0.00
Unraced	0%	1	49	2.0%	-0.90

ANALYSIS BY RUN NUMBER

Run No	Prop	Win	Runs	Wins%	£
FTO	0%	1	49	2.0%	-0.90
2nd Run	0%	0	66	0.0%	-1.00
3rd Run	0%	2	74	2.7%	-0.79
4th+ Run	99%	432	4162	10.4%	-0.28

ANALYSIS BY POSITION LAST TIME

Pos LT	Prop	Win	Runs	Wins%	£
Won	16%	68	238	28.6%	0.05
2nd or 3rd	24%	104	598	17.4%	-0.17
Unplaced	60%	262	3450	7.6%	-0.34
Not Compl	0%	1	65	1.5%	-0.92

OTHER FACTORS (WINS-RUNS, £)

Course Winner:	86-658	-£0.25
Distance Winner:	268-1881	-£0.18
Going Winner:	208-1277	-£0.16
Beaten Favourite:	34-189	-£0.28
BHA Top Rated:	86-382	-£0.11
Up in class:	59-913	-£0.41
Same class:	179-2005	-£0.28
Down in class:	196-1384	-£0.25
7-Day Winners:	14-50	£0.04
Colts and Geldings:	355-3286	-£0.34
Fillies:	80-1065	-£0.18
Absolute Favourites:	148-385	£0.03

TRAINERS (WINS-RUNS, £)

J C Fox 1-14 £6.21; R M Whitaker 8-46 £1.41; John A Harris 6-31 £1.62; J G Portman 3-13 £2.75; D Nicholls 40-147 £0.22; D W Thompson 1-21 £1.43; Miss L A Perratt 6-42 £0.66; J J Bridger 1-17 £1.41; P W Hiatt 5-30 £0.80; Miss Gay Kelleway 6-28 £0.56; J S Goldie 6-49 £0.27; N Tinkler 4-31 £0.42; N Wilson 3-19 £0.63; J G M O'Shea 4-24 £0.48; G A Swinbank 7-35 £0.29; Miss Tracy Waggott 4-33 £0.27; I Semple 11-58 £0.14; George Baker 2-13 £0.58; R A Fahey 28-94 £0.08; R Hannon 19-69 £0.07.

Claiming Races

All Age Races: Claiming Races – 2 to 7 runners

ANALYSIS BY AGE
Age	Prop	Win	Runs	Wins%	£
2yo	0%	0	0	0.0%	0.00
3yo	14%	16	142	11.3%	-0.63
4yo	30%	34	210	16.2%	-0.32
5yo	22%	25	114	21.9%	0.04
6yo	7%	8	73	11.0%	-0.30
7yo	12%	14	54	25.9%	-0.24
8yo	8%	9	41	22.0%	-0.12
9yo	4%	5	31	16.1%	-0.47
10yo	2%	2	14	14.3%	-0.53
11yo+	1%	1	14	7.1%	-0.88

ANALYSIS BY BHA RATING
Rating	Prop	Win	Runs	Wins%	£
120..139	0%	0	0	0.0%	0.00
110..119	0%	0	0	0.0%	0.00
100..109	1%	1	3	33.3%	-0.33
90..99	3%	3	7	42.9%	0.11
70..89	52%	59	218	27.1%	-0.18
50..69	36%	41	289	14.2%	-0.26
..49	8%	9	154	5.8%	-0.60
Unrated	1%	1	22	4.5%	-0.77

ANALYSIS BY WEIGHT CARRIED
Weight	Prop	Win	Runs	Wins%	£
10-01+	0%	0	0	0.0%	0.00
9-8 ..10-00	21%	24	82	29.3%	-0.08
9-0..9-07	41%	47	248	19.0%	-0.18
8-8..8-13	25%	29	198	14.6%	-0.37
8-0..8-07	11%	12	138	8.7%	-0.58
..7-13	2%	2	27	7.4%	-0.73

ANALYSIS BY DAYS SINCE LAST RUN
Days	Prop	Win	Runs	Wins%	£
1..7	17%	19	120	15.8%	-0.33
8..14	32%	36	186	19.4%	-0.17
15..28	37%	42	216	19.4%	-0.23
29..60	9%	10	101	9.9%	-0.61
61..100	2%	2	10	20.0%	-0.03
101+	4%	4	53	7.5%	-0.75
Unraced	1%	1	7	14.3%	-0.29

ANALYSIS BY TODAY'S STARTING PRICE
Price	Prop	Win	Runs	Wins%	£
Odds On	14%	16	26	61.5%	0.01
Ev - 2/1	32%	36	89	40.4%	0.02
9/4 - 4/1	33%	38	158	24.1%	-0.05
9/2 - 6/1	11%	12	85	14.1%	0.14
13/2-10/1	7%	8	102	7.8%	-0.34
11/1-16/1	4%	4	78	5.1%	-0.22
18/1-33/1	0%	0	80	0.0%	-1.00
40/1+	0%	0	75	0.0%	-1.00

ANALYSIS BY STARTING PRICE LAST TIME
Price	Prop	Win	Runs	Wins%	£
Odds On	2%	2	10	20.0%	-0.52
Ev - 2/1	15%	17	40	42.5%	0.36
9/4 - 4/1	19%	22	82	26.8%	-0.06
9/2 - 6/1	11%	12	81	14.8%	-0.43
13/2-10/1	18%	21	121	17.4%	-0.34
11/1-16/1	22%	25	138	18.1%	-0.10
18/1-33/1	8%	9	130	6.9%	-0.63
40/1+	4%	5	84	6.0%	-0.66
Unraced	1%	1	7	14.3%	-0.29

ANALYSIS BY DISTANCE BEATEN LAST TIME
Lengths	Prop	Win	Runs	Wins%	£
..-10	0%	0	0	0.0%	0.00
-10..0	24%	27	67	40.3%	0.33
0.1..2	14%	16	77	20.8%	-0.17
2.1..5	25%	29	134	21.6%	-0.09
5.1..10	8%	9	151	6.0%	-0.71
10.1..20	21%	24	152	15.8%	-0.31
20.0..30	4%	5	51	9.8%	-0.41
30.1+	3%	3	54	5.6%	-0.82
Not Compl	0%	0	0	0.0%	0.00
Unraced	1%	1	7	14.3%	-0.29

ANALYSIS BY RUN NUMBER
Run No	Prop	Win	Runs	Wins%	£
FTO	1%	1	7	14.3%	-0.29
2nd Run	0%	0	5	0.0%	-1.00
3rd Run	0%	0	13	0.0%	-1.00
4th+ Run	99%	113	668	16.9%	-0.31

ANALYSIS BY POSITION LAST TIME
Pos LT	Prop	Win	Runs	Wins%	£
Won	24%	27	67	40.3%	0.33
2nd or 3rd	24%	27	122	22.1%	-0.15
Unplaced	52%	59	496	11.9%	-0.45
Not Compl	1%	1	8	12.5%	-0.38

OTHER FACTORS (WINS-RUNS, £)
Course Winner:	19-105	£0.05
Distance Winner:	68-315	-£0.12
Going Winner:	61-249	-£0.01
Beaten Favourite:	13-38	-£0.02
BHA Top Rated:	21-83	-£0.24
Up in class:	19-150	-£0.31
Same class:	42-295	-£0.31
Down in class:	52-241	-£0.35
7 Day Winners:	5-14	-£0.03
Colts and Geldings:	94-538	-£0.29
Fillies:	20-155	-£0.44
Absolute Favourites:	46-103	£0.01

TRAINERS (WINS-RUNS, £)
I Semple 4-10 £0.53; K A Ryan 4-14 £0.16; R Hannon 9-22 £0.03.

Race Profiles

All Age Races: Claiming Races – 8 to 14 runners

ANALYSIS BY AGE					
Age	Prop	Win	Runs	Wins%	£
2yo	0%	0	0	0.0%	0.00
3yo	17%	46	585	7.9%	-0.43
4yo	20%	55	790	7.0%	-0.31
5yo	17%	48	477	10.1%	-0.14
6yo	15%	41	344	11.9%	-0.30
7yo	10%	28	273	10.3%	-0.24
8yo	11%	29	204	14.2%	-0.14
9yo	4%	12	113	10.6%	-0.38
10yo	3%	7	73	9.6%	-0.48
11yo+	4%	10	78	12.8%	-0.43

ANALYSIS BY BHA RATING					
Rating	Prop	Win	Runs	Wins%	£
120..139	0%	0	0	0.0%	0.00
110..119	0%	0	0	0.0%	0.00
100..109	0%	0	2	0.0%	-1.00
90..99	3%	8	30	26.7%	0.12
70..89	39%	109	570	19.1%	-0.10
50..69	44%	121	1167	10.4%	-0.26
..49	13%	37	1020	3.6%	-0.37
Unrated	0%	1	144	0.7%	-0.98

ANALYSIS BY WEIGHT CARRIED					
Weight	Prop	Win	Runs	Wins%	£
10-01+	1%	3	33	9.1%	0.36
9-8..10-00	26%	72	374	19.3%	-0.16
9-0..9-07	35%	97	977	9.9%	-0.47
8-8..8-13	24%	67	871	7.7%	-0.15
8-0..8-07	12%	34	600	5.7%	-0.29
..7-13	1%	3	82	3.7%	-0.77

ANALYSIS BY DAYS SINCE LAST RUN					
Days	Prop	Win	Runs	Wins%	£
1..7	23%	63	439	14.4%	-0.23
8..14	31%	86	781	11.0%	-0.14
15..28	27%	74	798	9.3%	-0.32
29..60	10%	28	450	6.2%	-0.57
61..100	4%	10	134	7.5%	-0.42
101+	5%	15	304	4.9%	-0.24
Unraced	0%	0	31	0.0%	-1.00

ANALYSIS BY TODAY'S STARTING PRICE					
Price	Prop	Win	Runs	Wins%	£
Odds On	5%	14	22	63.6%	0.09
Ev - 2/1	18%	50	141	35.5%	-0.08
9/4 - 4/1	33%	90	392	23.0%	-0.08
9/2 - 6/1	15%	41	290	14.1%	-0.13
13/2-10/1	14%	39	449	8.7%	-0.20
11/1-16/1	9%	24	429	5.6%	-0.23
18/1-33/1	5%	14	546	2.6%	-0.33
40/1+	1%	4	668	0.6%	-0.65

ANALYSIS BY STARTING PRICE LAST TIME					
Price	Prop	Win	Runs	Wins%	£
Odds On	2%	6	21	28.6%	-0.19
Ev - 2/1	5%	15	81	18.5%	-0.26
9/4 - 4/1	17%	48	256	18.8%	-0.19
9/2 - 6/1	16%	43	254	16.9%	0.16
13/2-10/1	26%	71	554	12.8%	-0.14
11/1-16/1	17%	46	548	8.4%	-0.43
18/1-33/1	13%	37	617	6.0%	-0.11
40/1+	4%	10	575	1.7%	-0.75
Unraced	0%	0	31	0.0%	-1.00

ANALYSIS BY DISTANCE BEATEN LAST TIME					
Lengths	Prop	Win	Runs	Wins%	£
..-10	0%	0	1	0.0%	-1.00
-10..0	12%	32	139	23.0%	-0.20
0.1..2	16%	43	257	16.7%	-0.18
2.1..5	22%	62	515	12.0%	-0.31
5.1..10	24%	65	684	9.5%	-0.28
10.1..20	18%	51	778	6.6%	-0.47
20.0..30	4%	12	264	4.5%	0.17
30.1+	4%	11	268	4.1%	-0.38
Not Compl	0%	0	0	0.0%	0.00
Unraced	0%	0	31	0.0%	-1.00

ANALYSIS BY RUN NUMBER					
Run No	Prop	Win	Runs	Wins%	£
FTO	0%	0	31	0.0%	-1.00
2nd Run	0%	0	48	0.0%	-1.00
3rd Run	1%	2	51	3.9%	-0.70
4th+ Run	99%	274	2807	9.8%	-0.27

ANALYSIS BY POSITION LAST TIME					
Pos LT	Prop	Win	Runs	Wins%	£
Won	12%	32	140	22.9%	-0.21
2nd or 3rd	25%	70	413	16.9%	-0.16
Unplaced	63%	174	2341	7.4%	-0.31
Not Compl	0%	0	43	0.0%	-1.00

OTHER FACTORS (WINS-RUNS, £)		
Course Winner:	58-454	-£0.31
Distance Winner:	167-1261	-£0.20
Going Winner:	121-834	-£0.20
Beaten Favourite:	17-132	-£0.42
BHA Top Rated:	59-253	-£0.02
Up in class:	33-627	-£0.47
Same class:	117-1354	-£0.31
Down in class:	126-925	-£0.15
7-Day Winners:	8-29	£0.05
Colts and Geldings:	226-2237	-£0.35
Fillies:	50-700	-£0.12
Absolute Favourites:	90-242	£0.06

TRAINERS (WINS-RUNS, £)

R M Whitaker 7-32 £2.18; J G Portman 3-12 £3.07; D W Thompson 1-15 £2.40; Miss L A Perratt 4-28 £1.21; D Nicholls 28-98 £0.27; Miss Tracy Waggott 3-24 £0.63; N Wilson 3-17 £0.25; R A Fahey 15-55 £0.25; J G M O'Shea 3-17 £0.77; R Hannon 10-39 £0.31; P W Hiatt 2-17 £0.68; B G Powell 3-16 £0.58; N Tinkler 1-20 £0.30; A G Newcombe 2-15 £0.35; Miss Gay Kelleway 2-16 £0.30; John A Harris 4-18 £0.24; J S Goldie 2-29 £0.09; B Palling 1-10 £0.10; G A Harker 1-11 £0.09; Mrs L J Mongan 1-10 £0.10.

Claiming Races

All Age Races: Claiming Races – 15 runners or more

ANALYSIS BY AGE

Age	Prop	Win	Runs	Wins%	£
2yo	0%	0	0	0.0%	0.00
3yo	13%	6	145	4.1%	-0.69
4yo	22%	10	201	5.0%	-0.54
5yo	9%	4	108	3.7%	0.46
6yo	16%	7	94	7.4%	-0.52
7yo	11%	5	67	7.5%	0.07
8yo	18%	8	44	18.2%	0.22
9yo	7%	3	39	7.7%	-0.64
10yo	4%	2	12	16.7%	0.58
11yo+	0%	0	11	0.0%	-1.00

ANALYSIS BY BHA RATING

Rating	Prop	Win	Runs	Wins%	£
120..139	0%	0	0	0.0%	0.00
110..119	0%	0	0	0.0%	0.00
100..109	0%	0	0	0.0%	0.00
90..99	0%	0	0	0.0%	0.00
70..89	31%	14	78	17.9%	-0.21
50..69	56%	25	309	8.1%	-0.36
..49	13%	6	297	2.0%	-0.19
Unrated	0%	0	37	0.0%	-1.00

ANALYSIS BY WEIGHT CARRIED

Weight	Prop	Win	Runs	Wins%	£
10-01+	2%	1	16	6.3%	-0.59
9-8..10-00	16%	7	50	14.0%	-0.41
9-0..9-07	40%	18	234	7.7%	-0.53
8-8..8-13	27%	12	231	5.2%	-0.11
8-0..8-07	9%	4	164	2.4%	-0.26
..7-13	7%	3	26	11.5%	-0.04

ANALYSIS BY DAYS SINCE LAST RUN

Days	Prop	Win	Runs	Wins%	£
1..7	33%	15	110	13.6%	1.41
8..14	47%	21	189	11.1%	-0.31
15..28	11%	5	167	3.0%	-0.75
29..60	7%	3	133	2.3%	-0.56
61..100	0%	0	37	0.0%	-1.00
101+	2%	1	74	1.4%	-0.93
Unraced	0%	0	11	0.0%	-1.00

ANALYSIS BY TODAY'S STARTING PRICE

Price	Prop	Win	Runs	Wins%	£
Odds On	2%	1	2	50.0%	-0.09
Ev - 2/1	13%	6	13	46.2%	0.17
9/4 - 4/1	27%	12	49	24.5%	0.01
9/2 - 6/1	13%	6	49	12.2%	-0.21
13/2-10/1	24%	11	104	10.6%	-0.05
11/1-16/1	7%	3	109	2.8%	-0.61
18/1-33/1	7%	3	171	1.8%	-0.64
40/1+	7%	3	224	1.3%	-0.14

ANALYSIS BY STARTING PRICE LAST TIME

Price	Prop	Win	Runs	Wins%	£
Odds On	0%	0	0	0.0%	0.00
Ev - 2/1	9%	4	13	30.8%	0.49
9/4 - 4/1	16%	7	45	15.6%	-0.12
9/2 - 6/1	7%	3	48	6.3%	-0.78
13/2-10/1	29%	13	122	10.7%	-0.07
11/1-16/1	27%	12	159	7.5%	-0.18
18/1-33/1	9%	4	185	2.2%	-0.82
40/1+	4%	2	138	1.4%	0.10
Unraced	0%	0	11	0.0%	-1.00

ANALYSIS BY DISTANCE BEATEN LAST TIME

Lengths	Prop	Win	Runs	Wins%	£
..-10	0%	0	0	0.0%	0.00
-10..0	20%	9	31	29.0%	0.59
0.1..2	11%	5	49	10.2%	-0.54
2.1..5	29%	13	133	9.8%	-0.10
5.1..10	16%	7	184	3.8%	-0.57
10.1..20	18%	8	187	4.3%	-0.39
20.0..30	7%	3	66	4.5%	0.74
30.1+	0%	0	60	0.0%	-1.00
Not Compl	0%	0	0	0.0%	0.00
Unraced	0%	0	11	0.0%	-1.00

ANALYSIS BY RUN NUMBER

Run No	Prop	Win	Runs	Wins%	£
FTO	0%	0	11	0.0%	-1.00
2nd Run	0%	0	13	0.0%	-1.00
3rd Run	0%	0	10	0.0%	-1.00
4th+ Run	100%	45	687	6.6%	-0.27

ANALYSIS BY POSITION LAST TIME

Pos LT	Prop	Win	Runs	Wins%	£
Won	20%	9	31	29.0%	0.59
2nd or 3rd	16%	7	63	11.1%	-0.28
Unplaced	64%	29	613	4.7%	-0.34
Not Compl	0%	0	14	0.0%	-1.00

OTHER FACTORS (WINS-RUNS, £)

Course Winner:	9-99	-£0.32
Distance Winner:	33-305	-£0.16
Going Winner:	26-194	-£0.19
Beaten Favourite:	4-19	£0.17
BHA Top Rated:	6-46	-£0.42
Up in class:	7-136	-£0.24
Same class:	20-356	-£0.16
Down in class:	18-218	-£0.55
7 Day Winners:	1-7	£0.14
Colts and Geldings:	35-511	-£0.36
Fillies:	10-210	-£0.17
Absolute Favourites:	12-40	-£0.14

TRAINERS (WINS-RUNS, £)

D Nicholls 5-20 £0.70.

Race Profiles

All Age Races: Claiming Races – good or faster going

ANALYSIS BY AGE

Age	Prop	Win	Runs	Wins%	£
2yo	0%	0	0	0.0%	0.00
3yo	16%	53	644	8.2%	-0.48
4yo	22%	71	891	8.0%	-0.36
5yo	17%	55	519	10.6%	-0.06
6yo	14%	47	398	11.8%	-0.28
7yo	11%	35	318	11.0%	-0.22
8yo	11%	37	217	17.1%	-0.09
9yo	4%	14	137	10.2%	-0.57
10yo	3%	10	78	12.8%	-0.23
11yo+	2%	8	82	9.8%	-0.56

ANALYSIS BY BHA RATING

Rating	Prop	Win	Runs	Wins%	£
120..139	0%	0	0	0.0%	0.00
110..119	0%	0	0	0.0%	0.00
100..109	0%	1	3	33.3%	-0.33
90..99	2%	5	24	20.8%	-0.25
70..89	44%	144	651	22.1%	-0.05
50..69	42%	138	1319	10.5%	-0.30
..49	12%	40	1147	3.5%	-0.38
Unrated	1%	2	137	1.5%	-0.94

ANALYSIS BY WEIGHT CARRIED

Weight	Prop	Win	Runs	Wins%	£
10-01+	1%	4	49	8.2%	0.05
9-8..10-00	25%	81	407	19.9%	-0.18
9-0..9-07	38%	124	1110	11.2%	-0.42
8-8..8-13	24%	80	975	8.2%	-0.17
8-0..8-07	12%	38	646	5.9%	-0.33
..7-13	1%	3	97	3.1%	-0.82

ANALYSIS BY DAYS SINCE LAST RUN

Days	Prop	Win	Runs	Wins%	£
1..7	23%	77	511	15.1%	0.04
8..14	33%	110	901	12.2%	-0.23
15..28	27%	89	882	10.1%	-0.33
29..60	10%	32	496	6.5%	-0.56
61..100	2%	6	132	4.5%	-0.55
101+	5%	15	328	4.6%	-0.43
Unraced	0%	1	34	2.9%	-0.85

ANALYSIS BY TODAY'S STARTING PRICE

Price	Prop	Win	Runs	Wins%	£
Odds On	7%	22	38	57.9%	-0.02
Ev - 2/1	21%	69	187	36.9%	-0.08
9/4 - 4/1	33%	108	452	23.9%	-0.04
9/2 - 6/1	13%	44	327	13.5%	-0.17
13/2-10/1	14%	47	490	9.6%	-0.13
11/1-16/1	8%	25	438	5.7%	-0.21
18/1-33/1	3%	10	598	1.7%	-0.57
40/1+	2%	5	754	0.7%	-0.55

ANALYSIS BY STARTING PRICE LAST TIME

Price	Prop	Win	Runs	Wins%	£
Odds On	1%	3	24	12.5%	-0.76
Ev - 2/1	9%	31	113	27.4%	0.00
9/4 - 4/1	19%	64	300	21.3%	-0.09
9/2 - 6/1	13%	43	285	15.1%	-0.19
13/2-10/1	25%	81	596	13.6%	-0.18
11/1-16/1	17%	56	622	9.0%	-0.39
18/1-33/1	11%	36	711	5.1%	-0.27
40/1+	5%	15	599	2.5%	-0.55
Unraced	0%	1	34	2.9%	-0.85

ANALYSIS BY DISTANCE BEATEN LAST TIME

Lengths	Prop	Win	Runs	Wins%	£
..-10	0%	0	1	0.0%	-1.00
-10..0	16%	54	183	29.5%	0.04
0.1..2	16%	53	297	17.8%	-0.20
2.1..5	24%	80	590	13.6%	-0.27
5.1..10	18%	61	787	7.8%	-0.41
10.1..20	16%	52	823	6.3%	-0.48
20.0..30	5%	18	278	6.5%	0.36
30.1+	3%	11	291	3.8%	-0.48
Not Compl	0%	0	0	0.0%	0.00
Unraced	0%	1	34	2.9%	-0.85

ANALYSIS BY RUN NUMBER

Run No	Prop	Win	Runs	Wins%	£
FTO	0%	1	34	2.9%	-0.85
2nd Run	0%	0	45	0.0%	-1.00
3rd Run	1%	2	52	3.8%	-0.71
4th+ Run	99%	327	3153	10.4%	-0.28

ANALYSIS BY POSITION LAST TIME

Pos LT	Prop	Win	Runs	Wins%	£
Won	16%	54	184	29.3%	0.03
2nd or 3rd	26%	86	470	18.3%	-0.12
Unplaced	57%	189	2583	7.3%	-0.35
Not Compl	0%	1	47	2.1%	-0.89

OTHER FACTORS (WINS-RUNS, £)

Course Winner: 69-502 -£0.22
Distance Winner: 207-1419 -£0.18
Going Winner: 170-1092 -£0.22
Beaten Favourite: 29-153 -£0.25
BHA Top Rated: 61-283 -£0.19
Up in class: 45-696 -£0.41
Same class: 139-1521 -£0.28
Down in class: 145-1033 -£0.25
7-Day Winners: 9-37 -£0.04
Colts and Geldings: 272-2483 -£0.34
Fillies: 58-801 -£0.20
Absolute Favourites: 112-290 £0.03

TRAINERS (WINS-RUNS, £)

J C Fox 1-11 £8.18; R M Whitaker 5-30 £2.31; John A Harris 4-16 £3.20; J G Portman 3-13 £2.75; D W Thompson 1-18 £1.83; D Nicholls 30-118 £0.20; P W Hiatt 4-26 £0.88; N Tinkler 4-23 £0.91; Miss Tracy Waggott 4-26 £0.62; N Wilson 3-15 £1.07; I Semple 8-38 £0.28; George Baker 2-10 £1.05; Miss L A Perratt 4-30 £0.26; R C Guest 2-17 £0.44; B G Powell 3-18 £0.40; Ollie Pears 6-25 £0.26; Ian Williams 6-13 £0.48; J R Boyle 6-18 £0.30; R A Fahey 19-69 £0.06; C J Teague 1-11 £0.36.

Claiming Races

All Age Races: Claiming Races – good to soft or softer going

ANALYSIS BY AGE

Age	Prop	Win	Runs	Wins%	£
2yo	0%	0	0	0.0%	0.00
3yo	14%	15	228	6.6%	-0.58
4yo	27%	28	310	9.0%	-0.34
5yo	21%	22	180	12.2%	0.12
6yo	9%	9	113	8.0%	-0.55
7yo	11%	12	76	15.8%	-0.04
8yo	9%	9	72	12.5%	-0.04
9yo	6%	6	46	13.0%	-0.11
10yo	1%	1	21	4.8%	-0.86
11yo+	3%	3	21	14.3%	-0.52

ANALYSIS BY BHA RATING

Rating	Prop	Win	Runs	Wins%	£
120..139	0%	0	0	0.0%	0.00
110..119	0%	0	0	0.0%	0.00
100..109	0%	0	2	0.0%	-1.00
90..99	6%	6	13	46.2%	0.79
70..89	36%	38	215	17.7%	-0.36
50..69	47%	49	446	11.0%	-0.21
..49	11%	12	324	3.7%	-0.28
Unrated	0%	0	66	0.0%	-1.00

ANALYSIS BY WEIGHT CARRIED

Weight	Prop	Win	Runs	Wins%	£
10-01+	0%	0	0	0.0%	0.00
9-8..10-00	21%	22	99	22.2%	-0.10
9-0..9-07	36%	38	349	10.9%	-0.47
8-8..8-13	27%	28	325	8.6%	-0.19
8-0..8-07	11%	12	256	4.7%	-0.31
..7-13	5%	5	38	13.2%	-0.11

ANALYSIS BY DAYS SINCE LAST RUN

Days	Prop	Win	Runs	Wins%	£
1..7	19%	20	158	12.7%	-0.04
8..14	31%	33	255	12.9%	0.04
15..28	30%	32	299	10.7%	-0.46
29..60	9%	9	188	4.8%	-0.59
61..100	6%	6	49	12.2%	-0.44
101+	5%	5	103	4.9%	-0.37
Unraced	0%	0	15	0.0%	-1.00

ANALYSIS BY TODAY'S STARTING PRICE

Price	Prop	Win	Runs	Wins%	£
Odds On	9%	9	12	75.0%	0.22
Ev - 2/1	22%	23	56	41.1%	0.12
9/4 - 4/1	30%	32	147	21.8%	-0.12
9/2 - 6/1	14%	15	97	15.5%	-0.05
13/2-10/1	10%	11	165	6.7%	-0.41
11/1-16/1	6%	6	178	3.4%	-0.52
18/1-33/1	7%	7	199	3.5%	-0.13
40/1+	2%	2	213	0.9%	-0.57

ANALYSIS BY STARTING PRICE LAST TIME

Price	Prop	Win	Runs	Wins%	£
Odds On	5%	5	7	71.4%	1.29
Ev - 2/1	5%	5	21	23.8%	-0.05
9/4 - 4/1	12%	13	83	15.7%	-0.37
9/2 - 6/1	14%	15	98	15.3%	0.23
13/2-10/1	23%	24	201	11.9%	-0.10
11/1-16/1	26%	27	223	12.1%	-0.13
18/1-33/1	13%	14	221	6.3%	-0.50
40/1+	2%	2	198	1.0%	-0.73
Unraced	0%	0	15	0.0%	-1.00

ANALYSIS BY DISTANCE BEATEN LAST TIME

Lengths	Prop	Win	Runs	Wins%	£
..-10	0%	0	0	0.0%	0.00
-10..0	13%	14	54	25.9%	0.10
0.1..2	10%	11	86	12.8%	-0.29
2.1..5	23%	24	192	12.5%	-0.14
5.1..10	19%	20	232	8.6%	-0.33
10.1..20	30%	31	294	10.5%	-0.30
20.0..30	2%	2	103	1.9%	-0.25
30.1+	3%	3	91	3.3%	-0.73
Not Compl	0%	0	0	0.0%	0.00
Unraced	0%	0	15	0.0%	-1.00

ANALYSIS BY RUN NUMBER

Run No	Prop	Win	Runs	Wins%	£
FTO	0%	0	15	0.0%	-1.00
2nd Run	0%	0	21	0.0%	-1.00
3rd Run	0%	0	22	0.0%	-1.00
4th+ Run	100%	105	1009	10.4%	-0.26

ANALYSIS BY POSITION LAST TIME

Pos LT	Prop	Win	Runs	Wins%	£
Won	13%	14	54	25.9%	0.10
2nd or 3rd	17%	18	128	14.1%	-0.38
Unplaced	70%	73	867	8.4%	-0.30
Not Compl	0%	0	18	0.0%	-1.00

OTHER FACTORS (WINS-RUNS, £)

Course Winner:	17-156	-£0.36
Distance Winner:	61-462	-£0.19
Going Winner:	38-185	£0.16
Beaten Favourite:	5-36	-£0.43
BHA Top Rated:	25-99	£0.11
Up in class:	14-217	-£0.42
Same class:	40-484	-£0.27
Down in class:	51-351	-£0.24
7-Day Winners:	5-13	£0.20
Colts and Geldings:	83-803	-£0.36
Fillies:	22-264	-£0.11
Absolute Favourites:	36-95	£0.03

TRAINERS (WINS-RUNS, £)

J S Goldie 3-16 £2.16; Miss Gay Kelleway 4-13 £1.72; Miss L A Perratt 2-12 £1.67; K R Burke 4-14 £1.03; A G Newcombe 2-10 £1.03; G A Swinbank 3-10 £0.75; R Hannon 8-24 £0.27; D Nicholls 10-29 £0.10; R A Fahey 9-25 £0.11.

Race Profiles

All Age Races: Claiming Races – 5 to 6 furlong races

ANALYSIS BY AGE

Age	Prop	Win	Runs	Wins%	£
2yo	0%	0	0	0.0%	0.00
3yo	12%	14	247	5.7%	-0.65
4yo	24%	28	324	8.6%	-0.34
5yo	19%	22	202	10.9%	-0.25
6yo	8%	9	127	7.1%	-0.58
7yo	11%	13	97	13.4%	0.49
8yo	11%	13	90	14.4%	-0.07
9yo	5%	6	45	13.3%	-0.55
10yo	3%	4	40	10.0%	-0.01
11yo+	6%	7	45	15.6%	-0.26

ANALYSIS BY BHA RATING

Rating	Prop	Win	Runs	Wins%	£
120..139	0%	0	0	0.0%	0.00
110..119	0%	0	0	0.0%	0.00
100..109	0%	0	0	0.0%	0.00
90..99	3%	4	11	36.4%	0.32
70..89	37%	43	206	20.9%	-0.04
50..69	48%	56	543	10.3%	-0.32
..49	11%	13	429	3.0%	-0.66
Unrated	0%	0	27	0.0%	-1.00

ANALYSIS BY WEIGHT CARRIED

Weight	Prop	Win	Runs	Wins%	£
10-01+	0%	0	0	0.0%	0.00
9-8 ..10-00	16%	19	92	20.7%	-0.05
9-0..9-07	40%	46	359	12.8%	-0.40
8-8..8-13	26%	30	403	7.4%	-0.39
8-0..8-07	16%	19	316	6.0%	-0.45
..7-13	2%	2	47	4.3%	-0.78

ANALYSIS BY DAYS SINCE LAST RUN

Days	Prop	Win	Runs	Wins%	£
1..7	29%	34	211	16.1%	-0.14
8..14	29%	34	346	9.8%	-0.36
15..28	31%	36	331	10.9%	-0.35
29..60	8%	9	184	4.9%	-0.59
61..100	2%	2	45	4.4%	-0.58
101+	1%	1	97	1.0%	-0.78
Unraced	0%	0	3	0.0%	-1.00

ANALYSIS BY TODAY'S STARTING PRICE

Price	Prop	Win	Runs	Wins%	£
Odds On	5%	6	12	50.0%	-0.15
Ev - 2/1	19%	22	56	39.3%	0.08
9/4 - 4/1	36%	42	170	24.7%	0.03
9/2 - 6/1	13%	15	112	13.4%	-0.19
13/2-10/1	13%	15	184	8.2%	-0.23
11/1-16/1	11%	13	179	7.3%	0.04
18/1-33/1	3%	3	237	1.3%	-0.71
40/1+	0%	0	267	0.0%	-1.00

ANALYSIS BY STARTING PRICE LAST TIME

Price	Prop	Win	Runs	Wins%	£
Odds On	1%	1	5	20.0%	-0.20
Ev - 2/1	9%	10	33	30.3%	0.01
9/4 - 4/1	18%	21	95	22.1%	-0.12
9/2 - 6/1	11%	13	110	11.8%	-0.31
13/2-10/1	27%	31	218	14.2%	0.02
11/1 16/1	22%	25	258	9.7%	-0.28
18/1-33/1	12%	14	291	4.8%	-0.62
40/1+	1%	1	204	0.5%	-0.93
Unraced	0%	0	3	0.0%	-1.00

ANALYSIS BY DISTANCE BEATEN LAST TIME

Lengths	Prop	Win	Runs	Wins%	£
..-10	0%	0	0	0.0%	0.00
-10..0	14%	16	56	28.6%	0.13
0.1..2	16%	19	125	15.2%	-0.32
2.1..5	31%	36	294	12.2%	-0.29
5.1..10	18%	21	339	6.2%	-0.53
10.1..20	15%	17	290	5.9%	-0.55
20.0..30	3%	3	62	4.8%	-0.50
30.1+	3%	4	48	8.3%	0.06
Not Compl	0%	0	0	0.0%	0.00
Unraced	0%	0	3	0.0%	-1.00

ANALYSIS BY RUN NUMBER

Run No	Prop	Win	Runs	Wins%	£
FTO	0%	0	3	0.0%	-1.00
2nd Run	0%	0	9	0.0%	-1.00
3rd Run	0%	0	12	0.0%	-1.00
4th+ Run	100%	116	1193	9.7%	-0.39

ANALYSIS BY POSITION LAST TIME

Pos LT	Prop	Win	Runs	Wins%	£
Won	14%	16	56	28.6%	0.13
2nd or 3rd	27%	31	168	18.5%	-0.09
Unplaced	59%	69	987	7.0%	-0.48
Not Compl	0%	0	6	0.0%	-1.00

OTHER FACTORS (WINS-RUNS, £)

Course Winner:	23-178	-£0.24
Distance Winner:	88-714	-£0.26
Going Winner:	57-385	-£0.18
Beaten Favourite:	7-41	-£0.42
BHA Top Rated:	21-104	-£0.02
Up in class:	10-218	-£0.62
Same class:	51-593	-£0.39
Down in class:	55-403	-£0.29
7-Day Winners:	4-16	£0.12
Colts and Geldings:	94-881	-£0.39
Fillies:	22-336	-£0.42
Absolute Favourites:	31-95	£0.07

TRAINERS (WINS-RUNS, £)

D Nicholls 23-63 £0.70.

Claiming Races

All Age Races: Claiming Races – 7 to 9 furlong races

ANALYSIS BY AGE

Age	Prop	Win	Runs	Wins%	£
2yo	0%	0	0	0.0%	0.00
3yo	16%	26	322	8.1%	-0.45
4yo	22%	37	470	7.9%	-0.41
5yo	17%	29	297	9.8%	0.22
6yo	19%	31	235	13.2%	-0.25
7yo	9%	15	174	8.6%	-0.05
8yo	9%	15	115	13.0%	-0.13
9yo	5%	9	66	13.6%	-0.45
10yo	1%	2	29	6.9%	-0.79
11yo+	2%	3	22	13.6%	-0.48

ANALYSIS BY BHA RATING

Rating	Prop	Win	Runs	Wins%	£
120..139	0%	0	0	0.0%	0.00
110..119	0%	0	0	0.0%	0.00
100..109	0%	0	2	0.0%	-1.00
90..99	2%	3	8	37.5%	-0.06
70..89	45%	75	363	20.7%	-0.11
50..69	41%	69	690	10.0%	-0.30
..49	11%	19	585	3.2%	-0.16
Unrated	1%	1	81	1.2%	-0.96

ANALYSIS BY WEIGHT CARRIED

Weight	Prop	Win	Runs	Wins%	£
10-01+	1%	1	16	6.3%	-0.59
9-8 ..10-00	24%	40	205	19.5%	-0.21
9-0..9-07	40%	66	603	10.9%	-0.40
8-8..8-13	26%	44	551	8.0%	0.02
8-0..8-07	8%	14	316	4.4%	-0.38
..7-13	1%	2	39	5.1%	-0.54

ANALYSIS BY DAYS SINCE LAST RUN

Days	Prop	Win	Runs	Wins%	£
1..7	27%	45	287	15.7%	0.45
8..14	34%	56	473	11.8%	-0.24
15..28	23%	39	460	8.5%	-0.40
29..60	10%	17	278	6.1%	-0.48
61..100	2%	4	65	6.2%	-0.51
101+	4%	6	144	4.2%	-0.46
Unraced	0%	0	23	0.0%	-1.00

ANALYSIS BY TODAY'S STARTING PRICE

Price	Prop	Win	Runs	Wins%	£
Odds On	7%	11	18	61.1%	0.08
Ev - 2/1	21%	35	93	37.6%	-0.06
9/4 - 4/1	31%	52	235	22.1%	-0.11
9/2 - 6/1	13%	21	157	13.4%	0.17
13/2-10/1	14%	24	254	9.4%	-0.18
11/1-16/1	7%	12	243	4.9%	-0.32
18/1-33/1	4%	7	321	2.2%	-0.45
40/1+	3%	5	409	1.2%	-0.24

ANALYSIS BY STARTING PRICE LAST TIME

Price	Prop	Win	Runs	Wins%	£
Odds On	3%	5	13	38.5%	-0.03
Ev - 2/1	7%	11	46	23.9%	0.09
9/4 - 4/1	18%	30	142	21.1%	-0.06
9/2 - 6/1	15%	25	151	16.6%	-0.11
13/2-10/1	23%	38	321	11.8%	-0.22
11/1-16/1	19%	32	339	9.4%	-0.28
18/1-33/1	11%	18	378	4.8%	-0.31
40/1+	5%	8	317	2.5%	-0.31
Unraced	0%	0	23	0.0%	-1.00

ANALYSIS BY DISTANCE BEATEN LAST TIME

Lengths	Prop	Win	Runs	Wins%	£
..-10	0%	0	0	0.0%	0.00
-10..0	16%	27	90	30.0%	0.10
0.1..2	19%	31	158	19.6%	0.05
2.1..5	20%	34	299	11.4%	-0.27
5.1..10	17%	28	421	6.7%	-0.55
10.1..20	20%	34	459	7.4%	-0.36
20.0..30	7%	12	142	8.5%	1.30
30.1+	1%	1	138	0.7%	-0.89
Not Compl	0%	0	0	0.0%	0.00
Unraced	0%	0	23	0.0%	-1.00

ANALYSIS BY RUN NUMBER

Run No	Prop	Win	Runs	Wins%	£
FTO	0%	0	23	0.0%	-1.00
2nd Run	0%	0	24	0.0%	-1.00
3rd Run	1%	2	29	6.9%	-0.47
4th+ Run	99%	165	1654	10.0%	-0.22

ANALYSIS BY POSITION LAST TIME

Pos LT	Prop	Win	Runs	Wins%	£
Won	16%	27	89	30.3%	0.12
2nd or 3rd	23%	39	209	18.7%	0.02
Unplaced	60%	101	1403	7.2%	-0.29
Not Compl	0%	0	29	0.0%	-1.00

OTHER FACTORS (WINS-RUNS, £)

Course Winner:	41-304	-£0.25
Distance Winner:	101-724	-£0.22
Going Winner:	85-519	-£0.16
Beaten Favourite:	10-71	-£0.39
BHA Top Rated:	35-147	-£0.14
Up in class:	29-407	-£0.25
Same class:	72-784	-£0.25
Down in class:	66-516	-£0.20
7-Day Winners:	7-21	£0.17
Colts and Geldings:	141-1345	-£0.28
Fillies:	26-385	-£0.12
Absolute Favourites:	60-153	£0.06

TRAINERS (WINS-RUNS, £)

J C Fox 1-14 £6.21; R M Whitaker 4-30 £1.80; John A Harris 3-13 £4.00; Miss L A Perratt 4-30 £1.17; Miss Gay Kelleway 5-14 £1.85; Miss Tracy Waggott 3-20 £0.95; R C Guest 2-10 £1.45; Ollie Pears 4-13 £1.00; K R Burke 4-20 £0.61; I Semple 7-32 £0.35; P W Hiatt 2-11 £1.00; P F I Cole 3-12 £0.56; P Monteith 1-10 £0.20.

Race Profiles

All Age Races: Claiming Races – 10 to 14 furlong races

ANALYSIS BY AGE

Age	Prop	Win	Runs	Wins%	£
2yo	0%	0	0	0.0%	0.00
3yo	19%	28	296	9.5%	-0.44
4yo	22%	32	397	8.1%	-0.29
5yo	17%	24	191	12.6%	-0.12
6yo	11%	16	139	11.5%	-0.23
7yo	12%	18	116	15.5%	-0.17
8yo	12%	17	78	21.8%	0.00
9yo	3%	4	66	6.1%	-0.37
10yo	3%	5	28	17.9%	-0.36
11yo+	1%	1	32	3.1%	-0.95

ANALYSIS BY BHA RATING

Rating	Prop	Win	Runs	Wins%	£
120..139	0%	0	0	0.0%	0.00
110..119	0%	0	0	0.0%	0.00
100..109	1%	1	3	33.3%	-0.33
90..99	3%	4	18	22.2%	0.07
70..89	44%	64	295	21.7%	-0.21
50..69	40%	58	506	11.5%	-0.18
..49	12%	18	433	4.2%	-0.33
Unrated	0%	0	86	0.0%	-1.00

ANALYSIS BY WEIGHT CARRIED

Weight	Prop	Win	Runs	Wins%	£
10-01+	2%	3	33	9.1%	0.36
9-8..10-00	28%	41	190	21.6%	-0.13
9-0..9-07	32%	47	471	10.0%	-0.51
8-8..8-13	23%	33	341	9.7%	-0.24
8-0..8-07	12%	17	262	6.5%	-0.09
..7-13	3%	4	46	8.7%	-0.50

ANALYSIS BY DAYS SINCE LAST RUN

Days	Prop	Win	Runs	Wins%	£
1..7	12%	18	168	10.7%	-0.47
8..14	34%	50	323	15.5%	0.11
15..28	30%	43	376	11.4%	-0.33
29..60	10%	15	212	7.1%	-0.65
61..100	4%	6	70	8.6%	-0.48
101+	9%	13	176	7.4%	-0.14
Unraced	0%	0	18	0.0%	-1.00

ANALYSIS BY TODAY'S STARTING PRICE

Price	Prop	Win	Runs	Wins%	£
Odds On	8%	12	17	70.6%	0.12
Ev - 2/1	23%	34	90	37.8%	-0.05
9/4 - 4/1	30%	43	188	22.9%	-0.13
9/2 - 6/1	16%	23	149	15.4%	-0.03
13/2-10/1	12%	18	204	8.8%	-0.19
11/1-16/1	4%	6	186	3.2%	-0.56
18/1-33/1	5%	7	227	3.1%	-0.19
40/1+	1%	2	282	0.7%	-0.58

ANALYSIS BY STARTING PRICE LAST TIME

Price	Prop	Win	Runs	Wins%	£
Odds On	1%	2	13	15.4%	-0.60
Ev - 2/1	10%	14	54	25.9%	-0.29
9/4 - 4/1	17%	24	140	17.1%	-0.27
9/2 - 6/1	13%	19	118	16.1%	0.18
13/2-10/1	23%	34	245	13.9%	-0.22
11/1-16/1	18%	26	240	10.8%	-0.42
18/1-33/1	12%	18	252	7.1%	0.01
40/1+	6%	8	263	3.0%	-0.66
Unraced	0%	0	18	0.0%	-1.00

ANALYSIS BY DISTANCE BEATEN LAST TIME

Lengths	Prop	Win	Runs	Wins%	£
..-10	0%	0	1	0.0%	-1.00
-10..0	17%	24	88	27.3%	-0.07
0.1..2	9%	13	98	13.3%	-0.54
2.1..5	22%	32	184	17.4%	-0.09
5.1..10	21%	31	247	12.6%	0.04
10.1..20	22%	32	355	9.0%	-0.42
20.0..30	3%	5	167	3.0%	-0.42
30.1+	6%	8	185	4.3%	-0.43
Not Compl	0%	0	0	0.0%	0.00
Unraced	0%	0	18	0.0%	-1.00

ANALYSIS BY RUN NUMBER

Run No	Prop	Win	Runs	Wins%	£
FTO	0%	0	18	0.0%	-1.00
2nd Run	0%	0	29	0.0%	-1.00
3rd Run	0%	0	33	0.0%	-1.00
4th+ Run	100%	145	1263	11.5%	-0.24

ANALYSIS BY POSITION LAST TIME

Pos LT	Prop	Win	Runs	Wins%	£
Won	17%	24	90	26.7%	-0.09
2nd or 3rd	21%	31	211	14.7%	-0.41
Unplaced	62%	90	1017	8.8%	-0.26
Not Compl	0%	0	25	0.0%	-1.00

OTHER FACTORS (WINS-RUNS, £)

Course Winner:	22-172	-£0.26
Distance Winner:	79-436	£0.03
Going Winner:	64-359	-£0.13
Beaten Favourite:	15-74	-£0.25
BHA Top Rated:	28-123	-£0.14
Up in class:	20-287	-£0.47
Same class:	54-595	-£0.19
Down in class:	71-443	-£0.26
7-Day Winners:	3-13	-£0.28
Colts and Geldings:	115-1016	-£0.38
Fillies:	30-327	£0.00
Absolute Favourites:	53-130	£0.04

TRAINERS (WINS-RUNS, £)

D W Thompson 1-13 £2.92; N Wilson 2-10 £1.90; G A Swinbank 4-13 £1.19; P W Hiatt 3-18 £0.78; R M Whitaker 3-11 £1.12; R A Fahey 11-31 £0.33; R Hannon 6-20 £0.38; Ian Williams 4-11 £0.43; P T Midgley 1-10 £0.30; D Nicholls 4-17 £0.13; D Carroll 2-13 £0.02.

Claiming Races

All Age Races: Claiming Races – 15+ furlong races

ANALYSIS BY AGE
Age	Prop	Win	Runs	Wins%	£
2yo	0%	0	0	0.0%	0.00
3yo	0%	0	7	0.0%	-1.00
4yo	29%	2	10	20.0%	-0.50
5yo	29%	2	9	22.2%	-0.29
6yo	0%	0	10	0.0%	-1.00
7yo	14%	1	7	14.3%	0.57
8yo	14%	1	6	16.7%	-0.25
9yo	14%	1	6	16.7%	-0.60
10yo	0%	0	2	0.0%	-1.00
11yo+	0%	0	4	0.0%	-1.00

ANALYSIS BY BHA RATING
Rating	Prop	Win	Runs	Wins%	£
120..139	0%	0	0	0.0%	0.00
110..119	0%	0	0	0.0%	0.00
100..109	0%	0	0	0.0%	0.00
90..99	0%	0	0	0.0%	0.00
70..89	0%	0	2	0.0%	-1.00
50..69	57%	4	26	15.4%	-0.66
..49	29%	2	24	8.3%	-0.35
Unrated	14%	1	9	11.1%	-0.44

ANALYSIS BY WEIGHT CARRIED
Weight	Prop	Win	Runs	Wins%	£
10-01+	0%	0	0	0.0%	0.00
9-8 ..10-00	43%	3	19	15.8%	-0.71
9-0..9-07	43%	3	26	11.5%	-0.26
8-8..8-13	14%	1	5	20.0%	-0.10
8-0..8-07	0%	0	8	0.0%	-1.00
..7-13	0%	0	3	0.0%	-1.00

ANALYSIS BY DAYS SINCE LAST RUN
Days	Prop	Win	Runs	Wins%	£
1..7	0%	0	3	0.0%	-1.00
8..14	43%	3	14	21.4%	0.28
15..28	43%	3	14	21.4%	-0.54
29..60	0%	0	10	0.0%	-1.00
61..100	0%	0	1	0.0%	-1.00
101+	0%	0	14	0.0%	-1.00
Unraced	14%	1	5	20.0%	0.00

ANALYSIS BY TODAY'S STARTING PRICE
Price	Prop	Win	Runs	Wins%	£
Odds On	29%	2	3	66.7%	0.05
Ev - 2/1	14%	1	4	25.0%	-0.41
9/4 - 4/1	43%	3	6	50.0%	1.13
9/2 - 6/1	0%	0	6	0.0%	-1.00
13/2-10/1	14%	1	13	7.7%	-0.15
11/1-16/1	0%	0	8	0.0%	-1.00
18/1-33/1	0%	0	12	0.0%	-1.00
40/1+	0%	0	9	0.0%	-1.00

ANALYSIS BY STARTING PRICE LAST TIME
Price	Prop	Win	Runs	Wins%	£
Odds On	0%	0	0	0.0%	0.00
Ev - 2/1	14%	1	1	100.0%	10.00
9/4 - 4/1	29%	2	6	33.3%	-0.06
9/2 - 6/1	14%	1	4	25.0%	-0.55
13/2-10/1	29%	2	13	15.4%	-0.55
11/1-16/1	0%	0	8	0.0%	-1.00
18/1-33/1	0%	0	11	0.0%	-1.00
40/1+	0%	0	13	0.0%	-1.00
Unraced	14%	1	5	20.0%	0.00

ANALYSIS BY DISTANCE BEATEN LAST TIME
Lengths	Prop	Win	Runs	Wins%	£
..-10	0%	0	0	0.0%	0.00
-10..0	14%	1	3	33.3%	0.50
0.1..2	14%	1	2	50.0%	0.19
2.1..5	29%	2	5	40.0%	-0.37
5.1..10	14%	1	12	8.3%	-0.08
10.1..20	0%	0	13	0.0%	-1.00
20.0..30	0%	0	10	0.0%	-1.00
30.1+	14%	1	11	9.1%	-0.70
Not Compl	0%	0	0	0.0%	0.00
Unraced	14%	1	5	20.0%	0.00

ANALYSIS BY RUN NUMBER
Run No	Prop	Win	Runs	Wins%	£
FTO	14%	1	5	20.0%	0.00
2nd Run	0%	0	4	0.0%	-1.00
3rd Run	0%	0	0	0.0%	0.00
4th+ Run	86%	6	52	11.5%	-0.53

ANALYSIS BY POSITION LAST TIME
Pos LT	Prop	Win	Runs	Wins%	£
Won	14%	1	3	33.3%	0.50
2nd or 3rd	43%	3	10	30.0%	-0.45
Unplaced	29%	2	43	4.7%	-0.67
Not Compl	14%	1	5	20.0%	0.00

OTHER FACTORS (WINS-RUNS, £)
Course Winner:	0-4	-£1.00
Distance Winner:	0-7	-£1.00
Going Winner:	2-14	-£0.51
Beaten Favourite:	2-3	£3.46
BHA Top Rated:	2-8	-£0.48
Up in class:	0-1	-£1.00
Same class:	2-33	-£0.81
Down in class:	4-22	-£0.18
Colts and Geldings:	5-44	-£0.00
Fillies:	2-17	-£0.16
Absolute Favourites:	4-7	£0.26

Race Profiles

All Age Races: Selling Races

ANALYSIS BY AGE

Age	Prop	Win	Runs	Wins%	£
2yo	0%	0	0	0.0%	0.00
3yo	22%	101	1394	7.2%	-0.22
4yo	32%	142	1658	8.6%	-0.31
5yo	18%	82	779	10.5%	-0.00
6yo	9%	40	413	9.7%	-0.19
7yo	5%	22	252	8.7%	-0.33
8yo	5%	21	204	10.3%	-0.48
9yo	6%	25	144	17.4%	0.01
10yo	2%	10	67	14.9%	-0.13
11yo+	1%	6	65	9.2%	-0.31

ANALYSIS BY BHA RATING

Rating	Prop	Win	Runs	Wins%	£
120..139	0%	0	0	0.0%	0.00
110..119	0%	0	0	0.0%	0.00
100..109	0%	0	0	0.0%	0.00
90..99	3%	14	96	14.6%	-0.07
70..89	23%	105	571	18.4%	-0.03
50..69	54%	241	2111	11.4%	-0.19
..49	18%	81	1980	4.1%	-0.33
Unrated	2%	8	210	3.8%	-0.10

ANALYSIS BY WEIGHT CARRIED

Weight	Prop	Win	Runs	Wins%	£
10-01+	1%	5	31	16.1%	-0.10
9-8..10-00	12%	54	371	14.6%	-0.27
9-0..9-07	51%	231	2315	10.0%	-0.18
8-8..8-13	24%	110	1420	7.7%	-0.18
8-0..8-07	10%	47	778	6.0%	-0.38
..7-13	0%	2	61	3.3%	-0.41

ANALYSIS BY DAYS SINCE LAST RUN

Days	Prop	Win	Runs	Wins%	£
1..7	20%	89	760	11.7%	-0.29
8..14	27%	122	1166	10.5%	-0.22
15..28	28%	126	1400	9.0%	-0.11
29..60	13%	59	772	7.6%	-0.29
61..100	4%	16	218	7.3%	-0.45
101+	8%	36	604	6.0%	-0.30
Unraced	0%	1	56	1.8%	0.45

ANALYSIS BY TODAY'S STARTING PRICE

Price	Prop	Win	Runs	Wins%	£
Odds On	6%	25	34	73.5%	0.25
Ev - 2/1	13%	57	158	36.1%	-0.07
9/4 - 4/1	33%	150	613	24.5%	0.02
9/2 - 6/1	14%	64	521	12.3%	-0.25
13/2-10/1	17%	77	942	8.2%	-0.27
11/1-16/1	9%	39	837	4.7%	-0.32
18/1-33/1	5%	24	964	2.5%	-0.35
40/1+	3%	13	907	1.4%	-0.15

ANALYSIS BY STARTING PRICE LAST TIME

Price	Prop	Win	Runs	Wins%	£
Odds On	1%	4	11	36.4%	-0.13
Ev - 2/1	6%	26	85	30.6%	0.15
9/4 - 4/1	15%	66	380	17.4%	-0.15
9/2 - 6/1	14%	61	441	13.8%	-0.24
13/2-10/1	23%	103	852	12.1%	-0.17
11/1-16/1	20%	90	961	9.4%	-0.21
18/1-33/1	15%	69	1165	5.9%	-0.14
40/1+	6%	29	1025	2.8%	-0.47
Unraced	0%	1	56	1.8%	0.45

ANALYSIS BY DISTANCE BEATEN LAST TIME

Lengths	Prop	Win	Runs	Wins%	£
..-10	0%	0	0	0.0%	0.00
-10..0	10%	44	202	21.8%	-0.20
0.1..2	16%	72	418	17.2%	-0.22
2.1..5	19%	86	790	10.9%	-0.39
5.1..10	26%	117	1295	9.0%	-0.26
10.1..20	21%	94	1308	7.2%	-0.10
20.0..30	6%	25	472	5.3%	-0.01
30.1+	2%	10	435	2.3%	-0.52
Not Compl	0%	0	0	0.0%	0.00
Unraced	0%	1	56	1.8%	0.45

ANALYSIS BY RUN NUMBER

Run No	Prop	Win	Runs	Wins%	£
FTO	0%	1	56	1.8%	0.45
2nd Run	1%	4	67	6.0%	-0.62
3rd Run	1%	5	98	5.1%	-0.04
4th+ Run	98%	439	4755	9.2%	-0.23

ANALYSIS BY POSITION LAST TIME

Pos LT	Prop	Win	Runs	Wins%	£
Won	10%	44	202	21.8%	-0.20
2nd or 3rd	22%	99	633	15.6%	-0.20
Unplaced	68%	305	4074	7.5%	-0.23
Not Compl	0%	1	67	1.5%	0.21

OTHER FACTORS (WINS-RUNS, £)

Course Winner:	64-513	-£0.29
Distance Winner:	218-1650	-£0.19
Going Winner:	134-1088	-£0.32
Beaten Favourite:	39-175	£0.09
BHA Top Rated:	72-442	-£0.08
Up in class:	60-828	-£0.24
Same class:	242-2765	-£0.25
Down in class:	146-1327	-£0.18
7-Day Winners:	13-44	£0.02
Colts and Geldings:	343-3397	-£0.21
Fillies:	106-1579	-£0.24
Absolute Favourites:	151-395	£0.19

TRAINERS (WINS-RUNS, £)

David Pinder 2-16 £4.00; Miss L A Perratt 1-27 £2.00; B R Johnson 5-14 £3.49; C J Teague 1-22 £2.05; J Howard Johnson 1-10 £4.10; B J Meehan 3-16 £2.33; W R Swinburn 5-11 £3.30; Mrs A Duffield 5-33 £1.08; M S Saunders 3-18 £1.72; J M Bradley 9-125 £0.22; Miss Gay Kelleway 8-45 £0.60; J Alston 6-26 £1.03; G Prodromou 2-14 £1.39; P T Midgley 6-54 £0.29; G L Moore 5-33 £0.46; D Carroll 6-32 £0.44; John A Harris 2-20 £0.60; R Bastiman 2-26 £0.46; M D I Usher 3-17 £0.65; Ollie Pears 5-25 £0.44.

Selling Races

All Age Races: Selling Races – 2 to 7 runners

ANALYSIS BY AGE

Age	Prop	Win	Runs	Wins%	£
2yo	0%	0	0	0.0%	0.00
3yo	27%	22	145	15.2%	0.03
4yo	30%	24	137	17.5%	-0.02
5yo	11%	9	78	11.5%	-0.61
6yo	9%	7	57	12.3%	-0.32
7yo	2%	2	30	6.7%	-0.69
8yo	11%	9	32	28.1%	0.71
9yo	9%	7	19	36.8%	-0.05
10yo	1%	1	4	25.0%	0.00
11yo+	0%	0	5	0.0%	-1.00

ANALYSIS BY BHA RATING

Rating	Prop	Win	Runs	Wins%	£
120..139	0%	0	0	0.0%	0.00
110..119	0%	0	0	0.0%	0.00
100..109	0%	0	0	0.0%	0.00
90..99	9%	7	36	19.4%	0.06
70..89	48%	39	179	21.8%	0.01
50..69	35%	28	187	15.0%	-0.12
..49	7%	6	97	6.2%	-0.48
Unrated	1%	1	8	12.5%	-0.25

ANALYSIS BY WEIGHT CARRIED

Weight	Prop	Win	Runs	Wins%	£
10-01+	0%	0	0	0.0%	0.00
9-8 ..10-00	6%	5	29	17.2%	-0.56
9-0..9-07	60%	49	259	18.9%	-0.04
8-8..8-13	25%	20	136	14.7%	-0.03
8-0..8-07	9%	7	77	9.1%	-0.38
..7-13	0%	0	6	0.0%	-1.00

ANALYSIS BY DAYS SINCE LAST RUN

Days	Prop	Win	Runs	Wins%	£
1..7	26%	21	100	21.0%	-0.18
8..14	28%	23	150	15.3%	-0.31
15..28	30%	24	128	18.8%	0.34
29..60	7%	6	66	9.1%	-0.58
61..100	0%	0	16	0.0%	-1.00
101+	9%	7	46	15.2%	0.20
Unraced	0%	0	1	0.0%	-1.00

ANALYSIS BY TODAY'S STARTING PRICE

Price	Prop	Win	Runs	Wins%	£
Odds On	16%	13	17	76.5%	0.25
Ev - 2/1	21%	17	51	33.3%	-0.13
9/4 - 4/1	35%	28	133	21.1%	-0.12
9/2 - 6/1	10%	8	64	12.5%	-0.22
13/2-10/1	10%	8	92	8.7%	-0.20
11/1-16/1	5%	4	62	6.5%	-0.03
18/1-33/1	4%	3	52	5.8%	0.40
40/1+	0%	0	36	0.0%	-1.00

ANALYSIS BY STARTING PRICE LAST TIME

Price	Prop	Win	Runs	Wins%	£
Odds On	2%	2	3	66.7%	0.77
Ev - 2/1	9%	7	21	33.3%	-0.11
9/4 - 4/1	17%	14	55	25.5%	-0.26
9/2 - 6/1	14%	11	79	13.9%	-0.54
13/2-10/1	25%	20	94	21.3%	0.03
11/1-16/1	21%	17	99	17.2%	0.20
18/1-33/1	10%	8	85	9.4%	0.24
40/1+	2%	2	70	2.9%	-0.76
Unraced	0%	0	1	0.0%	-1.00

ANALYSIS BY DISTANCE BEATEN LAST TIME

Lengths	Prop	Win	Runs	Wins%	£
..-10	0%	0	0	0.0%	0.00
-10..0	17%	14	53	26.4%	-0.22
0.1..2	19%	15	70	21.4%	-0.29
2.1..5	22%	18	98	18.4%	-0.23
5.1..10	17%	14	116	12.1%	0.04
10.1..20	19%	15	107	14.0%	0.19
20.0..30	5%	4	42	9.5%	-0.49
30.1+	1%	1	20	5.0%	-0.81
Not Compl	0%	0	0	0.0%	0.00
Unraced	0%	0	1	0.0%	-1.00

ANALYSIS BY RUN NUMBER

Run No	Prop	Win	Runs	Wins%	£
FTO	0%	0	1	0.0%	-1.00
2nd Run	1%	1	8	12.5%	-0.44
3rd Run	0%	0	6	0.0%	-1.00
4th+ Run	99%	80	492	16.3%	-0.12

ANALYSIS BY POSITION LAST TIME

Pos LT	Prop	Win	Runs	Wins%	£
Won	17%	14	53	26.4%	-0.22
2nd or 3rd	23%	19	97	19.6%	-0.35
Unplaced	59%	48	356	13.5%	-0.06
Not Compl	0%	0	1	0.0%	-1.00

OTHER FACTORS (WINS-RUNS, £)

Course Winner:	16-72	-£0.33
Distance Winner:	50-244	-£0.14
Going Winner:	29-176	£0.45
Beaten Favourite:	5-26	-£0.45
BHA Top Rated:	20-95	-£0.16
Up in class:	11-76	-£0.26
Same class:	47-288	-£0.08
Down in class:	23-142	-£0.17
7-Day Winners:	5-11	£0.49
Colts and Geldings:	71-397	£0.00
Fillies:	10-110	-£0.62
Absolute Favourites:	34-72	£0.14

TRAINERS (WINS-RUNS, £)

D Nicholls 7-14 £1.73.

Race Profiles

All Age Races: Selling Races – 8 to 14 runners

ANALYSIS BY AGE

Age	Prop	Win	Runs	Wins%	£
2yo	0%	0	0	0.0%	0.00
3yo	22%	63	875	7.2%	-0.22
4yo	29%	85	1097	7.7%	-0.36
5yo	22%	63	537	11.7%	0.23
6yo	10%	30	281	10.7%	-0.09
7yo	6%	17	168	10.1%	-0.30
8yo	4%	11	134	8.2%	-0.68
9yo	5%	15	93	16.1%	0.04
10yo	2%	5	48	10.4%	-0.33
11yo+	1%	4	47	8.5%	-0.60

ANALYSIS BY BHA RATING

Rating	Prop	Win	Runs	Wins%	£
120..139	0%	0	0	0.0%	0.00
110..119	0%	0	0	0.0%	0.00
100..109	0%	0	0	0.0%	0.00
90..99	2%	6	47	12.8%	-0.03
70..89	21%	61	351	17.4%	0.00
50..69	56%	164	1416	11.6%	-0.19
..49	20%	58	1332	4.4%	-0.28
Unrated	1%	4	127	3.1%	-0.20

ANALYSIS BY WEIGHT CARRIED

Weight	Prop	Win	Runs	Wins%	£
10-01+	1%	4	25	16.0%	-0.16
9-8 ..10-00	13%	37	251	14.7%	-0.32
9-0..9-07	50%	146	1492	9.8%	-0.11
8-8..8-13	25%	74	970	7.6%	-0.26
8-0..8-07	10%	30	500	6.0%	-0.35
..7-13	1%	2	42	4.8%	-0.14

ANALYSIS BY DAYS SINCE LAST RUN

Days	Prop	Win	Runs	Wins%	£
1..7	19%	55	493	11.2%	-0.35
8..14	26%	76	760	10.0%	-0.21
15..28	29%	85	926	9.2%	-0.03
29..60	14%	42	526	8.0%	-0.19
61..100	4%	13	144	9.0%	-0.36
101+	7%	21	396	5.3%	-0.52
Unraced	0%	1	35	2.9%	1.31

ANALYSIS BY TODAY'S STARTING PRICE

Price	Prop	Win	Runs	Wins%	£
Odds On	3%	10	15	66.7%	0.18
Ev - 2/1	12%	35	94	37.2%	-0.04
9/4 - 4/1	35%	103	419	24.6%	0.02
9/2 - 6/1	16%	46	356	12.9%	-0.21
13/2-10/1	17%	49	627	7.8%	-0.30
11/1-16/1	9%	25	555	4.5%	-0.34
18/1-33/1	5%	16	648	2.5%	-0.35
40/1+	3%	9	566	1.6%	-0.01

ANALYSIS BY STARTING PRICE LAST TIME

Price	Prop	Win	Runs	Wins%	£
Odds On	1%	2	6	33.3%	-0.29
Ev - 2/1	6%	18	53	34.0%	0.44
9/4 - 4/1	13%	39	260	15.0%	-0.18
9/2 - 6/1	14%	42	274	15.3%	-0.11
13/2-10/1	22%	63	575	11.0%	-0.21
11/1-16/1	19%	55	613	9.0%	-0.41
18/1-33/1	17%	50	769	6.5%	-0.03
40/1+	8%	23	695	3.3%	-0.39
Unraced	0%	1	35	2.9%	1.31

ANALYSIS BY DISTANCE BEATEN LAST TIME

Lengths	Prop	Win	Runs	Wins%	£
..-10	0%	0	0	0.0%	0.00
-10..0	8%	23	122	18.9%	-0.31
0.1..2	16%	48	277	17.3%	-0.17
2.1..5	19%	56	521	10.7%	-0.35
5.1..10	28%	81	855	9.5%	-0.22
10.1..20	20%	58	849	6.8%	-0.22
20.0..30	6%	18	305	5.9%	0.28
30.1+	3%	8	316	2.5%	-0.51
Not Compl	0%	0	0	0.0%	0.00
Unraced	0%	1	35	2.9%	1.31

ANALYSIS BY RUN NUMBER

Run No	Prop	Win	Runs	Wins%	£
FTO	0%	1	35	2.9%	1.31
2nd Run	1%	3	38	7.9%	-0.45
3rd Run	1%	2	55	3.6%	-0.77
4th+ Run	98%	287	3152	9.1%	-0.21

ANALYSIS BY POSITION LAST TIME

Pos LT	Prop	Win	Runs	Wins%	£
Won	8%	23	122	18.9%	-0.31
2nd or 3rd	23%	68	416	16.3%	-0.11
Unplaced	69%	201	2699	7.4%	-0.23
Not Compl	0%	1	43	2.3%	0.88

OTHER FACTORS (WINS-RUNS, £)

Course Winner:	39-339	-£0.30
Distance Winner:	140-1087	-£0.16
Going Winner:	86-701	-£0.32
Beaten Favourite:	30-122	£0.31
BHA Top Rated:	41-276	-£0.21
Up in class:	40-511	-£0.16
Same class:	157-1848	-£0.22
Down in class:	95-886	-£0.26
7-Day Winners:	6-28	-£0.28
Colts and Geldings:	216-2204	-£0.23
Fillies:	77-1076	-£0.16
Absolute Favourites:	96-261	£0.19

TRAINERS (WINS-RUNS, £)

Miss L A Perratt 1-18 £3.50; B R Johnson 5-11 £4.72; C J Teague 1-18 £2.72; Mrs A Duffield 5-23 £1.99; B J Meehan 3-13 £3.10; J M Bradley 6-85 £0.84; E J Alston 4-15 £1.82; G Prodromou 2-12 £1.79; G L Moore 4-25 £0.82; Miss Gay Kelleway 6-32 £0.63; R Hollinshead 4-24 £0.83; John A Harris 2-13 £1.46; R Bastiman 2-19 £1.00; M Johnston 3-11 £1.59; M Brittain 1-11 £1.36; Miss A Stokell 1-13 £1.00; R M Whitaker 7-34 £0.30; J Pearce 3-24 £0.42; J Akehurst 2-15 £0.53; G A Swinbank 7-25 £0.31.

Selling Races

All Age Races: Selling Races – 15 runners or more

ANALYSIS BY AGE

Age	Prop	Win	Runs	Wins%	£
2yo	0%	0	0	0.0%	0.00
3yo	21%	16	374	4.3%	-0.32
4yo	44%	33	424	7.8%	-0.27
5yo	13%	10	164	6.1%	-0.46
6yo	4%	3	75	4.0%	-0.45
7yo	4%	3	54	5.6%	-0.24
8yo	1%	1	38	2.6%	-0.76
9yo	4%	3	32	9.4%	-0.05
10yo	5%	4	15	26.7%	0.48
11yo+	3%	2	13	15.4%	1.00

ANALYSIS BY BHA RATING

Rating	Prop	Win	Runs	Wins%	£
120..139	0%	0	0	0.0%	0.00
110..119	0%	0	0	0.0%	0.00
100..109	0%	0	0	0.0%	0.00
90..99	1%	1	13	7.7%	-0.62
70..89	7%	5	41	12.2%	-0.50
50..69	65%	49	508	9.6%	-0.22
..49	23%	17	551	3.1%	-0.42
Unrated	4%	3	75	4.0%	0.08

ANALYSIS BY WEIGHT CARRIED

Weight	Prop	Win	Runs	Wins%	£
10-01+	1%	1	6	16.7%	0.17
9-8..10-00	16%	12	91	13.2%	-0.06
9-0..9-07	48%	36	564	6.4%	-0.45
8-8..8-13	21%	16	314	5.1%	-0.03
8-0..8-07	13%	10	201	5.0%	-0.45
..7-13	0%	0	13	0.0%	-1.00

ANALYSIS BY DAYS SINCE LAST RUN

Days	Prop	Win	Runs	Wins%	£
1..7	17%	13	167	7.8%	-0.15
8..14	31%	23	256	9.0%	-0.21
15..28	23%	17	346	4.9%	-0.49
29..60	15%	11	180	6.1%	-0.47
61..100	4%	3	58	5.2%	-0.50
101+	11%	8	162	4.9%	0.09
Unraced	0%	0	20	0.0%	-1.00

ANALYSIS BY TODAY'S STARTING PRICE

Price	Prop	Win	Runs	Wins%	£
Odds On	3%	2	2	100.0%	0.78
Ev - 2/1	7%	5	13	38.5%	-0.01
9/4 - 4/1	25%	19	61	31.1%	0.39
9/2 - 6/1	13%	10	101	9.9%	-0.39
13/2-10/1	27%	20	223	9.0%	-0.23
11/1-16/1	13%	10	220	4.5%	-0.35
18/1-33/1	7%	5	264	1.9%	-0.50
40/1+	5%	4	305	1.3%	-0.31

ANALYSIS BY STARTING PRICE LAST TIME

Price	Prop	Win	Runs	Wins%	£
Odds On	0%	0	2	0.0%	-1.00
Ev - 2/1	1%	1	11	9.1%	-0.76
9/4 - 4/1	17%	13	65	20.0%	0.05
9/2 - 6/1	11%	8	88	9.1%	-0.40
13/2-10/1	27%	20	183	10.9%	-0.12
11/1-16/1	24%	18	249	7.2%	0.12
18/1-33/1	15%	11	311	3.5%	-0.52
40/1+	5%	4	260	1.5%	-0.58
Unraced	0%	0	20	0.0%	-1.00

ANALYSIS BY DISTANCE BEATEN LAST TIME

Lengths	Prop	Win	Runs	Wins%	£
..-10	0%	0	0	0.0%	0.00
-10..0	9%	7	27	25.9%	0.32
0.1..2	12%	9	71	12.7%	-0.35
2.1..5	16%	12	171	7.0%	-0.60
5.1..10	29%	22	324	6.8%	-0.45
10.1..20	28%	21	352	6.0%	0.10
20.0..30	4%	3	125	2.4%	-0.56
30.1+	1%	1	99	1.0%	-0.48
Not Compl	0%	0	0	0.0%	0.00
Unraced	0%	0	20	0.0%	-1.00

ANALYSIS BY RUN NUMBER

Run No	Prop	Win	Runs	Wins%	£
FTO	0%	0	20	0.0%	-1.00
2nd Run	0%	0	21	0.0%	-1.00
3rd Run	4%	3	37	8.1%	1.19
4th+ Run	96%	72	1111	6.5%	-0.33

ANALYSIS BY POSITION LAST TIME

Pos LT	Prop	Win	Runs	Wins%	£
Won	9%	7	27	25.9%	0.32
2nd or 3rd	16%	12	120	10.0%	-0.39
Unplaced	75%	56	1019	5.5%	-0.30
Not Compl	0%	0	23	0.0%	-1.00

OTHER FACTORS (WINS-RUNS, £)

Course Winner:	9-102	-£0.21
Distance Winner:	28-319	-£0.36
Going Winner:	19-211	-£0.20
Beaten Favourite:	4-27	-£0.38
BHA Top Rated:	11-71	£0.53
Up in class:	9-241	-£0.40
Same class:	38-629	-£0.43
Down in class:	28-299	£0.06
7-Day Winners:	2-5	£0.65
Colts and Geldings:	56-796	-£0.28
Fillies:	19-393	-£0.37
Absolute Favourites:	21-62	£0.28

TRAINERS (WINS-RUNS, £)

R A Harris 2-26 £1.92; P T Midgley 2-20 £1.88; B Palling 1-10 £2.40; R E Barr 1-16 £1.13; G A Swinbank 2-10 £0.75; N Tinkler 1-16 £0.31; T D Barron 2-10 £0.13.

Race Profiles

All Age Races: Selling Races – good or faster going

ANALYSIS BY AGE					
Age	Prop	Win	Runs	Wins%	£
2yo	0%	0	0	0.0%	0.00
3yo	23%	80	1076	7.4%	-0.31
4yo	32%	109	1298	8.4%	-0.33
5yo	18%	63	596	10.6%	0.05
6yo	9%	31	324	9.6%	-0.11
7yo	5%	18	202	8.9%	-0.29
8yo	5%	16	150	10.7%	-0.50
9yo	5%	18	107	16.8%	-0.04
10yo	2%	8	47	17.0%	0.04
11yo+	1%	2	47	4.3%	-0.55

ANALYSIS BY BHA RATING					
Rating	Prop	Win	Runs	Wins%	£
120..139	0%	0	0	0.0%	0.00
110..119	0%	0	0	0.0%	0.00
100..109	0%	0	0	0.0%	0.00
90..99	3%	10	69	14.5%	0.04
70..89	23%	81	426	19.0%	-0.07
50..69	54%	186	1654	11.2%	-0.24
..49	18%	61	1539	4.0%	-0.31
Unrated	2%	7	156	4.5%	-0.22

ANALYSIS BY WEIGHT CARRIED					
Weight	Prop	Win	Runs	Wins%	£
10-01+	1%	4	19	21.1%	-0.05
9-8..10-00	13%	46	306	15.0%	-0.26
9-0..9-07	51%	175	1801	9.7%	-0.17
8-8..8-13	23%	79	1081	7.3%	-0.33
8-0..8-07	12%	40	598	6.7%	-0.26
..7-13	0%	1	42	2.4%	-0.83

ANALYSIS BY DAYS SINCE LAST RUN					
Days	Prop	Win	Runs	Wins%	£
1..7	19%	66	585	11.3%	-0.37
8..14	26%	91	918	9.9%	-0.33
15..28	28%	97	1108	8.8%	-0.14
29..60	14%	50	587	8.5%	-0.16
61..100	3%	12	153	7.8%	-0.36
101+	8%	28	454	6.2%	-0.33
Unraced	0%	1	42	2.4%	0.93

ANALYSIS BY TODAY'S STARTING PRICE					
Price	Prop	Win	Runs	Wins%	£
Odds On	5%	16	23	69.6%	0.17
Ev - 2/1	13%	46	130	35.4%	-0.10
9/4 - 4/1	35%	120	479	25.1%	0.03
9/2 - 6/1	13%	46	397	11.6%	-0.28
13/2-10/1	17%	60	700	8.6%	-0.23
11/1-16/1	8%	29	649	4.5%	-0.34
18/1-33/1	6%	19	739	2.6%	-0.33
40/1+	3%	9	730	1.2%	-0.28

ANALYSIS BY STARTING PRICE LAST TIME					
Price	Prop	Win	Runs	Wins%	£
Odds On	1%	3	8	37.5%	-0.10
Ev - 2/1	6%	19	63	30.2%	0.11
9/4 - 4/1	15%	52	298	17.4%	-0.20
9/2 - 6/1	14%	49	332	14.8%	-0.17
13/2-10/1	24%	82	657	12.5%	-0.18
11/1-16/1	20%	69	739	9.3%	-0.15
18/1-33/1	14%	47	913	5.1%	-0.26
40/1+	7%	23	795	2.9%	-0.49
Unraced	0%	1	42	2.4%	0.93

ANALYSIS BY DISTANCE BEATEN LAST TIME					
Lengths	Prop	Win	Runs	Wins%	£
..-10	0%	0	0	0.0%	0.00
-10..0	11%	38	158	24.1%	-0.10
0.1..2	17%	60	333	18.0%	-0.17
2.1..5	17%	60	600	10.0%	-0.46
5.1..10	26%	89	1006	8.8%	-0.24
10.1..20	21%	71	1022	6.9%	-0.22
20.0..30	6%	19	357	5.3%	0.12
30.1+	2%	7	329	2.1%	-0.63
Not Compl	0%	0	0	0.0%	0.00
Unraced	0%	1	42	2.4%	0.93

ANALYSIS BY RUN NUMBER					
Run No	Prop	Win	Runs	Wins%	£
FTO	0%	1	42	2.4%	0.93
2nd Run	1%	4	50	8.0%	-0.49
3rd Run	1%	4	68	5.9%	-0.61
4th+ Run	97%	336	3687	9.1%	-0.25

ANALYSIS BY POSITION LAST TIME					
Pos LT	Prop	Win	Runs	Wins%	£
Won	11%	38	158	24.1%	-0.10
2nd or 3rd	21%	71	492	14.4%	-0.29
Unplaced	68%	235	3145	7.5%	-0.26
Not Compl	0%	1	52	1.9%	0.56

OTHER FACTORS (WINS-RUNS, £)

Course Winner:	45-385	-£0.41
Distance Winner:	170-1291	-£0.21
Going Winner:	114-949	-£0.34
Beaten Favourite:	30-137	£0.07
BHA Top Rated:	59-330	-£0.01
Up in class:	42-570	-£0.40
Same class:	191-2199	-£0.27
Down in class:	111-1036	-£0.16
7-Day Winners:	12-40	£0.07
Colts and Geldings:	259-2615	-£0.26
Fillies:	86-1232	-£0.21
Absolute Favourites:	114-302	£0.17

TRAINERS (WINS-RUNS, £)

David Pinder 2-14 £4.71; B R Johnson 5-12 £4.24; C J Teague 1-18 £2.72; B J Meehan 3-14 £2.81; J M Bradley 7-104 £0.36; W R Swinburn 5-11 £3.30; M S Saunders 3-17 £1.88; Mrs A Duffield 4-26 £1.22; G L Moore 5-24 £1.01; G A Swinbank 10-34 £0.54; E J Alston 3-16 £1.13; R Bastiman 2-21 £0.81; John A Harris 2-16 £1.00; Miss Gay Kelleway 6-35 £0.46; D Nicholls 18-76 £0.19; M Brittain 1-14 £0.86; J Akehurst 2-12 £0.92; M D I Usher 2-13 £0.85; M Johnston 3-18 £0.58; B Palling 1-24 £0.42.

Selling Races

All Age Races: Selling Races – good to soft or softer going

ANALYSIS BY AGE

Age	Prop	Win	Runs	Wins%	£
2yo	0%	0	0	0.0%	0.00
3yo	20%	21	318	6.6%	0.09
4yo	32%	33	360	9.2%	-0.23
5yo	18%	19	183	10.4%	-0.16
6yo	9%	9	89	10.1%	-0.49
7yo	4%	4	50	8.0%	-0.52
8yo	5%	5	54	9.3%	-0.40
9yo	7%	7	37	18.9%	0.15
10yo	2%	2	20	10.0%	-0.52
11yo+	4%	4	18	22.2%	0.31

ANALYSIS BY BHA RATING

Rating	Prop	Win	Runs	Wins%	£
120..139	0%	0	0	0.0%	0.00
110..119	0%	0	0	0.0%	0.00
100..109	0%	0	0	0.0%	0.00
90..99	4%	4	27	14.8%	-0.36
70..89	23%	24	145	16.6%	0.10
50..69	53%	55	457	12.0%	0.00
..49	19%	20	441	4.5%	-0.42
Unrated	1%	1	54	1.9%	0.24

ANALYSIS BY WEIGHT CARRIED

Weight	Prop	Win	Runs	Wins%	£
10-01+	1%	1	12	8.3%	-0.17
9-8 ..10-00	8%	8	65	12.3%	-0.33
9-0..9-07	54%	56	514	10.9%	-0.22
8-8..8-13	30%	31	339	9.1%	0.27
8-0..8-07	7%	7	180	3.9%	-0.76
..7-13	1%	1	19	5.3%	0.53

ANALYSIS BY DAYS SINCE LAST RUN

Days	Prop	Win	Runs	Wins%	£
1..7	22%	23	175	13.1%	0.00
8..14	30%	31	248	12.5%	0.17
15..28	28%	29	292	9.9%	0.01
29..60	9%	9	185	4.9%	-0.71
61..100	4%	4	65	6.2%	-0.65
101+	8%	8	150	5.3%	-0.21
Unraced	0%	0	14	0.0%	-1.00

ANALYSIS BY TODAY'S STARTING PRICE

Price	Prop	Win	Runs	Wins%	£
Odds On	9%	9	11	81.8%	0.40
Ev - 2/1	11%	11	28	39.3%	0.08
9/4 - 4/1	29%	30	134	22.4%	0.01
9/2 - 6/1	17%	18	124	14.5%	-0.13
13/2-10/1	16%	17	242	7.0%	-0.38
11/1-16/1	10%	10	188	5.3%	-0.25
18/1-33/1	5%	5	225	2.2%	-0.42
40/1+	4%	4	177	2.3%	0.41

ANALYSIS BY STARTING PRICE LAST TIME

Price	Prop	Win	Runs	Wins%	£
Odds On	1%	1	3	33.3%	-0.21
Ev - 2/1	7%	7	22	31.8%	0.26
9/4 - 4/1	13%	14	82	17.1%	0.02
9/2 - 6/1	12%	12	109	11.0%	-0.47
13/2-10/1	20%	21	195	10.8%	-0.10
11/1-16/1	20%	21	222	9.5%	-0.38
18/1-33/1	21%	22	252	8.7%	0.30
40/1+	6%	6	230	2.6%	-0.37
Unraced	0%	0	14	0.0%	-1.00

ANALYSIS BY DISTANCE BEATEN LAST TIME

Lengths	Prop	Win	Runs	Wins%	£
..-10	0%	0	0	0.0%	0.00
-10..0	6%	6	44	13.6%	-0.57
0.1..2	12%	12	85	14.1%	-0.39
2.1..5	25%	26	190	13.7%	-0.18
5.1..10	27%	28	289	9.7%	-0.32
10.1..20	22%	23	286	8.0%	0.34
20.0..30	6%	6	115	5.2%	-0.41
30.1+	3%	3	106	2.8%	-0.19
Not Compl	0%	0	0	0.0%	0.00
Unraced	0%	0	14	0.0%	-1.00

ANALYSIS BY RUN NUMBER

Run No	Prop	Win	Runs	Wins%	£
FTO	0%	0	14	0.0%	-1.00
2nd Run	0%	0	17	0.0%	-1.00
3rd Run	1%	1	30	3.3%	1.23
4th+ Run	99%	103	1068	9.6%	-0.17

ANALYSIS BY POSITION LAST TIME

Pos LT	Prop	Win	Runs	Wins%	£
Won	6%	6	44	13.6%	-0.57
2nd or 3rd	27%	28	141	19.9%	0.10
Unplaced	67%	70	929	7.5%	-0.16
Not Compl	0%	0	15	0.0%	-1.00

OTHER FACTORS (WINS-RUNS, £)

Course Winner:	19-128	£0.06
Distance Winner:	48-359	-£0.15
Going Winner:	20-139	-£0.16
Beaten Favourite:	9-38	£0.17
BHA Top Rated:	13-112	-£0.30
Up in class:	18-258	£0.10
Same class:	51-566	-£0.20
Down in class:	35-291	-£0.24
7-Day Winners:	1-4	-£0.54
Colts and Geldings:	84-782	-£0.05
Fillies:	20-347	-£0.38
Absolute Favourites:	37-93	£0.27

TRAINERS (WINS-RUNS, £)

R A Harris 2-15 £3.77; P T Midgley 3-14 £2.92; D Carroll 3-15 £1.23; Miss Gay Kelleway 2-10 £1.10; E J Alston 3-10 £0.89; R M Whitaker 4-16 £0.36; M Dods 3-16 £0.34; R A Fahey 4-14 £0.25; A B Haynes 2-10 £0.20.

Race Profiles

All Age Races: Selling Races – 5 to 6 furlong races

ANALYSIS BY AGE
Age	Prop	Win	Runs	Wins%	£
2yo	0%	0	0	0.0%	0.00
3yo	14%	15	279	5.4%	-0.34
4yo	30%	31	366	8.5%	-0.24
5yo	20%	21	183	11.5%	-0.37
6yo	9%	9	108	8.3%	0.09
7yo	5%	5	61	8.2%	0.10
8yo	8%	8	71	11.3%	-0.56
9yo	10%	11	41	26.8%	0.72
10yo	3%	3	25	12.0%	-0.06
11yo+	2%	2	26	7.7%	-0.21

ANALYSIS BY BHA RATING
Rating	Prop	Win	Runs	Wins%	£
120..139	0%	0	0	0.0%	0.00
110..119	0%	0	0	0.0%	0.00
100..109	0%	0	0	0.0%	0.00
90..99	1%	1	10	10.0%	0.50
70..89	32%	34	152	22.4%	-0.05
50..69	46%	48	452	10.6%	-0.22
..49	21%	22	518	4.2%	-0.23
Unrated	0%	0	26	0.0%	-1.00

ANALYSIS BY WEIGHT CARRIED
Weight	Prop	Win	Runs	Wins%	£
10-01+	1%	1	13	7.7%	-0.23
9-8..10-00	10%	10	51	19.6%	-0.19
9-0..9-07	57%	60	553	10.8%	-0.17
8-8..8-13	28%	29	383	7.6%	-0.14
8-0..8-07	5%	5	147	3.4%	-0.54
..7-13	0%	0	13	0.0%	-1.00

ANALYSIS BY DAYS SINCE LAST RUN
Days	Prop	Win	Runs	Wins%	£
1..7	23%	24	225	10.7%	-0.37
8..14	32%	34	295	11.5%	-0.31
15..28	25%	26	312	8.3%	0.20
29..60	13%	14	155	9.0%	-0.05
61..100	1%	1	35	2.9%	-0.93
101+	6%	6	133	4.5%	-0.68
Unraced	0%	0	5	0.0%	-1.00

ANALYSIS BY TODAY'S STARTING PRICE
Price	Prop	Win	Runs	Wins%	£
Odds On	6%	6	9	66.7%	0.09
Ev - 2/1	14%	15	35	42.9%	0.12
9/4 - 4/1	33%	35	147	23.8%	0.00
9/2 - 6/1	10%	11	119	9.2%	-0.45
13/2-10/1	13%	14	219	6.4%	-0.40
11/1-16/1	14%	15	196	7.7%	0.10
18/1-33/1	7%	7	230	3.0%	-0.20
40/1+	2%	2	205	1.0%	-0.42

ANALYSIS BY STARTING PRICE LAST TIME
Price	Prop	Win	Runs	Wins%	£
Odds On	1%	1	1	100.0%	1.38
Ev - 2/1	5%	5	19	26.3%	-0.12
9/4 - 4/1	17%	18	87	20.7%	-0.04
9/2 - 6/1	15%	16	106	15.1%	0.02
13/2-10/1	22%	23	207	11.1%	-0.15
11/1-16/1	19%	20	204	9.8%	-0.08
18/1-33/1	11%	12	292	4.1%	-0.62
40/1+	10%	10	239	4.2%	-0.07
Unraced	0%	0	5	0.0%	-1.00

ANALYSIS BY DISTANCE BEATEN LAST TIME
Lengths	Prop	Win	Runs	Wins%	£
..-10	0%	0	0	0.0%	0.00
-10..0	12%	13	54	24.1%	-0.22
0.1..2	14%	15	102	14.7%	-0.32
2.1..5	22%	23	231	10.0%	-0.43
5.1..10	30%	32	362	8.8%	-0.24
10.1..20	16%	17	280	6.1%	-0.03
20.0..30	4%	4	74	5.4%	-0.05
30.1+	1%	1	52	1.9%	-0.02
Not Compl	0%	0	0	0.0%	0.00
Unraced	0%	0	5	0.0%	-1.00

ANALYSIS BY RUN NUMBER
Run No	Prop	Win	Runs	Wins%	£
FTO	0%	0	5	0.0%	-1.00
2nd Run	0%	0	6	0.0%	-1.00
3rd Run	0%	0	12	0.0%	-1.00
4th+ Run	100%	105	1137	9.2%	-0.20

ANALYSIS BY POSITION LAST TIME
Pos LT	Prop	Win	Runs	Wins%	£
Won	12%	13	54	24.1%	-0.22
2nd or 3rd	19%	20	136	14.7%	-0.30
Unplaced	69%	72	962	7.5%	-0.20
Not Compl	0%	0	8	0.0%	-1.00

OTHER FACTORS (WINS-RUNS, £)
Course Winner:	20-146	-£0.27
Distance Winner:	78-595	-£0.12
Going Winner:	39-310	-£0.34
Beaten Favourite:	10-42	£0.30
BHA Top Rated:	16-102	£0.17
Up in class:	13-132	£0.01
Same class:	57-667	-£0.28
Down in class:	35-356	-£0.17
7-Day Winners:	5-21	-£0.27
Colts and Geldings:	83-796	-£0.22
Fillies:	22-364	-£0.20
Absolute Favourites:	33-93	£0.03

TRAINERS (WINS-RUNS, £)
C J Teague 1-14 £3.79; R Bastiman 2-10 £2.80; Miss A Stokell 1-10 £1.60; N Tinkler 2-10 £1.40; I A Wood 2-12 £1.00; R Hollinshead 1-12 £0.75; T D Barron 3-10 £0.50; D W Barker 3-12 £0.40; J J Quinn 2-11 £0.23; M R Bosley 1-11 £0.18; T D Easterby 2-12 £0.04.

Selling Races

All Age Races: Selling Races – 7 to 9 furlong races

ANALYSIS BY AGE

Age	Prop	Win	Runs	Wins%	£
2yo	0%	0	0	0.0%	0.00
3yo	20%	35	536	6.5%	-0.34
4yo	30%	54	667	8.1%	-0.23
5yo	21%	38	331	11.5%	-0.01
6yo	8%	15	184	8.2%	-0.24
7yo	7%	13	130	10.0%	-0.31
8yo	6%	10	89	11.2%	-0.40
9yo	4%	8	66	12.1%	-0.59
10yo	2%	3	20	15.0%	-0.14
11yo+	1%	2	21	9.5%	-0.29

ANALYSIS BY BHA RATING

Rating	Prop	Win	Runs	Wins%	£
120..139	0%	0	0	0.0%	0.00
110..119	0%	0	0	0.0%	0.00
100..109	0%	0	0	0.0%	0.00
90..99	3%	5	46	10.9%	-0.42
70..89	24%	42	219	19.2%	-0.04
50..69	56%	100	924	10.8%	-0.20
..49	16%	28	775	3.6%	-0.39
Unrated	2%	3	77	3.9%	0.05

ANALYSIS BY WEIGHT CARRIED

Weight	Prop	Win	Runs	Wins%	£
10-01+	2%	3	16	18.8%	-0.11
9-8 ..10-00	12%	21	151	13.9%	-0.24
9-0..9-07	58%	104	998	10.4%	-0.14
8-8..8-13	18%	32	582	5.5%	-0.39
8-0..8-07	10%	18	273	6.6%	-0.31
..7-13	0%	0	24	0.0%	-1.00

ANALYSIS BY DAYS SINCE LAST RUN

Days	Prop	Win	Runs	Wins%	£
1..7	22%	39	301	13.0%	-0.05
8..14	22%	40	467	8.6%	-0.19
15..28	29%	52	593	8.8%	-0.44
29..60	12%	21	314	6.7%	-0.31
61..100	3%	6	94	6.4%	-0.55
101+	11%	20	251	8.0%	0.13
Unraced	0%	0	24	0.0%	-1.00

ANALYSIS BY TODAY'S STARTING PRICE

Price	Prop	Win	Runs	Wins%	£
Odds On	6%	10	12	83.3%	0.44
Ev - 2/1	13%	23	62	37.1%	-0.06
9/4 - 4/1	31%	56	234	23.9%	0.02
9/2 - 6/1	15%	26	205	12.7%	-0.22
13/2-10/1	19%	33	372	8.9%	-0.21
11/1-16/1	9%	16	359	4.5%	-0.34
18/1-33/1	4%	8	402	2.0%	-0.47
40/1+	3%	6	398	1.5%	-0.20

ANALYSIS BY STARTING PRICE LAST TIME

Price	Prop	Win	Runs	Wins%	£
Odds On	1%	1	3	33.3%	-0.48
Ev - 2/1	5%	9	32	28.1%	0.23
9/4 - 4/1	12%	21	146	14.4%	-0.28
9/2 - 6/1	13%	24	179	13.4%	-0.23
13/2-10/1	27%	48	343	14.0%	-0.10
11/1-16/1	21%	37	415	8.9%	-0.14
18/1-33/1	16%	29	496	5.8%	-0.12
40/1+	5%	9	406	2.2%	-0.62
Unraced	0%	0	24	0.0%	-1.00

ANALYSIS BY DISTANCE BEATEN LAST TIME

Lengths	Prop	Win	Runs	Wins%	£
..-10	0%	0	0	0.0%	0.00
-10..0	8%	14	69	20.3%	-0.21
0.1..2	19%	33	184	17.9%	-0.25
2.1..5	15%	26	308	8.4%	-0.53
5.1..10	26%	46	526	8.7%	-0.25
10.1..20	28%	49	564	8.7%	0.13
20.0..30	4%	7	204	3.4%	-0.47
30.1+	2%	3	165	1.8%	-0.65
Not Compl	0%	0	0	0.0%	0.00
Unraced	0%	0	24	0.0%	-1.00

ANALYSIS BY RUN NUMBER

Run No	Prop	Win	Runs	Wins%	£
FTO	0%	0	24	0.0%	-1.00
2nd Run	1%	1	24	4.2%	-0.81
3rd Run	2%	3	32	9.4%	1.53
4th+ Run	98%	174	1964	8.9%	-0.26

ANALYSIS BY POSITION LAST TIME

Pos LT	Prop	Win	Runs	Wins%	£
Won	8%	14	69	20.3%	-0.21
2nd or 3rd	19%	34	253	13.4%	-0.40
Unplaced	73%	130	1694	7.7%	-0.21
Not Compl	0%	0	28	0.0%	-1.00

OTHER FACTORS (WINS-RUNS, £)

Course Winner:	25-236	-£0.29
Distance Winner:	84-661	-£0.23
Going Winner:	66-497	-£0.23
Beaten Favourite:	12-61	£0.15
BHA Top Rated:	27-183	-£0.38
Up in class:	15-319	-£0.48
Same class:	103-1179	-£0.17
Down in class:	60-522	-£0.25
7-Day Winners:	5-17	£0.19
Colts and Geldings:	138-1447	-£0.22
Fillies:	40-597	-£0.32
Absolute Favourites:	60-153	£0.24

TRAINERS (WINS-RUNS, £)

J M Bradley 4-41 £1.16; R A Harris 3-41 £0.99; D Nicholls 14-48 £0.80; P T Midgley 3-26 £1.40; B J Meehan 1-10 £2.40; Ollie Pears 4-14 £1.36; M Johnston 3-11 £1.59; Stef Liddiard 2-11 £1.32; E J Alston 2-15 £0.73; G A Swinbank 6-22 £0.49; B Smart 4-12 £0.78; K A Ryan 4-12 £0.75; R E Barr 1-25 £0.36; Mrs A Duffield 2-13 £0.38; David Pinder 1-10 £0.30; P D Evans 4-32 £0.06; A Berry 2-19 £0.05; A B Haynes 3-16 £0.06; R Hollinshead 2-14 £0.04; I Semple 4-16 £0.01.

Race Profiles

All Age Races: Selling Races – 10 to 14 furlong races

ANALYSIS BY AGE

Age	Prop	Win	Runs	Wins%	£
2yo	0%	0	0	0.0%	0.00
3yo	31%	50	560	8.9%	-0.05
4yo	34%	55	602	9.1%	-0.44
5yo	13%	21	245	8.6%	0.00
6yo	9%	15	116	12.9%	-0.38
7yo	3%	4	60	6.7%	-0.80
8yo	2%	3	44	6.8%	-0.51
9yo	4%	6	37	16.2%	0.28
10yo	3%	4	22	18.2%	-0.20
11yo+	1%	2	18	11.1%	-0.48

ANALYSIS BY BHA RATING

Rating	Prop	Win	Runs	Wins%	£
120..139	0%	0	0	0.0%	0.00
110..119	0%	0	0	0.0%	0.00
100..109	0%	0	0	0.0%	0.00
90..99	5%	8	40	20.0%	0.17
70..89	18%	29	200	14.5%	-0.00
50..69	58%	93	723	12.9%	-0.15
..49	16%	26	640	4.1%	-0.37
Unrated	3%	4	98	4.1%	-0.73

ANALYSIS BY WEIGHT CARRIED

Weight	Prop	Win	Runs	Wins%	£
10-01+	1%	1	2	50.0%	0.88
9-8..10-00	12%	19	143	13.3%	-0.38
9-0..9-07	41%	66	742	8.9%	-0.34
8-8..8-13	31%	49	451	10.9%	0.04
8-0..8-07	14%	23	343	6.7%	-0.40
..7-13	1%	2	23	8.7%	0.57

ANALYSIS BY DAYS SINCE LAST RUN

Days	Prop	Win	Runs	Wins%	£
1..7	16%	26	227	11.5%	-0.49
8..14	29%	47	395	11.9%	-0.18
15..28	29%	47	478	9.8%	0.08
29..60	14%	22	289	7.6%	-0.41
61..100	5%	8	82	9.8%	-0.13
101+	6%	10	210	4.8%	-0.54
Unraced	0%	0	23	0.0%	-1.00

ANALYSIS BY TODAY'S STARTING PRICE

Price	Prop	Win	Runs	Wins%	£
Odds On	6%	9	13	69.2%	0.18
Ev - 2/1	12%	19	61	31.1%	-0.18
9/4 - 4/1	36%	58	221	26.2%	0.08
9/2 - 6/1	16%	25	188	13.3%	-0.18
13/2-10/1	18%	29	337	8.6%	-0.25
11/1-16/1	5%	8	271	3.0%	-0.57
18/1-33/1	5%	8	319	2.5%	-0.34
40/1+	3%	4	294	1.4%	-0.13

ANALYSIS BY STARTING PRICE LAST TIME

Price	Prop	Win	Runs	Wins%	£
Odds On	1%	2	7	28.6%	-0.19
Ev - 2/1	8%	12	34	35.3%	0.23
9/4 - 4/1	17%	27	146	18.5%	-0.08
9/2 - 6/1	13%	20	151	13.2%	-0.45
13/2-10/1	20%	32	295	10.8%	-0.23
11/1-16/1	20%	32	333	9.6%	-0.37
18/1-33/1	16%	26	362	7.2%	0.22
40/1+	6%	9	353	2.5%	-0.58
Unraced	0%	0	23	0.0%	-1.00

ANALYSIS BY DISTANCE BEATEN LAST TIME

Lengths	Prop	Win	Runs	Wins%	£
..-10	0%	0	0	0.0%	0.00
-10..0	11%	17	79	21.5%	-0.17
0.1..2	15%	24	132	18.2%	-0.10
2.1..5	23%	37	246	15.0%	-0.16
5.1..10	23%	37	394	9.4%	-0.28
10.1..20	16%	26	450	5.8%	-0.48
20.0..30	9%	14	179	7.8%	0.61
30.1+	3%	5	201	2.5%	-0.53
Not Compl	0%	0	0	0.0%	0.00
Unraced	0%	0	23	0.0%	-1.00

ANALYSIS BY RUN NUMBER

Run No	Prop	Win	Runs	Wins%	£
FTO	0%	0	23	0.0%	-1.00
2nd Run	2%	3	34	8.8%	-0.38
3rd Run	1%	2	51	3.9%	-0.75
4th+ Run	97%	155	1596	9.7%	-0.21

ANALYSIS BY POSITION LAST TIME

Pos LT	Prop	Win	Runs	Wins%	£
Won	11%	17	79	21.5%	-0.17
2nd or 3rd	28%	45	242	18.6%	0.07
Unplaced	61%	98	1356	7.2%	-0.29
Not Compl	0%	0	27	0.0%	-1.00

OTHER FACTORS (WINS-RUNS, £)

Course Winner:	19-130	-£0.30
Distance Winner:	56-393	-£0.25
Going Winner:	29-275	-£0.05
Beaten Favourite:	16-71	-£0.15
BHA Top Rated:	28-151	£0.10
Up in class:	32-375	£0.12
Same class:	79-882	-£0.34
Down in class:	49-424	-£0.10
7-Day Winners:	3-6	£0.56
Colts and Geldings:	119-1117	-£0.19
Fillies:	41-587	-£0.34
Absolute Favourites:	57-144	£0.27

TRAINERS (WINS-RUNS, £)

G L Moore 2-19 £0.99; J Pearce 2-14 £0.65; Miss Gay Kelleway 3-19 £0.26; D Carroll 4-21 £0.22; R M Whitaker 4-21 £0.21; G A Swinbank 4-18 £0.10.

Selling Races

All Age Races: Selling Races – 15+ furlong races

ANALYSIS BY AGE
Age	Prop	Win	Runs	Wins%	£
2yo	0%	0	0	0.0%	0.00
3yo	17%	1	19	5.3%	0.11
4yo	33%	2	23	8.7%	-0.37
5yo	33%	2	20	10.0%	3.35
6yo	17%	1	5	20.0%	-0.20
7yo	0%	0	1	0.0%	-1.00
8yo	0%	0	0	0.0%	0.00
9yo	0%	0	0	0.0%	0.00
10yo	0%	0	0	0.0%	0.00
11yo+	0%	0	0	0.0%	0.00

ANALYSIS BY BHA RATING
Rating	Prop	Win	Runs	Wins%	£
120..139	0%	0	0	0.0%	0.00
110..119	0%	0	0	0.0%	0.00
100..109	0%	0	0	0.0%	0.00
90..99	0%	0	0	0.0%	0.00
70..89	0%	0	0	0.0%	0.00
50..69	0%	0	12	0.0%	-1.00
..49	83%	5	47	10.6%	-0.03
Unrated	17%	1	9	11.1%	8.00

ANALYSIS BY WEIGHT CARRIED
Weight	Prop	Win	Runs	Wins%	£
10-01+	0%	0	0	0.0%	0.00
9-8 ..10-00	67%	4	26	15.4%	-0.06
9-0..9-07	17%	1	22	4.5%	2.68
8-8..8-13	0%	0	4	0.0%	-1.00
8-0..8-07	17%	1	15	6.7%	0.40
..7-13	0%	0	1	0.0%	-1.00

ANALYSIS BY DAYS SINCE LAST RUN
Days	Prop	Win	Runs	Wins%	£
1..7	0%	0	7	0.0%	-1.00
8..14	17%	1	9	11.1%	-0.33
15..28	17%	1	17	5.9%	0.24
29..60	33%	2	14	14.3%	0.04
61..100	17%	1	7	14.3%	-0.43
101+	0%	0	10	0.0%	-1.00
Unraced	17%	1	4	25.0%	19.25

ANALYSIS BY TODAY'S STARTING PRICE
Price	Prop	Win	Runs	Wins%	£
Odds On	0%	0	0	0.0%	0.00
Ev - 2/1	0%	0	0	0.0%	0.00
9/4 - 4/1	17%	1	11	9.1%	-0.64
9/2 - 6/1	33%	2	9	22.2%	0.44
13/2-10/1	17%	1	14	7.1%	-0.46
11/1-16/1	0%	0	11	0.0%	-1.00
18/1-33/1	17%	1	13	7.7%	0.62
40/1+	17%	1	10	10.0%	7.10

ANALYSIS BY STARTING PRICE LAST TIME
Price	Prop	Win	Runs	Wins%	£
Odds On	0%	0	0	0.0%	0.00
Ev - 2/1	0%	0	0	0.0%	0.00
9/4 - 4/1	0%	0	1	0.0%	-1.00
9/2 - 6/1	17%	1	5	20.0%	0.20
13/2-10/1	0%	0	7	0.0%	-1.00
11/1-16/1	17%	1	9	11.1%	-0.22
18/1-33/1	33%	2	15	13.3%	-0.23
40/1+	17%	1	27	3.7%	-0.22
Unraced	17%	1	4	25.0%	19.25

ANALYSIS BY DISTANCE BEATEN LAST TIME
Lengths	Prop	Win	Runs	Wins%	£
..-10	0%	0	0	0.0%	0.00
-10..0	0%	0	0	0.0%	0.00
0.1..2	0%	0	0	0.0%	0.00
2.1..5	0%	0	5	0.0%	-1.00
5.1..10	33%	2	13	15.4%	-0.23
10.1..20	33%	2	14	14.3%	1.04
20.0..30	0%	0	15	0.0%	-1.00
30.1+	17%	1	17	5.9%	-0.59
Not Compl	0%	0	0	0.0%	0.00
Unraced	17%	1	4	25.0%	19.25

ANALYSIS BY RUN NUMBER
Run No	Prop	Win	Runs	Wins%	£
FTO	17%	1	4	25.0%	19.25
2nd Run	0%	0	3	0.0%	-1.00
3rd Run	0%	0	3	0.0%	-1.00
4th+ Run	83%	5	58	8.6%	-0.22

ANALYSIS BY POSITION LAST TIME
Pos LT	Prop	Win	Runs	Wins%	£
Won	0%	0	0	0.0%	0.00
2nd or 3rd	0%	0	2	0.0%	-1.00
Unplaced	83%	5	62	8.1%	-0.27
Not Compl	17%	1	4	25.0%	19.25

OTHER FACTORS (WINS-RUNS, £)
Course Winner:	0-1	-£1.00
Distance Winner:	0-1	-£1.00
Going Winner:	0-6	-£1.00
Beaten Favourite:	1-1	£5.00
BHA Top Rated:	1-6	£0.25
Up in class:	0-2	-£1.00
Same class:	3-37	-£0.45
Down in class:	2-25	£0.00
Colts and Geldings:	3-37	-£0.50
Fillies:	3-31	£2.48
Absolute Favourites:	1-5	-£0.20

Race Profiles

All Age Races: Handicaps (Class 1..3)

ANALYSIS BY AGE

Age	Prop	Win	Runs	Wins%	£
2yo	0%	0	0	0.0%	0.00
3yo	20%	295	2518	11.7%	-0.16
4yo	38%	576	6298	9.1%	-0.14
5yo	21%	322	4033	8.0%	-0.22
6yo	11%	166	2691	6.2%	-0.33
7yo	5%	77	1674	4.6%	-0.49
8yo	3%	52	924	5.6%	-0.33
9yo	1%	9	417	2.2%	-0.61
10yo	0%	5	170	2.9%	-0.68
11yo+	1%	8	75	10.7%	1.34

ANALYSIS BY BHA RATING

Rating	Prop	Win	Runs	Wins%	£
120..139	0%	0	0	0.0%	0.00
110..119	0%	0	30	0.0%	-1.00
100..109	7%	100	1488	6.7%	-0.28
90..99	34%	517	6383	8.1%	-0.27
70..89	58%	876	10697	8.2%	-0.21
50..69	1%	17	202	8.4%	-0.05
..49	0%	0	0	0.0%	0.00
Unrated	0%	0	0	0.0%	0.00

ANALYSIS BY WEIGHT CARRIED

Weight	Prop	Win	Runs	Wins%	£
10-01+	1%	8	109	7.3%	0.05
9-8..10-00	15%	229	2568	8.9%	-0.29
9-0..9-07	41%	622	6905	9.0%	-0.24
8-8..8-13	28%	418	5734	7.3%	-0.25
8-0..8-07	15%	220	3117	7.1%	-0.15
..7-13	1%	13	367	3.5%	-0.57

ANALYSIS BY DAYS SINCE LAST RUN

Days	Prop	Win	Runs	Wins%	£
1..7	12%	181	2046	8.8%	-0.24
8..14	22%	333	4434	7.5%	-0.31
15..28	35%	532	6460	8.2%	-0.22
29..60	16%	246	3113	7.9%	-0.27
61..100	3%	47	609	7.7%	-0.17
101+	11%	169	2058	8.2%	-0.09
Unraced	0%	2	80	2.5%	-0.68

ANALYSIS BY TODAY'S STARTING PRICE

Price	Prop	Win	Runs	Wins%	£
Odds On	2%	23	44	52.3%	-0.11
Ev - 2/1	6%	88	302	29.1%	-0.24
9/4 - 4/1	23%	348	1501	23.2%	-0.02
9/2 - 6/1	19%	282	2014	14.0%	-0.14
13/2-10/1	25%	385	4325	8.9%	-0.19
11/1-16/1	17%	252	4572	5.5%	-0.21
18/1-33/1	8%	116	4360	2.7%	-0.35
40/1+	1%	16	1682	1.0%	-0.48

ANALYSIS BY STARTING PRICE LAST TIME

Price	Prop	Win	Runs	Wins%	£
Odds On	2%	25	151	16.6%	-0.09
Ev - 2/1	6%	87	630	13.8%	-0.19
9/4 - 4/1	19%	284	2386	11.9%	-0.16
9/2 - 6/1	15%	231	2493	9.3%	-0.22
13/2-10/1	25%	371	4538	8.2%	-0.18
11/1-16/1	18%	270	4066	6.6%	-0.30
18/1-33/1	13%	194	3316	5.9%	-0.28
40/1+	3%	46	1140	4.0%	-0.34
Unraced	0%	2	80	2.5%	-0.68

ANALYSIS BY DISTANCE BEATEN LAST TIME

Lengths	Prop	Win	Runs	Wins%	£
..-10	0%	1	16	6.3%	-0.59
-10..0	20%	307	2575	11.9%	-0.24
0.1..2	21%	310	3205	9.7%	-0.23
2.1..5	23%	346	4329	8.0%	-0.24
5.1..10	19%	291	4362	6.7%	-0.26
10.1..20	12%	178	2838	6.3%	-0.18
20.0..30	3%	46	745	6.2%	-0.19
30.1+	2%	29	650	4.5%	-0.34
Not Compl	0%	0	0	0.0%	0.00
Unraced	0%	2	80	2.5%	-0.68

ANALYSIS BY RUN NUMBER

Run No	Prop	Win	Runs	Wins%	£
FTO	0%	2	80	2.5%	-0.68
2nd Run	1%	14	106	13.2%	1.28
3rd Run	2%	23	176	13.1%	-0.27
4th+ Run	97%	1471	18438	8.0%	-0.24

ANALYSIS BY POSITION LAST TIME

Pos LT	Prop	Win	Runs	Wins%	£
Won	20%	308	2592	11.9%	-0.24
2nd or 3rd	24%	361	3800	9.5%	-0.25
Unplaced	55%	838	12291	6.8%	-0.23
Not Compl	0%	3	117	2.6%	-0.75

OTHER FACTORS (WINS-RUNS, £)

Course Winner:	323-3957	-£0.26
Distance Winner:	1012-12805	-£0.28
Going Winner:	786-9951	-£0.29
Beaten Favourite:	164-1282	-£0.07
Up in class:	605-7291	-£0.23
Same class:	623-8279	-£0.23
Down in class:	280-3150	-£0.26
7-Day Winners:	34-272	-£0.35
Colts and Geldings:	1285-16445	-£0.24
Fillies:	103-1273	-£0.20
Absolute Favourites:	304-1322	-£0.16

TRAINERS (WINS-RUNS, £)

Jane Chapple-Hyam 4-44 £1.88; M Blanshard 8-86 £0.85; N J Henderson 7-30 £2.40; T P Tate 16-129 £0.50; C G Cox 27-187 £0.28; D W P Arbuthnot 7-42 £1.06; J H M Gosden 25-141 £0.30; J L Spearing 5-44 £0.93; R C Guest 7-33 £1.23; Peter Grayson 1-27 £1.48; P R Webber 5-25 £1.58; B W Hills 36-286 £0.41; W J Haggas 29-209 £0.18; R Bastiman 3-11 £3.09; J A Geake 5-55 £0.59; R A Harris 8-86 £0.37; J Gallagher 4-35 £0.85; Ernst Oertel 1-12 £2.42; D Carroll 4-26 £1.11; Tom Dascombe 5-25 £1.04.

Handicaps (Class 1..3)

All Age Races: Handicaps (Class 1..3) – 2 to 7 runners

ANALYSIS BY AGE

Age	Prop	Win	Runs	Wins%	£
2yo	0%	0	0	0.0%	0.00
3yo	27%	60	279	21.5%	0.02
4yo	37%	83	438	18.9%	-0.03
5yo	18%	39	277	14.1%	-0.16
6yo	11%	25	164	15.2%	0.08
7yo	4%	8	94	8.5%	-0.51
8yo	1%	3	60	5.0%	-0.78
9yo	0%	1	28	3.6%	-0.75
10yo	1%	2	10	20.0%	0.10
11yo+	0%	1	6	16.7%	0.33

ANALYSIS BY BHA RATING

Rating	Prop	Win	Runs	Wins%	£
120..139	0%	0	0	0.0%	0.00
110..119	0%	0	1	0.0%	-1.00
100..109	4%	8	34	23.5%	0.60
90..99	28%	62	283	21.9%	0.16
70..89	67%	149	1021	14.6%	-0.22
50..69	1%	3	17	17.6%	0.56
..49	0%	0	0	0.0%	0.00
Unrated	0%	0	0	0.0%	0.00

ANALYSIS BY WEIGHT CARRIED

Weight	Prop	Win	Runs	Wins%	£
10-01+	0%	0	0	0.0%	0.00
9-8 ..10-00	26%	58	296	19.6%	0.03
9-0..9-07	45%	99	510	19.4%	0.01
8-8..8-13	18%	41	345	11.9%	-0.33
8-0..8-07	10%	22	188	11.7%	-0.29
..7-13	1%	2	17	11.8%	0.24

ANALYSIS BY DAYS SINCE LAST RUN

Days	Prop	Win	Runs	Wins%	£
1..7	14%	30	144	20.8%	0.13
8..14	22%	49	312	15.7%	-0.17
15..28	34%	76	493	15.4%	-0.16
29..60	16%	35	226	15.5%	-0.27
61..100	3%	7	43	16.3%	0.04
101+	11%	24	131	18.3%	0.14
Unraced	0%	1	7	14.3%	0.57

ANALYSIS BY TODAY'S STARTING PRICE

Price	Prop	Win	Runs	Wins%	£
Odds On	6%	13	28	46.4%	-0.20
Ev - 2/1	15%	33	121	27.3%	-0.30
9/4 - 4/1	43%	95	397	23.9%	0.00
9/2 - 6/1	18%	40	233	17.2%	0.06
13/2-10/1	11%	25	296	8.4%	-0.26
11/1-16/1	6%	14	181	7.7%	0.06
18/1-33/1	1%	2	89	2.2%	-0.53
40/1+	0%	0	11	0.0%	-1.00

ANALYSIS BY STARTING PRICE LAST TIME

Price	Prop	Win	Runs	Wins%	£
Odds On	2%	5	18	27.8%	0.42
Ev - 2/1	9%	19	66	28.8%	0.19
9/4 - 4/1	21%	46	215	21.4%	0.01
9/2 - 6/1	17%	37	218	17.0%	-0.14
13/2-10/1	20%	44	310	14.2%	-0.28
11/1-16/1	19%	43	259	16.6%	-0.01
18/1-33/1	9%	21	197	10.7%	-0.32
40/1+	3%	6	66	9.1%	0.10
Unraced	0%	1	7	14.3%	0.57

ANALYSIS BY DISTANCE BEATEN LAST TIME

Lengths	Prop	Win	Runs	Wins%	£
..-10	0%	0	3	0.0%	-1.00
-10..0	27%	59	248	23.8%	-0.02
0.1..2	20%	44	221	19.9%	0.02
2.1..5	20%	45	285	15.8%	-0.08
5.1..10	16%	36	272	13.2%	-0.26
10.1..20	12%	26	201	12.9%	-0.19
20.0..30	3%	6	58	10.3%	-0.01
30.1+	2%	5	61	8.2%	-0.32
Not Compl	0%	0	0	0.0%	0.00
Unraced	0%	1	7	14.3%	0.57

ANALYSIS BY RUN NUMBER

Run No	Prop	Win	Runs	Wins%	£
FTO	0%	1	7	14.3%	0.57
2nd Run	1%	3	17	17.6%	0.32
3rd Run	2%	5	22	22.7%	-0.17
4th+ Run	96%	213	1310	16.3%	-0.12

ANALYSIS BY POSITION LAST TIME

Pos LT	Prop	Win	Runs	Wins%	£
Won	27%	59	250	23.6%	-0.03
2nd or 3rd	24%	54	305	17.7%	-0.15
Unplaced	49%	108	793	13.6%	-0.13
Not Compl	0%	1	8	12.5%	0.38

OTHER FACTORS (WINS-RUNS, £)

Course Winner:	42-276	-£0.25
Distance Winner:	133-819	-£0.20
Going Winner:	104-673	-£0.22
Beaten Favourite:	22-90	£0.20
Up in class:	98-627	-£0.10
Same class:	68-425	-£0.20
Down in class:	55-297	-£0.03
7-Day Winners:	6-25	-£0.22
Colts and Geldings:	159-976	-£0.13
Fillies:	18-98	£0.01
Absolute Favourites:	64-201	-£0.14

TRAINERS (WINS-RUNS, £)

M Johnston 16-66 £0.43; J J Quinn 3-15 £1.27; G A Swinbank 7-23 £0.67; M H Tompkins 7-21 £0.62; W R Swinburn 4-13 £0.79; J H M Gosden 4-14 £0.70; B Ellison 3-15 £0.63; M A Jarvis 5-14 £0.56; Sir Mark Prescott 5-10 £0.78; H R A Cecil 5-14 £0.52; K R Burke 1-14 £0.50; L M Cumani 4-20 £0.33; J R Fanshawe 5-14 £0.47; R M Beckett 2-10 £0.38; W R Muir 3-12 £0.27; D Nicholls 4-21 £0.14; T D Barron 3-21 £0.05; A M Balding 3-12 £0.04.

Race Profiles

All Age Races: Handicaps (Class 1..3) – 8 to 14 runners

ANALYSIS BY AGE

Age	Prop	Win	Runs	Wins%	£
2yo	0%	0	0	0.0%	0.00
3yo	21%	174	1318	13.2%	-0.14
4yo	34%	287	3019	9.5%	-0.23
5yo	23%	196	1886	10.4%	-0.13
6yo	10%	85	1254	6.8%	-0.33
7yo	6%	47	786	6.0%	-0.40
8yo	5%	38	430	8.8%	-0.12
9yo	1%	6	207	2.9%	-0.41
10yo	0%	2	76	2.6%	-0.67
11yo+	0%	4	44	9.1%	0.10

ANALYSIS BY BHA RATING

Rating	Prop	Win	Runs	Wins%	£
120..139	0%	0	0	0.0%	0.00
110..119	0%	0	5	0.0%	-1.00
100..109	4%	35	378	9.3%	-0.29
90..99	31%	260	2595	10.0%	-0.23
70..89	63%	531	5906	9.0%	-0.23
50..69	2%	13	136	9.6%	0.10
..49	0%	0	0	0.0%	0.00
Unrated	0%	0	0	0.0%	0.00

ANALYSIS BY WEIGHT CARRIED

Weight	Prop	Win	Runs	Wins%	£
10-01+	0%	3	37	8.1%	0.18
9-8..10-00	15%	126	1389	9.1%	-0.32
9-0..9-07	43%	360	3366	10.7%	-0.17
8-8..8-13	26%	217	2711	8.0%	-0.28
8-0..8-07	15%	125	1387	9.0%	-0.15
..7-13	1%	8	130	6.2%	-0.46

ANALYSIS BY DAYS SINCE LAST RUN

Days	Prop	Win	Runs	Wins%	£
1..7	13%	107	967	11.1%	-0.13
8..14	23%	196	2277	8.6%	-0.28
15..28	36%	299	3051	9.8%	-0.20
29..60	15%	127	1407	9.0%	-0.33
61..100	3%	25	276	9.1%	-0.15
101+	10%	85	1002	8.5%	-0.14
Unraced	0%	0	40	0.0%	-1.00

ANALYSIS BY TODAY'S STARTING PRICE

Price	Prop	Win	Runs	Wins%	£
Odds On	1%	10	16	62.5%	0.06
Ev - 2/1	6%	51	168	30.4%	-0.20
9/4 - 4/1	25%	213	919	23.2%	-0.01
9/2 - 6/1	21%	177	1272	13.9%	-0.14
13/2-10/1	27%	229	2525	9.1%	-0.19
11/1-16/1	14%	118	2172	5.4%	-0.22
18/1-33/1	5%	38	1555	2.4%	-0.42
40/1+	0%	3	393	0.8%	-0.57

ANALYSIS BY STARTING PRICE LAST TIME

Price	Prop	Win	Runs	Wins%	£
Odds On	2%	13	79	16.5%	-0.18
Ev - 2/1	6%	49	314	15.6%	-0.14
9/4 - 4/1	19%	160	1170	13.7%	-0.13
9/2 - 6/1	15%	125	1171	10.7%	-0.18
13/2-10/1	24%	200	2195	9.1%	-0.26
11/1-16/1	17%	146	1905	7.7%	-0.28
18/1-33/1	14%	118	1592	7.4%	-0.18
40/1+	3%	28	554	5.1%	-0.35
Unraced	0%	0	40	0.0%	-1.00

ANALYSIS BY DISTANCE BEATEN LAST TIME

Lengths	Prop	Win	Runs	Wins%	£
..-10	0%	1	7	14.3%	-0.07
-10..0	19%	163	1186	13.7%	-0.24
0.1..2	19%	160	1498	10.7%	-0.25
2.1..5	23%	191	2049	9.3%	-0.28
5.1..10	21%	178	2149	8.3%	-0.18
10.1..20	12%	100	1399	7.1%	-0.16
20.0..30	3%	28	378	7.4%	-0.11
30.1+	2%	18	314	5.7%	-0.36
Not Compl	0%	0	0	0.0%	0.00
Unraced	0%	0	40	0.0%	-1.00

ANALYSIS BY RUN NUMBER

Run No	Prop	Win	Runs	Wins%	£
FTO	0%	0	40	0.0%	-1.00
2nd Run	1%	5	50	10.0%	1.38
3rd Run	2%	16	110	14.5%	-0.14
4th+ Run	97%	818	8820	9.3%	-0.23

ANALYSIS BY POSITION LAST TIME

Pos LT	Prop	Win	Runs	Wins%	£
Won	20%	164	1194	13.7%	-0.24
2nd or 3rd	23%	189	1793	10.5%	-0.26
Unplaced	58%	485	5974	8.1%	-0.21
Not Compl	0%	1	59	1.7%	-0.94

OTHER FACTORS (WINS-RUNS, £)

Course Winner:	190-1976	-£0.22
Distance Winner:	566-6116	-£0.27
Going Winner:	446-4656	-£0.24
Beaten Favourite:	86-601	-£0.10
Up in class:	352-3772	-£0.22
Same class:	329-3615	-£0.24
Down in class:	158-1593	-£0.20
7-Day Winners:	19-141	-£0.31
Colts and Geldings:	712-7681	-£0.21
Fillies:	57-653	-£0.29
Absolute Favourites:	179-738	-£0.12

TRAINERS (WINS-RUNS, £)

T P Tate 10-65 £1.08; B W Hills 21-116 £0.51; R C Guest 6-18 £2.38; S Gollings 4-19 £1.95; J A Geake 2-19 £1.89; D W P Arbuthnot 4-19 £1.61; B G Powell 5-26 £1.15; C G Cox 14-76 £0.39; Tom Dascombe 4-15 £1.93; C F Wall 13-68 £0.34; H Morrison 10-56 £0.38; J H M Gosden 13-65 £0.28; Mrs J R Ramsden 2-16 £1.13; W Jarvis 5-24 £0.71; R M H Cowell 3-17 £0.94; J R Jenkins 2-11 £1.36;W J Musson 5-48 £0.31; C E Brittain 8-76 £0.17; Mrs A J Perrett 9-99 £0.13; Jamie Poulton 3-19 £0.63.

Handicaps (Class 1..3)

All Age Races: Handicaps (Class 1..3) – 15 runners or more

ANALYSIS BY AGE
Age	Prop	Win	Runs	Wins%	£
2yo	0%	0	0	0.0%	0.00
3yo	14%	61	921	6.6%	-0.25
4yo	46%	206	2841	7.3%	-0.06
5yo	19%	87	1870	4.7%	-0.32
6yo	12%	56	1273	4.4%	-0.37
7yo	5%	22	794	2.8%	-0.58
8yo	2%	11	434	2.5%	-0.48
9yo	0%	2	182	1.1%	-0.82
10yo	0%	1	84	1.2%	-0.77
11yo+	1%	3	25	12.0%	3.76

ANALYSIS BY BHA RATING
Rating	Prop	Win	Runs	Wins%	£
120..139	0%	0	0	0.0%	0.00
110..119	0%	0	24	0.0%	-1.00
100..109	13%	57	1076	5.3%	-0.31
90..99	43%	195	3505	5.6%	-0.33
70..89	44%	196	3770	5.2%	-0.19
50..69	0%	1	49	2.0%	-0.65
..49	0%	0	0	0.0%	0.00
Unrated	0%	0	0	0.0%	0.00

ANALYSIS BY WEIGHT CARRIED
Weight	Prop	Win	Runs	Wins%	£
10-01+	1%	5	72	6.9%	-0.01
9-8 ..10-00	10%	45	883	5.1%	-0.34
9-0..9-07	36%	163	3029	5.4%	-0.35
8-8..8-13	36%	160	2678	6.0%	-0.20
8-0..8-07	16%	73	1542	4.7%	-0.13
..7-13	1%	3	220	1.4%	-0.70

ANALYSIS BY DAYS SINCE LAST RUN
Days	Prop	Win	Runs	Wins%	£
1..7	10%	44	935	4.7%	-0.41
8..14	20%	88	1845	4.8%	-0.37
15..28	35%	157	2916	5.4%	-0.26
29..60	19%	84	1480	5.7%	-0.22
61..100	3%	15	290	5.2%	-0.21
101+	13%	60	925	6.5%	-0.06
Unraced	0%	1	33	3.0%	-0.55

ANALYSIS BY TODAY'S STARTING PRICE
Price	Prop	Win	Runs	Wins%	£
Odds On	0%	0	0	0.0%	0.00
Ev - 2/1	1%	4	13	30.8%	-0.14
9/4 - 4/1	9%	40	185	21.6%	-0.07
9/2 - 6/1	14%	65	509	12.8%	-0.21
13/2-10/1	29%	131	1504	8.7%	-0.19
11/1-16/1	27%	120	2219	5.4%	-0.22
18/1-33/1	17%	76	2716	2.8%	-0.30
40/1+	3%	13	1278	1.0%	-0.45

ANALYSIS BY STARTING PRICE LAST TIME
Price	Prop	Win	Runs	Wins%	£
Odds On	2%	7	54	13.0%	-0.11
Ev - 2/1	4%	19	250	7.6%	-0.36
9/4 - 4/1	17%	78	1001	7.8%	-0.24
9/2 - 6/1	15%	69	1104	6.3%	-0.28
13/2-10/1	28%	127	2033	6.2%	-0.09
11/1-16/1	18%	81	1902	4.3%	-0.35
18/1-33/1	12%	55	1527	3.6%	-0.37
40/1+	3%	12	520	2.3%	-0.39
Unraced	0%	1	33	3.0%	-0.55

ANALYSIS BY DISTANCE BEATEN LAST TIME
Lengths	Prop	Win	Runs	Wins%	£
..-10	0%	0	6	0.0%	-1.00
-10..0	19%	85	1141	7.4%	-0.29
0.1..2	24%	106	1486	7.1%	-0.24
2.1..5	24%	110	1995	5.5%	-0.23
5.1..10	17%	77	1941	4.0%	-0.34
10.1..20	12%	52	1238	4.2%	-0.19
20.0..30	3%	12	309	3.9%	-0.33
30.1+	1%	6	275	2.2%	-0.33
Not Compl	0%	0	0	0.0%	0.00
Unraced	0%	1	33	3.0%	-0.55

ANALYSIS BY RUN NUMBER
Run No	Prop	Win	Runs	Wins%	£
FTO	0%	1	33	3.0%	-0.55
2nd Run	1%	6	39	15.4%	1.58
3rd Run	0%	2	44	4.5%	-0.64
4th+ Run	98%	440	8308	5.3%	-0.28

ANALYSIS BY POSITION LAST TIME
Pos LT	Prop	Win	Runs	Wins%	£
Won	19%	85	1148	7.4%	-0.30
2nd or 3rd	26%	118	1702	6.9%	-0.26
Unplaced	55%	245	5524	4.4%	-0.26
Not Compl	0%	1	50	2.0%	-0.70

OTHER FACTORS (WINS-RUNS, £)
Course Winner:	91-1705	-£0.32
Distance Winner:	313-5870	-£0.30
Going Winner:	236-4622	-£0.35
Beaten Favourite:	56-591	-£0.07
Up in class:	155-2892	-£0.28
Same class:	226-4239	-£0.23
Down in class:	67-1260	-£0.39
7-Day Winners:	9-106	-£0.43
Colts and Geldings:	414-7788	-£0.29
Fillies:	28-522	-£0.12
Absolute Favourites:	61-383	-£0.23

TRAINERS (WINS-RUNS, £)
Jane Chapple-Hyam 2-22 £3.93; M Blanshard 4-42 £1.93; N J Henderson 3-19 £3.26; R A Harris 6-43 £1.42; W J Haggas 7-88 £0.52; K G Reveley 1-11 £3.64; B J Meehan 7-73 £0.49; R Charlton 13-86 £0.41; G M Moore 2-12 £2.92; J L Spearing 1-18 £1.83; Ian Williams 3-31 £0.84; J Gallagher 1-16 £1.56; N Wilson 5-42 £0.58; P R Webber 3-17 £0.65; M Quinn 2-12 £1.83; A J Martin 3-19 £1.11; Paul Green 1-13 £1.62; C G Cox 11-103 £0.19; Sir Michael Stoute 15-97 £0.21; A G Foster 1-16 £1.13.

Race Profiles

All Age Races: Handicaps (Class 1..3) – good or faster going

ANALYSIS BY AGE

Age	Prop	Win	Runs	Wins%	£
2yo	0%	0	0	0.0%	0.00
3yo	18%	191	1633	11.7%	-0.19
4yo	40%	417	4428	9.4%	-0.11
5yo	20%	214	2830	7.6%	-0.27
6yo	11%	116	1919	6.0%	-0.37
7yo	5%	56	1187	4.7%	-0.49
8yo	4%	42	644	6.5%	-0.21
9yo	1%	6	285	2.1%	-0.61
10yo	0%	4	113	3.5%	-0.56
11yo+	1%	7	45	15.6%	2.61

ANALYSIS BY BHA RATING

Rating	Prop	Win	Runs	Wins%	£
120..139	0%	0	0	0.0%	0.00
110..119	0%	0	22	0.0%	-1.00
100..109	7%	76	1044	7.3%	-0.29
90..99	33%	352	4344	8.1%	-0.27
70..89	58%	616	7546	8.2%	-0.21
50..69	1%	9	128	7.0%	-0.06
..49	0%	0	0	0.0%	0.00
Unrated	0%	0	0	0.0%	0.00

ANALYSIS BY WEIGHT CARRIED

Weight	Prop	Win	Runs	Wins%	£
10-01+	1%	7	98	7.1%	0.11
9-8..10-00	16%	170	1866	9.1%	-0.26
9-0..9-07	41%	431	4871	8.8%	-0.25
8-8..8-13	28%	293	3919	7.5%	-0.20
8-0..8-07	13%	142	2075	6.8%	-0.25
..7-13	1%	10	255	3.9%	-0.51

ANALYSIS BY DAYS SINCE LAST RUN

Days	Prop	Win	Runs	Wins%	£
1..7	13%	134	1425	9.4%	-0.22
8..14	21%	219	3092	7.1%	-0.35
15..28	37%	387	4617	8.4%	-0.22
29..60	16%	167	2135	7.8%	-0.27
61..100	3%	28	379	7.4%	-0.17
101+	11%	117	1381	8.5%	-0.03
Unraced	0%	1	55	1.8%	-0.73

ANALYSIS BY TODAY'S STARTING PRICE

Price	Prop	Win	Runs	Wins%	£
Odds On	2%	17	31	54.8%	-0.05
Ev - 2/1	5%	51	203	25.1%	-0.35
9/4 - 4/1	24%	254	1031	24.6%	0.04
9/2 - 6/1	19%	204	1434	14.2%	-0.12
13/2-10/1	25%	259	3019	8.6%	-0.23
11/1-16/1	17%	174	3181	5.5%	-0.21
18/1-33/1	8%	83	3056	2.7%	-0.32
40/1+	1%	11	1129	1.0%	-0.50

ANALYSIS BY STARTING PRICE LAST TIME

Price	Prop	Win	Runs	Wins%	£
Odds On	2%	17	110	15.5%	-0.17
Ev - 2/1	6%	62	417	14.9%	-0.19
9/4 - 4/1	19%	202	1694	11.9%	-0.17
9/2 - 6/1	15%	159	1759	9.0%	-0.24
13/2-10/1	26%	270	3135	8.6%	-0.15
11/1-16/1	18%	186	2833	6.6%	-0.29
18/1-33/1	12%	126	2311	5.5%	-0.31
40/1+	3%	30	770	3.9%	-0.36
Unraced	0%	1	55	1.8%	-0.73

ANALYSIS BY DISTANCE BEATEN LAST TIME

Lengths	Prop	Win	Runs	Wins%	£
..-10	0%	1	9	11.1%	-0.28
-10..0	20%	215	1804	11.9%	-0.25
0.1..2	21%	222	2286	9.7%	-0.24
2.1..5	22%	232	2984	7.8%	-0.28
5.1..10	19%	196	3034	6.5%	-0.25
10.1..20	13%	136	1978	6.9%	-0.07
20.0..30	3%	30	514	5.8%	-0.24
30.1+	2%	20	420	4.8%	-0.53
Not Compl	0%	0	0	0.0%	0.00
Unraced	0%	1	55	1.8%	-0.73

ANALYSIS BY RUN NUMBER

Run No	Prop	Win	Runs	Wins%	£
FTO	0%	1	55	1.8%	-0.73
2nd Run	1%	6	60	10.0%	1.00
3rd Run	1%	12	114	10.5%	-0.47
4th+ Run	98%	1034	12855	8.0%	-0.24

ANALYSIS BY POSITION LAST TIME

Pos LT	Prop	Win	Runs	Wins%	£
Won	21%	216	1813	11.9%	-0.25
2nd or 3rd	24%	250	2652	9.4%	-0.28
Unplaced	56%	585	8539	6.9%	-0.22
Not Compl	0%	2	80	2.5%	-0.77

OTHER FACTORS (WINS-RUNS, £)

Course Winner:	221-2760	-£0.27
Distance Winner:	715-9001	-£0.29
Going Winner:	632-7997	-£0.28
Beaten Favourite:	119-887	-£0.04
Up in class:	421-5064	-£0.22
Same class:	427-5719	-£0.26
Down in class:	204-2246	-£0.22
7-Day Winners:	24-184	-£0.27
Colts and Geldings:	904-11416	-£0.24
Fillies:	59-866	-£0.30
Absolute Favourites:	212-914	-£0.14

TRAINERS (WINS-RUNS, £)

T P Tate 11-79 £0.97; M Blanshard 5-54 £1.34; C G Cox 24-152 £0.43; N J Henderson 4-18 £3.17; B J Meehan 12-97 £0.51; H Morrison 15-100 £0.44; R A Harris 7-69 £0.62; J A Geake 3-31 £1.19; B W Hills 27-199 £0.18; P R Webber 4-19 £1.87; D Carroll 3-19 £1.79; K G Reveley 1-18 £1.83; W Jarvis 7-43 £0.70; B G Powell 6-43 £0.70; Ernst Oertel 1-11 £2.73; J H M Gosden 17-97 £0.29; J L Spearing 2-29 £0.93; J R Jenkins 3-15 £1.73; S Gollings 3-23 £1.09; Tom Dascombe 4-20 £1.20.

Handicaps (Class 1..3)

All Age Races: Handicaps (Class 1..3) – good to soft or softer going

ANALYSIS BY AGE

Age	Prop	Win	Runs	Wins%	£
2yo	0%	0	0	0.0%	0.00
3yo	23%	104	885	11.8%	-0.10
4yo	35%	159	1870	8.5%	-0.21
5yo	24%	108	1203	9.0%	-0.11
6yo	11%	50	772	6.5%	-0.21
7yo	5%	21	487	4.3%	-0.50
8yo	2%	10	280	3.6%	-0.62
9yo	1%	3	132	2.3%	-0.61
10yo	0%	1	57	1.8%	-0.91
11yo+	0%	1	30	3.3%	-0.57

ANALYSIS BY BHA RATING

Rating	Prop	Win	Runs	Wins%	£
120..139	0%	0	0	0.0%	0.00
110..119	0%	0	8	0.0%	-1.00
100..109	5%	24	444	5.4%	-0.27
90..99	36%	165	2039	8.1%	-0.27
70..89	57%	260	3151	8.3%	-0.21
50..69	2%	8	74	10.8%	-0.02
..49	0%	0	0	0.0%	0.00
Unrated	0%	0	0	0.0%	0.00

ANALYSIS BY WEIGHT CARRIED

Weight	Prop	Win	Runs	Wins%	£
10-01+	0%	1	11	9.1%	-0.45
9-8 ..10-00	13%	59	702	8.4%	-0.36
9-0..9-07	42%	191	2034	9.4%	-0.21
8-8..8-13	27%	125	1815	6.9%	-0.34
8-0..8-07	17%	78	1042	7.5%	0.05
..7-13	1%	3	112	2.7%	-0.70

ANALYSIS BY DAYS SINCE LAST RUN

Days	Prop	Win	Runs	Wins%	£
1..7	10%	47	621	7.6%	-0.28
8..14	25%	114	1342	8.5%	-0.21
15..28	32%	145	1843	7.9%	-0.24
29..60	17%	79	978	8.1%	-0.27
61..100	4%	19	230	8.3%	-0.17
101+	11%	52	677	7.7%	-0.20
Unraced	0%	1	25	4.0%	-0.56

ANALYSIS BY TODAY'S STARTING PRICE

Price	Prop	Win	Runs	Wins%	£
Odds On	1%	6	13	46.2%	-0.23
Ev - 2/1	8%	37	99	37.4%	-0.01
9/4 - 4/1	21%	94	470	20.0%	-0.14
9/2 - 6/1	17%	78	580	13.4%	-0.17
13/2-10/1	28%	126	1306	9.6%	-0.10
11/1-16/1	17%	78	1391	5.6%	-0.20
18/1-33/1	7%	33	1304	2.5%	-0.40
40/1+	1%	5	553	0.9%	-0.44

ANALYSIS BY STARTING PRICE LAST TIME

Price	Prop	Win	Runs	Wins%	£
Odds On	2%	8	41	19.5%	0.15
Ev - 2/1	5%	25	213	11.7%	-0.20
9/4 - 4/1	18%	82	692	11.8%	-0.15
9/2 - 6/1	16%	72	734	9.8%	-0.18
13/2-10/1	22%	101	1403	7.2%	-0.24
11/1-16/1	18%	84	1233	6.8%	-0.32
18/1-33/1	15%	68	1005	6.8%	-0.21
40/1+	4%	16	370	4.3%	-0.32
Unraced	0%	1	25	4.0%	-0.56

ANALYSIS BY DISTANCE BEATEN LAST TIME

Lengths	Prop	Win	Runs	Wins%	£
..-10	0%	0	7	0.0%	-1.00
-10..0	20%	92	771	11.9%	-0.22
0.1..2	19%	88	919	9.6%	-0.19
2.1..5	25%	114	1345	8.5%	-0.17
5.1..10	21%	95	1328	7.2%	-0.26
10.1..20	9%	42	860	4.9%	-0.43
20.0..30	4%	16	231	6.9%	-0.09
30.1+	2%	9	230	3.9%	-0.01
Not Compl	0%	0	0	0.0%	0.00
Unraced	0%	1	25	4.0%	-0.56

ANALYSIS BY RUN NUMBER

Run No	Prop	Win	Runs	Wins%	£
FTO	0%	1	25	4.0%	-0.56
2nd Run	2%	8	46	17.4%	1.65
3rd Run	2%	11	62	17.7%	0.09
4th+ Run	96%	437	5583	7.8%	-0.25

ANALYSIS BY POSITION LAST TIME

Pos LT	Prop	Win	Runs	Wins%	£
Won	20%	92	779	11.8%	-0.22
2nd or 3rd	24%	111	1148	9.7%	-0.18
Unplaced	55%	253	3752	6.7%	-0.25
Not Compl	0%	1	37	2.7%	-0.70

OTHER FACTORS (WINS-RUNS, £)

Course Winner:	102-1197	-£0.25
Distance Winner:	297-3804	-£0.25
Going Winner:	154-1954	-£0.32
Beaten Favourite:	45-395	-£0.12
Up in class:	184-2227	-£0.25
Same class:	196-2560	-£0.18
Down in class:	76-904	-£0.35
7-Day Winners:	10-88	-£0.51
Colts and Geldings:	381-5029	-£0.26
Fillies:	44-407	£0.02
Absolute Favourites:	92-408	-£0.20

TRAINERS (WINS-RUNS, £)

Jane Chapple-Hyam 2-13 £7.62; Peter Grayson 1-13 £4.15; R M Whitaker 4-47 £1.03;W J Musson 6-44 £0.99; D W P Arbuthnot 5-19 £2.03; W J Haggas 7-54 £0.60; E A L Dunlop 6-43 £0.66; J R Fanshawe 10-42 £0.56; A G Foster 1-13 £1.62; P T Midgley 2-10 £2.00; R C Guest 3-10 £2.00; P R Chamings 2-23 £0.74; N J Henderson 3-12 £1.25, J H M Gosden 8-44 £0.33; J L Spearing 3-15 £0.93; J A R Toller 2-13 £1.00; R Charlton 6-51 £0.21; Jamie Poulton 3-21 £0.48; W G M Turner 2-10 £0.85; G A Butler 2-14 £0.43.

Race Profiles

All Age Races: Handicaps (Class 1..3) – 5 to 6 furlong races

ANALYSIS BY AGE
Age	Prop	Win	Runs	Wins%	£
2yo	0%	0	0	0.0%	0.00
3yo	11%	46	616	7.5%	-0.31
4yo	36%	157	1772	8.9%	-0.07
5yo	26%	114	1325	8.6%	-0.18
6yo	14%	59	913	6.5%	-0.35
7yo	6%	28	603	4.6%	-0.62
8yo	6%	25	375	6.7%	-0.30
9yo	1%	4	195	2.1%	-0.71
10yo	0%	1	95	1.1%	-0.80
11yo+	1%	3	47	6.4%	-0.21

ANALYSIS BY BHA RATING
Rating	Prop	Win	Runs	Wins%	£
120..139	0%	0	0	0.0%	0.00
110..119	0%	0	7	0.0%	-1.00
100..109	6%	28	529	5.3%	-0.45
90..99	38%	165	2102	7.8%	-0.26
70..89	54%	238	3242	7.3%	-0.24
50..69	1%	6	61	9.8%	0.05
..49	0%	0	0	0.0%	0.00
Unrated	0%	0	0	0.0%	0.00

ANALYSIS BY WEIGHT CARRIED
Weight	Prop	Win	Runs	Wins%	£
10-01+	0%	0	2	0.0%	-1.00
9-8..10-00	13%	56	684	8.2%	-0.34
9-0..9-07	43%	188	2238	8.4%	-0.27
8-8..8-13	28%	121	1890	6.4%	-0.29
8-0..8-07	16%	68	1027	6.6%	-0.15
..7-13	1%	4	100	4.0%	-0.22

ANALYSIS BY DAYS SINCE LAST RUN
Days	Prop	Win	Runs	Wins%	£
1..7	19%	84	978	8.6%	-0.26
8..14	27%	118	1582	7.5%	-0.25
15..28	33%	146	1869	7.8%	-0.23
29..60	10%	45	830	5.4%	-0.41
61..100	1%	6	136	4.4%	-0.53
101+	9%	38	539	7.1%	-0.15
Unraced	0%	0	7	0.0%	-1.00

ANALYSIS BY TODAY'S STARTING PRICE
Price	Prop	Win	Runs	Wins%	£
Odds On	0%	2	2	100.0%	0.65
Ev - 2/1	5%	20	59	33.9%	-0.10
9/4 - 4/1	18%	78	358	21.8%	-0.07
9/2 - 6/1	18%	80	618	12.9%	-0.19
13/2-10/1	30%	133	1379	9.6%	-0.12
11/1-16/1	20%	87	1540	5.6%	-0.19
18/1-33/1	7%	32	1468	2.2%	-0.49
40/1+	1%	5	517	1.0%	-0.48

ANALYSIS BY STARTING PRICE LAST TIME
Price	Prop	Win	Runs	Wins%	£
Odds On	1%	3	15	20.0%	0.23
Ev - 2/1	4%	18	131	13.7%	-0.22
9/4 - 4/1	14%	60	586	10.2%	-0.28
9/2 - 6/1	15%	64	777	8.2%	-0.22
13/2-10/1	29%	126	1474	8.5%	-0.17
11/1-16/1	19%	83	1377	6.0%	-0.38
18/1-33/1	14%	63	1167	5.4%	-0.33
40/1+	5%	20	407	4.9%	-0.14
Unraced	0%	0	7	0.0%	-1.00

ANALYSIS BY DISTANCE BEATEN LAST TIME
Lengths	Prop	Win	Runs	Wins%	£
..-10	0%	0	0	0.0%	0.00
-10..0	15%	64	667	9.6%	-0.38
0.1..2	24%	103	1123	9.2%	-0.24
2.1..5	28%	123	1598	7.7%	-0.25
5.1..10	22%	94	1523	6.2%	-0.27
10.1..20	10%	45	828	5.4%	-0.23
20.0..30	2%	8	135	5.9%	0.04
30.1+	0%	0	60	0.0%	-1.00
Not Compl	0%	0	0	0.0%	0.00
Unraced	0%	0	7	0.0%	-1.00

ANALYSIS BY RUN NUMBER
Run No	Prop	Win	Runs	Wins%	£
FTO	0%	0	7	0.0%	-1.00
2nd Run	0%	2	12	16.7%	1.33
3rd Run	1%	4	20	20.0%	0.28
4th+ Run	99%	431	5902	7.3%	-0.27

ANALYSIS BY POSITION LAST TIME
Pos LT	Prop	Win	Runs	Wins%	£
Won	15%	64	668	9.6%	-0.38
2nd or 3rd	22%	98	1082	9.1%	-0.26
Unplaced	63%	275	4173	6.6%	-0.24
Not Compl	0%	0	18	0.0%	-1.00

OTHER FACTORS (WINS-RUNS, £)
Course Winner:	107-1340	-£0.29
Distance Winner:	387-5186	-£0.28
Going Winner:	268-3507	-£0.30
Beaten Favourite:	45-384	-£0.04
Up in class:	154-2121	-£0.24
Same class:	190-2674	-£0.27
Down in class:	93-1139	-£0.28
7-Day Winners:	10-107	-£0.52
Colts and Geldings:	369-5189	-£0.27
Fillies:	38-500	-£0.22
Absolute Favourites:	79-386	-£0.18

TRAINERS (WINS-RUNS, £)
M Blanshard 6-57 £1.26; Peter Grayson 1-25 £1.68; D W Barker 12-85 £0.44; R A Harris 8-82 £0.44; R Bastiman 3-11 £3.09; J Gallagher 4-34 £0.90; W J Haggas 9-60 £0.50; C F Wall 6-41 £0.59; B G Powell 4-27 £0.85; C G Cox 12-84 £0.25; E S McMahon 4-25 £0.76; Tom Dascombe 3-19 £1.00; N Wilson 5-45 £0.39; K R Burke 3-47 £0.36; H Morrison 7-37 £0.43; R M H Cowell 4-24 £0.58; J L Spearing 3-19 £0.53; R J Price 6-61 £0.13; Miss Gay Kelleway 2-17 £0.41.

Handicaps (Class 1..3)

All Age Races: Handicaps (Class 1..3) – 7 to 9 furlong races

ANALYSIS BY AGE
Age	Prop	Win	Runs	Wins%	£
2yo	0%	0	0	0.0%	0.00
3yo	20%	101	985	10.3%	-0.20
4yo	42%	212	2258	9.4%	-0.07
5yo	18%	91	1335	6.8%	-0.37
6yo	10%	52	873	6.0%	-0.32
7yo	6%	30	609	4.9%	-0.34
8yo	3%	15	315	4.8%	-0.42
9yo	0%	2	108	1.9%	-0.76
10yo	0%	2	27	7.4%	-0.07
11yo+	0%	1	6	16.7%	2.83

ANALYSIS BY BHA RATING
Rating	Prop	Win	Runs	Wins%	£
120..139	0%	0	0	0.0%	0.00
110..119	0%	0	13	0.0%	-1.00
100..109	7%	33	506	6.5%	-0.18
90..99	31%	158	2203	7.2%	-0.30
70..89	61%	310	3711	8.4%	-0.19
50..69	1%	5	83	6.0%	-0.43
..49	0%	0	0	0.0%	0.00
Unrated	0%	0	0	0.0%	0.00

ANALYSIS BY WEIGHT CARRIED
Weight	Prop	Win	Runs	Wins%	£
10-01+	0%	2	37	5.4%	0.11
9-8 ..10-00	15%	78	831	9.4%	-0.16
9-0..9-07	39%	197	2384	8.3%	-0.27
8-8..8-13	29%	148	2011	7.4%	-0.22
8-0..8-07	15%	78	1133	6.9%	-0.18
..7-13	1%	3	120	2.5%	-0.71

ANALYSIS BY DAYS SINCE LAST RUN
Days	Prop	Win	Runs	Wins%	£
1..7	12%	63	677	9.3%	-0.14
8..14	21%	106	1540	6.9%	-0.35
15..28	36%	184	2318	7.9%	-0.20
29..60	17%	85	1023	8.3%	-0.20
61..100	3%	15	214	7.0%	-0.16
101+	10%	53	709	7.5%	-0.18
Unraced	0%	0	35	0.0%	-1.00

ANALYSIS BY TODAY'S STARTING PRICE
Price	Prop	Win	Runs	Wins%	£
Odds On	2%	10	16	62.5%	0.11
Ev - 2/1	4%	20	92	21.7%	-0.43
9/4 - 4/1	24%	119	481	24.7%	0.05
9/2 - 6/1	17%	88	680	12.9%	-0.20
13/2-10/1	25%	125	1497	8.4%	-0.25
11/1-16/1	18%	92	1563	5.9%	-0.16
18/1-33/1	9%	47	1547	3.0%	-0.24
40/1+	1%	5	640	0.8%	-0.59

ANALYSIS BY STARTING PRICE LAST TIME
Price	Prop	Win	Runs	Wins%	£
Odds On	1%	7	44	15.9%	-0.07
Ev - 2/1	6%	28	207	13.5%	-0.16
9/4 - 4/1	20%	102	828	12.3%	-0.12
9/2 - 6/1	15%	76	848	9.0%	-0.23
13/2-10/1	21%	108	1561	6.9%	-0.27
11/1-16/1	19%	98	1398	7.0%	-0.20
18/1-33/1	15%	74	1178	6.3%	-0.20
40/1+	3%	13	417	3.1%	-0.50
Unraced	0%	0	35	0.0%	-1.00

ANALYSIS BY DISTANCE BEATEN LAST TIME
Lengths	Prop	Win	Runs	Wins%	£
..-10	0%	0	2	0.0%	-1.00
-10..0	23%	116	888	13.1%	-0.12
0.1..2	17%	88	1078	8.2%	-0.28
2.1..5	21%	104	1477	7.0%	-0.27
5.1..10	20%	103	1546	6.7%	-0.27
10.1..20	13%	64	1034	6.2%	-0.16
20.0..30	4%	20	268	7.5%	-0.12
30.1+	2%	11	188	5.9%	-0.34
Not Compl	0%	0	0	0.0%	0.00
Unraced	0%	0	35	0.0%	-1.00

ANALYSIS BY RUN NUMBER
Run No	Prop	Win	Runs	Wins%	£
FTO	0%	0	35	0.0%	-1.00
2nd Run	2%	9	39	23.1%	3.91
3rd Run	2%	8	60	13.3%	-0.28
4th+ Run	97%	489	6382	7.7%	-0.25

ANALYSIS BY POSITION LAST TIME
Pos LT	Prop	Win	Runs	Wins%	£
Won	23%	116	892	13.0%	-0.12
2nd or 3rd	20%	103	1269	8.1%	-0.31
Unplaced	57%	286	4305	6.6%	-0.22
Not Compl	0%	1	50	2.0%	-0.93

OTHER FACTORS (WINS-RUNS, £)
Course Winner:	110-1536	-£0.33
Distance Winner:	341-4528	-£0.32
Going Winner:	258-3411	-£0.27
Beaten Favourite:	54-435	-£0.04
Up in class:	209-2514	-£0.19
Same class:	211-2999	-£0.25
Down in class:	86-968	-£0.25
7-Day Winners:	15-98	-£0.13
Colts and Geldings:	430-5647	-£0.24
Fillies:	24-364	-£0.20
Absolute Favourites:	95-434	-£0.19

TRAINERS (WINS-RUNS, £)
T P Tate 6-40 £1.65; B W Hills 24-183 £0.28; R Charlton 15-70 £0.73; J A Geake 3-23 £1.96; R C Guest 5-15 £2.53; W J Haggas 11-70 £0.51; B J Meehan 6-63 £0.50; W Jarvis 5-34 £0.93; C G Cox 9-55 £0.54; J H M Gosden 11-65 £0.43; S Gollings 3-20 £1.40; G A Swinbank 8-65 £0.37; J R Best 1-11 £2.09; R M Whitaker 3-65 £0.35; M Johnston 28-218 £0.10; A G Foster 1-16 £1.13; H Morrison 6-40 £0.38; G A Butler 5-39 £0.37; D M Simcock 2-27 £0.36; S C Williams 1-17 £0.53.

Race Profiles

All Age Races: Handicaps (Class 1..3) – 10 to 14 furlong races

ANALYSIS BY AGE

Age	Prop	Win	Runs	Wins%	£
2yo	0%	0	0	0.0%	0.00
3yo	28%	128	827	15.5%	-0.02
4yo	38%	177	1913	9.3%	-0.29
5yo	21%	97	1108	8.8%	-0.10
6yo	8%	37	679	5.4%	-0.40
7yo	3%	13	312	4.2%	-0.54
8yo	2%	8	153	5.2%	-0.21
9yo	1%	3	66	4.5%	0.20
10yo	0%	0	27	0.0%	-1.00
11yo+	0%	2	8	25.0%	6.06

ANALYSIS BY BHA RATING

Rating	Prop	Win	Runs	Wins%	£
120..139	0%	0	0	0.0%	0.00
110..119	0%	0	10	0.0%	-1.00
100..109	8%	36	409	8.8%	-0.20
90..99	35%	163	1706	9.6%	-0.27
70..89	56%	262	2936	8.9%	-0.21
50..69	1%	4	32	12.5%	1.06
..49	0%	0	0	0.0%	0.00
Unrated	0%	0	0	0.0%	0.00

ANALYSIS BY WEIGHT CARRIED

Weight	Prop	Win	Runs	Wins%	£
10-01+	1%	6	70	8.6%	0.05
9-8..10-00	16%	76	845	9.0%	-0.34
9-0..9-07	44%	203	1910	10.6%	-0.21
8-8..8-13	26%	122	1486	8.2%	-0.23
8-0..8-07	12%	55	702	7.8%	-0.05
..7-13	1%	3	80	3.8%	-0.69

ANALYSIS BY DAYS SINCE LAST RUN

Days	Prop	Win	Runs	Wins%	£
1..7	6%	29	322	9.0%	-0.30
8..14	18%	82	1037	7.9%	-0.34
15..28	36%	169	1869	9.0%	-0.26
29..60	20%	95	1003	9.5%	-0.22
61..100	5%	23	201	11.4%	-0.09
101+	14%	65	628	10.4%	0.08
Unraced	0%	2	33	6.1%	-0.21

ANALYSIS BY TODAY'S STARTING PRICE

Price	Prop	Win	Runs	Wins%	£
Odds On	2%	9	23	39.1%	-0.36
Ev - 2/1	9%	42	133	31.6%	-0.17
9/4 - 4/1	27%	124	545	22.8%	-0.03
9/2 - 6/1	20%	95	589	16.1%	-0.01
13/2-10/1	23%	105	1177	8.9%	-0.19
11/1-16/1	13%	60	1203	5.0%	-0.27
18/1-33/1	5%	25	1070	2.3%	-0.43
40/1+	1%	5	353	1.4%	-0.16

ANALYSIS BY STARTING PRICE LAST TIME

Price	Prop	Win	Runs	Wins%	£
Odds On	3%	13	76	17.1%	-0.10
Ev - 2/1	8%	35	230	15.2%	-0.08
9/4 - 4/1	22%	103	778	13.2%	-0.11
9/2 - 6/1	17%	80	686	11.7%	-0.10
13/2-10/1	24%	113	1227	9.2%	-0.13
11/1-16/1	14%	67	1036	6.5%	-0.39
18/1-33/1	9%	44	785	5.6%	-0.33
40/1+	2%	8	242	3.3%	-0.44
Unraced	0%	2	33	6.1%	-0.21

ANALYSIS BY DISTANCE BEATEN LAST TIME

Lengths	Prop	Win	Runs	Wins%	£
..-10	0%	0	6	0.0%	-1.00
-10..0	22%	101	809	12.5%	-0.27
0.1..2	22%	103	818	12.6%	-0.10
2.1..5	20%	93	1020	9.1%	-0.32
5.1..10	18%	83	1064	7.8%	-0.19
10.1..20	12%	58	782	7.4%	-0.10
20.0..30	3%	13	266	4.9%	-0.38
30.1+	3%	12	295	4.1%	-0.31
Not Compl	0%	0	0	0.0%	0.00
Unraced	0%	2	33	6.1%	-0.21

ANALYSIS BY RUN NUMBER

Run No	Prop	Win	Runs	Wins%	£
FTO	0%	2	33	6.1%	-0.21
2nd Run	0%	2	45	4.4%	-0.61
3rd Run	2%	10	84	11.9%	-0.36
4th+ Run	97%	451	4931	9.1%	-0.22

ANALYSIS BY POSITION LAST TIME

Pos LT	Prop	Win	Runs	Wins%	£
Won	22%	101	813	12.4%	-0.28
2nd or 3rd	29%	134	1139	11.8%	-0.12
Unplaced	49%	228	3100	7.4%	-0.24
Not Compl	0%	2	41	4.9%	-0.37

OTHER FACTORS (WINS-RUNS, £)

Course Winner:	85-865	-£0.14
Distance Winner:	254-2769	-£0.23
Going Winner:	211-2466	-£0.34
Beaten Favourite:	61-369	£0.07
Up in class:	200-2073	-£0.20
Same class:	183-2129	-£0.22
Down in class:	80-858	-£0.26
7-Day Winners:	6-58	-£0.44
Colts and Geldings:	393-4464	-£0.23
Fillies:	32-304	-£0.12
Absolute Favourites:	102-412	-£0.16

TRAINERS (WINS-RUNS, £)

Jane Chapple-Hyam 2-17 £5.59; W J Musson 8-60 £0.71; K G Reveley 1-16 £2.19; J R Boyle 5-34 £0.90; P R Webber 3-11 £2.45; T D Barron 4-24 £0.94; G G Margarson 4-25 £0.85; J H M Gosden 13-66 £0.31; C E Brittain 7-80 £0.25; D Carroll 3-11 £1.35; R M Beckett 6-35 £0.40; Sir Michael Stoute 28-147 £0.09; Saeed Bin Suroor 17-103 £0.11; B G Powell 2-15 £0.53; P G Murphy 1-10 £0.70; W M Brisbourne 1-19 £0.37; R C Guest 2-14 £0.48; B J Meehan 4-37 £0.16; S Kirk 1-15 £0.40; Ian Williams 3-32 £0.16.

Handicaps (Class 1..3)

All Age Races: Handicaps (Class 1..3) – 15+ furlong races

ANALYSIS BY AGE

Age	Prop	Win	Runs	Wins%	£
2yo	0%	0	0	0.0%	0.00
3yo	20%	20	90	22.2%	0.01
4yo	29%	30	355	8.5%	-0.20
5yo	20%	20	265	7.5%	-0.18
6yo	18%	18	226	8.0%	-0.03
7yo	6%	6	150	4.0%	-0.52
8yo	4%	4	81	4.9%	-0.40
9yo	0%	0	48	0.0%	-1.00
10yo	2%	2	21	9.5%	-0.48
11yo+	2%	2	14	14.3%	3.21

ANALYSIS BY BHA RATING

Rating	Prop	Win	Runs	Wins%	£
120..139	0%	0	0	0.0%	0.00
110..119	0%	0	0	0.0%	0.00
100..109	3%	3	44	6.8%	-0.11
90..99	30%	31	372	8.3%	-0.13
70..89	65%	66	808	8.2%	-0.23
50..69	2%	2	26	7.7%	-0.40
..49	0%	0	0	0.0%	0.00
Unrated	0%	0	0	0.0%	0.00

ANALYSIS BY WEIGHT CARRIED

Weight	Prop	Win	Runs	Wins%	£
10-01+	0%	0	0	0.0%	0.00
9-8 ..10-00	19%	19	208	9.1%	-0.38
9-0..9-07	33%	34	373	9.1%	0.10
8-8..8-13	26%	27	347	7.8%	-0.26
8-0..8-07	19%	19	255	7.5%	-0.27
..7-13	3%	3	67	4.5%	-0.69

ANALYSIS BY DAYS SINCE LAST RUN

Days	Prop	Win	Runs	Wins%	£
1..7	5%	5	69	7.2%	-0.67
8..14	26%	27	275	9.8%	-0.28
15..28	32%	33	404	8.2%	-0.14
29..60	21%	21	257	8.2%	-0.30
61..100	3%	3	58	5.2%	0.40
101+	13%	13	182	7.1%	-0.06
Unraced	0%	0	5	0.0%	-1.00

ANALYSIS BY TODAY'S STARTING PRICE

Price	Prop	Win	Runs	Wins%	£
Odds On	2%	2	3	66.7%	0.20
Ev - 2/1	6%	6	18	33.3%	-0.17
9/4 - 4/1	26%	27	117	23.1%	-0.09
9/2 - 6/1	19%	19	127	15.0%	-0.09
13/2-10/1	22%	22	272	8.1%	-0.26
11/1-16/1	13%	13	266	4.9%	-0.29
18/1-33/1	12%	12	275	4.4%	0.16
40/1+	1%	1	172	0.6%	-0.70

ANALYSIS BY STARTING PRICE LAST TIME

Price	Prop	Win	Runs	Wins%	£
Odds On	2%	2	16	12.5%	-0.39
Ev - 2/1	6%	6	62	9.7%	-0.63
9/4 - 4/1	19%	19	194	9.8%	-0.22
9/2 - 6/1	11%	11	182	6.0%	-0.59
13/2-10/1	24%	24	276	8.7%	0.05
11/1-16/1	22%	22	255	8.6%	-0.05
18/1-33/1	13%	13	186	7.0%	-0.17
40/1+	5%	5	74	6.8%	-0.27
Unraced	0%	0	5	0.0%	-1.00

ANALYSIS BY DISTANCE BEATEN LAST TIME

Lengths	Prop	Win	Runs	Wins%	£
..-10	1%	1	8	12.5%	-0.19
-10..0	25%	26	211	12.3%	-0.23
0.1..2	16%	16	186	8.6%	-0.38
2.1..5	25%	26	234	11.1%	0.26
5.1..10	11%	11	229	4.8%	-0.39
10.1..20	11%	11	194	5.7%	-0.34
20.0..30	5%	5	76	6.6%	-0.22
30.1+	6%	6	107	5.6%	-0.10
Not Compl	0%	0	0	0.0%	0.00
Unraced	0%	0	5	0.0%	-1.00

ANALYSIS BY RUN NUMBER

Run No	Prop	Win	Runs	Wins%	£
FTO	0%	0	5	0.0%	-1.00
2nd Run	1%	1	10	10.0%	-0.50
3rd Run	1%	1	12	8.3%	-0.50
4th+ Run	98%	100	1223	8.2%	-0.19

ANALYSIS BY POSITION LAST TIME

Pos LT	Prop	Win	Runs	Wins%	£
Won	26%	27	219	12.3%	-0.23
2nd or 3rd	25%	26	310	8.4%	-0.45
Unplaced	48%	49	713	6.9%	-0.07
Not Compl	0%	0	8	0.0%	-1.00

OTHER FACTORS (WINS-RUNS, £)

Course Winner:	21-216	-£0.06
Distance Winner:	30-322	-£0.21
Going Winner:	49-567	-£0.09
Beaten Favourite:	4-94	-£0.82
Up in class:	42-583	-£0.44
Same class:	39-477	£0.09
Down in class:	21-185	-£0.16
7-Day Winners:	3-9	-£0.12
Colts and Geldings:	93-1145	-£0.19
Fillies:	9-105	-£0.28
Absolute Favourites:	28-90	£0.13

TRAINERS (WINS-RUNS, £)

N J Henderson 4-24 £1.88; A J Martin 4-10 £3.35; M R Channon 3-32 £0.88; G M Moore 2-24 £0.96; M L W Bell 6-15 £1.50; Ian Williams 2-29 £0.62; D W P Arbuthnot 1-11 £0.91; Jamie Poulton 3-19 £0.42; H Morrison 2-19 £0.32; M A Jarvis 1-12 £0.42; J S Goldie 2-16 £0.22; T P Tate 3-25 £0.12; M H Tompkins 5-32 £0.02; Jane Chapple-Hyam 2-14 £0.04.

Race Profiles

All Age Races: Handicaps (Class 4..7)

ANALYSIS BY AGE

Age	Prop	Win	Runs	Wins%	£
2yo	0%	0	0	0.0%	0.00
3yo	15%	834	8769	9.5%	-0.20
4yo	34%	1916	20952	9.1%	-0.22
5yo	21%	1194	12809	9.3%	-0.22
6yo	13%	746	8200	9.1%	-0.17
7yo	8%	458	5462	8.4%	-0.16
8yo	4%	224	3315	6.8%	-0.32
9yo	2%	109	1846	5.9%	-0.46
10yo	1%	46	876	5.3%	-0.43
11yo+	1%	34	739	4.6%	-0.44

ANALYSIS BY BHA RATING

Rating	Prop	Win	Runs	Wins%	£
120..139	0%	0	0	0.0%	0.00
110..119	0%	0	0	0.0%	0.00
100..109	0%	0	0	0.0%	0.00
90..99	0%	5	14	35.7%	0.30
70..89	37%	2040	19621	10.4%	-0.18
50..69	58%	3203	37394	8.6%	-0.23
..49	6%	313	5937	5.3%	-0.33
Unrated	0%	0	2	0.0%	-1.00

ANALYSIS BY WEIGHT CARRIED

Weight	Prop	Win	Runs	Wins%	£
10-01+	5%	252	2643	9.5%	-0.18
9-8 ..10-00	16%	884	8190	10.8%	-0.23
9-0..9-07	41%	2275	23061	9.9%	-0.20
8-8..8-13	25%	1365	17182	7.9%	-0.25
8-0..8-07	13%	729	10674	6.8%	-0.22
..7-13	1%	56	1218	4.6%	-0.28

ANALYSIS BY DAYS SINCE LAST RUN

Days	Prop	Win	Runs	Wins%	£
1..7	18%	999	8666	11.5%	-0.20
8..14	29%	1596	16934	9.4%	-0.23
15..28	31%	1740	19304	9.0%	-0.20
29..60	12%	652	8874	7.3%	-0.26
61..100	2%	136	2121	6.4%	-0.28
101+	8%	430	6911	6.2%	-0.25
Unraced	0%	8	158	5.1%	-0.43

ANALYSIS BY TODAY'S STARTING PRICE

Price	Prop	Win	Runs	Wins%	£
Odds On	1%	74	141	52.5%	-0.11
Ev - 2/1	7%	395	1109	35.6%	-0.05
9/4 - 4/1	26%	1422	6582	21.6%	-0.09
9/2 - 6/1	20%	1106	7963	13.9%	-0.14
13/2-10/1	25%	1403	15162	9.3%	-0.16
11/1-16/1	14%	757	14523	5.2%	-0.25
18/1-33/1	6%	356	12331	2.9%	-0.29
40/1+	1%	48	5157	0.9%	-0.52

ANALYSIS BY STARTING PRICE LAST TIME

Price	Prop	Win	Runs	Wins%	£
Odds On	1%	53	256	20.7%	-0.27
Ev - 2/1	4%	218	1391	15.7%	-0.24
9/4 - 4/1	18%	992	7180	13.8%	-0.13
9/2 - 6/1	17%	937	8255	11.4%	-0.20
13/2-10/1	27%	1485	15054	9.9%	-0.16
11/1-16/1	19%	1069	14047	7.6%	-0.24
18/1-33/1	11%	634	11642	5.4%	-0.28
40/1+	3%	165	4985	3.3%	-0.41
Unraced	0%	8	158	5.1%	-0.43

ANALYSIS BY DISTANCE BEATEN LAST TIME

Lengths	Prop	Win	Runs	Wins%	£
..-10	0%	10	28	35.7%	0.04
-10..0	17%	922	5890	15.7%	-0.13
0.1..2	21%	1161	8864	13.1%	-0.20
2.1..5	24%	1328	13659	9.7%	-0.21
5.1..10	21%	1168	16246	7.2%	-0.23
10.1..20	13%	712	12074	5.9%	-0.22
20.0..30	3%	150	3228	4.6%	-0.28
30.1+	2%	102	2821	3.6%	-0.45
Not Compl	0%	0	0	0.0%	0.00
Unraced	0%	8	158	5.1%	-0.43

ANALYSIS BY RUN NUMBER

Run No	Prop	Win	Runs	Wins%	£
FTO	0%	8	158	5.1%	-0.43
2nd Run	0%	9	176	5.1%	-0.76
3rd Run	1%	37	278	13.3%	-0.01
4th+ Run	99%	5507	62356	8.8%	-0.22

ANALYSIS BY POSITION LAST TIME

Pos LT	Prop	Win	Runs	Wins%	£
Won	17%	930	5919	15.7%	-0.13
2nd or 3rd	28%	1537	11989	12.8%	-0.19
Unplaced	55%	3080	44770	6.9%	-0.24
Not Compl	0%	14	290	4.8%	-0.36

OTHER FACTORS (WINS-RUNS, £)

Course Winner:	1202-11411	-£0.22
Distance Winner:	3156-33117	-£0.22
Going Winner:	2231-22850	-£0.23
Beaten Favourite:	493-3697	-£0.20
Up in class:	1112-13283	-£0.24
Same class:	3048-34099	-£0.23
Down in class:	1393-15428	-£0.20
7-Day Winners:	240-1119	-£0.00
Colts and Geldings:	4089-46608	-£0.23
Fillies:	1002-11950	-£0.22
Absolute Favourites:	1262-4876	-£0.05

TRAINERS (WINS-RUNS, £)

B P J Baugh 9-172 £0.90; R J Price 39-287 £0.35; C A Cyzer 4-74 £1.00; D W Whillans 3-24 £3.00; P W D'Arcy 14-56 £1.28; Dr J R J Naylor 10-114 £0.60; W J H Ratcliffe 12-116 £0.48; P M Phelan 8-47 £1.17; Miss V Haigh 6-49 £1.19; J E Long 8-74 £0.72; Miss T Jackson 1-15 £3.47; W J Haggas 32-134 £0.36; A J Lockwood 6-52 £0.91; C N Kellett 1-35 £1.31; Jamie Poulton 13-101 £0.43; Miss B Sanders 14-85 £0.50; W J Knight 7-61 £0.66; G Woodward 5-67 £0.58; T T Clement 7-76 £0.50; P Bowen 6-37 £1.00.

Handicaps (Class 4..7)

All Age Races: Handicaps (Class 4..7) – 2 to 7 runners

ANALYSIS BY AGE

Age	Prop	Win	Runs	Wins%	£
2yo	0%	0	0	0.0%	0.00
3yo	19%	145	754	19.2%	-0.12
4yo	37%	287	1652	17.4%	-0.11
5yo	20%	155	921	16.8%	-0.03
6yo	12%	90	667	13.5%	-0.29
7yo	7%	54	387	14.0%	-0.20
8yo	3%	25	253	9.9%	-0.40
9yo	2%	12	116	10.3%	-0.14
10yo	1%	7	65	10.8%	-0.13
11yo+	1%	6	48	12.5%	0.27

ANALYSIS BY BHA RATING

Rating	Prop	Win	Runs	Wins%	£
120..139	0%	0	0	0.0%	0.00
110..119	0%	0	0	0.0%	0.00
100..109	0%	0	0	0.0%	0.00
90..99	0%	0	2	0.0%	-1.00
70..89	55%	428	2333	18.3%	-0.07
50..69	44%	341	2351	14.5%	-0.18
..49	2%	12	177	6.8%	-0.55
Unrated	0%	0	0	0.0%	0.00

ANALYSIS BY WEIGHT CARRIED

Weight	Prop	Win	Runs	Wins%	£
10-01+	1%	5	34	14.7%	0.00
9-8 ..10-00	21%	164	899	18.2%	-0.13
9-0..9-07	41%	323	1860	17.4%	-0.15
8-8..8-13	24%	185	1226	15.1%	-0.07
8-0..8-07	12%	94	750	12.5%	-0.28
..7-13	1%	10	94	10.6%	0.03

ANALYSIS BY DAYS SINCE LAST RUN

Days	Prop	Win	Runs	Wins%	£
1..7	17%	136	730	18.6%	-0.21
8..14	29%	224	1360	16.5%	-0.21
15..28	32%	250	1552	16.1%	-0.09
29..60	12%	91	610	14.9%	-0.05
61..100	2%	18	133	13.5%	-0.23
101+	8%	61	465	13.1%	-0.11
Unraced	0%	1	13	7.7%	-0.08

ANALYSIS BY TODAY'S STARTING PRICE

Price	Prop	Win	Runs	Wins%	£
Odds On	5%	42	73	57.5%	-0.04
Ev - 2/1	20%	160	425	37.6%	-0.01
9/4 - 4/1	40%	312	1439	21.7%	-0.12
9/2 - 6/1	16%	122	862	14.2%	-0.14
13/2-10/1	12%	95	1009	9.4%	-0.18
11/1-16/1	5%	36	588	6.1%	-0.13
18/1-33/1	2%	13	363	3.6%	-0.19
40/1+	0%	1	104	1.0%	-0.61

ANALYSIS BY STARTING PRICE LAST TIME

Price	Prop	Win	Runs	Wins%	£
Odds On	2%	18	46	39.1%	0.01
Ev - 2/1	6%	47	193	24.4%	-0.15
9/4 - 4/1	23%	178	795	22.4%	-0.05
9/2 - 6/1	15%	118	738	16.0%	-0.20
13/2-10/1	24%	190	1169	16.3%	-0.14
11/1-16/1	17%	132	934	14.1%	-0.12
18/1-33/1	10%	80	709	11.3%	-0.07
40/1+	2%	17	266	6.4%	-0.50
Unraced	0%	1	13	7.7%	-0.08

ANALYSIS BY DISTANCE BEATEN LAST TIME

Lengths	Prop	Win	Runs	Wins%	£
..-10	0%	1	3	33.3%	-0.33
-10..0	22%	173	687	25.2%	-0.13
0.1..2	23%	176	822	21.4%	-0.11
2.1..5	20%	160	1004	15.9%	-0.15
5.1..10	19%	145	1132	12.8%	-0.17
10.1..20	13%	98	769	12.7%	0.06
20.0..30	2%	15	218	6.9%	-0.46
30.1+	2%	12	215	5.6%	-0.50
Not Compl	0%	0	0	0.0%	0.00
Unraced	0%	1	13	7.7%	-0.08

ANALYSIS BY RUN NUMBER

Run No	Prop	Win	Runs	Wins%	£
FTO	0%	1	13	7.7%	-0.08
2nd Run	0%	2	21	9.5%	-0.50
3rd Run	1%	9	40	22.5%	-0.15
4th+ Run	98%	769	4789	16.1%	-0.14

ANALYSIS BY POSITION LAST TIME

Pos LT	Prop	Win	Runs	Wins%	£
Won	22%	174	690	25.2%	-0.13
2nd or 3rd	29%	230	1130	20.4%	-0.10
Unplaced	48%	375	3022	12.4%	-0.16
Not Compl	0%	2	21	9.5%	-0.19

OTHER FACTORS (WINS-RUNS, £)

Course Winner: 176-1031 -£0.13
Distance Winner: 417-2488 -£0.14
Going Winner: 332-1923 -£0.13
Beaten Favourite: 77-359 -£0.19
Up in class: 203-1354 -£0.12
Same class: 391-2459 -£0.19
Down in class: 186-1037 -£0.07
7-Day Winners: 47-130 £0.06
Colts and Geldings: 531-3307 -£0.13
Fillies: 120-748 -£0.23
Absolute Favourites: 246-701 -£0.06

TRAINERS (WINS-RUNS, £)

I Semple 15-55 £0.96; M Johnston 31-121 £0.29; E A L Dunlop 9-24 £1.10; M F Harris 2-10 £2.60; J W Hills 10-37 £0.68; E J Alston 6-33 £0.72; Ian Williams 3-22 £1.00; Peter Grayson 4-10 £2.20; J R Jenkins 3-35 £0.57; K R Burke 8-37 £0.50; H Morrison 10-31 £0.60; M A Barnes 5-14 £1.29; Mrs C A Dunnett 5-17 £1.05; J R Boyle 9-41 £0.37; B J Meehan 5-17 £0.78; A C Whillans 2-10 £1.32; J G M O'Shea 2-11 £1.09; L M Cumani 9-26 £0.45; Dr J R J Naylor 1-11 £0.91; J A R Toller 5-14 £0.71.

Race Profiles

All Age Races: Handicaps (Class 4..7) – 8 to 14 runners

ANALYSIS BY AGE

Age	Prop	Win	Runs	Wins%	£
2yo	0%	0	0	0.0%	0.00
3yo	15%	537	5496	9.8%	-0.17
4yo	34%	1244	13086	9.5%	-0.21
5yo	22%	788	8244	9.6%	-0.23
6yo	14%	512	5160	9.9%	-0.08
7yo	9%	312	3510	8.9%	-0.14
8yo	4%	150	2150	7.0%	-0.34
9yo	2%	70	1203	5.8%	-0.48
10yo	1%	26	527	4.9%	-0.52
11yo+	1%	22	481	4.6%	-0.45

ANALYSIS BY BHA RATING

Rating	Prop	Win	Runs	Wins%	£
120..139	0%	0	0	0.0%	0.00
110..119	0%	0	0	0.0%	0.00
100..109	0%	0	0	0.0%	0.00
90..99	0%	5	9	55.6%	1.02
70..89	35%	1299	12535	10.4%	-0.18
50..69	59%	2156	23827	9.0%	-0.21
..49	5%	201	3484	5.8%	-0.29
Unrated	0%	0	2	0.0%	-1.00

ANALYSIS BY WEIGHT CARRIED

Weight	Prop	Win	Runs	Wins%	£
10-01+	5%	178	1652	10.8%	-0.16
9-8..10-00	16%	590	5344	11.0%	-0.22
9-0..9-07	41%	1492	14509	10.3%	-0.19
8-8..8-13	24%	880	10542	8.3%	-0.23
8-0..8-07	13%	482	6990	6.9%	-0.21
..7-13	1%	39	820	4.8%	-0.23

ANALYSIS BY DAYS SINCE LAST RUN

Days	Prop	Win	Runs	Wins%	£
1..7	18%	655	5503	11.9%	-0.19
8..14	29%	1061	10808	9.8%	-0.20
15..28	32%	1168	12354	9.5%	-0.18
29..60	11%	415	5549	7.5%	-0.26
61..100	2%	84	1324	6.3%	-0.31
101+	7%	271	4211	6.4%	-0.22
Unraced	0%	7	108	6.5%	-0.27

ANALYSIS BY TODAY'S STARTING PRICE

Price	Prop	Win	Runs	Wins%	£
Odds On	1%	29	61	47.5%	-0.17
Ev - 2/1	6%	206	613	33.6%	-0.10
9/4 - 4/1	26%	967	4488	21.5%	-0.08
9/2 - 6/1	23%	824	5797	14.2%	-0.12
13/2-10/1	25%	930	10214	9.1%	-0.18
11/1-16/1	13%	468	8878	5.3%	-0.24
18/1-33/1	6%	211	6970	3.0%	-0.25
40/1+	1%	26	2836	0.9%	-0.53

ANALYSIS BY STARTING PRICE LAST TIME

Price	Prop	Win	Runs	Wins%	£
Odds On	1%	30	174	17.2%	-0.29
Ev - 2/1	4%	142	923	15.4%	-0.24
9/4 - 4/1	17%	636	4662	13.6%	-0.12
9/2 - 6/1	18%	660	5337	12.4%	-0.17
13/2-10/1	27%	976	9482	10.3%	-0.15
11/1-16/1	19%	711	8944	7.9%	-0.20
18/1-33/1	11%	396	7119	5.6%	-0.27
40/1+	3%	103	3108	3.3%	-0.45
Unraced	0%	7	108	6.5%	-0.27

ANALYSIS BY DISTANCE BEATEN LAST TIME

Lengths	Prop	Win	Runs	Wins%	£
..-10	0%	4	18	22.2%	-0.45
-10..0	16%	582	3803	15.3%	-0.14
0.1..2	21%	762	5572	13.7%	-0.18
2.1..5	24%	895	8702	10.3%	-0.19
5.1..10	21%	755	10071	7.5%	-0.24
10.1..20	13%	470	7652	6.1%	-0.22
20.0..30	3%	107	2062	5.2%	-0.20
30.1+	2%	79	1869	4.2%	-0.33
Not Compl	0%	0	0	0.0%	0.00
Unraced	0%	7	108	6.5%	-0.27

ANALYSIS BY RUN NUMBER

Run No	Prop	Win	Runs	Wins%	£
FTO	0%	7	108	6.5%	-0.27
2nd Run	0%	5	115	4.3%	-0.80
3rd Run	1%	22	181	12.2%	0.01
4th+ Run	99%	3627	39453	9.2%	-0.21

ANALYSIS BY POSITION LAST TIME

Pos LT	Prop	Win	Runs	Wins%	£
Won	16%	584	3822	15.3%	-0.14
2nd or 3rd	28%	1020	7733	13.2%	-0.19
Unplaced	56%	2047	28104	7.3%	-0.22
Not Compl	0%	10	198	5.1%	-0.27

OTHER FACTORS (WINS-RUNS, £)

Course Winner:	811-7595	-£0.22
Distance Winner:	2085-21002	-£0.20
Going Winner:	1449-14591	-£0.22
Beaten Favourite:	326-2389	-£0.19
Up in class:	742-8936	-£0.24
Same class:	2032-21500	-£0.21
Down in class:	880-9313	-£0.18
7-Day Winners:	141-713	-£0.06
Colts and Geldings:	2674-29318	-£0.23
Fillies:	674-7366	-£0.05
Absolute Favourites:	813-3189	-£0.05

TRAINERS (WINS-RUNS, £)

B P J Baugh 8-120 £1.39; R J Price 26-192 £0.51; P W D'Arcy 11-38 £1.61; N Tinkler 21-214 £0.20; P M Phelan 7-38 £1.57; P L Gilligan 9-38 £1.41; P Bowen 5-21 £2.38; T T Clement 5-45 £1.03; M Quinn 13-75 £0.61; Mrs R A Carr 17-139 £0.31; Miss B Sanders 10-61 £0.69; J D Bethell 29-207 £0.20; S Woodman 7-27 £1.41; G Woodward 4-36 £1.00; G M Moore 16-121 £0.27; W J Haggas 18-83 £0.39; J R Weymes 8-152 £0.21; G A Harker 10-89 £0.35; Dr J R J Naylor 5-74 £0.42; K King 20-111 £0.27.

Handicaps (Class 4..7)

All Age Races: Handicaps (Class 4..7) – 15 runners or more

ANALYSIS BY AGE

Age	Prop	Win	Runs	Wins%	£
2yo	0%	0	0	0.0%	0.00
3yo	14%	152	2519	6.0%	-0.28
4yo	34%	385	6214	6.2%	-0.26
5yo	22%	251	3644	6.9%	-0.25
6yo	13%	144	2373	6.1%	-0.32
7yo	8%	92	1565	5.9%	-0.22
8yo	4%	49	912	5.4%	-0.25
9yo	2%	27	527	5.1%	-0.48
10yo	1%	13	284	4.6%	-0.32
11yo+	1%	6	210	2.9%	-0.57

ANALYSIS BY BHA RATING

Rating	Prop	Win	Runs	Wins%	£
120..139	0%	0	0	0.0%	0.00
110..119	0%	0	0	0.0%	0.00
100..109	0%	0	0	0.0%	0.00
90..99	0%	0	3	0.0%	-1.00
70..89	28%	313	4753	6.6%	-0.25
50..69	63%	706	11216	6.3%	-0.27
..49	9%	100	2276	4.4%	-0.37
Unrated	0%	0	0	0.0%	0.00

ANALYSIS BY WEIGHT CARRIED

Weight	Prop	Win	Runs	Wins%	£
10-01+	6%	69	957	7.2%	-0.22
9-8 ..10-00	12%	130	1947	6.7%	-0.31
9-0..9-07	41%	460	6692	6.9%	-0.24
8-8..8-13	27%	300	5414	5.5%	-0.33
8-0..8-07	14%	153	2934	5.2%	-0.23
..7-13	1%	7	304	2.3%	-0.50

ANALYSIS BY DAYS SINCE LAST RUN

Days	Prop	Win	Runs	Wins%	£
1..7	19%	208	2433	8.5%	-0.20
8..14	28%	311	4766	6.5%	-0.29
15..28	29%	322	5398	6.0%	-0.26
29..60	13%	146	2715	5.4%	-0.30
61..100	3%	34	664	5.1%	-0.23
101+	9%	98	2235	4.4%	-0.34
Unraced	0%	0	37	0.0%	-1.00

ANALYSIS BY TODAY'S STARTING PRICE

Price	Prop	Win	Runs	Wins%	£
Odds On	0%	3	7	42.9%	-0.23
Ev - 2/1	3%	29	71	40.8%	0.13
9/4 - 4/1	13%	143	655	21.8%	-0.04
9/2 - 6/1	14%	160	1304	12.3%	-0.23
13/2-10/1	34%	378	3939	9.6%	-0.13
11/1-16/1	23%	253	5057	5.0%	-0.28
18/1-33/1	12%	132	4998	2.6%	-0.34
40/1+	2%	21	2217	0.9%	-0.49

ANALYSIS BY STARTING PRICE LAST TIME

Price	Prop	Win	Runs	Wins%	£
Odds On	0%	5	36	13.9%	-0.54
Ev - 2/1	3%	29	275	10.5%	-0.32
9/4 - 4/1	16%	178	1723	10.3%	-0.17
9/2 - 6/1	14%	159	2180	7.3%	-0.29
13/2-10/1	29%	319	4403	7.2%	-0.17
11/1-16/1	20%	226	4169	5.4%	-0.35
18/1-33/1	14%	158	3814	4.1%	-0.33
40/1+	4%	45	1611	2.8%	-0.32
Unraced	0%	0	37	0.0%	-1.00

ANALYSIS BY DISTANCE BEATEN LAST TIME

Lengths	Prop	Win	Runs	Wins%	£
..-10	0%	5	7	71.4%	1.44
-10..0	15%	167	1400	11.9%	-0.11
0.1..2	20%	223	2470	9.0%	-0.26
2.1..5	24%	273	3953	6.9%	-0.27
5.1..10	24%	268	5043	5.3%	-0.24
10.1..20	13%	144	3653	3.9%	-0.28
20.0..30	3%	28	948	3.0%	-0.40
30.1+	1%	11	737	1.5%	-0.73
Not Compl	0%	0	0	0.0%	0.00
Unraced	0%	0	37	0.0%	-1.00

ANALYSIS BY RUN NUMBER

Run No	Prop	Win	Runs	Wins%	£
FTO	0%	0	37	0.0%	-1.00
2nd Run	0%	2	40	5.0%	-0.77
3rd Run	1%	6	57	10.5%	0.04
4th+ Run	99%	1111	18114	6.1%	-0.27

ANALYSIS BY POSITION LAST TIME

Pos LT	Prop	Win	Runs	Wins%	£
Won	15%	172	1407	12.2%	-0.10
2nd or 3rd	26%	287	3126	9.2%	-0.23
Unplaced	59%	658	13644	4.8%	-0.30
Not Compl	0%	2	71	2.8%	-0.68

OTHER FACTORS (WINS-RUNS, £)

Course Winner:	215-2785	-£0.24
Distance Winner:	654-9627	-£0.26
Going Winner:	450-6336	-£0.27
Beaten Favourite:	90-949	-£0.23
Up in class:	167-2993	-£0.29
Same class:	625-10140	-£0.28
Down in class:	327-5078	-£0.25
7-Day Winners:	52-276	£0.10
Colts and Geldings:	884-13983	-£0.26
Fillies:	208-3836	-£0.33
Absolute Favourites:	203-986	-£0.04

TRAINERS (WINS-RUNS, £)

C A Cyzer 1-15 £5.73; J J Quinn 18-166 £0.42; C N Kellett 1-12 £5.75; Miss V Haigh 2-19 £3.21; Miss L A Perratt 9-74 £0.66; M Brittain 4-52 £0.74; J E Long 2-24 £1.58; Jamie Poulton 2-24 £1.52; Ms Deborah J Evans 2-15 £2.40; M L W Bell 7-43 £0.76; Miss Gay Kelleway 7-92 £0.35; E A Wheeler 4-31 £1.00; J W Unett 2-18 £1.72; Mrs P N Dutfield 2-30 £0.98; Dr J R J Naylor 4-29 £0.93; W J H Ratcliffe 3-35 £0.77; P R Chamings 5-39 £0.68; T P Tate 3-23 £1.09; D Burchell 2-12 £2.00.

Race Profiles

All Age Races: Handicaps (Class 4..7) – good or faster going

ANALYSIS BY AGE

Age	Prop	Win	Runs	Wins%	£
2yo	0%	0	0	0.0%	0.00
3yo	14%	576	6082	9.5%	-0.24
4yo	35%	1430	15422	9.3%	-0.23
5yo	22%	879	9425	9.3%	-0.23
6yo	13%	547	6018	9.1%	-0.16
7yo	9%	351	4047	8.7%	-0.13
8yo	4%	162	2470	6.6%	-0.35
9yo	2%	75	1371	5.5%	-0.47
10yo	1%	31	611	5.1%	-0.42
11yo+	1%	24	530	4.5%	-0.42

ANALYSIS BY BHA RATING

Rating	Prop	Win	Runs	Wins%	£
120..139	0%	0	0	0.0%	0.00
110..119	0%	0	0	0.0%	0.00
100..109	0%	0	0	0.0%	0.00
90..99	0%	4	10	40.0%	0.62
70..89	36%	1475	13920	10.6%	-0.19
50..69	58%	2361	27377	8.6%	-0.23
..49	6%	235	4668	5.0%	-0.37
Unrated	0%	0	1	0.0%	-1.00

ANALYSIS BY WEIGHT CARRIED

Weight	Prop	Win	Runs	Wins%	£
10-01+	5%	198	2045	9.7%	-0.18
9-8 ..10-00	16%	663	6221	10.7%	-0.25
9-0..9-07	42%	1698	16792	10.1%	-0.18
8-8..8-13	23%	946	12208	7.7%	-0.29
8-0..8-07	13%	528	7791	6.8%	-0.23
..7-13	1%	42	919	4.6%	-0.23

ANALYSIS BY DAYS SINCE LAST RUN

Days	Prop	Win	Runs	Wins%	£
1..7	18%	740	6483	11.4%	-0.21
8..14	29%	1185	12662	9.4%	-0.23
15..28	31%	1277	14182	9.0%	-0.21
29..60	11%	466	6278	7.4%	-0.25
61..100	2%	89	1490	6.0%	-0.32
101+	8%	312	4784	6.5%	-0.25
Unraced	0%	6	97	6.2%	-0.50

ANALYSIS BY TODAY'S STARTING PRICE

Price	Prop	Win	Runs	Wins%	£
Odds On	1%	57	110	51.8%	-0.12
Ev - 2/1	8%	306	808	37.9%	0.01
9/4 - 4/1	26%	1046	4883	21.4%	-0.09
9/2 - 6/1	20%	816	5856	13.9%	-0.14
13/2-10/1	25%	1019	11014	9.3%	-0.16
11/1-16/1	13%	547	10521	5.2%	-0.25
18/1-33/1	6%	252	8970	2.8%	-0.31
40/1+	1%	32	3814	0.8%	-0.56

ANALYSIS BY STARTING PRICE LAST TIME

Price	Prop	Win	Runs	Wins%	£
Odds On	1%	44	198	22.2%	-0.24
Ev - 2/1	4%	169	1012	16.7%	-0.18
9/4 - 4/1	17%	712	5176	13.8%	-0.13
9/2 - 6/1	17%	706	6045	11.7%	-0.19
13/2-10/1	27%	1094	11046	9.9%	-0.16
11/1-16/1	19%	785	10234	7.7%	-0.24
18/1-33/1	11%	452	8533	5.3%	-0.31
40/1+	3%	107	3635	2.9%	-0.46
Unraced	0%	6	97	6.2%	-0.50

ANALYSIS BY DISTANCE BEATEN LAST TIME

Lengths	Prop	Win	Runs	Wins%	£
..-10	0%	4	13	30.8%	-0.29
-10..0	17%	679	4312	15.7%	-0.13
0.1..2	21%	860	6490	13.3%	-0.18
2.1..5	24%	994	10113	9.8%	-0.21
5.1..10	21%	839	11882	7.1%	-0.26
10.1..20	13%	523	8771	6.0%	-0.21
20.0..30	2%	99	2275	4.4%	-0.36
30.1+	2%	71	2023	3.5%	-0.47
Not Compl	0%	0	0	0.0%	0.00
Unraced	0%	6	97	6.2%	-0.50

ANALYSIS BY RUN NUMBER

Run No	Prop	Win	Runs	Wins%	£
FTO	0%	6	97	6.2%	-0.50
2nd Run	0%	6	118	5.1%	-0.80
3rd Run	1%	22	193	11.4%	-0.34
4th+ Run	99%	4041	45568	8.9%	-0.23

ANALYSIS BY POSITION LAST TIME

Pos LT	Prop	Win	Runs	Wins%	£
Won	17%	681	4326	15.7%	-0.14
2nd or 3rd	28%	1121	8714	12.9%	-0.20
Unplaced	56%	2263	32748	6.9%	-0.25
Not Compl	0%	10	188	5.3%	-0.48

OTHER FACTORS (WINS-RUNS, £)

Course Winner:	888-8360 -£0.22
Distance Winner:	2316-24463 -£0.23
Going Winner:	1860-19035 -£0.22
Beaten Favourite:	365-2655 -£0.18
Up in class:	804-9707 -£0.25
Same class:	2248-24980 -£0.23
Down in class:	1017-11192 -£0.21
7-Day Winners:	178-837 -£0.04
Colts and Geldings:	3013-33909 -£0.23
Fillies:	713-8749 -£0.24
Absolute Favourites:	936-3566 -£0.05

TRAINERS (WINS-RUNS, £)

B P J Baugh 8-135 £1.34; Dr J R J Naylor 10-93 £0.96; C A Cyzer 3-62 £0.97; Miss T Jackson 1-11 £5.09; Miss V Haigh 5-41 £1.34; W J Knight 7-49 £1.07; P L Gilligan 12-57 £0.85; G A Butler 15-81 £0.58; John Berry 9-65 £0.60; Miss B Sanders 12-76 £0.51; W J Haggas 27-108 £0.35; P W D'Arcy 10-44 £0.84; M A Jarvis 15-71 £0.51; F P Murtagh 3-24 £1.46; Mrs P N Dutfield 9-72 £0.47; S Woodman 8-41 £0.77; D J Coakley 7-43 £0.72; B Palling 19-157 £0.20; J R Weymes 12-172 £0.17; H Morrison 42-257 £0.11.

Handicaps (Class 4..7)

All Age Races: Handicaps (Class 4..7) –good to soft or softer going

ANALYSIS BY AGE

Age	Prop	Win	Runs	Wins%	£
2yo	0%	0	0	0.0%	0.00
3yo	17%	258	2687	9.6%	-0.11
4yo	33%	486	5530	8.8%	-0.18
5yo	21%	315	3384	9.3%	-0.22
6yo	13%	199	2182	9.1%	-0.19
7yo	7%	107	1415	7.6%	-0.26
8yo	4%	62	845	7.3%	-0.24
9yo	2%	34	475	7.2%	-0.44
10yo	1%	15	265	5.7%	-0.44
11yo+	1%	10	209	4.8%	-0.47

ANALYSIS BY BHA RATING

Rating	Prop	Win	Runs	Wins%	£
120..139	0%	0	0	0.0%	0.00
110..119	0%	0	0	0.0%	0.00
100..109	0%	0	0	0.0%	0.00
90..99	0%	1	4	25.0%	-0.50
70..89	38%	565	5701	9.9%	-0.18
50..69	57%	842	10017	8.4%	-0.22
..49	5%	78	1269	6.1%	-0.20
Unrated	0%	0	1	0.0%	-1.00

ANALYSIS BY WEIGHT CARRIED

Weight	Prop	Win	Runs	Wins%	£
10-01+	4%	54	598	9.0%	-0.19
9-8 ..10-00	15%	221	1969	11.2%	-0.17
9-0..9-07	39%	577	6269	9.2%	-0.25
8-8..8-13	28%	419	4974	8.4%	-0.15
8-0..8-07	14%	201	2883	7.0%	-0.20
..7-13	1%	14	299	4.7%	-0.44

ANALYSIS BY DAYS SINCE LAST RUN

Days	Prop	Win	Runs	Wins%	£
1..7	17%	259	2183	11.9%	-0.16
8..14	28%	411	4272	9.6%	-0.21
15..28	31%	463	5122	9.0%	-0.17
29..60	13%	186	2596	7.2%	-0.27
61..100	3%	47	631	7.4%	-0.20
101+	8%	118	2127	5.5%	-0.25
Unraced	0%	2	61	3.3%	-0.31

ANALYSIS BY TODAY'S STARTING PRICE

Price	Prop	Win	Runs	Wins%	£
Odds On	1%	17	31	54.8%	-0.05
Ev - 2/1	6%	89	301	29.6%	-0.21
9/4 - 4/1	25%	376	1699	22.1%	-0.06
9/2 - 6/1	20%	290	2107	13.8%	-0.14
13/2-10/1	26%	384	4148	9.3%	-0.17
11/1-16/1	14%	210	4002	5.2%	-0.24
18/1-33/1	7%	104	3361	3.1%	-0.24
40/1+	1%	16	1343	1.2%	-0.39

ANALYSIS BY STARTING PRICE LAST TIME

Price	Prop	Win	Runs	Wins%	£
Odds On	1%	9	58	15.5%	-0.38
Ev - 2/1	3%	49	379	12.9%	-0.40
9/4 - 4/1	19%	280	2004	14.0%	-0.12
9/2 - 6/1	16%	231	2210	10.5%	-0.23
13/2-10/1	26%	391	4008	9.8%	-0.16
11/1-16/1	19%	284	3813	7.4%	-0.24
18/1-33/1	12%	182	3109	5.9%	-0.20
40/1+	4%	58	1350	4.3%	-0.28
Unraced	0%	2	61	3.3%	-0.31

ANALYSIS BY DISTANCE BEATEN LAST TIME

Lengths	Prop	Win	Runs	Wins%	£
..-10	0%	6	15	40.0%	0.32
-10..0	16%	243	1578	15.4%	-0.12
0.1..2	20%	301	2374	12.7%	-0.24
2.1..5	22%	334	3546	9.4%	-0.19
5.1..10	22%	329	4364	7.5%	-0.18
10.1..20	13%	189	3303	5.7%	-0.27
20.0..30	3%	51	953	5.4%	-0.08
30.1+	2%	31	798	3.9%	-0.38
Not Compl	0%	0	0	0.0%	0.00
Unraced	0%	2	61	3.3%	-0.31

ANALYSIS BY RUN NUMBER

Run No	Prop	Win	Runs	Wins%	£
FTO	0%	2	61	3.3%	-0.31
2nd Run	0%	3	58	5.2%	-0.68
3rd Run	1%	15	85	17.6%	0.76
4th+ Run	99%	1466	16788	8.7%	-0.21

ANALYSIS BY POSITION LAST TIME

Pos LT	Prop	Win	Runs	Wins%	£
Won	17%	249	1593	15.6%	-0.12
2nd or 3rd	28%	416	3275	12.7%	-0.17
Unplaced	55%	817	12022	6.8%	-0.23
Not Compl	0%	4	102	3.9%	-0.16

OTHER FACTORS (WINS-RUNS, £)

Course Winner:	314-3051	-£0.22
Distance Winner:	840-8654	-£0.17
Going Winner:	371-3815	-£0.29
Beaten Favourite:	128-1042	-£0.25
Up in class:	308-3576	-£0.19
Same class:	800-9119	-£0.23
Down in class:	376-4236	-£0.16
7-Day Winners:	62-282	£0.10
Colts and Geldings:	1076-12699	-£0.23
Fillies:	289-3201	-£0.14
Absolute Favourites:	326-1310	-£0.06

TRAINERS (WINS-RUNS, £)

K A Ryan 32-181 £0.63; R J Price 14-76 £1.05; T T Clement 2-18 £3.28; Lady Herries 9-34 £1.61; A G Newcombe 9-56 £0.94; J L Spearing 18-78 £0.67; M Quinn 8-38 £1.35; K R Burke 14-149 £0.34; P T Midgley 9-77 £0.64; A J Lockwood 3-19 £2.16; Jamie Poulton 4-31 £1.26; W R Swinburn 8-65 £0.57; P D Evans 21-163 £0.23; P W D'Arcy 4-12 £2.92; W J H Ratcliffe 4-38 £0.88; A G Foster 5-30 £1.03; C R Wilson 1-10 £3.10; J E Long 3-24 £1.21; R E Barr 6-61 £0.48; R M Beckett 11-47 £0.56.

Race Profiles

All Age Races: Handicaps (Class 4..7) – 5 to 6 furlong races

ANALYSIS BY AGE

Age	Prop	Win	Runs	Wins%	£
2yo	0%	0	0	0.0%	0.00
3yo	11%	173	2507	6.9%	-0.26
4yo	34%	533	5900	9.0%	-0.16
5yo	23%	357	3955	9.0%	-0.24
6yo	14%	218	2487	8.8%	-0.15
7yo	9%	137	1662	8.2%	-0.22
8yo	4%	66	1060	6.2%	-0.35
9yo	2%	35	619	5.7%	-0.50
10yo	1%	19	330	5.8%	-0.37
11yo+	1%	16	317	5.0%	-0.47

ANALYSIS BY BHA RATING

Rating	Prop	Win	Runs	Wins%	£
120..139	0%	0	0	0.0%	0.00
110..119	0%	0	0	0.0%	0.00
100..109	0%	0	0	0.0%	0.00
90..99	0%	1	4	25.0%	0.13
70..89	35%	548	5922	9.3%	-0.23
50..69	59%	922	11180	8.2%	-0.20
..49	5%	83	1730	4.8%	-0.36
Unrated	0%	0	1	0.0%	-1.00

ANALYSIS BY WEIGHT CARRIED

Weight	Prop	Win	Runs	Wins%	£
10-01+	2%	34	418	8.1%	-0.28
9-8 ..10-00	14%	225	2069	10.9%	-0.21
9-0..9-07	41%	638	6879	9.3%	-0.19
8-8..8-13	27%	419	5572	7.5%	-0.26
8-0..8-07	14%	224	3524	6.4%	-0.25
..7-13	1%	14	375	3.7%	-0.14

ANALYSIS BY DAYS SINCE LAST RUN

Days	Prop	Win	Runs	Wins%	£
1..7	25%	393	3602	10.9%	-0.19
8..14	32%	498	5530	9.0%	-0.20
15..28	27%	421	5265	8.0%	-0.25
29..60	8%	132	2366	5.6%	-0.29
61..100	2%	25	504	5.0%	-0.33
101+	5%	85	1567	5.4%	-0.20
Unraced	0%	0	3	0.0%	-1.00

ANALYSIS BY TODAY'S STARTING PRICE

Price	Prop	Win	Runs	Wins%	£
Odds On	0%	5	15	33.3%	-0.39
Ev - 2/1	5%	77	205	37.6%	0.00
9/4 - 4/1	24%	368	1658	22.2%	-0.05
9/2 - 6/1	21%	320	2311	13.8%	-0.14
13/2-10/1	27%	425	4651	9.1%	-0.17
11/1-16/1	15%	228	4614	4.9%	-0.29
18/1-33/1	7%	113	3871	2.9%	-0.29
40/1+	1%	18	1512	1.2%	-0.38

ANALYSIS BY STARTING PRICE LAST TIME

Price	Prop	Win	Runs	Wins%	£
Odds On	0%	6	41	14.6%	-0.38
Ev - 2/1	3%	46	303	15.2%	-0.09
9/4 - 4/1	16%	246	1908	12.9%	-0.12
9/2 - 6/1	16%	245	2417	10.1%	-0.27
13/2-10/1	29%	452	4615	9.8%	-0.13
11/1-16/1	21%	320	4421	7.2%	-0.22
18/1-33/1	13%	200	3667	5.5%	-0.30
40/1+	3%	39	1462	2.7%	-0.44
Unraced	0%	0	3	0.0%	-1.00

ANALYSIS BY DISTANCE BEATEN LAST TIME

Lengths	Prop	Win	Runs	Wins%	£
..-10	0%	0	0	0.0%	0.00
-10..0	15%	234	1631	14.3%	-0.09
0.1..2	26%	397	3122	12.7%	-0.18
2.1..5	26%	408	4989	8.2%	-0.27
5.1..10	22%	339	5359	6.3%	-0.26
10.1..20	9%	147	2969	5.0%	-0.20
20.0..30	1%	22	494	4.5%	-0.12
30.1+	0%	7	270	2.6%	-0.54
Not Compl	0%	0	0	0.0%	0.00
Unraced	0%	0	3	0.0%	-1.00

ANALYSIS BY RUN NUMBER

Run No	Prop	Win	Runs	Wins%	£
FTO	0%	0	3	0.0%	-1.00
2nd Run	0%	0	9	0.0%	-1.00
3rd Run	0%	3	21	14.3%	-0.05
4th+ Run	100%	1551	18804	8.2%	-0.23

ANALYSIS BY POSITION LAST TIME

Pos LT	Prop	Win	Runs	Wins%	£
Won	15%	233	1630	14.3%	-0.10
2nd or 3rd	27%	419	3398	12.3%	-0.23
Unplaced	58%	900	13779	6.5%	-0.24
Not Compl	0%	2	30	6.7%	0.57

OTHER FACTORS (WINS-RUNS, £)

Course Winner:	389-3900	-£0.21
Distance Winner:	1225-13742	-£0.21
Going Winner:	718-8222	-£0.07
Beaten Favourite:	150-1115	-£0.07
Up in class:	328-3956	-£0.19
Same class:	812-10067	-£0.25
Down in class:	414-4811	-£0.19
7-Day Winners:	71-411	-£0.05
Colts and Geldings:	1154-13737	-£0.20
Fillies:	264-3730	-£0.32
Absolute Favourites:	329-1362	-£0.02

TRAINERS (WINS-RUNS, £)

B P J Baugh 5-77 £2.44; Mrs R A Carr 15-110 £0.64; R J Price 14-45 £1.50; P L Gilligan 10-40 £1.37; M Mullineaux 9-72 £0.74; J R Boyle 11-76 £0.68; M W Easterby 13-170 £0.28; Mrs P N Dutfield 5-35 £1.29; W J H Ratcliffe 9-87 £0.47; I A Wood 5-59 £0.64; M Quinn 13-71 £0.45; C R Wilson 1-13 £2.15; B R Millman 16-130 £0.20; A D Brown 6-72 £0.34; A P Jarvis 8-38 £0.64; R C Guest 3-29 £0.83; Paul Green 10-62 £0.37; J Howard Johnson 3-27 £0.83; Ms Deborah J Evans 1-12 £1.83; P D Evans 26-205 £0.10.

Handicaps (Class 4..7)

All Age Races: Handicaps (Class 4..7) – 7 to 9 furlong races

ANALYSIS BY AGE

Age	Prop	Win	Runs	Wins%	£
2yo	0%	0	0	0.0%	0.00
3yo	15%	256	3128	8.2%	-0.27
4yo	35%	595	6849	8.7%	-0.25
5yo	22%	371	3908	9.5%	-0.16
6yo	13%	215	2420	8.9%	-0.18
7yo	8%	143	1641	8.7%	-0.11
8yo	4%	69	951	7.3%	-0.26
9yo	2%	29	525	5.5%	-0.49
10yo	0%	6	203	3.0%	-0.58
11yo+	0%	5	115	4.3%	-0.27

ANALYSIS BY BHA RATING

Rating	Prop	Win	Runs	Wins%	£
120..139	0%	0	0	0.0%	0.00
110..119	0%	0	0	0.0%	0.00
100..109	0%	0	0	0.0%	0.00
90..99	0%	1	4	25.0%	0.38
70..89	39%	653	6605	9.9%	-0.21
50..69	57%	960	11772	8.2%	-0.23
..49	4%	75	1358	5.5%	-0.20
Unrated	0%	0	1	0.0%	-1.00

ANALYSIS BY WEIGHT CARRIED

Weight	Prop	Win	Runs	Wins%	£
10-01+	4%	60	622	9.6%	-0.07
9-8..10-00	17%	281	2583	10.9%	-0.20
9-0..9-07	44%	736	7743	9.5%	-0.21
8-8..8-13	25%	422	5473	7.7%	-0.22
8-0..8-07	11%	178	3000	5.9%	-0.30
..7-13	1%	12	319	3.8%	-0.35

ANALYSIS BY DAYS SINCE LAST RUN

Days	Prop	Win	Runs	Wins%	£
1..7	18%	302	2614	11.6%	-0.19
8..14	28%	478	5354	8.9%	-0.21
15..28	32%	540	6252	8.6%	-0.19
29..60	13%	216	2811	7.7%	-0.24
61..100	2%	39	658	5.9%	-0.30
101+	7%	112	2025	5.5%	-0.36
Unraced	0%	2	26	7.7%	-0.38

ANALYSIS BY TODAY'S STARTING PRICE

Price	Prop	Win	Runs	Wins%	£
Odds On	1%	18	33	54.5%	-0.07
Ev - 2/1	5%	87	271	32.1%	-0.15
9/4 - 4/1	24%	412	1917	21.5%	-0.08
9/2 - 6/1	22%	367	2469	14.9%	-0.07
13/2-10/1	26%	436	4813	9.1%	-0.18
11/1-16/1	14%	238	4724	5.0%	-0.27
18/1-33/1	7%	119	4007	3.0%	-0.25
40/1+	1%	12	1506	0.8%	-0.60

ANALYSIS BY STARTING PRICE LAST TIME

Price	Prop	Win	Runs	Wins%	£
Odds On	1%	13	65	20.0%	-0.25
Ev - 2/1	4%	66	425	15.5%	-0.25
9/4 - 4/1	16%	267	2085	12.8%	-0.14
9/2 - 6/1	17%	287	2537	11.3%	-0.19
13/2-10/1	27%	457	4768	9.6%	-0.17
11/1-16/1	21%	355	4650	7.6%	-0.23
18/1-33/1	11%	192	3762	5.1%	-0.32
40/1+	3%	50	1422	3.5%	-0.33
Unraced	0%	2	26	7.7%	-0.38

ANALYSIS BY DISTANCE BEATEN LAST TIME

Lengths	Prop	Win	Runs	Wins%	£
..-10	0%	2	3	66.7%	1.06
-10..0	17%	287	1822	15.8%	-0.08
0.1..2	19%	326	2719	12.0%	-0.24
2.1..5	26%	436	4315	10.1%	-0.17
5.1..10	22%	371	5207	7.1%	-0.20
10.1..20	12%	211	3907	5.4%	-0.28
20.0..30	2%	38	1005	3.8%	-0.30
30.1+	1%	16	736	2.2%	-0.63
Not Compl	0%	0	0	0.0%	0.00
Unraced	0%	2	26	7.7%	-0.38

ANALYSIS BY RUN NUMBER

Run No	Prop	Win	Runs	Wins%	£
FTO	0%	2	26	7.7%	-0.38
2nd Run	0%	3	35	8.6%	-0.53
3rd Run	1%	14	82	17.1%	-0.28
4th+ Run	99%	1670	19597	8.5%	-0.22

ANALYSIS BY POSITION LAST TIME

Pos LT	Prop	Win	Runs	Wins%	£
Won	17%	288	1826	15.8%	-0.08
2nd or 3rd	26%	442	3632	12.2%	-0.19
Unplaced	57%	956	14217	6.7%	-0.25
Not Compl	0%	3	65	4.6%	-0.35

OTHER FACTORS (WINS-RUNS, £)

Course Winner:	379-3838	-£0.28
Distance Winner:	993-10474	-£0.20
Going Winner:	686-7142	-£0.19
Beaten Favourite:	134-1129	-£0.30
Up in class:	322-4023	-£0.27
Same class:	941-10795	-£0.20
Down in class:	424-3866	-£0.23
7-Day Winners:	74-321	£0.08
Colts and Geldings:	1233-14511	-£0.24
Fillies:	269-3466	-£0.18
Absolute Favourites:	349-1474	-£0.09

TRAINERS (WINS-RUNS, £)

M C Chapman 5-47 £1.63; D W Whillans 3-22 £3.36; Miss V Haigh 6-29 £2.54; R J Price 15-112 £0.54; W J Knight 4-26 £2.19; J R Weymes 9-90 £0.54; F P Murtagh 4-16 £3.03; S Woodman 7-26 £1.60; W J Haggas 13-41 £0.91; A J Lockwood 2-10 £3.70; G Woodward 4-44 £0.82; G A Harker 5-40 £0.88; R F Johnson Houghton 7-27 £1.21; R E Barr 9-85 £0.38; J E Long 1-13 £2.15; A Bailey 6-59 £0.42; S R Bowring 7-47 £0.52; Jim Best 5-18 £1.33; T J Etherington 2-28 £0.86; R Allan 6-39 £0.61.

Race Profiles

All Age Races: Handicaps (Class 4..7) – 10 to 14 furlong races

ANALYSIS BY AGE

Age	Prop	Win	Runs	Wins%	£
2yo	0%	0	0	0.0%	0.00
3yo	18%	342	2782	12.3%	-0.10
4yo	34%	658	7070	9.3%	-0.24
5yo	20%	391	4116	9.5%	-0.27
6yo	14%	259	2670	9.7%	-0.15
7yo	7%	143	1707	8.4%	-0.07
8yo	3%	64	989	6.5%	-0.40
9yo	2%	34	532	6.4%	-0.38
10yo	1%	17	252	6.7%	-0.36
11yo+	1%	10	234	4.3%	-0.47

ANALYSIS BY BHA RATING

Rating	Prop	Win	Runs	Wins%	£
120..139	0%	0	0	0.0%	0.00
110..119	0%	0	0	0.0%	0.00
100..109	0%	0	0	0.0%	0.00
90..99	0%	3	5	60.0%	0.63
70..89	37%	714	6166	11.6%	-0.13
50..69	57%	1085	11965	9.1%	-0.24
..49	6%	116	2216	5.2%	-0.37
Unrated	0%	0	0	0.0%	0.00

ANALYSIS BY WEIGHT CARRIED

Weight	Prop	Win	Runs	Wins%	£
10-01+	7%	143	1442	9.9%	-0.17
9-8 ..10-00	16%	298	2866	10.4%	-0.28
9-0..9-07	40%	768	7176	10.7%	-0.19
8-8..8-13	23%	433	5114	8.5%	-0.28
8-0..8-07	13%	256	3369	7.6%	-0.12
..7-13	1%	20	385	5.2%	-0.54

ANALYSIS BY DAYS SINCE LAST RUN

Days	Prop	Win	Runs	Wins%	£
1..7	13%	250	2113	11.8%	-0.25
8..14	27%	510	5086	10.0%	-0.27
15..28	34%	654	6514	10.0%	-0.16
29..60	13%	252	3056	8.2%	-0.25
61..100	3%	59	796	7.4%	-0.26
101+	10%	189	2683	7.0%	-0.18
Unraced	0%	4	104	3.8%	-0.63

ANALYSIS BY TODAY'S STARTING PRICE

Price	Prop	Win	Runs	Wins%	£
Odds On	2%	38	67	56.7%	-0.02
Ev - 2/1	9%	180	511	35.2%	-0.06
9/4 - 4/1	28%	545	2494	21.9%	-0.09
9/2 - 6/1	17%	333	2595	12.8%	-0.21
13/2-10/1	24%	458	4783	9.6%	-0.13
11/1-16/1	13%	248	4422	5.6%	-0.19
18/1-33/1	5%	99	3743	2.6%	-0.36
40/1+	1%	17	1737	1.0%	-0.48

ANALYSIS BY STARTING PRICE LAST TIME

Price	Prop	Win	Runs	Wins%	£
Odds On	1%	26	116	22.4%	-0.23
Ev - 2/1	5%	92	564	16.3%	-0.29
9/4 - 4/1	21%	403	2647	15.2%	-0.11
9/2 - 6/1	17%	331	2724	12.2%	-0.16
13/2-10/1	25%	470	4757	9.9%	-0.18
11/1-16/1	17%	320	4189	7.6%	-0.29
18/1-33/1	11%	209	3536	5.9%	-0.19
40/1+	3%	63	1715	3.7%	-0.41
Unraced	0%	4	104	3.8%	-0.63

ANALYSIS BY DISTANCE BEATEN LAST TIME

Lengths	Prop	Win	Runs	Wins%	£
..-10	0%	5	19	26.3%	-0.27
-10..0	17%	323	2018	16.0%	-0.20
0.1..2	19%	355	2539	14.0%	-0.19
2.1..5	22%	418	3753	11.1%	-0.17
5.1..10	21%	394	4812	8.2%	-0.23
10.1..20	15%	289	4329	6.7%	-0.20
20.0..30	4%	73	1395	5.2%	-0.28
30.1+	3%	57	1383	4.1%	-0.34
Not Compl	0%	0	0	0.0%	0.00
Unraced	0%	4	104	3.8%	-0.63

ANALYSIS BY RUN NUMBER

Run No	Prop	Win	Runs	Wins%	£
FTO	0%	4	104	3.8%	-0.63
2nd Run	0%	6	108	5.6%	-0.76
3rd Run	1%	15	139	10.8%	0.09
4th+ Run	99%	1893	20001	9.5%	-0.22

ANALYSIS BY POSITION LAST TIME

Pos LT	Prop	Win	Runs	Wins%	£
Won	17%	328	2038	16.1%	-0.21
2nd or 3rd	29%	547	4056	13.5%	-0.19
Unplaced	54%	1036	14098	7.3%	-0.22
Not Compl	0%	7	160	4.4%	-0.63

OTHER FACTORS (WINS-RUNS, £)

Course Winner:	377-3145	-£0.13
Distance Winner:	833-7946	-£0.24
Going Winner:	687-6324	-£0.23
Beaten Favourite:	176-1210	-£0.19
Up in class:	372-4280	-£0.24
Same class:	1086-11216	-£0.23
Down in class:	456-4752	-£0.17
7-Day Winners:	73-333	-£0.09
Colts and Geldings:	1403-15204	-£0.24
Fillies:	368-3871	-£0.17
Absolute Favourites:	473-1689	-£0.05

TRAINERS (WINS-RUNS, £)

C A Cyzer 2-29 £2.86; J J Quinn 31-189 £0.39; J D Bethell 24-153 £0.39; Miss T Jackson 1-10 £5.75; P W D'Arcy 9-23 £2.39; Jamie Poulton 5-30 £1.59; D J Coakley 8-29 £1.63; N Bycroft 11-79 £0.59; T T Clement 1-22 £2.05; P M Phelan 6-27 £1.65; Dr J R J Naylor 6-66 £0.59; A King 26-136 £0.27; C F Wall 13-61 £0.60;J T Stimpson 6-42 £0.87; Miss B Sanders 7-43 £0.81; E F Vaughan 7-33 £1.05; John Berry 6-44 £0.77; P Bowen 2-20 £1.70; P D Evans 24-181 £0.18; J R Weymes 3-22 £1.45.

Handicaps (Class 4..7)

All Age Races: Handicaps (Class 4..7) – 15+ furlong races

ANALYSIS BY AGE

Age	Prop	Win	Runs	Wins%	£
2yo	0%	0	0	0.0%	0.00
3yo	16%	63	352	17.9%	0.10
4yo	33%	130	1133	11.5%	-0.18
5yo	19%	75	830	9.0%	-0.24
6yo	14%	54	623	8.7%	-0.23
7yo	9%	35	452	7.7%	-0.48
8yo	6%	25	315	7.9%	-0.16
9yo	3%	11	170	6.5%	-0.49
10yo	1%	4	91	4.4%	-0.50
11yo+	1%	3	73	4.1%	-0.42

ANALYSIS BY BHA RATING

Rating	Prop	Win	Runs	Wins%	£
120..139	0%	0	0	0.0%	0.00
110..119	0%	0	0	0.0%	0.00
100..109	0%	0	0	0.0%	0.00
90..99	0%	0	1	0.0%	-1.00
70..89	31%	125	928	13.5%	-0.09
50..69	59%	236	2477	9.5%	-0.25
..49	10%	39	633	6.2%	-0.37
Unrated	0%	0	0	0.0%	0.00

ANALYSIS BY WEIGHT CARRIED

Weight	Prop	Win	Runs	Wins%	£
10-01+	4%	15	161	9.3%	-0.41
9-8..10-00	20%	80	672	11.9%	-0.26
9-0..9-07	33%	133	1263	10.5%	-0.25
8-8..8-13	23%	91	1023	8.9%	-0.22
8-0..8-07	18%	71	781	9.1%	-0.23
..7-13	3%	10	139	7.2%	0.23

ANALYSIS BY DAYS SINCE LAST RUN

Days	Prop	Win	Runs	Wins%	£
1..7	14%	54	337	16.0%	-0.04
8..14	28%	110	964	11.4%	-0.22
15..28	31%	125	1273	9.8%	-0.22
29..60	13%	52	641	8.1%	-0.28
61..100	3%	13	163	8.0%	-0.22
101+	11%	44	636	6.9%	-0.35
Unraced	1%	2	25	8.0%	0.44

ANALYSIS BY TODAY'S STARTING PRICE

Price	Prop	Win	Runs	Wins%	£
Odds On	3%	13	26	50.0%	-0.20
Ev - 2/1	13%	51	122	41.8%	0.08
9/4 - 4/1	24%	97	513	18.9%	-0.21
9/2 - 6/1	22%	86	588	14.6%	-0.10
13/2-10/1	21%	84	915	9.2%	-0.18
11/1-16/1	11%	43	763	5.6%	-0.21
18/1-33/1	6%	25	710	3.5%	-0.13
40/1+	0%	1	402	0.2%	-0.87

ANALYSIS BY STARTING PRICE LAST TIME

Price	Prop	Win	Runs	Wins%	£
Odds On	2%	8	34	23.5%	-0.31
Ev - 2/1	4%	14	99	14.1%	-0.41
9/4 - 4/1	19%	76	540	14.1%	-0.21
9/2 - 6/1	19%	74	577	12.8%	-0.21
13/2-10/1	27%	106	914	11.6%	-0.06
11/1-16/1	19%	74	787	9.4%	-0.11
18/1-33/1	8%	33	677	4.9%	-0.46
40/1+	3%	13	386	3.4%	-0.54
Unraced	1%	2	25	8.0%	0.44

ANALYSIS BY DISTANCE BEATEN LAST TIME

Lengths	Prop	Win	Runs	Wins%	£
..-10	1%	3	6	50.0%	0.49
-10..0	20%	78	419	18.6%	-0.16
0.1..2	21%	83	484	17.1%	-0.05
2.1..5	17%	66	602	11.0%	-0.24
5.1..10	16%	65	868	7.4%	-0.32
10.1..20	16%	65	869	7.5%	-0.14
20.0..30	4%	17	334	5.1%	-0.42
30.1+	6%	22	432	5.1%	-0.41
Not Compl	0%	0	0	0.0%	0.00
Unraced	1%	2	25	8.0%	0.44

ANALYSIS BY RUN NUMBER

Run No	Prop	Win	Runs	Wins%	£
FTO	1%	2	25	8.0%	0.44
2nd Run	0%	0	24	0.0%	-1.00
3rd Run	1%	5	36	13.9%	0.26
4th+ Run	98%	393	3954	9.9%	-0.23

ANALYSIS BY POSITION LAST TIME

Pos LT	Prop	Win	Runs	Wins%	£
Won	20%	81	425	19.1%	-0.15
2nd or 3rd	32%	129	903	14.3%	-0.10
Unplaced	47%	188	2676	7.0%	-0.29
Not Compl	1%	2	35	5.7%	0.03

OTHER FACTORS (WINS-RUNS, £)

Course Winner:	57-528	-£0.34
Distance Winner:	105-955	-£0.25
Going Winner:	140-1162	-£0.17
Beaten Favourite:	33-243	-£0.35
Up in class:	90-1024	-£0.30
Same class:	209-2021	-£0.24
Down in class:	99-969	-£0.15
7-Day Winners:	22-54	£0.33
Colts and Geldings:	299-3156	-£0.26
Fillies:	101-883	-£0.11
Absolute Favourites:	111-351	£0.00

TRAINERS (WINS-RUNS, £)

B Ellison 12-91 £0.61; G M Moore 8-34 £1.37; Dr J R J Naylor 4-38 £1.03; M H Tompkins 16-61 £0.55; M F Harris 5-22 £1.45; J L Spearing 4-22 £1.39; C R Dore 2-11 £2.36; D E Cantillon 6-17 £1.47; R M Beckett 4-16 £1.41; T P Tate 4-24 £0.94; C A Cyzer 2-14 £1.57; R A Fahey 4-27 £0.63; W Storey 3-27 £0.61; P R Webber 3-16 £0.98; Ian Williams 4-34 £0.46; E J Creighton 1-11 £1.36; B G Powell 4-38 £0.36; N B King 3-15 £0.90; Mrs P Sly 3-14 £0.89; D R C Elsworth 3-13 £0.85.

Notes

Notes